WRITING GENDER INTO THE CARIBBEAN

Selected Essays 1988 to 2020

OTHER BOOKS BY THE AUTHOR

Connecting the Dots: Life. Work. Balance. Ageing
Patricia Mohammed and Cheryl Ann Boodram (Eds.)
Ian Randle Publishers, Jamaica, 2020

Travels with a Husband
by Patricia Mohammed and Rex Dixon,
Hansib Publications, United Kingdom. 2016

Imaging the Caribbean: Culture and Visual Translation
Oxford, New York: Macmillan 2010

Gendered Realities: Essays in Caribbean Feminist Thought
Patricia Mohammed (Ed.)
Kingston: University of the West Indies Press and Centre
for Gender and Development Studies, Jamaica, 2002

Gender Negotiations Among Indians in Trinidad: 1917-1947.
London and The Hague: Palgrave / Institute of Social Studies, 2001

Caribbean Women at the Crossroads: The Dilemma of Decision-making Among Women of Barbados, St. Lucia and Dominica
by Patricia Mohammed and Althea Perkins UNFPA/IPP.F/WHR and
Canoe Press: University of the West Indies, Jamaica 1999

Gender in Caribbean Development
Patricia Mohammed and Catherine Shepherd (Eds.)
Originally published in Women and Development Studies, 1988
Second Edition, The University of the West Indies Press, Jamaica, 1999

WRITING GENDER INTO THE CARIBBEAN

Selected Essays 1988 to 2020

Patricia Mohammed

First published in Great Britain by Hansib Publications in 2021

Hansib Publications Limited
P.O. Box 226, Hertford, SG14 3WY, United Kingdom

info@hansibpublications.com
www.hansibpublications.com

Copyright © Patricia Mohammed, 2020

Cover image: Agostino Brunias (Italian, ca. 1730-1796). *Free Women of Color with Their Children and Servants in a Landscape*, ca. 1770-1796. Oil on canvas, 20 x 26 1/8 in. (50.8 x 66.4 cm). Brooklyn Museum, Gift of Mrs. Carll H. de Silver in memory of her husband, by exchange and gift of George S. Hellman, by exchange, 2010.59.

Author image on inside back cover flap by Owen Bruce

ISBN 978-1-912662-33-3

A CIP catalogue record for this book
is available from the British Library

All rights reserved.
Without limiting the rights under copyright reserved above, no part of this publication may be reproduced, stored in or introduced into a retrieval system, or transmitted, in any form or by any means (electronic, mechanical, photocopying, recording or otherwise), without the prior written permission of both the copyright owner and the publisher of this book.

Layout and Design: Anya Pierre, Seaview Graphic Design Studio
Printed in Great Britain

www.hansibpublications.com

For my father
Ayoob Mohammed

CONTENTS

ACKNOWLEDGEMENTS ix

INTRODUCTION 1

ORIGINARY NARRATIVES AND A POLITICAL   10
GRAMMAR FOR CARIBBEAN FEMINISM

1. Nuancing the Feminist Discourse in the Caribbean   13
2. Towards Indigenous Caribbean Feminist Theorizing   47
3. But Most of all Mi Love Mi Browning': The Emergence in 18th and 19th Century Jamaica of the Mulatto Woman as the Desired.   79
4. Like Sugar in Coffee: Third Wave Feminism and the Caribbean   111
5. The Pedagogy of Difference: Co-producing Feminist Consciousness across Borders   141

INDO-CARIBBEAN FEMINIST INTERSECTIONS   162

6. The Creolization of Indian Women in Trinidad   165
7. Structures Of Experience: Gender, Ethnicity And Class In The Lives Of Two East Indian Women   187
8. Writing Gender into History: The Negotiation of Gender Relations among Indian Men and Women in Post-indenture Trinidad Society, 1917–47   219
9. Negotiating with Myth and Symbols: The Historical Reconfiguration of Indian Masculinity and Femininity in Trinidad   255
10. Changing Symbols of Indo-Caribbean Femininity   305

3 INVITING MASCULINITY — 332

11. Deconstructing Patriarchy through Feminist Epistemology — 335
12. A Very Public Private Man: Sketches in a Biography of Eric Eustace Williams — 355
13. The Harder they Fall: Masculinity and the Cinematic Gaze — 441
14. Re-calibrating Male Gender Identity: A Dialogue with Men and Masculinity — 471

4 DRAFTING GENDER EQUALITY FRAMEWORKS — 494

15. Gender Politics and Global Democracy: Insights from the Caribbean — 497
16. Profiling the Gender Sensitivity of Nations — 527
17. The Metricizing of Gender in State Intervention — 551

5 GENDER AND CULTURAL STORYTELLING — 574

18. A Blueprint for Gender in Creole Trinidad: Exploring Gender Mythology through Calypsos of the 1920s and 1930s — 577
19. "Who taking Advantage ah who: Sparrow and Caribbean man woman relations" — 623
20. The Indian Snake Charmer and other Tales: The Image as Story — 655
21. Morality and the Imagination: Mythopoetics of Gender and Culture in the Caribbean: The Trilogy — 681

ACKNOWLEDGMENTS

I am grateful to the University of the West Indies (UWI), an institution in which I spent most of my salaried working life. As a regional Caribbean institution, The UWI provided the best vantage point for encountering geographical differences and the complexity of our related yet varied social histories. The regional Institute for Gender and Development Studies (IGDS) of The UWI and the collegiality of my colleagues are central to the existence of this book of selected essays. All writing requires a critical audience of readers. The use of this work by students and colleagues in teaching and research inspired their inclusion in this collection. As I write this, a new generation of scholars at the IGDS are busily expanding the scholarship among them Gabrielle Hosein, Halimah De Shong, Tonya Haynes, Sue Ann Barratt, Angelique Nixon, Deborah McFee and Dalea Bean. I thank them for taking on the task of driving the scholarship and excellence forged by the first generations of gender scholars and writers. Academic exchanges and enduring friendships of colleagues across the globe have been valuable in shaping these essays that are oftentimes a Caribbean response to global issues or claims. It would take many pages to fill the names of those with whom I have interacted, so rather than causing errors of omission, I embrace that sorority and fraternity of colleagues from all corners of the globe for over four decades. Among these, my sincere gratitude to the editors of the various books and journals for readily agreeing to my republishing of essays in this collected volume. I thank my colleagues Jane Parpart, Canada and Aisha Khan, New York for warmly agreeing to provide the back cover blurbs.

I sincerely thank Erica Williams-Connell for providing me with photographs from her own albums and for her permission to use images from the Eric Williams Memorial Collection, West Indiana Division, The UWI Library, St. Augustine that are contained in Chapter 12 of this book. At the West Indiana Division Aisha Baptiste, Assistant Librarian, was extraordinarily supportive in helping me to access this material.

This book was partially funded by a grant from the Campus Research and Publications Fund, The UWI, St Augustine, Trinidad. Tessa Ottley, copy editor of this volume, bore with me patiently throughout a lengthy process of resending revisions. It is a pleasure to work with Anya Pierre of Seaview Graphic Design Studio. She aims for economy of lines and a perfect balance between the content and design and always achieves this. I thank Arif and Kash Ali of Hansib Publications, United Kingdom for their willingness to publish my work and for allowing me great control over its aesthetic finish.

My husband Rex Dixon probably has a fixed image of me silhouetted against a computer screen rather than sharing a glass with him on an evening. I thank him for his sincere appreciation that writing is a reclusive occupation, one he understands well as an artist himself. Our friends Graham Gingles and Jude Stephens from the beautiful Antrim coast of Northern Ireland, have over the last two decades given me an environment that has continuously invigorated my thought and energy to write. My family have always been supportive of my somewhat antisocial existence as a writer and academic and have left me alone to it, with my sister Ramona Lisa Mohammed-Ramnarine being the one with whom I communicate most to test out an idea. From the vantage point of her legal training, she has been an intellectual sounding board outside the academy.

I dedicate this book to my father Ayoob Mohammed who turned eighty nine years old this year. He has seen three full generations of change and many mores, customs and practices transform in his lifetime. He has always taken a profound interest in my scholarship proudly buying and distributing copies of my books to his friends. He was among the early group of Indo-Trinidadian primary school teachers trained for rural schools in Trinidad and along with my mother, Zuleikha, (deceased), a champion for the education of his four daughters and a son. His interest in writing and painting unconsciously inspired me very early in life, while his earlier involvement in community work without a doubt infected the activist in my soul.

INTRODUCTION

ETCHINGS

The cover image of this book is Agostino Brunias's painting *Free Women of Color with Their Children and Servants in a Landscape*,[1] (circa 1764-96). A glimpse of the eighteenth-century colonial elite of the island of Dominica in the West Indies, it is thought that the painting depicts two mixed race women, one of whom was possibly the wife of the artist's patron with their children, accompanied by eight African servants on the grounds of a sugar plantation. The remote pink of the fading tropical evening sun throws a rosy light on to this leisurely stroll that reveals no hint of the labours of plantation life or the hierarchies of status and privilege, other than that signified by the positioning and costumes of the characters on the canvas.

Although the Italian born Brunias's works on the Caribbean have been critically analyzed as representing "a radical, hypothetical representation of a free, anti-slavery society" it is argued that, "he also painted black and mixed-race subjects with a kind of dignity and reverence rarely seen before in European art history."[2] David Dabydeen pointed out that only in William Hogarth's paintings in the eighteenth century is the black figure presented other than as a mere background figure. Generally they were portrayed as either serving or used as a literary device.[3] Brunias became possibly the first artist to paint the people he encountered in the West Indies *en plenair*. He had been recruited by Sir William Young, the newly appointed Governor of Dominica who was also an inveterate scholar and diarist. Brunias was brought to the West Indies in 1764 as Young's illustrator and remained in the islands until his death. However much these scenes were contrived by the artist and his patron as pro-slavery advocacy, Brunias's paintings are indisputably among the few visual insights into this period of historical transformation in the West Indies and provide layers of data that can be critically cross-examined. As the centuries roll by, it has become clearer to many that while "Brunias was originally commissioned to promote upper-class plantation life, his works soon assumed a more subversive, political role throughout the Caribbean as endorsements of a free, anti-slavery society, exposing the artificialities of racial hierarchies in the West Indies".[4]

A close encounter with Brunias's original paintings in an exhibition of works on loan to the Barbados museum in the 1990s piqued my interest in what they revealed about West Indian dress styles, body language, stances of individuals, the demarcation of status between the characters represented, and the way in which the paintings allowed me to imagine a sensibility of the region at this time. In the absence of other painterly works in a pre-photography era, these works have come to be viewed as archetypal of a Caribbean past. Brunias's paintings represent an iconic glimpse into Caribbean culture and gender relations in the eighteenth century, not unlike for instance the way in which Andy Warhol's repetitive Campbell's soup cans ushered in the era of pop art and underscored the advent of mass production and the consumer culture that surfaced in the 1960s in the United States.[5] I have used the selected painting on the cover as an allegory on how gender itself had to be made visible in the region. By extension, and similarly, other racial and ethnic groupings who were left out of the EuroAfrican script of the region also needed to be painted into the unfolding history. Like pictorial depictions of sex and sexuality, writing gender requires new lens, a decoding and reading between the lines of existing texts and images for what these have concealed or kept invisible. Looking back, I suspect my essay on the emergence of the mulatto woman as the desired in Chapter 3 "*But most of all mi love mi browning*" of this book was first envisaged through the recurrent signals in a number of Brunias's paintings, alongside historical documents that referred to sexual desire and conceptions of beauty in the region. Brunias consistently placed white, mixed race and black women in aesthetic counterpoint to each other on his canvases.[6] Masculinity is also a subject of much of his work and still remains an area to be treated with visual intelligence from a gender lens.

Many of the essays in this selection draw on paintings, myths, songs, photography, films, biographies, other historical works and personal testimonies. These are the texts that mould a foundational understanding of gender by which we might unburden Caribbean society of its colonial lens. Coming to grips with gender as a primary conceptual category that illuminates the past must help us to fashion ourselves a self-sufficient and brighter future.

The last two decades of the twentieth century marked a founding moment for gender scholarship in the Caribbean. The act of writing and publishing was as much a political strategy as it was a necessity. My earliest colleagues in this fellowship of the pen and keyboard all knew that we had to lay claim to our knowledge, to our women's and gendered histories, our culturally shaped gender tropes, to refine the literary canon, genderize (yes it is now a word) the classrooms and boardrooms, and excavate a parallel political economy of the region. Perhaps the closest affinities developed among those of us who headed the first Centres for Gender and Development Studies from 1993, a shared history that united us on many fronts, among many others I signal Eudine Barriteau, Elsa Leo Rhynie, Rhoda Reddock and Barbara Bailey.[7] Above all other objectives, we had to erect a foundational and conceptual scaffold that was apposite for a Caribbean centered conversation in the midst of a competitive global discourse that could otherwise subsume us as island girls inhabiting a minor demographic exception. In scribbling gender into different formats we had to reach the widest group of constituents whether they were students, gender scholars regionally and internationally, sceptical colleagues, feminist activists, government officials, media personnel or public consumers. Writing styles and rhetoric varied, forcing us to refine our gender arguments, expand our disciplinary range and sharpen our wits to suit the audience. While I have titled this book *Writing Gender into the Caribbean*, I certainly do not claim to be the only or even original scribe and pay homage to those who have also been very much part of this project alongside me.[8]

This year marks four decades and counting of my involvement in both activism and scholarship in feminism. Although gender as a concept was absent from our early schooling, I was reasonably perceptive about racial and national identities, a feature clearly evident in a short story that I wrote for the Naparima Girls' High School magazine in 1971 about the Black power riots in Trinidad in 1970. I had lived through and remembered our transition as a society from colonialism to independence and would later also write about this.[9] As an adolescent, I was very influenced by the music, photographic images and art of the sixties, and inspired by the heady sentiments of democracy and sexual freedoms presented in the "hippie" or flower power and anti-Vietnam movement. I came of age during the Allen Ginsberg era and was optimistic that non-violent advocacy, also previously prescribed by Mahatma Gandhi would shape a more positive global future. By the mid-seventies when I had completed an undergraduate degree, I had absorbed somewhere in the last decade, that feminism was glaringly absent in the isms - positivism, capitalism, Marxism, socialism we were taught. I related immediately to the messages sent in the first international women's day (1975) theme song belted out by Helen Reddy "*I am woman, hear me roar, In numbers too big to ignore, And I know too much to go back and pretend.*"[10] The idea of women's increasing visibility, voice and agency in shaping this new world would plant themselves firmly into my consciousness and I wanted to be among them.

The second wave feminist movement in the west had infected young women in countless nations with the possibilities of limitless futures and choices to have it all – career, marriage, children and recognition of our worth. By 1979 I was a member of a socialist feminist group while also beginning a University of the West Indies MSc Sociology thesis on understanding the rise of women in education in Trinidad.[11] Looking back on my academic journey as a "career feminist", the stereotyping and subtle diminishment of those of us who have devoted much of our scholarly life to the construction of gender knowledge has been challenging. Many of us strategically building the scholarship and curricula in gender and development studies opted to use gender as a more polite and persuasive descriptor of our multi-disciplinary undertaking rather than the more incendiary term feminism that lost our listeners before we uttered a sentence. Perhaps this is evident in both the language and tone of some of the papers included in this book.

What is now referred to in the popular western press as third wave and fourth wave feminism marches on.[12] This third wave is described as "me-ness", a prescription of a personal feminism that is self-serving, a movement characterized by greater solipsism than altruism. The fourth wave refocuses on women's empowerment globally through broad based activism that draws on the use of internet tools.[13] Each of these waves benefit from the experience of the previous ones whether this is acknowledged or not. The fallout of the consistent bad press that has dogged feminism through much of its history is a repudiation of gender and feminism which has percolated into the disciplines and classroom. Doctoral candidates in other disciplines systematically distance themselves from the term feminism and the theoretical constructs of this area of study, even while it is obvious that their topics of research or the problem they have set out to solve could only have been coined as a result of gender studies - a significant component of the feminist movement. There clearly have been gains in mainstreaming gender into academic, state and popular discourses. To deny this would be misleading. Over two decades ago Elsa Leo Rhynie's inaugural lecture as the first Professor in Women's Studies appointed at the University of the West Indies was hopeful about "moving from the periphery".[14] The passage of a gender policy for the regional University of the West Indies and a sexual harassment policy that is actively endorsed by the second decade of the twenty first century, along with several national gender policies rolled out by governments in the wider Caribbean region, markedly progressive gender legislation and the UN global insistence on gender parity are markers of real progress. As I write this introduction the messages that the COVID 19 pandemic has sent about the value of the caring and nurturing sector hopefully has erased more of this artificial separation between public and private spheres and has demonstrated instead the absolute interdependence of the two, imprinting the value of professions involved with caring, nursing and domestic labour.

COMPOSITIONS

"Writing has nothing to do with communication between person and person, only with communication between different parts of a person's mind" says Rebecca West. Writing has been my method of resolving issues and ideas and my primary form of expression. Following a genealogy of one's own writing and thought requires a certain fidelity to the state of mind when an essay was being composed. Accessing work from over three decades I recognize in my own thought an evolutionary approach to feminism and have attempted to retain the currency of academic concepts and ideas in the feminist struggle at the time of original writing. It is important to preserve the science of knowledge in any disciplinary area to be able to map how ideas change, thus allowing us to trace the etymology of concepts in the discipline. Resisting the urge to rewrite with contemporary consciousness and experience, each essay has nonetheless undergone some editing while retaining the original spirit of the piece. The twenty one essays selected include seven unpublished works drawn from conference presentations or keynote addresses. These have benefitted from being presented, from discussions or circulation as drafts for comments. In general within each of the five sections in the book, the papers follow a chronology of publication or presentation. I used the process of assemblage, juxtaposing theoretical ideas with empirical flows of data, to assess a possible legacy in thought that hopefully has contributed to our knowledge economy of gender in the Caribbean and elsewhere.

Each of the twenty-one papers distributed into five sections establishes some original thought or aproached its subject from an idiosyncratic stance. *Section 1*, 'Originary Narratives and a Political Grammar for Caribbean Feminism' disembeds ideas of race, class and colour that inform the language and politics of Caribbean gender relations and feminism, reminding us of the centrality of the region in the discovery of the new world. The section progresses from early concerns with Caribbean feminism to a consideration of current questions that the movement and concepts now raise globally. *Section 2* 'Indo-Caribbean Feminist Intersections' explores the creation of gender identities, gender performance and symbols among the Indo-Caribbean descended populations due to different cultural geographies and historical antecedents, arguing that this cross-cultural fertilization of experience enriches our understanding of Caribbean womanhood and manhood, and offers this expansion of ideas as fruitful for continued exploration of feminist strategies. In *Section 3* 'Inviting Masculinity' speaks to the ongoing dialogue with masculinity and men which Caribbean feminism engaged in from the outset of the second wave feminist moment and from the earliest stages in the development of gender studies. Two of the essays included in this section, 'Sketches in a Biography of Eric Williams', the first Prime Minister of Trinidad and Tobago and a comparative reading of the films *The Harder They Come and Brokeback Mountain* straddle disciplinary enquiry in order to allow a contemplation of the mind of the masculine rather than an attempt to prescribe masculinity.

In 'Drafting Gender Equality Frameworks' *Section 4* I include three unpublished pieces from among the range of other published and policy documents that constitute my extensive work in this area.[15] Two are empirically based contemplative pieces on how gender projects are underpinned by a shared philosophy of gender equality while the third provides practical tools gained from experience in order to assist others with the process of creating gender equity policies or programmes. In the final *Section 5* 'Gender and Cultural Storytelling' I extricate a gender perspective from various creative forms demonstrating that gender norms, practices, ideas, traditions and belief systems of societies, ethnic groups or individuals are manifested in the performance of culture and that gender identities are negotiated in and through culture.

I recognize that a running theme throughout my work is an appeal to the concept of negotiating change gradually, incrementally, but firmly. Gender beliefs and ideologies are always catching up with actual gender practices and expanding ideas about gender equality. As Tonya Haynes[16] summed up my theoretical contribution a few years ago more eloquently than I can, the papers in this book serve to "highlight both the fluidity and fixity of gender relations as well as the salience of gender in cultural self-definition". As I still continue to work in gender scholarship and feminist activism, I have come to believe that feminism needs more advancing and less reproach, more solidarities and less fragmentation, a point that might well apply to all profound social movements that sustain and do good work. I hope that this book leaves the reader with the view that feminists have already left the world a better place than we found it, for both sexes.

ENDNOTES

[1] Acquired by The Brooklyn Museum from the London Gallery Robilant + Voena
[2] Lydia Figes, Content Creator at Art UK https://www.artuk.org/discover/stories/agostino-brunias-and depicting-people-of-colour-in-the-colonial-caribbean
[3] See David Dabydeen, (1987) *Hogarth's Blacks: Images of Blacks in Eighteenth Century English Art*, Manchester University Press, England
[4] https://repeatingislands.com/2011/01/19/brooklyn-museum-acquires-18th-century-painting-of-dominica-by-agostino-brunias/
[5] https://www.moma.org/learn/moma_learning/andy-warhol-campbells-soup-cans-1962/
[6] See Patricia Mohammed, *Imaging the Caribbean: Culture and Visual Translation*, Macmillan, Oxford, 2009 and very important contributions by Lennox Honeychurch "Chatoyer's Artist: Agostino Brunias and the Depiction of St Vincent," *Journal of the Barbados Museum and Historical Society* 50, 2004, pp 104 - 128, "Agostino Brunias: Italian Artist in Dominica" *in Dominica's Arts & Culture Magazine*, Division of Culture, 1994
[7] A good analysis of the emergence of gender studies at the University of the West Indies can be found in Joycelin Massiah, Elsa Leo-Rhynie and Barbara Bailey (Eds), *The UWI Gender Journey: Recollections and Reflections*, The University of the West Indies Press, and the Institute of Gender and Development Studies, Jamaica, Barbados, Trinidad and Tobago, 2016
[8] The Women in the Caribbean Project 1979 to 1982 (ISER, Barbados) might be counted as one of the earliest organized attempts to do this. There are many more colleagues I would like to acknowledge but one will inevitably forget some and the list is extensive so I have chosen only to name those who came together as the first heads of the Trinidad, Barbados and two Jamaica units as we were all entrusted with the institutionalization of gender and development studies at The University of the West Indies.
[9] See "Midnight's Children and the Legacy of Nationalism in Trinidad" In *Callaloo: Eric Williams and the Post-Colonial Caribbean*, Volume 20, No 4, 1998 Sandra Pouchet-Pacquet (Guest Editor), Baltimore: John Hopkins University Press. pp. 737-752, also published in *Small Axe, A Journal of Criticism*, Number 2, September, Small Axe Collective, David Scott (Ed.), Ian Randle: Kingston, pp. 19-37, 1997
[10] https://www.youtube.com/watch?v=V6fHTyVmYp4
[11] MSc. Sociology Dissertation: '*Women and Education in Trinidad 1838-1980*' University of the West Indies, St. Augustine, 1987
[12] https://globalnews.ca/news/3292948/redefining-the-f-word-what-does-feminism-look-like-today/

[13] https://www.pacificu.edu/magazine/four-waves-feminism
[14] Elsa Leo Rhynie "Women and Development Studies: Moving from the Periphery" in *Gendered Realities: Essays in Caribbean Feminist Thought*, Patricia Mohammed (Ed) UWI Press, Kingston, Ch 8, pp 147-163
[15] See for example "Gender Equality and Gender Policy Making in the Caribbean" in *Public Administration and Policy in the Caribbean*, Indianna D. Minto-Coy and Evan Berman, (Eds) Taylor and Francis, 2015. . London and New York, Ch 18, pp 415-442
[16] Tonya Haynes, Introduction to Patricia Mohammed at the 21st Annual Public lecture, Caribbean Women Catalyst for Change, series of the Dame Nita Barrow Institute for Gender and Development Studies, University of the West Indies, Cave Hill, Barbados 2015

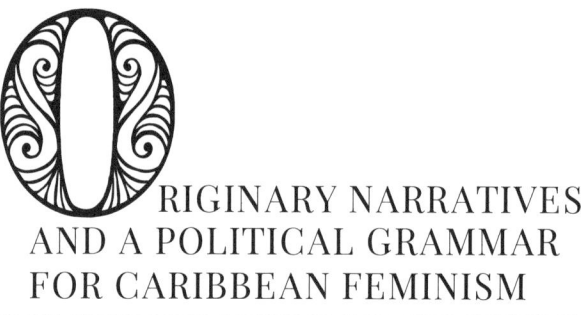RIGINARY NARRATIVES
AND A POLITICAL GRAMMAR
FOR CARIBBEAN FEMINISM

1
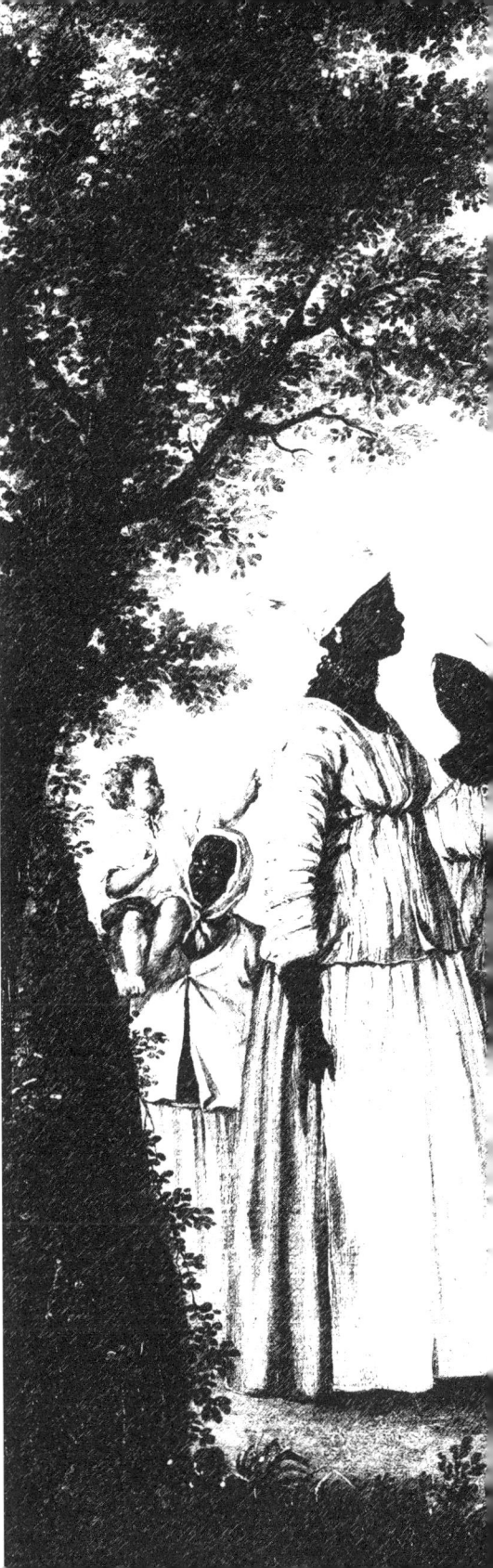

1

Nuancing the Feminist Discourse in the Caribbean†

INTRODUCTION

Feminism has increasingly entered the terminology of the twentieth century, yet there are many fears as to what it means for present and future relations between men and women. A large part of this fear stems from ignorance. What is popularly conceived of as feminism, and attributed to feminists, are the stereotypes of lesbianism, man-haters or women who are attempting to replace male power by female power. Despite the decades of serious feminist research and struggle, the myths and misgivings of feminism as a valid social movement still obtain. The first part of this paper addresses the wider goals of feminism and locates gender studies in the Caribbean within the global discourse of feminism. The essay argues, however, that despite the strides in feminist theory which feminist thought in the

---

† First published in *Social and Economic Studies,* 43 (3): 135-167 (1994).

Caribbean necessarily builds on, the challenge is still to nuance this discourse, to consider the subtle differences as it relates to the Caribbean region. We need for instance to understand the origins and manifestations of patriarchy in the Caribbean context and its interconnections with race and class. History is the best discipline through which patriarchy can be revealed in all its workings. The second part of the paper contributes to this understanding for Jamaican society by a rereading of an historical text, *Lady Nugent's Journal* of her residence in Jamaica from 1801 to 2805.

A MANDATE FOR GENDER STUDIES IN THE ACADEMY

The most significant if not the most meaningful stride in feminism in the twentieth century has been the formal entry of gender studies into the academy.[1] This has been contingent on another crucial development in feminism – the consolidation of a corpus of work which can be referred to as feminist theory. While some of the critical moments in the formulation of feminist theories have occurred away from the academy,[2] during the last three decades the sheer quantity of publications on women and gender, and the existence of innumerable scholars in departments in universities and research centres involved in women or gender studies, have created a body of work from which ongoing intellectual directions in feminism can be built.

Feminist thought has a tradition which now spans two centuries beginning with the writings of Mary Wollstonecraft in 1792 who argued for a vindication of women's rights. The origins of the word "feminist" can be traced back to French socialist Charles Fourier who, in the early nineteenth century, imagined a 'new woman' who would transform both herself and transform society and be driven by concerns for the collective well-being of a population rather than relying on a system based on competition and profits. His views influenced many women and combined self-emancipation and social emancipation. Changing oneself was part of changing the world."[3] The use of the term 'feminist' as a description of women active in the struggle for women's rights first appeared in English to describe women campaigning for the vote in 1890. By this time many organizations had begun to seek additional rights for women within an existing liberal framework which anticipated reform rather than revolution. It is interesting that contemporary applications of the term feminism have not moved radically away from Fourier's interpretation of the word. Feminism has retained the idea of transforming society, while focussing on the self-conscious emancipation of the agents of transformation – i.e. women themselves.

Feminism was originally coined to characterize women's struggles for rights and privileges which were perceived as somehow natural for men. But ongoing developments in the feminist movement have been rooted in the lived and social experiences of women, as were the theoretical ideas proposed for achieving equality. As it has developed from its early origins to contemporary times, feminism has followed the trajectory of theory and praxis, at times rubbing shoulders with other social movements which have also included men, and in the last few decades engaging in an uneasy alliance between academia and activism. This amalgam of theory and practice has given rise to different political perspectives in feminism and today feminism means different things to different people. Among the dominant political perspectives found in contemporary feminism are liberal, radical, socialist, black and post-modern feminism The origins of liberal feminist thought can be traced to the eighteenth century in the work of Mary Wollstonecraft, *A Vindication of the Rights of Women* (1792) and later in John Stuart Mill's famous essay "The Subjection of Women", (1869).

Liberal feminism argues that equality of opportunity for education and employment will end discrimination again women, its inherent assumptions ignoring the influence of class and racial discrimination. Radical feminists prefer to carve out a space for women's autonomy in society, emphasizing women's subordination to men as the key issue for social action. Socialist feminism sees female oppression as part of the matrix of other forms of subordination in society such as class and race inequality. They locate the fundamental cause of gender arrangements in the organization of production or the sexual division of labour. Thus they give primacy to the economic mode of production in both creating and perpetuating female subordination. None of these perspectives are mutually exclusive of the other, it is rather a question of different emphases derived from the ideological preferences (and usually lived experiences) of those who adhere to each school of thought. Black feminism arose in the context of other Third World' perspectives, and as a challenge to the universalism expressed by the dominant schools of thought attributed to white middle class women. Patricia Hill Collins writes that

> Theories advanced as being universally applicable to women as a group on closer examination appear greatly limited by the white, middle-class origins of their proponents. For example, Nancy Chodorow's (1974, 1978) work on sex role socialization and Carol Gilligan's (1982) study of the moral development of women both rely on white middle-class samples. While these two classics make key contributions to feminist theory, they simultaneously promote the notion of a generic woman who is white and middle class.[4]

Hill Collins stressed that while Black female intellectuals had long expressed "a unique feminist consciousness about the intersection of race and class in structuring gender", they were historically excluded from full participation in white feminist organizations.[5] What differentiates a Black feminist perspective is its reluctance to separate female oppression from the matrix of race and class oppression. Thus Hill Collins summarises the definition of Black feminism as "a process of self-conscious struggle that empowers women and men to actualise a humanist vision of community." In the latter respect and in its interconnections with race and class struggles, Black feminist thought provides a crucial point of departure for the development of Caribbean feminist theory. In my view, however, Caribbean feminism has to guard against the literal transfer of Black feminism onto Caribbean soil. Despite the parallel experience of slavery, subsequent historical developments in the Caribbean have made for differences in gender, class and race relations and statuses in the Caribbean from that of black men and women in the United States where black feminist thought largely originates.

Post-modern feminism derives its impetus from post-modern philosophy which provides a critique of the dominant paradigms established by the Enlightenment perspective. The post-modern discourses are all reconstructive in that they seek to distance us from and make us sceptical about beliefs concerning truth, knowledge, power, the self, and language that are often taken for granted within and serve as legitimation for contemporary Western culture.[6] Nonetheless feminism's engagement with postmodern philosophy is described by Rosemary Tong as an uneasy one. She suggests 'Postmodern feminists worry that because feminism purports to be an explanatory theory, it too is in danger of trying to provide the explanation for why woman is oppressed."[7] To guard against universal explanations which earlier feminist perspectives proffered, post modernism allows for plurality, multiplicity and difference. In fact, the articulation of a Black feminist perspective and the increasing development of indigenous feminisms have already challenged the universal claim of previous feminist theorizing.

Nonetheless, it seems to me that the development of feminist thought thus far has given rise to several questions which all theorists respond to from various angles. The earlier search for the origins of patriarchy - the overarching dominance of the male in society - has made way for an ongoing study of the reasons for the perpetuation of patriarchal ideology and practices in most cultures. Feminists are also concerned with the persistence of a sexual division of labour which relegates women to labour in the private and generally lower-valued spheres. Finally, feminism still adheres to a notion that in most societies and known cultures, woman retains the status of the "Other", the subordinate sex, a universalism that has not been shifted by the weight of feminist theorising, even if differences among women themselves by class and race have been cited in numerous empirical studies. In its substantive theoretical discourse however, as Jane Flax has observed 'The single most important advance in feminist theory is that the existence of gender relations has been problematized."[8] For those located in a radical feminist mode this has not represented an advance. For radical feminists the study of gender [9] – as a study of relations between men and women – de-emphasizes the earlier concentration on women, and ignores a fundamental point, that these relations are still hierarchical.

The question is, where does this place feminists in the academy in the Caribbean? The various political perspectives have all been reflected in the feminist agenda in the region. The activist movement has engaged in the liberal struggle to remove gender discrimination in education and to assert the rights of women in the laws, as for example those pertaining to inheritance, sexual violence and the family. Various women's groups which emerged in different territories, among them the Concerned Women for Progress in Trinidad (1979) and the Committee of Women for Progress in Jamaica in the early eighties, were integrally linked to socialist movements in both these countries. During the past two decades there has been a concerted effort by female and male scholars in the region to introduce programmes of research and teaching on women's studies at the University of the West Indies, a project which has resulted in the official establishment of a Centre for Gender and Development Studies at the University.[10] For activists engaged full time in the struggle to end discrimination in many spheres, the development of women's studies and its offspring, gender studies, is often seen as antithetical to the goals of feminism. The academy is viewed as another patriarchal institution in which women are expected to assume the subordinate position that such a hierarchy dictates. Some feminists have argued, however, that the objective of entering the halls of the academy is to create change by becoming part of the institution and posing challenges from within. This division between activism and the academy is at best a spurious one as the development of women's studies/gender studies provides an institutional memory for the feminist movement. In my view, the academy has a continuous and responsible mandate, that of giving theoretical guidance to and providing analytical perspectives on feminisms and the feminist movement.

This brings us to the second and related mandate posed by the development of feminist thought in the academy in the English-speaking Caribbean. What are the links between the feminist movement and the other social movements in the Caribbean and how can these be theoretically fused? This question arises from two fundamental concerns. First, if feminist theorising retains the "otherness" which has thus far characterised its trajectory, it runs the risk of continuously being marginalized, intended as a self-serving purpose - guarding a space for privileged women, or recreating another hierarchy in society. Second, I have come to believe that the further development of feminist theory in the Caribbean depends on locating our theorizing in a wider philosophical context. Despite its apparent focus, in practice, women's actions and concerns have been against interconnecting relations of inequality by class and race and not simply about gender. The poverty of theory, and limited gains of other social movements in the twentieth century in the Caribbean in addressing these other forms of inequality, forces the feminist agenda to apply itself seriously to other inequities. The degree to which feminist theory can both challenge as well as contribute to mainstream academia, and thereby to an understanding of societal problems, relies on the extent to which gender is understood as another conceptual tool that will allow for more robust social analysis of conditions faced in human society.

Eudine Barriteau began this task in her constrution of a postmodern feminist theory for Caribbean social science research in order to contribute to indigenous feminist theory building in the region. She argues that socialist feminist theorizing represents both theoretical and empirical contradictions of Caribbean realities while the "liberal feminist discourse can no more guarantee Caribbean women their equality than it can for their European and North American counterparts."[11] Barriteau suggests that while the multidisciplinary approach utilized by the Women and the Caribbean Project of the Institute of Social and Economic Research from 1979 to 1982 provided a valuable source of documentation and information on Caribbean women, it did not offer a theoretical frame work for analyzing Caribbean women's position from a feminist perspective. She acknowledges the contributions of empirical research thus far in identifying that Caribbean men and women are equally constructed as gendered beings, both sexes attempting "to work around this pervasive construct". She posits a framework for reconceptualizing gender, which requires investigating how historical, cultural, and social and economic issues impact differently on women and men. But she suggests that "It eschews using the same conceptual frames for women that are used for men. It sometimes requires a simultaneous focus on understanding what is happening to both women and men towards understanding what is happening with women, but it always maintains gender-specific distinctions."[12] Barriteau proposes the contours of this theorizing by operationalizing gender, race, class, sexual identity and political action within the Caribbean context, emphasizing that "all past generalizations of Caribbean women are 'subject to scrutiny and change'" to meet the requirements of this new construct. Simultaneously, my own work drew on both history and anthropology using the study of one ethnic group to unwrap the concept of gender to see how it works as an organizing principle under any historical period.

By examining the gender arrangements that would emerge with challenges to the original blueprint from which it derived in post-migrant Indian populations in Trinidad, I demonstrated the mechanics by which gender was constantly being negotiated at different levels, between the state and its citizens, among different gender systems in a society and within an ethnic group itself.

The Caribbean region is vested with a great deal of diversity. Class, race, ethnicity and gender are interlocked differently in each island or territory and as a result have given rise to different emphases in political and social struggles in each island or territory. For instance, in Trinidad and Guyana, the configuration of ethnic and political conflict differs considerably from that in Jamaica. Similarly, the different cultural composition of populations have made for differing gender arrangements. The discourse of post-modern feminism allows for investigating these differences through the construction of cogent indigenous feminist theories.

There are numerous ways of constructing social theory. The discourse of history provides one crucial entry point as the exploration of history provides an analytical base from which we can understand how race, class and gender divisions and relations are continuously being constructed and perpetuated. A feminist focus allows us to place gender theory and women at a central point of this inquiry, and at the same time making visible those interconnections of class and race that are affected by gender considerations. Feminist historian and theoretician Joan Scott describes these ideas most succinctly:

> We need a theory that can analyse the workings of patriarchy in all its manifestations – ideological, institutional, organizational, subjective — accounting not only for continuities but also for change over time. We need a theory that will let us think in terms of pluralities and diversities rather than of unities and universals. We need theory that will break the conceptual hold, at least of those long traditions of (Western) philosophy that have systematically and repeatedly construed the world hierarchically in terms of masculine universals and feminine specificities. We need theory that will enable us to articulate

alternative ways of thinking about (and thus acting upon) gender without either simply reversing the old hierarchies or confirming them and we need theory that will be useful and relevant for political practice.[13]

The term gender is often confusing but a useful definition of gender has evolved in feminist thinking. Gender is the social organization of sexual difference. The study of gender attempts to understand how the knowledge of sexual difference has been appropriated throughout centuries of human thought and development to render women in a status subordinate to that of men. In essence, the goal of gender studies has been to understand the origin and maintenance of patriarchy as ideology, and the patriarchal structures which support male domination. The term patriarchy, which is widely used to refer to male dominance, must also be viewed not only as the dominance of males in society, but the persistence of an ideology of male super-ordination which both men and women maintain consciously and unconsciously. To assume that feminist efforts are only directed at challenging patriarchy however, simplifies the wider goal of feminism – that is to redefine the parameters of maleness and femaleness so that some notion of sexual equality is achieved. This demands that we focus on patriarchy not as a fixed unchangeable entity found across time, space, class, ethnic group and generation, but as a moving, variable thing, open to contestation. We must be able to view patriarchy as ideas of superiority which function to control groups and classes in society, and that both men and women are victims of the dominant patriarchal contract. Only if patriarchal structures can be tampered with and the ideology shifted over time can the feminist movement continue to have validity, for there is no virtue in replicating the burden of Sisyphus. To understand gender as the ongoing construction of masculinity and femininity in which the boundaries of maleness and femaleness are not fixed and keep shifting overtime and are open to re-negotiations, appears to me to be a more optimistic, as well as analytically fruitful way to investigate gender in society.

The fertility of gender studies as it has evolved in the Caribbean lies in its inability to separate itself from other oppressive features endemic in society, that of discrimination created by class and race or ethnic differences. The systemic oppression of women and men has continuously varied by their class or ethnic affiliation and it makes little sense to understand the complexity of gender without this intersection of class and race. We can, through historical analysis, observe the workings of patriarchy in the class, race and gender relations which, rooted in the colonial legacy, still inform the present.[14] In this essay, I am attempting to develop an understanding of Jamaican society from a perspective which infuses gender as an integral part of how class and racial struggles are continuously being waged. Elizabeth Fox-Genovese further delineates this task of feminist history in her observation that such a history "must disclose and reconstruct consciousness and action, with conditions understood as systems of social relations, including relations between women and men, between rich and poor, between the powerful and the powerless; among those of different faiths, different races, and different classes."[15]

The data that gives insight into gender are both obvious and nebulous. The obvious sites have been those associated with women's domestic and reproductive roles and male and female sexuality. These remain the crucial areas from which a gender rereading can establish its point of departure as the sites for power and struggle in gender relations are generally located in the sphere of sexuality and reproduction. One has to also prise gendered data from unlikely sources as for instance diaries and letters written simply as records of daily life.[16] It is important to view history from a gender perspective not as a reconstruction of earth-shaking political movements or contributions of major historical characters, but as it allows one to see the evolution of relationships between peoples in a society who are, through the accidents of history, placed in positions of conflict, authority or subservience to each other. While gender is made a category for social analysis, it is not simultaneously invested with the burden of causality in history. Nor, in this approach, is it restricted to the study of one sex in isolation from the other.

ENTER LADY NUGENT

In this paper I begin to develop the lines of analysis for Jamaican society by a rereading of one historical text from a gender perspective. The text I have chosen is Lady Nugent's Journal of her residence in Jamaica from 1801 to 1805. The choice is deliberate in that I wanted to begin rereading Jamaican history with a gender lens, and this diary presented immediately accessible material, providing the insights into gender relations which other mainstream historical documents have rarely recorded.

Lady Maria Nugent's journal describes life in the household of the Governor of Jamaica, General George Nugent, during a four-year period of her residence in this country. The introduction to the published diary notes that "As the Governor's wife, the writer found herself at the centre of a slave-owning society, with a part to play there and no mere onlooker, yet observing its manners with the curiosity of a stranger. She met every one of importance in the colony..." Her accounts of domesticity in the household of the Governor as well as her commentary on the life and times of planters, slaves and free men and women are valuable insights into the structure of class, race and gender relations as they were already entrenched in Jamaican society from this time.

The population of Jamaica during Mrs. Nugent's residence in this island was comprised of three classes of persons, each with a distinct legal status. These were slaves, whites and "free coloured." The editor of Mrs. Nugent's journal writes that "Their numbers cannot be known for certain; contemporary guesses tended to approximate to some such figure as: 300,000 slaves, 20,000 to 30,000 whites, and perhaps twice that number of free coloured. The free coloured were the second class citizens with limited civil rights". There were already instruments built into the system in order to put an individual coloured person on the same legal footing as the child of English parents. For this a special Act of the Assembly was required; "most of the persons benefiting from such Acts were the natural children of well-to-do white men, like the group of coloured ladies whom Mrs. Nugent meets on her tour ("they are all daughters of Members of Assembly, Officers, &c. &c.). Coloured people were barred from government office and the professions" (p.xxix). Her life as Governor's wife required that she mixed socially with the white upper class and professionals, and with the Creole population of importance in the island. She displays an inordinate interest in the domestic lives of her servants as well as a real curiosity about slave and coloured society throughout Jamaica. She was also placed in a key position to satisfy this interest on her innumerable visits to various planters' houses where she and her husband enjoyed regal hospitality. Unlike others within the society, this gave her a bird's eye view of class, race and gender relations as they were being conducted on different terrain. Her own personality is of importance here in that she was an ambitious woman, not primarily on her behalf, but saw her interactions with the society as a valuable corollary to her husband's work. In addition, her concerns with Christian morality stem from her lifelong preoccupations with religious principles that extended beyond Jamaica. The editor of her journal introduces in this publication the words carved on the memorial tablet where she is buried in Little Marlow, England: "...in deepest affliction for the loss of one whose strictly religious principles, angelic temper and endearing qualities rendered her sincerely and universally beloved. She will long be mourned by the poor of the parish of whom she was for many years the devoted benefactress and friend (p.xiv).

Very early after her entry in this society Lady Nugent had already made the connections between class, colour and race. She comments on visits to Mr. Simon Taylor's house in Liguanea, on 5th March, 1802: "When I left the gentlemen, I took tea in my own room, surrounded by the black, brown and yellow ladies of the house, and heard a great deal of its private history" (p. 65). It was her access to a private history which she consistently chronicles that provides the historian with the most valuable material from which gender relations can be examined.[17]

Lady Nugent's comments on matters of state are less insightful than those pertaining to the intrigues of personal relationships. From her records we note that there was a clear sexual division of labour among the men and women in the class from which she emerged, a separation of the public and private spheres of life. As wife of the Governor she was expected to service the household, familial and entertainment needs required of this position. From the pen of this writer, drawn from the white elite, and informed by the patriarchal ideology of her class, these daily and seemingly mundane events, take on new meanings from a gender perspective.

A VIEW FROM THE TOP: EXPATRIATE WHITE SOCIETY

It must be recalled that constant problems of health threatened the lives of the population at the time, one of the worst being the high incidence of yellow fever. Mrs. Nugent is in perpetual fear for the lives of herself and her family and the people around her. There are very frequent references to deaths and they happen with such suddenness which perhaps accounts for the lack of morality she finds among the European population. A diary entry 17th September, 1802 notes "Am much shocked to hear of Captain Bartlett's being seized with the yellow fever. He only left us at 8 o'clock last night, in perfect health, and now they say that his life is almost despaired of. By 20th September she notes that "poor Captain Bartlett was given over" (p. 119). Another diary entry, 20th November 1802 states

> "Was told two melancholy circumstances. My poor little Cupid's mother (Venus) died at the King's House, on Thursday. They had kept her illness from me out of kindness, but everything had been done for her comfort, &c. I am assured. The other is the death of poor Mr. Blakeney, of the 85th. The chief cause of his death was the distress of his mind (poor fellow) for the loss of his brother officers. ...It is remarkable that poor Mr. Blakeney had scarcely any fever, and his death was almost sudden (p. 130).

The mortality rate of the white population instilled a sufficient amount of despair among those who either attempted to make their fortunes or serve His Majesty in the Colony. Perhaps this explained, in part, their frantic desire to enjoy the fruits of their labour, for it could prove to be a very limited period of enjoyment. She remarks on this on many occasions as for instance the following:

> It is indeed melancholy, to see the general disregard of both religion and morality, throughout the whole island. Everyone seems solicitous to make money, and no one appears to regard the mode of acquiring it. It is extraordinary to witness the immediate effect that the climate and habit of living in this country has upon

the minds and manners of Europeans, particularly of the lower orders. In the upper ranks, they become indolent and inactive, regardless of everything but eating, drinking, and indulging themselves, and are almost entirely under the dominion of their mulatto favourites. In the lower orders, they are the same, with the addition of conceit and tyranny; considering the negroes as creatures formed merely to administer to their ease, and to be subject to their caprice; and I have found much difficulty to persuade those great people and superior beings, our white domestics, that blacks are human beings, or have souls (p. 98).

The white population lived in constant fear of rebellion. The power of this class clearly had to be consistently maintained both by physical force and the ideology of the superiority of their race. Mrs. Nugent writes on 22nd November, 1801:

Very much shocked in the evening, by a sad account of the massacre of three hundred and seventy white persons in St. Domingo. How dreadful and what an example to the island. In the evening, many unpleasant and alarming reports, respecting the French prisoners on parole and the negroes of this town. One of the black men, a Dutch negro, had absented himself from prayers, and it was observed, by one of the staff, that he was seen making signs to one of the sentries, from a window. ...I cannot describe the anxiety I suffered, nor the thousand horrid ideas that pressed upon my mind; and, especially as there has appeared of late a general apprehension throughout the country, and various reports have been made, within the last few weeks, of the alarming state of the negro population, &c. Before we went to bed, General N. secured his own arms (p. 187).

On April 1st 1805, the year she and General Nugent left the island, she still lives with this fear:

Dear Clifford[18] returned here yesterday and she is so courageous that she is a great comfort to me; but

> she tells me that, before she left Spanish Town, the negroes appeared to be inclined to riot, and to make a noise in the streets, when the troops marched out, but they were soon dispersed by the militia. The black servants here seem to rejoice at the bustle, but, as they profess to hate the French, their pleasure is only that of change; for, like children, they are fond of fuss and noise, and have no reflection (p. 226).

> 4th March 1804 ...People here are so very imprudent in their conversation. The splendour of the black chiefs of St. Domingo, their superior strength, their firmness of character, and their living so much longer in these climates, and enjoying so much better health, are the common topics at dinner; and the blackies in attendance seem so much interested, that they hardly change a plate, or do anything but listen. How very imprudent and what it must all lead to! (p. 198).

Despite their will to rebel and their obvious capacity to organize rebellion as displayed by the Maroon rebellion which predates this period, the constitution of the black character was implanted as irresponsible and childlike. She nonetheless supported the sentiments of the nineteenth century humanitarians, that although childlike and like children, black people possessed souls and deserved to be humanely treated and not brutalized as she observed in the following instances.

> The Vicomte de Noailles' conversation was chiefly on the subject of St. Domingo ...He told General N. the French plan was, to put to death every negro who had borne arms, and to hamstring the others! General N. then asked him, what would the colony be worth in that case; but that he was not prepared for an answer. In short, it appears, that, though the French may have had a great deal of monkey in their composition and character formerly, they have now more than a double proportion of the tiger. For never were there such a set of cruel heartless wretches, and I rejoiced to see them depart at eight (p. 138).

Or the following diary entry:

> 10th January, 1802 – In the morning a carpenter, from Spanish Town applied to General N. to respite a slave, sentenced to be hanged to-morrow. The law of the land is, it seems, that three magistrates may condemn a slave to death. This case was, that two slaves, one, an old offender, the other, a boy of sixteen, robbed a man of his watch, &c. The old man shewed the boy how to get in at the window, and gave him all his instructions, while he remained on the outside, and received the things stolen. The old man has been condemned to hard labour, and the boy to be hanged. General N. made every exertion, but in vain, to save the life of the boy, and sent him out of the country; but it appears that it could not be done, without exercising his prerogative very far, and giving great offence and alarm to the white population. This law of three magistrates appears to me abominable, but I am too little versed in such matters to do more than feel for the poor sufferer (p. 51).

Despite the censure she obviously experienced, she adhered to both her Christian ethics and to a sense of the duties of her class position as this would be displayed if they were resident in England. For instance, on several occasions she clearly offended the sensibilities of the white population of Jamaica. "21st May, 1804 - Saw a number of black and brown ladies in the evening to please the old housekeeper; but I don't know whether the white ladies, whom I left in the drawing room when I gave audience, quite approved of my conduct" (p. 203). White women of the elite in Jamaica were also keepers of this class position and in many instances the patriarchal practices which it sustained.

THOSE WHO LABOUR

Maria Nugent held one of the highest status positions in the land. Her personal convictions of Christianity also give her the liberal and humane ideas which emerges when she considers the situation of the slave and black population. It was clearly one of *noblesse oblige* and the patronage expected of those of her class. On a visit to Merton and met by Mr. Milner the agent of absentee owner Mr. Bryan who lived in England, she remarks on this visit:

> I walked about the lawn, and talked to the negro children who were weeding, superintended by an old woman. I gave them a little money, and this brought almost all the negroes of the estate about us; but I found that the works were stopped and the negroes had been given a holiday in consequence of our arrival. Poor creatures they seemed much pleased and talked a great deal, but I could scarcely understand a word they said. On 12th October, 1803 she records in her journal "This day, my dearest little George is one year complete. ...Before we took our coffee, we went to see the blackies enjoying themselves, who had also a grant entertainment. After which they drank young Massa, with a sort of shout, that was more like an Indian war-whoop than anything else. Then came the young Missis, with the same vociferation, Old Massa and Old Missis came next; in short they were very merry (p. 178).

Notions of superiority and inferiority were supported by ideas of mental superiority and by the irresponsibility of this group whom she continuously likens to children. For instance, she writes on 26th December, 1803:

> The general negro masquerade began at daylight, and nothing could exceed the noise and bustle of the day. Little G. was delighted with Johnny Canoe, and with throwing money for the blackies to scramble for. ...Scolded General N. for being as silly as his little boy, in throwing money for the blackies to scramble for, as really some of them had all their finery torn to pieces in the struggle, and very narrowly escaped in whole skins (p. 188).

The condition of slavery clearly perturbed her, even if from the elevated position from which she could view it, and her journal records persistently reflect the indignities of slavery and her efforts to ameliorate the conditions which slaves experienced. She notes on 6th August, 1801 "Reflect all night upon slavery, and make up my mind that the want of exertion in the blackies must proceed from that cause. Assemble them together after breakfast, and talk to them a great deal, promising every kindness and indulgence. We parted excellent friends, and I think they have been rather more active in cleaning the house ever since" (p. 14). She is convinced, there being an accepted division of society into superior whites and inferior blacks, that the Negro population had themselves accepted the natural order of things. "Amused myself with reading the Evidence before the House of Commons, on the part of the petitioners for the Abolition of the Slave Trade. As far as I at present see and can hear of the ill-treatment of the slaves, I think what they say upon the subject is very greatly exaggerated. Individuals, I make no doubt, occasionally abuse the power they possess; but generally speaking, I believe slaves are extremely well used" (p. 86). On April 7th, 1803 she notes "After dinner explore the negro houses. Most of them neat, and very comfortable, with poultry &c. &c. about them." On 4th February, 1802 she describes a visit to Bushy Park Estate, owned by Mr. Mitchell as follows: "His house is truly Creole. The wood-work mahogany galleries, piazzas, porticoes, &c. In front a cane-piece, and sugar works, with plenty of cocoa-nut trees and tamarind trees, &c. He seems particularly indulgent to his negroes, and is I believe, although a very vulgar, yet a very humane man" (p. 56). She supports this rosy view with another journal entry of 22nd February, 1804:

> Notes on returning home from our drive this morning, we met a gang of Eboe negroes, just landed, and marching up the country. I ordered the postillions to stop, that I might examine their countenances as they passed, and see if they looked unhappy; but they appeared perfectly the reverse. I bowed, kissed my hand, and laughed; they did the same. The women, in particular, seemed pleased, and all admired the carriage, &c. ...They were all dressed in in new clothes, and the women had tied their coloured petticoats round their waists as aprons, and the rest had very little covering (p. 220).

What concerned her more than the actual physical or mental conditions of slavery was the moral turpitude of the slave population and during her entire stay on the island she makes a consistent attempt to correct this. Shortly after taking up residence in Kings House, 25 of her black domestics were converted to Christianity. If we calculate that in 1803 there were 33 servants at King's House, then clearly in her first few months of residence she assumed she had successfully converted almost her entire staff at the time. She diligently records, throughout her journal, her joy at the conversion or Christian behaviour of the slave population, or as she refers to them at different times – blackies, darkies or negroes. "Delighted to see black servants look so well, so orderly and behave so properly during the church service" (p. 39). It must be noted that she spent a considerable amount of time and effort in this vocation. In 1801 she remarks "I will begin the new year at the Perm, by instructing the poor negroes, and if I do but succeed in making them the better understand their duties as Christians, I shall be happy indeed!" (p. 49).

Nonetheless, it is certain that Mrs. Nugent never accepted or even understood this sentiment at the level of equality, reflecting at all times the shared sentiments of those of her class. Thus her descriptions of the slave population are always shaped by her perception of their diminished difference. They were human souls to be reclaimed for God, (according to Christian belief Christ died to save us all) but still belonging to some lower realm of existence which placed them both physically and intellectually as inferior to those of her race. She writes for instance:

> The few moments of fresh air between the dinner and the ball-rooms were a real treat; but when we arrived at the latter, the crowd was so great, that the heat if possible surpassed the former. However, the smell of the blackies and of the hot meats was absent, and that was some comfort. But never shall I forget the combination of a crown of Creoles, and a mob of blackies, with turtle soup, pepper-pot, and callipash and callipee at Mr. Mowat's as long as I live in this world (p. 90).

Her description of the appearance of the slave population inscribes in the history of race the imbedded notions of beauty as determined from a white and European perspective:

> December 1st, 1801: One of the black women produced two boys this morning. Went to see them, and they were exactly like two little monkeys (p. 42). 13th August 1804: I must now describe his little savage Majesty (The King of the Musquito Indians and his uncle) – he is about six or eight years old, a plain puny looking little child, but seems to have a very high and determined spirit. His features are rather better than those of negro, and his hair is so much straighter, that he is evidently of a mixed breed; but his uncle has the woolly hair of the negro, with flat features, and a very wide mouth. – It is said that many years ago, a large slave ship, from Africa, was wrecked on the Musquito shore, and no doubt this may account for the hair and features of the uncle, and for the mixture of the breed (p. 211).

The fear of the white and creole population that self-sufficiency could lead to rebellion was interconnected with the idea that the slaves were easily given to celebration and "slackness". Thus for instance she is perturbed in her entry on 6th March, 1802 when in her carriage she passes "innumerable parties of negroes, laughing, dancing, and singing, and dressing their food on the roadside, and all hurrying to get to Kingston; for alas! Sunday is the great market day. It is a sad custom, but I fear difficult to reform or alter in any way" (p. 65).

Not only were there differences in their moral conditioning, but physically, slave women were viewed as being able to endure much more pain than white or creole women in the labour of childbearing. Race and class differences had bred another "natural order". White and upper class women were viewed as more weakly, thus strangely attaining a superiority over black women who could not afford the luxury of pain. This sentiment is succinctly brought out in her journal entry of 10th March, 1802 when she makes a visit to Mr. Simon Taylor's estate at Golden Grove.

According to the usual custom, when I went to my bed room, I was surrounded by all the mulatto ladies the neighbourhood afforded. One little black girl came to beg that I would take her with me. She was a remarkably thick-lipped and ugly, but intelligent child. She could say the Lord's Prayer perfectly, but she could not say how she had learnt it. Both her father and mother field negroes, could not say prayers ...This led her to talk of field negroes, "with my friend Nelly Nugent who told me that Saturday and Sunday were allowed them to work in their own gardens, and to raise provisions for themselves. The smallest children are employed in the field, weeding and picking the canes, for which purpose they are taken from their mothers at a very early age. Women with child work in the field till the last six weeks, and are at work there again in a fortnight after their confinement. Three weeks in very particular cases are allowed but this is the very longest time since. Nelly Nugent remarked, however, that it was astonishing how fast these black women bred, what healthy children they had, and how soon they recovered after lying in. She said it was totally different to mulatto women, who were constantly liable to miscarry, and subject to a thousand little complaints, cold, coughs &c. Indeed I have heard medical men make the same observation (p. 69).

The construction of femininity of the different races was gradually being entrenched in social perception and in historical records and used as the basis for racial stereotyping rather than the ideas culled from class prejudices.

CREOLE SOCIETY

If foreign born whites fitted snugly into the top rungs of the social ladder[19] and slaves were to be found at the bottom, then creole society was demarcated a position secondary to those foreign born. Lady Nugent again reflects the attitudes of the upper class to this group who from this time were engaged in forging an identity based on a clearly recognised separation from the coloured and black working population. A footnote to the term 'creole' by the editor of the journal notes that it refers to a white West Indian; properly speaking a person born in the West Indies of white parents. Being born in the Colony rather than in the metropole already determined class status, despite the colour of one's skin. But more than this, it appears that birth and residence in the Colony was clearly detrimental to character building as for instance seen in the following entry. 15th January, 1802:

> Write, &c. till breakfast; then Major and Mrs. Cookson, their two daughters, and a little boy, a black maid, and two men on a West India visit, to spend the day. Mrs. C. is a perfect Creole, says little, and drawls out that little, and has not an idea beyond her own Penn. (Major Cookson was one of those Royal Artillery officers whom Nugent described as useless, chiefly as a result of their long residence in the country, and the connections they have formed) (p. 52).

Philip Curtin also supports this shift in the character of those who had lived long in the colony which was described as becoming creolized. He writes "During the eighteenth century, the creole whites had built up a body of social habits and customs that had come to be quite different from the nineteenth century standards in Britain. While only about three white Jamaicans in every five had been born on the island, a higher proportion were creole in outlook, having been "creolized" by their years of living in Jamaica" (p. 51). The derivation and connotations attached to the term creole which have all become part of the discourse and struggle of creole society are reflected variously in the entries which Maria Nugent again makes on her interaction with members of this class. In them we find her constantly amused and sometimes distraught at their behaviour, which she clearly saw as distinctly removed from her own. She is aware of the 'creolized' population's wish to establish a distance from the blacks and coloured, but sees them at the same time as exhibiting some of the habits of the lower class.

> 20th March, 1802: Visit to Mr. Sheriff's coffee estate. "We found Mrs. Sheriff, her mother Mrs. Strachan, and a Miss Cumming, dressed ready to receive us, all

in their best. Mrs. S. is a fat, good-humoured Creole woman, saying dis, dat, and toder; her mother a vulgar old Scotch dame; and Miss C. a clumsy awkward girl (p. 76). The Creole language is not confined to the negroes. Many of the ladies, who have not been educated in England, speak a sort of broken English, with an indolent drawling out of their words, that is very tiresome if not disgusting. I stood next to a lady one night, near a window, and by way of saying something, remarked that the air was much cooler than usual; to which she answered, "Yes ma-am, him rail-ly too fra-ish. (p. 98)

June 2nd, 1803: The Misses Murphy were afraid of the damp air. Mr. Clement, from America, Mrs. Dolmage, and Mrs. Ramsay, dined with us. A great deal of Creole conversation, and many prejudices that amused me, but I cannot enter into them (p. 160).

The word creole was already being used as a pejorative adjective when applied to the local born whites and had also entered daily speech as a verb. A footnote in the Journal notes: "Creolizing is an easy and elegant mode of lounging in a warm climate; so called, because much in fashion among the ladies of the West Indies: that is, reclining back in one arm chair, with their feet upon another, and sometimes upon the table". (John McLeod, Narrative of a voyage in his Majesty's late ship Alceste, to the Yellow Sea, 1817) (p. 117) and Lady Nugent herself remarks on 13th September 1804 that "Refreshments were ready, and then we all creolized till 5 o'clock" (p. 213). But the *noblesse oblige* of those of her class seemed to have been misplaced by those who were born in the Colony and she is frequently appalled at the prejudices and attitudes of the creoles, especially the creole women, towards the black population. On 27th March, 1802, in a visit to Sevilla she has cause to remark on the attitudes of the coloured to their own servants: "This is really a most uncomfortable house; the servants awkward and dirty, the children spoiled, and screaming the whole day. As for the ladies, they appear to me perfect viragos; they never speak but in the most imperious manner to their servants, and are constantly finding fault" (p. 80). On 26th May, 1803 she writes:

As soon as that ceremony was over, I began the ball with an old negro man. The gentlemen each selected a partner, according to rank, by age or service, and we all danced. However, I was not aware how much I shocked the Misses Murphy by doing this; for I did exactly the same as I would have done at a servant's hall birthday in England. They told me afterwards, that they were nearly fainting, and could hardly forbear shedding a flood of tears, at such an unusual and extraordinary sight; for in this country, and among slaves, it was necessary to keep up so much more distant respect! They may be right. I meant nothing wrong, and all the poor creatures seemed so delighted, and so much pleased, that I could scarcely repent it. I was nevertheless, very sorry to have hurt their feelings, and particularly too as they seemed to think the example dangerous; as making the blacks of too much consequence, or putting them at all on a footing with the whites, they said, might make a serious change in their conduct, and even produce a rebellion in the island. There was an unspoken agreement of the measures which had to be installed to ensure that each group could be differentiated from the other, and class positions rigidly maintained.

Mrs. Nugent is nonetheless a product of class society and sees the prospect of the mixing of bloods and the formation of a group of coloureds as having unfortunate consequences for the society. She remarks on 28th October, 1804 "In my drive this morning, met several of the unfortunate half-black progeny of some of our staff; all in fine muslin, lace, &c. with wreaths of flowers in their hats. What ruin for these worse than thoughtless young men! But advice is of no use, and they must stand the consequences; yet I cannot help pitying their families, and it makes me truly melancholy to think of their future distress" (p. 214). Bridget Brereton remarks in her reading of this text that Lady Nugent herself "spared few thoughts for the young men's willing or coerced prey". There is, as in all of these interpretations, the consistent superimposition of the binary opposition of Western philosophical thought. The leading class or term is accorded primacy, whiteness being superior to blackness meant that white was despoiled as against black themselves being soiled by closer contact with whites.

SEXUALITY AND REPRODUCTION: SPHERES OF NEGOTIATION IN GENDER RELATIONS

Mrs. Nugent is very concerned throughout the journal with the immorality displayed by the resident population at large in Jamaica. For instance, she is disapproving of the sexual liaisons between white men and black women, the product of which is the coloured offspring, which she clearly finds an unattractive prospect. In this context we can read into her interpretation a consciousness of female oppression from which women of her class were not exempt, and from her voice we can see the other side of the coin as well. Generally, white men were the culprits in extending their sexual favours, rather than white or creole women. Her attack on white immorality was directed against the males, not the females. The sexual norms expected of women in her social class limited their possibilities for shifting notions of white femininity. As part of this white group herself she no doubt sympathised with the invidious position in which this placed white women. Here was another race of women who presented an alternative sexuality to the white men, yet white women were virtually powerless to compete with the patriarchal order within their own class. She records a visit to Hope estate in which we see some of these reservations.

> October 1st, 1801: About 10 we drove to the Hope estate. ... As you enter the gates, there is a long range of negro houses, like thatched cottages, and a row of cocoa nut trees and clumps of cotton trees. The sugar-house, and all the buildings, are thought to be more than usually good, and well taken care of. The overseer, a civil, vulgar, Scotch officer, on half-pay, did the honours to us; but, when we got to the door of the distillery, the smell of the rum was so intolerable, that, after a little peep at the process, I left the gentlemen, and went to the overseer's house, about a hundred yards off. I talked to the black women, who told me all their histories. The overseer's *chere amie*, and no man

> here is without one, is a tall black woman, well made, with a very flat nose, thick lips, and a skin of ebony, highly polished and shining. She shewed me her three yellow children, and said with some ostentation, she should soon have another. The marked attention of the other women, plainly proved her to be the favourite Sultana of this vulgar, ugly, Scotch Sultan, who is about fifty, clumsy, ill made and dirty. He had a dingy, sallow brown complexion, and only two yellow discoloured tusks, by way of teeth (p. 29).

On 10th March, 1802 she visits Golden Grove, one of the several estates owned by Mr. Simon Taylor and makes the following observation: "A little mulatto girl was sent into the drawing room to amuse me. She was a sickly delicate child, with straight light brown hair, and very black eyes. Mr. T. appeared very anxious for me to dismiss her, and in the evening, the housekeeper told me she was his own daughter, and that he had a numerous family, some almost on every one of his estates." She blames this degeneracy on the licentious behaviour of the white male population and during her stay in Jamaica she persistently attempted to resolve this moral decline by appealing to the white class to set different standards for the slave and coloured population. This is illustrated in the following entry in her journal:

> Yet it appears to me, there would be certainly no necessity for the Slave Trade, if religion, decency, and good order, were established among the negroes; if they could be prevailed upon to marry; and if our white men would but set them a little better example. Mrs. Bell told me today, that a negro man and woman of theirs, who are married, have fourteen grown up children, all healthy field negroes. This is the only one instance out of many, which proves, that, the climate of this country being more congenial to their constitutions, they would increase and render the necessity of the Slave Trade out of the question, provided their masters were attentive to their morals, and established matrimony among them; but white men of all descriptions, married or single, live in a state of licentiousness with their female slaves; and until a great

reformation takes place on their part, neither religion, decency nor morality can be established among the negroes. An answer that was made to Mr. Shirley, a Member of the Assembly (and a profligate character, as far as I can understand) who advised one of his slaves to marry, is a strong proof of this. "Hi, Massa, you telly me marry one wife, which is no good! You no tinky I see you buckra no content wid one, two, tree, or four wifes; no more poor negro". The overseers, &c. are in general needy adventurers, without either principle, religion, or morality. Of course their example must be the worst possible to these poor creatures (pp. 86-87).

Faced with the threat of abolition of the slave trade from Africa, the planters were interested in encouraging their slaves to breed, and the Slave Law of 1792 was designed to offer incentives to the proprietor and the overseer of any estate which could show a natural increase in its slave population during the year. Mrs. Nugent noted on a visit to the estate of Mr. C. that he gave two dollars to every woman who produced a healthy child. She bemoans the fact that legal and Christian marriages were not similarly encouraged between the slaves (p. 26-27). Mrs. Nugent pleads for marriage as an antidote to the evils caused by miscegenation as well as the pattern of sexual relations established on the plantations between slaves on religious and moral grounds, with an argument addressed to the slave-owners' material interest. It was possible that she felt, as did the planters, that marriage would lead to an increase in the number of slave children. The other side of the coin which has no grounding so far in any evidence seems to be a corollary of the planters' theory that the chief cause of infertility among slave women was their promiscuity.[20] By 1805 Mrs. Nugent seems to have made some gains in this respect. She records on 18th June:

> At dinner, Colonel Pollock (St. Mary's), and Mr. Vaughan (Trelawny). Had a long conversation with the latter, on the subject of making Christians of the negroes, and of his experience of the advantages of teaching them the consequent duties, &c. On his estate (Plumstead), he has christened all his negroes, and has induced many of them to marry, and lead regular lives. He says, they have in consequence

improved in all respects; are sober, quite, and well behaved; and the last year twelve children were born of parents regularly married. The new negroes are attended to, the instant they arrive on the estate, and are taught their prayers most zealously, by the oldest black Christians, and those best instructed and most capable. How delightful this is! I wish to God it could be made general, and I am sure the benefits arising from it, in every point of view, would be incalculable. I gave Mr. Vaughn several of my catechisms, made for our black servants, and several good little books for their instruction, with which he seemed much pleased (p. 242).

While Mrs. Nugent pursued the question of marriage as resolving the moral decay of the black population, one must recall that this naivete was consistently grounded in the values held on to firmly by her class, that of the preservation of whiteness, distance and status.

ADDING SOME MILK TO THE COFFEE: THE EVOLUTION OF COLOURED SOCIETY

Colour emerges as a crucial component in the way in which class and racial divisions became diluted. Since coloured folk were the product of liaisons between white men and black women, the issue of miscegenation speaks directly to the question of emergent gender, race and class relations in the evolving society of Jamaica. Whiteness signified upper class status, carried with it the privileges assigned to this class, and had already been demarcated as the standard by which beauty was determined. Blackness represented servitude, poverty, low status and, among many others at this time, a gross inequality in the law of the Colony as it existed then. If slave women were the object of white male attention, then it was obvious that this was the path through which their children after them would be relieved of the burden of both blackness and the indignities of slavery. Philip Curtin supports this observation:

> Since children followed the condition of the mother, the children of these unions were legally slaves, but in practice, planters usually secured the manumission of their children. In this aspect the Jamaican social

system differed sharply from the practice of other slave areas like the American south. Since there were few white women to prevent the open recognition of coloured children and their eventual freedom, Jamaica was divided into three, rather than two, racial castes. There were not simply whites and Negroes, but white, coloured, and black. Although the sexual union of master and slave did little to increase the mutual understanding between the two races on the plantations, it created a new class of racially mixed freemen – a group which heavily outnumbered the whites in the 1830s (p. 18).

Few if any black men had the opportunity of sexual relations with white women to exploit or improve their status, or relieve the burden of hard labour. The dynamic of gender relations between black men and women therefore begins to be interrupted by another variable, that black women have other means of challenging power relations between whiteness and blackness that black men do not have. This gender question must be pursued to its logical trajectory – how did the white exploitation of black female sexuality and the repressive conditions that limited family life among the black population, construct antagonistic notions of masculinity and femininity within black society? The relations, sexual and otherwise, which obtain between men and women, are always relations of power. The equations of power are by no means fixed and power as Michel Foucault has pointed out, is constantly being traded. Thus black women were also mediating power relations between black and white on the basis of their sexuality, companionship and childbearing. While the white planter or overseer was clearly still in a position of power over his slave, at the same time, the Hegelian master-slave dialectic could be equally invoked and he was as much a slave to his sexual desires. Thus we find that the lines of power and control and sexual relations between white men and black women were gradually being normalized as Philip Curtin also agrees:

> An additional feeling of impermanence was given to the lives of all the white planters by the traditional pattern of family life. The proprietor or the successful attorney might have a wife from England or might

have married a creole white, but below this social level the European wife was an extravagance, which neither the planter nor the estate could afford. Mainly because of the expense of keeping European women on the premises, but also, it was said, because a black mistress made a convenient spy of Negro affairs, the general policy of planting attorneys was to hire only unmarried men as overseers and book keepers. The bookkeeper was expected to find himself a "housekeeper" from among the slave women, while the overseer could either do the same or find a permanent "housekeeper" from the free coloured class. By the 1830s the custom of sexual union with the slaves was so well established that a new bookkeeper who failed to take a mistress was likely to meet with distrust for his holier-than-thou attitude.

CONCLUSION

Although definitive conclusions are premature from the point of view of a single diary, drawn from a particular class, from Maria Nugent's diary it has been possible to examine the contours of class, race and gender relations which had already emerged in Jamaican society from the eighteenth century onwards. We begin to see clearly the way in which the dominant ideas of race and class are implanted onto social identities. Concepts of beauty and ugliness, ideas of good speech and bad speech were all dependent on the closeness or distance to a white ideal. It was not only the whip and the economic vagaries of plantation economy which locked the blacks into a psyche of subservience, but the relations with their masters and mistresses who strove to preserve their superiority on a daily basis. This was happening equally in the private spheres of life among different groupings, as we see in the creole ladies disapproval of Lady Nugent's choosing to dance with the old negro man, or her entertaining the coloured ladies in her bedroom. In both public and private spheres, the distances were to be maintained to avoid too much familiarity lest the notions of superiority and inferiority were compromised.

The dominant ideas of the patriarchy at this time were those constructed by the white males. Black men are noticeably absent as patriarchal characters, prefiguring the sociological studies that would focus on the absence of black men in the African family. In fact an interesting picture which emerges of how black male sexuality is also being constructed as requiring multiple partners is seen in the example set by the dominant white group who "were not content with one, two tree, or four wifes." In addition, Lady Nugent's commentary helps us to understand, and with a feminist lens sympathize, with the concerns of white and coloured women as women who were also victims to an overarching patriarchy. A systematic perusal of other official and unofficial sources of this kind, documented histories and views from women and men of different classes can assist us in reconstructing a more complete picture of the workings of patriarchy. This task has already begun in the works of historians such as Lucille Mathurin Mair, Bridget Brereton and others, but much remains to be uncovered.

Constructs of masculinity and femininity are constantly revealed throughout this diary. White women are frail, petulant and need to be served, while black women can bear pain and perform hard labour. White men are immoral while women are the keepers of the morality and culture. Some of the nuances of masculinity and femininity have not fully emerged in the sections quoted in this text, but what is interesting though, and what has begun to surface, is that ideas of masculinity and femininity clearly differ by class and race, and that there is an ideal created by the dominant patriarchy, which may or may not represent the aspirations of all classes. The task of the feminist historian is to subject this to close scrutiny.

In nuancing this discourse in the Caribbean, I am intrigued by the silences in a feminist perspective that either creates a heterogeneous category of "woman" or establishes divisions by class, race and colour. It has always been an interesting omission, to my mind, that sexuality and reproduction have been major sites of controversy and control in systems of either forced or voluntary migration of peoples,[21] yet it is rarely intensely scrutinized as a key element through which these same identities - ethnic, class or gender, are disrupted. The creation and characteristics of another strata in Jamaican society, a class of coloured, formed by the mixing of blood of the two extremes, becomes the mediating point between the two polarized classes, a group which could be coerced into the political sentiments of the dominant group or form other political alliances. The extent to which this has informed the ongoing construction of masculinity and femininity, and poses challenges to patriarchal power and political alliances is a crucial question for gender to pursue in its search to fully understand the origins and ongoing development of Caribbean societies.

While Mrs. Nugent's diary confirms in many cases what other historians have already brought to light, her diary reveals a subtext in these relations, providing "elusive psychological"[22] insights which help us to understand the artificial distance between the public and private worlds, that emotions, sexuality and domesticity are equally involved in construction of class, race and gender identities. A gender perspective of history can guide us to building indigenous feminist theoretical understandings of how class, race and gender relations are configured within patriarchal ideology, and thus to more appropriate political solutions which address the ongoing and debilitating conflicts in the private and public areas of social life impacted upon by gender differences.

ENDNOTES

[1] The feminist movement is largely an activist one, intent on shifting negative attitudes and practices towards women and redressing their subordinate status in society. It is only during the twentieth century, and for that matter over the last three decades there has been a proliferation of women's studies and gender studies departments or institutions at various academic institutions. There has also been a shift over time in the emphasis. The early initiatives were primarily the study of women in society, but the theoretical developments which have fed into activism at the level of the academy certainly has shifted the emphasis to gender studies rather than a focus on women alone.

[2] Good examples of these are the contributions of the statement "the personal is political" a theoretical leap in the understanding of women's situation which came out of the consciousness raising groups which proliferated in the early seventies. Other contributions such as Kate Millett's *Sexual Politics*, and Betty Friedan's *The Feminine Mystique* were also written before the development of women's studies in the academy.

[3] This interpretation of Charles Fourier's writings is to be found in Sheila Rowbotham, (1998). *Women in Movement: Feminism and Social Action*, New York and London: Routledge, p.8.

[4] Patricia Hill Collins. (1991). *Black Feminist Thought*, New York and London: Routledge, pp. 7-8. Hill Collins refers to following work: Nancy Chodorow. (1974). "Family Structure and Feminine Personality" in *Woman Culture and Society*, (eds.) M. Rosaldo and L. Lamphere, Stanford University Press, and Nancy Chodorow. (1982). *The Reproduction of Mothering*, Berkeley: University of California Press, and Carol Gilligan. (1982). *In a Difference Voice*, Cambridge, MA.: Harvard University Press.

[5] One can note here that this exclusion was not only that of participation, but the lack of access to publishing etc. which not only Black American women suffered but so did the vast majority of third world women.
[6] Jane Flax. (1990). "Post-modernism and gender relations in feminist theory" In: L. Nicholson, ed., *Feminism/Post Modernism*, New York and London: Routledge, p. 40.
[7] Rosemary Tong. (1992). *Feminist thought: A comprehensive introduction*. London: Routledge, p.217
[8] Jane Flax, *op cit.*
[9] Gender is a much bandied about and overused word in scholarship at present, both internationally and in the Caribbean. Yet, in my view, the analytical capacity of this word means for many proponents and novices to merely "add women and stir".
[10] Now Institute for Gender and Development Studies with units on three campuses of the University of the West Indies, Trinidad, Barbados and Jamaica.
[11] E. Barriteau Foster. (1992). "The construct of a post-modernist feminist theory for Caribbean social science research", *Social and Economic Studies*, 41:2, p. 2
[12] E. Barriteau Foster, *op cit.* p. 16
[13] J. Scott. (1988). "Deconstructing equality-versus-difference: or the uses of poststructuralist theory for feminism" in *Feminist Studies*, 14: 1 Spring.
[14] This is not to suggest that patriarchal relations did not exist before colonial domination of the Caribbean. I feel that the present structure of race, class and gender relations have been tremendously shaped in the Caribbean by our history of migration and colonization. For instance, in India, gender relations between men and women are far more informed by Indian philosophy and mythology,
[15] E. Fox Genovese. (1989). "Literary criticism and the politics of the new historicism." In: A.A.Verseer, ed., *The New Historicism*, New York and London: Routledge, p. 217
[16] See Bridget Brereton's 1994 Elsa Goveia lecture "Gendered Testimony: Autobiographies, Diaries and Letters as sources for Caribbean History" for further understanding of the uses of such material for researching gender in history
[17] It is useful to note that while the new task of writing gender into history has become a formal part of the academy, women have always recorded history from the particular positions which they have found themselves and their letters, journals and diaries continuously provide us with some of the most valuable insights into gender relations in the past. Unfortunately, this is usually restricted to literate women with the leisure and luxury of being able to write or keep diaries and letters and in general to the educated rather than to the uneducated woman. The perspective is still, therefore, one-sided.
[18] Nurse Clifford who was made her nurse for the birth of her first child, remained very faithful to her during her stay in the island. Mrs. Clifford was the wife of an Irish soldier.
[19] It must be noted here, although this point is not developed in this paper than among the foreign-born whites themselves there was a distinct pecking order. I am grateful to Rex Dixon for his many observations and for the time he spent in discussion while writing this paper.
[20] A footnote on this page of the journal notes that "Perhaps the chief reason for the planters' opposition to marriage was that it would make the sale of slaves more difficult. The cost of marriage registration on a large scale may also have been a consideration", an argument which seems quite plausible in the circumstances, (p. 87).
[21] In my PhD Thesis *A social history of post-migrant Indians in Trinidad 1917-1947: A gender perspective*, (The Institute of Social Studies, The Hague, 1994), I found that the spheres of sexuality and reproduction are very crucial in the discussions

of power, ethnicity and identity between the various races and among Indians themselves.
[22] Bridget Brereton makes reference to this in her 1994 Elsa Goveia Lecture, already cited in this paper, see p. 2 of her lecture.

REFERENCES

Barriteau-Foster, V. Eudine. 1992. "The Construct of a Post-modernist Feminist Theory for Caribbean Social Science Research." *Social and Economic Studies*, 41 (2): 1-43

Brereton, Bridget. 1994. "Gender Testimony: Autobiographies, Diaries and Letters by Women as Sources for Caribbean History", 1994 Elsa Goveia Memorial Lecture, Department of History, University of the West Indies, Mona, Jamaica.

Curtin, Philip D. 1975. *Two Jamaicas: The Role of Ideas in a Tropical Colony 1830-1865*, *Studies in American Negro Life*, New York: Atheneum.

Fox-Genovese, E. 1989. "Literary Criticism and the Politics of the New Historicism". In *The New Historicism*, edited by A.A. Veeser. New York and London: Routledge.

Lady Nugent's Journal of her Residence in Jamaica from 1801 to 1805, A new and revised edition by Philip Wright, Institute of Jamaica, Kingston, Jamaica, 1966.

Mill, John Stuart. 1970. "The Subjection of Women", In *Essays on Sex Equality*, edited by John Stuart Mill and Harriet Taylor Mill, 123-242. Chicago: University of Chicago Press.

Scott, Joan W. 1988. "Deconstructing Equality-versus-Difference: Or, the Uses of Poststructuralist Theory for Feminism." *Feminist Studies* 14, no V, (Spring).

Scott, Joan W. 1988. *Gender and the Politics of History*. New York: Columbia University Press.

Tong, Rosemary. 1992. *Feminist Thought: A Comprehensive Introduction*. London: Routledge.

Wollstonecraft, Mary. 1975. A Vindication of the Rights of Women, edited by Carol Poston, New York: W. H. Norton (first published 1792).

2

Towards Indigenous Caribbean Feminist Theorizing[†]

INTRODUCTION

This attempt to develop an indigenous reading of feminism as activism and discourse in the Caribbean is informed by my own preoccupation with the limits of contemporary postmodern feminist theorizing both in terms of its accessibility as well as application to the specificity of a region. I cannot speak for or in the manner of a white middle class academic in Britain, or a black North American feminist as much as we share similarities which go beyond our individual societies and are fuelled by our commitment to gender equality. At the same time our conversations allow for intersections as a greater clarity of thought emerges in relation and perhaps in reaction to others. Ideas of difference and the epistemological standpoint of "Third World" women have been dealt with admirably by many feminist writers such as Chandra

---

[†] First published in *Feminist Review* No 59, Routledge Journals, UK, Special Issue edited by Patricia Mohammed, *Rethinking Caribbean Difference*, 1998.

Mohanty, Avtah Brah and Uma Narayan. In this article I draw on some debates emerging in contemporary western feminist thought pertaining to sexual difference and equality and continue my search for a Caribbean feminist voice which locates feminism and feminist theory in the region, not as a linear narrative that takes its cue from the north but one which has its own internal contradictions. Nonetheless, internal differences are consolidated by the denominator of a shared politics of identity in the region.

LOCATING THE CARIBBEAN

In the last decades of the twentieth century, for those who live on this stepping stone of islands and adjacent territories between the north and south Americas, the Caribbean represents a deep blue and verdant green space, sheltered from the icy cold wet winters of the north and far south, rain fed by the prevailing winds across the Atlantic and continually bronzed by the tropical sun. This contemporary image was in the making for over five hundred years. It was not these aspects, which initially encouraged the Dutch seafarers, the Spanish explorers, the French and British planters and officials, to settle and colonize the landmasses. The region represented virgin territory to be used, developed, exploited and governed by the trespassers. The indigenous Amerindian population had put up no gates or boundaries, no barbed-wire fences, and wore no armoured breastplates to protect their underpopulated villages and settlements.

The narratives of misuses and abuses of colonization are tired old ones which will not be retired. The secrets and disguises of the past will be constantly rendered up for public scrutiny by each new generation of Caribbean peoples, descendants of the myriad group of migrants, enslaved, bonded, coerced or encouraged to work and settle in these lands. The historical past will be constantly interpreted by those who have adopted the region as their permanent or temporary home, untangled by those who physically live in the region, and debated by those who have migrated out of the region. Both consciously and unconsciously, the interrogation of the past with the present is the process of creating continuity and tradition. This continuity and tradition - of families, buildings, institutions, art, music, song, dance, cuisine, of political systems and political struggles, of language, and of cultural beliefs – are markers of identity and difference. The different manifestations of these are the signature of the Caribbean on the world map – the way in which the circumstances of history, natural geography and resources of the region have evolved into something which is viewed as Caribbean, despite colonialism, and because of colonization.

To establish identity and difference is not simply to demarcate ownership or territorial rights, it is also an expression of the desire to belong (Moore 1994, 2). Situating difference establishes the boundaries of belonging. In his Nobel acceptance speech in 1992 the poet Derek Walcott describes the region as *The Antilles: Fragments of Epic Memory*. "Break a vase" writes Walcott "and the love that reassembles the fragments is stronger than that love which took its symmetry for granted when it was whole...it is such a love that re-assembles our African and Asiatic fragments, the cracked heirlooms whose restoration shows its white scars"(1992). The project of defining identity is a most insistent one in the postmodern discourse. This preoccupation with ethnic identity did not begin in the academy but in the cultural assertions during colonialism, and during the post-colonial period, in the nationalist and independence struggles in the region. The scars which must be healed are not only those of physical brutality and privation. The deeper gashes are the deprivation of ethnic customs, and loss of ethnic pride and dignity. Undoubtedly, the scars of enslavement of African peoples are deepest. No other group apart from the indigenous Amerindian population under colonization in the West Indies suffered so much in terms of inhumanity, both physical as well as in the disruption of its cultural memory.

Ethnicity is a collective word which in its political appeal to the group, ignores gender differences within a culture. Recognising the different ways in which men and women within any cultural group experience enslavement, indentureship or migration is integral to understanding ethnic identity. The psychological scars of emasculation or de-feminization caused by such uprooting are not skin deep and have residual effects on gender relations and gender struggles within a society far beyond the periods of disruption. Identity politics take the form not only of definitions against externalities, but are also about the internal and ongoing processes of re-constructing masculinity and femininity within the society. The dynamics of gender in each society or region operate not through grand revolutionary upheavals but through the ongoing negotiations between men and women at the individual and collectively organized levels. Masculinity and femininity exist not simply in opposition, but equally in relation to each other (Mohammed 1994, 32). In this process of reconstructing gender identities, the rhetoric - either nationalist or cultural - has generally been towards reinforcing an "ethnic" ideal which predates the disruptions of colonization. Markers such as dress or hairstyle are good examples of how these appeals are made to women. In studying the colonized subject, the tendency has been to see the burden of reconfiguring gender identities as primarily that of the colonized group. It is, also, a problem which confronts the colonizers. Women whether born in Europe or creole born,[1] were themselves ill at ease with the situation. This is best illustrated by the author Jean Rhys whose novel *Wide Sargasso Sea* and subsequent writings describe with more pathos than historical writings can achieve, the insecurity and fears which also underlay the perceived 'privileged' spaces. The construction of masculinity and femininity went on busily under colonization as it continues at present.[2] Within each society, the residual effects of Eurocentricism and elitism of the white planter class on the dynamics of race and gender in each society, still inform the ongoing construction of masculinities and femininities. Feminism within Caribbean society has therefore been involved in an unrelenting dialogue about what constitutes Caribbean manhood and masculinity and womanhood and femininity, as it has also been affected by the late twentieth century consciousness of and struggles for gender equality which is debated through the global discourse.

In this paper I select three aspects of difference which have led to the specific ways in which feminism in the Caribbean is both articulated in daily struggles and activism as well as debated within the academic discourse. The *first* "moment"[3] of difference is situated around the question of political struggles in the region and the stances taken by women, some of which might appear to be antithetical to contemporary feminist goals per se. My overall argument is that feminism as an expression of sexual equality must itself be historically located, despite the global discourse which feeds its growth. The *second* moment contemplates the linguistic meanings of gender inside the region. I suggest here that the presentation and re-presentation of masculinity and femininity have internalized meanings within a culture, differentiated further still by class or ethnic groupings, and is key in the reproduction of gender identities within a society or region in the way in which language informs thoughts, images and practices of what it is to be a man or woman, boy or girl, heterosexual or homosexual. The *third* moment is closely linked to the idea of linguistic difference but elaborating this in relation to the contemporary western feminist interrogation of "sexual difference". Here I am on more uneven ground as I am attempting to situate these debates in the language of the English-speaking Caribbean. It seems to me that the issues of sexual difference versus equality also preoccupy our societies, but they are not generally approached with the same theoretical stances. The concept of difference as it has been raised and deconstructed in feminist circles has generally focussed on sexual difference between man and woman, and differences between women themselves. "…the feminist analysis of gender has undone one version of a presumably basic difference, thought to be rooted in nature, and come up with another, albeit more debatably basic than the previous one" (di Stefano 1990, 64). If twentieth century second wave feminism has problematized gender (Flax 1990, 44), then the continuing goals of feminism depend on the further deconstruction of "difference" beyond the limits to which it has been already applied. I explore the overtones of difference for unpacking gender in the Caribbean and in an effort to indigenize Caribbean feminist theory.

In each of these sections I use illustrative examples to explain my points, outlining both my biases and assumptions. First, I am more familiar with the history, culture and struggles of the English-speaking Caribbean and therefore my theorization may have more relevance to these territories. Second, I am interested in feminism and the feminist movement as an historically progressive movement engaged in shifting human consciousness towards a greater acceptance of equality of the sexes, as well as a celebration of difference, both sexual and otherwise. I am interested in a feminism that does not merely pay lip service to women's status with empty promises of equality and celebration of difference, but that which is realized in state policies, community programmes and in individual human relationships. The feminist movement has largely emphasized women's subordination and the ongoing need for a consciousness of gender equality to be built into the process of constructing gender identity. But female gender identities are not constructed in isolation from other components of identity such as race, class, nation and from masculinity. How identities are being affirmed or even constructed are based on real struggles which people and groups are engaged in and which they communicate to each other in coded messages within a culture, much the same way that lovers communicate with words, signals and body language, the meanings of which are not immediately apparent to the outsider or onlooker. This preoccupation with different components of identity and my particular interpretation of feminism inform both my approach as well as the areas I select for interrogation.

CARIBBEAN FEMINISM AND THE POLITICS OF IDENTITY

Why is there this insistent desire to re-assemble the fragments of ethnic and gender identities and to belong to a space? Why has Caribbean society engaged in a continuous process of defining identity? In a contemporary sense the Caribbean appears more as a political space rather than a geographical entity, "When did the name Caribbean move from the sea to the imprecise geography of some or all the land masses surrounding it?" (Gaztambide-Geigel 1996, 1). One Puerto Rican historian traces the legend of the word *Caribe* as rebellious and/or enslaved native, a title assigned by the Spanish. The region was named the West Indies by the Spanish in the sixteenth century. There is a confusion of the name of the region in a Dutch map of West America dating back to 1594. It was the English-speaking Europeans who named the islands the *Caribby* or *Caribbee Islands* "thus transferring to the sea waters the name once given to the masters of the islands" and the French who underscored the direct heritage when they spoke of Mer des *Caraibes* or Sea of the Caribs. "Ironically" writes Gaztambide-Geigel, "when the Caribs, by then mixed with the Africans, had been reduced to "reservations" in Martinique and Dominica, or had been exiled by the British to the Mosquito Coast and Honduras, they became immortalized when the sea they had mastered was baptized with their name" (Gaztambide-Geigel 1996, 6-7).

Like a child, unsexed, named after the parents it has lost, the region and its peoples continue to examine the past. Edward Braithwaite also interprets the region similarly when he writes "But we are really involved with two mothers (more as we grow younger)" (Braithwaite 1985, 6). This process of becoming Caribbean persisted past the abolition of slavery into the twentieth century with the addition of different ethnic groups. Each language group continues its association with its colonizer even while it constructs new destinies from within. The nationalist or independence struggles have differed for each society. In August 1791, two years after the French Revolution, the African slaves of the French West Indian Colony of San Domingo revolted, a struggle which lasted for twelve years and led in 1803 to the formation of the negro state of Haiti (James 1963). Over two hundred years later, in 1998 the islands of Martinique and Guadeloupe are still *departements* of France. The once Spanish colony of Puerto Rico exchanged hands and is now administratively linked to the United States of America but Spanish remains its mother tongue. The Spanish-speaking island of Cuba has forged its distinctive struggle for socialism befriended and heralded in part by the region for its decisive political stance against the imperialism of the United States. By the twentieth century the English-speaking colonies, with the exception of the islands of Montserrat, Bermuda and the British Virgin Islands, are all independent states.

The region is imagined differently by the different groups who have settled into this space. The demographic distribution of races and ethnic groups brought together from east and west varies by territory and has led to different political tensions within each society founded on race or class/colour. In this demographic balance African-descended peoples are the dominant group in most of the territories. This demographic dominance has largely posited the region as an African diaspora. Yet the writings of the second half of the twentieth century tell of other dispersions of peoples who feel the need to equally define their belonging within the region. Mary Noel Menezes records that 1985 marked the 150th anniversary of the arrival of the Portuguese in Guyana. *The Still Cry* by Kumar Mahabir and *Survivors of Another Crossing* by Marianne Ramesar record the histories of the Indians who in 1995 celebrated 150 years in the island of Trinidad, as they did also in Jamaica. The story of Chinese migration to Trinidad was examined by Trevor Millette in Trinidad, and Sylvia Moodie-Kublalsingh adds the oral history of *panyols* or *espanoles*, Trinidadians of mixed

Spanish, Amerindian and African descent, to a burgeoning list of fiction and non-fiction writers who write on ethnic identity. All of these are expressions of the re-ordering of experience to continuously redefine identity. In the same breath, these are not primarily expressions of difference, but of different members of the same family. The Caribbean is not just one lost child but the children of many parents, who have made similar but different passages across the ocean – a sentiment best expressed by the Mighty Stalin, a Trinidadian calypsonian in the 1979 song: *To the Caribbean Man: "we take the same trip in the same ship"*.

History and experience move on incessantly and by the twentieth century development of capitalism, the Caribbean is no longer the site of plantations but the space from which labour can be re-appropriated. The *Mer des Caraibes* is a wide open mouthed river with currents which run back and forth across the Atlantic, to Africa and Europe, far east to India and China, and now especially northwards to the United States and Canada. The currents which continue this flow, the legacies of colonization and the influences of present imperialism, make the Caribbean equally open to global discourses. In this definition of regional, national and ethnic identities, the Caribbean finds itself poised between sovereignty and openness – a small eddy in a large stream, but an eddy all the same. The Caribbean is the community, the society is the village, and the ethnic group represents the family at home and abroad with whom we establish a past, find solace in the present and seek assurance for a future.

Political struggles for identity which have taken place in the Caribbean must themselves be historicized and culturally investigated if they are to have meaning. In 1791, two years after the French Revolution in Europe, and one year before Mary Wollstonecraft published *A Vindication of the Rights of Women* and situated the base from which the liberal feminist struggle for women's equality began, the Caribbean was in the midst of the Haitian Revolution, described by C.L.R. James as the only successful slave revolt in history (James 1963, ix). The class of women who would and could question the ideology of male dominance with the pen, was limited. Lucille Mathurin Mair commenting on the period 1655 to 1770 in Jamaican history writes that

The dominant creole values of a society "whose business was business" continued, during the classic slavery period of 1770 to 1834, to determine the condition and interrelationships of women. Racism and colonialism combined with sexism to shape their life patterns. Women's acceptance of prevailing norms confirm the orthodoxy of women as the silent, second sex, serving as a conservative if not reactionary social element.

At the same time, we should not conclude that women, black, white or brown, were indifferent or lacking in a consciousness of gender, however defined at that time in the Caribbean. Mathurin Mair concluded from her analysis of this period that "Counter-evidence also suggests women's capacity for criticism, modification, rejection even, of these norms, in ways often peculiarly available to them, as women" (Mathurin 1974, 1).

The peculiarity of women's situation is that they are at the same time inside and outside of politics. Mathurin Mair points to situation of white women in Jamaica during slavery. English law and custom dictated the status of the white woman in Jamaica. White women had no voice in the Parliament, could make no laws and the rule of primogeniture ensured that the eldest son inherited the estate of his father. A good marriage saved them from "unnatural" spinsterhood, possibly from destitution, an unmarried daughter was a burden and shame to the family:

> Edward Long breathed a sigh of relief at his daughter's "honourable alliance" to Mr. Howard in 1801 for he had "dreaded leaving her at large in the world, either to be subject to the multitude of inconveniences which generally attend the situation of the single woman, or else to experience the mortifications of a state of dependence on someone of their relations" (Mathurin 1974, 224).

Nonetheless, men of substance took good care of their daughters and white women furthermore had the advantage of being part of the elite by virtue of their whiteness. The shortage of white females did not necessarily give a white woman advantage over black and brown women as concubinage with the two latter groups was deeply entrenched in the creole way of life. Marriage itself also did not grant white women further independence since it place them in "coverture" restricting their capacity to act as free and rational beings. Yet, the white woman in Jamaica was in many ways the "classic creole consumer of prestige" ensuring that the status symbols of the ruling class maintained its distance from the middle and lower classes (Mathurin 1974, 248).

After slavery, in Trinidad and Guyana, the system of Indian indentured labour introduced another ethnic group into these societies, between 1845 and 1917. The majority of Indian women and men were wage labourers, some later becoming part of the land-owning peasantry, the minority were professionals or owned businesses of their own. The status of most Indian women was that of household or field labourer. Few Indian women had the luxury to be educated and to be involved in a debate on questions of female liberation and equality. At the same time such questions were already being raised by progressive Indian women in India, women such as Dr. Anandibai Joshi (1865-1887) and Pandita Ramabai (1858-1922) (Kosambi 1994). This tradition of an anti-colonial female militancy in India was conveyed to Trinidad through the medium of the newspapers in a section entitled "Indian News and Views" regularly featured in the *Trinidad Guardian* on Thursday and Sunday and produced by Indian journalist Seepersad Naipaul, father of V.S Naipaul. One feature, entitled "Indian Women Hold Parley", drew attention to the All-India Women's Conference held in 1936 whose goals were to "create a wider scope for the powers and responsibilities for Indian women, and to emphasize the value of women's work in every well-ordered State" (*Sunday Guardian*, 5th July, 1936). Visitors to Trinidad, among them Beatrice Grieg, drew local attention to the undeniably secondary status allocated to Indian womanhood in India and in Trinidad.[4] Both in India and in the West Indies, Indian women were inside and outside the political struggle. On the one hand, the allegiances to ethnicity were encouraged through the retention of a Brahminic ideal. Indian women were expected to mirror themselves after the image of Sita, the virtuous, longsuffering and faithful bride of Rama[5], the latter epitomizing the male patriarch in control of his household - in order to counteract the 'westernizing' influences of the colonizer. Within the ethnic group, women as a group suffered as a result of this expectation of their roles and behaviour as women. It was unrealistic for women who were themselves wage earners and homemakers to confront their men and assert their autonomy and ethnic identity. Indian women in Trinidad were caught in the dilemma of also desiring the re-establishment of "Indian" ethnicity as it was recalled from India and the reconstitution of community within Trinidad, therefore colluding at one level with the reconstruction of a notion of Indian femininity and masculinity. Nonetheless they were also engaged in renegotiating new ideas of Indian womanhood in Trinidad. With migration had come many opportunities to change some of the more gender-oppressive features of caste and religion. Newly found freedoms based on the demographic shortage of Indian women in the colony as well as a greater capacity for wage earning on estates allowed them to challenge the patriarchal expectations of Indian femininity.[6]

The questions which would be raised for all women by the second wave of feminism became more complex, adding to the issues of class, religion/ethnicity, were those of political nationhood, race, and sisterhood among women. What political alliances should they forge? What interests would compel them to act on behalf of other women, themselves, their families, or their ethnic groups? It is important to view the emergence of the women's movement as parallel to and intersecting with other struggles which are specific to each group and society. Another example serves to explain the multi-layered aspect of struggle.

In the Pan-African movement which had its origins in the Caribbean, there was no specific feminist rhetoric in a contemporary sense of the word. Marcus Garvey formed the Universal Negro Improvement Association (UNIA) in 1914, shortly after he returned from England. The first member of the association was Amy Ashwood, a young woman of seventeen who would in due course become his wife. Of the original list of members, it was revealed that over half of them were women. From the earliest phases, there were allocations for women as secretaries in each division and presidents of various divisions. The social welfare tradition of the period found these women and those of the UNIA involved in activities such as concerts, fundraising for the poor, visiting hospitals, setting up of an industrial school, trying to run a labour bureau and finding jobs for unemployed persons. At weekly meetings of the UNIA in which were then largely a debating society, topics pertaining to women such as "Is the intellect of woman as highly developed as that of man?" were also discussed. It is recorded that Garvey himself participated in this debate and argued in the affirmative. Another debate entitled "Women or men: Whose influence is more felt in the world?" shows a concern for issues of women's equality without the rhetoric of contemporary feminism.

Subsequently, when the UNIA moved to New York, women continued to play decisive and leading roles in the organization, although here more black American women seemed to have been involved. What is clear however, is that both in its name as well as focus, the issue was that of strengthening black nationalism. Garvey preached a doctrine of race first, self-reliance and nationhood, and linked the woman question to the race question. "Race first meant that black folks would have to put their racial self-interest first" writes Martin. "Garvey told black people, among other things, to take down the white "pin ups" from their walls. He was opposed to the gross advertisements for skin lighteners ... he encouraged through his organization a factory that made black dolls so that young black children would not have to deal with the question of beauty being seen through the eyes of white folk all the time". In contrast to Garvey's interpretation of progressiveness on the status of women, Claudia Jones, a famous black woman of the Communist Party of the United States in the 1940s and 1950s, lamented the position of black women in the party. If women supported Garvey as a leader, then it was also because from their perspective, Garvey supported women. Tony Martin affirms that the dignity of women was a crucial issue for Garvey and the UNIA (Martin 1988, 68). Honor Ford-Smith suggests that there is a close connection between the anti-colonial and feminist movement in many societies who have similarly experienced colonization and that "...the Jamaican feminist movement of the 1930s and 1940s was nurtured within the Garvey movement." Ford-Smith, however, identifies the contradiction of this 'feminist' stance at the time. "Strangely enough, the ideal image of womanhood upheld within the movement differed very little from the ideal image upheld by dominant colonial ideology in terms of the way it perceived women's position within the family, women's labour and sexuality" (Ford-Smith 1988).

Parallel with the emergence of the UNIA in Jamaica and the United States, was the preamble to the anti-colonial struggles which fed the later nationalist struggles in Trinidad. In 1928, Jim Headley, who had worked for years in the Trade Union Movement in the United States returned in 1934 to Trinidad to witness the eruption of hunger marches. Together with Dudley Mahon, of the Federated Workers Trade Union and Elma Francois,[7] a former member of the Trinidad Labour Party, Headley founded the National Unemployment Movement (NUM). Within weeks of holding public meetings, pamphleteering and recruiting unemployed persons to the organization, the NUM had on its list 1200 members and became a political pressure group in the society. The NUM suffered a quick death as Headley himself, one of the hungry unemployed who was additionally hassled by authorities, felt forced to leave the country. The other members of the group felt that the focus on unemployment was too limited as a basis for wider political mobilization and later the same year, the Negro Welfare Association founded by Elma Francois, Jim Barrat, Christina King, Payne and Rupert Gittens came into being. The militancy of this period has been matched since then by another equally powerful set of messages sent by the "Black Power" riots of the 1970s in which women also fought as hill guerillas alongside men. In the intervening period in Trinidad the co-optation of working class and middle-class black women by the nationalist demagogue who brought Trinidad to Independence, has come under close scrutiny in a rereading of the past.[8]

If women did not willingly support the national political struggle sometimes any autonomous movement was defeated by dictatorship regimes. This was the case of the Dominican Republic under the Trujillo regime which lasted for more than thirty years. The regime adopted a patronizing patriarchal attitude, ostensibly supporting women's difference and at the same time quelling any revolutionary tendencies among women. There were for instance pensions for prolific mothers and "demagogic concessions to "women's issues" such as women's suffrage and the enactment of a protective labour code." Combined with the general repression experienced by the entire society, this was no climate for the development of any major women's movement before 1961. Despite this repression, three women, Minerva, Patria and Maria Teresa Mirabal have emerged as icons for the contemporary women's movement in this society. The dictatorship had attempted to silence them through rape, and finally did silence them by assassination in 1960. Their deaths, however, accelerated the fall of Trujillo and his regime, although the succeeding regimes continued the manipulation of women and femininity for their own ends (Pineda 1984, 132).

Despite their allegiances to nationalist and independence struggles, an unarticulated consciousness of gender equality must have run through the veins of each woman, black, white, Indian, Portuguese and Chinese, coloured, Spanish, French, Haitian, Barbadian... the same way the idea of class and racial equality had occurred to men and women long before these claims erupted in revolutions. To speak of a feminist movement in the Caribbean which predates the contemporary second wave movement is to bring alive on paper the individuals who would not be silent, those who spoke or wrote on behalf of others who felt similarly,[9] much as we do today. To speak of a feminist movement in the Caribbean is to identify the contradictions which women faced in the post-colonial struggles and the contradictions of the men who welcomed their comradeship. There were different battles to be fought on Caribbean soil when the Suffragette movement in Britain at the turn of the nineteenth century began its path-breaking and victorious fight which eventually benefited all women. By the middle of the twentieth century, when masses of post-war unemployed and professional women in the United States felt the anger of rejection, women in the Caribbean were differently placed in their own societies, battling foes of poverty and patriarchal restraints on their freedoms. That first wave feminism in the region took on many strands of a liberal feminist discourse was an indication that women's rights were being fought for on the basis of an equal rights tradition which characterized both the anti-colonial and race struggles. That second wave feminism assumed other dimensions of thought: some radical, some Marxist, some liberal, is consistent with the expansion of identity politics which began to perceive individuals as belonging to different classes and different races. That feminism in general and the feminist movement in the Caribbean appears to be eclectic is a reflection of its manifold responses to the issues of class, race/ethnicity, nationhood and to gender and sexual identity. Only by the late twentieth century onwards was there both the global consciousness as well as the rapid spread of the ideas of gender equality among many. Nonetheless, as we have seen, Caribbean women's claims to recognition of their sex and to gender equality ran parallel to many of the struggles that ensued from the nineteenth century onwards in the region.

CREOLE - THE EXPRESSION OF CARIBBEAN DIFFERENCE

The struggles for political identity are generally overt statements of difference. Not all aspects of identity politics are so explicit or given to manifest expressions. Within any culture the meanings shared by those who speak the same language also provide another space in which identity is being shaped. Language itself is a crucial marker of identity, as it is also an indicator of continuity and tradition. In Trinidad for instance the French word *jour ouvert (day-break, or opening day)* describes the traditional opening of the two-day pre-Lenten carnival celebrations. Early Monday morning, before the sun has risen, the people who have been partying the night before spill out onto the streets and dance/walk to the slow steady rhythm of the steelbands around the towns. The word *jour ouvert* to a Trinidadian is never a literal reference to day-break on any day, but captures a mood, a feeling, a moment, of tired bodies entwined, an image of subdued light and rhythmic music pacing the motion of people taking possession of streets and sidewalks. Unless this has been experienced by someone for many years, the word when uttered could have no such connotation. *Jour overt* itself tells a large part of the history of this society, especially the influence of the French on language/culture. In the same vein as the term *creole* has become a metaphor for the Caribbean region, its people, language and culture. The genealogy of *creole* is interesting and the term itself has been 'creolized' in its Caribbean applications for it is by no means only applicable to, or uniquely used, in the context of the Caribbean.[10]

There is a continuing adaptation of the term, its use has varied over time in the Caribbean and has meant different things to different groups, sometimes simultaneously in the same society. Lady Nugent, wife of the English Governor of Jamaica from 1801 to 1805 described the white women born in the island as creole to distinguish them from the white women who came from "foreign", applying the word not only to describe their birth, but also to differentiate their behaviour, habits and customs which were different as a result of being born and raised in the island (Nugent 1805). Locally evolved habits, customs, cuisine and popular culture increasingly began to be defined as *creole*. In essence, *creole* customs and habits were viewed as departures from a norm established by the European colonizer and perceived as deficient in both form and content. Nonetheless, the term clearly had resonance for the peoples in the different territories of the Caribbean. In Trinidad for example, in the nineteenth and early twentieth century it was used to refer to the descendants of the French planter class born in the society, as well as to the local African population.[11]

Where language was key in the instrumentation of empire in the Caribbean, language has also been crucial in the definition of sovereignty. This battle was very early on appreciated by J.J. Thomas in his response to Anthony Froude's *The English in the West Indies: The Bow of Ulysses* published in 1887. Froude, a learned British scholar travelled to the West Indies and was warmly welcomed by the local population. His book, officially commissioned by the British government was a brutal and ignominious attack on the West Indians. Froude had been called upon by the West Indian colonists to block the efforts of the West Indian blacks, the first of the non-white colonial peoples who had become English-speakers themselves, from functioning in their society according to the principles of parliamentary government. He argued that the black population was seeking a self-government which they did not have the capacity to exercise. J. J. Thomas, a largely self-taught scholar responded to his defamation with *Froudacity: West Indian Fables Explained* published in 1889, displaying in his turn equal erudition and command of a language which was not his first tongue. J. J. Thomas was a young, black, educated man of Trinidad. In one of his jobs as a village schoolmaster in rural Trinidad he developed a facility for languages in order to communicate with students who spoke a variety of different tongues. Without any formal training in languages, Thomas mastered French, began to learn Spanish and understood the significance of the living dialect which he could observe in its evolution. He recorded the Creole grammar of the French language, the dominant stream which emerged from the Babel of different tongues at the time in Trinidad in a book entitled *The Theory and Practice of Creole Grammar*. Published in 1869, this book was said to have been better appreciated by philologists in England and Europe than at home at the time, unfortunately another aspect of creole culture.

Both of Thomas's contributions had immediate, and still has, far reaching implications for the continued evolution of Creole society.[12] More importantly, it appears to me that in his systematic study of *creole*, Thomas signalled not just the internal integrity of the grammar, but also the idea of language expressing the meanings shared within a culture. This emergence of a shared language revealed another aspect of the society's evolution – that people of different tongues had begun to communicate in a common language of their own, a language which excluded others, not consciously or deliberately but because the meanings of words and ideas are also derived from the lived experience of a territory. Though culled from the mixtures of languages which each of the different groups brought, the creole dialect in each region is predominantly influenced by the language of its chief colonizer. Within each society as well, the official language of the state and the elite continues to be the language of the main colonizing agent. In this relationship between two entities umbilically tied, we find the other dimension of creole society, the capacity to move back and forth between a language with its internal shared meanings, and the "mother" tongue from which it was created. This skill for double entendre is nicely illustrated in J. J. Thomas's response to Froude in *Froudacity: West Indian Fables explained*. He had the "audacity" to confront the master "using the master's tools."[13] In Trinidad, the importance assigned to a command of the language is evident in the early development of the calypso where the singer demolished his opponent with language by using either "big words" or *double entendre* which could be variously interpreted by the listeners.

The derivation from other tongues as well as the ongoing communication with its local audience created of *creole* not a mimetic culture,[14] but a constantly evolving syncretization and hybridity. This is best explained through music[15] and dance.

The Cuban *rumba* evolved partly through interaction of slaves of different African regions, with a European influence obvious in the use of the Spanish language. Where the *santeria* of Cuba is largely a transplanted Yoruba entity, the *rumba* is a distinctly creole or Cuban creation. The evolution and eventual acceptance of creole musics are closely interconnected with the internal and external political struggles for nationalism and elite recognition of Afro-Caribbean heritage (Manuel 1995, 15).

The way in which all these aspects of national identity struggles, economic deprivation or empowerment, popular culture and desire come together is in the *creole expression* of the body in Caribbean society, the language of intimacy. The language of intimacy is not only that of sexual desire, it is the expression of familiarity, tenderness, of mutual understanding or their bedfellows – antagonism,[16] conflict and antipathy. All of these are inscribed in the language of the body of masculinity and femininity, of man and woman, of gender and gender relations. There are subtle and indefinable ways in which a common language of the body and gender relations are shared within a culture, crossing race and class divides. These messages can be sought only in and through language as it is spoken and understood by people themselves. This element also explains the difficulty we have of understanding gender codes we encounter in a new society simply because we cannot immediately grasp the messages which are implicitly conveyed with and without words.[17]

What are such messages in the Caribbean?[18] A first message might be the ideas of what constitutes womanhood or manhood. When does a child move from being a girl into an "*ooman*" or from boyhood into "you tink you is *man*". Cultural rituals that begin to take place from adolescence sharpen the difference between male and female gender identity. There are numerous indicators of manhood as the research from Brown and Chevannes illustrate from an ethnographic project on gender socialization which spanned the societies of Dominica, Guyana and Barbados (Brown and Chevannes 1996). Starting with the inscribed religious doctrine

> From yu bawn yu is a man...De Bible did say, "Let's make man", and outa man dere cometh ooman, ...At all time yu mus' know seh yu is a man an' like yu is supreme. It go right back to religion y'know.

To biological criteria:

> From me bawn wid 'ood (hood or penis), me know seh me is a man.

To self-determined behaviour and roles:

> Him is man when him decide fe tek up responsibility. Like you start a relationship wid a girl. Suppose she get pregnant an she have a baby wid yu, yu start tek up dat responsibility. ...Yu can be a man from yu is a likkle bwoy. An yu can be a big ol' bwoy.

> When me really realized dat me turn a man was when me staat to work and hangle (handle) me own money, y'know. Buy my own clothes an t'ings like dat, me staat go out an' come in late, like look girlfrien' an t'ings like dat. Mi fadder used to tell me seh, me t'ink yu a man, yu come een dem hours ya a night.

Most importantly, male sexuality is a central definition of maleness, in relation to femininity,

> A wil' (wild) man always get ah enormous amount a respec' ...a wil' man normally have money. An yu know that respect is based on money. If yu don' have money ...yu get no ratings from nobody.

but perhaps more stridently in opposition to male homosexuality, the latter widely perceived as pure "wutlessness".

> Me love ooman bad, bad, bad, bad. Me hate gay wid a passion ...how me seet it is like de type a gay wha me hate is, him is man like me, or him bawn wid balls, but because of certain situations like all economics, like all money, an him waan look good an, him go tu'n gay ... (Brown & Chevannes 1996, 116-118).

The girl must be beaten into a young lady, to be a young "ooman" is unacceptable. Both the fiction of the region and other forms of popular culture are replete with these messages:

> All the same right is right and there is only one right way to bring up a (girl) child and that is by bus' ass pardon my French Miss Mary but hard things call for hard words. That child should be getting blows from the day she born. The she wouldn't be so force-ripe now …Little children have no right to have so many things in their brain. Guess what she ask me the other day nuh? - if me know how worms reproduce. …As Jesus is me judge. Me big woman she come and ask that (Senior 1986, 69).

The allusion to "force-ripe" – generally applied to prematurely ripened fruit is a powerful metaphor for the construction of femininity. It situates the young girl in opposition to the "big woman" who is mature and has the "knowing" which the young girl should not possess before her time. The attainment of one's femininity is a process of grooming before attainment of sexual knowledge.

While these processes of constructing masculinity and femininity take place in all societies, how they do so are both historically and culturally shaped and continue to be so, despite external influences. Like most culture, they are also passed on from one generation to the next, and the terms and conditions are changed by the struggles between masculinity and femininity to define boundaries. For example the ideal of the "browning" – the mixed light skinned woman – in Caribbean society is currently undergoing change, but these notions are the direct legacy of a colonial history of opposition between white and black sexualities. How does each culture agree on acceptable norms and practices of gender, for example that in Trinidad "a deputy is essential" or in Jamaica "a man is entitled to his matie on the side". The 'deputy' and 'matie' are the idiomatic references to the "other woman", the "bit on the side". Is this a mutual agreement between men and women in society? Who determines the boundaries of what is permitted in sexual relations and in the range of sexualities openly allowed to individuals within a society? How power and control mechanisms in gender relations are put in place in each society and how these are negotiated is also based on an internal dialogue which is constantly taking place about sexual difference and equality.

SEXUAL DIFFERENCE AND THE CARIBBEAN

The word "feminism" has itself been part of the problem of feminism and writing on gender in the region. While such struggles and negotiations are and have been ongoing in the course or our history, as they are in most societies, the importation of a word brings with it the messages of gender in another culture. The image of the strident British suffragette has not been part of the history of Caribbean society, even while equally strident women have fought here for nationhood and equality. The image of the "bra-burning sexually liberated" North American white woman in the sixties has negative resonances in these parts. Where the word is used, as it must be, for a thing has to be named, it has to be constantly defined in context as "I am a not a feminist like those ..." or "I am a feminist but I am not one of those man-hating ..." This is an ongoing irritant in this area of work and struggle in the Caribbean and the problem will no doubt persist.

At the same time, a crucial debate in feminist theory is itself being discussed within the region, but perhaps with a different vocabulary. The post-colonial, national and ethnic contestations for identity have been forced to create a place for the interrogation of gender identity, leading one to agree with Irigaray that "Sexual difference is one of the major philosophical issues, if not the issue, of our age" (Irigaray 1993, 5). The current debates in learned feminist circles are focussed on the issues of equality and difference. I think there is more or less agreement among scholars, north, south, east and west, that equality between the sexes can only be achieved if femininity and masculinity are both valued for their difference. That the opposition in sexual difference has proved to be a constraint now for further theorizing as well as activism (De Lauretis 1989) has also become quite evident. Instead of reproducing these binary oppositions which we are simultaneously engaged in breaking down, I believe feminist writing supports the idea that difference or equality between the sexes can be approached pragmatically. There are instances in which sexual difference must be argued for rather than gender equality across the board, as in the case of maternity leave in employment. The difference-equality concepts and debate can be more usefully applied as an heuristic device to generate new questions about gender and new research issues (Hermsen and

Van Lenning 1991), thus leading to novel insights. Like the early feminist search for the "origins of patriarchy" this debate cannot be resolved at this point. Whether we are naturally different as a species, or whether we have control over the construction of our identities and potentialities, remain part of the ongoing evolution of sex and gender. The problem of gender for each society becomes a process of understanding its own constructions of masculinity and femininity, identifying the legacies and issues which are recalled in the reconstruction of gender and intersected ethnic identities and ensuring that these proceed without further contractions of status or power between and among the sexes.

The language of this struggle is also culturally specific. For the rest of this essay I briefly situate ways in which this debate is carried out in the region. First, a large number of women, if not the majority, have always worked outside the home and if not fully, then certainly have been prime supporters of their households. As central figures in nurturing and production, women have provided the continuity to household and family life. The burden of class differences and uneven privilege of women is a more recently acquired twentieth century concern among the majority of black, Indian and coloured peoples. The region has inherited a generalized stereotype of woman in society as *matrifocal* or mother-centred, often confused for matriarchal and matrilineal both of which are not at all applicable. In this stereotyping, women are not only assumed to possess extreme strength and resilience, but also to be responsible for the increasing *marginality* of the male. The paradox of both stereotypes rarely surface in popular discussions, although this has been debated to some degree at the level of scholarship (R. T. Smith 1996; Barrow 1996; Momsen 1993). Matrifocality has not led to greater gender equality. Women's power in the home is equated with power in the society at large. Marginalization is rarely depicted as the relations between men and men, which is in fact the underlying subtext of two books by Errol Miller's *Marginalization of the Black Male*, and *Men at Risk*, both published in the eighties, and popular butts for feminist attacks in the region. Instead marginalization is assumed to be the fault of female (over) achievers. Slavery was initially blamed for the emasculation of the male. The fact that women have emerged from the same system with their femininity and strength reasonably intact is often glossed over. Black men were shown little mercy or respect by the white elite and managerial class in matters pertaining to their personal lives. In Thomas Thistlewood's Jamaican diary between 1750 and 1786,[19] at least one record exists about the extent to which black masculinity suffered at the hands of another male grouping. Emasculation was tendered by extreme humiliation and pain as for instance seen in the following entry:

> Friday, 30th July 1756: Punch catched at Salt River and brought home. Flogged him and Quacoo well, and then washed and rubbed in salt pickle, lime juice and bird pepper; also whipped Hector for losing his hoe, made New Negro Joe piss in his eyes & mouth &c. (Hall 1992, 73)

The conditions under which intimacy between black men and women in the new setting was persistently invaded by the assumed rights over their body by the master:

> On the domestic scene, Mrs. Cope was brought to bed of a girl on the night of Saturday 26th; Mr. Cope was paying frequent nightly visits to Egypt where he would summon Little Mimber, for whom he had a passion until mid-April when he transferred his attentions to Sancho's wife, Cubbah (Hall 1992, 93)

This legacy, together with that of being commodified, sold and bartered as property and the host of other indignities, has continued in other ways, in the stereotyping of black masculinity in the Caribbean and also evident in the United States of America. The question of why, out of this legacy, blame has been conferred on to black women, and women in general, for a persistent emasculation of the male, needs to be investigated thoroughly. The facile notions pervasive as an explanation in the Caribbean is that due to the presence of "female headed households" in which women are both provider and nurturer, women are consistently themselves blamed for the "spoiling" of their sons and husbands by inculcating irresponsible male behaviour as the norm. The feminist or women's attempt to achieve parity with men in various spheres is viewed, here as elsewhere, as an antagonistic measure to gain control over the other sex. The fact that women's struggles thus far in the region's political arena have been more than conciliatory, reconciling the need for ethnicity, nation and community and family with that of desire and intimacy, remains a persistently elusive part of the discussions which take place in the societies. At the same time, one must record that there have always been supportive male colleagues or partners in this struggle for gender equality.

While this is the dominant discourse of the black diaspora, there is a continued interface with the gender systems of other groups who also live in the region, such that the idea of matrifocality and marginality, though still applicable in part, may take different forms in different societies. For instance, the presence of a large number of Indians and Indian family systems in Trinidad and Guyana which has held firm to an ideology of patriarchal gender relations, creates differences in the dominant Caribbean perception of ideas of masculinity and femininity. Societies such as Dominican Republic and Cuba with large European Spanish populations have other distinctions in gender systems as do societies influenced by the French such as Haiti, Martinique and Guadeloupe. Belize is another uniquely developing situation, where, despite its similarity in the past to the English-speaking Caribbean islands, has had in the twentieth century a continuous influx of migrants from the neighbouring Spanish-speaking Central American populations, introducing into the society a Mayan group with an extremely patriarchal system of gender relations.[20] Much systematic research needs to be undertaken in these societies to establish a more comprehensive and accurate picture of the ongoing constructions of masculinity and femininity into the present.

If sexual difference in relation to economic survival and production is couched in largely antagonistic categories, the ideas of different licences allowed male and female sexualities is a firmly implanted one. In general men are allowed many partners, women are to be monogamous, although serial monogamy is acceptable as women are not expected to remain unmarried after the death of, or separation from, a husband or partner. This different expectation of male and female sexuality is continually debated. Femininity is still defined in relation to virtue, motherhood and being a wife, while masculinity is at the same time bounded by expectations, as for instance that of being a provider, but allowed indefinite boundaries and privileges because "he is man". The debate on sexuality is by no means restricted to differences between men and women, but equally between same sex relations or women of different classes or ethnic groups, all of which militates against a unified platform for gender consciousness. Much of this debate is contradictory. One Dancehall lyricist appeals to a notion of working-class female sexuality as being free, exuberant and untamed and therefore the most desired. The downtown girl is presumed to be the most libidinous "Gimme the girl wid the wickedess slam" (Beanie Man, 1995) in opposition to the "browning" who represents the "uptown' middleclass ideal woman of mixed race who is limited in her performance by the control and reserve which she is made to assume. In Trinidad the idiom of the 'red' woman has fairly similar applications although perhaps not so sharply contested as in the Jamaican context where class differences are more defined by colour. The origin of this ideal from the 'mulatto' woman bred in slavery needs to be traced insofar as both sexuality and power over other men clearly were intersected in the historical construction of sexuality within the region.

The commitment to sexual difference in the English-speaking Caribbean in terms of the opposition between masculinity and femininity is very fertile ground for gender analysis. In societies where black masculinity constantly seeks to assert itself, where it is defined as power over other men and in relation to multiple relationships with the other sex, where monogamy and fidelity are perceived as signs of weakness or of being a "soft man" masculinity remains simultaneously macho and a very fragile thing. Fragility is especially evident in the antagonism and distance which must be maintained from male homosexuality and from homosexuality itself, the latter which is in general unacceptable as an alternative sexuality in these parts. My understanding of the non-English speaking territories, especially that of the Dominican Republic, suggest that the 'machismo' culture is very similar. Ironically, again because of the shared legacies of colonization and continuing imperialism in which both masculinity and femininity have had to be defined in relation to the other, feminism has largely been, in my view, a nurturing one, a recognition of a shared condition, despite sexual difference and despite obvious inequalities. In the region, the construction of masculinity has emerged as an issue which is tackled by women and feminist scholars and is now being treated seriously by some men.[21]

I have argued in this paper that indigenous feminist theorizing requires a comprehensive grounding of the construction of gender identities in an historical perspective, an appreciation of the linguistic meanings applied to gendered categories within a culture to establish the boundaries and implicit sources of discrimination that are kept in place through language and a Caribbean claiming and adaptation of terminologies such as sexual difference that are traded in the global discourse of feminism and gender. Theoretically I have attempted to demonstrate most insistently the foundation on which a Caribbean feminist discourse must be built. If the struggles for identity have also been about the desire to enrich the space and group to which we belong, then Caribbean feminism is an expression of the new conditions of that desire. In the last decades of the twentieth century, for those who live in this stepping stone of islands and adjacent territories, between the North and South Americas, feminism provides a new lens to interrogate the past and renders new challenges and opportunities to establish boundaries of identity and difference with respect to equality.

ENDNOTES

[1] As will later be more fully explained, 'creole'-born here refers to those born in the region itself.

[2] This interpretation of the ongoing construction of gender identities under colonization is consistent with the ideas put forward in Teresa de Lauretis (1987) *Technologies of Gender*

[3] I use this term to signify this point of difference, and also as it resonates with the Marxist use of the word, building here on Ken Post's explanation in *Arise Ye Starvelings, the Jamaican Labour Rebellion of 1938 and its Aftermath* 1978, The Hague: Martinus Nijhoff. Post writes that "each moment of antagonistic contradiction continually recreates the other and is the condition of its existence, but their relationship is such that both cannot develop equally" p. 28

[4] References to Beatrice Greig's visits and activism in Trinidad is found in Reddock (1994) and Mohammed (1994b).

[5] These stories are evident in the Ramayana, and are told and retold by the pundits or hindu priests in Trinidad to each generation of Hindu men and women. These ideas, though part of Hindu mythology were pervasive among all Indians in Trinidad despite religion. I have examined the recurrence and pervasiveness of mythology in informing gender ideals and roles, despite migration in an article entitled "Ram and Sita: The Reconstitution of Gender Identities among Indians in Trinidad through Mythology" in *Gendered Ideologies*, Christine Barrow ed., (1998). Kingston: Ian Randle Publishers.

[6] These ideas are more fully developed in Patricia Mohammed *Gender Negotiations in Trinidad 1917-1947*. Palgrave/ Institute of Social Studies

7 Discussions on Elma Francois and other women involved in the early labour struggles in Trinidad are well developed in Reddock (1994). Reddock also draws attention to the existence of branches of the UNIA in Trinidad, indicating another aspect of struggle within the region which I have not sufficiently developed in the text - that is the way in which the ideas and activism in one territory often affected and influenced the others creating its own internal dynamic. The labour struggles of the 1930s is a good example of how this takes place, as is the Grenada Revolution in the late 70s early 80s which affected the Caribbean in ways still being revisited by political scientists such as Brian Meeks.

8 There have been different interpretations of women's roles in the People's National Movement led by Eric Williams to the extent which they brought and helped to sustain his power for near three decades, from 1956 to 1981. My own analysis of history leads me to a partial leniency with the 'consciousness' of gender in the past. While leaders and politicians have no doubt been aware of women's importance or crucial roles in various platforms, the consciousness of the time did not lead women themselves to demand equal treatment or recognition as the unspoken ideology of patriarchy affected both men and women.

9 In the Caribbean there is an extensive literature which is growing on the women of the past who have been active in many different ways in these struggles for gender equality. See for instance Linnette Vassal (1993). *Voices of Jamaican Women 1898-1939*. Kingston Jamaica: Department of History, University of the West Indies.

10 Richard Allsop discusses its etymology in the Region. It was first used "with pride by European colonists, especially the French, to refer to themselves as born and bred in the "New World". It later came to distinguish local breeds of livestock from imported, and by extension, in a system where slaves were viewed as property as well, to refer to locally born slaves to differentiate them from the original Africans brought under the system. Allsop notes that the status of the word then took a nose dive among the white population, but rose among the local population, thus creating two further distinctions. It was a label applied to a class of non-white persons of "breeding" or an excluded class of "ill-bred blacks". In the latter sense, while unfairly applied, the word appeared to have returned to its original source. Two Spanish etymologists Corominas and Pascual, who have traced its origins to Portuguese also indicated that the word may have originally been of African origin used among the Negroes(sic) "born in the Indies" to distinguish those "born in Guinea from those born in America because they consider themselves more honourable and of better status than their children because they are born in the fatherland, while their children are born at home.(Allsop,1996: 176-7).

11 When I was growing up as a child in the late 1950s in a village of Lengua in South Trinidad, a village primarily inhabited by Indians, the few persons of African descent who lived in this village, were referred to as Creoles by all the Indians. For Indians it had become synonymous with Africans. To my knowledge its use then as now, was not pejorative, but rather to define difference of race, as everyone was accustomed to doing in this society to distinguish the many different groups which co-existed.

12 While this analysis focuses on the etymology of the term and its meaning for English speaking societies in the Region, I am aware that the mutation of language is similar for all societies. In Haiti a French creole patois is the langue parole, in the Dominican Republic and Cuba as well as Puerto Rico, the Spanish varies from that spoken in Europe although the common base still exists. An

Argentinian colleague once commented to another Dominican colleague in my hearing that he thought that the Dominicanas spoke a "bad Spanish" in the very same way that the various dialects of English spoken by those of us in the English-speaking Caribbean were thought to be "bad English". Near the end of writing this paper I have just come across a book entitled *Caribbean Creolization: Reflections on the Cultural Dynamics of Language, Literature and Identity* Kathleen M. Balutansky and Marie-Agnes Sourieau, eds., 1998, Jamaica: The Press, UWI. The collection of essays in this book bears out some of my suggestions in this section on a definition of the Caribbean as *creole*.

13 The allusion here to black US feminist Audre Lorde's famous statement of using the master's tools to demolish the master's house is deliberate and relevant for feminism in the Caribbean.

14 Yet there is mimicry inherent in its evolution. Many of the words we used in an Indian household in Trinidad to describe kitchen implements were derived from Bhojpuri Hindi, the dialect which was shared by the largest groups which came and therefore became the dominant one. For example, we 'balayed' the roti, meaning to roll out the dough. None of these have any meaning for a Hindi speaking Indian from India as it is the creation of a verb from a noun through the rules of English grammar and not those of Hindi. Yet this and other such terms are still widely used today in many Indian households. The emergence in Trinidad of the genre of music referred to as chutney/soca is itself a blend of the Indian with the soul music which emerged out of the United States and the calypso of Trinidad.

15 The work of Carolyn Cooper, (1993). *Noises in the Blood.* London: Macmillan is useful and more highly developed on these themes. From my reading, Cooper's work largely supports the points I am making. She looks at the emergence of the dancehall artist in Jamaica, examining the African resonances of this genre and arguing in this and subsequent writings that this popular culture form is an oral expression of nationalism from a hitherto silenced group.

16 By antagonism here I acknowledge that gender relations are also extremely ridden with conflicts and antagonism between men and women, women and women and men and men. My particular approach in this essay has been admittedly a bit one sided, dwelling on the mutually negotiated aspects of gender relations as compared to the confrontations caused by its opposition. This was pointed out to me by Yaba Badoe who also made many other very insightful comments on a draft of this paper, for which I am very grateful. I attempt to deal with the antagonism which results from women's challenges to male patriarchy through the matrifocal/marginality debate in the region.

17 I lived for several years in the Netherlands. Before that I had also lived in the UK for some time. While in Britain because I shared a language and past history, the messages of gender were clearer and more accessible. For the entire period of my stay in the Netherlands, because I had no real knowledge of the language, it was difficult for me to understand either the business of intimacy between men and women, or the subtle aspects of racism which were no doubt part of the black migrant's lived existence in this society.

18 I realise that from this point onwards, much of my analysis speaks directly to the English-speaking Caribbean. Nonetheless, from my understanding of the other territories, as well as close association with persons from the different societies, I argue that many of these ideas of masculinity and femininity and the body are applicable across the Region. For instance Huguette Dagenais in her paper "Women of Guadeloupe: The Paradoxes of Reality" in (Momsen 1993)

comes to the same conclusion about paradoxical status of the Guadeloupean woman as studies in the English speaking do.

[19] Douglas Hall selected and published extracts from Thomas Thistlewood's diary in a book entitled *In Miserable Slavery: Thomas Thistlewood in Jamaica, 1750-86*, Macmillan, UK, 1989. Thistlewood lived in western Jamaica as a small landowner for 36 years. He was an inveterate diarist and he chronicled during this time, almost daily, the activities of himself and those around him, thus leaving a legacy which, despite its obvious limitations or personal biases etc, also provide us with information which was otherwise not recorded in historical documents of the time.

[20] While I have not studied this systematically, recently I worked in Belize with community-based workers involved in a project on Sexual and Reproductive Health sponsored by the International Planned Parenthood Federation, New York. Some of the problems and issues which confront women in the society are those expressed by the rural Mayan women of a very patriarchal control over their sexuality and lives.

[21] See for instance articles in the First Symposium on Masculinity in the Caribbean hosted by The Centre for Gender and Development Studies at St. Augustine, Trinidad in January 1996. Published as *Interrogating Caribbean Masculinities*, Rhoda Reddock (ed.). Kingston: University of the West Indies Press, 2004.

REFERENCES

Alexander, Jacqui. M. and Chandra Talpade Mohanty. 1997. *Feminist Genealogies: Colonial Legacies, Democratic Futures*. New York: Routledge.

Allsop, Richard. 1996. *A Dictionary of Caribbean Usage*. Oxford and New York: Oxford University Press.

Barrow, Christine. 1996. *Family in the Caribbean: Themes and Perspectives*. Kingston and Oxford: Ian Randle Publishers and James Currey Publishers.

Brah, Avtar. 1996. *Cartographies of Diaspora: Contesting Identities*. London and New York: Routledge.

Braithwaite, Edward. 1985. *Contradictory Omens: Cultural Diversity and Integration in the Caribbean*. Kingston, Jamaica: Savacou Publications.

Brown, Janet and Barry Chevannes. 1995. Report to UNICEF on the Gender Socialization Project of the University of the West Indies, Jamaica: University of the West Indies.

de Lauretis, Teresa. 1987. *Technologies of Gender: Essays on Theory, Film and Fiction*, bloomingtob, IN: Indiana University Press.

Di Stefano, Christine. 1990. "Dilemmas of Difference: Feminism, Modernity, and Postmodernism." In *Feminism/Postmodernism*, edited by Linda J, Nicholson. New York and London: Routledge.

Flax, Jane. 1990. "Postmodernism and Gender Relations in Feminist Theory." In *Feminism/Postmodernism*, edited by Linda J, Nicholson. New York and London: Routledge.

Ford-Smith, Honor, 1988. "Women in the Garvey Movement in Jamaica." In *Garvey, His Work and Impact*, edited by Rupert Lewis and Patrick Bryan. Kingston, Jamaica: Institute of Social and Economic Research, University of the West Indies.

Gaztambide-Geigel, Antonio. 1996. "The Invention of the Caribbean in the Twentieth Century." Paper presented to the 28th Annual Conference of the Association of Caribbean Historians, Barbados.

Hall, Douglas, 1992. *In Miserable Slavery: Thomas Thistlewood in Jamaica, 1750-86*. London and Basingstoke: Macmillan Caribbean.

Hermsen, Joke J. and Alkeline Van Lenning. 1991. *Sharing the Difference: Feminist Debates in Holland*. London and New York: Routledge.

Irigaray, Luce. 1984. *An Ethics of Sexual Difference*. New York: Cornell University Press.

James, C.L.R. 1963. *The Black Jacobins: Toussaint L'Ouverture and the San Domingo Revolution*. New York: Vintage Books.

James, C.L.R. 1969. "The West Indian Intellectual" Introduction in *Froudacity* by J.J. Thomas. London and Port of Spain: New Beacon Books.

Language 1982. *Caribbean Quarterly*, 28 (4) (December). Jamaica: University of the West Indies: Department of Extra-Mural Studies.

Mahabir, Noor Kumar. 1985. *The Still Cry: Personal Accounts of East Indians in Trinidad and Tobago during Indentureship*. Trinidad: Caloux Publications.

Manuel, Peter. 1995. *Caribbean Currents: Caribbean Music from Rumba to Reggae*. Philadelphia: Temple University Press.

Martin, Tony. 1988. "Women in the Garvey Movement." In *Garvey, His Work and Impact*, edited Rupert Lewis and Patrick Bryan. Kingston, Jamaica: Institute of Social and Economic Research, University of the West Indies.

Mathurin, Lucille. 1974. "A Historical Study of Women in Jamaica from 1655 to 1844" PhD Dissertation, University of the West Indies, Mona, Kingston, Jamaica.

Menezes, Mary Noel. 1992. *The Portuguese of Guyana: A Study in Culture and Conflict*. Gujarat, India: Anand Press.

Mohammed, Patricia, 1994. "Gender as a Primary Signifier in the Construction of Community and State among Indians in Trinidad". *Caribbean Quarterly*, 40 (3-4).

Mohammed, Patricia. 1994. "Nuancing the Feminist Discourse in the Caribbean" Social and Economic Studies, Special Issue edited by Brian Meeks: Jamaica: Institute of Social and Economic Research, University of the West Indies.

Momsen, Janet, ed. 1993. *Women and Change in the Caribbean*. London, Kingston, Bloomington: James Currey Ltd., Ian Randle Publishers and Indiana University Press.

Moore, Henrietta. 1994. *A Passion for Difference*. Cambridge: Polity Press.

Pineda, Magdalena. 1984. "The Spanish-Speaking Caribbean: We Women Aren't Sheep." In *Sisterhood is Global*, edited by Robin Morgan. New York: Anchor Books.

Ramesar, Esmond, ed. 1974. "Language and Society." *Caribbean Issues. A Journal of Caribbean Affairs*. Trinidad: Extra Mural Studies Unit, University of the West Indies.

Reddock, Rhoda. 1994. Women Labour & Politics in Trinidad and Tobago: A History, Kingston: Ian Randle Publishers.

Rennie, Bukka. 1973. *History of the Working Class in the Twentieth Century*. Trinidad: New Beginning Movement.

Rhys, Jean. 1966. *Wide Sargasso Sea*. Great Britain: Richard Clay Ltd.

Senior, Olive. 1986. *Summer Lightning and Other Stories*. London: Longman Group Ltd.

Senior, Olive. 1991. *Working Miracles: Women's Lives in the English Speaking Caribbean*. Barbados: Institute of Social and Economic Research.

Smith, R.T. 1996. *The Matrifocal Family: Power, Pluralism and Politics*. New York and London: Routledge.

Thomas, J. J. 1889. *Froudacity: West Indian Fables*. London: New Beacon Books Ltd.

Vassell, Linnette. 1993. Voices of Women in Jamaica. Kingston, Jamaica: Department of History, University of the West Indies.
Weeks, Jeffrey. 1986. *Sexuality*. London: Ellis Horwood Ltd.

Walcott, Derek. 1992. "The Antilles: Fragments of Epic Memory." Nobel Acceptance Speech, *Trinidad and Tobago Review* Jan-Feb 1993, pp. 23-26

3

"But Most of all Mi Love Mi Browning"

The Emergence in 18th and 19th Century Jamaica of the Mulatto Woman as the Desired[†]

INTRODUCTION

The subject of miscegenation between the black and white populations has provided prurient data for the observers and diarists of slave society in Jamaica (such as Thomas Thistlewood (1750-86) and Lady Nugent (1801-1805), crucial information for the critics of slavery on the inhumane nature of slave/master relations, diverting data for the historical researcher in general, and colourful material for the historical fiction writer. In employing the term "slave society" I am using the concept as it applies to the Caribbean experience in particular. The meaning here is drawn from Goveia (1965) in her reference to the Leeward Islands – the coherence of the whole system within each territory, more specifically, the division of peoples into groups separated by differences of legal and social status, possessing different

---

[†] "'But most of all me love me browning': The Emergence of the Mulatto Woman as Desired in 18th and 19th century Jamaica." In *Feminist Review: Reconstructing Femininities: Colonial Intersections of Gender, Race, Religion and Class*, Special Issue # 65, June 2000, Meera Kosambi (Guest Editor – India) and Jane Haggis (Guest Editor- Australia), London: Routledge Journals. pp. 22-48

political rights and economic opportunities, and differentiated by racial origin and culture.

A mixed-race population was one of the early by-products of colonization and slavery, but one which was problematic to a system which thrived on distinctions of race, class and colour. Mixed races were at first perceived as a cross between two species and therefore as "hybrids". While anti-slavery adherents stressed the idea that all peoples belonged to a single family, the dissenters laid the claim that "hybridity" fostered infertility. In 1774, Edward Long (1774), a Jamaican slave-owner, argued strenuously that the 'White and the Negro' were two distinct species. Despite the evidence of fertility of the "mulatto" and mixed races in Jamaica, Long pursued his argument, deliberately highlighting the linguistic connection between mulatto and mule, the latter an infertile offspring of the horse and ass:

> Some few of them (Mulattos) have intermarried here with those of their own complexion: but such matches have generally been defective and barren. They seem in this respect to be actually of the mule-kind, and not so capable of producing one from the other.[1]

The mixing of races that facilitated continued fertility was referred to as "amalgamation". It was not until 1864, that the term "miscegenation" was applied. Yet the debates on hybridity and infertility persisted throughout the nineteenth century and into the twentieth century. There were clearly underlying currents behind these debates which were not openly confronted in the eighteenth and nineteenth, nor early twentieth centuries. Young (1995) suggests that "what has not been emphasized is that the debates about theories of race in the nineteenth century, by settling on the possibility or impossibility of hybridity, focussed explicitly on the issue of sexuality and the issue of sexual unions between whites and blacks. Theories of race were thus also covert theories of desire."[2]

The major theme of this essay, the emergence of the mulatto woman – the product of cross breeding between black and white peoples – as desired, is stimulated by the theoretical debates which have taken place under the rubric of colonial desire. While Michel Foucault's (1980) work advanced the notions that from the seventeenth century onwards and gathering momentum in the eighteenth century, there was a "multiplication of discourses concerning sex in the field of exercise of power itself,"[3] Foucault's analysis, based on observations in Europe, accentuated a need to appreciate the parallel set of discourses also unfolding in colonized societies. Peter Hulme for instance depicted the encounter between Inkle, an English sailor, and Yarico, the indigenous (coloured) woman, as the archetypal love story between the colonizer and the colonized. The pregnant Yarico is deserted and sold into slavery by her lover Inkle when he is rescued from the Caribbean island where he has been shipwrecked.[4] Similar analyses have proliferated on the experiences of the British in India, the dilemma of the Anglo-Indian offspring or the creation of categories such as "prostitutes" out of temple dancers (*Devdasis*) adding to the stream of outcasts in the highly regulated caste structure of Hindu society (Chatterjee 1992). The seminal theoretical contributions by Young's *Colonial Desire* (1995) and Anne McClintock's *Imperial Leather* (1995) have been critical in advancing the debates in this area.

There is much scattered historical data on miscegenation (or cross breeding and hybridization which will be used interchangeably in this essay), and the creation of a mixed race of peoples in the Caribbean. My own lived experience and gender scholarship throughout the region has fine-tuned my perception of the legacies of our historical past on the contemporary connection between gender, class, race and colour. It was as a result of cross breeding that another aesthetic of beauty and desirability evolved in Creole society. As regards to femininity in particular, the mixed or mulatto woman disrupted the notions of a Victorian purity of the white woman versus a "hot constitution'd black female sexuality" (Bush 1990). Recognizing that desirability of the mulatto or mixed race woman in Jamaica and elsewhere in the Caribbean still obtains, I want to investigate the conditions in the past which may have influenced ideas and constructions of desire then and into the present. This exploration is an asymmetrical interplay between past and present, and despite its title, must be viewed as neither historical nor sociological, but rather contemplative of how contemporary gender relations need to be processed through the ongoing constructions of gender and sexuality in the past.

The term "mulatto" is not an undisputed one in the literature. The definition of who constitutes a mulatto has varied over time and is clearly differentiated by location since different admixtures make for the state of being mulatto. There are nonetheless synonymous terms employed by writers, or those who live in various societies to describe women and men of mixed race. At present, the mulatto woman is referred to as "browning" in Jamaica, the "red woman" in Trinidad, the "mulata" in Latin societies and the "woman of colour" in the United States of America. Men in Trinidad who are mixed are described as 'red'. If this diverse nomenclature exists at present, in the past there was also confusion about which population was being referred to by the writer or the historian. Lady Nugent (1966) applied the term "creole women" to both the "yellow" (mixed) women and to the whites born in Jamaica. Thome and Kimball (1969),[5] observers from the United States of America supported by the Anti-Slavery society, employed the term "coloured" in their report, a term which is more commonly applied in the USA.

The *Dictionary of Caribbean English Usage*, (Allsop 1996) interestingly does not have an entry for "browning". The entry which comes closest is "brown skin" (adj). *"A person of light or dark brown skin; a person whose skin is noticeably less than quite black..."* The entry "red" is more revealing. In reference to a person's skin colour, this entry reads:

> Being of any colour from brown to near white, showing varying mixtures of Black and White races. ...
> (b) Barbadians often speak about 'red people' alluding to persons of fair skin complexion. Even though the word red is used here to denote a certain colour, it carries with it a strong connotation namely that persons involved are the end products of cross breeding between Caucasians and Negroes.

The entry of "mulatto" in the dictionary, however, indicates the ambiguity of this term in British West Indian society, possibly dating its widespread use in the period of slavery and early emancipation. The author notes:

> The term which was historically meant to be derogatory barely passes as acceptable in writing in the Caribbean today as a recognized description of a person of mixed (white/black) race; but its offensive connotation, especially with the pronunciation malata, easily surfaces as insult.[6]

The Guyanese referent as cited by Allsop (1996) needs scrutiny. "I ain want no white man cause I ain able with no mulatta chile" she said", suggests that the mulatta woman was not always acceptable to either group, black or white, illustrating that there has been a shifting set of attitudes to colour and race under slave society.[7] The category "coloured" is of more recent vintage (early twentieth century) in describing peoples of mixed race and not to my knowledge used widely by Caribbean peoples.

Earliest constructions of racial mixing in slave society were very precise, with an elaborate colour scale found in the Caribbean. The lighter the shade, the higher was the person's rank on the social ladder. The sambo was the mixture between the mulatto and black, the mulatto was the offspring of white and black, the quadroon the offspring of mulatto and white and so on (Shepherd 1971; Braithwaite 1971). Terborg-Penn (1995a) points to the different use of the terms "mulatto" and "coloured" in past and contemporary United States and Caribbean society. The mulatto woman in the British West Indies does not identify herself as black. In the United States, the same kind of woman may have no choice in defining herself other than as black. The variations in terminology applied to skin colour in different societies coupled with the sometimes misleading measurement of mixed race populations led Terborg-Penn to suggest that "The key to historical reconstruction in such cases must rest first upon how women identify themselves, and second, on whom they are identified as by the society in which they live. In addition, the perceptions about race and colour of scholars who have written previously about the subject must be considered."[8] This unclarity of the terms being applied is one of the theoretical problems inherent in discussing the group which I am generically referring to as mulatto in eighteenth- and nineteenth-century Jamaica. "Creole society" here refers to a society evolving from a colonized space, where elements of the society are mixing, blending and changing its manners, customs, habits, inhabitants, cuisine and so on. The complication arises where people from creole society are also referred to as "creole", and often times the simultaneous use of the term creole to mean born into or native to a society rather than foreign born. This term is a very disputed and a chameleon-like one. For this reason creole as descriptive or process has been very applicable to the dynamics of population and cultural change in the Caribbean (and elsewhere). Because I move back and forth in time and draw on different sources in which varied terms were applied, there is a necessary confusion. Where possible in the text this will be clarified. In general "coloured" is synonymous with "mulatto", while "creole" and creole society may be read from the context of its use.

In studying the generic mulatto woman in relation to the concept of desire, I am also attempting to further engender Caribbean history by concentrating on the category "mulatto woman" rather than Black, White or Indian as precise racial categories and as the primary foci of inquiry. In writing women into the history of the second wave feminist project, the category "woman" had at first been treated largely unproblematically. Women were viewed in relation to their ethnic group and as a racialized category, representative of the class into which they were born and recognized by societal and cultural difference but under the skin we were collectively linked by biological make up. Yet from the inception of this task in the Caribbean we see that the mulatto was already signified as a category to be reckoned with. Lucille Mathurin Mair's (1974) pioneering work examines women in Jamaican society from 1655 to 1844 and was literally the first attempt by a scholar to legitimize the writing of women's history within the academy.[9] Mathurin Mair had initiated this task of differentiating women from men, but her analysis records the distinction between different groups of women she encounters in the historical records. She identified three main groups of women, white, black and mulatto, examining the status and conditions of each during the selected period. Barry Higman's (1976, 1984) demographic studies of slaves provide a vast fount of data and insights already being tapped by gender historians.

Later on, works by Hilary Beckles, Marietta Morrissey, Barbara Bush, Verene Shepherd, Rhoda Reddock, Bridget Brereton and Patricia Mohammed continued this first layer of making visible the women who inhabited the region.[10] In a more recent publication entitled *Centering Woman*, Hilary Beckles (1999) still remarks, however, that the primary focus of historical research in gender in the Caribbean has been "the black woman, with the brown (coloured) woman running a competitive second and the white woman trailing behind at a distance." In this book Beckles places women in slave society, black, white and coloured (brown) in relation to each other, thus advancing one of the trajectories now accelerating in gender historiography in the region.

Before Beckles's effort, in 1995 the edited collection of papers in *Engendering History: Caribbean Women in Historical Perspective* (Shepherd, Brereton and Bailey 1995) had begun to record some theoretical developments in gender historiography in the Caribbean. Three essays in this book Terborg-Penn, Mohammed and Hall "focus[ed] on the problematic issue of discursively constructing a women's history which is representative of the multiple experiences of national and racial groups in the Caribbean ..."[11] Terborg-Penn (1995b) proposed an African feminist theoretical lens through which Caribbean women may be viewed cross-culturally. While drawing on the work of Filomena Chioma Steady, Terborg-Penn places "black" and African-descended women at the centre of her framework, yet she also focuses attention on the need to establish colour stratification as an analytical variable in the study of African-descended women Drawing primarily on the study of (East) Indian women and men in Trinidad in the post-slavery period of Indian indentureship and settlement, my own approach to engendering history has tended to pose the problem of gender in terms of the construction of gender roles and the negotiation of gender identities, at the same time embracing the need for scholars to place women as central actors in historical revisioning. Interestingly the question of the mulatto mixture of Indian and Caucasian never emerged as an issue although that of African and Indian mixtures had already been pejoratively named as *dougla*[12] (Mohammed 1995). In dealing with any one group in British West Indian history, it is virtually impossible to ignore the intra- and inter- group negotiations which take place in the political and social struggle of identity formation, as Beckles (1999) also illustrates in *Centering Women*. Signalling that gender politics must intrude on imperial politics, Catherine Hall (1995) supports the need to challenge the narratives of empire, urging scholars in gender to "rethink ways of writing imperial histories."[13] Thus this attempt to understand present constructions of desire in relation to the past continues the task of rewriting the colonial narratives with a Caribbean insider lens.

The problem of colonial desire is not a new one and has preoccupied writers and scholars for many centuries. Young (1995) cites the poet Tennyson who captured the paradox of the colonial quite succinctly: "I will take some savage woman; she shall rear my dusky race," following in the same verse with, "Could I wed a savage woman steept perhaps in monstrous crime?"[14] Attraction and repulsion are always bedfellows in desire, and is doubly complicated by the element of racial power imbalances. In *Roll Jordan Roll: The World the Slaves Made*, Eugene Genovese (1976), citing W.B. Dubois, observes that in the United States antebellum miscegenation was "stark, ugly, painful, beautiful, ...The coloured slave woman became the medium through which two great races were united". Genovese adds about the interracial unions of the southern United States that "many white men who began by taking a slave girl in an act of sexual exploitation ended by loving her and the children she bore. They were not supposed to, but they did ...."[15]

Anthony Trollope (1859) also echoes ambivalence in the attitudes to sexual relations between black and white, possibly voicing the thoughts of many others at the time. He proposed the advantages of racial "amalgamation", on the grounds of economy. He theorized that the race which emerged from an amalgam of black and white would be more suited to physical labour in the tropics. He couples the white man's intolerance of the tropical climate with a low opinion of the labouring or organizational capacity of the African, and provides a solution to the empire "without stain to our patriotism, to take off our hats and bid farewell to the West Indies."[16] Women and men, black or white, and their personal and emotional responses to cross breeding, are absent from Trollope's equation and solution.

IMAGES OF BODY AESTHETIC IN "CREOLE SOCIETY"

That an aesthetic related to gradation in skin colour was emerging in creole society is supported by references in poetry, art and festivals in the Caribbean. Michael Scott (1833) records a John Canoe (Jonkunnu) song that expresses the ambiguities of desire as it attaches to skin colour and race.

>...But Massa Buccra have white love,
>Soft and silken like one dove,
>To brown girl - him barely shivel!
>To black girl - ho, Lord, de Devil!
>
>But when him once two tree year here,
>Him tink white lady wery great boder(bother)!
>De coloured peoples, never fear,
>Ah. him lob him (love her) de morest nor any oder
>
>But top - one time had fever catch him,
>Coloured peoples kindly watch him -
>In sick-room, nurse voice like music -
>From him (her) hand tastes sweet de physic
>
>So alway come - in two tree year,
>And so wid you, massa - never fear -
>Brown girl for cook - for wife - for nurse,
>Buccra - poo - no wort a curse[17]

Carolyn Cooper (1994) interprets the song as tracing "...Massa Buccra's gradual path from the soft silken dove of his white love, to the brown girl, and ultimately, we may presume, to the black devil herself."[18] While both the mulatto and black women are eventually desired by the white "Massa Buccra" for different reasons, the white woman fades as an object of desire. The verse also suggests a certain fear of the black woman, (black devil herself) and of black female sexuality which both Cooper and Bush (1990) have also discussed in their works. What it also hints at is that the mulatto woman, for reasons which were perhaps not always rational ones, grew to be a more acceptable intermediary between the oppositional categories of black and white as sexual partner options for the white male in slave creole society.

Some parallels are also evident in June Carter's (1985) discussion of the various metaphoric constructions of female beauty by colour and race in the Hispanic Caribbean: *la negra* as an object of sensuality and evil, *la mulata* as highly sensuous and at the same time linked to the imagery of fruit: "cultivated not for their beauty, as is a flower, but to carry out the more utilitarian function of nourishing and sustaining the consumer. ... (to) ... perform its duty, it is handled, squeezed, tasted and finally devoured. ...Her counterpart, *la blanca*, is traditionally associated with flowers, *la rosa, el lirio, el jazmin* – objects of adoration and beauty, underlines the society's assumptions about the cultural and aesthetic inferiority of the black female."[19] Interestingly a corresponding aesthetic for masculinity was not developed for mulatto men. Patriarchal power relations between men and men were also being contested in creole society, so perhaps mulatto men would have already been perceived as more threatening to the power and superiority of the white male. Constituted with less power anyway, as all women were at the time, mulatto women did not as yet pose similar threats to the hierarchy. The perception of power is confused by sexual objectification and desire as one would expect.

The mulatto women by the late eighteenth century and early nineteenth century were also becoming subjects for painters who worked in the region. Agostino Brunias, an Italian-born and British-trained painter accompanied Sir William Young, the first Governor of Dominica to the island in 1773. He also travelled to the other islands with Young officially during his office. From 1773 to 1796, Brunias continued to paint in the region. Several of Brunias's better known works place the mulatto woman as the central figure - *The Barbados Mulatto Girl, 1780, A Negro Festival drawn from Nature in the Island of St. Vincent and The West Indian Washerwoman.*[20] The positioning of the mulatto woman as the focus of the viewer's eye and the centre of attention of the others in the picture plane already signifies (though possibly only imagined by the painter), the elevated position in which the mulatto woman was attaining in slave society compared to black women (Pereira 1992).

In Trinidad and Cuba, two nineteenth century painters, Jean Michel Cazabon (1813- 888) and Victor Patricio Landaluze (1825-1889), also selected the mulatto woman as subjects. Cazabon's painting *Seated Mulatto Beauty*[21] is singular in that it admits the aesthetic view of the painter – that she is a beauty, and possibly also reflecting the view of the society in the title of the painting. Landaluze's depiction of the *calesero* or the liveried Cuban servant - held in high prestige because he was chosen from among the most handsome and proportioned of male servants to drive the two-wheeled carriages - shows him flirting with the mulatto woman as his improved class status allowed. Mulatto women were able to be more discriminating about their choice of male partners. She is described by Guellermo de Zendegui (1975) in his discussions of Landaluze's paintings as the feminine counterpart of the *calesero* "born of a forbidden dalliance by the scion of some rich house, who was usually emancipated and kept with the family servants as a maid, seamstress ...or to work at other minor occupations or crafts of her own account. On a decreasing scale of colour, the quadroon revealed only the slightest tinge of cinnamon that served to increase the feminine attractions seductively..."[22]

EXPRESSIONS OF DESIRE FROM PAST TO PRESENT

By the eighteenth century, clearly there had emerged a critical mass of men and women who would today fit the description of brown but whose mixture of blood was measured with much concern, agitation and attempt at accuracy at the time. The precision of statistical data on the coloured population is questionable, as the categories and censal measurements were themselves imprecise, particularly for a group "whose ethnic and legal condition tended to be fluid". According to Mathurin Mair (1974), the mulatto population of Jamaica, both enslaved and free, numbered approximately 60,300 in the 1830s rising from 23,000 in the 1770s. One estimate of the population in Jamaica in 1801 puts the slave population at 300,000, the white population at 20,000 to 30,000 and the free coloured at perhaps twice this number (Wright 1966). Barry Higman (1976) estimates that 10% of Jamaica's slaves were coloured in 1832. The census of 1844, (the first official census to take place in the colonies of Jamaica and Trinidad), enumerated a total population of 377,433, comprised of 293, 128 persons or 77.7 % black, 15,776 or 4.2% white, and 68,529 or 18.1% brown. Coloured ex-slaves were concentrated in the urban areas of Jamaica. Higman notes that in Lucea 56% of births in the period 1829-32 were coloured, in Savanna la Mar, 50% were coloured, in Montego Bay, 46%, Spanish Town

41% and in Kingston 34%. There were roughly equal numbers of males and females in the coloured population. Both Higman and Mathurin Mair agree that the coloured women were more concentrated in the urban environment where they had more economic opportunities and a freer lifestyle. In Mathurin Mair's words the "melting pot" of the urban centres allowed them more personal liberties and achievements.

Not all evidence on mulatto women supports a thesis of desirability. Mathurin Mair (1974) remarks that the idea that the white man felt a sense of obligation towards his coloured dependents is an overrated one in slave society and that the majority of white fathers did not manumit their children. Among the mulatto population could be found poverty, drunkenness, disorder and some were present among society's vagabonds. There is ample evidence however to indicate that mulatto women were also fortunate because of their colour and were often enough considered attractive in slave society. For instance, comparing women of different groups in slave society, Bryan Edwards (1801) observed: "In one of the principal features of beauty, however, few ladies surpass the Creoles (mulattos), for they have in general, the finest eyes of any women in the world, large, languishing and expressive and sometimes beaming with animation, and sometimes melting with tenderness...combined with other systems of life and manners - (sequestered, domestic, and unobtrusive) it is doubtless owing that no women on earth make better wives or better mothers."[23] In Tom Cringle's Log, there is a description of the Christmas holiday festival of John Canoe (Jonkunnu) on the streets of Jamaica, and a comparison of women in the street parade:

> But the beautiful part of the exhibition was the Set Girls. They danced along the streets in bands of from fifteen to thirty. There were brown sets, and black sets and sets of all intermediate gradations of colour. Each set was dressed pin for pin alike, ...I had never seen more beautiful creatures than there were amongst the brown sets – clear olive complexions, and the fine faces, elegant carriages, splendid figures – full, plump, and magnificent[24] (Scot 1833).

Mathurin Mair (1974) observed that during the eighteenth and nineteenth centuries already there had emerged a group of women who were neither black nor white and who had a different bargaining power in the context of emerging Creole society. She writes of the attractions of these women; of the fact that that one William Hickey was captivated by the lovely young mulattos and quadroons who attended a Spanish Town ball. Hickey reportedly noted: "Girls of this description are frequently to be procured, though at a monstrous expense, far exceeding what frail ones in London cost."[25] Mathurin Mair develops at length and with some detail the more attractive bargains which mulatto women could make or had made with the more privileged white male planters or managerial class: "The mulatto female was relatively well placed in Creole Society to name a high price for her favours; for the dominant male group, applying its racist aesthetic, made it clear that browns, being closer in physical appearance to whites than black, were the more desirable mates. In the absence of white women, the law of supply and demand thus gave mulatto women some bargaining power."[26] Deals were made for the trading of mulatto daughters. One, Reverend Barry claimed: "I have known an instance of a woman as fair as I am who voluntarily surrendered her daughter for a consideration in doubloons, and handed her into the chaise with her own hands."[27] The attractiveness of the mulatto woman went beyond the skin-deep fairness. Mathurin Mair notes that the brown mistress provided a family and home away from home for those who lived away from their relatives, and her skills both as housekeeper and nurse could not be underrated in a climate and period in which a high rate of morbidity and death required good and careful nursing. This appeal of the mulatto woman in slave society as "domesticated" and as nurses or caregivers is also supported in the findings of Bush (1990) who noted that "White men remained infatuated, particularly with light-skinned coloured women. This preference was rewarded by the great attachment and devotedness of coloured women to the white men who chose them as companions or housekeepers."[28]

Mary Seacole of Jamaica represents one lived example of such a woman, although her life is a uniquely different one by any standards. She was born early in the nineteenth century and is referred to in the literature as the "yellow doctress." Seacole

(1858) describes herself in her autobiography as "a few shades of deeper brown upon my skin which shows me related – and I am proud of the relationship – to those poor mortals whom you once held enslaved, and whose bodies America still owns."[29] Craig (1984) analyzes Seacole as "visibly neither black nor white, who could, therefore, to some extent, experience both worlds."[30] Seacole can be considered Jamaica's first published woman writer, a woman of word and deed. She devoted much of her life to caring for the sick, and was in the Crimea for some of the most intense fighting of that war. Her mixed race more than likely allowed her the opportunities which were probably unavailable to black women at the time.

Although the mulatto women were valuable as mistresses, housekeepers and partners of white men, white women did not similarly embrace the presence of the mulatto women and ensured that this distance between white and brown was kept intact. The mulatto woman may have enjoyed some social preference as for instance a visit from a white woman, or been introduced to her husband's peers. Mathurin Mair (1974) comments that those who had the wherewithal to do so frequently outdid the white women in fashion and adornment, a point also well supported in Lady Nugent's diary. Lady Nugent was not averse to being the houseguest of planters who kept mulatto women as their mistresses, as she records at various intervals in her diary, but: "It is doubtful whether a coloured person ever sat down to dinner with Mrs. Nugent. When staying at planters' houses, she receives the coloured ladies apart from the rest of the company, usually in her bedroom"[31] (Wright 1966). According to the missionary Gardner, it was not until some thirty years after her time, when Lord Mulgrave was Governor (and free coloured people had achieved full citizenship) that coloured guests were invited to functions at Kings's House (Wright 1966). Lady Nugent is often disparaging about the mixed women, although she clearly allocates the blame for the emergence of this "class of women" and for their intermediate position in slave society to the white men of "lower orders". She wrote: "It is extraordinary to witness the immediate effect that the climate and habit of living in this country have upon the minds and manners of Europeans, particularly of the lower orders. In the upper ranks, they become indolent and inactive, regardless of everything but eating, drinking, and indulging themselves, and are almost entirely under the dominion of their mulatto favorites"[32]

By the middle of the twentieth century, Henriques (1953) supports the view that while the importance of colour had diminished, it was still an important ingredient in the structure of gender relations. Henriques quotes "A black peasant proprietor of more than average standing" as saying:

> In the old days the mother or a black or coloured daughter felt a sort of pride in her daughter living with the slave master – "Gone to buckra (master) house, gone live". That feeling still applies. The black girl who cohabits with a white man "Gone lift the colour." Mothers would rather their daughters lived with a brown or white man than married a black man.[33]

He noted also that successful black men

> ...seek out and marry women of 'higher colour' in order to improve their social status, leading to a class of well-educated and often well-off black spinsters (sic). These women are unable to get married to the type of man they would like to as such men would like to marry only women lighter than themselves. The only men available as mates are those belonging to a socially inferior group with whom they will have nothing to do.[34]

To understand the tenacious constructions of race, gender and sexuality in society, it is useful to look at these expressions of desire based on race and colour one step further into contemporary Jamaican society. The title of this paper is appropriated from a dancehall song of Jamaica, released in 1992 by the popular Jamaican Dancehall recording artiste Buju Banton. Buju Banton sings:

Mi love mi car, mi love mi bike, mi love mi money and ting
But most of all, mi love mi browning,
Love mi car, love mi, bike, love mi money and ting
But most of all mi love mi browning

The term browning in Jamaican society, coined in the 1980s,[35] represents a collective range of skin colours which would in the eighteenth century have been broken down into smaller subgroups each denoting as far as possible the amount of black blood that had been added to the white. Purity of blood (*limpieza de sangre*) afforded the greatest access to resources, but in this case purity was viewed as closer to whiteness. The idea of race as a dialectical discourse did not preoccupy adherents of scientific racism. The focus on hybridity, centred around purity and breeding, nonetheless inadvertently inscribed the categories of gender and sexuality, without acknowledging the "ambivalent axis of desire and aversion: a structure of attraction where people and cultures intermix and merge, transforming themselves as a result, and a structure of repulsion, where the different elements remain distinct and are set against each other dialogically."[36] This process of dialectical shifting yet stasis is still evident in contemporary Jamaica but manifested in different ways. The browning in Jamaica comprises a recognizable combination of black and white (and/ or other ethnic groups such as Chinese or Jews). More apposite, the browning in Jamaica also represents a class of people, the post-colonial inheritors of privilege and status passed on by the white upper class. Blacks are still perceived as occupying the lowest rung of the class pyramid in Jamaica, although there have been considerable changes since the nineteenth century.[37] It is no longer simple to pin down class and status by colour. Nonetheless, the legacies of the colonial past are still evident, and the clear skinned or fair skinned, straight (*"tall"*) haired woman still figures as a desirable catch. In this song, Buju Banton also promises marriage and monogamy to his browning. The song created a sufficient stir among the black population, particularly the black female population, to force Buju Banton to immediately release another song in 1993 entitled "Mi nu stop cry fi all black woman".

Mi nu stop cry fi all black woman
Respect all di gal with dark complexion
Whole heap ah things a gwaan for oonu complexion
Black is beauty, oonu colour is one inna million
Have it from birth, a natural suntan, smooth like a lotion
Take care of your complexion
Don't get me wrong, mi respect black woman

The interpretation of Buju's *volte face* here by a young Jamaican female student of gender studies at the University of the West Indies was that of the two-facedness of men, having to ensure that he pleased both sets of women at the same time. This is no doubt one explanation as there have emerged others. What is observable in the first song is the depiction of the browning as property.[38] The possession of property situates one's position in post-colonial capitalist society as it removes one far away from the taint of poverty and all that this implies. Status for the black Jamaican male however is not simply owning the house, car, bike and capital, but to display a woman who is lighter skinned as a trophy of success. In the second song, the singer is less concerned with 'owning' the woman, as much as with underscoring respect for a colour which incidentally, he shares equally with them. Respect in the Jamaican context may signify a political awareness of blackness, national and racial identification, but does not necessarily imply sexual attraction or desire. Despite Buju Banton's protestations, one gets the impression that the browning still emerges as a prize for the black man. This importance of lighter skin colour is constantly underscored in Jamaica by the debates over the sale of skin whiteners and in the history of beauty contest where light-skinned straight-haired contestants are generally the winners. Barnes (1997) notes that skin colour still serves as a handicap in access to good service, securing decent jobs, housing and other social amenities. A similar point was also made earlier by Gordon (1991) who found a close correlation between skin colour and occupational status in Jamaica. Reddock (1999), quoting Barnes, also points out that not only skin colour is of importance in national beauty contests in Jamaica, but a key ingredient is whether facial features approximate the Caucasian or are closer to African stereotypes.

Desire is always imbued with historical meanings and constructed from the material of economy and polity as this blends human bodies together. How the present constructions of aesthetics and desire in Jamaica are informed by the past constructions of race, colour and sexuality needs to be uncovered from many more angles and perspectives than can be completed in this exploratory investigation. As this essay continues, I merely make an entrance into, and inconclusive exit from these ongoing and complex debates, drawing on other insights gleaned from secondary historical data.

COLOUR, STATUS AND FAMILY

Skin colour was such a crucial signifier of parentage, status and position in slave society and later in Creole society, that colour gradations were closely measured and taken account of in the business of marriage and family. Edwards (1801) cites one Don Antonio de Uloa who identifies the colour schema as follows:

> Among the tribes which are derived from an intermixture of the whites with the Negroes, the first are the mulattoes, next to these are the tercerones, produced from a white mulatto, after these are the quarterones, proceeding from a white and terceron, the last are the quinterons i.e. white and quarteron. This is the last gradation, there being no visible difference between them and the whites either in colour or features. Between mulatto and negro the intermediary is the sambo. Every one of these are jealous of the order of their tribe or caste.[39]

In the United States, all persons of African ancestry were lumped together as Negro both socially and legally and later referred to as coloured. In the Hispanic American colonies the range of gradations of colour and racial mixtures are worked out to their infinitesimal detail (Stolcke 1995). Since the colour scheme was introduced and invoked by the whites, it is fair to say that the gradations were also under close scrutiny by the white population. Nonetheless, the significance of the subtle difference in status assigned to each gradation would not have been lost on the black slave population. The resulting system of hypergamy which functioned during the period confirms that colour was in fact one of the criteria by which mating, if not marriages, took place. Higman (1976) notes that it was very rare for a mulatto slave woman to bear children darker than herself. The quadroon women had all of their children by white men while it was more common for the sambo women to have children by black men. In other words, the sambo women were more likely to mate with darker men than themselves, while the mulatto and quadroon women would more than likely have children lighter than themselves. Some mulatto women had all of their children by whites, some having up to seven registered births over a 25-

year period. While it is difficult to deduce that these women had stable unions, it appears that none of the black or sambo slave women had long term relationships with whites, although a few black women had long-term unions with mulatto men.

The pattern of interbreeding was reversed for coloured or slave men. In fact, as Higman (1976) observed, "The lighter his colour, the less likely was he to father children lighter than himself, or even of his own colour. When mulatto women lost their white mates, in general they took up with other mulatto or quadroon men."[40] The pattern was a very distinctive and consistent one. Miscegenation followed rules which were obeyed as much by whites as it was by blacks. Individual preferences were less important than the unwritten rules which had begun to govern the system of marriage and mating to produce a new mixed breed in Creole Society. Reddock (1999) observes that well into the twentieth century the practice of hypergamy, of women marrying or forming relations with men "superior" in status to themselves, continues to inform the system of marriage and mating in Jamaica and Trinidad. She writes that "notions of beauty and the tyranny of colour affect women dis-proportionately, as compared to men, but at the same time are central to patriarchal relations, ensuring that men's position and power is continuously ensured."[41]

The power wielded by white men was likely to be more preserved in the eighteenth and nineteenth centuries if mulatto women married or mated with men whiter than themselves, thus lightening the colour of the skin while retaining the white male in a dominant patriarchy. The same could not apply to mulatto men who did not have similar opportunities for marrying or mating with women of a lighter skin colour, much less for mating with white women. The white women were in shorter supply and secondly, those who lived in the region would definitely have been closeted and controlled by the ideologies of femininity of the time, and by the white men in authority and position. Where mulatto men had access to economic and political advancement, this was also blocked by white men. For instance Thome and Kimball (1969) note of the coloured (mulatto) men in 1838 that "they have by no means evinced a determination to claim more than their share of office and influence. On the contrary, they stop very far short of what they are entitled to. Having an extent of suffrage, but little less than the whites, they might fill one third of the seats in the Assembly, whereas they now return but four members out of forty-five."[42] The assumption of white superiority over black or mixed was a very strong one in the minds of the free coloured male population who were by then granted suffrage. No women, of any class or colour, had such rights or privileges. Thome and Kimball observed:

> It is a fact that the portion of the coloured people continued to return white members to the Assembly, and to vote for white aldermen and other city officers. The influential men among them have always urged them to take up white men, unless they could find competent men of their own colour. As they remarked to us, if they were obliged to send an ass to the Assembly, it was far better for them to send a white ass, than a black one.[43]

LEGAL STATUS OF THE MULATTO POPULATION

Where whiteness denoted both freedom and higher status, colour was a tangible measure by which freedom could be sought under slavery, both coloured men and women used this, where possible, to their advantage. It was by no means an automatic or easy process as Higman (1976) and Mathurin Mair (1974) have both underscored in their analyses. During the period 1829 to 1832, the latter years of slavery, 1,363 slaves were manumitted, of which 797 or 58% were coloured. Of these, 450 were coloured women. Manumissions in Jamaica were heavily weighted on the side of women. Of 309 slaves freed in 1826, 92 were males and 217 females. Both black and mulatto female slaves were better placed to benefit from their intimate associations with whites, one benefit including the granting and purchase of freedom, although accounts of this have also been exaggerated. The majority of white fathers, however, did not manumit their offspring. Some of them clearly could not afford to do so, the less well-off white fathers having to negotiate other means by which this could be done. For instance, the overseer of Amity Hall offered at first to exchange his own slaves for members of his mulatto family. It would seem that this was not a priority of the more prosperous men. Where they took greater care to do so was in the rural rather than the urban environment, in which "the white parent may have had a stronger sense of responsibility to some of his coloured relations, than in the more flexible environment of the town, where relationships could be more transient and less demanding."[44] Mathurin Mair suggests that where the economic opportunities were roughly equal in the urban setting, and the black slave woman had nearly the same access as the brown to skilled and non-praedial occupations, the mulatto slave woman was equally placed as her black counterpart in acquiring freedom. The suggestion is that the closeness of the domestic and household relationship in the great house created the basis of a more intimate relationship of dependence and commitment between slave woman and master. Mathurin Mair concludes, however, that on an overall island assessment, the mulatto slave was more likely than the black or male slave to not only buy her freedom, but "to receive her liberty as a gift."[45]

Mulatto and black women were restricted as beneficiaries from white men's bequests, however, by the 1761 Act of Devizes which limited the value of such legacies. According to Edward Long (1774), an inquiry into wills in 1762 revealed to the Jamaican Assembly that between two and three thousand pounds, as well as four sugar estates, thirteen houses and unspecified amounts of land were left to mulatto children. To prevent this pattern of bequests occurring with regularity, the law therefore declared null and void any sum over £2,000. There was apparently fervent objection to this law, clearly from men who did the bequeathing. They claimed that it deprived them of their rights to dispose of their possessions based on their personal inclinations. The matter of property and savings being left in the hands of either black or mulatto women clearly disturbed the gentry considerably. Both Edward Long and Thomas Atwood were emphatically opposed to the white men who they felt appeared content with negro or mulatto mistresses and who produced a "spurious race of children". Long went so far as to accuse some of the higher status men as being "under the dominion of their mulatto favourites,"[46] implying that they were being ruled by their genitals and not their heads. The contradictory emotions of the men who were themselves involved in these cross racial liaisons were very rarely discussed, or openly invoked as Genovese (1976) suggests. Judging from the controversies which raged in the matter of bequests, such liaisons could not be simply reduced to convenience or carnal desires on the part of men. The bequests also serve as a recognition of lasting relationships between black and white men and women, in other words, an acknowledgment of humanness, unimaginable in the earliest periods of slavery.

Nonetheless, the laws worked consciously at preventing ownership of property by coloured and black folk. Jamaica's Deficiency Laws were largely designed to provide an adequate militia by ensuring that each slave owner employed at least one white for every twenty slaves or to pay a fine for each person in which he or she was deficient. Thus the law was discriminatory against coloureds who had great difficulty in employing whites. This law against coloured males was relaxed in 1813 but was maintained against females, thus accounting for the few coloured women who would actually own plantations.

Free coloured women still suffered all the legal disabilities of their group. Like coloured men, until 1823 they were not allowed to give evidence in courts of law, thus restricting them from protecting either their person or their property. While coloured men were restricted in different ways to coloured women, for instance, until 1831 free coloured men were not eligible to become vestrymen, jurors, Members of Council or Assembly, they could not vote in elections or hold a public office. All women – white, black and coloured, suffered these disabilities at the time.

OCCUPATIONAL STATUS AND MOBILITY OF MULATTO POPULATION

Within the rural plantation, for those still bound as slaves, the coloured female or male slave clearly had a status a notch above the field slaves as they were employed in largely domestic non-praedial occupations. It is difficult to separate the domestic coloured slave from her sexual and familial association with the household, but it is clear that on the plantation at least this was a more sought after position and one which brought more possibilities for improvement of status, and certainly freedom from the heat, sun and the rigours of field labour.

Mathurin Mair's analysis of the economic status of the free coloured male and female population indicates that while they did suffer many disabilities, there were some opportunities available to them. Coloured women and men engaged in agricultural activities such as ownership of small coffee plantations, and she finds evidence for instance of three mulatto women who between them owned 22 slaves and others who owned a proportion of stock and slaves. These were largely very small concerns as the tenor of agricultural production at the time did not support small non-white farmers in the least, much less coloured female managers and owners. The free mulatto female was more likely to be the urban dweller than the agricultural farmer where the opportunities were more available for entrepreneurship. In Jamaica, the towns lured mulatto women who were inclined to be entrepreneurs. Montego Bay contained more than one half of the registered coloured inhabitants of the parish of St. James according to a 1774 estimate of Edward Long (1774) and in 1838, Thome and Kimball's (1969) remark on the prevalence of coloured folk whom they visited or saw in Kingston. The male progeny of white and black were not so fortunate in setting up themselves as masters of industry. Thome and Kimball commented that "White men drove their coloured sons from their houses, and subjected them to every indignity and suffering, in order to deter them from prosecuting an enterprise which was seen by the terrified oppressors to be fraught with danger to themselves."[47]

They noted in their visit to Kingston in 1837 that people of colour were generally employed as porters, watermen, draymen, "and servants of all grades, from him who flaunts in livery, to him who polishes shoes. ...The market, which is the largest and best in the West Indies, is almost entirely supplied and attended by coloured persons, mostly females (Thome and Kimball 1969." The artisan trades were all dominated by coloured persons. While the main occupations of the coloured women on the plantations were those of domestic workers, the urban centres offered the coloured women economic opportunities. They recorded a brief conversation they had with a brown woman whom they passed "driving an ass laden with a great variety of articles."[48] She told them she had been to Kingston and with a load of provisions, and in return had purchased items to sell to apprentices.

The social distance between the white and coloureds was clearly still inscribed in 1801 when Lady Nugent took up residence in Jamaica.

While coloureds were not invited to sit at the Governor's table, at the same time they hosted their own balls, some of these organized by the mulatto mistresses of lodging houses. The towns offered the mulatto women some degree of independence and the means by which they could begin to affirm their own status in the society, quite apart from being viewed as (generally) illegitimate issue of a white man, or low caste appendage to a white household. Mathurin Mair notes that the mulatto women were "acknowledged to be leading domestic entrepreneurs of accommodation: white male visitors were their chief customers."[49] She identifies a few of these women, the courteous and lively Miss Polly Vidal of Falmouth, Miss Bessy McClean of Black River, Eliza Thompson of Rio Bueno and the highly praised Judy James of Montego Bay. Many of these establishments were very handsome as the inventory of the lodgings house of Elizabeth Sutton of Kingston showed. She had over seven bedrooms, fully equipped with over 100 household articles including mahogany furnishings, and was said to have been worth over £2,820. In the early nineteenth century as the main centre of government, Spanish Town offered numerous possibilities for the lodging of jurymen, witnesses and visiting dignitaries and Miss Charlotte Beckford's lodging house provided a salubrious accommodation for these men. Mathurin Mair also notes that the grog-shops of Trelawny towns were entirely run by mulatto women, their taxes from sale of liquor contributing between £2,000 and £3,000 annually.

While some mulatto women were successful as urban and rural entrepreneurs, not all were so successful in business. Their colour debarred them from the kind of relief normally given from poor houses, and from making their destitution more public. They were also among the debtors, vagrants, poor and destitute in the towns and in the countryside. At the same time they were viewed as proud and indolent people, some of whom refused to work on the land. Many of the free coloured were bound by the contradictions of the time, being too light skinned to be a slave to agriculture, and still unacceptable to the pure white class. The evidence of the period points to the fact that the distance between the brown and white was still firmly entrenched in terms of social status. It was very unlikely that the Jamaican mulatto woman at the beginning of the nineteenth century would have been able to rise above her station, having been born on the wrong side of the track.

CONCLUSION: THE TRAFFIC IN MULATTO WOMEN

In concluding her assessment of the general status of mulatto women Mathurin Mair (1974) noted:

> Women of interracial unions, heads of their households, frequently engaged in multiple mating, guided the upward mobility of their families, and in the process, inculcated socio-racial values applicable to a much wider world than that of the domestic circle. From the perspective of the ruling group in the society, such women were persons of influence and authority. In so far as females who were non-white had any access to power in a power structure which was white and male, they were these women. The original creole matriarch may well have been not black, but brown.[50]

That mulatto women posed a social and economic threat in slave society is illustrated by the limitations imposed on them in the legal and economic frameworks. While there were roughly equal numbers of mulatto males and females, the literature of the eighteenth and nineteenth centuries is in general more taken up with the women than the men, although there are scattered references to the employment of and the political posts which mulatto men had begun to occupy. These references rarely focus on the private lives of these men as it does on women. Lady Nugent (1966) for example refers in passing in her diary to the fact that a mulatto man, named Rogers, was engaged as her husband's *valet de chamber* and she "rejoices" that her dear N. would be much more comfortable with this man with little reflection on him personally. Throughout her diary, however, there is a continuous stream of remarks about the coloured women she encounters, and many of her references to coloured folk are somewhat disparaging. Her attitude surfaces in her passing comments as for instance when she refers to the "three yellow children of the 'vulgar Scotchman's chere amie" or in her diary entries, as in this example of 26 August 1803: "A long conversation with my dear N, about the misconduct of some of our young men, in forming improper connections, and thus involving themselves in future - poor foolish Captain Johnson is in great distress, about an ugly mulatto favourite, who has been accused of theft."[51] Lady Nugent's attention to the mulatto (and creole) women may be merely because she is also a woman and attentive to the details of women's lives and the representations of femininity in the society. At the same time, this scrutiny of the sexuality and desirability or undesirability of mulatto women is repeated by many male observers of slave and creole society. By the eighteenth and nineteenth centuries, black women's centrality in production and reproduction may have very well been shared or supplanted by mulatto women.

We cannot assume that the "browning", as the mulatto woman later came to be called in the Jamaican context, emerged as the 'desired' primarily on the more acceptable mix of skin colour and features which she presented to the white race, though this clearly contributed to her status. It is not exclusively so, as black women clearly then as now, continued to retain their appeal for white, black and coloured men. A combination of aesthetic 'acceptability' from the point of view of white male society, together with the economic and social entrepreneurship of the more fortunate in this class of women, however, contributed to the heightened attractiveness of the mulatto woman. If mulatto women were beginning to be viewed by a number of white men as desirable partners or mistresses, in time they would also come to represent the improvement in status to men who were less 'fortunate' in the colour scheme of things, thereby providing one means for such men to emerge out of the derided status which they had inherited because of the complexion of their skin. Perhaps a primary element of desire was rooted in the belief that mulatto woman represented a distance from the indignities of poverty and enslavement. Cross breeding had created between the periods of slavery and freedom a graduated continuum of colour which compromised, in different ways, the superiority and opposition of whiteness to blackness. Mulatto women were central to this process of change. In *Centering Woman*, Beckles (1999) argues that the slave (black) woman's location at the apex of "power pyramid of the slave order was secured essentially by sex and gender representation ...where the requirement of production and reproduction merged, that the black woman's experience, identity and consciousness gave structural form to what represented the central characteristic features of the slave mode of production."[52] If the black woman represented the womb of slavery, and the white woman the body politic, what then did the mulatto woman represent?

ENDNOTES

[1] Long, Edward, *The History of Jamaica*, 3 vols. (London: T Lowndes, 1774), p. 335
[2] Young, Robert J.C., *Colonial Desire: Hybridity in Theory, Culture and Race* (London and New York: Routledge, 1995), p. 9.
[3] Foucault, Michel, *The History of Sexuality, Volume 1: An Introduction* (New York: Vintage Books, 1980) p. 18
[4] Resonances of *"Brown skin girl stay home and mind baby, Brown skin girl stay home and mind baby, I going away on a sailing ship and if I don't come back throw way the damn baby"* a popular ditty now graduated into a folk song, the origins of which are relatively unknown in the region.
[5] Thome, James and Horace Kimball. *Emancipation in the West Indies*, first published in 1838, edition 1969 used.
[6] All references to Allsop, Richard, *Dictionary of Caribbean English Usage* (Oxford: Oxford University Press, 1996, pp 118, 469, and 394
[7] Cynthia Miller works as a household helper in Kingston, the equivalent of domestic worker in other societies. She is of mixed race, brown, but in Jamaica would not be considered a 'browning' which also indicates class position. Miller moved from rural St. Elizabeth to downtown overpopulated working-class Kingston and recalls that in the early years after here arrival, she was shunned and ill-treated because she was of a lighter complexion than others around her.
[8] Terborg-Penn, Roslyn, 'African feminism: a theoretical approach to the history of women in the African diaspora' in Rosalyn Terborg-Penn et al, *Women in Africa and the African Diaspora* (Washington, DC: Howard University Press, 1995), p. 10
[9] The vast body of data and findings uncovered by Lucille Mathurin in her work carried out for a PhD dissertation on which this paper draws heavily was published as *A Historical Study of Women in Jamaica, 1655–1844* Lucille Mathurin Mair, Edited and introduced by Hilary McD. Beckles and Verene A. Shepherd, (Kingston: University of the West Indies Press, in association with the Centre for Gender and Development Studies, 2006). The dissertation was completed in 1974 and at the time of writing this paper in 2000 it was only available in the West Indian reference sections of the three libraries of The University of the West Indies.
[10] See Beckles, H. McD, (1989) *Natural rebels: A social history of enslaved black women in Barbados*, London: Zed Books Ltd. Morrissey, M. (1990). "Female headed households in Latin America and the Caribbean" *Sociology Spectrum*, 9, p. 197-210, Bush, B. (1990). *Slave Women in Caribbean Society* 1650-1838; Shepherd, V. (1993). "Emancipation through servitude?: Aspects of the condition of Indian women in Jamaica, 1845-1945." In H. Beckles and V. Shepherd (eds.) *Caribbean Freedom: Society and Economy from Emancipation to the Present*, Kingston: Ian Randle Press; Reddock, R. (1986). "Indian Women and Indentureship in Trinidad and Tobago 1845-1917: Freedom Denied" *Caribbean Quarterly* Vol. 32 No. 3 &4;, Reddock, R. (1985). "Women and Slavery in the Caribbean: A Feminist Perspective" *Latin American Perspectives*, 44 vol.12, no.1; Reddock, R. (1994). *Women, Labour and Politics in Trinidad and Tobago: A History*, London: Zed Books; Brereton, B. (1988). "General Problems in studying the history of Women" In P. Mohammed and C. Shepherd eds., *Gender in Caribbean Development*, Centre for Gender and Development Studies,

University of the West Indies; Bridget B. (1994). "Gendered Testimonies" Elsa Goveia Lecture, Department of History, University of the West Indies, Kingston Jamaica; Mohammed, P. (1988). "The 'Creolization' of Indian Women in Trinidad" In Selwyn Ryan ed., *Trinidad and Tobago: The Independence experience*, 1962-1987. St. Augustine, Institute of Social and Economic Research; Mohammed, P. (1994). "Nuancing the Feminist Discourse in the Caribbean" *Social and Economic Studies* Vol. 43, no. 3, and Mohammed, P. (2002). *Gender Negotiations Among Indians in Trinidad 1917-1947*, United Kingdom and The Hague: ISS/Macmillan.

11 Shepherd, Verene, Bridget Brereton and Barbara Bailey (editors) *Engendering History: Caribbean Women in Historical Perspective*, 1995, p. xv

12 Studies of the dougla in Trinidad would become another focus of sociological enquiry from the late twentieth century.

13 Hall, Catherine. "Gender politics and Imperial Politics: Rethinking the Histories of Empire" Shepherd, Verene, Bridget Brereton and Barbara Bailey (editors) *Engendering History: Caribbean Women in Historical Perspective* ,1995. p. 48

14 Young, Robert J.C., *Colonial Desire: Hybridity in Theory, Culture and Race*, 1995, p. 90

15 Genovese, Eugene Roll, *Jordan, Roll: The World the Slaves Made* (New York: Random House, 1976.), pp. 413-415

16 Trollope, Anthony. *The West Indies and the Spanish Main* (London: Chapman and Hall, 1859), cited in Robert Young, *Colonial Desire Hybridity in Theory, Culture and Race* 1995, p.142

17 Scott, Michael, *Tom Cringles Log* (London: George Routledge and Sons, 1833), p. 200-201

18 Cooper, Caroline. *Noises in the Blood: Orality, Gender and the 'Vulgar' Body of Jamaican Popular Culture* (Warwick University Caribbean Studies, London: Macmillan Education Limited, 1994) p. 23

19 Carter, June. "La Negra as Metaphor in Afro-Latin American Poetry", *Caribbean Quarterly*, 31 (1): 73-82, 1985

20 See: http://slaveryimages.org/s/slaveryimages/item/2433

21 See references to Jean Michel Cazabon's work and discussions on his paintings in Patricia Mohammed, "The Visual Grammars of Race, Class and Gender in the paintings of four 18th and 19th century painters, Agostino Brunias, Isaac Bellisario, Jean Michel Cazabon and Patricio Landaluze", Paper presented to Association of Caribbean Historians Conference, Martinique, 1997. Jean Michel Cazabon's work has been covered in Geoffrey MacLean, *An Illustrated Biography of Trinidad's Nineteenth Century Painter Michel Jean Cazabon* (Trinidad and Tobago: Aquarela Galleries, 1986).

22 de Zendegui, Guellermo L. "Painter of Nineteenth Century Cuba" *Americas*. Vol.27, no. 9, 1975, p. 19

23 Edwards, Bryan, *The History, Civil and Commercial of the British Colonies in the West Indies*. 3 vols., London, 1801. p. 13)

24 Scott, Michael, *Tom Cringles Log*, 1833, p. 200-201

25 Mathurin, Lucille, *A Historical Study of Women in Jamaica from 1655 to 1844*, 1974, p. 420

26 Mathurin, Lucille, *op cit*, p. 422

27 Mathurin, Lucille, *op cit*, p. 422

28 Bush, Barbara, *Slave Women in Caribbean Society 1650-1838* (London: James Currey, 1990, p. 115.

29 Seacole, Mary. *Wonderful Adventures in Many Lands*. (London: 1858), p. 14

30 Craig, Christine. "Wonderful Adventures of Mrs. Seacole in Many Lands: Autobiography as literature and genre and a window to character" In *Caribbean Quarterly*, Vol. 30, no. 2 (1984): 33-47. p. 34.

31 Wright, Philip. *Monumental Inscriptions of Jamaica*, 1966, p. xxix, in Lady Nugent's Journal

32 Nugent, Maria. *A Journal of a Voyage to and Residence in the Island of Jamaica 1801 – 1805*, 1966, p. 98

33 Henriques, Fernando. *Family and Colour in Jamaica* (London: Eyre and Spottiswoode), 1953, p. 50.
34 Henriques, Fernando. *Op. cit.* p.50.
35 The topic of "The Browning was one of the selected themes in a weekly lecture series organized by the Institute of Caribbean Studies, University of the West Indies, Jamaica, from September to December, 1999. The discussion revealed that (a) the etymology of the term is unclear, but more than likely derived from dance hall lyrics coined largely by working class male singers. One suggestion by Joseph Pereira was that the term only gained currency in the 1980s, a moment of greater political consciousness about the growing imbalances in class and status in Jamaican society.
36 Young, Robert J.C., *Colonial Desire: Hybridity in Theory, Culture and Race*, 1995, p.19
37 As I am editing this paper in 2020 I think the current situation has undergone change again and the class/colour hierarchy has again shifted considerably.
38 It must be noted that this association with brown skin or browning as property is not restricted to Jamaican society. In a discussion on calypsos in Trinidad in the 1930s Gordon Rohlehr comes to a similar finding, that the brown woman was viewed as property and the prize for the black calypso singer as a signifier of his success in the face of his peers and with other men. See "Images of Men and Women in the 1930s Calypsos: The sociology of food acquisition in the context of survivalism" In P. Mohammed and C. Shepherd eds., *Gender in Caribbean Development*, Canoe Press, University of the West Indies, Kingston, Jamaica: Canoe Press, 2nd edition, 1999 pp. 223-289.
39 Edwards, Bryan, *The History, Civil and Commercial of the British Colonies in the West Indies*. 1801, .p. 19
40 Higman, Barry. *Slave Population and Economy in Jamaica 1807-1834*, 1976, p. 152.
41 Reddock, Rhoda. "Ethnicity, Class and Gender in the Anglophone Caribbean: A Conceptual History" 1999
42 Thome, James and Horace Kimball. *Emancipation in the West Indies* (New York: Arno Press, 1969), p. 89
43 Thome, James and Horace Kimball. *Emancipation in the West Indies* (New York: Arno Press, 1969), p. 89
44 Mathurin, Lucille, *A Historical Study of Women in Jamaica from 1655 to 1844*, 1974 p. 410
45 *Ibid* p. 410
46 Edward Long, and Thomas Atwood, in Bush, Barbara, *Slave Women in Caribbean Society 1650-1838*, 1990, p.115
47 Thome, James and Horace Kimball. *Emancipation in the West Indies*, 1969, p. 88
48 *Ibid*, p.89
49 Mathurin Mair, *op cit* p 415
50 Mathurin, Lucille, *A Historical Study of Women in Jamaica from 1655 to 1844*, 1974, p. 440-441
51 Nugent, Maria. *A Journal of a voyage to and residence in the island of Jamaica 1801 – 1805*, 1966, p.173
52 Beckles Hilary McD. *Centering Woman: Gender Relations in Caribbean Slave Society*. 1999, p.xx

REFERENCES

Allsop, Richard. 1996. *Dictionary of Caribbean English Usage*. Oxford: Oxford University Press.

Barnes, Natasha. 1997. "Face of the nation: Race, nationalisms and identities in Jamaican beauty pageants." In *Daughters of Caliban: Caribbean Women in the Twentieth Century*, edited by C. Lopez Springfield. Bloomington, IN and London: Indiana University Press and the Latin American Bureau.

Beckles, Hilary McD. 1999. *Centering Woman: Gender Relations in Caribbean Slave Society*. Kingston, Jamaica: Ian Randle Publishers.

Braithwaite, Kamau. 1971. *The Development of Creole Society in Jamaica 1770-1820*. Oxford: Clarendon Press.

Bush, Barbara. 1990. *Slave Women in Caribbean Society 1650-1838*. London: James Currey.

Carter, June. 1985. "La Negra as metaphor in Afro-Latin American poetry". *Caribbean Quarterly* 31(1): 73-82.

Chatterjee, Ratnabali. 1992. *The Queen's Daughter: Prostitutes as an Outcast Group in Colonial India*. Occasional Publication of Department of Social Sciences and Development, Michelsen Institute Bergen, December.

Cooper, Carolyn. 1994. *Noises in the Blood: Orality, Gender and the 'Vulgar' Body of Jamaican Popular Culture*. London: Macmillan Education: Warwick University Caribbean Studies.

Craig, Christine. 1984. "Wonderful Adventures of Mrs. Seacole in Many Lands: Autobiography as Literature and Genre and a Window to Character." *Caribbean Quarterly*, 30 (2): 3-47.

de Zendegui, Guellermo L. 1975. "Painter of Nineteenth Century Cuba" *Americas*. 27 (9): 19

Edwards, Bryan. 1801. *The History, Civil and Commercial, of the British Colonies in the West Indies*. 3 vols. London.

Foucault, Michel. 1980. *The History of Sexuality, Volume 1: An Introduction*. New York: Vintage Books. p. 18.

Genovese, Eugene. 1976. *Roll, Jordan, Roll: The World the Slaves Made*. New York: Random House.

Gordon, Derek. 1991. "Race, class and social mobility." In *Garvey: His Work and Impact*, edited by Rupert Lewis and Patrick Bryan. Trenton: Africa World Press.

Goveia, Elsa. 1965. Slave Society in the British Leeward Islands at the End of the Eighteenth Century. London: Yale University Press.

Hall, Catherine. 1995. "Gender politics and imperial politics: Rethinking the histories of empire." In *Engendering History: Caribbean Women in Historical Perspective*, edited by Verene Shepherd, Bridget Brereton and Barbara Bailey. Kingston, Jamaica: Ian Randle Publishers.

Hall, Douglas. 1992. *In Miserable Slavery: Thomas Thistlewood in Jamaica*, 1750-86. London: Macmillan Caribbean.

Henriques, Fernando. 1953. *Family and colour in Jamaica*. London: Eyre and Spottiswoode.

Higman, Barry. 1976. *Slave Population and Economy in Jamaica 1807-1834*. London: Cambridge University Press.

Higman, Barry. 1984. *Slave Populations of the British Caribbean 1807-1834*. Baltimore and London: The Johns Hopkins University Press.

Long, Edward. 1774. *The History of Jamaica*, 3 vols. London: T. Lowndes.

Mathurin Mair, Lucille. 1974. *A Historical Study of Women in Jamaica from 1655 to 1844*. PhD, The University of the West Indies.

McClintock, Anne. 1995. *Imperial Leather: Race, Gender and Sexuality in the Colonial Conquest*. London: Routledge.

Mohammed, Patricia. 1995. "Writing gender into history: The negotiation of gender relations among Indian men and women in post-indenture Trinidad society, 1917-47." In *Engendering History: Caribbean Women in Historical Perspective*, edited by Verene Shepherd, Bridget Brereton and Barbara Bailey. Kingston, Jamaica: Ian Randle Publishers.

Nugent, Maria. 1966. *A Journal of a Voyage to and Residence in the Island of Jamaica 1801-1805*. Kingston, Jamaica: Institute of Jamaica.

Pereira, Mark. 1992. *Agostino Brunias 1730 – 1796*. Trinidad: Tragarete Road. An Art Gallery.

Reddock, Rhoda. 1999. "Ethnicity, class and gender in the Anglophone Caribbean: A conceptual history." Paper presented at the Lecture Series, University Women's Group and Mona Unit, Centre for Gender and Development Studies, University of the West Indies.

Scott, Michael. 1833. *Tom Cringles Log*. London: George Routledge and Sons.

Seacole, Mary. 1858. *Wonderful Adventures in Many Lands*. London: James Blackwood.

Shepherd, Verene, Bridget Brereton and Barnara Bailey. eds. 1995. *Engendering History: Caribbean Women in Historical Perspective*. Kingston, Jamaica: Ian Randle Publishers.

Stolcke, Verena. 1995. "Invaded women: Sex, race and class in the formation of colonial society." In *Ethnicity, Gender and the Subversion of Nationalism*, edited by Fiona Wilson and Bodil Folke Frederiksen. London: Frank Cass.

Terborg-Penn, Roslyn. 1995a. "African feminism: a theoretical approach to the history of women in the African diaspora." In *Women in Africa and the African Diaspora*, edited by Rosalyn Terborg-Penn et al. Washington, DC: Howard University Press.

Terborg-Penn Roslyn. 1995b. "Through an African feminist theoretical lens: Viewing Caribbean women's history cross-culturally." In: *Engendering History: Caribbean Women in Historical Perspective*, edited by Verene Shepherd, Bridget Brereton and Barbara Bailey. Kingston, Jamaica: Ian Randle Publishers.

Thome, James A. and J. Horace Kimball. 1969. *Emancipation in the West Indies*. New York: Arno Press.

Trollope, Anthony. 1859. *The West Indies and the Spanish Main*. London: Chapman and Hall, cited in Robert Young, *Colonial Desire: Hybridity in Theory, Culture and Race*.

Young, Robert J. C. 1995. *Colonial Desire: Hybridity in Theory, Culture and Race*. London and New York: Routledge.

Wright, Philip. 1966. *Monumental Inscriptions of Jamaica*. London: Society of Genealogists.

4

Like Sugar in Coffee: Third Wave Feminism and the Caribbean[†]

> Feminism is the movement for social, political and economic equality of men and women.
>
> Feminism is undeniably at a generational crossroads, with many young women declining to even call themselves feminists.
>
> Jenifer Baumgardner and Amy Richards *Manifesta: Young Women, Feminism, and the Future*, 2000

PROLOGUE

I would like to connect with a younger generation of women and men, those who are already seriously engaged in feminism, gender and women's studies, those who flirt and flit on the margins, those who have inherited from the feminist struggles without recognizing what they owe to these struggles, those who would stay the course to become the new scholars and activists in our midst, and those who may not ever avow feminism but in their daily lives and actions are eminent practitioners. There are different interpretations of epochs in feminist activism. The ideas and periodization in this essay emerge from my own experience and perceptions of feminism in the Caribbean and gleaned from societies I have been fortunate to study. Second wave feminism was founded on some weighty aphorisms that united many women

---

[†] First published in the thematic Issue of *Social and Economic Studies*, 52 (3):.5-30 commemorating the 10th Anniversary of the Centre for Gender and Development Studies, Rhoda Reddock (ed.), Sir Arthur Lewis Institute for Social and Economic Studies, UWI, Mona. 2003.

cross-culturally: "speaking one's piece", "the personal is political" and a standpoint and reflexive methodology which tells another truth, however we define this truth in and out of the academy. I attempt to reach rather than teach; my approach is more lyrical than academic at times, more stream of consciousness than apparently structured. It is a monologue written as a conversation with an imaginary set of individuals, drawing in different trajectories; some things are left unsaid, some asked, others suggested. It disputes in both form and content the discourse of universality or contrived similitude which had defined the emergence of second wave feminism.

Yet there is of course a structure.[1] The main title, 'Like sugar in coffee'[2] describes my contemporary perception and guarded optimism about feminism today. Unlike three or four decades ago, a gender consciousness, if not a feminist consciousness has filtered throughout society. I locate a gender consciousness here as the self-awareness and confidence of one's rights and privileges as female or male in society as well as the limits or oppressiveness which being male or female still imposes on the individual to realize their potential. But this sweetened moment is not to be taken lightly or unadvisedly. If young women and men have benefited unwittingly from struggles waged by their foremothers and fathers so that they are aware of these rights and privileges, then what are their imperatives to avow feminism or to engage in old and new feminist concerns today, particular when it might seem that they have more to lose by joining another "ism"? It is always difficult to put oneself in the place of another. It is even more difficult to span the generational gap. Nonetheless, I attempt in this piece to speak through my (hopefully our) experience to do just that. The sub-sections of this essay are titled after selected feminist authored texts of the first and second wave which have planted theoretical or programmatic issues still relevant to third wavers. Second wave is also in the process of becoming third wave. Each wave is not just a chronology of events but is continually engaged in a dialogue with former history and thought, and optimistically moving on cumulatively.

OF WOMAN BORN

"Nana rolled herself another cigarette. I liked the smell of sulfur when she outed her match and was fascinated by the way she cupped the cigarette in both hands and sucked erratically before she got a good enough light". This vignette from Shani Mootoo's *Cereus Blooms at Night* rescues a memory of old Indian women I had known in the village in which I was raised in south Trinidad. These women were most unlike the svelte and sophisticated white young lasses in the Virginia Slims advertisements "you've come a long way baby" that we knew from American magazines. For one thing they smoked the harsh tobacco of Trinidad's Broadway cigarettes. Not unlike their rural menfolk, they generally bought these two or five at a time from a jar on the shop counter. Then they would wrap the cigarettes in worn cotton handkerchiefs, and tuck them into the bosoms of their shapeless cotton frocks, to be retrieved for a smoke when they sat among their women friends. Interestingly, cigarette smoking was never a public activity for women in the Caribbean, and to this day is not, despite the passage of years and ideas.

Nonetheless, like the Virginia Slims models, one wondered what long ways had these women also come? Their eyes were full of mischief when they talked amongst themselves. Rheumy eyes, the twinkle kept wonderfully alive by shared memories. Their laughter and conversation would grow secretive when we came too close, switching to the Hindi which they knew we could not fully understand. I was too young to listen except in passing, as the young always are, too busy discovering life to recognize it unfolding in the everyday and commonplace events. Subconsciously, I expect, one constantly noticed things. I sided with the livelier souls especially when they were set against other women who were so bent over double by life that you could barely see their eyes. If you did catch sight of the latter's eyes, they were piercing, unflinching, almost accusing in their gaze, as if willing you to choose between two alternatives. Shani Mootoo recognizes these differences among the women. She called the irreverent one "Cigarette Smoking Nana", the other is dubbed "Bible Quoting Nana", of whom says her protagonist, "I couldn't bring myself to get too close to, nor she to me since I was not turning out to be boyly enough for her church going satisfaction" (Mootoo 1996, 24).

The Bible Quoting Nanas too had their stories to tell. Perhaps there were only two alternatives for women in the fifties. After all the choices were either marriage or spinsterhood, motherhood or barrenness, acceptance or ostracism. Were you going to be a good serious woman, well respected in the community, or one of the fallen, who laughed too loudly, drank and smoked like men, dressed gaudily, wore too much eye makeup and Moscow red lipstick? Good women stayed by their men, loyal and faithful, in martyred polygamous unions as brides of Christ or with allegiances to the Prophet Mohammed or aspiring to emulate the holy dyad of Sita and Lord Rama. Others who did not, had strayed from the paths of righteousness.

Many of these women, bible quoting and cigarette smoking both, would not have heard of feminism or gender as we talk about it freely today. Yet they would have made the most of their lives, flaunting or following rules when they had to. Let us not dismiss them as cardboard characters on a stage in which they played preordained roles. Any notions of gender equality which we, the generation who came of age in the wake of the sixties' women's liberation movement entertained in our heads, were planted there by the examples of our foremothers and fathers. To speculate on what has influenced third wave feminism I think one should return to the mother lode, that of trying to figure out what is conveyed to each generation by the previous ones as they come of age. We should not also, in considering third wave feminism, think that it is only women who influence the shape of a feminist and gender consciousness. Such ideas are transmitted or influenced equally by the actions, or reactions, of men and masculinity.

Caribbean fiction, including women's writing which grew in stature in the last few decades of the twentieth century, is valuable in representing these coded messages between generations of women. There are fewer examples of the ways in which manhood and ideas of masculinity are being transmitted between men and men, although this is by no means an absent theme in the fiction of the region. Femininity had first to discover and map itself. The relationships between women - young and old, book educated and life taught, rural and urban, mother and child, grandmothers and granddaughters, between women of different ethnic groups and classes - are never untroubled. Much of the fiction of the region which has dealt with coming of age, has pointed to the uneasy processes by which gender, race and class identities are ascribed, acquired and maintained.[3]

In the Martiniquan novel *The Bridge of Beyond*, Simone Schwartz-Bart deals with the competition between women and, at the same time, the wisdom gained from the knowledge of their physical bodies. Toussine was once a beauty, "...when she was fifteen, she stood out from all the other girls, with the unexpected grace of red canna growing on the mountain, so that the old folk said she in herself was the youth of L'Abandonnee" (Schwarz-Bart 1982, 4). Her beauty is disturbing to the other women. "The breeze blowing over Minerva's (her mother's) cottage embittered the women, made them more unaccountable than ever, fierce, fanciful, always ready with some new shrewishness, "What I say is, Toussine's more for ornament than for use. Beauty's got no market value. The main thing is not getting married, but sticking together year in and year out" (Schwarz-Bart 1982, 7). When luck deserts Toussine, when she becomes a grandmother, she refuses to prop sorrow and instills in her grand-daughter Telumee the principles of self-reliance, which she has come to learn, because of and despite her beauty. Beauty is another curse for women to bear, even while it presents opportunities for happiness or sexual fulfilment. A 1970s US pop song by Janis Ian comes to mind, "*I learnt the truth at seventeen, that love was meant for beauty queens, and high school girls with clear skin smiles, who married young and then retired.*" Beauty is not to be scoffed at, and young women are not fooled by the idea that 'good looks', however this is constituted in each society, are not important. They have not been blindly cajoled that they can make up for "good looks" by being achievers or by being sanctimoniously proper and therefore loved or chosen for themselves rather than their bodies. The young know that the currency of the body matters. Feminism has not provided a panacea for such social beliefs, and cannot do so, even while it creates the space for other possibilities for the feminine and masculine selves and a range of gender identities to emerge and find fulfillment.

In Olive Senior's "The Two Grandmothers" (1989) Grandma Del has baby chickens, lives in a pretty house with white lace curtains which cover the jalousied windows, sends her granddaughter to Sunday school, is appalled that she comes to visit her with only jeans and shorts and has no respectable church dress. Grandma Del has no television, and so she tells her granddaughter stories at night. Grandma Elaine refuses to be called "grandma", dresses elegantly, is always rushing off to the gym and pool and dinners and cocktails. While she is fun, she has no time for her granddaughter. Yet she makes her granddaughter very self-conscious about her darker skin and curly hair. The messages are mixed, she likes both grandmothers and cannot and does not want to choose between homely one who stifles yet comforts her and the other whose lifestyle suggests excitement but who is disquieting to her spirit.

Expanding the breath of gender possibilities does not necessarily make for an easier choice. Today young women are faced with multiple choices, of marriage or motherhood or career or all three, and therefore have a harder time in determining the avenues they will choose. Marx's often cited quote, "the satisfaction of basic needs, creates other needs" seems to hold equally true for feminism as it does for other material concerns. The fact that women have more possibilities of expressing their femininity today than the cigarette-smoking and bible-quoting nanas had in the past, does not mean that they will yet comprehend the repercussions of their choices. One example of how this conflict of choice was understood in retrospect is valuable here. While women were busily proving equal performance in employment outside of the home, the burden of housework and childcare was not being similarly shared. The increasing satisfaction of a need for recognition as workers and professionals, has not reduced the double burden which most women still undertake as workers and mothers/homemakers.

Older women recognize and celebrate the opportunities which have now been made available to younger women, compared to those they would have had in their lifetimes. "Befo' time," her Gran remarked towards nightfall, "Beka would never have won that contest ... And long befo' long time, you wouldn't be at no convent school" writes Zee Edgehill in *Beka Lamb* (1982, 1). Beka had just won an essay contest at St. Cecilia's Academy in Belize City, a victory which changed her overnight from "a flat-rate Belize creole into a person with a high mind" in her family's view. Not only is educational access for girls recognized and treasured by older women, nationhood also represents the possibilities for their granddaughters to achieve the things which were never available to them under an alien regime. Education also marked out other territorial borders and boundaries for women. In Merle Hodge's *Crick Crack Monkey* (1970), Tee's winning of a scholarship draws her out of rural sanctity to experience discrimination by colour and class at the hands of her urbanized Aunt Beatrice, cold comfort for progress after her country aunt - Tantie's enveloping warmth and unconditional love. In Claude McKay's *Banana Bottom* (1986), Bita Plant is placed in a similar quandary. "Rescued" from poverty and a peasant class future by the English missionaries, educated in England and returned like polished fruit to her native environment, Bita's choices are between the identity and comfort of the native self and the presumed benefits of respectability, education and the church. Educational access created more barriers between women, more choices for how they adjust to the same women they have loved and depended on, but who now have become more distant. It has created more spaces between women, another basis for establishing gender oppression within the sex.

In Jamaica Kincaid's *Annie John*, the individuation of mother and daughter is a tortured path between childhood and adolescence. The sexual awakening of young girls is recurrently traumatic it seems, whether in fiction or real life, or precisely as fiction expresses reality. "As if that were not enough, my mother informed me that I was on the verge of becoming a young lady, so there were quite a few things I would have to do differently. She didn't say exactly just what it was that made me on the verge of becoming a young lady, and I was so glad of that, because I didn't want to know" (Kincaid 1986, 26). We are drawn palpably into this growing distance between mother and daughter at the onset of puberty and the utter self-consciousness of the young girl at this time, in the spare prose of Jean Rhys' *Smile, Please*. "I remembered the dress she (her mother) was wearing, so much prettier than anything I had now, but the curls, the dimples surely belonged to somebody else. The eyes were a stranger's eyes. The forefinger of her right hand was raised as if in warning. ...Why I didn't know, she wasn't me any longer. It was the first time I was aware of time, change and the longing for the past. I was nine years of age. Catching sight of myself in the long looking-glass I felt despair, I had grown into a thin girl, tall for my age. My straight hair was pulled severely from my face and tied with a black ribbon. I was fair with a pale skin and huge staring eyes of no particular colour" (Rhys 1979, 19-20).

In Edwidge Danticat's *Breath, Eyes and Memory* (1994), the protagonist Sophie is excruciatingly forthcoming, more fitting to the times in which there is greater openness with the subject of sex and the possibilities of the sexual expression open to men and women. Yet for the Caribbean female protagonist in this novel, guarding, preserving, or discovering female sexuality is a painful business, both a legacy as well as burden, to be passed from mother to daughter. How is this to be handled by mother and received by daughter?

> When I was a girl, my mother used to test us to see if we were virgins. She would put her finger in our very private parts and see if it would go inside. Your Tante Atie hated it. She used to scream like a pig in a slaughter house. The way my mother was raised, a mother is supposed to do that to her daughter until the daughter is married. It is her responsibility to keep her pure….My mother stopped testing me early", she said. "Do you know why?" …"The details are too much", she said. "But it happened like this. A man grabbed me from the side of the road, pulled me into a cane field, and put you in my body. I was still a young girl, just barely older than you".
> "You need to concentrate when school starts, you have to give that all your attention. You're a good girl, aren't you?"
> By that she meant if I had ever been touched, if I had ever held hands, or kissed a boy.
> "Yes", I said, "I have been good".
> "You understand my right to ask as your mother, don't you?"
> I nodded" (Danticat 1994, 60).

Adrianne Rich's work, couched in the metaphor "of woman born', pointed to the new feminine ethic required of feminism and of women. She writes "Patriarchal lying has manipulated women both through falsehood and silence …and so we must take seriously the question of truthfulness between women, truthfulness among women. As we cease to lie with our bodies … (there) …is a truly womanly idea of honour in the making?" (Rich 1993, 446). Third wave feminism must take this idea of honour in the making further, dispute by action rather than words the convenient patriarchal cliché, that women have been their own worst enemies and push the boundaries of sisterhood further than second wave feminism did. We continue to be, both male and female, of woman born.[4]

A VINDICATION OF THE RIGHTS OF WOMAN

By the beginning of the twenty-first century, gender awareness has placed its stamp on human self-consciousness, indelibly so. If, in the nineteenth century, the black ex-slave woman Sojourner Truth had the temerity to ask a group of white men and women "And ain't I a woman?" and the twentieth century dawned with the British suffragettes chaining themselves to Parliament railings to demand civil rights, then that visibility of womanhood, if not unchained power, has been partially won. To the casual onlooker or observer, sexual difference as a conceptual tool of social analysis might not appear to be a valuable one, but it is one which cannot be ignored, just as we cannot take for granted the validity of people's ethnic and cultural differences and practices, imbalances in development between societies, political machismo and dictatorships, or the persistence of pockets of extreme poverty in an excessively wealthy over consumerist contemporary world. The young are born today, in most societies, with entitlements and rights, one of which includes rights that accrue to them as members of a particular sex.

Wollstonecraft, who authored *Vindication of the Rights of Woman* in 1792, is cited as the mother of first wave liberal feminism. With all the limits of her time, class and race, she established some common ideas which fed into first wave and remains on the agenda today. She underscored that apart from being given free access to education, women were not to be excluded, without a voice, from "a participation of the natural rights of mankind" (1982:88). The first feminist wave was categorized as a movement for women to have rights within and alongside men, and be linked to other social movements. In both Europe and America this wave emerged out of abolitionist platforms, but also led to a demand for rights under liberalism and socialism.

The second wave has been viewed as the twentieth century movement for women to have sexual rights, legal rights and legal equality. The early second wave was perceived as a far more organized and intensive moment of social realization and change from the decades of the sixties to the eighties. Accomplishments of this movement included the demand for legal abortion and reproductive rights, equal employment laws, sexual offences bills, equal education, equal opportunity in the workplace, recognition of housework and childcare as work. Again, these may seem commonplace today because they have filtered into everyday language, policy documents of companies and governments' political agendas. This wave also brought women and gender studies into the university classroom and created both a globalized feminist movement and a thriving non-governmental business of feminist and women's organizations. The latter deals with matters ranging from ensuring rights for prostitutes or sex workers, to training women for political leadership.

The emerging Third Wave appears more diffused, less programmatically organized, and at present less confrontational than the first and second waves. On the one hand, in an organized sense it has been viewed as having already been co-opted by institutions, organizations and states, conservatively channeled into universities, non-governmental organizations, government bureaucracies and political agendas for votes, and international funders with tax-free funds to disburse. On the other hand, what is less known, is that its scholarship will continue as with the second wave to be quietly subversive within the university curricula, disputing existing epistemologies and inviting critical thought. This feature remains more elusive, not by choice, but by virtue of the project in which it engages - that of reconstructing androcentric knowledge. Two other key components form part of the third wave though, and how this is being expressed is not yet quite clear. First is that young women (admittedly not all but many that I know) today are well aware and quite articulate about their gender rights in an everyday sense and willing to stand up for these rights, in their homes, with their partners, in their workplaces. This has had its obvious effect in challenging masculinity on many fronts, and thus the third wave is equally the adjustments or retaliations being made by masculinity and men, not the least it is argued with increasing forms of gender-based violence. The third wave has also benefited from another kind of diffusion: that of disrupting the essentialism of social if not biological gender. No longer can we with reason hold on to notions of fixed gender and sexual roles and attributes. Ideas of transgender, transsexual identities and shifting gender identities throughout one's lifetime are already the currency of thought in gender and feminism.

Perhaps the main problem which first and second wave feminists have with the Third Wave is that there is less evidence of a militant organization around specific issues or themes, such as those which fed the struggles before. First and second wave feminisms were grounded in praxis rather than separated from theory and benefited from the articulated relationship between these. This dispersion of Third Wave feminist activisms and ideas in my view emerged because the effects of the first and second waves were widely felt and received. As one feminist ally reminded me over dinner one night, daughters today have grown up with mothers who taught them by their actions to expect a certain set of rights and possibilities as a way of life, without even questioning this, just as our mothers transmitted ideas of their generation to us. Women today have more social freedoms, more privileges, more access to occupations, more scope for expression of their dissatisfaction and of their sexuality than that allowed their mothers and grandmothers and great grandmothers before them. By the end of the second wave, masculinity has also re-examined itself, offering men further possibilities for performance of masculinity, if not always reaching all men. Patriarchy has been forced into a new collective reckoning about gender roles because of women's greater agency in contemporary society.

At the root of these shifts are the changes in mode of production, technology and divisions of labour which have over time drawn men and women differently into the labour force, thus creating different needs of each sex at any time. The ideas of gender equality did not simply emerge from the ideological meanderings of a subversive minority. They were impelled by concrete factors. Among these have been women's demands for reproductive rights, for freedom from consistent child bearing and rearing and its effects on their health, for equal wages for work which they did outside of the home, many also serving as heads and single wage earners in their households. It has emerged from the lived experience of oppressive acts such as domestic violence, and from the persistent threat of rape as social control over their sexuality. Ideas about gender equality are also fundamentally influenced by other social and political movements which demand freedoms of one sort or another. The emergence of the first and second wave movements cannot be delinked from accepted philosophical notions of development: that the level of 'development' of a society may be measured by the status of its women.

But these new gender rights and reconfigurations in the twentieth century, though inalienable for many societies, are still alien in others. The un-education of girls in Afghanistan was counteracted by brave women within the society who worked underground, at risk of death, to continue teaching young girls. Nor do we condone that a woman may be stoned to death under Sharia law in Nigeria for committing adultery. She is castigated as a sinner, while the adulterous male walks free. Such instances of lack in women's rights in "Third World" societies are emblazoned across the globe on internet and media networks as evidence of underdevelopment of such societies. Third wave feminism must be far more politically sophisticated and astute as to how these are used and misused on political agendas of nations. Michelle Rowley comments personally on these two examples:

> ... even as we speak to Afghanistan and Nigeria, it is important to note simultaneously that these manifestations of misogyny are not only national but also tools in a geo-political battle where the West draws attention to the Rest as a way of re-establishing old political markers of Third Worldism. So it is not accidental that concern re-emerged for Afghanistan's women on U.S.-based Women's Studies List serves around the threat of terrorism. The point is that the notion of sisterhood is still riddled with sinister nationalistic agendas where the only thing of colour in the "South" that seems to matter to the West is the black of oil.[5]

While Third Wave feminism will continue to rethink what "sisterhood means", it also has to consider how it may deal with geo-political arrangements that underpin cultural inconsistencies across the globe in respect of those rights that we now hold to be indisputable? What has Third Wave feminism to offer in those instances where rights once gained may be just as easily retracted?

WOMAN'S CONSCIOUSNESS, MAN'S WORLD

A short while after I had begun an activist and scholarly involvement in the area of socialism and feminism in the late seventies, I was introduced to Sheila Rowbotham's *Woman's Consciousness, Man's World*. She wrote:

> When I was seventeen feminism meant to me shadowy figures in long old-fashioned clothes ho were somehow connected with headmistresses who said you shouldn't wear high heels and make up. It was all very prim and stiff and mainly concerned with keeping you away from boys. From dim childhood memories I had the stereotype of emancipated women: frightening people in tweed suits and horn-rimmed glasses with stern buns at the back of their heads. (Rowbotham 1974, 12)

Although separated by miles of cultural differences in a little Caribbean island, I understood the sentiments.[6] The images she evoked were similar to those I had of older unmarried Presbyterian female teachers at Naparima Girls High School in San Fernando, Trinidad. Among these were two elderly white Canadian teachers who earned my great respect along with a youthful compassion for their singleness. I thought that although rewarded as career women, their lives must be very lacking without children and husbands and family outings. There were of course other married women on the teaching staff, some of whom looked happy, but others who looked harassed and tired in front of the classroom. Was this the burden of a career? Were these the new choices available to us when we grew up? Again, these were never clear-cut scenarios. The younger teachers on the staff were glamorous and seemed to lead very rich social lives, some not beyond reproach by the respectable, or so it seemed to the prurient young. Curiously, I was not put off by these contradictions; rather life seemed to offer a range of possibilities to the map of a future. Looking at these female role models in the sixties, I can understand Sheila Rowbotham's question and response: "Why did it take so long to make a movement like women's liberation? ... To start with we had consciously to recognize our femaleness and see through the existing versions of femininity which surrounded us" (Robowtham, 1974: 3). Young women, and young men, in the beginning of the twenty-first century, are placed in a similar dilemma; they must navigate between old and new constructions of femaleness and maleness around them and come to terms with the convictions of their choices. Like all choices pertaining to identity building, these are not simple or linear ones, for they tread a path of great uncertainty and are still controlled by social sanctions about male and female roles which defy time. What are the imperatives to avow feminism today, either for the young woman or for the young man? Many argue and believe that younger women have far less to lose by becoming feminists, but what they have to lose is not so clear to those already past their prime.

Fear of Feminism
I think we need to examine carefully this seeming apathy to feminism among the young. I use 'seeming' deliberately. There is far more here than meets the eye in the lifestyles of the young and restless. "Young women today have been profoundly affected by the demonization of feminism during ...the time when they formed their understanding of political possibility and public life" writes Lisa Marie Hogeland. "...Young women may experience their situation as extremely precarious – too precarious to risk feminism" (1994, 1). Hogeland argues that this fear of feminism is a fear of politics, the latter understood as "a fear of living in consequences, a fear of reprisals" as there are powerful interests opposed to feminism. What are these powerful interests against feminism or the ideas which feminism advances? It is not in the interest of men that women insist on abortion and reproductive rights. It is not in the interest of capitalism that women demand economic equality in the marketplace. It is not in the interest of consumer culture that women demand that their bodies are less exploited for sale of products. It is not in the interest of men that women demand an end to sexual abuse in the home and workplace. It is not in the interest of men that women begin to compete evenly with them in the once male-dominated spheres of governance and politics, of high finance and corporate business. It is not in the interest of the family and society that women choose careers over childbearing, and are more selective in their

choice of partners. It is not in the interest of men that women ask them to give up the privilege of multiple partners (a "deputy" or "matie" being essential in the Caribbean) or the freedom from domestic routines which tie one partner, in general the female, to a routine tied to home and workplace.

There are other repercussions of second wave feminism now visited on the young. A declared feminist, unless otherwise known and proven to be heterosexual, is assumed to be a lesbian – the two go together as once love and marriage went together with a horse and carriage. At a time in which the young are self-consciously involved in discovering and constructing their identities and when romantic and sexual relationships are primary arenas for selfhood, the institution of heterosexuality provides the safety net of normalcy. In their early twenties few young women have begun professional or community careers that provide another venue through which alternative identities are being shaped. They know that being a feminist limits their chances with the pool of men available for partnerships.

Engaging men
Masculinity, occupied in a defence of its patriarchal rights, is only slowly lowering its rose-coloured lens on traditional ideas of companionship and sexual partnership. In the view of a young Canadian man Ramesh Dharan, the word feminism

> ...strikes a chord of terror in the heart of young males. Images of an army of young feminist activists, clutching proposed legislative amendments and burning Barbie dolls in effigy, leap forth at night from the dark recesses of the male mind. ...Though perhaps not strong enough to paralyze us with fear, accepting feminism is often an especially problematic proposal for many young males.

One young Caribbean man had a slightly different take on the subject:

> I c'yar mess with dem liberated woman. Dem want you to wash up and stay home with them and do everything they say. You cyar make a wrong note around them

but they down on yuh case. I prefer woman I could fool a lil bit. I still want to feel like I'se man.

Feminism appears to be a direct attack not on phallogocentricism, but on the male phallus, an observation supported by Rhoda Reddock, that "One of the most intriguing, although little noticed developments on the 1998 calypso scene in Trinidad was a significant increase in the number of songs dealing with the phallus" (Reddock 2002, 161). Reddock points out that references to phallic imagery have always been an important component in the calypso genre, yet from 1997, the songs dealing with the phallus "did not express that triumphal tone" (Reddock 2002, 162). The angle had changed. The use of humour was now self-directed and unassertive and for Reddock, pointing tenuously to a male reflection of an uncertainty affecting men in general.

It is not difficult to appreciate the male response: not all men are batterers, delinquents, bad fathers, parents and lovers. Not all men are powerful in the workplace or public sphere. While these qualifications of masculinity are implicit or explicit in feminist literature, particularly from the Caribbean where it was the systemic nature of patriarchy rather than individual males who were being targeted, the second wave feminist analysis of patriarchy was viewed as a collective attack on all manhood. Even today, this particular message of feminism has never got very far. The fear of "women taking over" looms large as a threat of the feminist movement and seemed to have merged with symbolic processes associated with manhood and emasculation. Dharan questions this response.

> Having grown up in a post-civil rights, politically correct, and morally conscientious society, what could young males possibly find fault with in feminism, at least in the most popular "liberal emancipatory" part of the movement? I have come to realize that many of my male peers are uncomfortable and antipathetic to the continual advancement of feminism and the consequences of this advancement. The causes for this for the most part can be traced back to a common thread: a lack of understanding and a narrow-minded view

of feminism, and the accompanying fear which the movement has made possible... In my own personal experience, a typical response of teenage males when confronted with an expression of feminist views has been to dismiss the debate as irrelevant, since women and men supposedly possess equal rights and freedoms in our society (Dharan 1998).

In the face of this debate, the young woman who publicly avows feminism runs the risk of being denounced as going against women's essential nature, therefore, not the right "wife material". Masculine methods of control over the freedoms now available to young women are both clever and efficient. One young woman in my gender studies class jokingly proffered that a favorite gift of young men to their girlfriends was that of cellular phone. Why? "Miss, so they could check up on you anytime, anywhere".

Michael Flood who teaches in Women and Gender Studies at the Australian National University agrees that men's lives have changed in profound ways over the last three decades. He writes:

> The women's movement and feminism have questioned the meanings given to being male and female. Their efforts, plus other social changes, have shifted the possibilities of men's lives. Men now face new expectations from their girlfriends and partners, their friends, their sisters and daughters and other men. Some traditional forms of manhood – based on being emotionally shut-down, dominating others, work obsessed and aggressive – are often seen as out of date and unhealthy. Men are being encouraged to change their behaviour in the kitchen, the bedroom, the classroom and on the street. Men are expected to treat the women in their lives with respect and to avoid sexist behaviour such as date rape and domestic violence (Flood 2001).

Recognizing that this change is also being asked of Caribbean men, Linden Lewis observes that "social change presupposes some degree of concession and compromise, and it is very often accompanied by some notion – however articulated – of struggle and resistance" (Lewis 2002, 512). Lewis suggests that given the imbalance of power between men and women, "It is fairly axiomatic that men ought to play a pivotal role in the reconfiguration of gender relations" since men everywhere, benefit from the "patriarchal dividend in society" (Lewis 2002, 513).

If men are being asked to change their expectations of femininity, to reshape their practices of masculinity and so on, then what is being asked of young women in their own behaviour and attitudes to young and older men. If one reads between the lines of what young women are saying, they have been presented with a gender consciousness of their equal status, a right to expect equality in all spheres, public and private, collectively and individually. But masculinity itself has not been fully primed or even collectively receptive to the kind of changes in gender relations which Linden Lewis points to. Thus younger women, who are less experienced, are faced with the question of how to manage this new equality which has been offered to them. The younger men, some of whom appear to understand and respect these changes, are trying to adjust; others react more harshly and resentfully, after all the rights of the father were also expected by the son; the Freudian connections cannot be so summarily dismissed.

More feminist bogeys

For those who teach or work in gender studies or feminist organizations of one kind or another, feminism has not by any means been easy work. Both intellectual and activist work required much reading, thinking, time, energy and courage to defy accepted norms, to challenge institutional arrangements, and to take a leap of faith if you like that this was a valid enterprise towards engendering both new knowledge and new sources of empowerment for the young and the society at large. The study of gender, unlike many other disciplines which have emerged in the academy over centuries, is constantly forced to explain its relevance over and over again. Most unfortunately, it acquired a reputation in the early days of its introduction as a "soft" option, as if both the students and those who taught and worked in this area, had compromised quality for some puttied quantity. In many ways, gender studies, like much of feminist activism, has become ghettoized. Why should we assume that young women and men will voluntarily sign up for labelling, hardship, censorship, and reprisals which are associated with this area of work or study?

Women's studies and gender studies have now existed in the academy in the Caribbean for at least twenty years, more formally with the setting up of the Centre for Gender and Development Studies at the three campuses of The University of the West Indies since 1993.[7] Students who venture into the gender studies curriculum come with a range of misconceptions and simultaneously have to contend with a range of perceptions about themselves. Why on earth are they doing courses in gender studies they are asked, by their female and male peers, parents and relatives? What are they going to do with this after they leave university? The undertones are they must be closet lesbians and man haters to have made such choices, they must be foolhardy as gender studies is not a professional degree linked to an obvious occupational choice or career, or worst yet, simple minded as gender studies is soft and available for those who "cannot take learning." Needless to say, many critics have never bothered to discover the content of such courses but assume that the curriculum must be filled with male-bashing topics – a school for feminist scandal and intrigue. The questions we are faced with, those who teach and work in the area, and those who choose to follow, have become too tiresomely repetitive, but nonetheless gnawing and annoying ones.

In the context of the English-speaking Caribbean, two features emerged dominantly at the end of the twentieth century fuelling this fear of feminism and of its proliferation through the teaching of women and gender studies. *First* among these has been the introduction of a clause related to marital rape in the Sexual Offences Act and second the establishment of the Domestic Violence Act in several societies. While in practice these pieces of legislation are by no means unproblematic in themselves, they serve the more profound purpose of signaling that age-old ideas thought to be founded on the 'essential nature' of male and female can and do undergo change. The marital rape clause questions the conjugal rights of a man over a woman within the institution of marriage. In the case of the Domestic

Violence Act, it is no longer possible for the court to dismiss domestic violence as "man-woman business" which should be settled outside of the judiciary and policing system. The signal to masculinity is loud and clear and frightening, destabilizing to what has constituted masculinity for centuries. Residual notions of chattel slavery which have "kept femininity in its place" are slowly eroding. For the layman and laywoman, this shift in what comprises woman's and man's rightful place in society, is an intimidating one raising everyday questions and concerns – How do we bring up our children? How must they be socialized? What moral values must apply to each sex? Who will be responsible for the home? These are very legitimate concerns and questions, which first wave feminism could not have anticipated, and second wave feminism assumed would be ironed out in provisions and services by state and community, by accommodations within households and by an increasing conscientized society which would accept the inevitability and logic of changing gender roles and ideologies. Third wave feminism must consider carefully the implications of what real gender equality and equity means to relations between and among the sexes in general, the sexual division of labour in the family and the workplace, and relations within the household. Third Wave feminism must also consider how ideologies, even more than practices, are most resistant to change.

The *second* feature, a global occurrence, is the entry of more women into the formal education system, particularly at secondary and tertiary levels. In the Caribbean, this increased visibility of women in education, albeit dominantly in the 'softer' areas of humanities and social sciences" and in professions such as teaching, law and medicine, has come under serious scrutiny, echoing perhaps a fear which the eighteenth and nineteenth century educators had when they opened the schoolroom to women *en masse*. Ironically, the far fewer numbers of educated women until the last decades of the twentieth century had created no such panic among policy makers and planners. The ideas of and assumed male marginality in the household have now been further underscored by a panic about the underachievement of men in education, and consequently, in the workplace and in public office. Both spoken and unspoken are the directives to women, that feminism has bred disfigurement and chaos to the natural order of society, that once again, like the biblical Eve in the garden of Eden, women have compromised the "true course of nature." The convenient bogey is *feminism*, rather than the circumstances which had given rise to a new social order.

Gender consciousness versus feminist consciousness

It is not a lack of gender consciousness which is the problem now, it is the lack of a feminist consciousness. To admit or embrace a feminist consciousness, by definition, one has to work actively and consciously at dealing with the problem, not just acknowledging it. More to the point, to admit a feminist consciousness requires moving beyond the clichéd ideas of supporting gender equity and equality, to more informed and articulated ideas of how these may be achieved – it demands a level of intellectual and political engagement which few are really prepared to deal with. In the past, things pertaining to gender were thought to be grasped naturally because of each individual's experience of having male and female bodies, and by simply being man and women. So too, ideas of feminism are thought to be easily understood, and worse yet static, as if there has been no progression in its theory and praxis over the last few decades.

Teresa de Lauretis (1989) observed that the technology of gender is both its presentation and re-presentation. Once we become self-conscious of our gender identities, we are also busily engaged in consciously re-presenting them. This proceeds daily in many spheres, but it is most evident for instance in the business of the film industry. Contemporary television and big screen films are rife with examples of how gender representation has come a long way from the first half of the twentieth century. Films in the eighties and nineties which pecked at the issues such as *An Unmarried Woman* (Jill Clayburgh) and *Working Girl* (Sigourney Weaver and Meg Ryan) have grown far more explicit and precise. Among these are the remaking of the old television series Charlie's Angels – the Angels, though "angelic", are by no means pushovers and docile pawns of the mysterious Charlie again. Both the contemporary "Sex and the City" and "Mind of the Married Man" dissect from different viewpoints the new morality which informs each sex, and "Will and Grace" take homosexuality, one of feminism's best bedfellows in activism, as its theme in a family situation comedy. Nor are these interrogations restricted to a white middle-class morality only. Ideas of race and gender differences and representation have become generous fodder for the financially conscious mill of the film industry, tapping on to new themes which engage the modern mind. If "Guess who's coming to dinner" forced the old white couple of the screen Spencer Tracy and Katherine Hepburn to accept the black Sidney Poitier as their daughter's spouse, Spike Lee's "She's gotta have it" examines the flexibilities allowed the new young black woman of the 1980s in her choice of sexual partners, and the more recent "Save the last dance" (2001) pits a black young man and white young woman in a close encounter of another kind. The latest James Bond release "Die another day", even admits the black femme fatale heroine in the form of Halle Berry, suggesting that racially as well, black women too have come a long way. In the western dominated media which influences the everyday consciousness of the young, these are not incidental in reshaping ideas pertaining to gender, race and sexuality, obfuscating sometimes, yet representing new dimensions of race, gender and sexual relations.

Third wave feminism is surfing in different waters than that of the second wave. There has emerged a gender confidence without an attendant political consciousness. Hogeland observes of the contemporary situation that "Gender consciousness is a necessary precondition for feminist consciousness, but they are not the same" (Hogeland 1994, 1). Others have suggested that this is actually the other way around, that we need to separate gender consciousness and feminist consciousness, understanding the successes of the first as a victory of feminism itself, and the limits of the other as the limits of social movements themselves. Eudine Barriteau (2002) suggests that "gender has consumed its feminist mother." Third wave feminism must continue to pose the question this raises: has gender consciousness been at the expense of a feminist consciousness? Is there a difference and is this difference key to the future of feminism?

'MY MOTHER WHO FATHERED ME' AND THE RISE OF A NEW MATRIARCHY

There has begun to be bad blood between younger and older women and this does not augur well for the future of feminism.

At the *Re-Centring Caribbean Feminist Workshop* in Barbados, June 2002, one young woman had this to say "We need to broaden the scope of feminism. At this point it is crafted in such a way that it can be marginalizing to young women."[8]

It is easy to blame the early feminists and founding mothers of feminism for this or that flaw in the feminist agenda. The reasons for this lack of obvious activism may lie outside feminism itself in that second wave feminism actually emerged alongside a period of great social resistance and turmoil, including black power, civil rights and student movements and anti-war sentiments, whereas third wave feminism, though emerging in very troubled times, did so when there were no grand narratives of resistance or subordination such as capitalism versus socialism and a cold war narrative on which it could hang its hat - nor has terrorism versus the rest convinced us that this is how the west must be won.

It is easy to overlook what older feminists or conscious women have created as a body of thought to which the young are invited to polemicize, critique and ultimately to enhance. Recently, a colleague at the University of the West Indies expressed her sadness at the incapacity of younger scholars to appreciate the pathbreaking scholarship of women like Lucille Mathurin Mair.[9] We who have worked directly with and under Lucille Mathurin Mair and understood the battle she waged, with the support of Elsa Goveia to do the first Ph.D history dissertation at the University of the West Indies on the study of women in Jamaica in the 1970s, cannot take this for granted. Just as today we must also recognize and appreciate the path breaking efforts of young women who are at the forefront of projects such as ASPIRE: *Advocates for Safe Parenthood: Improving Reproductive Equity* in Trinidad which confront subjects still taboo or inflammatory such as abortion rights. The subject matter of women and gender has become fit material for activism and scholarly investigations, even if there is still baggage and derision attached. Gains achieved are taken for granted, with little knowledge sometimes of the inconveniences experienced to arrive at this place. Memories are very short, especially in an accelerated world, although this is by no means applicable to feminism alone, a feature that is often overlooked by those who rise to its defense.

It is easy to blame the young women and men for lacking a feminist consciousness and for not becoming part of the "women's movement." But what is not clear to many of them is to what precise "movement" should they be admitted. The second wave women's movement in the sixties was admittedly a more defined and public feminism. There were visible characters, activities and public proclamations of varying sorts. There were, as noted above, other social movements that both used and supported women's growing activism. But feminism has for some time now, in the popular discourse, become immersed with and consumed by an amorphous set of ideas and practices and less difficult to pin down other than in its most direct statements pertaining to women's continuing struggle for ascendancy to political power, equal treatment in the home and workplace, persistent fight against sexual violence, control of reproductive rights, and a growing dialogue with masculinity. As with all political change, some of the spokespersons are not convincing that they represent all women, even if this is not intended. As with all social change, each generation, by definition, challenges and resists the other, reinventing the wheel until they learn that the revolutions can simply continue if we add more spokes and spokespersons.

Within feminism the distance of older and younger women is more worrying because second wave feminism itself was built on ideas of sisterhood.

> There is not enough continuity being built with a new cadre of up and coming feminist, women. We have to guard against a mistrust hardening to the point it prevents our strategic solidarities around the agendas with which we identify. We the ones who are established, who have paid some dues, cling to power in all its manifestations and often frustrate younger women. Similarly, younger women anxious and eager to make their mark, often arrive before they have reached. They dismiss the wisdom, the experiences, even the mistakes of the women who walked before them as irrelevant to feminist politics and scholarship of the twenty first century (Barriteau 2002, 14).

There is need for understanding and appreciation on both sides, a willingness to share knowledge, power and resources, an openness to unlearn and to learn.

If feminism has perchance thrown up a new matriarchy, there have been other female regimes and authority figures in the past which younger women and men have had to reckon with. The relations between mother and son, mother and daughter have to be individuated. The power of the mother-in-law over new daughters-in-law, of first wives over younger wives, all of these are built on similar ideas of ascendancy through experience or the crucial roles one has played, as ways of establishing power bases. The rise of a new matriarchy in feminism may be read as both, with its problems but also its pathways. The resolution once more lies in the feminist solution. Many young women are mindful of the lessons of the past and are interested in the foundations laid by second wave Caribbean feminist thinkers. Gabrielle Hosein (Trinidad), for instance observes:

> I feel I need to know – about the gains won, the setbacks and the original issues that Caribbean women organized around – to be able to differentiate specifically Caribbean concerns. To tell the truth, as a young person, I have major concerns about how much more my generation needs to know about our history since independence – that history of what has been achieved and how and where we need to still follow through. I think this has major consequences for the future of the feminist movement and for changing generational roles.

Shakira Maxwell (Jamaica), comments:

> I think as feminists we cannot necessarily believe that our concerns are so vastly different from others around the world, despite the region or country they may come from. However, I do believe that Caribbean feminists have had to fight for the rights of Caribbean women in different ways than those which have been undertaken in other "first world" countries. For instance, class and racial concerns have had to be tackled from a different

standpoint, similar to that of countries such as Africa and Latin America and this I think binds us together.[10]

'from margin to centre': Challenges for Third Wave feminism

The young have a lot to give. Many of them do not yet have binding responsibilities of families or careers, they have energy, idealism and time. The challenge is for the older feminists to support and encourage initiatives of the young. Activism and political consciousness, however, seem driven by factors other than a promoting or receptive group. Feminist activism will arise out of the specific experiences and problems which confront the young and their will to create change. Although I do not dare to speak for a new generation, it appears to me that some of the issues are already apparent. Among these are:

1. The paradox of choice

Women are presented with a range of acceptable choices, of motherhood or career, to have or not have children and still lead full and productive lives, to lead single lives, to have families in same sex relations. Those who do have children are faced with the problem of feeling left out of the brave new world experienced by those who choose otherwise. With the freedom to choose comes the responsibility of this choice and of their future lives. The blame for unfulfilled professional or family lives cannot be put onto men, or masculinity, or patriarchy for that matter. This responsibility for self must be accepted by women. Women have been writing themselves out of the victimhood script, but what is the next scene?

2. Deconstructing masculinity

Feminism has shaken masculinity to its core. Masculinity is already rethinking itself. What are the implications for new and more equitable gender relations and for the reshaping of patriarchal structures? What are the benefits to masculinity for taking on such a challenge? In addition, will patriarchy, like the amoeba recreate itself from the spore of a damaging masculinist discourse?

3. The institutionalization of feminism

Feminism has moved into the academy but what is its true goal in the academy? Is it about jobs for the girls or about reshaping epistemologies? That feminism has moved into the classroom should not be viewed as conservatism but as a new site from which activism takes place. But what theoretical directions and guidance will academic Third Wave feminism bring to feminist thought and practice? One of the challenges is already there. How do we move Caribbean feminist scholarship and indigenous material to the centre from the margins where it is still to be found?

4. The geopolitical challenge of feminism
The real political challenge of feminism, through its reconstruction of knowledge and understanding of power, is to intervene in global and international political and economic threats to peace and survival of the species, to openly engage in areas and issues that appear unrelated to specific gender interests. How may this be achieved and what new internationalist movements must this give rise to in feminism?

EPILOGUE

The title of the last section of this paper is an adaptation of bell hooks' book, *Feminist theory: from margin to centre*. hooks establishes a rewarding relationship between margin and centre, a symbiotic one, as if to say the centre is continuously shifting and cannot hold for all time. The margin too has its standpoint: "To be part of the margin is to be part of the whole but outside the main body." Third wave may be on the margins now, but it is part of the whole. The full effects of each wave are not felt until they have completely washed over us. We should not assume by an apparent lack of militancy that the present gender consciousness will not create another form of the feminist movement, even while it appears today that, like sugar in coffee, feminism has dissolved throughout society. That the second wave has achieved this diffusion must be celebrated as one of its many victories, as we wait for the third wave to rise to its own crescendo.

ENDNOTES

[1] I am very grateful to Michelle Rowley, then Lecturer, Centre for Gender and Development Studies, who carefully read the first draft of this paper and gave me valuable comments on its structural improvements as well as some of its errors and contradictions. The views retained in this essay are, however, idiosyncratically mine, and are not meant to represent a collective voice nor those of the institution to which I belong.

[2] The title is borrowed from a line from Doris Anderson "Feminism's future is secure", an optimistic reading which I partially share, that if there is no future for feminism, then there is no future for the world. http://ww2.mcgill.ca/uro/Rep/r3105/anderson.html

[3] The imperative to write this essay comes out of the experience of attending a workshop organized by Tracy Robinson, Michelle Rowley and Eudine Barriteau and facilitated by the Cave Hill Centre for Gender and Development Studies at UWI, Barbados in June 2002 entitled Re-*Centring Caribbean Feminism*. After over two decades in the 'feminist" movement, as both an activist and academic, the intergenerational differences emerged at this workshop with a certain forcefulness which left me uncertain about the future of feminism. I understand that the climate improved just before the end, as if the "speaking bitterness" had cleansed the air momentarily. Perhaps it did. This essay is a response to the mood which this workshop left me with, as it is a dialogue with the students who each year come into our gender courses and force a continued questioning.

[4] This brief foray into the rich fiction of the region can in no way represent the complex themes dealt with by these writers. It is by way of homage to such writers of fiction who, some without claiming themselves feminists, have left profound legacies for us in the region.

[5] Extracted from Comments by Michelle Rowley on a first draft of this paper, June, 2003

[6] In my second year of my doctoral studies in The Netherlands I had the pleasure of meeting Sheila Rowbotham and remarked to her how influential her book had been to me. She was very pleased to hear this and observed that hearing comments like this justified the act of writing for her.

[7] For further reading on the introduction of women's studies and gender studies into the academy in the Caribbean, readers are referred to Elsa Leo Rhynie, "Women and Development Studies: Moving from the Periphery" Ch 8, pp 147-163, In: P. Mohammed ed., *Gendered Realities: Essays in Caribbean Feminist Thought*, University of the West Indies Press, Kingston, 2002.

[8] Comments taken from the Report of the Re-Centring Caribbean Feminism Workshop under "Intergenerational Concerns".

[9] I would like to keep the anonymity of this colleague but thank her for sharing this insight with me.

[10] Responses taken from emailed questionnaire sent in February 2003 to a group of scholars in Caribbean feminism and gender studies.

REFERENCES

Barriteau, Eudine. 2002. "Issues and Challenges of Caribbean Feminisms" Keynote Address, Caribbean Feminisms Workshop: Recentring Caribbean Feminisms, June 17, University of the West Indies, Cave Hill, Barbados.

Baumgardner, Jenifer and Amy Richards. 2002. *Manifesta: Young Women, Feminism, and the Future*. New York: Farrar, Straus and Giroux.

Danticat, Edwidge. 1994. *Breath, Eyes, Memory*. New York: Vintage Books.

De Lauretis, Teresa. 1989. *Technologies of Gender: Essays on Theory, Film and Fiction*. Bloomington, IN: Indiana University Press.

Dharan, Ramesh. 1998. "Feminism from the Sidelines: A Young Male's Perspective" http://www.youthactionnetwork.org/forum/spring_summer1998/Feminism_from_the_Sidelines.html

Edgehill, Zee. 1982. *Beka Lamb*. London, Kingston and Port of Spain: Heinemann.

Flood, Michael. 2001. "Can Men be Feminists?" Australian National University Women's Handbook, Canberra, Australia. Also see http://www.xyonline.net/Canmenbefeminists.shtml

Hodge, Merle. 1970. *Crick Crack Monkey*. London and Kingston, Jamaica: Heinemann Educational Books.

Hogeland, Lisa Maria. 1994. "Fear of Feminism Why Young Women get the Willies" *Ms. Magazine* November/December.

hooks, bell. 1984. *Feminist Theory: From Margin to Centre*. Boston: South End Press.

Kincaid, Jamaica. 1986. *Annie John*. New York: Plume Books.

Lewis, Linden. 2002. "Envisioning a Politics of Change within Caribbean Gender Relations." In *Gendered Realities: Essays in Caribbean Feminist Thought*, edited by Patricia Mohammed, 512-530. Kingston, Jamaica: University of the West Indies Press, Kingston.

McKay, Claude. 1986. *Banana Bottom*. London: Pluto Press (first published 1933).

Mootoo, Shani. 1996. *The Cereus Blooms at Night*. New York: Avon Books.

Reddock, Rhoda. 2002. "Man Gone, Man Stay!": Masculinity, Ethnicity and Identity in the Contemporary Sociopolitical Context of Trinidad and Tobago." In *Caribbean Masculinities: Working Papers*, edited by Rafael

Ramirez, Victor Garcia-Toro and Ineke Cunningham, 147-172. San Juan, Puerto Rico: HIV/AIDS Research and Education Center, University of Puerto Rico.

Rich, Adrienne. 1993. "On Lies, Secrets and Silences." In *Women's Studies, Essential Readings*, edited by Stevi Jackson, 445-446. New York: New York University Press.

Rowbotham, Sheila. 1974. *Woman's Consciousness, Man's World*. London: Pelican Books.

Schwarz-Bart, Simone. 1982. *The Bridge of Beyond*. London, Kingston and Port of Spain: Heinemann Caribbean Writer Series.

Senior, Olive. 1989. *Arrival of the Snake-Woman and Other Stories*, London; Longman Caribbean Writers.

Wollestoncraft, Mary. 1992. *A Vindication of the Rights of Woman*. London: Penguin Books. (First published 1792).

5

The Pedagogy Of Difference: Co-Producing Feminist Consciousness Across Borders[†]

INTRODUCTION

How has a movement built on the consciousness of sisterhood become so fragmented between the end of the twentieth and into the second decade of the twenty-first century? As different political tendencies, widely varying economic conditions and cultural dissimilarities emerged in global struggles to achieve diverse visions of women's and gender equality, the current feminist movement appears to be characterized by chasms between the east, west, north and south rather than viewed as a movement whose basic tenets are parallel across racial, geographic and social barriers. By looking at lived examples of confrontations, and through a deliberate process of self-reflexive questioning, I look at elements that might sustain the global nature of the feminist movement into the future. Through a re-examination of

---

[†] First published in the *Journal of International Women's Studies* 19 (3). Selected Papers of the Third World Conference on Women's Studies, Colombo, Sri Lanka, May 2017 Article 2, 2018.

key authors who have identified differences wrought by geography and culture, among them Mohanty's (1986) *Under Western Eyes*, and in conversation with two feminist scholars from North America and India, I interrogate the concept of difference and argue that confronting and accepting difference might teach us more about our "sameness under the skin" and about the continued building of consciousness across borders.

REGARDING DIFFERENCE

In May 2017 I was asked to do a keynote address to the Third World Conference on Women's Studies, held in Colombo, Sri Lanka on the theme of "Building Resilience: Dialogue, Collaboration and Partnerships across Our Differences". The conference triggered a conundrum that I believe feminism faces as a movement as it reconstitutes itself into twenty-first century modernity. One of the dominant ideas of second wave feminism was *sisterhood*, a sense of a common cause in women's equality, if not gender equality, shared by women. All movements begin with inspiration and innocence so it was not unusual that as the demands of feminists expanded globally, the movement also began to render up fissures. One of the primary cracks in the edifice of feminism is that of handling differences among women. Whose authoritative voice represented all women? Did cultural, geographic and economic differences create new hierarchies between and among women? Feminism aims for an eradication of inequalities yet it has itself produced an unevenness of perception or ranking among women and between societies and cultures. "Through the inequalities, the criteria for evaluating liberation become defined by the powerful" writes Diana Fox, "ultimately rendering them a neo-colonial trap rather than a true engagement of differences and explorations of potential solidarities."[1] The shadow of the west dominates the feminist landscape, and the benchmark for equality emerges as a western-defined set of gender practices, roles, attributes and behaviours. Rather than creating a singular or shared vision or feminist goal, this feminist monopoly on ideas, has infused dissension, fragmentation and downright rejection. It is not unusual to still hear in countries as far as Belize, Guyana and Namibia the refrain that "feminism" is foreign, meaning imported from the west and not relevant to the women (and men) of these societies.

The experience of attending the Colombo conference and meeting women from across the world, especially a critical mass drawn from the East, forced anew a reckoning with some fundamental questions that have preoccupied me. "What brings feminists together and what keeps the feminist movement fragmented and undermined globally?" "What sustains a movement and what causes its disintegration?" Niveditha Menon, one of the delegates at this conference, wonderfully framed the root cause of this fragmentation at the Colombo setting: "How can we talk to each other through difference? What language can we share when we are coming from different subject positions and, nowadays, what comes down to identity position? How do we build a shared political feminist emancipatory imagination when we are functioning from spaces radically different (geographically or otherwise) from each other?"

I engaged Diana Fox from Providence, USA and Niveditha Menon of India, both of whom were centrally involved in this conference, in discussions during and after the conference, and interrogated the works of other authors to stimulate thought and explore the consciousness-producing effects that allow us a serious reckoning with some idealistic notions that, for many of us, have sustained the feminist movement. I write this as a polemical paper, in conversation with many scholars and with no attempt to arrive at rarefied conclusions.[2]

The goal of feminist knowledge is not that of essentializing gender politics or universalizing global sisterhood. I would like to think that we, scholars and thinkers and activists, feminist and sympathetic others, can place ourselves in the second decade of the twenty-first century into what Yuval Davis (1999) calls "transversal politics" This is politics informed by "First, standpoint epistemology, which recognizes that from each positioning, the world is seen differently, and thus any knowledge based on just one positioning is 'unfinished' – … that the only way to approach 'the truth' is by a dialogue between people of differential positionings". The second relevant concept within transversal politics is "the encompassment of difference by equality. This means the recognition, on the one hand, that differences are important…that notions of difference should encompass, rather than replace, notions of equality". And Yuval Davis stresses, "Such notions of difference are not hierarchical."[3]

Fully supportive of its aims to meld differences within the feminist movement, my keynote address in Colombo was titled "Other People's Lives: Exploiting Difference". I argued that while difference among groups, geography and culture had been "exploited" in the past to separate peoples, and thus had itself created distances and divergencies in the feminist movement, we could also view differences as valuable to comprehending a new feminist order, employ what the knowledge of this difference brings to us as variations of struggle rather than assuming we must all march to the beat of the same feminist drum. Styled for more emotive delivery, the paper was an impassioned plea for placing ourselves in the condition of the other, and accepting this difference as the first reality we must contend with, to bridge the divide between and among different cultural and racial groupings. I argued that the firm acknowledgment and acceptance of difference would allow for partnerships based on a philosophical platform of equality. Individually and within societies, nonetheless "We would continue to perform our race, class and gender through society's mechanisms of gender construction, processes that are largely learnt in context…while we move to accept difference, or as Jacques Derrida would have this, a "sameness that is not identical."[4]

Diana Fox pointed to the obvious flaw in this statement: "It is a bit of an irony to argue for differences yet to also assert that we can in fact place ourselves empathetically in the position of the other."[5] There is some resonance in this response with Maria Lugones proposal for "an identification based not on presumed sameness, but on recognition of the other, and an openness to transformation of the self."[6] Agency in change is the prerogative of the individual, a western liberal concept that does not hold water even in the west. Maria Lugones argues that current western modernity "implemented European understandings of gender and sex, erasing the various conceptualizations of sex and gender that pre-existed European modern/colonial gender systems". I emphatically do not agree that the concept of gender was absent from a binary opposition that existed in all societies at all periods, and not always with a hierarchy of privilege and status. The evidence of both gender and of cultural resistance shows that there were not only erasures, but syncretisms, as well as resistance to erasure via underground practices, the responses were neither monolithic nor passive.[7] To accept that western modernity could suppress all that came under its hammer is to assume that *we*, meaning individual groups of women and men, *we* meaning a global feminist movement, and *we* meaning disparate individuals, do not and have not exhibited individual or collective autonomy, and an inherent capacity to resist manipulation by distorting external forces. The history of continuous global unrest and individual or group challenges for centuries is ample evidence of this.

What was in retrospect missing from my Colombo keynote address was a robust counter argument acknowledging the uneven nature of power relations that mitigated against group resistance or the individual will to change.[8] I agree fully and as argued by Iris Marion Young, that symmetrical reciprocity cannot be achieved simply by imagining ourselves in place of the other, as asymmetries are themselves created because of variances in histories, culture, sex, ability and, among other elements, age. As Weir (2008) sums this up, "...transformative identity politics are politics of self-critique and self-transformation of a we", placing the burden of transformation more on ourselves as on the "other" we want to reach.[9] Diana Fox readily admits to the positions that "northern feminists find themselves in. I am continually involved in this process" she writes, "and it is always necessary for those of us who, because of national origin, are a part of the source of the asymmetry, to be reminded of this".

Niveditha Menon considers how she has contended with difference from an ethical perspective as an activist and scholar.

> From the time that I started working in the area of gender studies, the conversation of feminism has been dominated by the idea of difference – working through difference, engaging with difference, or transcending difference. I don't think we have found a satisfactory answer to the question of difference. I think this is primarily because of the way in which difference presents itself. Because difference is relational and is defined by power, there is always a contextual creation of difference that, perhaps, cannot be expressed by an abstraction of it. The theorising of difference has always highlighted the importance

of context, precisely because regardless of how we might 'want' to theoretically engage with difference, the lived experience of it is very different.

My central engagement with difference therefore comes in the field. For the past three years, I have been interviewing women who have been part of collectives in Mahila Samakhya (a woman's empowerment programme). They are strong, articulate and spirited women who are always willing to talk about their lives, the interesting and difficult things that they have done, and the various ways in which they resisted the patriarchy in big ways and small. I am often amazed at the open way in which the women share their stories with me, and I always come back inspired by their lives.

However, it is very clear to me, even in writing this, that I am representing them – that in doing so, I am drawing so much power over the way people can know them. Based on my class, caste, my English writing capabilities and the access to an academic space, I have the power to mould the way people perceive them. So, in the very act of meeting them and documenting their lives, the difference between us is drenched in power, something I am very conscious of when I am writing about them.

And yet, when I think about my interactions with them – when they hug me, when they bless me, when we laugh together about the silly things that both of us have done, or the silly things that I say (and I say a lot of silly things), I don't *feel* the difference. Recently, when a woman hugged me at the end of a very emotional interaction, I didn't feel the yawning social gap that exists between us. I felt like we had travelled together and the hug was a marker of this journey. It doesn't feel like she and I are different.

And yet, I know that we are. Yet, I know that in writing about them, I am usurping their right to represent themselves in the spaces where I am writing about them. Yet, I know that they share these stories with me so that people do know about them. And yet, I know that while I get to tell their stories, they do not get to tell theirs (or even mine, for that matter). And yet. . .

And it is in these continuous loops of *And Yets* that any understanding of the relationship between us can be had. It is the understanding that we have to be constantly conscious of the fact that no matter how close our relationships might be, there is a social world outside of our interaction (that gets recreated in our interaction) that dictates the rules of our interaction. Those rules assign both of us to different sets of experiences that I cannot change, even if I desperately might wish to.[10]

I am particularly moved by Menon's revelations as they echo perfectly with many moments of connection with women and groups whom I have encountered in various settings, either in the classroom, in activist work in communities, or in several Caribbean islands while carrying out consultations towards the formulation of national gender equality and equity policies. The engagement with the rules of difference across boundaries of class, ethnicity, nation, economic divides and across masculinity itself forces a reflexivity about the inevitability of power in social relations, and at the same time must also free us from becoming immobilized as a result of such complexity.

In the Colombo keynote address, I had short-circuited the moral and philosophical debates on transformative identity politics in the theme by shunting aside, for the moment, the main binary implicit in difference feminism (Gilligan 1993; MacKinnon 2006), i.e. that located in the difference of women from men and the binary of nature versus nurture, to another concept of difference, that which differentiated groups of women (and men) based on the unequal ethnic relations wrought by nation history and systems of patriarchy, all of these sometimes combined. The latter conception of difference has also generated even more persistent binaries: developed versus underdeveloped, civilized versus the barbarian, Christian versus pagan, the leading term underscored as evidence of western superiority in eighteenth-century western enlightenment thought.

These precepts undoubtedly influenced the geopolitics of feminism and were perhaps the primary trigger for Chandra Mohanty's classic essay *Under Western Eyes: Feminist Scholarship and Colonial Discourses* which was first published in 1986. The clause "under western eyes" which formed the first part of the title of Mohanty's essay was a brilliant one, capturing the essential theoretical and political crux of relations between western women and the rest of the world. Mohanty's *"Under Western Eyes"* had seized on this signifying capacity of the west to homogenize and diminish huge blocks of culture into another essentialist binary: that of the west in relation to the rest of us in the global feminist movement.

Mohanty demonstrated that by constituting a category of women as Third World and assuming this category as a "single monolithic subject", Western feminism has been guilty of another form of colonizing, erasing historical and geographical differences and establishing dominance through a moral standpoint of informed knowledge and progressive praxis. For example, compared to cultures where there are more restrictions on women's sexual and reproductive autonomy, those societies where women have more obvious rights and access to services appear as superior to those who do not. Though Mohanty is careful not to paint "Western feminism" as itself monolithic, the primary signifiers of western versus non-western that are invoked reinforce the binary of the west versus the rest, the same binary that it attempts to deflate. Thus the questions that are raised by activists and scholars remain still bound by the binary that the dominant western discourse has imprinted on mentalities. In my keynote address I used the example of Muslim women wearing the *burkha* as an example of how this binary is reproduced. The wearing of the *burkha* in public by Muslim women in France was banned by the European Court of Human Rights in the interests of everyone "living together" in 2010. Shami Chakrabarti, director of the UK human rights pressure group Liberty, said the ban "has nothing to do with gender equality and everything to do with rising racism in Western Europe."[11] The wearing of the *burkha* or *chador* remains a problematic one not only in France but in different societies, and are viewed by western women in particular as extreme control over women's bodies and mobility rather than as protections that are offered to women within Islamic culture. Beyond this, there is much written by women who wear the *burkha* or *chador* who have redefined its use in a multiplicity of ways, claiming agency over its definition and reclaiming the symbolic referents that make sense within their cultural frameworks.

MADE IN THE WEST

A refusal to be categorized or homogenized prompts Paravisini-Gebert (1997) to write in a finely crafted essay "Decolonizing Feminism: The home-grown roots of the Caribbean Women's Movement":

> It is commonplace …to speak of our history, our literature, the quality of our feminism or lack thereof, as if we constituted a homogeneous block, an undivided, unfragmented and unfragmentable entity – a knowable, understandable, whole. Caribbean feminism is often discussed in much the same way, as something graspable, perceptible, complete – perhaps different from US and European variables but nonetheless comprehensible, unequivocal.[12]

How could differences that were so palpably evident in the anthropology of nations well into the early twentieth century become so evaded and erased in a relatively short time? In its appeal to the universality of gender inequality and discrimination, there were major elisions that have not served feminism as a social movement at all well.

In the 2017 Colombo conference site, Niveditha Menon had in fact raised the ethical dilemma that still troubles the epistemic space of Indian scholars and activists from the Asian subcontinent. Menon asked "How can narratives of violence not be used as indicative of backward women, and not reinforce the idea of South Asian women as victims of underdeveloped countries to be rescued by developed ones?" She elaborates further:

> My point is also about how we, as South-based scholars who have come to represent 'other' South-

based survivors of violence – have to constantly move against the dominant discourse of 'death by culture' (as poignantly referenced by Uma Narayan) when we speak of violence. What thin lines do we have to walk, then, given our own power of representation over the 'other' – the survivor' – to Western Eyes, as well as the culpability that we have in evoking a particular form of 'survivor' that provides no space for multiplicity of experience and agency?[13]

Not only are feminists within societies separated or differentiated by class, ethnicity or cultural groupings, but across nations, the burden of being "under western eyes" still obtains for those who carry the designation of "Third world women" in current geopolitical formation. The main ideas outlined in Mohanty's now classic paper persist as a powerful conceptual framework or point of departure for those who write and work from small or culturally marginal societies.[14] Mohanty's critique had nonetheless extracted a moral responsibility on those who used, funded or generated research projects or data collection and those who underwrote feminism in the western publishing houses for societies deemed "developing and under-developed". In her new publication *Feminism without borders: Decolonizing theory, practicing solidarity* (2003), written nearly two decades after the first landmark essay, Mohanty shifted the focus of her preoccupation with how "the "West" colonizes gender" to "the way that gender matters in the racial, class, and national formations of globalization". She focuses attention more specifically on the emancipatory potential of the feminist project globally for social justice, racial, class and gender equality by appealing for a transcendence of borders that preoccupy feminist scholars and activists within the silos of their societies or institutions. As Diana Fox puts this:

> I perceive Mohanty as levying an on-going critique of Morgan's assumed global sisterhood, and instead issuing a call to generate coalitions and solidarities across borders anchored in conversations that build mutual understanding, producing analyses that are simultaneously situated and systemic—systemic critiques of institutions and structures of global

capitalism and hierarchies of the corporate academy that produce a flattening of differences.[15]

Such ideas for crumbling boundaries and rejecting a flattening of differences present a twenty-first century manifesto for feminism that one can have little quarrel with. It advances the mantra of the second wave feminist movement, "sisterhood is powerful" (Robin Morgan 1970) which Morgan herself updated with "sisterhood is forever" to ensure that despite divergences and differences, there is a global call to unity. I wonder about the processes by which these optimistic declarations can be translated into collaborative, cross-cultural possibilities for global transformations and the necessary resilience required of the feminist movement both within a society and across borders.

In *Feminism without borders,* Mohanty (2003) presents a rational visionary framework within which she proposes feminist goals can be achieved. She identifies two projects to be tackled: *first,* dismantling the distinctions and hierarchies that have been made between Western feminism and Third World feminism in order to solidify the global project as one without borders. The *second* retains the need for autonomous feminist concerns and strategies to be applied, a recognition that there were no universal prescriptions for gender oppression or discrimination, although she stresses that transnational feminist solidarity remains the cornerstone of a struggle that must transcend time and space.

Writing from an African feminist perspective, Amina Mama (2017) endorses this position:

> It takes integrity and courage to listen across boundaries, to hear and respect the multiple languages of gender and sexuality, marked by the striations of other dimensions of power and status. Unless we link collective organising with coherent feminist consciousness informed by sound theories of gender oppression and change, we easily become subject to an identity politics that will keep us divided. By strengthening feminist consciousness, we strengthen the collective will to change.[16]

Mama proposes that feminist writing and publishing is a key route to conscientization, to engage the collective consciousness within societies or regions and claim ownership of theoretical explanations and cultural specificities, while also proposing common grounds for solidarity with others. A review of journal issue titles of *Feminist Africa* of which Mama is the Editor, affirms this exercise of inward looking, outward stretch:

> *Feminist Africa*
> 3: "National Politricks" (2004);
> 10: "Militarism, Conflict and Women's Activism" (2008);
> 11: "Researching for Life: Paradigms and Power" (2008);
> 12: "Land, Labour and Gendered Livelihoods" (2009);
> 13: "Body Politics and Citizenship" (2009);
> 14: "Rethinking Gender and Violence" (2010);
> 17: "Researching Sexuality with Young Southern Africa Women" (2012);
> 19: "Pan-Africanism and Feminism" (2014) and
> 22: "Feminists Organizing - Strategy, Voice, Power" (2017).

All of these journal issues grapple with concerns that are raised within the context of feminist struggles and through an African feminist epistemological lens. In *Feminist Africa* 11, "Researching for Life: Paradigms and Power", Hanan Sabea

> demands re-engagement with the paradigmatic "order of things" through which questions of Africa, nation, gender, and location are imagined. Her invitation is to see past the prefixes of "trans" (-national, -continental), "inter" (-disciplinary, -dialogic) and "post" (-feminist, -colonial, -state) to discover the operation of homogenizations which recolonize, re-monopolize, the gaze on the sheer complex and multi-gendered realities of work, mobilities, and meaning.[17]

This journal is incisive in its intent. The journal policy establishes that it is

> ...guided by a profound commitment to transforming gender hierarchies in Africa, and ...targets

gender researchers, students, educators, women's organizations and feminist activists throughout Africa. It works to develop a feminist intellectual community by promoting and enhancing African women's intellectual work.

One might of course ask the question, where do the boundaries of Africa lie, and where might we find its feminist intellectual community located. The Africa referenced above is by no means the homogeneous terrain constructed by the west. Yet even in the journal, there is an emblematic Africa that has been conscripted across borders.

There is an inescapable contradiction in the call for a collective consciousness without an interrogation of the basis for this collective position. The default position of feminism is an essentialist one when collectivities congregate. By virtue of being female the appeal is to sisterhood, by virtue of being female from a geographical location often there is a silencing of difference in order to represent the idea of communal strength or national identities that the media finds easier to handle, and the global metrics of inequality can better grasp. Mohanty's "feminism without borders" admits to these complex realities and argues for the need to *construct* similarities or perhaps solidarities—that they are not inevitable, but are built and elicited through dialogue and engagement in the creation of relationships. She argues that the process of engagement creates points of intersection that are necessary to combat the very powerful forces of oppression, neo-colonialism and neoliberal assumptions that infringe upon individual and group rights and freedoms.

To some extent this addresses Menon's ethical dilemma because it allows for women across borders to acknowledge that violence is not exclusive to underdeveloped nations but is systemic across class, race, colour, and nation. In this respect the issues of violence against women and the claims for sexual and reproductive rights have certainly been two primary platforms which have admitted to universality with difference, as the cultural manifestations of violence and sexual and reproductive rights have much in common yet also differ in their varied contexts due to diverse cultural expectations and practices.

"Feminism without borders is not the same as "border-less" feminism" writes Mohanty. "It acknowledges the fault lines, conflicts, differences, fears, and containment that borders represent. It acknowledges that there is no one sense of a border, that the lines between and through nations, races, classes, sexualities, religions, and disabilities, are real…" How these ideas are translated in different settings must be part of this dialogue of difference towards the dismantling of borders. Diana Fox elucidates the multiplicity of interpretations by example. She writes "Mohanty published an article in *Signs* in 2013, ten years after *Feminism without borders*, which is a fascinating reflection on how that book has been interpreted in three distinct settings – Sweden, Mexico, and Palestine, and how, in each context, there were distinct takes on her message. Interestingly, the Palestinian feminist view saw a justification for militant feminism—they rejected any suggestion of coalition building with both Israeli and Palestinian women who sought mutuality, highlighting a complete rejection even in the construction of a global sisterhood. Indigenous feminists in Mexico, by contrast, highlighted the importance of transcultural feminism and the politics of solidarity to create alliances, work which depends for its success on difficult conversations that articulate differences and actively construct points of intersection. Building solidarities must be contingent on explicating differences; however, there is simultaneously an assertion of overlapping conditions that surface through systemic analyses."[18]

BUILDING SOLIDARITIES: "Even this conversation in which we are currently engaged is a product of that concept" [19]

To deconstruct the monolith of feminism itself requires a close circuit assessment of how gender scholarship and knowledge production in feminism have emerged, how activisms are framed within borders and across global boundaries, what theoretical insights are gleaned and what bridges were crossed that maintain the global connectivity and political relevance of feminism, not as a single movement but as a multiplicity of movements still underscored by some common goals. A Herculean task at the very least! What does all of this bring to the feminist tactical boardroom or to the groups of isolated feminist organizations and grassroots movements, to gender studies scholars struggling away with definitions, concepts and theories in universities across the world?

For one thing I think it defuses the underlying philosophy through which global gender equality is calibrated, that gender equality has gained ascendancy in first world countries because the gender violations experienced by women in south Asia, Africa, poorer communities in the south and in the Caribbean persist as the benchmarks of inequality. Recent developments in the United States, more so in the "Me Too"[20] phenomenon that has targeted sexual politics within the film industry, has demonstrated that sexual harassment remains a seething area of gender inequity that the west has openly disclosed and vented globally.[21]

Fox notes:
> There is a feeling about the fragility of gains that have been made that is emerging and it serves as a reminder that assumptions of a huge gap between the western feminist self and the so-called third world other is not as large as once thought. ...From my standpoint in the U.S., I think this is absolutely true—particularly in the current political climate of opposition to Trumpism where not only the "Me Too" movement, but women's marches, anti-gun marches, climate change marches, and "Time's Up" movements are recalibrating assumptions about so-called western advancement vis-á-vis women's oppression in the rest of the world. US hypocrisy is stark for participants in these movements—it is not possible to see gender equality again only in relationship to the "non-western other.
>
> The solidarities in marches around the world underscore the ways in which our realities are a bricolage, an increased interlinking of local, national, and international networks. For increasing numbers of people there is a global framing of the meaning of community – constant and intense interconnections based on communications and movements of people.[22]

This strikes a real chord. We wondered in the Caribbean (at least I did) how the "Me Too" movement would ignite. Sexual harassment is one of the more difficult areas to legislate. Yet as if the mood of no nonsense had caught on through a process of osmosis, around the 2018 Carnival season the public was warned by a police spokesman that "Thiefing a wine," translated as gyrating on someone's else's body in public fetes, (especially at Carnival when the assumption in this libidinous festival is that everything is allowed), is behaviour which is now considered assault under the Summary Offences Act in Trinidad and Tobago, with penalties that could lead to imprisonment for three to six months.[23] There is of course a lot of discussion and disagreement on how a "wining" assault can be proved. Nonetheless, the actual passage of such an act is a definite signal of how this society is dealing with the increasing demand by women and some men, that ultimately, the individual's right over their body is sacrosanct. The acknowledgement of the state demonstrates how enlightenment values of individual rights are constantly being introduced and becoming embedded in once taken for granted cultural contexts. It builds imperceptibly on the famous Clause Four of the Sexual Offences Act, debated in 1986, which created the offence of rape within marriage. This is an evolutionary step for a Caribbean society to take in the 1980s, borrowing heavily from the Sexual Offences Act previously passed in Canada as a result of the militancy of feminists in that society. In Trinidad the passage to the act engaged the population with the debate that again challenged the conjugal contract with individual human rights. This example attests to the fact that one action leads to another and another and these often cross geographic boundaries. It is the result of incremental societal or national responses, a syncretism of the application of struggle in a new setting involving resistance and responses that are culturally acceptable, and does not have to be regarded as the imposition of western individualism over collectivism.

In another incident that occurred also in February 2018, a public lecture delivered by the Prime Minister of St. Vincent and the Grenadines on The University of the West Indies, Cave Hill campus in Barbados was disrupted by a group of female protesters. "The protest came in the wake of recent controversy and criticism over the handling of a case in St Vincent involving

22-year old former model Yugge Farrell who was charged with using abusive language towards the wife of Finance Minister Camilo Gonsalves who is the son of PM Gonsalves. The young woman, who alleged that she was involved in an extramarital affair with Camilo Gonsalves, was twice sent to the country's mental health centre for evaluation though the prosecutor did not present any evidence that such an evaluation was needed."[24] The protesters were self-acclaimed feminist scholars, members of two women's groups in Barbados, the 'National Organization of Women' and 'Life in Leggings' movement. "We do not like misuse of power, we will not show deference to politicians or prime ministers because we are in solidarity with our sisters and our brothers across the region"[25] protested the women, while security intervened to silence them. This public shaming and naming, specific to the context, might also be read as the ripple effect of the "Me Too" movement, gathering storm across boundaries.[26]

Is it possible to develop geographically grounded feminist theory and responses to struggle and at the same time to forge transnational feminist links? Sue Ann Barratt's paper (2017), presented at the Colombo conference, addresses the now global problem that women face of online sexual harassment and misogyny. Her analysis of the specific comments men make in an online forum required interpretation of Caribbean notions of respectability which polices female respectability by pejorative linguistic and idiomatic expressions. For example in one of the cases Barratt deals with, the female character Therese Ho suffered for having this surname in typical Trinidadian male tongue-lashing. "Never trust a girl with the last name ho."[27] This paper renders up new methods by which struggles are being waged in the contemporary period not only within societies but globally by a complex and sophisticated set of media networks that have found new means to define and reify differences of all kinds. In this brave new world, the optimism of feminist struggle continues as we create new ways to establish and maintain difference and at the same time build bridges of solidarity.

Constructing a "new sisterhood" across all sorts of borders that is not based on naïve notions of sameness under the skin, must confront the real limits still posed by the power that some people possess and exert over others.

> Paying attention to difference, then, is critical, as long as the real contours of power in shaping discourse are made clear, at least, to those who wield the power. Precisely because of the power differentials between women, it is easier to create horizontal alliances than to engage vertical alliances. ... Of course, the vertical alliances are much more difficult to navigate because I have to constantly be aware of and question the complicity of feminist privilege in these [academic] spaces. And that is sometimes a harder battle. It is sometimes harder to deal with one's own role as an oppressor than it is to deal with the ramifications of being oppressed. And it is precisely because of this reason that one has to constantly engage with the way in which we create solidarity.[28]

The two components, difference and power, remain central not just to feminist battles, but to a range of current global confrontations. Feminisms are not exempt from these erupting forces, they are transformed and implicated in ways that continue to create the basis for further difference. Yet solidarity and sisterhood underpin the concept of equality that the Global Gender Gap and the UN CEDAW committee calibrate. And in individual societies, small and large feminist groups, women's organizations, LGBTQI movements and politically motivated politicians continue to stretch the boundaries of gender to reach a goal that is continuously envisioned around acceptance of difference.

> What would this acceptance of difference look like?" asks Diana. Niveditha responds "To be truly honest, I do not know. ...I sometimes think it is an idea – an idea of a better world. And I think what keeps us fragmented is the very same idea - the idea of a better world – because our better worlds are, and perhaps have to be different".

What continues to elude are the lessons to be conveyed through difference. What do we hear when we ask or learn about other peoples' experiences? What are the expectations that we subconsciously require of those we encounter? In the intricate network of surfaces that connect us as individuals, academics, writers, feminists, travellers, conference goers, internet explorers and the multiple identities we possess, difference remains the central motif. When will difference become inauthentic and create the pathways for genuinely reciprocal solidarities?

ENDNOTES

[1] Email conversation with Diana Fox, Wednesday 4th April, 2018.

[2] The final version of this paper was recast as a dialogue with two feminists, one from North America (Diana Fox) and one from India (Niveditha Menon) in an effort to straddle the boundaries of difference. I am grateful to both of them for sharing their comments and thoughts openly with me, and as far as possible I have integrated their responses in their own words. The idea of framing the paper in this way came from Diana Fox who read the first draft and suggested that this format of an open ended conversation was itself a unique way of presenting these ideas in order to invite reflection and further discussion.

[3] Nira Yuval Davis *Soundings* Issue 12 summer 1999 pp. 94-95.

[4] Excerpt from Keynote Address, Patricia Mohammed, Colombo conference, "Other People's Lives: Exploiting Difference" May 2017

[5] Email Conversation with Diana Fox, April 4th, 2018.

[6] Lugones, M. (2003). "Playfulness, "world"-traveling and loving perception." In: *Pilgrimages/Peregrinajes: Theorizing coalition against multiple oppressions*. Lanham, Md.: Rowman & Littlefield, cited in A.Weir, "Global Feminism and Transformative Identity Politics, Project Muse, Hypatia vol. 23, no. 4 (October-December 2008), p. 112.

[7] The best example I can draw on, unrelated to gender specifically but clearly illustrative of syncretism and adaptation is the emergence of *vodun, santeria* and *candomble* as blends of Catholicism and African religions when the latter was outlawed under periods of colonial slavery in the Haiti, Cuba and Brazil.

[8] Not because I am unaware of the presence of power in every exchange, but because some speaking occasions require us to present visionary possibilities beyond the limits of our human frailties.

[9] Alison Weir "Global Feminism and Transformative Identity Politics, Project Muse, Hypatia vol. 23, no. 4 (October–December 2008), p. 112.

[10] Email correspondence Niveditha Menon, Centre for Budget and Policy Studies, Bangalore, India 16th April, 2018

[11] https://www.theguardian.com/world/2014/jul/01/french-muslim-women-burqa-ban-ruling

[12] Lizabeth Paravisini Gebert, "Decolonizing Feminism: The Homegrown roots of Caribbean Women's movements" in, *Daughters of Caliban: Caribbean Women in the Twentieth Century*, Consuelo Lypez Springfield (Ed), Indiana University Press, Bloomington, USA, p. 4.

[13] Email correspondence with Niveditha Menon, Centre for Budget and Policy Studies, Bangalore, India November 27th, 2017.

[14] See for example Abeer Al-Sarrani and Alaa Alghamdi "Through Third World Women's Eyes: The Shortcomings of Western Feminist Scholarship on the Third World" Taibah University, Saudi Arabia, *Analize – Journal of Gender and Feminist Studies*

- New Series • Issue No 2 / 2014, http://www.analize-journal.ro/library/files/alaa. pdf, and Kvinna till Kvinna (Sweden) and Women for Women International (USA), 2013. "Western NGOs representation of 'Third World women' – A comparative study." http://www.divaportal.org/smash/get/diva2:632032/fulltext01.pdf

[15] Email with Diana Fox November 8, 2017.

[16] Amina Mama *Feminist Africa* Feminists Organizing – Strategy, Voice, Power, Special Editorial "The Power of Feminist Pan-African Intellect", Issue 22, 2017, p. 1.

[17] Jane Bennett, "Editorial: Researching for Life: Paradigms and Power" *Feminist Africa*, Issue 11, December 2008, p. 7.

[18] Email conversation Diana Fox, November 2017.

[19] Email Niveditha Menon 16th April 2018.

[20] https://www.theguardian.com/commentisfree/2017/dec/31/the-guardian-view-on-metoo-what-comes-next

[21] Although we must not assume that only women in the west take up the mantle on behalf of others. See for example https://www.hindustantimes.com/india/it-s-a-man-s-world-7-sexual-harassment-cases-that-rocked-india/story-TJ4sebHtBlmn2oEkJpJCHO.html

[22] Email Diana Fox, April 4, 2014.

[23] http://newsday.co.tt/2018/01/20/reckless-outburst-by-machel/; http://newsday.co.tt/2018/01/18/you-could-getcharged-fined-for-wining-like-that/

[24] Gonsalves interrupted by protesters during Cave Hill lecture, Amanda Lynch-Foster, amandalynchfoster@nationnews.com, Added 23 February 2018.

[25] *Ibid.*

[26] The first MeToo statement was made by an African American woman. https://www.theguardian.com/world/2018/jan/15/me-too-founder-tarana-burke-women-sexual-assault

[27] In the event that this needs further translation, *ho* is the bastardization of the word *whore* in Trinidadian dialect.

[28] Email conversation Niveditha Menon, 16th April 2018.

REFERENCES

Barratt, Sue Ann. 2017. "Reinforcing Sexism and Misogyny: Social Media, Symbolic Violence and the Construction of Femininity-as-Fail." Paper presented at 3rd World Conference on Women's Studies – 2017 "Building Resilience; Dialogue, Collaboration and Partnerships across Our Differences", 04th - 06th May 2017, Colombo, Sri Lanka.

Bennett, Jane. 2008. "Editorial. Researching for Life: Paradigms and Power." *Feminist Africa* Issue 11, p. 7.

Gilligan, Carol. 1993. "February Meeting at the Crossroads: Women's Psychology and Girls' Development." *Feminism & Psychology* 3 (1): 11-35.

MacKinnon, Catharine A. 2006. "Difference and Domination: On Sex Discrimination." In *Theorizing Feminisms: A Reader*, edited by Elizabeth Hackett and Sally Anne Haslanger. New York: Oxford University Press.

Mama, Amina. 2017. "The Power of Feminist Pan-African Intellect." Editorial in *Feminist Africa: Feminists Organizing - Strategy, Voice, Power*, Special Issue 22.

Mohanty, Chandra Talpade. 1986. *Under Western Eyes: Feminist Scholarship and Colonial Discourses*. Bloomington, IN: Indiana University Press.

------. 2003. *Feminism without Borders: Decolonizing Theory, Practicing Solidarity*. Raleigh, NC: Duke University Press.

Morgan, Robin. 1970. *Sisterhood is Powerful: An Anthology of Writings from the Women's Liberation Movement*. New York: Random House.

Paravisini-Gebert, Lizabeth. 1997. "Decolonizing Feminism: The Homegrown Roots of Caribbean Women's Movements." In *Daughters of Caliban: Caribbean Women in the Twentieth Century*, edited by Consuelo Lopez Springfield, 4. Bloomington, IN: Indiana University Press.

Weir, Allison. 2008. "Global Feminism and Transformative Identity Politics." *Hypatia* 23 (4): 112.

Yuval Davis, Nira. 1999. *Soundings*, [Special issue on transversal politics]. Issue 12 Summer, pp. 94-95

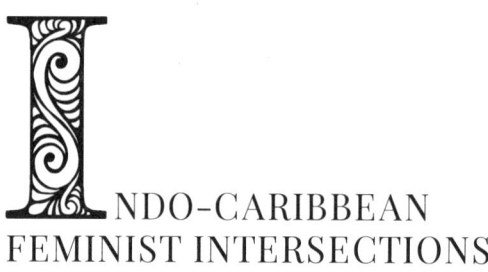
INDO-CARIBBEAN FEMINIST INTERSECTIONS

2

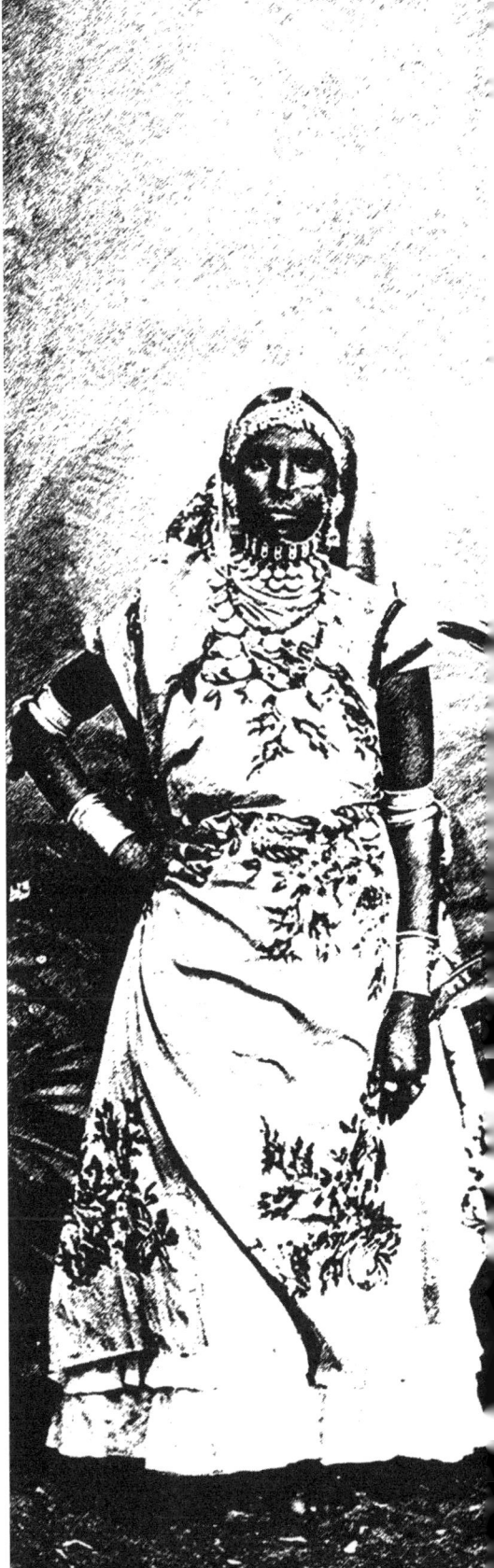

6

The "Creolization" of Indian Women in Trinidad[†]

PREFACE

This paper was originally published in 1988. The changes to the original paper have been deliberately few, although my own work on the area of gender relations in the Indian community grew substantially in both scope and depth. On rereading I feel convinced that it captures a sentiment and component of creolization which, if I were to adjust, would not convey the mood or the moment which the paper expresses at the time if its writing. After three decades, I also still agree with most of what I wrote as a younger scholar. It has been republished many times but remains the first bold strokes of feminist thought that I contributed to the Caribbean and thus is included in this book.

[†] First published in Selwyn Ryan, ed., 1988. *Trinidad and Tobago: The Independence Experience 1962 - 1987*, ISER, St Augustine. Reprinted in Rhoda Reddock and Christine Barrow, eds., 2000. *Reader in Caribbean Sociology*, Kingston: Ian Randle Publishers and in Verene Shepherd and Glen Richards, eds., 2002. *Questioning Creole: Creolisation Discourses in Caribbean Culture*, 130-142. Kingston and Oxford: Ian Randle Publishers and James Currey Publishers

INTERPRETING 'CREOLIZATION'

"Creolization" is a troublesome but useful term. Troublesome because there are so many interpretations of the word; useful because it confronts the issues related to ethnicity and ethnic relations in a multi-racial society. It is a daring, perhaps even an offensive word to use in reference to Indian women in Trinidad for it was used popularly to refer to those women who mixed or consorted with people, especially men, of African descent; Indian women who changed their eating and dress habits and who adopted non Indian social customs. But this draws perhaps on a more popular interpretation of the term. A derivative of the word "creole" used in Trinidad to refer to descendants of African slaves to distinguish them from indentured Indian immigrants, "creolization" was viewed as synonymous with the absorption of black culture at the expense of one's own – a process referred to as acculturation. Anyone appreciative of the history of the relations between the two majority ethnic groups in this society – Blacks and Indians, understands immediately the anathema which greets the suggestion of acculturation, especially from the Indian population.

The term has a vastly richer meaning and it is in the more expansive framework of the concept that I want to discuss the changing status of Indian women in the post independence period in Trinidad and Tobago. I am drawing first on the original Spanish sense of the word, from "criollo" which meant born in and committed to the area in which one lives. In Trinidad and Tobago we have been accustomed to using it in this sense, for instance when we refer to French creoles or Spanish creoles. Creole society has also resulted from some colonial arrangement with a metropolitan power, so that there is the additional dimension of an internal reaction against external metropolitan pressures. There are simultaneously internal adjustments taking place between the cultures interacting in the society. This is a more reciprocal relationship between cultures – an "intermixture and enrichment, each to each" as it has been formulated by Edward Braithwaite (1985), or inter-culturation as opposed to acculturation.[1] Included in the latter process is also the acceptance of the values inherent in creole society, in this instance its preoccupation with class and colour. My discussion is focussed on these ongoing and dynamic processes – acculturation, commitment to one's country of birth, reactions against external cultures and inter-culturation.

There are two other concerns though which are important to any consideration of movement and cultural change in society. First is the impact of political movements which influence attitudes and practices among competing ethnic groups; second, the effect of "modernization" on the competing cultures.

Where and how do Indian women fit into this matrix of cultural change? How do they contribute to the process and how are they affected by it? That they comprise a significant proportion of the population is a demographic fact worth noting. In the 1980 census of the population Indian women accounted for 39.6% of the total female population of Trinidad and Tobago while women of African descent comprised 39.9%, thus accounting for just under one quarter of the total population of this country at this time. We should also not forget a very salient point – that Indian is not synonymous with Hindu. In 1980 Hindu women comprised 24% of the total female population, while Muslim women comprised 6%, Presbyterians 4% and other Christians just under 6%. Although Hindu women predominate, there are subtle differences to be found between Indian women of different religions, differences which transcend their ethnic similarity

THE PRE-INDEPENDENCE PERIOD

Post-independence changes are clearly meaningless if they are not measured against the pre independence era. From all accounts, Indian women's introduction into the new society was dramatic to say the least and made for the rather paradoxical situation in which the first Indian female immigrants found themselves in the new society. First of all, consider the sexual imbalance between Indian males and females which existed for the entire period of indenture – 1845 to 1917, and well into the post indenture period. Between 1881 and 1891 there were 2,117 males to every 1,000 females. Being in short supply females were at the same time more in demand and freer to make choices yet internally policed because of their scarcity. Not given to celibacy, Indian men found the situation unsatisfactory. Planters were also concerned about accretions to their labour supply especially when it seemed that the system of indenture would be discontinued. Thus efforts to increase female immigration resulted in a ratio of 1,354 males to every 1,000 females by 1911. Despite these efforts, at no time during the indentureship system did the number of females equal the number of males imported into the Colony. By 1931 there was still an imbalanced ratio of 1,135 men to 1,000 women.

Second, consider the type of woman who was indentured. Reddock (1984) has suggested that those women who came would have already been drawn from a more independent breed; it is calculated that two thirds of the women who were recruited were single, widows who would have been forbidden to remarry in India, women who had separated from or been abandoned by their husbands and other women of "easy virtue." I think the origin status of the migrant women needs more conclusive research but the fact remains that under the new and more promising conditions, the Indian woman could challenge her former role in India. She was now in the enviable position of being a valuable resource and like her male counterpart, a wage earner on the estate, even if paid less for her labour.

These factors obviously created conditions for a more independent and less passive role for Indian women. This was more easily said than done however. Indian men could no longer rely on the rules which entrenched patriarchy in India in both the Hindu and Muslim family. On the estate they could not make recourse to the rules governing Hindu life, *karma* and *dharma* which, while glorifying womanhood, also placed femininity in a passive role as chattel to masculinity, ensuring female subservience and passivity. Indian men in Trinidad violently coerced their women into submission. Bridget Brereton (1979) notes that between 1872 and 1900, 87 murders of Indian women occurred of which 65 were wife murders. This legacy of institutionalized violence persisted and appears to have been one of the features of the relations between Indian men and women when they were married, such as those typified in the cruel and dehumanized relationship between Pa and Ma in Tola Trace in 1905 in Harold Sonny Ladoo's (1972) *No Pain Like this Body*.

Yet in the face of this kind of coercion it is believed that Indian women were the keepers of the culture, establishing in the new society many of the traditions and cultural practices of the motherland. Why would Indian women have voluntarily recreated a pattern of life which was restricting and oppressive to them in India? We need to ask, as sociologist Kim Johnson (1984) has done, if Indian women sought independence in the first place, then who was it from? His explanation appears to me to be a logical one. He suggests that, like Indian men, Indian women clung to their remembered culture as the only solace and strength: there was nothing in the new culture which replaced the old. It was possible, proposes Johnson, that Indian women were not "struggling for chimeric independence but for an altered balance of power within the family," a balance which was altered in their favour.

Neither Indian men nor women attempted in the earliest periods to become integrated or even familiar with the new society. Loyalties were first to India to which they hoped to return some day. They lived culturally apart from the rest of the "creole" society. Geographical and occupational separation, combined with mutual contempt and misunderstanding, kept the various races apart. For their part, Blacks, who had internalized the values of creole society had a reciprocal contempt for this group of immigrants who spoke "barbarous" languages, dressed differently, and worked for cheaper wages than they did. Indians arrived with their caste and religious rules and regarded Africans as untouchables and polluted as they ate the flesh of pigs and cattle and engaged in occupations which they considered ritually impure. Despite the scarcity of Indian women, sexual relations between Indian men and African or Creole women were extremely rare. Twenty-six years after Indian indenture had begun, the Protector of Immigrants could note that there "was not a single instance of an indentured immigrant who cohabits with one of the negro race."

The last thirty years of the 19th century marked a turning point in Indian integration into the wider island community. The sugar market grew depressed, more and more Indians were still being introduced and improved technology in the sugar industry lessened the availability of jobs in the factories. Indians sought jobs which were formerly held by Africans. In addition, Crown lands were being sold to them in lieu of repatriation to India.

They began to recreate on these settlements the Indian villages which they were unable to do under conditions in the estates.

This movement out of the estates into little villages, and the knowledge that they would no longer be returning to Mother India must have clearly had an impact on the way in which Indians began to relate to the wider non-Indian community. Certainly, the movement out of cloistered estates and housing settlements and intermixing as a result of job diversification led to greater contact between the Indians and non-Indians. While our sociologists may have been less observant on the subject of acculturation, some calypsonians, as early as 1939, had begun to notice and comment on the changes which were taking place in attitudes to Indian women.

In 1939 the calypsonian Lord Invader sang:

> I want everybody to realize
> I want a nice Indian girl that is creolise
> I don't want no parata or dhal water
> I want my potato and cassava

In a calypso entitled *Marajh Daughter,* Rohlehr (1988) comments, and accurately so, that this calypso does not provide a true portrait of the Indian woman, revealing instead the rejection of Indian women's culture. We can also deduce though, that there must have been a growing tendency on the part of Indian women to become "creolised" for this calypsonian to begin to comment, in less than complimentary fashion, on the phenomenon. By the 1940s however, we see more conclusive evidence of cultural change among Indian women. Killer, leader of the Young Brigade Calypso Tent, commented:

> ... But I notice there is no Indian again
> Since the women and them taking Creole name
>
> Long ago was Sumintra, Ramnawalia...
> But now is Emily, Jean and Dinah...
>
> Long ago you hadn't a chance
> To meet an Indian girl in a dance

> But nowadays it is big confusion
> Big fighting in the road for their Yankee man
> And see them in the market they ain't making joke
> Pushing down nigger people to buy dey poke
> And see them in the dances in Port of Spain
> They wouldn't watch if you call an Indian name

Reference to the Yankee men in this calypso is very significant. The expansion of employment opportunities on the American bases erected from 1942 provided an option for some Indian women to find jobs and also mix with men who were thought, perhaps especially by their parents, to be more acceptable than men of African descent. But movement out of the rural villages and socializing with non-Indian men created gaps between the expectations of the older generation of Indians and their daughters.

From 1957-1958 Morton Klass (1961) carried out anthropological fieldwork in Amity, the fictional name for an existing Indian village in Trinidad. If we view this village as generally but not entirely representative of Indian attitudes and lifestyles in other parts of Trinidad, especially rural Trinidad where Indians were largely concentrated, a brief look at some aspects of its social organization is very revealing of the prevailing condition and status of Indian women in the society at the time. Klass subtitled his research, "A study of cultural persistence," and this is precisely what he found. Kinship relations were still binding; in fact Klass (1961) was struck by what he termed the "East Indian capacity for indefinite extension of kinship" and by the important observance of the rules and regulations which governed kin relations.

Rather than early marriages before puberty arranged between parents with no consent sought from the boy or the girl, a major concession had been made. Boys and girls were now introduced to each other before the marriage and had a right to veto the proposed match. While a boy was considered of marriageable age from the time he was sixteen until around thirty, and even over thirty he was still very eligible, the Indian girl was still considered marriageable between the ages of fifteen and seventeen. An unmarried girl over age eighteen became a serious problem for the father if not a disgrace to the entire family. No one wished to have an unmarried daughter in the house. Apart from being an economic liability, it was feared that she would lose her virginity or become pregnant before she could be married, or worse yet, consort with the dreaded polluted race of African men bringing utter shame and disgrace on the family. The notion of an untrammelled female sexuality was used as another rationale for the close vigilance of Indian girls and women by Indian men. On this Klass (1961) noted "It is a generally held assumption in the village that no female has any capacity to resist sexual advances. Only the continually watchful eyes of her family can protect her." This clearly had the effect of restricting the freedom which Indian women could otherwise have had. But it also had the contradictory effect of perpetuating a vibrant women's culture based on the separate spaces in which they could vent their creative and sexual expression – a factor which, perhaps, despite their outward subservient and passive role, undoubtedly made for greater female self-confidence. The ritual of "*lawa*" in the *maticore* ceremony before the Hindu marriage is illustrative of this point. In this ceremony there is a frank and ribald sharing and enjoyment between older women with the younger ones, of the joys or otherwise of the sexual experience. In addition, the bride (and separately the groom) are anointed with a mixture of yogurt and turmeric to prepare their bodies for the first nights of their sexual union. I speculate that on the basis of a more reserved yet inherent confidence in their sensuality, Indian women were geared for better adjustment to the mixed and multi racial society when they attained greater freedoms in the society of Trinidad in the decades which followed.

Restrictions had been imposed before marriage to ensure their purity while they were schooled in the art of pleasing their menfolk. This schooling clearly did not entail an education out of the home and only a small proportion of Indian women by this time had had access to any formal schooling, mainly those who had been converted to Christianity. For many young Indian brides in both the Hindu and Muslim households, marriage represented simply a changing of the guards. The bride was now under the protection of a new extended household in which other oppressive conditions were the norm. While the "*doolaha*" or bridegroom could expect to be served by his new "*doolahin*" in addition to his mother, the new *doolahin* was expected to shoulder the full burden of the household chores, greater acceptance into the new family only coming with the birth of her first child. She was also expected to display ample evidence of her fertility by producing many sons, another activity which ensured her total domestication and restricted her involvement in any activity in the wider society. It was not uncommon for instance to find Indian women in the rural areas at age 21 already having five or six children. Harewood (1975) had found that the level of fertility of women of Indian descent in Trinidad and Tobago was for a long time appreciably higher than that of non-Indian women as a group, and more specifically than that of women of African descent, so much so that in the analysis of fertility in this society demographers often separated the rest of the female population from women of Indian descent. Between 1946 and 1960, the completed fertility of Indian women was still in the vicinity of 40% to 50% higher than that of women of African descent.

While this unfolding picture for Indian women can be generalized across Indian women of different religions, there were subtle differences between Hindu, Muslim and women converted to Christianity. For instance, in Amity, Morton Klass (1961) noted that the Muslim young people, being in the minority, exhibited some indication of a sense of alienation from the community. Two young Muslim girls who had become converted to Presbyterianism professed a certain distance from the community in terms of its "backwardness" and the "ignorance of its inhabitants."[2] And in Amity, between those who had been converted to Christianity and those who had not, there was a feeling of mutual contempt. Clearly, the process of creolization whether acknowledged or not, had been internalized within and the Indian population had begun to embrace the values of cultured versus uncultured inherent in creole society.

Although there began to be qualitative changes in the relationship of Indians to the wider community, on the political front, if conditions under the period of indentureship ensured separatism between the dominant cultures along with a certain degree of hostility, other features which emerged in the society up to the period of independence also kept much of this distance alive. This data is highly schematized and so omits much of the detail of the underlying political struggle between the two dominant cultures.

But it is interesting to note that the period of decolonization in Trinidad and Tobago did not also coincide with a growing nationalist consciousness among the majority of peoples of Indian descent. Selwyn Ryan (1974) notes for instance that between 1919 and 1939, the bulk of the Indian population did not identify with the nationalist movement, while Marianne Ramesar (1976) makes the point that the development of a group consciousness among Indians during the period 1921 to 1946 in fact contributed to friction with other groups developing similar nationalism. In addition, the movement to self-government and the coming to power of the Peoples National Movement was characterized by differences and rifts among the Indian community itself, and certainly not wholehearted support for a party which they felt would take advantage of them when in power. Apart from a few urbanized Muslims and Christian Indians, the Hindu population were largely anti-PNM.

Evidence of Indian integration, though limited, could be seen in the greater occupational diversification among the Indian population. Although the Tyson report shows that in 1931 only a small percentage of Indians comprised the non-agricultural work force in Trinidad, we see evidence of both male and female inroads into various professions. There is no question that there is a clear predominance of Indian men over Indian women in the gainfully occupied work-force – for instance, of the 637 men and women recorded under the category, professions, only 72 were women and these were all teachers. Women comprised 29.2% of the total work force of Indians and, of this, 25% were in the lowest paid, lowest status jobs - that of agricultural labourers or domestic servants.[3]

Despite their increasing integration of one sort or another in the wider community, actual racial intermixing was very limited. A crude indicator of the degree of intermixing with non-Indians is seen in the following figures. In 1911 there were 1.47 mixed Indians for every 100 unmixed Indians. In 1921, this figure had increased to 1.87 per 100 unmixed Indians and, by 1946, to 4.29. On the other hand, intermixing in the urban areas was greater for the 1946 census calculated at a rate of 21.37 Indian creoles per 100 unmixed Indians in the main city of Port of Spain. Thus another factor which contributed to the gap between the two major cultures was the geographical separation from each other, with Indians viewed as a rural population and Africans and others as urbanized.

When greater integration into the community developed for Indian men and especially for Indian women, it came through educational and employment opportunities away from the home or family farm. Education at first was mainly for boys. It was thought unwise to educate your girls. In Seepersad Naipaul's (1976) *Adventures of Gurudeva* (written in the 1940s) we see some of the reasons why this is so. Gurudeva is impatient with his new child bride Ratni's proclivity to answer back and seeks advice from his father Jaimungal.

> Gurudeva: I have not patience with her. She is rude and crude and gives me back-answers.
> Jaimungal: I know that. But she is only a woman and will ever be foolish, no matter what you do: but you must keep your temper, for you can read and write, and know good from bad... But she – well to her letters are like dirt.

Indian women had not been given early opportunity to access the rudimentary education system available then. In 1899, after 30 years of Canadian missionary schooling, girls comprised only 28% of total enrolment in primary schools and were mainly kept at home to do domestic chores. Even where and when they were educated by the Canadian missionaries, this was initially meant to prepare them to make good wives for the converted Indian men who had become teachers in the Presbyterian schools. Illiteracy rates were relatively high compared to the rest of the population. A look at the proportions of females of various ethnic groups in Trinidad and Tobago who were illiterate according to the 1946 census gives a very good idea of the extent of the problem. 65.7% of Indian females ten years and older were illiterate, compared with 10.1% for women of African descent, 3.4% for women of European descent and 8.3% for women of Chinese descent. By the 1950s there was an organized attempt to catch up with the rest of the population and by this time too it had become more acceptable to educate daughters as well as sons. The *Indian Centenary Review* of 1945 for instance includes entries of 16 women in professions or business and, of those, one Gladys Ramsaran was a barrister. It is again significant that these women were all Christians and most came from families which had attained professional status a generation before. The Muslim and Hindu communities opened their own schools or expanded existing facilities to include secondary education. With the easier acceptance of education offered by the Presbyterians, very soon the effects would be seen on the educational attainment level of the female Indian population.

Given their delayed access to formal education it is interesting to note the diametric effects of these opportunities among Indian girls five years before independence. In 1957, Vera Rubin and Marisa Zavalloni (1969) carried out a survey among a relatively large sample of secondary school students on their aspirations in the developing society of Trinidad and Tobago. In correlating university orientation with expectations of becoming full time housewives, they found that only 17% of the Indian girls compared with 50% of the White girls intended to make home a post career focal point. The researchers concluded from other indicators as well that whereas higher education had become a normative expectation for middle and upper class girls as preparation for marriage, for Indian girls securing an education entailed greater sacrifice and more of a break with their culture and consequently was seen as a channel to a career and personal independence rather than as preparation for a housewife's role.

It is again ironic or, on the other hand, perhaps perfectly understandable and inevitable that in a culture which had suppressed women for too long, Indian women would readily embrace opportunities to engage with the rest of the society. Consider for example the aspirations of one Indian girl in Rubin and Zavalloni's (1969) study:

> I will go in for the Legislative Council Elections. If I am successful I can then help the people of my country most of all whether I am the Minister of Health or not, though I would be extremely happy if I am the Minister of Health or Education.

To my knowledge there were no Indian women involved in politics at the time of this study. Even within this striving for individual expression and ambition, one sees evidence of those qualities which were traditionally expected of Indian women in the society in the aspirations of another young Indian girl:

> I want to be a doctor, yet everything is against me... I get no real encouragement. They think it is foolish that a girl should sacrifice so many years to study and then at the end of it she'll get married. And even if I decide to go ahead with this idea there is the very real difficulty of finding fees. My father has four children to provide for, two of them are boys who really need a good start in life.

This epitomizes the role which Indian women were expected to perform in the Indian community. They were keepers of the culture, they were assumed to be passive and submissive, they were expected to sacrifice their own ambitions for the benefit of their brothers and husbands. Despite all of this, we can see that some Indian women had begun to commit themselves to goals which identified with the national interest. These aspirations are clear indications though that at least some Indian women had begun to become integrated into the creole society and to fracture the boundaries of their restricted domain.

THE POST-INDEPENDENCE YEARS

Independence itself meant very little to many Indians. An interview with Savitri Pargass, who had had the experience of a rural Indian girl who had come from a small village and had won a scholarship to a prestige grammar school in Port-of-Spain was insightful. Ms Pargass said quite frankly, that for most of the Indians she knew at this time, independence appeared to be another victory for the Blacks and not for Indians themselves.[4]

Despite indifference from some Indians, guarded participation from others and outright support from few, certain values had become common to the various ethnic groups in the larger society, to peoples of both African and Indian descent. One of these was the importance of education as a means for attaining social mobility. Developments in various areas of the economy and society were to benefit all groups even if it did benefit some more than others. Developments in the education system and economic expansion in the post independence period in fact accelerated the integration of Indian women into creole society.

The rapid expansion in the provision of free secondary education for both rural and urban Trinidad and Tobago was clearly important for Indians, a large percentage of whom still lived in rural Trinidad as noted before. Of the total Hindu population in 1960, 68.3% lived in a rural district. The introduction of the Common Entrance Examination which offered equal chances to boys as well as girls created major differences in the attitudes to the education of girls and attitudes to their later employment out of the home. The establishment of the Junior Secondary and Senior Comprehensive school system later on also contributed to changing attitudes and practices between young people of different ethnic groups, perhaps through contact with each other at earlier ages. And free university education, somewhat still limited in its early offering, also became available to the local population.

The second factor which was of major importance was the opening up and expansion of the cash economy in the sixties and seventies. New developments in the economy especially from the seventies made jobs available in the various sectors – commercial, petroleum and other industrial and public sectors and allowed for greater geographical shifting and displacement in the rural based Indian female population. Indian women began to enter the Public Service and mix with the African men and women who had predominated in this sector. Many Indian women joined the teaching profession – a profession in which they were encouraged as it was an extension of their nurturing role. Other Indian women who had had access to a university education began to move into other professions - the legal profession proving to be one of the most attractive. The main outcomes of all of this were the changes which began to occur in the traditional Indian family setting. In the shift to a greater consumer economy, the women's wage or salary earning contribution was now being viewed as important.

Changes which occurred in the Indian family in the post independence period appear to be more sudden than they in fact were as these had been slowly evolving over the last few decades. The extended family network had become eroded over time and replaced more and more by the nuclear family. Researchers and other insightful observers now freely commented on the somewhat oppressive nature of the extended Indian family despite the glorified notions of support and security which it purported to offer. Pariag's extended family network dominated by a rich uncle in Earl Lovelace's *The Dragon can't Dance* (1972) illustrates the relations of economic dependence which ensured kin allegiances. Some research has revealed a shift to more nuclear-type families among Indians in urban settings – for instance in San Fernando in 1980, 88% of Indian families were nuclear; in Arouca and El Dorado 48% and 44% of the families were extended and these were based primarily on economic cooperation.

A study on social and cultural change in the Indian community of El Dorado from 1960 1980 is also useful. Sharmatee Sieunarine (n.d.) finds this Indian community not at all homogeneous either by religion or by generational attitudes and practices. With regard to the question of marriage, most of the older women she interviewed aged between 50 and 60 indicated that they were married by age 12. One woman recounted that she had never seen her husband before the wedding and she only knew she was going to be married on the Sunday when on Thursday her mother took her to town to buy some new clothes. The situation had by the 1980s changed drastically. There was a significant decrease in arranged marriages, and the unmarried girls above 20 felt and said there was no disgrace attached to being unmarried at that age.

Some of the changes that occurred showed a startling shift for only a few decades. For instance, Jack Harewood (1975) had noted a remarkable reduction in the Crude Birth Rate among Indians, from 45.9% to 29.1% from 1960 to 1970. This appreciable decline among the Indian population was due in part to the greater availability and accepted use of contraceptive practices, lower fertility among more educated women and later childbearing among women who also deferred their age of marriage. It might be pointed out here that despite many changes in mating and fertility practices of Indian women, there is still little cultural acceptance for unmarried pregnancies especially for women resident in their parents' homes.

At some point we need, however, to differentiate between creolization and modernization. In the post independence era the two are necessarily linked. Creolization has been interpreted to mean a political and social commitment to the new society, as well as physical engagement with the society so that the existent cultures are mixed and enriched in the process; modernization is taken to mean the intrusion of the external and metropolitan. V. S. Naipaul (1962) in *The Middle Passage* is incisive on this; modernity in Trinidad means more than the trappings-air conditioned bars and supermarkets, night clubs and restaurants, "It means a constant willingness to change, a readiness to accept anything which films, magazines and comic strips appear to indicate as American."

Modernization and petroleum revenues had been the major democratizing agents in the society in the last twenty years or so. The creolization process thus became interlocked with modernization as new values were formed and shared between and among the various groups. To speak of the "creolized" Indian woman in 1987 was to employ both concepts of creolization and modernization at the same time. If we compare some of the obvious changes in the pre-independence and post-independence periods the picture is a more accurate reflection of the time. For instance, the staple diet of Indian women or the meals they prepared in Indian households could no longer be said to be comprised of a traditional cuisine but included many other "creole" dishes as well as the more modern fast food of the American variety.

It became very uncommon to see even older Indian women wearing their *ohrnis*, the traditional muslin cover which it was incumbent on them to wear as a form of respect in the presence of menfolk or the public. In fact, like the *sari*, the *ohrni* and forms of Indian dress have become traditional wear for religious or ceremonial functions. Among younger Indian girls I detected little difference in their trendy style of dress with women of other ethnic groups. Similar findings, but always with exceptions for age, class and location, can be stated for linguistic patterns, musical preferences and leisure time activities. To gauge the extent to which there have been changes among Indian women, I thought a useful exercise would be to assess my theory against the views of some younger women of Indian descent who were born in and are products of the post-independence era. I asked fourth and fifth form girls from two secondary schools, one school predominantly Indian and the other mixed, to write short essays on growing up in the multi-racial society of Trinidad and Tobago. The responses were encouraging yet troubling. The early paradox which Indian women faced had now been replaced by others and in the more complicated society today by a series of growing contradictions. One Indian girl of fourteen admits:

> As an Indian girl I feel fairly well adjusted lo being in a multi-racial society. I don't consider myself as being superior to anyone else. Although at times I tend to feel a bit inferior when I hear people say 'look a coolie,' but I don't let this keep me down. Being an Indian has given me a fairly good opportunity to break the tradition that my grandmother and mother followed. I mean I don't have to quit school at an early age for the purpose of learning to handle a household so that I can get matched for marriage. But quite differently, I can pursue a career ahead of me. I think having a career is important because then I would be less dependent on a man.[5]

This independence of thought and action is a source of conflict between many younger and older women as this youngster's predicament tells us:

> Anytime I get into a quarrel with my mother, she gets into a rage and says its time for me to get married... anytime I want to go somewhere, for example to the cinema or a bazaar, my mother has to bring up some "nancy" story and say that when she was my age, she never wanted to go anywhere or she never quarrelled with her parents. I know I can't cook, but I try and then at that moment my mother begins her "nancy" stories again, and says that when she was my age she already knew how lo cook, wash and take care of a house. She totally hates to see me talking to a boy in person or talking to him on the phone... then and there she starts to talk about marriage again. While I am on the topic of marriage, she says she doesn't

mind who I marry as long as he's rich, has a good job, does not smoke or drink and is not a Muslim.

Young Indian girls today are also keenly aware of the conflicts in male/female relationships which have arisen from greater female autonomy, but it seems that they are also ready to deal with these situations. Another young girl thought:

> A lot of Indian women today are working women. The Indian men, however, do not like the idea of this because they like to be the superior one. I think that people expect too much from an Indian woman and that they have a lot of changes to make in their lives. Indian women have to have the right to their say!

CONCLUSIONS

It has obviously not been possible to deal with every factor or every qualification in presenting these arguments for the creolization of Indian women in Trinidad and Tobago. In fact, I know I have run the risks of over-generalizations and over-simplifications. I summarize my conclusions to incorporate some observations about the present trend and its implications for the future.

My first conclusion is that there has been a tremendous shift in the status of Indian women in this society from their early introduction to the present time. The stereotype of Indian woman as primarily keeper of the culture, sacrificial and passive, can no longer apply to all Indian women; Indian women have become more integrated into the society, a process accelerated in the post independence era by the increased opportunities available to them in education and employment out of the home. Indian women who embraced Christianity fairly early were among the first to become creolized, but there is a distinct and growing trend for women of the Hindu and Muslim faiths to assert their presence in the society.

The second conclusion I would draw attention to is that contemporary creolization has been a selective one. While it has involved a necessary degree of interculturation there is also a qualitative change. Indian women's affirmation of their national identity does not automatically mean a negation of ethnic or religious identity. On the one hand there is a greater political "national" consciousness among both Indian men and women especially evident perhaps in recent political events over the last decade of the twentieth century, although clearly, women are grossly under represented in national politics. An Indo-Trinidadian Prime Minister governed the society for the first time in its history, obviously allowing for greater self confidence among an ethnic group who were considered interlopers at the beginning of and well into this century. But a growing confidence in national assertiveness has also reinforced a confidence in ethnic and religious identity. This might explain for instance the recent attention being paid by the more fundamentalist Hindu groups to the roles expected of Hindu women and in this society. Even for those who do not subscribe to the Hindu faith, or blindly follow the path of ethnic politics, Indian women and men are very reluctant to relinquish the source of their cultural strength, and rightfully so, for it is not clear that the answer to the ethnic problems of plural societies is that of cultural homogenization.

Finally, what has this meant for Indian women themselves? A process of change which was in my view inevitable has created a number of severe contradictions for Indian women today in their relationships with the rest of the society.

Accustomed to the stereotype of the passive and submissive female role Indian men have reacted to the growing confidence of Indian women in a confused and sometimes violent fashion. This violence is not always manifested physically but can take the form of vicious, degrading or obscene insults slung at Indian women who choose to be friendly with men outside of their ethnic group. Without fail, all of my interviewees repeated the theme "Indian men are traumatized by the new and assertive Indian woman they are now seeing." Several felt that the phenomenon of a relatively large proportion of professional Indian women who were unmarried today was a result of their increasing outspokenness and assertiveness. The reasons for this reaction on the part of Indian males certainly need to be researched to complete this picture.

Several respondents also hinted at the uneasy relationship which existed between Indian women and women of other ethnic groups in the society. They suggested that this was due to their growing assertiveness in the professions, in an area in which they were historically lagging compared to non-Indian men and women. I cannot claim to substantiate any of these statements as they can only be subjective and impressionistic at the moment. They reveal nonetheless the new contradictions and paradoxes faced by Indian women who have become "creolized."

One can only be optimistic about change which creates possibilities for developing the potential of a group or a sex. I think that the qualities traditionally ascribed to Indian women have been turned in the direction of becoming virtues. Indian women have not become embittered by their history. Thus subservience has become discipline, submissiveness turned into passion, and sacrifice into diligence. Wedded with intelligence, these have only served to propel those Indian women who are prepared to challenge the imposed limits fast forward into a rewarding future.

ENDNOTES

[1] The use of the term creolization does not fully appreciate the concept as it employed by Edouard Glissant, the idea of a culture born through "free assented sharing" rather than co-erced into accepting dominant ideas and values. Caribbean culture emerges as the opposition between Europe and Africa. That "Indian" culture has remained outside of this Caribbean composition of culture has resulted from another set of ideas which had not entered popular or academic thinking at the first writing of this paper. Indian-ness provides an intermediary component in this binary opposition, but one which to date is insufficiently recognized in the region.

[2] In *Callaloo Nation: Metaphors of Race and Religious Identity among South Asians in Trinidad*, (Duke University Press, 2004) while author Aisha Khan reinforces that religion has functioned as an crucial point of reference for the boundary inscription Indo-Trinidadianess, her study demonstrates the internal differences between these two communities with far greater detail and is recommended as a substantively important body of work for understanding the dynamics of religious and racial identities of Indians in the Caribbean.

[3] Memorandum of the evidence for the Royal Commission to the West Indies presented by J. D. Tyson, Esq. C.B.E on behalf of the Government of India, HMSO, 1938-39.

[4] From an interview carried out with Savitri Pargass in 1987. She went to McGill for her scholarship and returned to Trinidad serving as a teacher, university lecturer and Vice President of the Trinidad and Tobago Teachers Union for

several years. I did not disclose her identity at the time of writing the paper. Ms Pargass is now deceased and I have the permission of her family to do so.

[5] This and subsequent quotes were taken from essays written by fifth form students of the San Juan Senior Comprehensive School. I wish to thank Vasanti Boochoon, a teacher of this school, who carried out this exercise for me in 1987 to assist me with writing this paper.

REFERENCES

Braithwaite, Edward. 1985. Contradictory Omens. *Savacou Publications*. Monograph 4. Mona, Jamaica.

Brereton, Bridget. 1979. *Race Relations in Colonial Trinidad, 1870-1900* Cambridge: Cambridge University Press.

Census of the Population of Trinidad and Tobago, Port of Spain. (1946).

Census of the Population of Trinidad and Tobago. (1982), Central Statistical Office, Port of Spain.

Harewood, Jack. 1975. *The Population of Trinidad and Tobago*. CICRED Series. St. Augustine, Trinidad and Tobago: Institute of Social and Economic Research.

Johnson, Kim N. 1984. "Considerations on Indian Sexuality" Paper presented to the Third Conference on East Indians, August 29-September 4, 1984, University of the West Indies, St. Augustine, Trinidad.

Klass, Morton. 1961. *East Indians in Trinidad. A Study of Cultural Persistence*. New York; Columbia University Press.

Ladoo, Harold S. 1972. *No Pain Like this Body*. UK: Heinemann.

Lovelace, Earl. 1972. *The Dragon Can't Dance* UK: Heinemann.

Maharaj, A. M. (n.d.). "The Changing Pattern of the East Indian Family in Trinidad." Caribbean Studies Thesis, UWI, St. Augustine.

Mohammed, Patricia. 1987. Women and Education in Trinidad and Tobago, 1938-1980. MSc diss., Department of Sociology, University of the West Indies, St. Augustine.

Naipaul, Seepersad. 1976. *The Adventures of Gurudeva and Other Stories* N.p.: Andre Deutsch, 33.

Naipaul, V.S. 1962. *The Middle Passage*. England: Penguin Books, 48.

Poynting, Jeremy. 1987. "East Indian Women in the Caribbean: Experience and Voices." In (eds.) *India in the Caribbean*, edited by David Dabydeen and Brinsley Samaroo, 231-263. London: Hansib Publishing Ltd.

Quevedo, Raymond. 1983. *Atilla's Kaiso*. Trinidad and Tobago: Extra Mural Dept., University of the West Indies, p.88.

Ramesar, Marianne. 1976. The Integration of Indian Settlers in Trinidad after the Indenture Period, *Caribbean Issues* 11 (3): 52 -70.

Reddock, Rhoda. 1984. "Women, Labour and Struggle in 20th Century Trinidad and Tobago 1898-1960." PhD diss,. Institute of Social Studies, The Hague.

Rohlehr, Gordon. 1988. "Images of Men and Women in the Calypsos of the 1930s on the Sociology of Food Acquisition in the Context of Survivalism." In *Gender in Caribbean Development*, edited by Patricia Mohammed and Catherine Shepherd, 232-306. Trinidad and Tobago: Women and Development Studies.

Rubin, Vera and Marisa Zavalloni. 1969. *We Wish to be Looked upon*, New York: Teacher's College Press, 89-91.

Ryan, Selwyn. 1974. *Race and Nationalism in Trinidad and Tobago*. Jamaica: Institute of Social and Economic Research, University of the West Indies.

Sieunarine, Sharmatee. (n.d.) "The Social and Cultural Change in the East Indian Community of El Dorado in 1960-1980." Caribbean Studies Thesis, UWI, St. Augustine.

7

Structures of Experience: Gender, Ethnicity and Class in the Lives of Two East Indian Women[†]

INTRODUCTION

There comes a time in the work of a sociologist when one loses sight of the fact that sociology is about people; that all of the classes, genders and ethnic groups are comprised of real people who are engaging with the world and its problems and living their ordinary lives. And while all of these structures and concepts – class, gender, ethnicity – may influence a person in this or that direction to make this or that decision, the simple fact is that people live their lives by gaining experience and, hopefully, learning from that experience. Our intellectual vocabulary may mean little to them in their daily existence. In this essay I use the experiences narrated by two women to appreciate how they have lived their own understandings or come to terms with these concepts of ethnicity and class and

---

[†] Originally published in *Trinidad Ethnicity*, edited by Kevin Yelvington, 208 - 234. Coventry: Macmillan: Warwick University Caribbean Series. (1992).

gender, in the latter especially how they understood their gender roles and Indian patriarchal practices which underpinned the culture. In approaching the subject in this way, I draw on John Dewey's philosophy that as human beings we make sense of everyday life and re-organize our knowledge on the basis of this experience[1] alongside the insights from second wave feminist philosophy: that the subjective experience of individual woman and the collective experiences of all women[2] - standpoint theory and "the personal is political" are central to our unwrapping of femininity and the female experience.

Debates on ethnicity and class had long preoccupied scholars of the region. Gender was acknowledged as an important concept which can help us to analyze and understand our societies. Feminism had added gender as another sociological concept, another prism through which we can view the historical process of growth and change. The challenge which gender analysis puts to mainstream academia is to examine how "gender" works in human social relationships. Analyses of class and ethnicity have attempted a similar exercise, usually focusing on the aggregate societal level. Class, gender and ethnicity are themselves intricately related. Seen through the lens of gender analysis, concepts like ethnicity and class also undergo change in perception and analysis. Gender is not just another "additive" concept: "Like race, it is a conceptual understanding of a social reality which transforms our very perception of class" (Reddock, 1988: 3).

Statements such as these are no doubt revealing about the conceptual relationship that exists between the constructs of ethnicity, class and gender. One is still left, however, wondering how the dynamics of ethnicity, class and gender operate in the real life experiences of men and women. A point made by Sheila Rowbotham comes to mind: "It is worth remembering every time we use words like "class" and "gender" that they are only being labelled as structures for our convenience, because human relations move with such complexity and speed that our descriptions freeze at the point of understanding" (Rowbotham, 1981:365). As sociologists, when we use these external constructs to analyze human lives, we sometimes ignore the existential dilemma which all human beings face: while they may be born into a certain set of social arrangements not of their choice, their lives can be viewed in terms of how they use these arrangements to get the best out of them; to fight against them or be defeated by them; how they may use parts and reject others. For instance, within the constraints of ascribed norms which they must observe, some men and women choose, or circumstances may force them, to redefine the accepted notions of their gender, class or ethnicity, but, presumably at all times, attempting to satisfy their basic physical and psychological needs.

"Experience" is itself an ambiguous term. On the one hand it denotes "passing through any event or course of events by which one is affected" and on the other, common sense usage suggests also learning from such events or course of events and subsequently altering or modifying behaviour. Writing on *The Poverty of Theory*, E.P. Thompson makes an important observation. "Experience", he says, "is a necessary middle term between social being and social consciousness". But at the same time "for any living generation, in any "now," the ways in which they "handle" experience defies prediction and escapes from any narrow definition of determination" (Thompson, 1978:363). People experience "experience" both as a feeling and also as ideas in a collective consciousness, be it of class, ethnicity or gender. Class consciousness may be described as the way in which experience is handled in cultural terms, through traditions, values, ideas and institutional practices. There are two additional factors, however, which are equally important in understanding "experience". First is the notion of history – the moment in which an incident occurs. What are the economic, political and social considerations which will predispose consciousness and action? The second is the age of the individual when it occurs. At what point are they in their life cycle, what previous experiences do they draw on, and what are their options as a result of both age and experience? Ethnicity and gender are determined by birth, class by circumstances at birth, and how these are shaped in subsequent years is perhaps a complex mix of experience and collective consciousness, the latter being itself modified by experience and so on.

In trying to understand the gender, ethnicity and class dialectic from this perspective the questions we might begin to ask of a woman for instance are: How does the fact of being born female to a poor working class African or East Indian family influence a woman's life? How does this affect the decisions she makes about marriage and family? What factors influence the jobs she takes? What are her relations to other ethnic groups in the society at different points in her life? The subjects of this chapter are East Indian women simply because, as a starting point, I can draw on my own experience of being East Indian and female. I propose to look at the life experiences of two Indian women of Trinidad as gleaned from taped interviews carried out with each of them separately.[3] The choice of subjects is deliberate. The first interview was carried out with Mrs. Droapatie Naipaul, mother of the authors V.S. and Shiva Naipaul, primarily because of my interest in the works of V. S. Naipaul and also because she is by birth a member of one of the oldest and most prestigious high caste Indian families in Trinidad. My second interview was with Mrs. Dassie Parsan,[4] whose life history, class and caste position contrasted sufficiently with Mrs. Naipaul's, thus allowing further insights. The two women are deceased. Mrs Parsan died in May 1990 and Mrs Naipaul in December 1990. This chapter is written in the present tense in order to emphasize the relevance of their lives in contemporary times, and the continuing salience of gender, ethnicity and class in Trinidad society.

Mrs. Droapatie Naipaul
Mrs. Droapatie Naipaul lives in the small two-storied house in St James, a suburb of Port of Spain. Her house is painted white inside and out. The drawing room is spotless and all around the room clean white lace curtains hang from the top of the windows to the floor. An oil painting of her late husband Seepersad Naipaul dominates the room; on her dining table a covered Bhagavad Gita rests on a carved sandalwood book stand; intricately filigreed and polished miniature brass Indian vessels and ornaments rub shoulders with red cushioned Morris chairs and a vase of red plastic poinsettias; they give the room its peculiarly Trinidadian aesthetic of a blended culture. At first glance, Mrs. Naipaul epitomizes the Trinidadian idea of the traditional old East Indian woman. She is dressed simply in a white cotton dress, with three little bows down the bosom, the hemline of the skirt reaching near to her ankles; her almost white hair is pulled into a small bun at the back of her head. Her manner, however, belies this traditional appearance of simplicity and passivity; at age 75 she lives alone

and carries out her daily chores briskly and independently. Her answers are always alert, sometimes aggressively so. She is a confidant and self-assured woman.

In 1926, when Droapatie was 13 years old, her father Pundit Capildeo made his second visit to India. He died during this visit leaving Droapatie fatherless and Mrs. Capildeo with the responsibility of looking after the rest of her family. She was lucky though. Pundit Capildeo, besides being a well-respected Hindu priest, was also a businessman and the family possessed some land and a commercial enterprise in Chaguanas, the small town located in central Trinidad where they lived. There was no need for any of the family to work in agriculture, the typical occupation of most Indian men and women at the time.

Pundit Capildeo was one of the more than 144,000 Indians who were brought to Trinidad from India between 1845 and 1917 under the system of indentured labour. He had come, like the others, for five years, bound to the sugar cane estates during this time. Like many, he did not return to live in India, choosing to remain instead and marry a young Trinidad-born East Indian girl. He had been an educated man in India and of Brahmin stock – belonging to the most revered caste, class and occupation in India. The Brahmins were the priestly caste and their lives were regulated by a collection of rules and restrictions. They were either the priests or intelligentsia in the Hindu community, their food had to be prepared by Hindus of a particular caste. As with all Hindus they were obligated to marry into their caste.

Droapatie's childhood days, spent with nine sisters and three brothers, were bounded by expectations of her caste and gender. She recalled:

> We were under strict Hindu parentage and we were not allowed to go anywhere. Anywhere you want to go, you have to go with an elder person or sister or if your mother is taking you and you only go to family if you are going. Even when you go to school she is counting the minutes when school is over and you should be home, and you better be home on time. Sometimes you find yourself running home.

Until she was 12 years old Droapatie could mix with the other children at school. She was sent to the Canadian Mission school in Chaguanas which was established since the late-nineteenth century by the Presbyterian missionaries and catered primarily for the Indian population. Without this provision the majority of Indian parents would have been reluctant to send their children to the government or Catholic schools for fear of them mixing with non-Indians. The other children in the school were all Indians – either Muslims or Hindus - and they would mix indiscriminately. But this was always restricted to school time alone: when school "broke off" they all went their separate ways.

It was unusual during those years for East Indian parents to agree to educate their daughters, even at primary level. Perhaps it was because Mrs Capildeo was Trinidad- and not India-born that she insisted that her girl children as well as her boy children be given at least the benefit of a primary school education.

PM: Why did they allow you to go to school?
DN: My mother tell my father we must go to school. He said no school, but she wanted all of us to go to school. She went to school as well, though. All of my sisters and brothers went to school. You see we had the store and my mother wanted us all to work in the family business 'till we get married. You had to learn to sign your name at least and count. But you had to stop school at age 11 or 12 years. Then the girls have to get married and the boys went to college.
PM: Why did your mother decide to send only the boys to college?
DN: Don't ask me that question. Don't ask me that question again. She decided to educate them and I think she was very correct in educating them.

She agreed with the correctness of this view just as she accepted that the next stage in her life would be a marriage arranged by her elders.

PM: What did you feel about entering an arranged marriage?
DN: It's a routine you have to follow. You don't see nobody before you get married. And after you leave school everybody know that in a year or so you have to be married – it was just that routine.

PM: Why did you feel that in a year's time you had to get married?
DN: Don't ask me that question again.

I realized by now that it was not that she was offended by my questions as much as astounded by the idea that one could challenge these traditions. She added:

> I didn't have to feel anything. As I said you have to do what you are told. That was their opinion, this is what we have to do and we were children in the age when you could not ask questions, but just obey and listen. You felt that was the routine of life, because all the sisters elder than me were married at the same age or younger even.

By 1928, at age 15, Droapatie's marriage to Seepersad Naipaul was arranged. Seepersad also came from central Trinidad from a poor Brahmin family. He was a sign painter by occupation but being a Brahmin by birth he was qualified to be the spouse of a young Brahmin girl even though she came from a prestigious and wealthy family. Pundit Capildeo had always provided well for his family. In fact they were one of the more privileged and respected Indian families in Trinidad at this time. The large and imposing house in which they lived in Chaguanas was known far and wide as the "Lion House", nicknamed after the stone statues of lions which guard the two sharp front corners of the building. One of her brothers, Rudranath, was duly sent to college as was the custom for boys, and having won an open island scholarship, on to university in London, becoming an internationally known mathematician. He was also to become the leader of the Democratic Labour Party in Trinidad, a primarily East Indian party which opposed the People's National Movement (PNM) for many years.

Droapatie recognized that the circumstances of her life were different to that of many other East Indian women around her.

> We never really had to work in the fields, we had a lot of lands. My father find he could maintain us because we had no right to work in the fields. Anybody who had enough to maintain their wife and children didn't let them go to work.

Seepersad had married a young girl who had clear notions of her role as a wife, and the importance of her high class and caste status in Indian society in Trinidad. Unlike her sisters though, she did not move into her in-laws' home after marriage. Instead the young couple migrated to Tunapuna where Seepersad was a sign painter with the bus company.

PM: So you had to rent an apartment in Tunapuna after you got married?
DN: *He* had to rent all of these things darling, not me. *He* had to rent it, *he* had to furnish it, I only have to move in. I make my life very comfortable,

They continued to live in Tunapuna for several years. The town itself grew up around the Pasea Estate which was not far from the Tacarigua and Golden Grove estates. Its population was a mixed one comprising some whites and French Creoles, Indians and Africans. During the years of World War II they moved to Luis Street in Woodbrook, to a house owned by the Capildeo family. Seepersad had by this time changed his profession as well, and Mrs. Naipaul had given birth to six of her seven children. She had decided that all of her children must receive a sound education and the older ones had to attend college in Port of Spain. Woodbrook was one of the several districts within the wider Port of Spain area and attracted a different kind of settler. Shiva Naipaul, her youngest son, recollects in *Beyond the Dragon's Mouth* the district to which the family had now moved:

> Woodbrook with its quiet streets, its sprinkling of tiny squares, its neat wooden houses fronted by verandahs with fretted eaves from which were suspended orchids and ferns in wire baskets, was definitely more respectable, more desirably "residential" in every respect than was St James. Lighter-skinned folk, families of clerkly status, schoolteachers, they all showed a marked preference for Woodbrook. Not surprisingly it was also a favourite haunt of Presbyterians. There must have been more pianos per square acre in Woodbrook than in any other district of Port of Spain .... It had, predictably enough, many fewer steelbands; while

the Hispanic bias of its street names – Luis, Carlos, Alberto, Cornelio, Rosalino – further emphasized its pretensions (S. Naipaul, 1985:29).

Moving to Woodbrook, therefore, the family lived surrounded by upwardly mobile neighbours from all ethnic groups – Africans, Chinese, Portuguese, Syrians and East Indians. All these changes – from childhood to womanhood, from semi-rural Chaguanas in Central Trinidad to semi-urban Tunapuna in the east and urban Port of Spain in the north – must have begun to change her awareness of the society around her and theirs towards her. East Indians had entered Trinidad society on peculiarly disadvantageous terms, as indentured labourers replacing African slaves, and a mutual antagonism had developed between them and the rest of society. Bridget Brereton writes that:

> The essential reality was that the Indians came to a society that was hostile to them, a society whose attitudes ranged from fear to contempt to indifference. They reacted defensively. Geographical, residential and occupational separation was reinforced by the Indians' protective use of caste, religion, village community and traditional family organization to cushion them from contacts with a hostile society. This would be the pattern of race relations long after the system of indentured immigration was ended in 1917 (Brereton, 1981:115).

East Indians were seen as occupying the lowest status jobs and had been stereotyped as being overly thrifty if not miserly, a condition borne out of their need during indentureship to save their meagre wages and sacrifice present comforts for future security. This way of life contrasted greatly with the lower-class Creole population of the day who were reputed to be profligate whenever they had money. Many Indians continued to dress and eat modestly so that much of this stereotyping persisted. Some movement out of the failing estate agriculture, the development of a small elite of Indians through the influence of the Presbyterian church and the general movement of Indians into occupations such as teaching, had nonetheless created changes in the relations between Indians and the other major ethnic group, the Africans.

"Did you get along well with your neighbours?" I asked. I was searching for something of this change.

> I had nothing to do with anybody I don't know", she replied. "Because my home, my life was very filled with work – I had to take care of my children and my house and that was a lot of work to do. I got a little help to do the washing and ironing but I alone have to do my cooking ... they can't cook for me, their food is tasteless.

I persisted again. "Do you remember who were your neighbours in Woodbrook though? What were they like? " By this time I was not surprised at the characteristic response:

DN: Don't ask me anything about other people, ask me nothing about other people. I cannot answer anything about other people. The things that they would do – the gossip in the street – I can't do those things. I never could, and furthermore my husband can't come home and see me gossiping in the street neither. He will find "what happen" if anybody come they must come and sit down inside and talk.
PM: Did you find any change in your lifestyle because of moving?
DN: No, no. I never changed my lifestyle. I didn't change it at all because I copy nobody, because I believe that what I am doing is the best, I copy nobody lifestyle because I find that their lifestyle *cyar* (can't) be as good as mine. They could never be a good example.

By the late 1930s, Seepersad was no longer a sign painter. He had changed jobs and had entered one which was very unusual for a male Indian of his time – journalism.

PM: How did your husband's new job affect you?
DN: He did not bother me at all. I had nothing to do with his work. He was writing for the Trinidad Publishing Company. I am a housewife. I am doing my duty as a wife and as a mother and that is where I draw my line.

There was nothing to suggest that she valued the role she had undertaken in life in her duties as wife and mother as in any way inferior to that of her husband's. There was a clear and unequivocal acceptance of this role. Was there something in the socialization of Indian girls which prepared them for this role? Mrs. Naipaul said:

> Well, they always tell you, you have to be obedient and do your duty, and not too much as the people say "backchat". If you feel sometimes something offend you, you go in your room or something and you sit down and cry and give vent to your feelings and then you come out.
>
> You see a woman has a place in this world and when she abuse that place, she has lost that thing they call womanhood because she is no more that woman. She is something else because a woman should always think very great of herself, she must always feel that I am a woman and must live to the name I have. I must do everything which uplifts womanhood and not degrade it ... decide that I would never fail in my duty. That is something that is very important and not every woman has that in them. I could afford to tell you – if they have it they wouldn't be as slack. My sisters all felt the same way about their duty as wife and mother. It was an honour to me – everyday practice meant that I have a duty to do every day and I must fulfil my duty every day and that was a very important duty which people fail to do now.

The next and last move Mrs. Naipaul was to make with her husband was from Woodbrook to St James where they had bought the small two-storeyed white house. She has lived here for the past 42 years. They moved to this house in 1946 and her husband Seepersad died in 1953. Two of their children had already gone to university abroad – her eldest daughter, Kamla, had gone to India on a scholarship, and her second child, a son Vidiadhar, had gone to Oxford having won an open island scholarship as well – a most prestigious acclaim in the country. Although most of them were grown, there were still two children at home to educate at college first and then at university.

By the time of her father's death, Kamla had completed her scholarship abroad and returned to Trinidad. She found a job easily and helped Mrs. Naipaul support the rest of the family at home. Droapatie looked after the last two until they were also independent of her. In 1962 she defied the previous pattern of her life so far – as daughter, wife and mother. Her brother offered her a job of managing his quarry for him – a quarry which employed 49 people. Mrs. Naipaul had never worked outside her home before she was married nor during the twenty six years of her marriage.

> "I said I would try", she explained. "I hadn't managed a quarry before. Not even thinking of quarry. Quarry is an unusual thing for you to think of going to".

She managed the quarry, however, for 22 years and kept the books successfully. The years of bringing up seven children on a limited budget proved a useful experience that she brought to the business. She retired in 1985 and lives now just as she lived with her husband and children, never bending her will to anyone. She never remarried. Her first thoughts were for her children, especially her girls. While it was still not possible for a Hindu widow to undergo a second religious marriage, the accepted practice was that widows could cohabit with another male partner. Often, women with children chose to live a life of celibacy, however, rather than introduce another male into the household for fear that her children would be mistreated or abused.

Mrs. Naipaul is still a devout and practicing Hindu, does not eat food cooked by anyone other than herself, and goes to the *mandir* (Hindu temple) every Sunday. In some ways she has changed very little from the confident young woman who got married over 60 years ago. In others, though, she has had to change.

> How could you change – I am so old fashioned that I can't change – it don't mean that I can't mix. But you see, if you don't have confidence in your life, when everybody is married and gone, your husband is dead, tell me who you want to lean on – I want to lean on nobody.

Mrs. Dassie Parsan

Mrs. Darsan is generous in the way of older Indian women, plying you with food and drink at every visit. Her house is always clean and well "put away". She views this business of housekeeping very seriously. It shows in the clean white embroidered tablecloth always draped over the dining table, in the ornaments placed carefully on crocheted doilies on side tables, in her healthy collection of plants which brighten up the front and back porch of the comfortable three-bedroom house. She is a short and slightly plump woman with a full head of wavy black hair. She is easy to talk to and willing to discuss her life story. Some memories are not easy to relive though and an anxious expression often lines her unwrinkled brown and pleasant face.

Ruth Dassie Singh was born in El Socorro on the 16 May 1930. Both her parents were Trinidad-born. Her grandparents on her mother's side were also born in Trinidad. They were from "Cane Field' on the Tacarigua estate and were estate workers. Her mother Sumintra worked briefly on the estate before she married Mahadeo Singh from El Socorro. His parents were India-born and were also agricultural workers all their lives. Tacarigua lies to the east of El Socorro along the Eastern Main Road – a road which links Trinidad's main city, Port of Spain – to a string of small towns all of which grew up around market centres, agricultural estates or railway stations at the foot of the Northern Range which itself spans the northern breadth of the island. El Socorro is an interesting town because it is both an active commercial centre and a very colourful and at times chaotic working class urban district comprised of both East Indians and Africans. It adjoins some extremely fertile agricultural land which belongs to the Arranguez Estate, once a thriving plantation as well.

Before the years of World War II, El Socorro was a swampy land mass with plenty of coconut trees. In 1941, when Dassie was around ten years old, the Americans began constructing the Churchill-Roosevelt Highway through El Socorro, thus extending the available land for housing, agriculture and commercial development. Estate lands from the Arranguez Estate and land from the El Socorro area were parceled out to farmers who specialized in small crops such as cabbages, cauliflower, sweet peppers, tomatoes and so on. It was rich agricultural land and attracted a large number of East Indian farmers who settled and worked the land. The town of San Juan which abuts onto El Socorro and Arranguez was one of the railway stops for the train which linked the towns along the eastern strip. El Socorro and the surrounding areas were therefore densely populated and with a very mixed population. Apart from the large proportion of East Indian farmers and their families, there was also a significant working-class population of African descent, many of whom worked in Port of Spain. Mahadeo Singh, Dassie's father, was one of the farmers who worked on leased estate lands from the Arranguez Estate. He built a small two-bedroomed house for his family in El Socorro.

He was not a very healthy man and suffered from "wheezing" (chest ailments) as far back as she could remember. Her mother Sumintra at first sold the vegetables he grew in the market at San Juan but when he became too ill to work full-time in the garden, she took over, and with the help of her older children looked after the family, worked in the garden and still sold produce in the market. When he died, aged 45, she continued doing this until she herself died at the age of 55, leaving three of her nine children unmarried. According to the hierarchy of the Hindu caste system, Mahadeo Singh was displaced in his occupation for although he was a gardener he also belonged to the second highest caste – the Chatriyas or the warrior caste – as his last name Singh denoted. Being a sickly man, however, he was dependent on his wife and children. Despite his illness and dependence on them, Mahadeo Singh seemed to have exerted a remarkable amount of control over his family. Dassie recalled this with a great deal of sadness:

DP: When my mother had four children, my mother and my father they couldn't get along well. So then my mother break up with my father and we went up to Tacarigua to live. I went to school in Tacarigua.
PM: Why couldn't she get along with him?
DP: You see the sickness had him so irritable that sometimes he used to be cruel. He used to beat her sometimes. She came out from a very nice home. I would say, my grandparents were very nice people and when she get married she didn't know about working hard and so on.

PM: You said that she couldn't get along with your father, this is the same father that died at 45? She had four more children with him though, so this means that she returned to him?
DP: Yes, they made back up and she came home.
PM: When they made back up you find the relationship was better?
DP: No, it wasn't better, it wasn't better at all. What she used to say is that seeing that she had all these children she have to try and make it because she wouldn't like to leave the children and go. And she try and make it with him. Although he was sick he used to still beat her.
PM: What did you all do about that?
DP: We couldn't do anything at the time because we were still small and at home – so we had to abide and stay with her and feel sorry for her and try to help out in whatever way we could. I find he was a little cruel knowing that she had to work so hard.

Her childhood freedom was also very restricted.

DP: We used to play with the children around, but my father were a very strict man. He never allow us to go to the neighbour's home. We have to stay in the house all the time and then we used to thief little chance when they not at home and go and play with the neighbour children.
PM: He was strict with the boys too?
DP: Yes, with the boys and girls also. And when six o'clock you can't go nowhere at all.
PM: You used to go out at all, what kind of things you used to go to if you were going out?
DP: Well, only theatre, to Ritz Cinema in San Juan. Theatre once in a while, not all the time.
PM: The boys go more often?
DP: Yes, the boys go more often than the girls.
PM: What you used to go and see?
DP: Well, we never used to go and see English pictures. Once in a while we used to go and see an Indian picture. Because as I tell you my father were a very strict man and he never want us to go. Whenever one of the elder heads going well then so we used to get to go with them.
PM: But you never used to go into town (Port of Spain) at all?
DP: No, I only know between San Juan, Tunapuna and Tacarigua. I only know that when you take a bus in San Juan it used to stop in Tacarigua – we used to take a bus or the train.

PM: But Port of Spain was not very far – you didn't know Port of Spain as well?
DP: No, even though we were so close I didn't know Port of Spain – only when I get married that I started going. Is only the older heads like when they wanted to bank money or pawn their jewels if anything crop up and they have to pawn their jewels they have to go to Port of Spain – we had no bank in San Juan here.

Her father's illness and consequently their poverty created other problems for the family as well.

PM: Did you and your brothers and sisters go to school?
DP: We went to school but as I tell you poverty again – we couldn't make it to go to school for too long. We went to San Juan Presbyterian school. The teacher who teach me, his name was Ramkissoon.
PM: For how many years … ?
DP: Well, I wouldn't say years, eh, because when you go to school you have to go to school like four times for the month, five times for the month, and then you stay home, you help out, and then next month you go four or five times for the month again and it's like that. We grow up in the hard way, we grow up knowing that my father was a sickly man.

Despite their relatively high caste status, Dassie's parents were hardly devout Hindus. Perhaps this fact, coupled with the influences of El Socorro with its semi-urban mixed population, allowed a certain flexibility in her religious practice.

PM: Your parents were Hindus. Were they practicing Hindus?

Dassie laughed as she started recounting the religious practices of her family:

> I'll tell you. My parents were never practicing Hindus. They used to have "*howan*" prayers – and we will go and join with them. That is the Arya Samaj – my father was a Singh but he was an Arya Samaj also and every Wednesday the Arya Samaj used to have a little prayers and sing bhajans and so on and I used

to go to that, my mother used to go sometimes, my father – he was a different kind of man, he never really go. And I remember too when we were small we used to go to the Catholic church, and we used to go to the Presbyterian Sunday school.

The Arya Samaj movement was an alternative Hindu sect being introduced into Trinidad by missionaries from India. It was a new movement and brought in more progressive ideas. It was especially critical of the ritualistic practices of Orthodox Hinduism and its unquestioning observance of a rigid caste system. Time and distance from India had eroded the memory and need for some of the excessively caste ridden rituals traditionally practiced. It was understandable perhaps, that some members of the Hindu population would respond to new ideas emerging out of India and to the freedoms from type caste boundaries offered in Trinidad. Simultaneously, the Presbyterian church had directed its attention to converting and saving the souls of the East Indians whom they had tended to view as pagans. But why did she go to the Catholic church as well?

DP: Well, I used to go to the Catholic church because we had a neighbour next door and they used to go to the church. They had bought my grandfather's property and since they come here to live I always used to be with them and whenever they go church I used to go with them.
PM: So you were more Catholic?
"Yes", she replied, laughing once again. There was no contradiction, no embarrassment or reservation in her response, just amusement as if laughing at herself. "Catholic, Presbyterian, Hindu – a mixture".

I was curious nonetheless about who were the neighbours next door and why, in the face of her father's strict upbringing, she was able to go the church with them. It turned out that they were African descended Trinidadians whom she referred to as creoles, not an impolitic way but in the descriptive way in which Trinidadians phenotypically defined each other.

"How did you live with them?", I asked, trying to get from her a sense of relations in the mixed community.

DP: The Indians and the Creoles, they used to live like one family in those days. You see if they have anything they would give you, and if you have anything you would give them. If you cook you will give them what you have, and if they know you are not eating certain things they will not give you.

Their next door neighbour with whom she was very friendly was a woman of African descent whose husband had died. She was bringing up her children single-handedly while working in an hotel in Port of Spain.

El Socorro was also well-known for its large and devout Muslim community. What did she know of them? Her picture was again an optimistic one:

> The Muslim people always keep up to their religion. El Socorro had a lot of church. Every Friday the Muslim people would go to church. And they used to live very, very nice with even the Hindus. They used to have prayers and invite them.

Despite her generous attitude and openness towards her African-descended neighbours and the Muslims in the community, it was clear that when it came to marriage, both Dassie and her parents had very strong preferences. She was married in 1949 at age 18, three years after she had left school. During those years she had stayed at home and helped her parents in the garden, sometimes selling in the market with her mother, sometimes at home taking care of the house and the younger brothers and sisters. She had chosen to discontinue school as she felt sorry for her mother and preferred to stay at home and help her. She did not have an arranged marriage. "Who decided you should get married?", I asked. For most Indian women marriage was a crucially important event in their lives as this was what they were groomed for from childhood. Dassie could recall the memories of her courtship and eventual marriage in great detail:

> I went to the garden one day with my eldest sister, she went to help pick some string beans and there is where I met my husband Gobin. He was talking to my big sister and I didn't say nothing because I didn't

know the person and he said to her "What happen, your sister like she don't speak to people?" Well I turn 'round and say that I don't talk to people who I don't know. My father was not there at the time. He (Gobin) did know my parents, not my mother, I think, but he had known my father. Then he started to come home to visit my father and he told my mother that he liked me and he wanted to get married to me. I didn't approve of it. I didn't want to get married to him.

"Why is that?", I prodded gently. She began to think aloud, almost as though she was reflecting and analyzing that part of her life for the first time.

> I don't know. I just feel that he was from a higher bracket and I was from a lower bracket. I think that we were very poor, and they were living right near the theatre on the Eastern Main Road, and I always had the feeling that they on top and I kind'a didn't know whether if that relationship would work. I told my mother no I didn't want to get married to him but I say to myself that if I had to get married I want to get married to somebody who would be on the same bracket with me. And then my mother say no he is a nice person, he is a nice boy, he come out from a nice home and so on and I should think about getting married and I told her no. before he, somebody had asked for me and he were a farmer also and I think to myself that that was the right person for I to get married to because seeing that he is a farmer and my father was a farmer I think that we would get along better.

PM: When you say Mr Parsan was from a higher bracket – he wasn't also a famer?
DP: He was a farmer also but what I mean, they own more land you know, they had this big house. I always had the feeling that they are very wealthy people, not knowing them so good, and a person like me to get married to him, I say to myself I don't think that it is right really, I should get married to someone poor like myself. And my mother told me no,

and she used to leave and go, and she know the time when he would come, only for us to talk and so on. And still I would just step aside, I don't want to see him at all and eventually he start coming and he start talking and then my mother she encourage me and I get married to him.

PM: Why you felt so strongly about him being of a different bracket – that means you didn't have anything to do with caste?

DP: Good thing you bring up that, that had a lot to do with it too, because we was from a higher caste – Singh – and they were from a lower caste. And my father, I heard him say they is from a lower class and we was from a higher class and that he don't think that I should get married in that home. But my father didn't know that I hear him say so, you see – I think all that too …

PM: So even though you weren't practicing Hindus you still thought the caste was important?

DP: Yes, and when I get married to him, my parents and his parents never meet you know. When I wanted to get married to him my father say that he will go but Gobin, knowing that my father from a higher caste and they from a lower caste, never wanted my father to go and so they never meet. He never wanted my parents to go and meet his parents – he say no that he would marry me without them meeting up.

PM: That would have been wrong for your father to have to go and meet his father because he was from a higher caste?

DP: Yes, but my father still wanted to go knowing that his daughter was going to get married and go in that home, but Gobin never really wanted it – and that is why they never really go. They never met, but the day I went to buy my clothes my mother drop in there and she met my mother-in-law and they talk and so on and we get married.

They were engaged for nine months before they got married. During the courtship period, however, Gobin Parsan, Dassie's future husband, had to prove to her father that his intentions were perfectly honourable: " He had to go and write my father a solicitor letter before he could'a enter and come there. The only time he could come there in that house is when my parents at home. He couldn't come any and any time". She did not question this request or in fact any of the restrictions imposed on the courtship. I pursued the point though.

PM: Why he had to write a solicitor's letter to them?
DP: Because my father was a very strict man and my father told him he had to write a solicitor letter before he could enter in this house and come, a solicitor letter promising that he would marry me and promising that he wouldn't come while they were not at

I didn't think of asking her if he ever broke his promise and visited when they were not at home. I wondered, however, if they had been out together during the nine months.

"Only once", she confided. "We went to the cinema to see an Indian picture".

PM: Did you go alone?
DP: No, we went with my cousin.

Dassie and Gobin were married first at her parents' home according to Arya Samaj rites. She likened it to the Muslim ceremony where "you sign up and say a few words and it is over". She underwent the entire ritual of the traditional Hindu marriage ceremony again when she went to her husband's home. Her parents were not invited to this ceremony. The new couple lived with her husband's parents for a while and she had her first two children over the next three years. These living arrangements did not work out well for the families. Too many people were living in the four-bedroom house on the Eastern Main Road, San Juan. When she had the children there was no place to put them. So they moved to Barataria in 1951.

Barataria is west of El Socorro and nearer to Port of Spain and was now becoming populated and developed. It was close enough to San Juan though for Mr. Parsan to rent lands from the Arranguez Estate, the land which he still cultivates with celery and other seasonings to this day. Barataria was mostly populated by Indians in those days, most of them working on leased estate lands. Later, with the coming to power of the PNM, more people of African descent moved in as a result of jobs being given out by the new government. Being on the outskirts of Port of Spain it attracted those who wanted to work in the main city but could not afford the rents there or those who could find no place to live in the already overcrowded streets. Barataria therefore developed as a curiously semi-urban district, with East Indians and Africans, rural dwellers and urban folk, who among them held a wide array of occupations, from civil servants to bus conductors, sales clerks to gardeners. The latter were still mainly East Indian men who planted vegetables which their wives marketed in the nearby San Juan market. It was the Barataria described by Samuel Selvon in *A Brighter Sun* (1979 [1952]), where Joe Martin and Rita moved in next to Tiger and Urmilla, the former an African couple from "town" the latter an East Indian couple from the "country".

"The men and women used to co-operate a lot?", I asked
DP: Some of them yes, but some used to beat their wives a lot.
PM: Why they used to beat their wives so much?
DP: Because they used to drink their lil' liquor, but I think now it is frustration.
PM: Why frustration?
DP: Because in those days they working for 25 cents a day. Money not circulating then as it is now, you see they couldn't get work.

She did not question why this frustration had to be taken out on the women who were themselves workers and also poor. Although her marriage had not been formally arranged, Dassie felt that such marriages, which many of the East Indian men and women had at that time, did work out well. Why did she feel so?

> You see long ago, it wasn't like nowadays. Long ago, even though you get married, no matter what you meet with your husband and you have to put up with it. Even though you go to your parents' home, they will take you and bring you back. And you have to stay, you have to remain. Whatever your licks you have to stay.

Unlike many women in her neighbourhood who had to "take licks", Dassie was one of the more fortunate. Mr. Parsan was a good husband and father, he provided well for her and their seven children, did not beat her, and, unlike most men at the time, he helped her out with the housework and children. The caste differences between herself and Mr Parsan had never been a problem for her. She feels very fulfilled now about her family but knows that she has given up a lot for them.

I sacrifice my whole life for my children. I never used to go nowhere at all, at all, at all. I never give nobody no problem with my children. Now that they get big I now start to go out. When they was young, if I go, I taking them with me. All the people from the district here, they used to dress and go to carnival, see Hosea[5] [Hosein, a Muslim celebration] and so on but I used to stay at home.

The family is no longer a Hindu family. When did this happen?
DP: When the children were small I used to send them to the Catholic church but then it was a problem to get them to go there. Not even a problem to go there but I think the Presbyterian church had some kind of thing and they invited the children and myself and we went and we find that they all were Indians there and everybody talk well and we find that it was a nice place where we could be with the children too, you know.
PM: So you prefer the Presbyterian church because more Indian people were there?
DP: The Catholic church it was nice too but then I go tell you in those days the Catholic people used to pray in Latin and then I find with the Presbyterian church everything in English so you could'a understand. So I think through the children we really leave our religion you know – like leaving the Hindu to go over to the Presbyterian. Because then we say the children can't be one way and we the other way.
PM: But they didn't have any kind of Hindu schools or churches nearby?
DP: Not in those days, no.
PM: Barataria was always very Presbyterian?
DP: No, no I wouldn't say so. Barataria was more Hindu. But seeing that probably before I get married I used to go to church and so on and I had that in me. When I was having the children I used to read the Bible and all this kinda thing so although we were Hindus and I think the children look like they take that from me.

She feels very fulfilled by the successes of her children now. One daughter has recently completed her doctorate in England and she is very proud of her achievement. One son has chosen to work with his father in the garden while the others have moved into professional or skilled jobs. Some of her children are married and she has several grandchildren as well. From a childhood of poverty and an over strict father she considers herself to be lucky in life. Her marriage continues to be a happy one despite her earliest misgivings.

PM: Did the caste difference make any problems in your life?
"I never bothered with it", she said. "The marriage was going well, and we never had anything. He never brought it up, I am the one to make it a problem and I didn't find it was a problem so I never did."

MITIGATING CIRCUMSTANCES
Mrs. Naipaul is over two decades older than Mrs Parsan. Their lives have varied, not only as a result of the circumstances of their birth – one is Brahmin and born into a wealthy and prestigious family, the other has known great poverty and deprivation and was born into a lower caste and class. They were born and grew up in different parts of Trinidad and at different times. The similar features are that they are both females of East Indian descent. In disentangling the relationship between class, gender and ethnicity in the lives of these two women we are presented with baffling contradictions.

Take their respective class positions. Commenting on the impact of the development of an East Indian community on class society in Trinidad from 1870 to 1900, Tikasingh writes:

> The development of that community had serious consequences for Trinidad society in that it made this society intractably divided and segmented. Hitherto, the society was stratified along the lines of race, colour, class and caste (between the upper class and the other classes) so that the society may be described briefly as a three-tiered system: the white upper class, the predominately coloured middle class, and the predominately black lower class ... an Indian community added a totally new dimension to the basic three-tiered social structure and may even be said to have established a structure outside the main structure (Tikasingh, 1973:46).

In 1953 Lloyd Braithwaite observed that immigrant groups, which included East Indians, Portuguese, Syrians and Chinese, remained largely outside the social system and were considered by the rest of the population to be on the lowest scale. Retaining their own culture and customs, he recognized that they constitute "a social system within the social system" (Braithwaite, 1975 (1953):47). In the published *West Indian Census* (1951), by 1946, Chinese comprised 1.01 per cent of the total population, Portuguese, who were not separated from the wider group of mixed or coloured, made up 14.15 per cent; blacks comprised 46.86 per cent; whites 2.74 per cent; and East Indians 35.08 per cent – over one third of the total population of 557,970. Relatively speaking we are therefore talking about a very significant number of migrants and post migrants who, under the conditions of their indentureship and later settlement, were able to recreate, both spatially and culturally, a social system within a social system. The fact is that they were largely set apart from the rest of Trinidad at this time: they intermarried, lived in separate villages or settlements, and reintroduced various aspects of their religion, popular culture, and their social structure.

Thus East Indians in Trinidad could conceivably have also reproduced a stratification system within own ethnic group, one which initially at least did not conflict with the wider class system, and which was based on criteria internal to this group. What were these criteria? They were mainly to do with the system of caste hierarchy which operated among the Hindu section of the ethnic group. Of East Indians in 1946, Hindus constituted 64.5 per cent, Muslims 16.7 per cent, Presbyterians 10.3 per cent, and other Christians 8.5 per cent. Much has been written and speculated about the opportunities provided in the new society to change or altogether relinquish the notion of caste. Of the four major divisions which denoted caste hierarchy, the Brahmin caste was the highest, followed by the Chatriyas, the Vaishas and the Sudras. Clearly there were opportunities to tamper with caste positions, but what is not generally discussed is the way in which a new caste system of one sort or another was in fact reproduced, and how much this was still adhered to well into the twentieth century. Within this system, such features as "untouchability" and degrees of pollution may have been jettisoned, but the idea of hierarchy remained deeply embedded among the Hindu population. Shifting one's religion or sect within Hinduism did not completely do away with the notion of caste. For example, a Chamar Presbyterian may have achieved higher status among members of his or her church group, or his educational status may have increased his, or her, respectability among the wider village population. S/he remained, nonetheless, a Chamar – a "low nation" as it was referred to disparagingly in the eyes of the Hindu community. One qualification here, though, is that Muslims tended to remain indifferent to the caste system since years of conversion to Islam in India itself had eroded its importance to them. Insofar as class among Indians was concerned in the first half of the twentieth century, they had retained among themselves a viable notion of hierarchy and privilege due to the highest castes. This situation was clearly not a static one for it coexisted unevenly with the class system and values of the wider society which were still based on criteria of race, colour, wealth and education, and with each increasing decade the values and traditions of one would collide more and more with the more dominant western and increasingly Afro-dominated culture.

Both a conscious and subconscious awareness of this coexisting class/caste system is conveyed in the life histories of these women. For instance, note Mrs. Parsan's use of class and caste interchangeably when she says "… because we was from a higher caste – Singh – and they were from a lower caste. And my father, I heard him say them is from a lower *class* and we was from a higher *class* and that he don't think I should get married in that home". Interestingly caste did not trump economics as her hesitancy in the first place to marry Mr. Parsan was based not on caste, but on the higher economic standing which his family had over hers. Similarly, in the case of Mrs. Naipaul, we see another aspect of the class/caste consciousness among Indians. Mrs. Naipaul's move to Woodbrook and later St James with its mixed population, her husband's occupation as a writer in the local press, the concerns to educate both her sons and daughters, are all circumstances which force on her an awareness of the values important to Trinidad society, some of which were different to those she had known in the wealthy and respected Brahmin family from which she came. What is remarkable, though, is the way in which she retains the distance of her Brahmin caste position, despite the twists and turns her own life has taken, while also confronting the value system observed by the wider society.

We also see the nuances of class/caste relations among Hindus as well. Mrs. Parsan, who has agreed to a marriage with a lower caste man, and whose father belonged to the Hindu sect that had underprivileged the importance of caste, appears to have greater flexibility than Mrs. Naipaul who was of the highest Brahmin caste, with Dassie going so far as to change religion as well. In Mrs Parsan's life story we see more clearly the possibilities extended to those who were less restricted by high caste constraints and the opportunities this allowed for flexibility in choice of places of worship, mixing with neighbours and, no doubt, tasting and expanding of cuisines.

Let us now consider gender and ethnicity. We find that gender and ethnicity are closely interlocked structures, barely separable during the earlier part of both women's lives. A strictly demarcated gender role is decreed for both these women, the responsibility of a girl child to parents, the obligations to both parents and husband, the duties expected of a woman and wife, the role of mother. The imagery of gender – that is the expectations, roles, responsibilities and so on of men and women – is firmly rooted in the ethnic consciousness of the women of this group. It is a consciousness that both women share, despite caste differences: "My sisters all felt the same way about their duty as wife and mother. It was an honour to me ...", as Mrs. Naipaul says. Or, as Mrs. Parsan says, "Long ago, no matter what you meet with your husband you have to put up with it. Even though you go to your parents they will take you and bring you back."

I would argue that in the case of East Indian women, gender and ethnic stereotypes were completely enmeshed. The scarcity of females in the early days of indentureship led to women's increased importance for it was not the general tendency of East Indian men to marry out of group. Women were a scarce resource at first and a necessary ally in reconstituting an East Indian community in Trinidad. Thus East Indian women were viewed as embodying the values of the group, not only because of their reproductive roles, but also because the bedrock of gender relations inherited from India appeared to be built on the primacy of the male role to that of the female in matters of religion, marriage and a sexual division of labour. To shift this would be viewed as endangering the survival of the entire cultural group. As can be seen from the life stories of both women, in an effort to retain the harmony of the group's concern, alternatives being unthinkable at the time, women colluded equally with men in reinforcing a particular gender and ethnic identity as observed by this group. Thus one would find liberally sprinkled in their representations of self, the acceptance of a notion of what it is to be an East Indian women. In the eyes of the society these women were viewed as subservient and passive while all East Indian men, thought to be patriarchal and dominant. Once we strip away the stereotypes and examine the details of each of their lives, there are variations on a theme both on the part of the women and the behaviour of the men in their lives.

The life stories of these women show that while there are stereotyped expectations of both sexes, actions very often go against the grain of these beliefs. Both women have very strict parents who guard their daughters zealously. "Patriarchal" control is not only exerted by the father, clearly, but is rather a system of values entrenched in the East Indian family itself. Mrs. Naipaul's father died when she was 13, yet her mother, and possibly brothers and elders, ensured the same control over her life – they determined the level of education she should receive and when and whom she should marry. But when her husband died in 1953, she made the choice to provide for her family, she chose to work and support them rather than rely on the income of another man. Mrs. Parsan's father did not provide for his family, yet his authority was unchallenged. She found herself in a very contradictory position. Conscious of her higher caste status and lower (economic) class situation, she was unsure of marrying Gobin whose family was from the lowest caste but who came from wealthier circumstances. She was also troubled by her father's disapproval of the match. Nevertheless, it was her mother who persuaded her and sanctioned the marriage to Gobin despite his lower caste status. Her mother's response was a pragmatic one. She had had to work hard and endure poverty because her husband could not provide for his family; she did not wish the same fate for her daughter. One could argue that Mrs. Singh, Dassie's mother, was also able to defy her husband's decision, not only because he was a weak provider, but also because the changes from India would have allowed her a greater flexibility in redefining gender roles and allowing women more latitude in Trinidad.

The relationship between class and caste is itself interesting one. High caste, like high class, predisposes certain patterns of behaviour and possibly preservation of an elite culture. Their caste differences by birth seemed to have lent themselves to a variation in class consciousness of Mrs. Naipaul and Mrs. Parsan. From their life stories and their personalities, one gets the impression that the two women emerged in their 50s with different perspectives and awareness of the same society they were inhabiting although it must be admitted that Dassie would be considered belonging to a new generation. For instance, Mrs. Naipaul is very rarely aware of people from other ethnic groups, even those who are her next door neighbours. Her concerns are primarily with her family. Although this might be because of a difference of personalities, Mrs. Parsan, on the other hand, is constantly aware of the relations between different ethnic groups, people of different religions, and of class divisions that exist within the society. In Mrs. Parsan's case, this awareness is articulated in many ways, as for instance her class/gender empathy of why men would beat their wives in the old days and not so much now: "Because in those days they working for 25 cents a day. Money not circulating then as it is now you see and they couldn't get work" or her empathy and closeness with her neighbour of African descent.

Nonetheless, it must be admitted that throughout their lives Mrs. Naipaul and Mrs. Parsan have retained "the thing they call womanhood" as defined by their ethnic group. Perhaps the circumstances of their lives, supportive husbands, responsibilities for home and family, and so on have guaranteed that their understanding of an ethnically-defined gender identity from early childhood did not undergo traumatic shifts, as for instance a situation in which an Indian woman enters a racially-mixed relationship and is forced to contend with competing or at least differing cultures and values. This is also facilitated by the period of their childhood and early womanhood in which there is still a considerable distance between East Indians and other ethnic groups in the society. The different ethnic groups of Trinidad may have lived side by side but there were fewer intermarriages and very little social mixing or knowledge of East Indian festivities or religions. And within this ignorance of each other, and the highly stratified class structure of a post-colonial society finding its feet, there were still far more prejudices floating in the ether of culture. In the triad of gender, ethnicity and class, class or adoption of behaviours expected of another class is the element that would most likely influence changes in either gender or ethnic identification. Only with the adoption of another set of values associated with moving into the mainstream of a class constructed society would East Indians begin to develop different ideas of ethnicity and consequently varying notions of what constituted male and female roles in the society. As with all culture however, there is no replacement or complete eradication, rather there are accretions and adaptations.

The growth of a peasant proprietary East Indian class, the benefits to be derived from adopting Christian and Western values, the importance of education from the early twentieth century, were among the significant factors which slowly but surely pervaded the East Indian community, factors which made them participants in the wider class society. But changes which these wrought were to be observed more so in the younger generations – not the trajectory of the lives of both families and the incremental break with tradition and custom which each new generation was able to make. Clearly one cannot generalize about the entire society on the basis of two life stories, nor am I attempting to do so. What is perhaps more germane to an understanding of gender, ethnicity and class among East Indian women in Trinidad is the way in which second and third generations of women and men would be influenced by the increasing concerns of class and values associated with mixing and becoming accepted as Trinidadians and thus be forced to confront and shape new gender and ethnic identities. Their experiences from birth would lead to more accelerated changes than those observed by their mothers and fathers who clung to the known and familiar, or whose options were limited.

There is, however, a message in the tale of the two women's lives, that we need to take account of as feminists and sociologists engaged in the reinterpretation of women's and men's realities. Mrs. Naipaul and Mrs. Parsan have both forged a happiness out of a given set of social circumstances. They maintain that they have no regrets of unfulfilled ambitions for themselves but have found satisfaction in loving their husbands and families, the gender role assigned them within their ethnic group. They took pride in carrying out what they saw as their responsibility. They have not been passive actors in all of this, at times conceding to circumstances that were beyond their control, at others determining their own goals. Each woman is clearly still the product of her ethnicity and class and assigned gender role. But they show us in their life experiences that they defy our expectations of them as stereotypes of a specific ethnic group, class and gender; that none of these categories are static but in real life are constantly being negotiated and renegotiated.

ENDNOTES

[1] See https://education.stateuniversity.com/pages/1914/Dewey-John-1859-1952.html

[2] See Dorothy Smith's very useful paper "Sociology from Women's Experience: A Reaffirmation" in https://www.d.umn.edu/cla/faculty/jhamlin/4111/2111-home/CD/TheoryClass/Readings/SmithWomen.pdf

[3] The original interviews are available in the now digitized Oral and Pictorial collections of the University of the West Indies Library at St Augustine, Trinidad.

[4] When this paper was initially written for the Second Disciplinary Seminar in Women and Development Studies, University of the West Indies, Barbados, 1989, Mrs. Naipaul and Mrs. Parsan consented to the use of their names, having also read the interviews before its presentation. Parts of the paper have been altered for publication but the original text of the interviews retained. It is dedicated to the memory of both these women. The suggestion to carry out interviews with East Indian women and to explore the relations between class, race and gender through life histories came from Kim Johnson. My gratitude also to Dr. Elizabeth Parsan for her introductions to Mr. and Mrs. Parsan for both of whom I had a sincere affection. All of these women and their spouses are deceased.

[5] Or Hosay, an Islamic festival in Trinidad, also celebrated in Jamaica, Guyana and Suriname, commemorates the martyrdom of Husayn in Karbala. Elaborately decorated models of mosques made of paper and tinsel called "tadjahs" are carried through the streets to the accompaniment of tassa drums. On the third day the tadjahs are thrown into the sea at sunset. It attracts all ethnic groups.

REFERENCES

Braithwaite, Lloyd. 1975 [1953]. *Social Stratification in Trinidad*. Mona: Institute of Social and Economic Research, University of the West Indies.

Brereton, Bridget. 1981. *A History of Modern Trinidad 1783-1962*. London: Heinemann.

Naipaul, Shiva. 1985. *Beyond the Dragon's Mouth*. New York: Viking.

Reddock, Rhoda. 1988. "Race, Class and Gender: Gender Issues and the Future of the Caribbean." St Augustine: Institute of Social and Economic Research, University of the West Indies, mimeo.

Rowbotham, Sheila. 1981. "The Trouble with Patriarchy." In *People's History and Socialist Theory*, edited by Raphael Samuel. London: Routledge and Kegan Paul.

Selvon, Samuel. 1979. [1972]. *A Brighter Sun*. London: Longman.

Thompson, Edward P. 1978. *The Poverty of Theory and Other Essays*. Harmondsworth: Penguin.

Tikasingh, G.I.M. 1973. *The Establishment of the Indians in Trinidad, 1870-1900*. PhD diss., University of the West Indies, Trinidad and Tobago.

West Indies Census 1946. 1951. Kingston, Jamaica: Central Bureau of Statistics

8

Writing Gender into History: The Negotiation of Gender Relations among Indian Men and Women in Post-indenture Trinidad Society, 1917–47[†]

THEORIZING GENDER AS A CATEGORY OF HISTORICAL ANALYSIS

The task of the feminist historian is not restricted to adding women – the sex whose history has been denied – to historical accounts of society. In order to engender history itself, the discipline must be challenged from both theoretical and methodological perspectives. To write gender into history, the historical construction of masculinity and femininity or the differentiated construction of gender identities must be posed as the problem. In this approach gender must be conceived of as another category of historical analysis in which the cadences in gender relations are juxtaposed and connected with the ongoing conflicts in society, especially with the confrontations of class, race and ethnic identities.[1]

[†] Adapted from my Ph.D thesis completed in 1994, this essay was first published in *Engendering History: Caribbean Women in Historical Perspective*, Bridget Brereton, Verene Shepherd and Barbara Bailey (Eds.). Kingston and Oxford: Ian Randle Publishers and James Currey Publishers. pp. 20-47, 1995. It has been edited and revised for this publication.

To make gender a category of historical analysis we must envision society continuously functioning around a recognizable gender system, or a series of gender systems. Gender as used in this essay takes its definition from Joan Wallach Scott (1988): "Gender is the social organization of sexual difference. But this does not mean that gender reflects or implements fixed and natural physical differences between men and women; rather gender is the knowledge that establishes meanings for bodily differences."[2] A gender system is defined as the accepted schema of gender relations which is deemed to exist at any time and around which the cultural construction of masculinity and femininity proceeds. The term gender relations, as I use it, refers to the social relations, both structured and unstructured, between men and women which are "guided by norms and values, underpinned by ideology, sanctioned by a range of mechanisms from social opprobrium to death."[3] A gender system is best perceived as the rules governing the social, sexual and reproductive behaviour of both sexes in any given society. The components of a gender system include the social roles assigned to men and to women; the cultural definitions of masculinity and femininity and prevailing societal attitudes to heteronormativity, the sexual division of labour; the rules regarding marriage and kinship behaviour between and among the sexes, as for example, whether monogamy or polygamy is an acceptable practice within a particular culture; the social significance of women's identification with the family; and women's position relative to men in political and economic life. Clearly these components vary with each society or culture so that the term "gender system" itself defies precise definition, and like gender, remains an elusive concept.

Gender systems in general function around a notion of patriarchal dominance. The concept of patriarchy is often applied in popular usage in its literal meaning "the rule of the father" and in its feminist usage as "the hierarchical relationship between men and women in which men are dominant and women are subordinate." Patriarchy has also been used to distinguish the forces maintaining sexism from other social forces, such as capitalism. It has been introduced through psychoanalysis in terms of the psychic and symbolic context of Oedipal socialization as opposed to that of a political and economic domination of men over women. In addition, anthropological, archaeological, historical and sociological studies have demonstrated that there are manifold variations of patriarchal systems in which the spheres of domination between men and women within the same society differ. What is clear is that once men established patriarchal dominance in our prehistory, it needed to be maintained. The ideology of patriarchy and its tributary branches are constantly retained and almost always evident in the power relations between and among the sexes. It is important to understand that patriarchy is not only a relationship of power between men and women, but also exists in the relationship between men and men and women and women. It is possible to extract and illustrate with direct reference to particular historical situations and events where and how patriarchal relations are manifested. In general, most societies exhibit both the ideology and practice of male super-ordination and female subordination. Thus, the ongoing construction of masculinity, femininity, the changing discourses on heteronormativity, and the shifting definitions of gender identity involve rewriting the patriarchal contract through negotiations in the sphere of gender relations, a process that I refer to as the "negotiation of gender relations." For each ethnic group or class in society the construction of gender and the negotiation of gender identities are carried out within the framework of a system of gender relations that may or may not be the dominant system in that society, depending on the ethnic composition of the population and historical circumstances of the society at a given period.

WOMEN'S HISTORY VERSUS GENDERED HISTORY

Writing gender into history rather than women's history requires first of all a challenge to traditional subjects and methods of data collection. Conventional history has concerned itself with the individual, the event, and the important social motors, which in some way shaped the world. Since men orchestrated many of these important world-shaking events, traditional history tended to focus on men. The development of social history has facilitated the narration and analysis of other rhythms of history, of groups and groupings excluded from these momentous processes. Defining another theoretical approach to writing gender into history also involves a disruption to the earliest feminist challenges to historiography. Stimulated by the political imperative of feminism, some writers of women's history, or "herstory" as it was referred to at one point, tended to celebrate and romanticize women in history, resulting in "volumes of sketches of great women, descriptions of their country childhood, and tributes to their mothers." Writing women's history also created new myths to serve the goals of the feminist movement; understandably and justifiably so since in any social movement the knowledge of one's history is a liberating experience.

Feminism embodies two simultaneous processes: a consciousness of the subordinate position in which women are viewed in society; and the actions which those who regard themselves as feminists take to redefine this unequal position. In their earliest attempts to record women's contributions in history, some writers of women's history concentrated on the issue of women's subordinate status. As Linda Gordon (1991) observed, feminist historians "felt impelled to document oppression, diagram the structures of domination, specify the agents and authors of domination, mourn the damages."[4] Inadvertently they maintained the notion of women as victims of history rather than as active agents. Substituting women for men in history also did not rewrite conventional history. What was seen as the subject matter of conventional history and the methods by which the evidence was retrieved and articulated remained unchanged for a while.[5]

The development of historiography from a gender perspective has demanded both a theoretical understanding of gender, as well as a notion of how gender works in history. Joan Kelly's essay entitled "The Social Relation of the Sexes" was written at a period when the feminist debates centered on whether sex, like class, was a social category in which women were seen as comprising a distinctive social group. Kelly's inquiry into a new periodization for feminist history led her to conclude that an assessment of historical change, in which sex is seen as a social category, should be broadened to include changes in the relation of the sexes. She suggested: "The activity, power, cultural evaluation of women simply cannot be assessed except in relational terms: by comparison and contrast with the activity, power, cultural evaluation of men, and in relation to the institutions and social developments that shape the sexual order."[6] Kelly cites a contribution of Natalie Zemon-Davis in support of her argument, a comprehensive statement which deserves full repetition:

> It seems to me that we should be interested in the history of both women and men, that we should not be working only on the subjected sex any more than an historian of class can focus exclusively on peasants. Our goal is to understand the significance of the sexes, of gender groups in the historical past. Our goal is to discover the range in sex roles and in sexual symbolism in different societies and periods, to find out what meaning they had and how they functioned to maintain the social order or to promote its change.[7]

Elizabeth Fox-Genovese (1982) cautioned that adding women to history as either victims or heroines had not challenged the discipline of history itself, but rather has carved out a space for another subject of history, assigning women to the status of the 'other' once more. Situating this task in the Caribbean context, Bridget Brereton (1995) also pointed to the limitations of a separate women's history and the need for understanding the shifts which occur in gender systems: "It is futile to try to pursue woman as an abstracted category, frozen in time, isolated from the great historical developments. There was never any single, uniform system of male dominance or female oppression nor any single gender system: each changes constantly as societies change."[8] Fox-Genovese stressed that "we must adopt gender systems as a fundamental category of historical analysis, understanding that such systems are historically, not biologically, determined" and that "the forms of male dominance vary historically and cannot be assimilated under the general rubric of patriarchy."[9] Fox-Genovese and Brereton emphasized that gender systems are by no means fixed, but vary historically, and that they are continuously being constructed over time.

When we depart from the use of *gender* as synonymous with *women*, we seek to answer several fundamental questions: What constitutes gender? How is it to be recognized? Why does it take the form it does? And how does it change over time? What are the component parts of gender? What parts of the society are involved in the construction of gender identity? What parts of the body are implicated in the construction of gender identity? In essence, the question that has perplexed feminists has been the way in which constructs of masculinity and femininity – gender identity – are determined from biological sex at birth and how one's gender identity continues to be shaped by economic, political, social, psychological and cultural factors.

The continuous unwrapping of gender in feminist thought has involved an analysis of gender in relationship to sex and sexuality. The word sex has two connotations, one the biological basis on which one's gender is determined as for instance school placements or official certification of one's sex at birth. The other is the colloquial use of the word that refers to an activity, hence the derivative term sexual relations that will be employed alongside that of gender relations in this essay. The colloquial dimension of sex was very quickly dropped from feminist theory. Gerda Lerner (1986) perceptively noted that the widespread public use of gender was "probably due to it sounding a bit more 'refined' than the plain word 'sex' with its 'nasty' connotations."[10] Joan Wallach Scott (1988) also pointed out that gender had become a particularly useful word as studies of human sexuality mushroomed from the 1970s onwards.[11] Gender offered a way in which sexual practice could be differentiated from the social roles assigned to men and women.

The use of sex as the biological determinant of masculinity and femininity created immediate problems in feminist theory, as it placed greater emphasis on the biological and psychological features than on the cultural and social factors shaping gender identity. Instead of making a distinction between sex and gender, Gayle Rubin (1975) employs the term "sex/gender system" and describes this as "a set of arrangements by which the biological raw material of human sex and procreation is shaped by human, social intervention and satisfied in a conventional manner."[12] Even if we begin to think in terms of a definition of gender that is not framed in oppositional categories of masculine versus feminine, sex versus gender, such a definition still embodies the notion of "sexual difference." One can argue that it is not one's sex, but sexual difference that has led to this skewed hierarchy between male and female in society. The fact that it is the difference derived from sex and the sexual that is appropriated to create and maintain an ideology of difference, and the controversial issues that arise with regard to homosexuality, gives rise to further questions. Maintaining a heteronormative set of ideologies and practices around sexual difference is deeply embedded in subterranean aspects of most cultures, supported by mythology and life cycle rituals, and thus least amenable to easy change. Decoding gender in history cannot ignore the dynamics of sex (as activity), sexual symbolism and imagery, which are included implicitly in the analytical category of gender. The area of sexuality has become a respectable area to research, and the amount of empirical data and theory which now exists on the subject is formidable. Yet for all our understanding, the area still remains elusive, not surprisingly, as Jeffrey Weeks has pointed out, "The more expert we become in talking about sexuality, the greater the difficulties we seem to encounter in trying to understand it."[13]

Michel Foucault's contribution to our understanding of sexuality has revolutionized the study of the subject and allowed us to see sexuality itself as an historical construction rather than as natural libido arising from biological urges "yearning to break free of social constraint." Rubin (1984) writes of Foucault's work on sexuality that "he emphasizes the generative aspects of the social organization of sex rather than its repressive elements by pointing out that new sexualities are constantly produced."[14] Foucault (1980) also points to a major discontinuity between kinship-based systems of sexuality and more modern forms. Thus sex, sexuality and sexual relations must also be examined with historical specificity. For instance, what was perceived as socially acceptable sexual behaviour for a woman of the middle class in nineteenth-century England is vastly different from that allowed at the end of the twentieth century.

This means that both sex and gender as historical categories must be examined in context. As Joan Wallach Scott (1988) observes, we must consider it

> ...a historical phenomenon, produced, reproduced, and transformed in different situations... The story is

no longer about the things that have happened to women and men and how they have reacted to them; instead it is about how the subjective and collective meanings of women and men as categories of identity have been constructed. If identities change over time and are relative to different contexts, then we cannot use simple models of socialization that see gender as the more or less stable product of early childhood education in the family and the school ...[15] The process by which gender identities change over time is the cumulated result of shifts in ideological thinking about men and women by men and women in society as they make culture. Men and women shape and define each other into a continuum of masculinities and femininities that exist not only as oppositional categories but especially in relation to each other.

Post-modern feminist thinker Teresa de Lauretis (1987) has demonstrated how gender can be conceived of as a process of construction and thus how gender identity is continuously being reconstructed. De Lauretis attempted to theorize gender beyond "sexual difference" and opposition. She approaches the construction of gender identity by employing the theoretical insights achieved by Michel Foucault (1980) in developing his theory of sexuality, which he referred to as the "technology of sex." De Lauretis proposed that it is equally possible to apply Foucault's genealogical method to developing a "technology of gender". She reveals the ongoing process of how gender is constantly at work in society, and how gender identity is simultaneously being constructed and deconstructed.

> The construction of gender is the product and the process of both representation and self-representation ... The ambiguity of gender must be retained – and that is only seemingly a paradox ... The construction of gender through its representation goes on today as much or more than in any other times ... Paradoxically, the construction of gender is also effected by its deconstruction.[16]

Thus we have a notion of the construction of gender identity as an ongoing process, creating, shifting and recreating new gender systems. By seeing gender as both a process of representation (how accepted gender stereotypes are presented) and self-representation (how gender is represented in practice), de Lauretis makes a break with earlier thought which tended to view women primarily as victims of a patriarchal contract determined to keep them in subservience. In other words, patriarchy does not only exist as a concrete set of rules and regulations which confine women to a secondary status, but it is also dominant as an ideology in the perception and interpretation of gender relations for both sexes, thus reinforcing its hegemony over thought and action.

While applying de Lauretis's technologies of gender in historical analysis, one has to be careful of not making further critical errors in writing feminist history. First, we cannot assume a similar feminist or gender consciousness in pre-twentieth century society as exists currently. Feminist consciousness of gender equality and equity were derived from decades of thought and struggle particularly over the twentieth century, even if human beings were instinctively conscious of wrongdoings or unfairness at all times in history. While women may have challenged their circumstances and the boundaries created around femininity at any time period, we also cannot assume that they have the same control over their construction of gender identity in any given time or space. With the current awareness we have of concepts of gender equality and equity and the rights of asexual or transgendered persons, we also cannot assume that gender identity was perceived as pre-eminent over other identities such as class and ethnicity, all of which, to quote de Lauretis, "go on as busily today as they did in earlier times."[17] We are made up of multiple identities that coexist and may do so in contradiction to each other at one and the same time. A "technology" of gender must explicitly convey the fact that one's class and/or ethnic identity may be determinant factors in shaping gender identity at any period, and perhaps more so in the past.

The problem of the feminist historian, therefore, is to discover how hierarchies of gender, like those of class, are constructed and legitimized under any historical period; how they vary by ethnic or racial group and are consciously being contested by individuals, institutions or structures. The implications of the discussion above are that both sex and gender must be viewed with historical specificity, and that we must see gender identities as continuously undergoing construction and deconstruction and forming new gender identities and new gender systems that are optimistically moving closer to an ideal of gender equality. In writing gender into history and employing gender as a category of historical analysis, the construction of gender occurs at the individual and collective levels and involves both material and ideological shifts. Eudine Barriteau pointed out that what is frequently missing is a "focus on the simultaneity of changes in the material and ideological relations of gender."[18]

THE CONCEPT OF GENDER NEGOTIATIONS

The idea of "patriarchal bargaining" suggested by Deniz Kandiyoti (1988) provides a critical point of departure from the accepted understanding of gender in terms of opposed sexual difference or as fixed non-malleable identities. She proposes a method by which women can deal with the patriarchal contract that they view as a fact of life. Kandiyoti interrupts the pessimistic grip of patriarchy on feminist thought by illustrating two active aspects of the concept. Firstly, while in general feminism has worked with a notion of classic patriarchy — the overarching rule of the father, the subordination of younger men by older men, the control which older women have over younger women and so on — she concludes from her analysis of concrete examples that the "material bases of classic patriarchy crumble under the impact of new market forces, of capital penetration in rural areas."[19] Secondly, she argues that while the patriarchal contract still influences women's gendered subjectivity and determines the prevailing gender ideology, women themselves strategize within a set of concrete constraints that reveal and define the patriarchal bargain of any given society, which may exhibit variations according to class, caste and ethnicity. She concludes that patriarchal bargains are not timeless or immutable entities and are susceptible to historical transformations that open up new areas of struggle and renegotiation of the relation between genders thus creating other technologies by which gender limits are transcended.

I have introduced, as Kandiyoti (1988) has done, the idea of a negotiation with patriarchy. The concept of negotiation, however, offers scope for different and more expansive configurations. This process is not only confined to a negotiation with patriarchy, but also to the negotiation of a new gender system, in which the patriarchal contract is being rewritten and in which the construction of new gender identities is taking place. The use of the term "negotiation" is innovative in the feminist vocabulary. It first occurred to me in terms of a commonsense understanding of how people actually live their daily lives, bargaining around their expected roles and expectations. Subsequently I found an application of the idea in Phyllis Rose's *Parallel Lives*. Rose (1988) recounts the life stories of five famous Victorian marriages "as unsentimentally as possible, with attention to the shifting tides of power between a man and a woman joined, presumably for life."[20] Admittedly, "negotiation" brings to mind trade union bargaining, or even the class struggle, but in the case of gender relations, at the individual or household level these negotiations are dependent on the levels of communication and willingness to resolve issues amicably or otherwise. At the societal level, these negotiations are not geared towards the abolition of one sex because both have expressed needs of each other.[21]

The problem with negotiation is that it implies a rational rather than accretional process, in fact it hints at a cohesive rationality that many aspects of gender relations do not possess. We must immediately conceive of a different setting for these negotiations, with different actors. They are not carried out over the boardroom table in a conference room confronting each other. Such negotiations are comprised of the compromises, the arguments, the conflicts in the domestic sphere that get ironed out over days of silences, arguments or violent confrontations. An interesting new dimension of this power to negotiate either through voicing or silences has been developed by Jane Parpart who argues that "the uncritical identification of silence with disempowerment ...dismisses and obscures the potential of many subtle strategies attempting to improve women's lives and to foster gender equality."[22] It is important to consider how these negotiations take place both in households and with the wider society by those who are thought to be without agency. Negotiations carried out in the wider society are generally done through legislation, media debates, representations of masculinity, femininity and queer politics in popular culture, or it may be perceived in other organized or unorganized forms of female or male resistance. These are the ongoing processes at work in most societies each day.

The negotiation of gender relations incorporates several dimensions. First is the idea that the negotiations are never static, they are always ongoing. Given that these negotiations are about gender relations and the construction of gender identity, they invariably start from basic assumptions about masculine and feminine roles in the specific class and culture, and from the knowledge of a system of gender relations which, in general, is familiar to all parties concerned. One can hypothesize that negotiations in gender relations involve collusions, compromise and accommodation, resistance and subversion, between men and women, between individuals and institutions. We must see collusion, compromise and accommodation as part of the construction of gender identities, and as the effort to retain many of the features from a gender system with which people are comfortable or familiar. Some of these that may seem oppressive to those outside a particular class or ethnic group have their internal rationale. For instance, the practice of polygamy among some tribes in Africa may appear abhorrent to adherents of Christianity who assume that monogamy must be the norm.

Secondly, where do these negotiations take place in society? There is a subdivision here. Negotiations in gender relations can take place at the individual level where men and women, men and men or women and women, work out their own gender boundaries and norms, in the privacy of their homes, bedrooms or in their workplaces or social gatherings. This level of negotiations I shall term for purposes of analysis, the micro-level. But there is also an ongoing set of negotiations being carried out at the cultural or aggregate level, where what is being negotiated are new components in the existing system of gender relations. For example, when a public debate is held about the passage of legislation concerning domestic violence or rape that affects the rights of women, we see an instance of a negotiation carried out at a collective level. This level of negotiation involves a macro-level institution of the state, which often reflects the prevailing dominant ideology - and therefore the cultural structures that have erected an accepted framework for masculinity and femininity. Cultural elements include norms, laws, ways of seeing, structures of emotion, caste, politics, and religion, and they are above the individual man or woman. We are born into and grow with greater or lesser discomfort in such structures. Very rarely can we change them, and if we do it is hardly ever as individuals.

What is the relationship between the two levels: the individual and the institution, the micro and the macro? The sources of power in each sphere are differently allocated to men and women. Thus, for example, within the household and family, women appear to have more power, and negotiate within the frame of reference provided by household relations. As childbearers and child-rearers, their knowledge of children may give them greater bargaining power for themselves and for benefits on behalf of their children. On matters pertaining to religion, politics, and a wider social interaction with society, which have not been expected to be part of women's knowledge, men have historically had greater influence and through institutionalized frameworks such as religion and politics they have historically made decisions about women's well-being.

How do the negotiations at the micro-level affect those at the macro-level? The rise of the women's movement in the 1960s and 1970s in the United States is a good example of how individual actions can and do affect the structural, not unlike termites eating away at the foundation of a building which must cause it to crumble. In the 1960s the expressed dissatisfaction of many individual women in homes, offices, universities, and so on, coalesced into a national organized women's movement, and collectively emerged in a slogan whose ideological message: "The personal is political", was to have tremendous influence on many women in different societies. This came about from the attempt to arrive at new gender identities.

The theoretical formulation of the concept of negotiation is being articulated at two connected levels. While institutions and cultural norms are built as a result of the accumulated convictions and decisions of individual men and women, by other metaphysical and material demands, there is a continuous dialectical relationship between individual action and group, community or state concerns. Theoretically, the relationship between the micro and macro disallows the tendency to "reify subjectively originating antagonism between males and females as the central fact of gender"[23] and allows instead a focus on questions of how gender systems are formulated and reproduced and the ultimate purpose this serves for harnessing women and men's labour for reproduction of the species and for economic production of goods and services. Christopher Lloyd (1986) supports this approach to the explanation of structural change:

> Society is a macro structure that endures, has powerful effects, and is partly opaque to common-sense knowledge. But it also changes due to social actions and their mental/cultural antecedents. It cannot change spontaneously ... In order to construct a viable approach to social change, therefore, it is essential to have a general theory of the dialectical interrelationships of the micro and macro "moments" of the social totality (personality, consciousness, action, culture and social structure) and "levels" of macro structure (economy, politics, state, culture, geography).[24]

The discourse of negotiations acknowledges that there is no easy acceptance for desired changes and that there will be counterattacks from those who actively seek to keep the patriarchy or status quo intact. Gender construction as a process is therefore a complex mix of material and mental factors; it is not stationary, nor is it uni-dimensional, and the multiple identities - class, ethnicity and gender – of which men and women are comprised, are being fashioned simultaneously, each interacting with the other. Women therefore have to constantly negotiate under a dominant patriarchal ideology for a position of greater equality. We need not see this in terms of present-day feminist consciousness of equality, but rather as a natural human response of rebellion. This negotiation may be viewed primarily as seeking greater freedoms of one kind or another still within the confines of a dominant patriarchal ideology. If these new ideas are inimical to the traditional patriarchal contract, then those who are most threatened by its erosion will obviously find ways in which to quell resistance and subversion. Those threatened may include not only men but women of a particular class or age group, the classic example in the Indian gender system being for instance the mother in law who expects devotion and duty from her daughter in law.

An implicit assumption of the concept of negotiation is that there is power to negotiate. Kate Young (1988) observes. "One of the basic premises of feminism is that the relation between men and women is essentially a power relation in which, in the majority of societies known to us, women have less power than men."[25] That power is structurally encoded in institutions, ideological superstructures and laws, and part of an all-embracing system of relations dominated by the interests of capital has been well documented and argued by Marxist scholars.[26] The preservation of a sexual division of labour that increasingly requires female labour both within and outside of the home works to the benefit of capital and state interests and maintains the ideology of the protective patriarchal male.

THE POWER TO NEGOTIATE

The nuances of power in gender relations are best understood through Michel Foucault's work (1980). Quite early in his thinking, Foucault pointed to the elusiveness of the concept of power and to its many functions:

> Power would be a fragile thing if its only function were to repress, if it only worked through the mode of censorship, exclusion, blockage and repression... If on the contrary, power is strong this is because, as we are beginning to realize, it produces effects at the level of desire — and also at the level of knowledge .... The fact that power is so deeply rooted and the difficulty of eluding its embrace are effects of all these connections.[27]

If patriarchal power in gender relations functioned only to repress, then the history of women in society would be one of a continuous slide into greater and greater oppression. Foucault

(1980) was attempting to derive a definition of the concept of power that would be useful in the analysis of social relationships. In this respect his disembodying of the power residing in a perceived omnipotence of the state is useful here. He argues that the state, like other relations of power, "can only operate on the basis of other, already existing power relations. The state is superstructural in relation to a whole series of power networks that invest the body, sexuality, the family, kinship, knowledge, technology and so forth."[28] Joan Wallach Scott (1988) brought all these issues into focus in her second proposition of a definition of gender when she states that "... gender is a primary way of signifying relationships of power."[29]

In other words, in examining the technology of gender in history I am asking, as Joan Wallach Scott (1988) has done, how significations of gender and power construct one another and how things change. The legitimizing function of power can work in many ways: Fox-Genovese (1982) and Scott's theories conclude that how gender and power are interconnected and construct each other can only be determined by examining the specific historical circumstances in which these relationships are functioning. It is unwise to assume that there is always an immediate or direct connection between the power relations immanent in sexual difference and the state. Scott observes that the relationship between the state and power in sexual relations "make little sense in themselves; in most instances the state had nothing immediate or material to gain from the control of women... Gender is one of the recurrent references by which political power has been conceived, legitimated, and criticized. It refers to but also establishes the meaning of the male/female opposition."[30]

There is also the idea of a dominant ideology of a gender system which is wielded by those in positions of public power or authority (in religion or education, for example) and which is established as the normative base on which the gender system is premised. It is important to consider who determines the dominant knowledge of gender, for this influences the negotiations of gender systems in the same country at the same time. For instance, it may reside in the authority of the state or religious institutions if secular interests hold sway over denominational ones. These interests may be, and often are, competing ones in respect of gender belief systems.

Where economic or political power is being traded or wielded, in general, men are the main actors. Thus we can find much clearer and direct lines among and between who presumably holds power, what kind of power is held and how it operates. The nuances of power in gender relations are far more difficult to identify as the ideology surrounding gender relations comes in a gift-wrapped package – notions of romantic love, reciprocity and partnerships etched onto unwritten emotional contracts. It is difficult to separate where simple power ends and abuse begins, for instance, or what are the sources[31] of power most utilized in gender relations and in the construction of gender identities. An important corollary must, however, be stated in examining power in gender relationships. In human society men and women have always expressed a need for the roles of both sexes to be present in pursuit of the larger goal of the preservation of the species. Power in gender relations should not be perceived as an abstract, ephemeral thing, or in the negative aphorism "battle of the sexes", but should be viewed as a resource which can be brought to bear on the process of negotiation. Power can be perceived of as strengths and consciousness which men and women are possessed of differently as a result of their different relationships to production and reproduction, and which each can and do exercise to their advantage in the arena of sexual and gender relations in the development of human society.

A METHOD FOR WRITING GENDER INTO HISTORY

How do the above theoretical explorations and propositions translate into a method for writing gender into history? The good starting point is to ask what are the spheres or spaces in which gender is negotiated under the particular historical circumstance. An approach that considers how women's resources and strengths have challenged the dominant order leads to an increasing visibility of women in history while allowing a continuous redefinition of concepts of femininity and masculinity in society. For instance, Lucille Mathurin Mair (1987) in her examination of women fieldworkers in Jamaica during slavery, observed that: "Motherhood with its biological and customary social applications is frequently perceived as a conservative force which imposes constraints on female activism. It became, however, in this instance, a catalyst for much of women's subversive and aggressive strategies directed against the might of the plantation."[32] Mathurin Mair describes how women not only deliberately depressed fertility, thus frustrating the planter's hopes for a self-reproducing labour force, but also withheld their labour and that of their children at crucial periods on the plantation. She notes: "By their actions during slavery and apprenticeship, they placed themselves in the very eye of the storm of Jamaica's post-emancipation crisis."[33]

In another example, Blanca Silvestrini (1990) analyses women's resistance to capitalism and multinational corporations in the first half of the twentieth century in Puerto Rico. She points out that women faced the new forms of capitalist growth in distinct ways from men:

> Subordination was enforced in powerful ways by the capitalist organizations that moved to the island, the local intermediaries that facilitated their enterprises, and the bureaucratic apparatus at their service. Women looked inside themselves to resist the many incongruities involved in the new changes... They clung to traditional ways of understanding family and community relations, sexuality, language, education, and health among other things. At the same time they dared to speak, to break their silence, looking to other women's groups for support and action, and in many cases breaking into the ranks of political and labor organizations.[34]

Both Silvestrini's (1990) and Mathurin Mair's (1987) contributions to "herstory" of Caribbean women provide valuable insights and data on sites where Caribbean women have constantly forged new gender identities.

To fully exploit the new approach I am proposing, however, we need to also investigate the tensions inherently caused by the imbalance of power in gender relations. If we ask what were the sites for accommodations, subversions, resistances and collusions of women in gender relations, then we need also to pursue the organized and unorganized resistances of the male patriarchy. What were the institutions or ideological instruments which ensured the persistence of patriarchy, as for example, areas of mythology, popular culture, religious doctrine and so on? Most crucially in the process of negotiation, we need to know what were the sources of power which women had at their disposal to subvert or resist male control when there was a wider patriarchal contract at stake? For historians interested in using gender as a category of historical analysis and seeing this as another rhythm in history, the theoretical considerations raised in the idea of a negotiation of gender relations provide both searching questions as well as tools for analysis. The methods by which this is carried out will vary for each historian and will also depend on the availability of data on the period being researched.

THE SPHERES OF NEGOTIATION BETWEEN INDIANS IN TRINIDAD, 1917–47

The theoretical and methodological approaches examined above are applied in this section of the essay as an illustration of the application of gender analyses to the study of the social history of post-migrant Indians in Trinidad from 1917 to 1947.[35] The objective is to find out how a new gender system was negotiated between Indian men and women in Trinidad, informed by that which they had left behind in India and the conditions in the new society which either allowed for changes or were resistant to transformations.

The system of indentured Indian labour introduced to Trinidad by the British Crown Government began in 1845 and lasted for over 70 years. In 1917, when the transportation of indentured labourers was brought to an end, 143,000 Indians[36] had been taken from India[37] to Trinidad. Those who relinquished their right to repatriation and those who were born in Trinidad entered another phase of their history in this society. From the time Indians chose to remain in Trinidad any time during their servitude rather than to be repatriated at the end of their indentureship, they began the process of forging an Indian community in this new setting. The negotiations among Indian men and women, and between Indian men and women and the rest of the society, were carried out in the context which may or may not have been hostile to them, but in which they felt and in fact were "different."[38] The construction of community, as with many migrant groups, was synonymous with the affirmation of ethnic identity in the new setting.[39]

Gerad Tikasingh's (1973) research reveals that the period 1870–1900 had seen the emergence and establishment of an Indian community in Trinidad, "the transformation of the Indians from a mere category of immigrants into a community." This process was both an economic and social one. First was the movement of Indians from essentially immigrant wage labourers in the export sector into a peasant proprietorship. Parallel with this was the social evolution of community as the Indians withdrew from estates into villages and here naturally attempted to reconstitute their known institutions and methods of social organization. Some of these institutions and customs had to be adapted to the new environment while others failed to survive. Studied from a gender perspective, community can be synonymous with ethnicity and gender identity, both of which were interlocked in the affirmation of an emerging Indian community.

The period of consistent transshipments of peoples from India in the nineteenth century did not see significant sexual rivalry or intermarriage between Africans and Indians. From 1900 onwards, however, this was no longer a dormant issue. While Tikasingh (1973) reported that in 1901 "it was probably true that there was no intermarriage between Negroes and Indians," by 1917 this had become another contentious dispute in the struggle to preserve racial purity. The Indian men who were at the forefront of this national struggle were quite open about this, as seen in F.E.M. Hosein's exhortation to Indian men to marry within their race. Hosein lamented:

> ...the growing tendency of cultured Indian gentlemen whom the impact of western influence has captivated to such an extent that they consider it the highest piece of wisdom to seek as suitable life partners ladies of a higher hue and of different race... Intermarriage in this Colony between Indians and others is becoming a social evil which must react on race.[40]

The spectre before Indian men was the loss of a separate Indian identity, an identity linked to the notion of ethnic purity. This fear could only have been founded on new practices in gender relations being recognized among both the male and female Indian population. As the primary spokespersons for the Indian community, men were actively against racial interbreeding. The Indian patriarchy required control over their women in the various spheres of life.

What was the patriarchal contract in Trinidad in 1917? There coexisted three patriarchal systems simultaneously in Trinidad at this time, all competing with each other. These were: the dominant white patriarchy which controlled state power as it existed then; the "creole" patriarchy of the Africans and the mixed group, functioning with and emerging from the dominant white group; and an Indian patriarchy found among the Indian population. How did these three systems interact, and why did they affect the consolidation of an Indian community? I am proposing that there was a hierarchy to be found among these three coexisting patriarchal systems, and that Indian men found themselves at the bottom of the patriarchal ladder as the last group of migrants into the society at this time. They were still largely agricultural labourers, even though they had already begun to establish themselves as landowners and peasant farmers. Among the Indian population itself, a dominant group of men who presented these ideas were emerging in Trinidad by 1917 in the form of religious leaders, educated men and large landowners or entrepreneurs. They were only now beginning to produce a significant crop of educated or professional men who could confront issues pertaining to their community either orally and or in writing. The period also evidenced patriarchal control over Indian women's voices. The records have substantiated a clear division between public and private spheres: Indian women were largely absent from the public records as mouthpieces of the Indian community.

The patriarchal contract was that of a competition between males of different racial groups, each jostling for power of one sort or the other – economic, political, social, sexual and so on. In the face of the hegemony of the white and "creole" population, and the increasing struggle on the part of the black and Indian populations to assert themselves, the stage was set for the emergence of a definition of masculinity between men of different races. For Indian men, this involved still a retrieval of their masculine pride from the demeaned status it had suffered during indentureship, in which the structure of classic patriarchy inherited from India had suffered a severe dislocation. Thus in their view, a consolidation of the traditional patriarchal system brought from India would place them in a better position to compete in the patriarchal race in Trinidad.

Why was a consolidation of an Indian patriarchy so important to the Indian community? The answer can be found in the conditions that affected all Indians, male and female, despite their internal divisions by language, religion, caste and area of origin. It was important for community to reconstitute itself in Trinidad, since it was only now emerging from the derided position that this ethnic group has suffered through the system of indentureship. In Trinidad the boundaries of a gender system based on the classic patriarchy from which Indians had emerged, became one of the significant markers which identified both the difference of the Indian community from others in the society and the consolidation of a unified ethnic community itself. Thus it was important for the Indian male to re-establish in the new society the resemblance of what this community represented in it ethnic gendered form - a system of power relations between the sexes which reinforced the old patriarchal order: male dominance and female subservience.

Under the system of indentureship, while the colonial state may have wielded a larger power over the community as a whole, with both Indian men and women as pawns in the chess game between capital and labour, the authorities were unwitting allies in this agenda, and continuously made adjustments to support the culturally specific gender system they understood as dominant in the Indian community. For instance, although stipendiary magistrates serviced districts, it was accepted by the colonial legal system that the village *panchayat*[41] would have jurisdiction over some types of problems, especially those pertaining to sexual relations between men and women. The primary power struggle in the wider political and economic sphere was that articulated through a male/male patriarchal contest among different racial groups of men. The dominant ideology regarding the roles, attitudes, practices and expectations of a gender system in Trinidad was determined by the ruling class which was comprised still of a European bourgeoisie. The gender negotiation that would take place therefore between Indian men and women was contained within their own patriarchal boundaries, even while contending with the influences of the wider society.

During the period of indentureship the majority of Indians under contract had lived in barracks on the estates. In the post-indentureship period, villages and communities were reconstructed, and with this came the re-emergence or consolidation of many of the customs and traditions that had been brought from India. In this period the sex ratio had not yet evened out from its imbalance throughout indenture when four times as many men as women were introduced as migrants. Women were therefore important both to the physical reproduction of this group as well as to the continuity of rituals, part of which was indisputably female: their relegation to the domestic sphere had made women vital to certain aspects of this culture.

The original function of the kinship systems in India was to organize and control production and reproduction, carried out in the context of a defined gender system that regulated sexual activity within marriage. Kinship systems constantly regenerate themselves and are not easily relinquished. Post-migrant Indians found themselves threatened by other cultural expectations in Trinidad, and as expected, the threatened group tightens its hold on the most endangered aspects of its culture. Thus, it became necessary to re-establish or reinforce rules that had governed the kinship and gender systems previously in India, in order to ensure the physical and cultural survival of the group. These rules upheld the preservation of a masculinity and femininity and a patriarchal order that the entire group took as given, would be recognized as "Indian" and which collectively deemed important for the continuity of Indian culture in Trinidad.

From 1917 onwards, with the movement of Indians to peasant proprietorship, there were other concerns that affected gender negotiations and these required compromise and accommodations between men and women. There were important areas of life to consolidate. Houses had to be built, food had to be grown, surpluses for the education and welfare of children had to be accumulated. While some migrants were India-born, some were first or second generation Indians who had to be socialized into the gender roles and norms that were being regulated by organized institutions such as religion and the *panchayat*. From the shreds of indentureship the patrilocal family was being reconstituted. The refashioning of the Indian community in Trinidad required co-operation between men and women in reconstructing homes and villages and maintaining the observance of kinship rules. Women were not indifferent to the re-establishment of their familiar culture and they colluded with men to a large extent, building institutions and re-establishing norms which appeared, to other groups in the society, to be particularly oppressive. Sheila Rowbotham (1992) observes that our needs as human beings, whether male or female, are "not determined by our gender alone."[42] Thus for instance, child marriages were arranged by both parents, mothers-in-law controlled their daughters-in-law, and sons were still given the best opportunities for advancement in the family. Men grew in patriarchal stature as they once more became the heads of households, village and community leaders, reviving the Indian patriarchy that had suffered a blow.

Both men and women had different sources of power in various areas of life and these were being negotiated each day in different spheres of interaction and at varied levels. The economic survival of individual families depended on the joint efforts of both man and wife when the extended family system, a remnant of the old kinship system, was not yet in place to buttress their efforts. Female labour in the household and in the kitchen gardens was an important economic source of power which women possessed, and which men, as a group, may have undervalued publicly but which they acceded to privately in their homes. In addition, the economic contribution of women's wage earning on nearby estates was also vital to the production of surplus value in the Indian community and to the consolidation of male power, thus providing a rationale for further entrenchment of the patriarchal system. Women also possessed knowledge of cuisine, domestic gardening, childbearing, child-rearing ritual practices of Hinduism and Islam. In such ways women were very important to the reconstitution of an Indian community in Trinidad and the history of the period 1917 to 1947 illustrates by and large the collusion and accommodations of Indian women in establishing this community in the new society.

Despite this, Indian women were not passive creatures, blindly accepting the oppressive features of the classic patriarchy from the original migrant culture. In defining gender in the context of the historical and cultural specificities of Indians and Trinidad in the early twentieth century, it is important to appreciate the nuances of a gender system which did not separate sexuality from gender. Both were closely interlocked. The rules and regulations which governed members of Indian society, their expected behaviours to each other in general and in their sexuality, marriages and family forms, were clearly demarcated in the kinship systems as practiced in India. Kinship structures were overseen by a patriarchy that regulated sex and sexuality within a closely controlled gender system. Sex as an activity did not, in principle, exist out of marriage, and neither young men nor women had a choice in the matter. Their spouses were chosen for them by their male kin. For Hindus especially, the choice of a marriage partner was carried out within the framework of another very tightly knit system which regulated all aspects of life, from birth to death: the caste system. Marriages were arranged only between persons of a similar caste. Monogamy was incumbent on women, while men had the option of remarriage on the death of their spouse. Fertility was an important signifier of purity aligned to femininity and female reproduction was closely controlled. The virginity of young girls was highly guarded.

Migration to Trinidad over a period of 70 years involving mostly single males or females, had nonetheless created a major disruption in the kinship rules which before had been observed by both sexes. The newly formed society of Trinidad, peopled by diverse ethnic groups and dominated by a western culture, did not provide a substitute kinship or family system to which Indians would easily assimilate. In their initial settlement into the new society it was assumed, if the colonial mindset went that far, that Indians would naturally recreate the kinship and gender systems with which they were familiar. But in Trinidad, while a kinship system was being re-established, this was already gradually shifting from its rigid control over female (and male) sexuality, adjusting to conditions which Indian men and women encountered in the different "Western" setting.

Significant modifications had already occurred in the pattern of gender relations among Indians during the period of indentureship in the nineteenth century. The system of indentureship had attracted many more males than it did females and women found themselves a very scarce resource. Another fundamental feature of Indian culture – caste taboos were tampered with in the crossing of the black water[43], contriving to also allow gender relations to swiftly undergo a major and rapid transformation. So while some Indian women colluded with men to keep the system intact, other Indian women began to wield a power that they did not and could not possess under the rigid conditions of life in India. They could and did challenge this system in Trinidad through their new wage-earning status and their sexuality, by moving from one male partner to another when it was in their own interests to do so. This was not without dire consequences, for it led to violent retaliations on the part of men who had viewed women as personal property.

A focus on sexual relations and sexuality provides a clue to a source of power that women in general possess, and which Indian women clearly utilized in nineteenth and early twentieth-century Trinidad. The fundamental reason why this sphere of sexuality could be exploited was an inordinate imbalance of male to female migrants. Table 1 shows the sex ratio of males per 1,000 females from 1891 until 1946, one year before this study terminates. Only by 1946 did the sex ratio in the Indian population in Trinidad begin to approximate a balance. The shortage of female migrants, from the first moment, provided Indian women with the most powerful tool for bargaining in sexual relations: an extreme scarcity of women among a migrant group which was largely averse to miscegenation.

Table 1: Sex Ratios (males per 1000 females) among Indian migrants to Trinidad, 1891—1946

Year	Sex ratio
1891	1,571
1901	1,410
1911	1,354
1921	1,234
1931	1,135
1946	1,066

Source: Jack Harewood, The Population of Trinidad and Tobago, 1975, Table 4H

Tikasingh has draws attention to the liberties which women began to have during indentureship, 1845–1917:

> Neither polygynous or polyandrous unions existed for long or to any great extent. The prevalent and extensive union was the keeper union, whose stability depended primarily upon the satisfaction of the female partner. For example, Mungaree had such an arrangement with Namoomarlala on Orange Field Estate who had given her $150 in silver and clothes and with whom she lived for eight years. She then went to live with Nageeroc with the understanding that she could return to her former keeper at any time; and at the time of her current court case, she was living with a shopkeeper. As soon as females were ill-treated by their "papa" as Sarah Morton put it, they were quite ready to break the existing union and form another.[44]

This kind of behaviour and personal choice would have been unthinkable if Mungaree had remained in India. A marriage would have been arranged for her from childhood and, even if dissatisfied with her spouse, she would have been committed to endure this state until his death, without the option of remarrying even then. Her sexuality would have been learnt within that marriage and she would have been confined to one sexual partner for the duration of her life. The disruptions to the gender system in Trinidad, which included radical shifts in sexual arrangements, allowed Mungaree opportunities to challenge this rigid set of rules, exploring both her expectations of a male partner and her sexuality.

The evidence available on female sexual "misdemeanours" during and after the period of indentureship suggests that this trend in female behaviour persisted throughout the seven decades of this labour system. Around 1915 or so, Batya, an only daughter of India-born parents of the Hindu religion, left the indentured man with whom she had had an arranged marriage. He was treating her badly and so she went to live with a man of African descent, who was then a driver at the McClean Estate in Rio Claro where she was employed. Shortly after, her father, mother, two brothers and her husband, armed with sticks, a flambeau and a gun, arrived at her new home and called out to her new partner Mr. Lewis, a man of African descent: "We come for Batya." Mr. Lewis put up no resistance. "Look she here. Come for she nah, look she here. She say she eh coming, I cyar drive she out." They were unsuccessful that night and later in bringing her back to the fold, for she ceased all contact with her family.[45]

Indian women continued to challenge the traditional expectations of their sex in other ways and evoked mixed responses from males. Due to the shortage of women as well as the contradictions in emotional and pragmatic responses in the sphere of sexual relations, evidence such as the following could be noted in public notices placed by men in the newspaper:

> Having been accused of ill treatment to my registered wife which she has failed to prove to the satisfaction of the court and no order of maintenance having been made against me in consequence, I beg to notify the public in general that although I am quite willing to receive her, she not consenting I shall have to take legal proceedings, not necessarily against her but against any other person who might harbour her later on, as I have not been cruel to her, nor have I divorced her.[46]

This is not to suggest that all women were straying from traditional roles expected of them, nor that all men were so easily appeased. In fact the incidence of physical violence and murders of Indian women by Indian men suggests that violence was being applied as a major method of control. But it is also true that a large number of men were led to take their own lives as a result of loss of face in relation to their masculinity among their peers. In the new setting, the expression of another sexuality was one of the greatest challenges to the Indian patriarchy. Sexuality was not being redefined apart from the negotiations taking place in other spheres of life, as they all were intimately connected at various levels, and with efforts to bring all under social control. For instance, the *panchayat* and the reconstituted family provided checks and balances on the extent to which any individual could challenge the norm. This challenge in sexual relations involved individual initiatives of change and could be interpreted in one sense as the negotiation of a new concept of Indian femininity, and by extension masculinity, in the setting of Trinidad.

The examples cited above provide a few examples only of the changes which emerged as sexual arrangements were being negotiated among this group, in the context of threats posed by the presence of another race of men who were available as alternative partners to Indian women. Yet the goal for the Indian community was to retain a singular notion of Indian masculinity and femininity, and a conception of sexual partnerships that would secure the consolidation of an Indian community in Trinidad. While the organisation of the major religions of Hinduism and Islam in the early twentieth century, and the presence of the *panchayat*, could attempt to shape masculine and feminine identities into parallel versions found in the Indian sub-continent, and by and large Indian men and women colluded on building a sound financial base for their offspring and communities, the greatest challenge to the received gender system which they sought to put back into place, nonetheless, was that encountered in the challenges to and renegotiation of choices in sexual partners and new freedoms that women and some men, sought as sexual beings.

During the period 1917-47 of Indian history in Trinidad, it was the dissatisfaction of individual women with the structured patriarchy in the spheres of kinship obligations and sexual relations, as well as the later benefits of education, which allowed them to challenge the dominant patriarchal tendency, resulting in a redefinition of its boundaries. Indian women had already carried out a "first negotiation" during the indentureship period, that of an affirmation of their sexual needs and the freedom of choice in partners. In addition, they had come to Trinidad not as dependent females but as wage-earners in their own right, and as such had other resources for bargaining for greater equality within the confines of a gender system.[47] Most importantly, they were not blind or indifferent to the other gender systems around them, thus incorporating new ideas into the map of possibilities for relations between the sexes.

Two conditions experienced by Indian women during indentureship – their scarcity as a sex and their wage-earning status - gave them certain freedoms and produced certain effects at the level of desire and knowledge. In the post-indentureship period this would resurface in other ways. During 1917–47, while collusion, accommodation and submission could be read into the actions of the majority of women who built houses and communities with their partners, their resistances could be more clearly seen in those negotiations they undertook for their daughters and sons, thus ensuring change in subsequent generations. For example, the education of males used to take pre-eminence over that of females who, viewed primarily in roles of wife and mother, were not given opportunities for education in the earlier period. By the 1940s education had emerged as another site for negotiation between men and women. The project of writing gender into history in this instance, therefore, leads to an understanding of how masculinity and femininity, while being reconstituted in presumed traditional forms, were also simultaneously undergoing major transformations.

CONCLUSION – THE ONGOING NEGOTIATION OF GENDER IN HISTORICAL CHANGE

The conclusion towards which this approach to writing gender into history propels us is to appreciate that gender systems are by no means fixed or immutable, that they are constantly shifting and changing through each historical period, and with each set of historical circumstances in which men and women find themselves. Gender systems are therefore consistently recreating themselves in different formations over every historical period, persistently defining and reshaping versions of femininity and masculinity, and facets of what is considered to be the purview of a gender system.

The question one might well ask though is how does this approach actually write gender into history? Perhaps it challenges fundamental questions posed by historians of gender relations. What comprises the discipline of history? Who were the main actors in human history and what were their contributions to historical development? What were the major themes with which history has concerned itself and what empirical evidence was considered the data of history? A writing of gender into history brings all of these questions into sharp focus and attempts to refute the traditional boundaries. It seems to me that a history in which gender inequality and sexual difference are posed as problematic, reveals another lens through which we can view the development of society. By unwrapping gender from the covers under which it has been hidden, we begin to disclose evidence which has hitherto not surfaced. Since gender allows us to make women the primary subjects of our enquiry, it sheds light on the invisible contributions which women have made to the development of a culture. By focusing on areas of life which are considered outside the conventional range of the discipline, we can deepen our analyses of the motors which lead to social change. By unearthing gender as another rhythm in society, we can lend an ear to the different conflicts and preoccupations which engage both sexes in the daily business of material existence. Most of all, writing gender into history can, optimistically, further the goal of the feminist struggle, which, in the final analysis, is to demonstrate that sexual difference should not provide a basis for yet another measure by which we can condone inequalities in human society.

ENDNOTES

[1] Currently termed intersectionality; at the time I was writing this piece, the concept had not yet surfaced.
[2] Joan Wallach Scott, *Gender and the Politics of History* (New York: Columbia University Press, 1988), Introduction, p. 2.

[3] Kate Young, 'Notes on the Social Relations of Gender', in Patricia Mohammed and Catherine Shepherd (eds.), *Gender in Caribbean Development*, Women and Development Studies Project (Jamaica, Trinidad and Tobago and Barbados: University of the West Indies, 1988), p. 99
[4] Linda Gordon, 'Rewriting Women's History', p. 75.
[5] This assessment of women's history is not at all meant to be dismissive of the real contribution that historians writing in this field have made thus far. The sheer quantity and approaches to writing women into history are themselves quite impressive. Two essays, Elizabeth Fox-Genovese's 'Placing Women's History in History', *New Left Review*, 133 (May-June 1982) and Olwen Hufton's 'Survey Articles Women in History – Early Modern Europe', *Past and Present*, 101 (1983), review the range of material presented in women's history over the past few decades.
[6] Joan Kelly-Gadol, 'The Social Relation of the Sexes: Methodological Implications of Women's History', *Signs: Journal of Woman in Culture and Society, 1: 4* (1976), pp.809-23.
[7] From an address by Natalie Zemon Davis to the Second Berkshire Conference on the History of Women, October 1975, later published in *Feminist Studies* (Winter 1975/76).
[8] Bridget Brereton, 'General Problems and Issues in Studying the History of Women' in Mohammed and Shepherd (eds), p. 125
[9] Elizabeth Fox-Genovese, "Placing Women's History in History", *New Left Review*, 133 : 5-29 (1982).
[10] Gerda Lerner, *The Creation of Patriarchy*, 238. New York and Oxford: Oxford University Press, 1986.
[11] Dating back to 1947 with the work of Alfred Kinsey, sexuality studies is an interdisciplinary field devoted to the analysis of human sexuality. It explores the historical, political, biological, cultural, sociological, educational, legal, health, aesthetic, and psychological contexts of human sexuality.
[12] Gayle Rubin, 'The Traffic in Women: Notes on the "Political Economy" of Sex' in Rayna Reiter (ed.), *Toward an Anthropology of Women* (New York: Monthly Review Press, 19/5), p. 165.
[13] Jeffrey Weeks, *Sexuality*, p. 11
[14] Gayle Rubin, 'Thinking Sex: Notes for a Radical Theory of the Politics of Sexuality', in Carol S. Vance (ed.), *Pleasure and Danger: Exploring Female Sexuality* (London: Routledge & Kegan Paul, 1984), p. 276.
[15] Joan Wallach Scott, *Gender and the Politics of History*, Introduction, p. 6.
[16] Teresa de Lauretis, *Technologies of Gender: Essays on Theory, Film, and Fiction* (Bloomington & Indianapolis: Indiana University Press, 1987).
[17] de Lauretis, *Technologies of Gender*, p. 3.
[18] The relationship between the material and the ideological is well developed in Eudine Barriteau, *The Political Economy of Gender in the Twentieth-Century Caribbean*, International Political Economy Series, Palgrave, Basingstoke, 2001, p. 28, her published Ph.D research. Interestingly, we were simultaneously doing doctoral studies at the same time. It useful to see the overlaps in thought as I rework this essay in 2019.
[19] Deniz Kandiyoti, 'Bargaining with Patriarchy', *Gender and Society, 3:2* (1988), (2), pp.274-89
[20] Phyllis Rose, *Parallel Lives: Five Victorian Marriages* (London: Penguin, 1988), p. 13
[21] Two meanings of the word negotiation, as defined in the *Concise Oxford Dictionary* (1988), give another measure as to the way in which it is being employed here. These are 'confer with another with view to compromise or agreement', and 'get over or through obstacle or difficulty'.

[22] Jane Parpart, "Choosing silence: Rethinking voice, agency and women's empowerment", Ch 1 in *Secrecy and Silence in the Research Process: feminist reflections*, Roisin Ryan-Flood and Rosalind Gill (Eds.) (Oxfordshire: Routledge, 2010) p. 15-16
[23] Joan Wallach Scott, *Gender and the Politics of History*, p. 39.
[24] Christopher Lloyd, *Explanations in Social History* (London: Basil Blackwell, 1986), p. 182.
[25] Kate Young, Towards a Theory of the Social Relations of Gender', London, *Womankind* (1988).
[26] See Mark C. J. Stoddart, "Ideology, Hegemony, Discourse: A Critical Review of Theories of Knowledge And Power", https://pdfs.semanticscholar.org/f66b/93d70a3ba41d23704c25d24f0e1a82935d0e.pdf
[27] Colin Gordon, (ed.), *Power/Knowledge Selected Interviews and other Writings 1972—77, Michel Foucault* (New York: Pantheon Books, 1979), p. 88.
[28] Colin Gordon *op cit* p. 122.
[29] Joan Wallach Scott, *Gender and the Politics of History*, p. 42.
[30] *Ibid.*, p. 49.
[31] I have introduced the notion of 'sources' of power into the concept of negotiation, in order to get away from the abstractions still evident in Foucault's brilliant insights. It is also based on my conviction that people, men and women, are sometimes very consciously aware of the sources of power which they possess which they can wield over a partner or colleague. For example, in gender relations, a knowledge of someone's emotional dependence on one can be used as a tool for manipulating the other. Economic power is also a major controlling element in gender relations, where in general women are deemed to be dependent on men, although this is not always the case since women's non-wage earning activities are equally important, even if undervalued. But I would also argue though that in gender relations these sources are not necessarily consciously or conspiratorially used.
[32] Lucille Mathurin-Mair, 'Women Field Workers in Jamaica During Slavery', *The 1986 Elsa Goveia Memorial Lecture* (Mona, University of the West Indies: Department of History, 1987), pp. 11-12.
[33] *Ibid* 11-12
[34] Blanca Silvestrini, 'Women and Resistance: Herstory in contemporary Caribbean History', *The 1989 Elsa Goveia Memorial Lecture*, (Mona, University of the West Indies: Department of History, 1990), p. 9.
[35] The larger study from which this theoretical framework has been excerpted, analyses, with supporting historical evidence, the spheres of negotiations in gender relations between Indian men and women during the period 1917—17. This discussion is extracted from Mohammed, 'A Social History of Post-Migrant Indians in Trinidad, 1917—47: A Gender Perspective,' PhD. Diss., Institute of Social Studies, The Hague, 1994. The statements presented here are therefore summaries of the findings of this research which drew on documented histories, archival and oral histories for the period 1917 to 1945 and are not to be interpreted as impressionistic.
[36] 'Indian' as used here refers to people who were either born in India or those whose ancestors were from India. It has been the custom in the Caribbean literature to describe this group as *East* Indians to distinguish them from other racial groups in the *West* Indies.
[37] The large majority of Indian migrants who were brought to Trinidad came from the United Provinces (Uttar Pradesh) in North India. Where India is referred to, unless otherwise specified, it refers to North India and more directly to those regions from which the migrants originated.

[38] To enter another discussion on the 'difference' of Indian culture from a Western culture here takes us into other dimensions of the study which it is not possible to develop fully, but a knowledge of their difference is important to convey when one considers the distinctive differences which existed between Indian culture, an Oriental culture, from that in which they were placed, which was primarily a Western setting.

[39] Kelvin Singh's discussion in Chapters 1 and 2 of *Race and Class Struggles in a Colonial State: Trinidad 1917—45* (Kingston: The Press, University of the West Indies, 1994), published after the completion of this study, serves to confirm the ideas expressed in this extract and in the dissertation that 1917—47 was a period in which there was little cooperation between the different racial groups in Trinidad and that each was involved in consolidating separate communities. His data also support my findings, expressed later in this article, that the Indian community had by 1917 begun to be represented by a group of men who represented the patriarchal front of this ethnic group. In addition, his listings of the various men who represented the other groups all confirm the point I am making here, that the confrontation between the different groups was, at one level, between the competing male patriarchies. Women of all races were nowhere to be seen in these struggles.

[40] F.E.M. Hosein, unpublished paper, 5 October 1928.

[41] A council consisting of five male elders chosen from within the community. With the grouping of Indians into villages, the *panchayat* selected by the village or community functioned as arbiters of moral and social conduct

[42] Sheila Rowbotham, *Women in Movement: Feminism and Social Action* (London & New York: Routledge, 1992), p. 12.

[43] Indians referred to this as *kala pani*, the crossing of the black water which meant that once they had left their towns and villages in India and entered this sea journey they already had tampered with the rigid rules and regulations which governed the caste system, and which defined Indian life from birth to death. This was a fundamental shift in Indian life which would have repercussions in many other areas of life, especially those associated with rules pertaining to gender. For instance caste endogamy was the rule. In Trinidad, where all castes were already polluted, the ideology of caste was immediately challenged when marriages or alliances on estates broke all caste rules of endogamy.

[44] Gerad Tikasingh, 'The Establishment of the Indians in Trinidad, 1870—1900', p. 270.

[45] This information was taken from one of the 65 oral history interviews carried out with Indian men and women in Trinidad as research material for this study. The reference is to be found in Tape 39 among the collection of tapes which is now lodged at the library of the University of the West Indies in St Augustine, Trinidad. For purposes of anonymity, the names of the respondents have been changed.

[46] *Trinidad Guardian*, 29 November 1918.

[47] Evidence of Indian women's struggles against patriarchy during indentureship can be found as well in Rhoda Reddock's 'Freedom Denied: Indian women and indentureship in Trinidad and Tobago 1845-1917', in *Economic and Political Review: Review of Women's Studies*, 20: 43 (1985), pp. 79-87.

REFERENCES

Brereton, Bridget. 1989. "General Problems and Issues in Studying the History of Women." In: *Gender in Caribbean Development*, edited by Patricia Mohammed and Caroline Shepherd, 125. Women and Development Studies Project, Jamaica, Trinidad and Tobago and Barbados: University of the West Indies.

de Lauretis, Teresa. 1987. *Technologies of Gender: Essays on Theory, Film, and Fiction.* Bloomington and Indianapolis: Indiana University Press.

Foucault, Michel. 1980. *The History of Sexuality: An Introduction*, vol. 1. New York: Vintage Books.

Fox-Genovese, Elizabeth. 1982. "Placing Women's History in History," *New Left Review*, 133: 5-29.

Gordon, Linda. 1991. "Rewriting Women's History." In *A Reader in Feminist Knowledge*, edited by S. Gunew. London and New York: Routledge.

Kandiyoti, Deniz. 1988. "Bargaining with Patriarchy." *Gender and Society*, 3 (2): 274-89.

Lerna, Gerda. 1986. *The creation of patriarchy*, 238. New York and Oxford: University of Oxford Press.

Lloyd, Christopher. 1986. *Explanations in Social History*. London: Basil Blackwell.

Mathurin-Mair, Lucille. 1987. "Women Field Workers in Jamaica during Slavery", *The 1986 Elsa Goveia Memorial Lecture.* Mona, University of the West Indies: Department of History.

Rose, Phyllis. 1988. *Parallel Lives: Five Victorian Marriages*. London: Penguin.

Rowbotham, Sheila. 1992. *Women in Movement: Feminism and Social Action.* London and New York: Routledge.

Rubin, Gayle. 1975."The Traffic in Women: Notes on the 'Political Economy' of Sex." In *Toward an Anthropology of Women*, edited by Rayna Reiter. New York: Monthly Review Press.

Rubin, Gayle. 1984. "Thinking Sex: Notes for a Radical Theory of the Politics of Sexuality." In *Pleasure and Danger: Exploring Female Sexuality*, edited by C. S. Vance, 276. London: Routledge and Kegan Paul.

Silvestrini, Blanca. 1990. "Women and Resistance: Herstory in Contemporary Caribbean History." *The 1989 Elsa Goveia Memorial Lecture.* Mona, University of the West Indies: Department of History.

Tikasingh, Gerad. 1973. "The Establishment of the Indians in Trinidad, 1870-1900". PhD diss., University of the West Indies, Trinidad and Tobago.

Wallach Scott, Joan. 1988. *Gender and the Politics of History*. New York: Columbia University Press.

Weeks, Jeffery. 1986. *Sexuality*, Ellis Horwood/Tavistock, p. 11.

Young, Kate. 1988. "Notes on the Social Relations of Gender." In: *Gender in Caribbean Development*, edited by Patricia Mohammed and Caroline Shepherd, 99. Women and Development Studies Project, Jamaica, Trinidad and Tobago and Barbados: University of the West Indies.

Young, Kate. 1988. *Towards a Theory of the Social Relations of Gender*. London, *Womankind*.

9

Negotiating with Myth and Symbols: The Historical Reconfiguration of Indian Masculinity and Femininity in Trinidad[†]

INTRODUCTION

Myth and symbol are the subterranean foundations on which gender systems are constructed and reinforced. They provide us with metaphors that permeate everyday understandings of gender.[1] The collective lexicon of gender is consciously and unconsciously acquired by both male and female, and derived in part from culturally specific myths, symbols, symbolic representations and rituals that express the gender order of a society. Myths "legitimate power structures, endorse and justify existing social arrangements. They explain politics through symbols and metaphors. They offer truth spiced with eternity." (Duncker 1992, 133)

[†] Originally extracted from a chapter of my 1994 doctoral thesis, other versions of this essay were published in *Portraits of a Nearer Caribbean: Gendered Ideologies*, edited by Christine Barrow. Kingston: Ian Randle Publishers. pp. 391- 413, 1998 and *Matikor: A Social History of Indian Women in the Caribbean*, edited by Rosanne Kanhai Brunton. St. Augustine: School of Continuing Studies, UWI, pp. 62-99, 1999.

Symbolic references are necessary for defining cultural and gender identity and are, for the most part, involuntary. Very rarely do people consciously interpret or decode myths. In some Hindu households in Trinidad, for instance, a stone representation of the *shiva lingam* is generally to be found in a secluded corner of the garden. This sculptured image representing the phallus of Shiva comprises a form in the shape of an elongated egg set in a shallow stone or concrete basin and is the site of morning and evening ritual worship for both men and women. Flowers are placed at its base, and *deyas* – small clay lamps – are lit there at sunset accompanied by ritual prayers. I questioned some of these worshippers, and none of them seemed to find it curious or extraordinary that the object of worship was a phallus. One man said that, for him, praying to this image every day allowed him to focus his thoughts away from evil and practice the discipline of his religion.[2] The women seemed fully aware that they were mediating their prayers through the male phallus. This was not incongruous, given that women were expected to observe the rule of *patidevata*, or worship of one's husband. How the phallus emerged as a symbol to be worshipped, and why this practice continued, is, to my knowledge, not questioned in Trinidad society. Possibly, it has different symbolic meanings for the different people involved. The message is dual, perhaps foremost it represents Shiva and is revered as an emblem of generative power of this deity. Nonetheless by its very form, it privileges male sexuality and, by extension, masculine power at the apex of biological reproduction and cultural renewal.

Over long periods, practices connected with myth and symbol undergo shifts, but only when circumstances force or permit such changes. In February 1868, for instance, 23 years after Indians began arriving in Trinidad, Sarah Morton observed that Indian women used veils in public, or when meeting strangers or male kinfolk. "When they go on the street (or speak to a stranger) they throw over them a straight piece of some light material (either white or coloured) covering the head and gracefully draping the whole figure" (Morton 1916, 51). Covering of one's head was a sign of respect for others, while it also symbolised aspects of femininity expected of an Indian woman - keeping one's body well covered, unexposed. By shrouding the head and obscuring the visage, women symbolically displayed acceptance of the norm that they should be shielded from the watchful eyes of men. By the time they had lived in the colony for a few years, this practice gradually declined, so that the *ohrni* (veil) was worn only on ceremonial or other occasions, when it was incumbent on the woman to defer to men or her elders. Symbolic practices regarding gender are kept alive by both women and men, although in the case of the covering of the head, it was clearly a signifier of male control. In 1940, for instance, Ethel converted from Hinduism to Christianity to marry Albert. She was sixteen at that time and always wore her *orhni*. She tried to relinquish this custom, but Albert, a converted Christian Indian of many years, was against this. For him, the loss of these customs by Indian women meant a loss of identity.

Such symbolic expressions of gender were not practised by women as part of an active political struggle – as "ethnic" dressing may represent today. On the other hand these symbolic expressions are informed by a common denominator; that of acknowledging racial difference. As Aisha Khan comments "For Indo-Trinidadians, racial emblems come from the marked category "Indian religion" which encompasses much of what is recognized as Indian cultural practices."[3] Nor were these signifiers of race or ethnicity always perceived as problematic by women themselves, but as necessary interpretations of the traditional beliefs that sustain familiarity and comfort within a culture. In Trinidad, the early Indian settlers simply resorted to known and customary practices. Recurrent gender practices drew heavily upon sexual imagery transmitted through myths, cultural symbols, artefacts, religious rituals and festivals that expressed ideas about what was expected of male and female characteristics and behaviour. By recurrent gender symbols I am referring on the one hand to the ideas of what constitutes masculinity and femininity – for instance that men hold patriarchal authority in the household and the role of women is to serve not only their men but their children. For instance, the concepts of *pativrata* and *patidevata*, the former referring to the devotion of husband, and the second to the worship of one's husband, were an inherent part of Hindu philosophy and religion, and upheld as an ideal by both men and women. There was, interestingly, no similar precept for men to worship their wives. Attitudes to women existed on a more metaphysical plane, that associated with the worship of female deities, or the reverence for *Ganga Mai* or the Ganges river as earth replenishing mother. Recurrent gender symbols are also expressed through the traditional sexual division of labour, premised on the original biological blueprint in which women are responsible for reproduction and by extension nature, while men are responsible for production and therefore control and shape culture. Often, these ideas are contrary to the actual gender behaviours both sexes display in their daily lives and actions. Ritual beliefs genuinely do undergo changes. The arena of myths and rituals must therefore be seen as a venue of domination, struggle, redefinition and ambivalence, shared and reinterpreted by both men and women, and another sphere in which notions of gender and patriarchy are themselves renegotiated.

In this essay I explore the importance of myth, symbol and ritual for the Indian migrants, the purposes which these myths served to preserve ideas of tradition, and the various channels through which they were renegotiated in Trinidad. These forms were transmitted through traditional sources such as habit and individual memories, ritual renditions by pundits of the sacred texts, literary readings and dramatic performances, and through the cinema.

CONTINUITIES AND CORRESPONDENCES

Indian mythology influenced all Indians in Trinidad despite religious differences, and provided a secure base for many aspects of what constituted Indian culture. It can be argued that Hindu religion and myth are closely entwined, and in conflating the two I am dismissing symbolic interpretations of gender characteristic of the Muslims and Christians. Nirad Chaudhuri argues that Hindu mythology

> has been the most serious obstacle in the way of understanding Hinduism as a religion' and that the relationship between Hindu mythology, cults and devotion are complex, sometimes coinciding, often independent of one another. This separation of religion from mythology is not at all confined to Hinduism, but can be found in all Indo-European religions, especially those of the Greek and Romans (Chaudhuri 1979, 221).

Hinduism was a religion as well as a philosophy and cultural inspiration which fed directly into the national identity of all

Indians. The religious texts of Hinduism were drawn from Sanskrit literature. This was, on the whole, a "romantic literature interwoven with idealism and practical wisdom, and with a passionate longing for spiritual vision" (Mascaro 1962, 10). Thus is derived the notion of Sanskritization, a process which "even brings groups outside of Hinduism into the fold and raises the cultural status of groups already within it" (Misra 1991, 10), and ensured the continuity and unity of Indian culture. Sudhil Kakar writes that "... the Indian celebration of the narrative (and the dramatic) has its roots in one of the more enduring and cherished beliefs of the culture. This particular belief holds that there is another, higher level of reality beyond the shared verifiable, empirical reality of our world, our bodies and our emotions" (Kakar 1989, 3). The importance of the spiritual text in making sense of the mundane realities and despair which survival requires, while providing continuity to generations of men and women about their roles and functions in life, cannot be underestimated. For the Indians who settled in Trinidad, what were regarded as holy texts were derived from both a classical and contextual mode, the classical based on the original literary sources, and the contextual offering variations depending on the areas from which the migrants had come. The deviations in myth, symbol and ritual, like that of language, moved towards standardization and selective adaptation by those who conveyed them and those who believed and practised them.

Clear differences or divergences among the three religious groupings meant that symbolic interpretations of written and orally transmitted customs would also be variously transformed. Those who had converted to Christianity were sometimes viewed as outsiders, "westernized" in dress and eating habits, who had relinquished the practices of Hindu culture. In April 1931, for example, the *East Indian Weekly* carried a letter from Pundit Sahadeo Tiwary to the *Trinidad Guardian* which attacked the Honourable Seeran Teelucksingh and A. C. B. Singh, both Christianized Indians who agreed with the Government-proposed Hindu Divorce Bill. Tiwary and 31 other pundits had signed a protest to the Governor against this bill, vilifying Teelucksingh and Singh for their interference. "If it is that they were tired of being Christians and want to be Hindus, well I invite them both to call upon me and I will teach them free of cost and at least make them honest and true Hindus. If they will not do this then I strongly advise them to keep out of the question which does not concern them. ...Take my advice Mr. Teelucksingh, keep out of the Hindu religion and Hindu customs" (*East Indian Weekly*, 4 April, 1931). There appeared to be greater cohesion between the Hindus and Muslims on some matters. Non-Christian education was one issue that brought them together. On Sunday 3rd November 1929, a mass meeting of Hindus and Muslims was scheduled to support the resolution on education as it affected non-Christians (*East Indian Weekly*, 25 October, 1929).

Despite the different paths along which Hinduism, Islam and Christianity had progressed from the period of indenture to the first half of the twentieth century, there was tremendous overlap in the cultural arena where ethnic identity was being expressed. Whether one was Hindu, Muslim or Christian, there were symbolic aspects of Indian culture which predated the development of contemporary Hinduism and affected all Indians. In August 1929, for instance, Reverend C. F. Andrews visited Princes Town as the guest of Dr. and Mrs. Frank Mahabir and later of the East Indian National Association. "A large and enthusiastic gathering of Indians and others attended to hear Mr. Andrews deliver to the Indian community messages from their brethren in other parts of the world. He brought messages of love and greetings to them from the three greatest Indians. The three greatest Indians were Mahatma Gandhi, Rabindranath Tagore and the greatest woman, poet and statesman of India, Sarojini Naidu" (*Trinidad Guardian*, 8 August, 1929).

In October 1934, the "Indian News and Views" of the *Trinidad Guardian* celebrated the life and work of the late Mian Syed Abdul Aziz Sahib, who had died in August 1927, as a pioneer of Islam in Trinidad. He was cited as a founder of the East Indian National Association in 1893, and of the Islamic Guardian Association in 1906. The report noted that his funeral in 1927 had been attended by "thousands of Muslims, Hindus and Christians, included about 300 ladies, and was testimony to the high estimation in which he was held." Among the other positions he had filled was that of the Presidency of the Tackveeyatul Islamic Association, on the basis of which he was often called upon to represent the entire Indian population. The report concluded that, "As an adviser, he possessed those sterling qualities which won for him the affection and respect of the entire East Indian community" (*Trinidad Guardian*, 21 October, 1934).

Another instance of a collective feeling can be seen in a visit by Pundit Bhaskaranand of Bihar, described as one of the Leaders of the Arya Samaj movement in India, a Missionary of the International Aryan League and a great Sanskrit scholar. "Under the auspices of the San Fernando Branch of the Tackveeyatul-Islamic Association of Trinidad and Tobago Inc., Pundit Bhaskara-nand will deliver an address tomorrow at Prince Albert Street Mosque Hall at 7.30 p.m., his subject being "India Today." This meeting, held in the Prince Albert Street Mosque Hall, attracted non-Muslims as well, including Pundit Harripersad Sharma of Trinidad. Pundit Bhaskaranand's lecture focused on the notion of Indian unity. He spoke of the "historical life of Mahatma Gandhi in his young days in Africa how he sincerely fought for the rights of Indians" and "also gave an outline of the history of the Congress, which is the most successful political organization of India" (*Sunday Guardian*, 5th July, 1936). Later reports of Pundit Bhaskaranand's visit noted that he delivered several lectures on interesting Indian topics at various places (*Trinidad Guardian*, 12 July, 1936).

In general, due to their demographic dominance, and because Hinduism symbolized the essence of Indianness, there was a tendency for Hinduism to be representative of Indian culture. Hinduism was itself a pantheistic religion, and allowed the inclusion of other icons, rituals and gods, thereby embracing the totality of the Indian experience. The following observation was made in 1893:

> It is curious to note that many immigrants who are not Christians visit annually a Catholic shrine at Siparia, which is not very far from the Indian settlements of "Faizabad" and "Roussillac." in the ward of Oropuche. ...As far as it can be ascertained, the statue of the Virgin Mary, which is in the Church at Siparia and honoured as the "Divina Pastora" was brought there by some Spanish monks of the Capuchin order in about the year 1730 (Comins 1893, 38).

Thomas Harricharan, a Roman Catholic priest, observed that, by 1890, the statue was attracting large numbers of East Indians, especially Hindus but also including Muslims. He suggests that their attraction to this symbol was understandable. The Goddess

Kali, who was superimposed onto La Divina Pastora, was the goddess of famine, destruction, plagues, epidemics, illnesses and other disasters. "Indentureship in Trinidad was a gruelling time for the East Indians ...when they saw that favours were granted through the intercession of Mary as represented by the statue, they readily came to her and saw her as Mother Kali." (Harricharan 1981). By the twentieth century, the festival of La Divina Pastora, held on Good Friday morning, became a full syncretic devotional event known as the Festival of Sipari Mai, with La Divina Pastora as Sipari Ke Mai representing the goddess Kali to the population of Trinidad (Khan 1990).

In such ways, the migrants and children of migrants in Trinidad drew on their past and reconstructed their present and future in Trinidad, negotiating with new symbols yet maintaining continuity.

DIRECT TRANSMITTERS OF MYTH AND SYMBOL

Ritual religious occasions
The most important venues for transmission were the religious prayer meetings and festivals where the pundits and imams would have before them a captive audience. A large proportion of the older men and women were illiterate in English, so debates carried on through newspapers or debating clubs appealed only to a limited group. The population census data for 1921 records that, of the total Indian population for that year, 13,563 were able to read and write, 1,829 were able to read only, and 106,028 could neither read nor write English, a language which was still secondary to the Indian population. It is doubtful whether many Indians could both read and write Hindi. The vast majority of the migrants were drawn from a class of uneducated labourers,[4] and their education in Trinidad, whether in Hindi or English, was not a priority of the Crown Colony government. Many of them continued their religious instruction through prayer meetings and festive occasions at which the teachings of the sacred texts were recited.

The recruitment system of indentureship made little distinction between the caste of Indians, other than to attract its majority from the lower castes, thought to be more suited to agricultural labour. On the estates and villages, those who claimed to be Brahmin, and were learned, were accepted by the indentured, and later free population, as religious leaders of the Hindu population. They were the repositories for Sanskrit, old Hindi, and the sacred scriptures (Jha 1985, 16). A third-generation pundit, Ragbir, whose grandfather is thought to have come to Trinidad in 1845, recalls when he worked on the Orange Grove Estate as a driver that, "there were few Brahmins on the barracks. The few educated ones who slipped through became pundits afterwards. (On the barracks) they kept Ramayan and readings among the Jehajis on evenings" (La Guerre 1985, 188). Jankey Tiwari Maharaj, who came to Trinidad as an indentured labourer in 1907 and was sent to the Waterloo estate, explained, "the Pundit on the barracks was the leader, someone to stand up as both father and mother." (La Guerre 1985, 193) Avinase, a female Indian, born in Freeport in 1904 to Brahmin parents, said that her father would bathe in the morning and read the Ramayan, perform Howan rituals and was sometimes late for work and harassed by the driver on the estate. "He taught the boys in the family to do puja each day." Sacred ritual knowledge, as was customary at the time, was being taught to men while being preached to women.

The development of Islam was similar. Those who could read the Koran became interpreters of the religion. Sadhul explained that the village of Lengua shared one imam with many surrounding villages since he was the only one who knew how to read Arabic. These interpreters of the texts were few, and male, and became the purveyors of religious doctrine in the new society, interpreting the scriptures for their eager flock with the fundamentalism of new converts. The texts were selectively shaped and moulded by the tellers of these myths, both consciously and unconsciously, in their own patriarchal interests.

The transmission of symbols through religion was largely carried out in pujas or prayer meetings and functions in which large audiences were addressed. As early as 1868, Reverend John Morton cites a visit to a "Mohammedan house of worship - a nice little place with galvanized roof."[5] These venues continued to grow in each village or were centrally located in the nearest town. By 1934, the venues had become more sophisticated and expansive communal meeting places. A newspaper report in September of this year indicates that:

At a meeting of San Fernando Hindus it was decided to hold a *Bhagwat* prayer meeting at the San Fernando Hindu Temple which was recently erected by public subscription among the Hindus of the South. As a result of this meeting the *Bhagwat* was started on Saturday, September 15 and will be completed today. The people of San Fernando and the neighbouring villages have contributed to this religious function. Every night there is a large gathering to be observed at this prayer meeting to which the public are invited. Ramnarine Pundit, a young Trinidadian is the officiating priest. This has been the third occasion on which the *Bhagwat* is being read at this temple. The first and second *Bhagwat* aided materially in the erection of the present temple, which is built upon modern lines with more accommodation than the previous one (*Sunday Guardian*, 23 September, 1934)

Symbolic and ritualistic reminders of the teachings of the sacred scriptures were also conveyed at the various festivals that were becoming an entrenched part of Indian culture in Trinidad by the second decade of the twentieth century. For instance, on Thursday 27th September, 1917 it was reported that the annual festival "in connection with the Mohammedan rites known as E-dud-do-ha was celebrated by the Mohammedans" of Chaguanas with Imam Niamat Meah officiating and offering a bull as sacrifice. The new society was just becoming aware of the rites and rituals of Indian society and integrating them into the cultural life of Trinidad. During the First World War, when the Hindu festival of Ramleela was celebrated in Chaguanas, a newspaper report noted: "This festival will depict the destroying of Rawan by Ram, and the East Indians sincerely hope that the same fate will be meted out to the Germans by our Allies" (*Trinidad Guardian*, 7 October, 1917).

By the next two decades, the celebration of this and other Hindu and Muslim festivals that conveyed the messages of these religions in a more accessible form was of tremendous importance to the Indian community and attracted large crowds. The Hindu festival of Divali and the Muslim festivals of Eid ul Adha and Eid ul Zohar were more private celebrations for the adherents of these faiths, while those of Ramleela for the Hindus and Hosay for the Muslims were more public events.[6]

Among the Hindu population, and other non-Hindu Indians who participated in village festivals, the Ramleela or Ramlilla was particularly outstanding in that it re-casted, through drama, a fundamental myth from the most important of the sacred texts, the Holy Ramayana. "People in this village know more about the Ramayana not from what they read, but from going to the Ramleela" (Maharaj 1987, 12). Many, if not all, of these festivals conveyed symbolic and social expectations of masculinity and femininity. Up to the 1950s, both male and female parts in the Ramleela were played by men. Women were not allowed to perform in public. There was participation by both Hindus and Muslims in festivals that required the construction of costumes and re-enactment of scriptural scenes, thus merging the influence and effects of both religions on the Indian population at large. One writer tells of an encounter with an old man in Dow Village, California. Enquiring about his intimate knowledge of the Ramleela story, she learnt that he was a Muslim, but a member of the group which organized the performances each year (Maharaj 1987, 11).

It is useful to examine the scope and effects of one festival in transmitting gender messages. The festival of Ramleela appealed to a considerable proportion of the Hindu and non-Hindu population as it was carried out as a large outdoor public theatre. Food and drink were sold on the grounds and there was a festive atmosphere for days while the *nataka* or folk theatre was performed.[7] Both the public performance, as well as the opportunity the occasion offered for mixing, assumed that it attracted huge crowds. On 21st October, 1934, the "Indian News and Views" column reported that "The Indian pageant known as the Ramlilla Festival ended with *eclat* on Thursday last at the Waterloo Estate Savannah where gaiety and enthusiasm ran free among thousands who took part in this ancient and sacred drama." A full and vivid description of the event was printed.

> This festival is held yearly by Hindus to commemorate the battle and victory of Ram and others as recited in the Lanka Kand of the Holy Book, the Ramayana.

The gigantic black demon Ravan, at the conclusion of the festival, was burnt to ashes. Ram, Latchman, Bharat, and Chatoorgoon, the four Princes, were gorgeously dressed in princely style. The other actors displayed costumes of striking and variegated colours. The atmosphere was filled with the melodious chanting and singing of sacred verses and songs from the Lanka Kand of the Ramayana (*Sunday Guardian*, 21 October, 1934).

The Ramayana relates the story of Rama, the eldest son of King Ayodhya. An envious stepmother, who covets the throne for her own son, causes Rama to spend 14 years in exile in the forest accompanied only by his loyal brother Laksmana and his devoted wife Sita, married to him at age six. Sita is kidnapped by Ravana (Rawan), the demonic king of Lanka (Gaur 1980, 23). Despite Rawan's clever advances, Sita maintains fidelity to Rama. Kelvin Singh has observed that, "the legend of Sita, wife of the epic hero, Ram, and the ideal of female fidelity, was chanted by the pundits, who expounded from the Scriptural verses of the Ramayana, the exploits of the hero and the constancy of the wife in the face of adversity. At the numerous household prayer-meetings, adults and children were religiously fed with the epic" (Singh 1985, 37). Up to the present, Sita is presented through the retelling of mythology as the ideal woman, possessing virtues of female love and devotion, a role model to all Hindu women on how they should behave in their daily lives.

By 1934, such festivals were an established part of Indian culture in Trinidad. The *Sunday Guardian* of 21 October, 1934, carried on one page: a commentary on the Ramleela festival held at Waterloo Estate Savannah; a notice that the festival at Dow Village, California, would end on 22nd October; another notice that the Ramleela festival which had begun on Tuesday, October 9th, at the Tacarigua Savannah, had come to an end on the Thursday before; and a report that read, "The Hindu festival of Ramlilla[8] had its final celebration at Cedar Hill Estate Savannah on Wednesday last, and in spite of the inclement weather there was a large gathering. The scene was reminiscent of an Oriental Pageant." A photograph was published showing the all-male officials and friends at the Ramlilla Festival in Waterloo including: Major C. L.

Hanington, Managing-Editor of the Trinidad Guardian, Mr. A. C. B. Singh, Rajoe Singh, Narad Moonee, Pundit Ramchand, Mr. C. B. Mathura, Pundit Seeram, Pundit Rambharose, Sadhu Kadarnath Singh, Pundit Bridgelal Maharaj, Pundit Rampersad (the officiating priest) and Tal Bahadur Maharaj. Women were captured in another photograph on this same page as part of the audience, never as the performers or organizers, visiting dignitaries, or religious leaders.

As the Pundits and Imams were the transmitters of these myths and ritual knowledge, it is no coincidence that the symbols and images of women were those that secured patriarchal control. One element of patriarchal control which was enforced was that Indian women were not allowed the freedom to have sexual encounters before marriage, and were not allowed to marry outside of their race. In Trinidad, this concern for preserving the virtue of Indian girls and women had possibly attained other dimensions than would have been encountered in nineteenth and early twentieth century India. The Rawan of the Ramayana was portrayed as a black man, as he was of Dravidian extract. The portrayal of the myth in public theatre form took on additional relevance in the setting of Trinidad, where Indian women could not help but come into contact with black men. One writer suggests: "How else can we explain the seeming preoccupation of Indian men with Indian women being seduced by black men long before such liaisons were commonplace. There must have always been a subconscious fear that the women would be unable to resist Rawan's advances" (Johnson 1984, 27).

Hindu philosophy depicts female sexuality with a duality frightening to the male while it presents a much less contradictory picture of male sexuality. Kalidasa's long epic poem, entitled *Kumara-Sambhava*, is the mythological story of the marriage of Siva and Parvati and the birth of their son, Kartikeya. Siva was one of the major deities, with no smear of imperfection on his characterization. Parvati is worshipped as the Mother Goddess, Durga-Kali, a mixture which evokes extremely contradictory images in Hindu religious practice – she is goddess of both wealth and destruction. Chaudhuri comments, "after describing how devotion and austerities brought about the marriage of Siva and Parvati and thus achieved what the arrows of Cupid could not, Kalidasa makes a staggering *volte face*, and in the eighth canto of the poem describes their sexual enjoyments with a frankness and gusto which is not surpassed even by Casanova" (Chaudhuri 1979, 224). The Siva of devotion has become a personal god of love, while the Siva of mythology is allowed the extremes of pleasure and passion.[9]

From the outset, whether in human form or as goddesses, women alone are possessed of feared dual characteristics. "On the one hand woman is fertile, benevolent, bestower of prosperity; on the other hand she is considered aggressive, malevolent and destructive. This dual character manifests itself in the goddesses as well; while there are dangerous, aggressive, malevolent goddesses like Kali and Durga; there are equally important goddesses like Laxmi, Saraswati and Mariamman who are benevolent" (Desai and Krishnaraj 1990, 28). The duality is explained through the logic of other cultural concepts embedded in Hindu philosophy. The female consists of *shakti* – energy/power, the energizing principle of the universe, and *prakti* – nature, the undifferentiated matter of the universe. The latter is uncultured and therefore dangerous, sustaining the idea that women are impure, easily polluting, and themselves polluted. In metaphorical terms, this has meant that the female, as uncultured nature, must be controlled by the male. At the same time, the alliance between male and female is presented through mythology as a complementary one. The male godhead is passive, abstract and powerless unless activated by the power of the goddess. Gaur explains that, "Benevolent goddesses are those who have transferred control of their sexuality (power-*shakti*, nature-*prakti*) to their husbands. ...Married the goddess is always good. Unmarried she can be good or bad. She can be good if she herself has achieved control of her power, either through extreme austerities or (particularly sexual) abstinence. But if she has failed to do so, she remains nature (*prakti*) and pure nature is always unpredictable and dangerous" (Gaur 1980: 18). Such ideas of femininity and masculinity are explicit in the lived culture of a people. They are subtle, understated but evident in all the unwritten roles and taboos which guard the boundaries of gender. They were transmitted in Trinidad and sustained by the religious retelling of mythology and philosophy in much the same way as the ongoing construction of gender in India itself was continuously built and rebuilt through the telling and elaboration of the myths originally derived from the ancient history of the subcontinent. When the migrants left the shores of India, these myths and symbols were part of their past. "The Ramayana sustained our forefathers in Trinidad. This journey they had taken was comparable to that of the temporary exile of Ram and thus women here were to be like Sita, self-suffering wives, faithful to the end."[10] The importance of securing references to the Ramayana, the idealization of characters of the Ramayana, was crucial. Placed in the lowest class in the new society, and deprived of the cultural sustenance to which they would have been accustomed, these myths and rituals helped to transform the mundane of the everyday to epic quality (Maharaj n.d.), and persisted as a reference point around which gender and ethnicity was demarcated.

It would be misleading to infer from all of this that the situation was a static one. It is precisely here that we find contradictions in mythology playing themselves out in real life among men and women in Trinidad, thereby shifting traditional notions of gender. Not all women were Sitas or Mother Lakshmis, nor were all men Ramas or Krishnas. Men had the power through the male dominated areas of religion and public life to constantly reinterpret their positions in their favour, and it served their interests to maintain a patriarchal lead. Mohania, the daughter of India-born Maharani, who came as a single indentured labourer in 1916, recalls that her knowledge of what was expected of her had come from hearing the Ramayana. "You see when you go to the Ramayan *yag* they had pundits reading and they will read part and explain and tell you this is so and that is so. They will read it in Hindi and explain it in English." The pundits had said that Raja Dasarath, King of the Kosalas and father of Rama, had had seven wives, implying that men could remarry up to seven times. While a widower was allowed to remarry, the life of a widow could be quite untenable – she was not allowed to participate in her children's weddings and other rituals as she was considered *asubh* or inauspicious. Mohania had carried out such rituals expected of her on the death of her first husband. However circumstances in Trinidad, both during indentureship and in the first decades of the twentieth century, had allowed changes to these ritual practices and expectations. Her own mother had remarried after completing her indentureship, and so did Mohania. She did not remarry in the traditional way but in the style frequently followed by the non-Indian population, that of a common-law or unregistered union, and, moreover, to a non-Indian man. While Mohania was aware of the ideals required of Indian femininity, she challenged these expectations in her further life choices and actions.

Orality and transmission of gender ideology
There were different oral sources for transmission of gender ideology. One was the collection of folk and religious songs[11] sung at weddings. Others were rituals associated with the birth of a child, birth and marriage being the two rites of passage in which women's presence was obviously necessary and acceptable. Sookhoo recollected that, "Long time ladies never go to funeral, never go to wedding, every lady keep home. When the wedding go, every lady merry theyself at home, they eh going to follow wedding, only men go." But he was referring to the fact that women were originally not allowed to follow the wedding procession from the house of the groom to that of the bride's where the actual ceremony would take place, a practice common to both Hindu and Muslim weddings. Instead, the extent to which they were allowed to participate in this public event was established by their stipulated female role. This was explained by Rupanee. Women's roles were ritualistic as well as functional, but never to be confused with the demonstration of responsibilities or coming into the public gaze which men had at such times:

> If it have a wedding somewhere, they invite you, house to house, the *nau*[12] come and tell you, you have invitation for three days ...or he tell you that you have invitation for one week to come and sing and come and do a little work and help them. When you go you have *dhal* to grind, after that we make mango *anchar*, we make *cuchela*, we make *kurma*, well that take a whole week. You going home, you coming sometime half night, ten o'clock, eleven o'clock night. In daylight you do your own work at your home, when evening come, you go again, a set of ladies.
>
> When from Friday now, you go from early time because today is *saffron*.[13] ...When the evening come, they bring the boy or the girl come, and the pundit would come and do the ceremony and all ah we ladies will sing and have a good time, and put the *saffron* for the boy or girl, and they sing and eat whatsoever they

have and spend until 11, 12 o'clock night and then we go home. Next day you go back again same helping doing everything for the night, because is cooking night tonight and it have plenty thing to do. People will sing and dance the whole night. A set of dancers you order – you have to pay a little money for this, is male dancers only, not no ladies - and the best dance you could ever see.

As singers rather than dancers in the background of wedding feasts and ceremonies, women were clearly important as transmitters of orality through song. One researcher recorded thirty songs surrounding wedding rituals (Maharaj n.d.). These strengthened ideas of community, reinforcing the value and respect accorded each person in the extended family, which had many gender specific implications. In each song, relationships among family members, kin members, and between male and female are clearly defined, both in terms of general interaction, and within the rituals of the wedding cycle. Forms of ritual respect and address were very specific. Particular titles were used for mother's sister, father's sister, mother's brother's wife, father's brother' wife and so on. In all lyrical allusions, the paternal grandfather was mentioned before the maternal grandfather, reflecting the patrifocal centering of the culture, which dictated that the boy or girl belonged in the household of the father and father's father. Several of the 30 songs recorded demonstrate the low status of the *bhowjee* or daughter-in-law, who was married into the household, compared to the visiting married sister. Many songs describe the tears of the mother and the satisfaction of the father at the marriage of the child. The stereotyping of desirable traits of the bride and groom are also to be found:

> My sister is walking hesitantly
> She is the daughter of a modest woman
> The bridegroom is rushing along
> He is the illegitimate son of a cattle-tender
> My daughter is like a gem, but the groom
> is black like a mole (Song 25, Maharaj n.d.).

The bride is young, virtuous, her mother is respected and she comes from a wealthy family, all the traits that make her desirable as a female, and material for a good wife. What of the male? His illegitimacy, references to "his rushing along" suggest a certain coarseness. He is, nonetheless, still acceptable as a bridegroom.

From the mid-1930s onwards, actual renditions of these songs by wedding guests and kin began to decline in importance, to be replaced by recorded film music. A chorus of human voices could not compete with the electronic speakers now being used on festive or religious occasions. The performed songs were rendered in Hindi by village amateurs, and lacked the verve of a large back-up orchestra. They could not compete with Bombay recordings. Technology began to replace customary tradition in the transmission of culture. There was also the declining importance of Hindi as a spoken language, and the influence of another Hindu sect – the Arya Samaj – which frowned upon folk-expressive forms (Maharaj n.d.). The result was that both these occasions and songs, as the conduit of symbols influencing the behaviour expected of women (and men), also diminished in impact over time. In general, how women internalized and either accommodated or challenged these symbols is much less evident in the written records. These are to be found in their actions. Especially, perhaps, in the sphere of individual sexual relations in which we find confrontations with the established and expected norms.

With the decline in ritual songs, there was the evolution of Indian folk tales – *kissas* – derived from old myths and stories, but also indigenous to Trinidad. These served a function similar to the stories rendered from the scriptures.[14] Prior to widespread access to cinema, radio and television, folk tales were important sources of evening entertainment. The *kissas* introduced the major characters of the ancient stories and new ones into Caribbean literature including fictional kings, queens, princes and princesses. Local experiences were grafted on to the tales recollected from India. In telling and retelling, these newly-derived tales fell into the category of "folk wisdom," distilling the collective experiences of reconstituted life among Indians in Trinidad into moral statements. Several collections exist, gathered primarily by male Indian scholars or activists, and published over the last two decades - an indication that their preservation is important for the continuing definition of Indian identity in Trinidad. In his introduction to a collection of folk tales entitled *Salt and Roti*, Kenneth Parmasad observes:

> In traditional Indian society, ...this crucial role of storyteller was performed by the women. This function of the women was decisive in ensuring cultural continuity. The fact that of all the folk tales which I have researched, more than eighty percent have come from the lips of women, is well in keeping with this tradition. Judging from the tales themselves, two trends may be identified in the process of the cultural consolidation of the Indians in the Caribbean. On the one hand, there is continuity, on the other, there is innovation (Parmasad 1984: xiv).

Commenting on another collection of Indo-Trinidadian folk-tales, collated by Ashram Maharaj, literary scholar Kenneth Ramchand identifies the reasons for such innovations: "consciously or unconsciously ...these tales register the new environment of the indentured Indian. The "Fisherman and the Conch-Shell"[15] for example, is a moral fable about how envy of our neighbour's prosperity makes us unable to be happy with our own good fortune" (Ramchand 1990, vii).

The themes of gender conflict and gender relations are recurrent ones in the older as well as the more recently created folk tales. Mahabir records one folk tale entitled "Oman" (woman) narrated by Sankar Ram, an ex-indentured Indian male born in 1879. This tale is essentially an illustration of the capacity of women to dupe men. The woman asks her husband if he knew "women's tricks." He replied he did not, and she proceeds to show him by carrying out a trick on him. While the tale may have been based on one recalled from India, the idiomatic expressions and local references used by the teller situate it in the new society (Mahabir 1988). In another tale, the promiscuity of women and distrust of men is revealed. Entitled, "*A Dishonest World*," it begins as follows:

> It had this man who had a pretty wife, when he go to wuk the wife saga[16] boy used to come and make joke and thing. When the wife see 4.00 o'clock she used to take she *datwan*[17] and sit down by the door to scrub she mouth. The husband say, "Hear nah you go dead you know, you now scrubbing you mouth." The wife

replied, "When ah doh see you ah does can't eat or do anything, ah can't live without you" (Maharaj 1990, 6).

The gist of the story is that the husband suspects his wife of having another lover, and confirms it by spying on her. He tells his employer, the Raja or King, that he wants a week off, and proceeds to traverse the country to see if he can find an honest person. At the end of his travels, he comes to the conclusion that no one was honest, having found that the sadhu or wise man he first met was dishonest, and the Rani, or King's wife, was cuckolding the King with his own groomsman. He concludes, "even god is worse." He decides he might as well stay with the dishonesty he knows.

At a subconscious level, this story might deal with the displacement of the individual trying to recreate his world in a culture that has been uprooted and transplanted. This man's journey to discover honesty and truth seems to be linked with the Brahminical ideal where, in man's four life stages, the last is a search for knowledge through abstinence and self-abnegation. It also might be linked to the hero (Rama) of the epic Ramayana, and his journey into the wilderness. Rama's 14-year-long banishment from the civilized world is caused by the undesirable traits of his stepmother, Queen Kaikeyi, who wanted her own son, Bharat, to be crowned instead of Rama, the eldest son of King Dasaratha. Sita, recently wed to Rama, refuses to part from him and goes off with him into the wilderness, fulfilling all the expectations of the dutiful and loving wife.

> For the faithful woman follows where her wedded lord may lead,
> In the banishment of Rama, Sita's exile is decreed
> (Ramayana 1978, 111: 1: 34).

In the stories as retold in Trinidad there is a major disruption in the configuration of the female protagonist. In "*A Dishonest World*," the tale is premised on the sure knowledge of his wife's infidelity. In several of the stories in this small collection of folk-tales, quite a few wives are depicted as cheating on their husbands. This is inconsistent with the image of the faithful and dutiful wives of Sanskrit mythology. The suggestion is that, with the loss of patriarchal control in Trinidad there emerges the other side of the duality which characterizes woman, which they are deemed capable of, due to their "untamed nature," and which men must vigilantly keep in check.

A different problem of gender is presented in the tale, "*The Challenge.*" Here, conflict arises between families when a Hindu boy wants to marry a Muslim girl. It seems that Muslims and Hindus lived together harmoniously in the established villages – until the problem of intermarriage cropped up. Esau, born in 1917 in Cane Farm Village, Tacarigua, of Muslim parents, was told that "the relationship was so close that when my mother had to go sometimes in the cane field and so and I was a little kid, this Hindu woman would nurse me." This folk-tale signifies the new challenges that were now being made to the rigidly structured system of gender relations:

> It had this Muslim family and this Hindu family. The musulman (muslim) had a daughter name Zalina. The Hindu man had a son name Kishan. Kishan and Zalina really like one another since they was small. The Muslim and Hindu parents never like that. The other part was that Kishan family was poor and Zalina family had plenty money. When Zalina and Kishan finish read in school the two ah dem get wuk. Now they feel they big they want to get married. But the parents doh want dem to marry. Kishan father say dat Zalina and dem is *madinga* (bastard) people. Zalina father say Kishan and dem is *chamar* (low caste) people and dem wouldn't turn muslim. Kishan and Zalina well like one another but they can't find no solution because they parents too stubborn. Kishan tell Zalina, "Dis eh go wuk, we go ha to run away or something." Zalina replied, "I go gladly do dat because I love you and I want to be with you all me life"[18]   (Maharaj 1990, 32).

Despite the fact that Zalina's father was a Muslim, he is dissatisfied with the low caste status of Kishan, illustrating that Muslims were themselves not indifferent to the caste system among Hindus. Especially significant is the fact that Zalina and Kishan, independently of their parents' notions of marriage by arrangement, had "fallen in love" and were willing to endure the censure of their families and village by eloping. It was clear, though, that both Zalina and Kishan also had independent means with which to challenge their parents' authority – both had "finish read in school and get wuk," echoing a fear which Indian parents had, of sending their girls to school alongside boys. This challenge to religious obligations, to the practice of caste endogamy, together with a shift to individual choice and a notion of romantic love, desired by both girl and boy, signalled the changes which were taking place in Trinidad.

TRANSMISSION THROUGH LITERARY SOURCES

Although women were the village story tellers, and the other occasions on which symbols were passed on were through the practices and festivals of the religions of Hinduism and Islam, men were the chief conveyors of myth and symbol in the more public sense up until the first half of the twentieth century. Visiting male missionaries from India lectured to audiences on the ancient culture of India, and many Trinidadian-born Indian men became carriers of symbolic messages in their own work, for example Seepersad Naipaul and C. B. Mathura in journalism, and lawyers and public officers like F. E. M. Hosein, Frank Mahabir and the Honourable S. Teelucksingh. Though the literacy rate was low, messages and news items from newspapers had a relatively wide reach. In fact, the low circulation and ultimate failure of the *East Indian Weekly* as a commercial enterprise was due to the fact that one newspaper could serve an entire village. The one or two persons who could read would buy and read the newspaper aloud to the others (Samaroo 1977) The newspapers reflected, as well as reinforced, ideas of gender and ethnic identity. In 1935, Asshia, an Indian man, was accused of the murder of his wife Poptee and Rampersad, her lover. The newspaper reports that "when Asshia arrived at Rampersad's house, Poptee knew that he would have seen her and why did she not open the back door of the house and run out. She did not do that but with the characteristics of an Indian woman went to make peace between the two men" (*Trinidad Guardian*, 11 July, 1935).

What were the "characteristics of an Indian woman"? Other articles, including some reprinted from India, throw light on such allusions. In an article entitled "Indian Womanhood" reproduced in the *Trinidad Guardian*, Mrs K. Shivpuri, BA, B.T. (Alwar) of India cites the ideals of the Brahminic tradition:

> Man has always been, so to say, incomplete without a woman. He cannot perform any religious rites (Yagna) without his wife taking part in it. ... People think that because an Indian wife sacrifices so much for her husband she is like a slave to him. This is of course far from the truth. The ideal Indian woman has always done her best to keep her husband very happy and comfortable, even at the risk of her happiness. If she makes any sacrifice it is because of her love of and devotion to her husband. ... She sacrifices because she gets pleasure in making her companion comfortable (*Trinidad Guardian*, 6 August, 1936).

Mrs. Shivpuri elaborates the sacrifices required of Indian women in relation to their male partners:

> If a modern girl ...wants real happiness, lasting love, she would not go after equality, nor crave for it but should behave in a better manner in the old Indian way, look after her husband's welfare, and when that educated man of today finds that his wife has the goodness and qualities of the ancient loving wife, he himself will come round and respect and love her more that she could ever expect (*Trinidad Guardian*, 6 August, 1936).

Indian womanhood is depicted here through the eyes of the male and defined only in terms of a relationship to the male. "It was their unbounded love and sacrifice for their husband that they were known for so far." According to Mrs Shivpuri and others around this time, the ideal Indian woman does not attempt to challenge this balance in gender relations, which requires that women always sublimate their needs to those of their husbands. As a consequence, this kind of presentation reinforces the Indian Brahminic ideal of men as masters and providers, women as commodity and possession of the male, whether as daughter, wife or mother (Desai and Khrishnaraj 1990, 27).

There was a stream of such reports. The "Indian News and Views" published the prescribed order of ceremony at Hindu marriages, its source cited as the *Sacred Book of the Hindu Matrimonial Ceremony*. At this time, this was generally relayed to the audience and the bride and groom in Hindi. Since the majority of Indians did not speak Hindi, the full impact of what was being said within the ritual marriage ceremony was lost. The publication of the text in English in the newspaper made the information more accessible to a larger majority of the Indian population. The expected reply of the bridegroom to the officiating pundit was reproduced along with the bride's promise.

Bridegroom:
I call upon Brahma, Vishnu and Mahase, known as Trimurthy, the Sun, the Moon, the Stars and the four winds of the Earth, and the vast assembly that is present here tonight, to bear witness of my promise to you. Having acceded to your request, it is but fair that I in return should expect from you (the bride) a similar promise for the upkeep of the five following conditions.

(1) You should so conduct yourself in society, as never to bring disgrace or dishonour to our honoured name.

(2) In my absence you are expected to accommodate and entertain any acquaintance or visitors to our home according to our means and their social standing; and your conduct towards them should at all times be beyond reproach.

(3) Should there ever occur at any time, any domestic difference or friction between us, you will ever bear in mind that such difference does not exist exclusively in our home; it is a curse or a blessing that exists in every human home. You are therefore, not supposed to leave my home for every such difference, for such an action will lead to public scandal and an ultimate separation which is not consistent with the domestic history of our forefathers.

(4) You are to be punctual, regular and careful in your domestic duties so that your husband not suffer any inconvenience.

(5) Tonight by the grace of God I hope to share with you a comfortable home but, should at any time adversity be our lot, you are expected to share it with me as readily and hopefully. Not that when adversity comes, you will leave me to my own devices and find a more comfortable home. As I have promised to cherish and work for your welfare, similarly, you are expected to do the same to me. Should it be my lot to suffer from any serious malady, or accident that would make me incapable of gaining a livelihood, you should also assist me.

The Bride replies:
I readily give you the required undertaking and call upon Brahma, Vishnu and Mahase, known as the Trimurty, and the Sun, the Moon, the Stars and the four winds of the Earth and the vast assembly that is present here tonight to bear witness of my promise (*Sunday Guardian*, 11 November, 1934).

That such ideas were internalized as much by women themselves, perhaps more so among the Brahmin or higher caste women, is seen in the following outburst by Mrs. Dropatie Naipaul, wife of Seepersad Naipaul and daughter of one of the earliest and most highly respected pundits in Trinidad, Pundit Capildeo.

You see a woman has a place in this world and when she abuse that place, she has lost the thing they call womanhood because she is no more that woman. ..I decided I would never fail in my duty. That is something very important and not every woman has that in them. I could afford to tell you – if they have it they wouldn't be as slack. I talking about Indian people, forget about the others. My sisters all felt the same way about their duty as wife and mother. It was an honour to me – everyday practice meant that I have a duty to do every day and I must fulfil my duty every day and that is a duty which people fail to do now.[19]

If women were expected to be dutiful, obedient, sacrificial and forgiving, what did the masculine role constitute? In 1926, when she was eleven years old, Phoolo, of the lower (*chamar*) caste, was married to a young man of fifteen. She had three children with him and was committed to the marriage until and after his death, never remarrying. He, unfortunately, did not reciprocate this loyalty. A few years after their marriage, when she had already had two of her three children, he began a lifelong habit of drinking and violent abuse, openly consorting with other women and even having children with them. He brought very little of his earnings into their household and she was forced to work in a nearby cotton plantation to support the family. Her reason for remaining with him was partly due to the children, and partly because her family expected this.

While, in general, the reproduction of traditional gender identity was only incumbent on women, in the collective ethnic identity being formulated by the literate Indian population, and in the actual reconstitution of Indian culture in Trinidad, both Indian men and women were expected to live up to the Brahminic ideal. Other articles were being printed in the newspapers to appeal to women to retain traditional roles, since these were changing fast both in India and in Trinidad itself, especially as there were also references to women and men who were not living out this prescribed ideal. Women dared to leave their partners, for instance. Khornali, of Caratal, Gasparillo, placed a notice in the newspaper stating that he would not be held responsible for any debt or debts contracted by his wife Saparan, "she having left my house and protection on 27th April, 1924" (*Trinidad Guardian*, 9 May, 1926). Dookhni, of Bamboo Village, also took the initiative to announce to the public through the print media that she was "no longer under the care and protection of my husband Ramnarine Maharaj of Woodland, La Fortune as I have left his home since April 1935" (*Trinidad Guardian*, 3 July, 1935).

There was nonetheless a growing acceptance among some sections of the Indian community that women could be part of the new group of articulate young Indians who were consciously fashioning their ethnic identity. In his inaugural address to the members of the Literary and Debating club at the Woodbrook C. M. I. School, P. L. Akal remarked:

> The old and mistaken idea of keeping the women in the background is happily being removed, for in India today it is the women who are not only stirring the men to greater efforts but are taking a very prominent and leading part among their people (*East Indian Weekly*, 15 August, 1931).

In their daily choices, some women had already challenged the roles strictly allocated to them. Before 1945, few Indian women had veered from this rigidly defined path to choose careers instead of the traditional roles of wife and mother. Though in the minority, several women were cited in the 1945 *Indian Centenary Review* as having careers. Among them were Celestina Lucky, who came from a wealthy Christian family in San Fernando. She chose to become an optician, went abroad to study in this field and returned to practice her profession in Trinidad. She also chose to remain unmarried. Her sister, Evelyn Josephine Lucky, born in 1917, also trained as an ophthalmic optician in Northampton, and later became part-time director of her father's business, continuing to travel widely in Europe and the West Indies, and becoming part of various clubs and societies for Indians such as the India Club and the Southern Indian Organization. Stella Abidh, the daughter of the Couva County Councillor, C. C. Abidh, completed her degree as a medical doctor in Toronto in 1930 and returned to become one of the first female doctors in Trinidad, as well as a pioneer in the field of public health. Gema Ramkeeson, born in 1910, completed her secondary education in Port of Spain, and, after her marriage to Canon J. D. Ramkeeson, continued to be intensely involved in initiatives in both Trinidad and the wider Caribbean regarding the development of social work and social welfare organizations for the poor and underprivileged (*Indian Centenary Who's Who*, 1945).

Such role models began to provide the newer generations of Indians born in Trinidad with some leverage for negotiation with their parents in terms of careers and marriage, thus challenging the images presented through mythology and ritual of a fixed role and place for women.

HEROES AND HEROINES OF THE SILVER SCREEN

While the traditional texts continued to provide symbols for gender identity, by the mid-30s these were reinforced by a new and equally compelling medium. The introduction of Indian films into Trinidad in 1935 was not just another form of entertainment. "Aged Indian people who recall the films of yester-age often feel it as a kind of ethnic ritual, an attempt to keep up one's forefather's love and yore. Ramdaye, an aged woman from what used to be called the "coolie block" up in Diego Martin, is an illustration of this. Her father came from India, while her mother was born in Trinidad of parents there. ...What does Ramdaye feel about Indian films. To her, they are more than frivolous entertainment. ...These films are an act of piety, a feeling of veneration towards her background ...almost a spiritual experience like a pilgrimage" (Golikeri 1977, 55).

In 1935, Ramjit Kumar, a London-trained engineer, originally from Lahore, India, introduced the film, *Bala Jobhan*, and followed this with others, including *Afzal, Chabukwali, Jungle Ka Chavan, Andaz,* and *Midnight Mail* (Samaroo 1979, 3). They were shown to packed houses. Silochan, a Hindu man born in Trinidad in 1914 recalls that when "*Bala Jobhan* the first Indian picture come down in Couva, it had plenty people, it eh even have place, people pushing so hard, I can't get a ticket." He used to walk from Freeport to the cinema in Couva every week as a rule, a distance of several miles, to see Indian shows. By 1936, the Yogi, a writer of the "Indian News and Views Column" was requesting the appointment of two Indians on the Film Censors Board, one for the Hindi language and one for the Urdu language. He justified his request on the basis that, "There are many Indians who are interested in the importation of these films which have undoubtedly won the fancy and admiration of the entire Indian community" (*Trinidad Guardian*, 6 August, 1936).

Sudhir Kakar sees the Indian cinema "as the primary vehicle for shared fantasies of a vast number of people living on the Indian subcontinent who are both culturally and psychologically linked." He explains: "I do not use "fantasy" in the ordinary sense of the word, with its popular connotations of whimsy, eccentricity, or triviality, but as another name for that world of imagination which is fuelled by desire and which provides us with an alternative world where we can continue our longstanding quarrel with reality" (Kakar 1989).

These observations were perhaps more applicable to Indians overseas, as distance from the reality of India created a romantic longing for its imagery. Until 1935, only English language films were available in Trinidad. Films like *The Scarlet Empress*, starring Marlene Dietrich, which was advertised at the Empire Theatre in Port of Spain on 9th December 1934, clearly had an appeal to the local audience which would have included more Indian men than women, for women were not generally allowed to go to the cinema. But such films could not bridge the gap between fantasy and reality for the generations of migrants still emotionally linked to India.

Almost every Indian man or woman in Trinidad over the age of 60 in the 1990s remembered *Bala Jobhan*, and the continuous stream of films brought in after 1935 cultivated other ideas of Indianness and Indian culture. Unlike the Indians on the subcontinent, who may have suspended disbelief during the actual viewing of the films, but were quite aware of their reality, Indians in Trinidad took these films quite seriously. For the children of migrants, born in Trinidad, this represented the India they had never seen. By the mid-30s, the majority of the Indian population in Trinidad were second and third generation Indians who would have lost first hand contact with India: the last group of migrants was brought in 1917. With the advent of Indian films, the epic grandeur of an India left behind was now being portrayed in the land of their adoption. They saw India in the landscape, the clothing, the religious practices transmitted on the screen, the fictional characters who lived out the morals they were counselled to replicate in their own lives. The images on the screen gave greater credence to their own practices. These mirrored and authorized the rituals carried out at wedding ceremonies by their own pundits and imams.

Just as the Indian "talkies" were responsible for a general cultural rejuvenation among Indians, they also had an impact on gender imagery. Kakar observes about Indian films that, in emphasizing the central features of fantasy, "the fulfilment of wishes, the humbling of competitors and the destruction of enemies" they are not unlike fairy tales. And like fairy tales, there is an:

oversimplification of situations and elimination of detail, unless the detail is absolutely essential. The characters of the film are always typical, never unique, and without the unnerving complexity of real people. The Hero and the Villain, the Heroine and Her Best Friend, the Loving Father and the Cruel Stepmother, are never ambivalent, never the mixed ticket we all are in real life (Kakar 1989, 29).

In this respect, the films continued the symbolic constructions of femininity and masculinity, for they also replayed the stereotypes which mythology had previously extolled. Before the 1950s, many of the Trinidad Indian population still spoke or understood some Hindi, so the messages of these films were less nuanced, retaining stark black-and-white renditions of morality. Subtitling in English did not begin until the 1970s and constituted another point in the rebirth of Indian culture in Trinidad through films. (Vertovec 1992, 229)

At the same time, these films also fashioned new ideas of femininity and masculinity, reflecting changes in caste relations that were emerging in India. For example, *Chandra Lekha* was promoted in the 1940's as a western-style Indian film. Its plot revolves around an organized revolt and reinstatement of the rightful heir to the throne by a very accomplished woman. She is a member of the lowest of the military castes of Kshyatrias who are dairy farmers during peacetime. "It was they who rallied around Lord Krishna to conquer the North India renowned Yasdava Army of Kansa, the demon king, around 5000 BC."[20] She refuses to marry the younger prince who has fallen in love with her. He has wrongfully seized the throne from his elder brother whom he forces to flee the kingdom. The young woman supplies the banished heir with weapons and an army to confront his brother who is massacred in a skirmish. The popular wish is that she marry the rightful heir and become queen. She obliges.

Another film, titled *Ann*, dealt with the touchy subject of caste. The caste system was already being contested by the Arya Samaj movement and by Mahatma Gandhi in India. Given the loosening of the caste structure in Trinidad, this resonated with the ideas of Trinidad-born Indians. In the film, the reigning monarch signs a parliamentary decree outlawing discrimination based on caste. The ensuing plot involves the imprisonment of the monarch and his queen by the prince who does not support this decree, the flight into the forest by the princess, a middle caste man who has won her regard and that of the lower and middle castes, in an effort to found a new society. A battle ensues between the latter group and the usurping prince, who is ousted from the throne he has seized by force and executed by the people. The throne is then assumed by the princess and the middle caste man whom she marries.

In the attempt to appeal to cinema-goers in a Western setting, local film advertisements often carried mixed messages even while the stories they related to retained the original mythical flavour. *Madhuri*, for instance, was advertised with a photo of the leading actress, captioned, "Sulochana, popularly known as the "Greta Garbo of India," who appears in *Madhuri* now showing at the Roxy Theatre." What did this new development do for gender identity? Clearly, it was a statement that Indian women could perform publicly, could display glamour, even take off their *orhnis*. On the other hand, some messages explicitly reinforced traditional conceptions of approved male and female behaviour. Despite the glamorous allurements of Sulochana, the character she portrays on screen is not unlike Sita in her fidelity to her husband, Rama. *Madhuri* remains faithful to Amber, the male protagonist of the film, in the face of many misadventures, resisting the advances of traitors and kings to save Amber from the gallows, yet encountering suspicion until she has repeatedly proved her virtue.

This diet of Indian films, enthusiastically digested by the Indian population, was contradictory in its effect. On the one hand, it provided a new opportunity for women to legitimately go out of their homes and, in fact, a new area for mixing between Indian boys and girls. Rajdaye, of Hindu parentage, who was engaged to a young Hindu man for nine months in 1945, was allowed to go out with him once in those nine months – to the cinema to see an Indian film, accompanied by a cousin. Attending Indian films together was one form of leisure which brought Indian men and women together after marriage as well. Silochan continued his weekly outing to the cinema in Couva with his wife, Etwaria, after his marriage while his mother took care of the children.

While conditions in the rural areas still kept Indian men and women largely apart in social settings, by 1938 things had begun to change in Port of Spain. Samlal, born in 1922 on the rural estate of Picton, recalls that "at that time in the rural areas only men would go to the cinema. A fortunate Indian woman may have gone if her husband wanted her to go, and if it was in the afternoon, not the night. But when I came into town (Port of Spain) in 1938 and shortly after that, Indian women had started going to the cinema to see Indian pictures." By the early forties, the young urban Indian girl was allowed to go to the matinee showing of Indian and sometimes even English films with her sisters, unchaperoned, while her mother and grandmother, if they did venture to the cinema at all, would only do so to see the Indian talkies. Their counterparts in the rural areas were still restricted by accessibility to cinemas.

Indian films were considered so much part of the revival of Indian culture that it was not incongruous to find film advertisements in the *Hindu Mahasaba Bulletin*, first published in 1940 to disseminate information on the religious organization in order to maintain and build its membership.[21] The cinemas that advertised were owned by Indian proprietors. There was no dearth of films which focused on female heroines, if the names are anything to go by. From May 1940 onwards, in various issues, the *Hindu Mahasaba Bulletin* advertised: *Bhabi*, starring Renuka Devi and P. Jairaj, *Jiva Naiya*, featuring Devika Rani and Ashok Kumar, *Our Darling Daughters* starring Rose Kumar, *Daughter of India* starring Khurshid, and *Hurricane Hausa* starring Fearless Nadia. Other films reinforced the stereotypical female role - as for instance, *Sansar - Woman thou Art Sacrifice*. *Mother India*, a famous and often repeated film, echoed a far more political message. In this film, an aged woman from a village in India commissions an irrigation canal for the benefit of the village peoples. Her son uses harsh methods, involving an armed revolution, to bring about equality and fair play between lender and borrower in the village and surrounding region. "It was not well organized and lacked both doctrine and dialogue. In a country with over 10,000 years of civilized rule, sobriety and dialogue are always better" records the caption on this highly popular film. To resolve the problem, the aged woman kills her son in order to prevent a massacre. The film promoted not only ideas of non-violent change, but the allegorical construction of woman as repository of nation and nationalism. Interestingly, by compromising the female nurturing role in terms of killing her own offspring, the film simultaneously pulls at the heartstrings of the viewer, reinforcing the traditional expectation of motherhood and femininity.

In many of these films, the themes of long-suffering and martyred mother, and the sari-clad femininity of the traditional passive bride, are continuously replayed, but others gave birth to a new kind of heroine. Fearless and intrepid, this heroine dances publicly, sings, has adventures, all of this with the film director still ensuring that female modesty is preserved, as she emerges from a pool or river with a drenched cotton sari seductively clutching her figure. While some of these new ideas were embryonic in the forties, the older films were still influencing generation after generation, and ensuring that the old ideals lived on. In 1944, for instance the first film to be shown in Trinidad in 1934 – *Bala Jobhan*, was still screening at the Palace Cinema in San Fernando and drawing large crowds.[22]

NEGOTIATING WITH SYMBOLS OF PATRIARCHY

"How a young lady ought to conduct herself was made clear to me in this story my mother told me – the story of Draupaudi from the Mahabharata" says Kamla, the protagonist of *Butterfly in the Wind*, an autobiographical novel describing the author's childhood in Tunapuna in the late 1930s and 1940s (Persaud 1990, 102).

> The Mahabharata tells, with innumerable interpolations, the story of the great war between the Kauravas and the Pandavas, two rival factions of one royal family. ...At one point in the story the Pandavas learned that the King of Panchala had proclaimed a svayamvara at which his daughter Draupadi was to select a husband from among the suitors. Disguised as Brahmins the Pandavas attended the svayamvara and Arjuna, a mighty bowman and warrior defeated everybody, including the hundred Kaurava brothers who were among the competitors. On their return home Arjuna's mother, when told he had won a great treasure, unwittingly advised him to share it with his brothers. Thus Draupadi became the common wife

of all the five Pandava brothers and to avoid jealousy it was decided that she should dwell for two days with each of them in turn (Gaur 1980, 21).

Basham notes that "The *locus classicus* of ancient Indian polyandry is the Mahabharat, where the heroes, the five Pandava brothers, share their wife Draupadi in common" (Basham 1967, 175). It is interesting, however, that in the retelling of this tale by pundits and others, the practice of polyandry was never promoted as a virtue for women, yet the second part of the myth is constantly invoked as another ideal of chastity, like that of Sita's virtue, to which women should aspire. This part tells of the attempted rape of Draupadi by Duhsasana, the most wicked of the Kaurava brothers, after the eldest Pandava brother has lost everything, including Draupadi, in a dice game, to Sakuni, the uncle of the Kaurava princes. Draupadi is dragged into the assembly and Duhsasana begins to peel of the layers of her sari. But Krishna intervenes and, although the king pulls and pulls at her sari, Draupaudi remains clothed and cannot be publicly stripped.

This tale is related to Kamla to stress the chastity and virtuous behaviour expected of a young girl and woman under any circumstances. The symbol of cloth, and the idea of being clothed and preserving purity, is a recurrent one, with deep roots in both Hindu and Indo-Muslim traditions. Bayly observes that:

> In the Mahabharata, for instance, the mythic female Draupadhi, under attack by demons, was endowed by the gods with a sari that had no end. The more cloth the demons unwrapped, the more remained to protect her virtue. A similar theme pervaded Indo-Muslim culture. According to the flowery Persian metaphor for creation and protection, "God clothes the bosom of nature with the mantle of existence" (Bayly 1986, 288).

The other side of the story is never examined as a violent invasion of a woman's privacy. It is accepted behaviour for a man to attempt to rape a woman, especially if the man is a powerful one.

> The assembly is a company of men. Draupadi's body is private property, the property of men. Like all

property, she can be bought, sold, exchanged. ...notice that Krishna's gesture does not alter her status; ...In the Mahabharata the woman is property, to be exchanged between men, she is held captured by the male gaze; her nakedness would be her shame; ...Shame is man's threat against women: a woman without shame is a woman without worth (Duncker 1992, 132).

Women must persistently be seen through male eyes and defined through male concerns. Indian feminist historian, Uma Chakravarti, also observes from her examination of various sources of the Ramayana story that, as the Sita legend develops in the historical context of India, "the emphasis on chastity and the assumption that ideal marriage is based on female devotion are aspects grafted on to an originally simple story. Over the centuries important details added to the story have had a crucial influence on the shaping of the feminine identity"[23] (Desai and Krishnaraj 1990, 24). While poetic licence is often taken in the retelling of these tales, there is no doubt that they continued to serve as moral fodder for the Indian migrants in Trinidad.

> In Tulsidas's retelling of Valmiki's Ramayana, there is an episode where Sita, wife of Rama, has just been freed by the capture of Lanka, and the death of the powerful king Ravana who has kept her captive. It has to be proved publicly that Sita has been faithful to her husband in both thought and deed. So she is put through what my mother described as her "trial by fire," "the proving of her purity" by the cleansing ritual of fire which consumes all human ugliness including woman's unfaithfulness. ...It was only when Sita stepped out of the fire, without a hair of her body singed, that she was able to return to her husband Rama. Young Hindu girls like myself, aged eight when I first heard this story, enjoyed the rich imagery and poetry of these epic adventures, without being aware that we were unconsciously absorbing the sentiments and values of Valmiki (Persaud 1990: 103).

When she was older, Kamla questioned the ordeal through which Sita had been placed, asking her mother: "If Rama was

God, shouldn't he have known that Sita was faithful? Didn't he trust her word?" While it seems that Lord Rama had complete faith in his wife, he needed to allay the fears of his subjects and assure them that Sita had remained a completely chaste woman during the period she was captured by Ravana, and that she was fit to be their Queen. Kamla was still unhappy with this response so her mother explained further: "You must remember Kamla, that as queen she held a position of responsibility and of trust. All wives hold positions of great trust." But Kamla, a generation removed from her mother, persisted "Do husbands hold positions of trust? I provoked" (Persaud 1990, 105).

An unusual re-interpretation through women's eyes of the classical mythology of the Ramayana is revealed in a 1930s short story by the Trinidadian journalist, Seepersad Naipaul, entitled, "The Adventures of Gurudeva."

> And thus they felt because they knew that such was their lot as well, and they wondered in a vague, resigned sort of way why the Deity had allowed them to be born at all. For they had heard it taught by their fathers, by the elders of the village, as well as by the pundits who often read the Ramayana on evenings, that the husband was to the wife God, lord and master – all in one – and that a woman's highest virtue lay in her absolute submission to her husband's will. ... 'But you see,' Dhira told Mira in Hindi, 'it is all a very one sided operation. They want us all to be like Sita ... but on the other hand, they are far from being like Rama, the incarnation of the great God Vishnu himself, it is not fair (S. Naipaul 1976, 26).

Naipaul had himself recognised the one-sided interpretation of the myths and tales which had emerged - that masculinity is invariably allocated the dominant and active role while women are allocated the submissive one and are seen as passive agents in change. Kim Johnson develops this observation in his examination of the mythical representations of female and male ethnic identities in Trinidad, observing about the story of Sita's ordeal, "This didactic tale of good triumphing over evil, virtue over morality, is told in drama in Trinidad as a lesson in morality especially aimed at women" (Johnson 1984, 27).

Between myth and reality, between India and Trinidad, some negotiations had already taken place. The symbols pertaining to masculinity and femininity which were derived from, and supported the retention of these myths, are many and varied and it would be difficult to discuss them all in detail. One example will suffice. On the occasion of her marriage, a Hindu woman was given a specially designed necklace, usually of gold, called a *mangalsutra*. *Mangal* means auspicious, *sutra* is thread. A red vermilion dot called the *sindoor* was pressed against her forehead signifying her married state and she was allowed to wear a set of bangles which was referred to as the *kangan*. On the death of her husband, she had to take off the *mangalsutra* and keep it safely in a box. She was no longer allowed to display a rich vermilion *sindoor* but had to wear a white one, and, on hearing of her husband's death, her *kangan* had, immediately, to be broken against the wall. These rituals clearly allowed the widow a symbolic outlet for her grief and were a form of respect for the dead. However, they also signify that, from the time of her husband's death, she was expected to have no adornment, never to remarry, and in fact to exist only to serve her children. The older practice of *suttee*, requiring that a wife allow herself to be burnt on her husband's funeral pyre, came to signify the extremes of monogamy expected of the Indian female. To our knowledge of Hinduism in Trinidad, this ritual sacrifice was never practised in the new society, while as noted, it had been banned by the British since 1829 in India itself.

Thus far, I have concentrated on the idea that the symbolism of Hinduism was the dominant one in influencing the construction of masculinity and femininity among Indians. But Islam, as it developed in Trinidad in the twentieth century, was sufficiently different in its gender imagery to warrant some inquiry. Islam was practised with a certain austerity. Unlike Hinduism, Muslims had a place of worship – a mosque – in which no graven images, pictures or symbols were permitted. Nor were the sermons derived from myths or Persian literature, but from the literal interpretation of the Holy Koran which, given the fact that the imams were male, were explicated in a manner that served to maintain male interests. Yet, as with Hinduism, Islam glorified motherhood and also placed a high value on the chastity of women. The dress code for Muslim women became a much more rigid one than that expected for Hindu women, requiring that women's bodies were covered from neck to toe while they were in public. Nonetheless, it must be stressed that during the early and later periods of indenture, there was little difference between Muslim and Hindu women. Hindu and Muslim weddings were very similar, providing one of the crucial spaces in which women would socialize, sing and dance. The influence of Christianity from the late nineteenth century, and the organized development of both religions from the 1930s had begun to differentiate and nuance notions of femininity and masculinity among this ethnic group.[24]

PATRIARCHAL SYMBOLS

What does this tell us of the changes emerging in the construction of femininity and masculinity in Trinidad? The stories of female duplicity suggest that the Indian male felt threatened about his capacity to control his wife's libidinous instincts. Certainly, notions of what constituted masculinity would have undergone change, and we may speculate that what is displayed here is a masculine concern with increased powerlessness in the sphere of sexual relations. It is necessary now to move backward in time and refocus on the early trauma experienced by Indian men during the period of indentureship to see how they responded and compare this to changes which women were undergoing, despite the stereotypes being transferred by mythology and the practice of gender relations in India. Only then can we appreciate the persistence of mythology together with the dissonance between mythological representations and the lived reality that allowed new and challenging possibilities for both sexes.

Since the period of indentureship, there was always a noticeably high rate of suicide among Indian men. Some of this was attributed to the unfaithfulness of their wives. "The man whose wife had been unfaithful suffered a disastrous loss of self-esteem, and in the absence of other mechanisms for expressing anger and self-assertion, violence directed against the other (murder or mutilation of the woman) or against self (suicide was almost as frequent in these situations) was the only way to recover his pride" (Brereton 1979, 183). On 4th December, 1917, for instance, one Sirju was found hanging by a rope and deemed to have committed suicide (*Trinidad Guardian*, 1 January, 1918). Two days later, another inquest was held on the death of Sookhoo, found hanging from a cocoa tree on 25th November 1917. A verdict of suicide was returned (*Trinidad Guardian*, 3 January, 1918). On the same day, the newspaper reported the trial and execution of Palakdharri, a young Indian man of about 26 years who was executed for the murder of Bajbahar, an Indian woman on the Non-Pareil Estate, Sangre Grande on Sunday 31st October 1917. Palakdharri was an indentured immigrant from India and had been resident in the colony for a period of years. The account of the murder is instructive.

> A short time before the crime took place Palakdharri and the murdered woman lived together in one of the barrack rooms on the estate and for some reason or another they fell out. It was suggested that the woman left him for some other man. ...His defence at the trial was that the woman, apart from being unfaithful, had him put off the estate and jeered at him when he was going away. He had a cutlass in his hand at the time and chopped her (*Trinidad Guardian*, 3 January, 1918).

The trauma among the male community, which resulted in a high rate of suicide and murder, persisted in other ways. One means of retaliation and dealing with their own derided selves and their women was by turning to the bottle.[25] Omatie was born in 1922 and married at the age of 16 to a young man her parents had chosen for her. She was from a wealthier family, as her parents had both land and commercial property, while her husband came from poor rural peasantry. In the earlier years of her marriage, she was beaten by her husband routinely, it seemed to her an action she did not dare to question.

> My husband used to drink but I really don't know if they had a reason. When he start working in the estate he never used to drink and it was after he start working in this government road, to me like when the fortnight reach and they go for the pay, and everybody meet up, and so they go and they buy a nip ah rum they drink and they get drunk, well I

say is through when they get the company and they meet up is so they drinking. ...They was different yes, if your husband drinking rum in a shop you can't go, you just have to stop home and till he come and if he come he quarrel or he eh quarrel, he beat you or he eh beat you, or he go and sleep. ...Women make their own happiness.

At the same time there is also evidence that fathers were willing to protect the interests of their daughters. For instance, Jangalee was charged for beating his father-in-law, Gopaul, on 22nd December 1917. "For the defence, Jangalee and three witnesses testified that Gopaul came to his house, called him out, and enquired whether he had beaten his wife, (Gopaul's daughter)." When Jangalee admitted this, the old man collared him and proceeded to inflict two blows on him with a piece of wood, upon which Jangalee in his turn seized the same weapon and reciprocated likewise (*Trinidad Guardian*, 12 January, 1918).

What such evidence confirms is that post-indentureship ideas pertaining to masculinity and femininity were constantly undergoing shifts, despite the collusion of women in the sphere of economic life, and the reinforcement of tradition through religion and ritual. It was clearly unacceptable to assume that one's wife or partner was property to be disposed of at will. Certainly the magistrate's court looked harshly on the extremes of this attitude to women as property.

Despite the overwhelming influence which mythology and symbols may have had on the construction of gender, the influences of the new society had an impact on both men and women, thus allowing a negotiation with the lived reality while retaining the symbolic representations through which gender was transmitted. If women encountered resistance from the male patriarchy in their efforts to negotiate freedoms appropriate to conditions in this new setting, what were the freedoms concurrently sought by men? Unfortunately, one finds that, in general, like any group that possesses a source of power, men assumed the rigidity of patriarchal ideology and wanted to hold on to control over their womenfolk. In doing so, they could only incorporate few incremental ideas onto their map of gender.

Pressure on the Indian male was not only generated within the Indian community by women, but also from external sources. Indian men now had to compete with other men in the masculine culture of Trinidad. While women had the dubious protection of the family, and were relatively sheltered within the private sphere, Indian men had to engage with the wider public. The symbolic representations of masculinity, the exploits of Rama, Rawan, Krishna and Shiva, could not so easily be superimposed onto the new setting, where other notions of maleness were clearly dominant. The class structure automatically placed white men at the top. African-descended men, the other majority, had also proven to be a threat to the Indian's masculine image in front of their own womenfolk. If the African male role models were well built sportsmen like Learie Constantine, or the urban "saga boy" of Laventille who had several women at the same time, then what did the new Indian masculine image in Trinidad begin to draw on? In sports, Indian men participated in areas like wrestling and cricket – which required greater skill than physical stamina or build. In 1918, there was a report of the wrestling contest at the Palladium Cinema in Tunapuna between Geerd, of Dutch Guiana, and Gaphoor Meah of Chaguanas (*Trinidad Guardian*, 4 October, 1918). By 1919, cricket had become one important area of organized sport among Indian men. The Sagar Cup competition for cricket, St Joseph vs. Tunapuna was advertised in the newspaper as featuring on the team A. Hamid and D. Narayansingh. Later on, the newspapers also avidly covered the fights of Mottee Kid Singh (Fighting Rajah of Amenea) (*Trinidad Guardian*, 8 February, 1931). Mannie Dookhan, dubbed the Trinidad Barefoot Runner, lone participant in the Empire Games of 1934, was given a hero's welcome on his return from London, personally congratulated by the Mayor and having an editorial devoted to his achievements (*Sunday Guardian*, 2 September, 1934). But these were still few and far between.

There were other shifts evident, such as the achievements of individuals such as Adrian Cola Rienzi who had travelled and studied abroad, and who returned with a self-confidence which could not be dampened by the dynamics of male-male relations in Trinidad. Movement into the professions, first as interpreters, then as doctors, lawyers, pharmacists and teachers, followed by appointments to the Legislative Council, offered Indian men opportunities to compete equally with non-Indian men at one level.

Meanwhile, day to day control over the Indian community itself and over women's lives was reinforced by more traditional and compelling methods. The *panchayat* or council of elders was a patriarchal institution that ensured male control not only of women, but of their own villages. The only way this institution could function was if its decisions were respected by all members of the village – male and female. Since the *panchayat* was invariably comprised of men, its existence also depended on respect for those men as the authoritative voice and conscience of the village. Mandelbaum points out that in village usage in India, the *panchayat* "refers not only to the group that convenes, but also to a set of processes for resolving conflict, for redressing transgressions, and for launching group enterprises. The pattern of *panchayat* action is triggered by a problem that people feel must be tackled and cannot be handled by individuals acting singly ...The responsible men of the group gather to discuss the issue" (Mandelbaum 1970, 278).

Reconstituted in Trinidad, the *panchayat* immediately took on different dimensions. In India, for instance, there could be a strong correlation between its membership and the *jati* group where the two coincided (Mandelbaum 1970, 278). In Trinidad, however, the *panchayat* might comprise men from all three religions. C. D. Lalla recalls in his biography that the *panchayat* at Balmain, Couva, consisted of a tribunal comprised of his father, a Presbyterian minister; Mohammed Hosein, a Muslim; Permanand Pundit, Ramjattan Pundit, Pundit Ajodya Persad, Babu Lalsingh and Sarran Teelucksingh, the three pundits being Hindus. The venue for the tribunals held by the panchayat was the ground floor of his father's house and these were usually held at night and in public. Disputes settled by the *panchayat* could range from the theft of garden produce, through marital disputes, to assault, rape and murder. Those who attended generally accepted and upheld the decisions taken (Lalla 1983, 4).

A similar pattern was also observed in another village. Both Jaipaul and Sadhul of Lengua village recall that no *panchayat* meeting could be held without Baboo Hosein, a Muslim, and invariably included Pundit Basdeo Misir, the Hindu priest of the district. Pundit Misir described the importance of the *panchayat* in relation to the existing judicial system.

There were two sets of *panchayat* in every area or it was mixed (by religion). If you do take a matter to court, Mr. Cazabon (the presiding magistrate) use to ask, did you all go to the panch, what did the panch say, and the person was charged double time if they did not follow the decision of the panch.

The range of problems brought before the *panchayat* was varied, but they were frequently associated with problems in gender relations. Pundit Misir illustrates:

Yuh take away a man's daughter, which is not right, they say that is wrong, they fine you; or some people take yuh daughter and don't want to marry, they say all yuh have to marry, yuh spoil the girl, you have to married, you say you don't want to, you have to listen, if you don't marry you'll have bastard children, nobody will want to marry bastard children.

The net of social control was finely meshed around each person in the village. Sadhul describes other areas in which the *panchayat* had control.

The *panchayat* would be for Hindu, Muslim, Negro too. They would call a woman if she do something out of the way, like if the woman left her husband and gone away with somebody else or quarrel with somebody, or destroy somebody garden. For punishment they put you out for a month or two. Nobody talk to you, you can't go to their house for water, or to the pond for water, they have nothing to do with you, and you have to pay something too.

The men who were chosen from among the villagers were those thought to have sound minds, who did not ill-treat their wives and children, sometimes men of education, or those who were felt to have strong religious convictions. The *panchayat* did not function only to control women, but would just as soon offer protection to women who were ill-treated by men. Boodoo, a Hindu man born in Trinidad in 1903, recalls that he was brought before the panchayat of Sangre Grande in 1929.

It had a time I did take up with another fella daughter while I had family in the house ...the panchayat stop invitation going and coming ...until it reach to the government ...well they get the girl in my house. They take out a warrant to arrest me.

Sookoo was made to spend one night in the jail at Manzanilla for his misdeeds, in this case the *panchayat* worked with the colony's legal system to protect the rights of a woman. Normally, however, *panchayat* methods of control were based on the imposition of ostracism and fines, the latter to be paid to the community. Some of the penalties could be very demeaning. Boodhoo, for instance, in addition to his fines, tells that "they make me walk around the village for days with the boots of five persons on my head." It was important to honour the decision of the *panchayat* for fear of complete isolation from the community. "If trouble overtake you, nobody will come and help you," explained Sookoo.[26]

Apart from consolidating and ensuring a sense of communality as opposed to individuality, the *panchayat* was very important in reinforcing the familiar parameters of masculinity and femininity outlined by the sacred texts and the religious leaders. It renewed the authority of masculinity even while it protected the rights of women, bestowing on patriarchy its finer points of benevolence. In time, the forms of punishment and control meted out by the *panchayat* began to clash with the rules emerging under the official judicial system, and its moral grip weakened. Pundit Misir, once a member of the *panchayat*, suggested that the authority of the *panchayat* faded when people who either had greater physical strength or wealth started to violate its decisions. The law was more amenable to bribery and corruption, and easier to resort to, than the *panchayat*, which relied on a collective social and moral responsibility within the community and a common belief system and tradition within the ethnic group.

Despite its waning control, *panchayats* existed in Trinidad in one form or other until the fifties. They constituted another measure by which patriarchy reared up to restore its power in a situation where the boundaries of Indian femininity had been extending differently since the start of the indentureship system.

CONCLUSION

Myth and ritual provide a venue for domination as well as struggle. Symbolic boundaries can be reinstated to redefine solid and seemingly protective walls. While new understandings of masculinity and femininity emerge from the cumulated and collective challenges of individuals in the group, and from other forms of mythmaking that begin to legitimize new behaviours deemed acceptable for men and women in any culture, the old foundations are perpetuated, allowing an arena for the continuous negotiations between men and women. Even if they vary some of the normative expectations in their lifetime, men and women who are born into a particular ethnic group are never indifferent to the boundaries defined by their community. The capacity of an individual man or woman to change the resonances of myth and symbol in his or her own lifetime is extremely rare.

ENDNOTES

[1] In *The Sexual Metaphor*, (Harvard University Press, MA, 1994), Helen Haste argues that the basis of gender construction is through metaphor and real change only occurs when there is profound change in the underlying metaphors of gender.

[2] I am grateful to a Hindu gentleman in Felicity Village, Chaguanas for allowing me to photograph his devotional area and discuss some of these ideas with me. I was simply passing by and he was extremely accommodating. During the entire period of my formal research for this study (1989-1992) when I questioned and approached Indian men and women in Trinidad about their lives and histories, I almost always found openness and willingness to share intimate details. The examples of lived practices employed in this essay were drawn from oral history interviews that were carried out for my doctoral research between 1989 and 1992. In this respect I found myself an anthropologist in my own land, and that Trinidadians always welcomed conversations about their rituals, confirming what non-local anthropologists who studied various aspects of culture in Trinidad had often told me.

[3] Aisha Khan, *Callaloo Nation: Metaphors of Race and Religious Identity among South Asians in Trinidad*, (Duke University Press, 2004) p. 14

[4] Reverend John Morton relates the story of Bhukhan who was born in India in 1856 and had learnt to read and write in school there. He came to Trinidad as a young man and recalls: `I was sent to a sugar estate called Ben Lomond, under the indenture for five years. There I met a man whose name was Balaram. He was the only one who could read and write on the estate. I asked him if he had any Hindi books. He said, "Yes I got some from an Indian minister who lives at Iere Village" (Morton 1916, 81).

[5] From Sarah Morton, *John Morton of Trinidad*, Toronto, 1916, p. 53, also cited in Brinsley Samaroo 1996, 208.

[6] Kelvin Singh, in *The Bloodstained Tombs*, has discussed the festival of Hosay as a site for resistance and as a festival which attracted non-Muslims in an urban setting.

[7] I recall the fascination I felt as a child and adolescent in the fifties and sixties when we would drive pass the grounds in Cedar Hill village where the Ramleela festival was annually staged. The play was performed in a natural sunken amphitheatre – a small flat plain surrounded by gently sloping hills on two sides. It was a time of great joy and merriment, an opportunity to buy and sell traditional Indian sweets and savouries, offering another sphere in which women could socialize outside their homes. Kumar Mahabir notes that along with the Ram Lila, the Krishna Lila was also an annual affair. I have not come across this festival in my research thus far (Mahabir 1988).

[8] Ramleela is the more contemporary spelling of the festival referred to as Ramlilla in the historical sources found in Trinidad.

[9] A similar case can be made for another major deity, Krishna, the worship of whom has created another principle in Hinduism, that known as *bhakti*, "which signifies the self-surrender of human beings to a personal god of love." (Chaudhuri 1979, 256) Krishna's escapades, as related in mythology, are beyond reproach: one famous episode has him conducting simultaneous affairs with milkmaids or the wives of milkmen. Later, this same Krishna becomes a heroic figure in portions of the Mahabharata, through the epic poem becoming the personal supreme deity of a monotheistic cult, and given an additional identification as the incarnation of the god Vishnu from the triad of Brahma, Siva and Vishnu from the Vedic religion, and generally worshipped as another supreme god, an ideal for all men to emulate.

[10] Information gleaned from an informal discussion with Dr. Rosabelle Seesaran, who was also one of my oral history interviewees.

[11] Many of these songs had their origins in India, as evidenced by the references in the lyrics made to such features as elephants and the river Ganges (Maharaj, 1974)

[12] The colloquial Hindu term for a messenger

[13] The ritual anointing of the groom and the bride with mixture of turmeric and dahi or yoghurt - turmeric was the same colour and perhaps general taste of saffron, the original spice used in this ritual which was both expensive and perhaps not available. The ritual was referred to as "saffron night."

[14] I have chosen here only to deal with folk tales, or *kissas*. Kumar Mahabir notes that among the oral tradition could be found chants, riddles, games, and proverbs (*kahawats or kahanis*) (Kumar Mahabir, "The Indo-Caribbean Oral Tradition," The Oral and Pictorial Records Programme, The University of the West Indies, St. Augustine, December 1988, No. 4).

[15] In the folk tale "The Fisherman and the Conchshell," a fisherman finds a conch shell which speaks to him and grants him all of his wishes. Every time he is granted a wish, the same thing is also granted to his neighbour twice over. His jealousy forces him to wish for misfortune to himself and therefore double misfortunes for his neighbour, eventually leading to the stage where he is both incapacitated and half blinded. The moral of the story is, of course, that his own jealousy of the good fortunes of others has led to his unhappiness (Maharaj 1990).

[16] Saga boy is the colloquial term used in Trinidad to refer to a man who dresses smartly and is generally known as a charmer of ladies. I am not aware of the derivation of the term.

[17] *Datwan* refers to a piece of strong vine used as a toothbrush.

[18] It is instructive to note as well while reading this passage that idioms pertaining to caste, race and religion were liberally sprinkled in the everyday language among Indians.

[19] A taped record of this interview is available in the Oral and Pictorial Records of the Alma Jordan Library, University of the West Indies, St Augustine

[20] Notes on the early Indian films were collected from an older Indian man in Trinidad who has an interest in film and who kept advertisements for old films which he had seen. I am grateful to my father, Ayoob Mohammed, born in 1931, who has continuously been a source of information for this and other items related to traditional Indian culture. He willingly carried out some research on films on my behalf. He located and transcribed some of the texts of these films from this informant.

[21] It was no coincidence that Ranjit Kumar, who became the first president of the Maha Sabha in Trinidad, was also responsible for importing these films.

[22] In my own childhood experience in the late fifties and into the sixties, Indian films were still the ones which my parents would go to and the ones to which we would be taken because it was safer to show children, i.e. they alluded to sex rather than were explicit about it, and secondly they always had a moral point to convey. While by this time a certain amount of distance from India would have been developed by my generation, the impact of such powerful images on femininity and masculinity were tremendous, and no doubt continued to influence and confuse us when we were being challenged with numerous other symbols from the West.

[23] This discussion, cited from Desai and Krishnaraj, is originally taken from Uma Chakravarti, "The Sita Myth" in *Samya Shakti*, Vol. 1, No. 1, July 1983, p. 70.

[24] The influences of Christianity and the differentiation between women and gender expectations and roles in the various religions has been alluded to from time to time. It has not been possible to qualify these differences or deal with them in great detail as this detracts from the main purpose of this particular study. Nonetheless, there were differences among women and men of these religions emerging during the period of this study, but I would argue that these manifested themselves much more in the latter half of the twentieth century. This clearly remains an area for further investigation and development.

[25] The problem of alcoholism among the Indian population, especially the male Indian population, has been studied and discussed by many writers. It also features as a theme in fiction which deals with Indians in Trinidad, for instance in Harold Sonny Ladoo's gripping novel, *No Pain Like this Body*, 1987, Toronto.

[26] Taken from an interview with Mrs. Narick of San Fernando carried out by Rosabelle Seesaran for her PhD research on Indians in Trinidad.

REFERENCES

Basham, A. L. 1967. *The Wonder that was India: As a Survey of the History and Culture of the Sub-continent before the Coming of the Muslims*. London: Sidgwick and Jackson

Bayly, C. A. 1986. "The origins of swasdeshi (home industry): cloth and Indian society, 1700-1930, in Arjun Appadurai (ed.) *The Social Life of Things: Commodities in cultural perspective*. London: Cambridge University Press

Brereton, Bridget. 1979. *Race Relations in Colonial Trinidad 1870-1900*. Cambridge: Cambridge University Press.

Chaudhuri, Nirad. 1979. *Hinduism*. Oxford: Oxford University Press.

Comins, D.W.D. 1893. *Note on Emigration from India to Trinidad*. London: British Library: Asian and African Studies

Desai, Neera and M. Krishnaraj, 1990. *Women and Society in India*. New Delhi: South Asia Books.

Duncker, P. 1992. *Sisters and Strangers: An Introduction to Contemporary Feminist Fiction*. Oxford, UK and Cambridge, USA: Blackwell.

Gaur, Albertine. 1980. *Women in India*, 22-23. London: British Library.

Golikeri, V. 1977. "Indian Films in Trinidad" People, (3) 21: 52-55

Harricharan, John Thomas. 1981. *The Catholic Church in Trinidad*, 1498-1852. Trinidad: Imprint Caribbean.

Jha, J.C. 1985. "The Indian Heritage in Trinidad" in J. la Guerre (ed) *From Calcutta to Caroni*. St. Augustine, Trinidad and Tobago: University of the West Indies, Extra Mural Unit.

Johnson, Kim N. 1984. "Considerations on Indian Sexuality." Paper presented to the Third Conference on East Indians, August 29-September 4, 1984, University of the West Indies, St. Augustine, Trinidad.

Kakar, Sudhir. 1989. *Intimate Relations: Exploring Indian Sexuality*. New Delhi: Viking.

Khan, Aisha. 1990. 'Sipari Mai', *Hemisphere: A magazine of Latin American and Caribbean Affairs*, (2) 2:40-41
Khan, Aisha. 2004. Call*aloo Nation: Metaphors of Race and Religious Identity among South Asians in Trinidad, North Carolina*: Duke University Press.

La Guerre, John. (ed.) 1985. *From Calcutta to Caroni*. St. Augustine, Trinidad and Tobago: University of the West Indies, Extra Mural Unit. Trinidad: C.D. Lalla

Lalla, C.D. 1983. Biography of the Late Rev. C.D. Lalla

Mahabir, N. K.1988. "The Indo-Caribbean Oral Tradition". The Oral and Pictorial Records Programme, The University of the West Indies, St. Augustine, No 4 (December)

Maharaj, N. K. n.d. "Hindu Festival, Ceremonies and Rituals in Trinidad", Chakra Publishing House

Maharaj, Ashram B. (comp.). 1990. *Indo-Trinidad Folk Tales in the Oral Tradition.*

Maharaj, Niala. 1987. "Ramleela, Truly Bigger and Better" in K. Johnson and N. Maharaj (eds) *Divali Magazine: Hinduism in Trinidad and Tobago*, Trinidad: Inprint Caribbean

Mandelbaum, David. 1970. *Society in India: Change and Continuity.* University of California Press.

Mascaro, Juan, (transl). 1962. *The Bhagavad-Gita.* Hounslow, Middx.: Pelican Books.

Misra, P. K. 1991. "Case of an Overlooked People", *Indian Arrival Aagaman Supplement: Sunday Guardian* (31 May).

Morton, Sarah E. 1916. *John Morton of Trinidad: Pioneer Missionary of the Presbyterian Church in Canada to the East Indians in the British West Indies (Journals, Letters and Papers).* Toronto: Westminster Company.

Naipaul, Seepersad. 1976.*The Adventures of Gurudeva and Other Stories*, 26. London: Deutsch.

Parmasad, Kenneth V. 1984. *Salt and Roti: Indian Folk Tales of the Caribbean.* Sankh Productions.

Persaud, Lakshmi. 1990. *Butterfly in the Wind.* Leeds, UK: Peepal Tree Press

Ramchand, Ken. 1990. "Introduction." In *Indo-Trinidad Folk Tales in the Oral Tradition*, compiled by Ashram B, Maharaj.

Samaroo, Brinsley. 1977. "The Vanguard of Indian Nationalism in Trinidad: The East Indian Weekly, 1928-1932", Paper presented to the Ninth Conference of the Association of Caribbean Historians, Cave Hill, Barbados

Samaroo, Brinsley. 1979. "The Indian Connection: The Influence of Indian Thought and Ideas on East Indians in the Caribbean", presented at the Symposium on Contemporary Economic and Political Issues of East Indians in the Caribbean, St. Augustine, Trinidad, University of the West Indies
Singh, K. 1985. "Indians and the Larger society" in J. la Guerre (ed) *From Calcutta to Caroni.* St. Augustine, Trinidad and Tobago: University of the West Indies, Extra Mural Unit.

Vertovec, Steven. 1992. *Hindu Trinidad: Religion, Ethnicity and Socio-Economic Change.* Basingstoke: Macmillan

10

Changing Symbols of Indo-Caribbean Femininity[†]

TRANSITIONS

Each culture, each ethnic or racialized grouping, or each nation, generates archetypes of femininity. These are convenient markers of difference that serve as codes for those internal or external to the culture. Such archetypes are not static, they undergo modifications with changes in technologies of production, are disrupted under various historical circumstances and are challenged as ideas of gender equality accumulate. This essay engages some of the seminal ideas that have shaped the symbols of Indo-Caribbean femininity, with specific reference to Trinidad. From the earliest concept of the *jehagin* or the sisterhood of the boat which surfaced during the migration crossings of the nineteenth century, moving to the more submissive perception of the woman as *dulahin*, or the caste-centred one of *maharajin*, I

[†] Extensively edited for this book in 2020, this essay was first published in Gabrielle Hosein and Lisa Outar, eds. 2012. Indo-Caribbean Feminisms: Charting Crossings in Geography, Discourse, and Politics, *Caribbean Review of Gender Studies: A Journal of Caribbean Perspectives on Gender and Feminism*, Issue 6, December

examine how a changing set of symbols and further signifiers, such as *matikor* and *bindi*, have by the twenty first century complicated the simple stereotypes and perceptions of either loose morality or passivity once attached to early twentieth century Indo-Caribbean femininity.

Indian femininity occupies an invidious position in Caribbean society. For one thing, while the Indo-Caribbean population is in the majority in both Trinidad and Guyana and is well represented in Suriname, this ethnic group is still viewed as having a "minority" status in the region being less visible in Jamaica, St. Lucia, Martinique and Guadeloupe, St Vincent and Barbados. Suffused in overtones of religion and family-bound cultural practices and expectations, Indo-Caribbean femininity is, as with other femininities, burdened with a repertoire of signifiers and associations. The Indo-Caribbean script begins during the entire period of indenture when it was difficult to get a suitable percentage of female migrants to match the number of male migrants. Those who were recruited and those who left their villages, those who abandoned violent or much older husbands, or those who fled from poverty and were adventurous enough to seek their fortunes in another land were immediately earmarked as licentious. Because of the new-found liberties they had in the Caribbean due to their scarcity as a sex as far more males than females were recruited, Indo-Caribbean women were soon being labelled as having a loose morality and many were presumed to have been drawn from the class of prostitutes in India, (Reddock 1985, Mohapatra 1995, Mohammed 2002). At the same time, drawing from their history of British rule for centuries, the colonial authorities dismissed Indian femininity as childlike or needing the protection of their men, who interestingly were also viewed as effeminate needing to pummelled into shape by the a rigid colonial patriarchy. Despite the established record of stridency and agency among Indian women in negotiating their gender, sexual and wage-earning status during indenture and in the post-Indenture period, the dominant characteristics that were attributed to Indo-Caribbean femininity by the end of indenture was that of submission, passivity, non-confrontational attitudes, collusive natures and under the thumb of a violent Indo-Trinidadian patriarchy.

By the last decades of the twentieth century when the Caribbean experienced its second wave feminism, this was perhaps still the lingering perception of all Indian women – they were considered largely outside of the mainstream struggle for female equality and equity, assumed to have been submerged in family or ethnic loyalties to a male patriarchy and indifferent to the exertions for community, welfare and national liberation that had enveloped the region since the 1950s. In *Diasporic (Dis)locations: Indo-Caribbean Women Writers Negotiate the Kala Pani*, Brinda Mehta (2004) remarked on the under-represented community of Indo-Caribbean women and observed "that there was 'a serious pedagogical and scholarly flaw' in Caribbean studies, in the form of "a wide theoretical and literary gap in the analysis of Indian constructions of female identity in Guyana and Trinidad and its determining impact on issues of race, class, gender and nationhood."[1] She disrupts this persistent skein of thought and proposes that the Indo-Caribbean diaspora might well be viewed through a *"kala pani*[2] discourse as an alternative analytic framework, or a way of thinking about Indo-Caribbean women writers and their work in order to reposition this marginalized community and its body of concerns as central to questions of national development."[3] Mehta argued that the contributions of Indo-Caribbean women had been filtered through an Afro-centric lens rather than moving beyond the fixed juxtaposition and formula of race-identity that characterized the colonial and postcolonial scholarship. She proposes that *kala pani* - the taboo or pollution of caste that stained everyone who crossed large expanses of water to reach the West Indies was instead a liberating one, likened to the shedding of a skin, a release of past encumbrances, the basis for a common solidarity among all who had made that journey even if through different migrant routes.

The marginality that Mehta addresses has not only applied to Indo-Caribbean female writers and feminist activism, but to the representations of the Indo-Caribbean in the literature of the region. One of the earliest references that captures the Indian immigrant population in the Caribbean is *Lutchmee and Dilloo: A Study of West Indian Life* by Edward Jenkins, first published in 1877. Jenkins was an Englishman, born in India. The novel is sympathetic to the concerns of the indentured Indian migrants in Guyana and the other colonies. It begins in India with a rivalry between Dilloo and Hanooman over Dilloo's young and beautiful wife Lutchmee. Dilloo fetches up in Guyana, Lutchmee follows on her own volition after she has not heard word from Dilloo and they manage, by luck, to find themselves bonded on the same estate. The novel deals with the challenges of estate life, with collusions between overseers, planters and magistrates and those like Hanooman who ends up in the same estate, all of which lead to a tragic end for the hero of the story Dilloo. Dilloo is characterized as both a leader of his people and a strong righteous man. Replete with archetypes of every sort and for every race, including whites and blacks, David Dabydeen writes in the introduction to the version published in 2003 that "Jenkins himself is not radical enough to give Lutchmee her own voice, her own emotional and intellectual control over the narrative of her experiences."[4] While C.L.R. James' *Minty Alley* published in 1936 has no reference to the Indian population in Trinidad, interestingly enough, the Guyanese born Edgar Mittelholzer's *A Morning at the Office* set in the 1940's Trinidad Office of Essential Products Ltd and first published in 1950, takes a comedic look at office politics in this small establishment and brings the Indo-Trinidadian into the plot as an equal actor as the characters negotiate sexual attraction and repulsion, comment on colonial rule, and demonstrate the racial tensions in this society at the time. By 1970 Merle Hodge's *Crick Crack Monkey* overrides racial difference in the close childhood friendship between Tee, the young black protagonist and Moonie, her young Indian friend. In Earl Lovelace's 1979 novel *The Dragon Can't Dance*, the male Indian character Pariag is also featured. Linden Lewis comments however that "Unlike the other central male characters in this novel Pariag, or Boya as he was more familiarly called, seems to be groping simultaneously with the definition of his masculinity and his ethnic identity. Pariag seems to be in search of himself in the world" (Lewis 1998, 177).

In the work of Indo-Trinidadian writers such as Samuel Selvon and V. S. Naipaul from the late 1950s we begin to see Indo-Trinidadian characters who were fleshed out with contradictions, humour, frailties, strengths and desires. Perhaps this delay in ushering fully rounded characterization of the Indo-Caribbean in literature was understandable as the system of Indian indenture continued until the second decade of the twentieth-century and the incoming and outgoing migration of these labourers until then signalled transience rather than rootedness even among those in this population. Forming part of the earlier wave of colonization, the system of African slavery brought European whites and African-descended populations into closer, if more antagonistic, relationships for a period of four hundred years before Asians began to figure on the landscape. Thus the gender symbols and metaphors in the region were the fusions of two primary groupings, the African or European descended population. The indigenous population appeared to have left few gender markers in this terrain. Characters like the African women *Nennen*, *Ma-Davis* and *Tantie* that Merle Hodge writes about in *Crick Crack Monkey* or the stereotyped, generally middle or upper class "white woman," were recognizable archetypes on the mental landscapes of the society. The Indo-Caribbean stereotypes that prevailed were primarily those fostered by the colonial script – the patriarchal male and the subservient or morally deficit female.

If one systematically scours the scholarship, fiction and popular songs from the twentieth-century, there begins to emerge a distinctive set of terms, stereotypes and archetypes that establishes the presence of the East Indian population, and in particular, notions of Indo-Trinidadian femininity. It is difficult to identify categorically when and how this evolution occurs. Foreign anthropologists in particular tended to pick up some of the earliest nuances. Morton Klass's *East Indians in Trinidad: A Study in Cultural Persistence*, first published in 1961, is very thorough in its inventory of kinship terms that were specific to the original settled groups. He demonstrates the persistence of these kinship forms of address as late as the fifth decade of the twentieth-century. The earliest form of address, generally internal to the collective ethnic group, to refer to both the women and men was *jahaji*, with the qualifier *bhai* (male) or *bahin* (female). These were abbreviated to *jahaji* and *jahajin*, the prefix derived from the Hindi *jahaj*, meaning ship. The transatlantic journey created a bond or a generic brotherhood among those who came on the same boat and who therefore crossed the *kala pani* together. The kinship of the boat trumped all other descriptors of family, religion or caste in the earliest settlements of migrants as this was the primary association of the ethnic family from India that began to populate the new territory. It was interesting for me to encounter, in 2001, an Indo-Caribbean association of women in Queens; New York who called themselves *Jahajee Sisters*. This was a double take and reference back to the earliest migration on to their own status as first generation female migrants in New York. The group Jehajee describes itself thus: "During the period of Indian Indentureship (1838-1917), *Jahajee Bhai* and *Jahajee Bahen* (Ship Brother and Ship Sister) were terms used by our ancestors to unify and support each other in the midst of the arduous voyage by sea from South Asia to the Caribbean. Despite adversity, they were able to forge bonds, survive and thrive. In this spirit, Jahajee Sisters seeks to build community and power to address critical issues challenging Indo-Caribbean women."[5] The terms *jehaji, jehagin* and *jahajee* carried and carries at present no pejorative connotations about and among the Indian population and has rather been claimed and reclaimed despite the negative undertow of the *kala pani* discourse.

Morton Klass's inventory of the kinship names is supported by my late 1950s childhood village memory of the forms of address between and among Indian families. All women of a senior age would be addressed as *didi* out of respect. There were differences between Hindu and Muslim titles. Since Hindus were in the majority, the Hindi/Bhojpuri titles became better known than those that were influenced by Urdu. Klass divides his inventory into first and second ascending generations and first descending generation with differences based on whether a male or female was doing the calling. These forms of address were adhered to fairly rigidly. A young man would not for instance take the liberty of calling his brother's wife or even his elder brother by name and instead would refer to his elder brother as *bhe* or *bhai* (phonetically) and his brother's wife as *bhowji*. Calling someone by their given first name was simply not done, again out of respect. Klass notes for instance that "many men say proudly they have never called their wife's name aloud" (p. 94). Pet or nick names could be applied but speaking someone's proper name was a sign of familiarity which was not sanctioned to ensure that respectful distances were still maintained within the confining single household of an extended family. Affectionate displays were frowned upon so as to diminish the possibilities of intimacy and thus the risk of sexual overtures or too close alliances that could lead to potential divisiveness in the family. Although it was thought that the extended family was the norm among Indians, Klass points out that at the time of his study of village life in the 1950s, East Indians had been living in

Trinidad for over one hundred years and at this time only few people had very large extended families.[6] The closeness of the *jehagi* relationship and the acknowledgement and willingness to claim kinship of any degree was still very important to Indians. There were valid reasons why this knowledge was important in a small population. To ensure marriage outside of the close kin group, it was necessary to recognise kin and avoid incest taboos. Klass commented on the "...East Indian capacity for indefinite extension of kinships."[7] The boat brother and sister relationship remained so binding that pseudo kin relationships allowed for the expansion of family networks and thus for a support system that was vital to a community which depended on its internal resources during the process of early resettlement.

From this early deployment of kinship and a re-invented family or brotherhood of the boat, some of the kinship terms have surfaced with remarkable recurrence. I draw attention to these terms as they enter the marketplace for exchange of language and gender symbolism among Indians in Trinidad, as well as those outside of the ethnic and cultural group. Klass records that for the second ascending generation, *nana* (referring to one's maternal father or maternal father's brother) and *nani* (referring to maternal mother or any second ascending female on one's mother's side) was generally used. For the first descending generation, *beta* and *beti* for son and daughter of any sibling or cousin, *dulahin* for a bride and *dolaha* for a bridegroom were generally used by all Indians. This was common practice among both Hindus and Muslims, whether rural or urban.

A lived example comes to mind on how binding these gender differentiations were in establishing both respect and rewards. In the 1960s an aged Indian woman moved from her rural village into a house across the street from ours in the relatively urban district of Princes Town. She was a Hindu of the Brahmin caste and her name was Mrs Maharaj. She had moved to be closer to her son and his family who lived a few miles away. Every now and then, when she wanted to attract my mother's attention, Mrs. Maharaj or *Nani*, as we children called her, would cry out sonorously and insistently from the top floor of her tall two-storied house to ours across the street: "*Dulahin... Dulahheen... Dulahheeeen.*" Her voice echoed along the slope of houses downwind to the rest of the street's occupants. It was her right, if you like, to demand this kind of attention. My mother who had by then been married for over twelve years remained a *dulahin* to her as the younger woman in this neighbourly relationship. Thus we were all complicit in this arrangement of running errands for her in respect of her age and caste status – as a Maharajin she was of the Brahmin caste so expected this response from those around her. The construct of *Dulahin* for the young wife and *Nani* for the older woman, the implicit acceptance of the power relations between them, were founded on lines of hierarchy and authority that were clearly drawn in the pre-partition India from which all Indo-Trinidadians were descended. It provided the structure and psychological base for the complex *jehagee* networks, village support and blood related family relationships while also ensuring that kinship ties and respect accorded to both women and for men. The primary signifiers within the ethnic community for allocating respect to women were age, caste standing and marital status. Men achieved respect on the basis of age and caste status but additional status was achieved by their occupational status or their possession of wealth.

For the non-Indians in particular who lived on our street, my mother was Mrs. Mohammed and Nani was Mrs. Maharaj. My father called her Maharajin in acknowledgement of her caste. In *A House for Mr. Biswas*, V.S. Naipaul describes a scene that although underlined with his typical irreverence, underscores the mutual respect that had to be shown between the different religious groups who comprised the Indian population.

> Seeing the group of three walking Indian file across the plank over the gutter, F. Z. Ghany got up, spat out the matchstick, and greeted them with good humoured scorn. '*Maharajin, Majarajin*, and little boy'. He made most of his money from Hindus but, as a Muslim, distrusted them (p. 42).

This mark of respect through kinship names, despite the difference in religion and in deference to age, was implicitly understood among the Indo-Trinidadian community well into the sixth and seventh decades of the twentieth century, just as Indians also understood and used the term *Tantie* as a form of respect for women in Afro-descended families. Well into the century, young Indian girls were still called *Beti*, and young Indian males *Beta*, perhaps as a form of affection rather than to emphasize their youthfulness.

By the middle to late twentieth century, a variety of kinship terms came to be understood and appreciated not only within the Indo-Trinidadian community but among the rest of the society. The relationships were clearly laid out – *nani* was one's maternal grandmother, *nana*, maternal grandfather. Even today, the legacy of this hierarchy that is established by age and gender may still be observed by many. Elders ranked above juniors, and among people of similar age, males invariably outranked females. How these kinship terms came to be major signifiers that were also used by those outside the Indian community and how other metaphors were added is relevant to the story of an evolving feminism among Indo-Caribbean populations. Honorific titles are important in human society and recognition of the etymologies of these terms are vital to understanding how they confer power or agency on the individual of either sex and maintain through naming, the symbolic markers of gender identity.

CONTINUITIES

Literature from the sixties onwards conveys the changing stream of consciousness and accompanying archetypes and tropes that would come to be associated with Indo-Caribbeanness. Harold Sonny Ladoo's *No Pain like this Body* (1972) is a novel about a rice-growing Indian family in Trinidad. Its compelling prose draws you into the appalling violence of the relation between Ma and Pa, demonstrating the failure of the Indo-Caribbean family to enact in real life circumstances the support that was expected of its protective kinship structures as previously analysed by Morton Klass. Nonetheless, in Ladoo's novel, the characters a generation before, Nana and Nani, Ma's parents, still stand out inherently as the keepers of older traditions of respect. Nani in particular is the female bearer of tradition and knowledge, skill even: she can beat the drums, she attempts to soothe the boy's pain, and Ma still turns to her in times of trouble. In *A Brighter Sun* by Samuel Selvon set in the 1950s, ideas have shifted yet again as Tiger and Urmilla are married and have moved to the suburban district of Barataria in their own home, away from the watchful eyes of the extended family. Selvon's subtle grasp of the complexities of

Indian masculinity and femininity and its changes are excellent – the young couple not only call each other by name but there is an acknowledgement of love and companionship. Despite having had a marriage arranged by their parents, they become friends and partners in this relationship, indicating that Selvon had picked up the subtle changes in the nature of the relations and insider power to negotiate changes that women in the Indo-Trinidadian family did possess.

Unfortunately, none or perhaps few of these nuances of kin, tradition, respect or evolution of gender relations emerges in the earlier song forms in Trinidad folk culture. The earliest calypsos that recognised Indian femininity tended to either romanticise the Indian woman as sexually attractive and attainable or, as Gordon Rohlehr writes, "The Indian woman was generally presented against the background of the Indian feast, and many calypsos in which such women appear are really not about the women at all, but about masked interracial conflict, in which the feast becomes a point of, or arena of, ethnic confrontation" (Rohlehr, 261). The generic Indian woman *Dookhani* featured in a number of calypsos in the 1930s. Interestingly enough, and perhaps not surprisingly, The Mighty Sparrow's *Marajihn*, first sung in 1982, captures the Indian woman in a package that was wrapped with sexual overtones while holding fast to all the stereotypes associated with Indo-Trinidadian women's dress styles and kinship associative terms:

> You are the genesis of my happiness
> You are the one I always dreamed off
> How can I exist without your sweet love
> When I see you in your sari or your ohrni
> I am captured by your innovative beauty
> If it wasn't for your nani or your bhowji
> I would marry you and tek you out of the country
> Marahjin, marajihn oh my sweet dulahin
> Saucy marajihn, racy marajihn, all right
> Dulahin dulahin
> Dulahin, hear the sweet music playing

The Mastana Bahar competition by the late 1960s "was aimed at encouraging competitors, the majority of whom were Indians, to produce innovative music rather than imitate film songs and the traditional folk songs."[8] Sundar Popo's 1971 song *Nana and Nani* first made popular through Mastana Bahar comes out from the belly of Indo-Trinidadian folk culture.

> Nana, Nani ghar se nikle
> Dheere dheere chalte hain
> Madura ke dukaan me
> Dono jaake baithe hai
> Nana peeye puncheon daaru,...
> Charlie's wine aur Gilby wine,
> Karire meri Nani
> Aga aga nana chale nani going behind
>
> Nana drinking white rum
> and nani drinking wine

Sundar Popo not only linguistically blends the Hindi with English but the introduction of this mixture of musics, language and content gives rise to the new form marketed as chutney, signifying its origins within this culture. As his first and what was to become his most popular song, the characters of Nani and Nana loom large. Unlike the still sacred or ancestral space in which Harold Sonny Ladoo holds the male and female ancestral presence, Popo humanizes and locates them squarely in the context of poverty and distorted gender and social relationships that occurred with the breakdown of kin and family structures as the society continued to evolve.

With the emergence of the first public female voice in chutney in the 1980s, some of these themes continued – the sauciness of the Indo-Trinidadian male and especially the female population which I return to later, are rendered in Drupatee Ramgoonai's popular *Roll up the Tassa* (1988). In this song Bissessar is referred to occasionally as *bayta/beta*, referencing that he is a young male, and there is the ubiquitous reference to the *dulahin*. By this time, the idea of the *nani* – the older, wiser woman to be respected in the family – had lost much of its earliest resonance and *nani* is now associated with both sexual overtones as well as raucous behaviour, as also found in Sundar Popo's tune.

When Sita and Parbati
Start a song now in Hindi
But meh nani get on baad
She get the old man stick all hard

Roll up de tassa
Roll up de tassa Bissessar
Oh Beta, roll up de tassa,
Roll up de tassa, Bissessar
Rip up de tassa, Bissessar
Ruff up de tassa, Bissessar
Oh Beta

Look at my nani
She real get on bad yuh no man[9]

While the emergence of popular discourse on Indo-Trinidadian femininity begins through music, it is to contemporary literature that we must turn for further disruption of the archetypes. In novels like Lakshmi Persaud's *Butterfly in the Wind* (1990), Shani Mootoo's *Cereus Blooms at Night* (1996) and *Valmiki's Daughter* (2009) and Ramabai Espinet's *The Swinging Bridge* (2003), the characters are modern, nuanced, liberated, more complex in both sexuality and in their needs and desires. In all of these novels, Indo-Trinidadian femininity is central, confrontational and certainly not the retiring stereotypes dictated by early rules of kinship and gender or that required of religious precepts. In Persaud's *Butterfly in the Wind* (1990), the character Kamla is a feisty and challenging young woman who will not accept homegrown truths or religious dictums without questioning their relevance to the current condition of women. In her subsequent novels including *Sastra* (1993) and *Daughters of Empire* (2012), we see a recurrent tendency to establish the potency of female power and to incise this against a previous grain that presented a more submissive female stance. Persaud draws on references to the characters in the holy scripts of the Ramayana, as models against which change is being confronted.

The gradually increasing visibility and audible presence of the Indo-Caribbean population in occupations, professions and entertainment by the last three decades of the twentieth century began to disrupt the homogeneity that characterized gender identity and gender relations among Indians and allowed for some agentic claiming over their own narratives. Group identity is shaped by the internal micro forces that are themselves mutating, by meso factors that intervene to create change and by macro factors that force community and national perception, action and responses. Identities are shaped by the social worlds in which people interact. The tension that arises in the lived construction of identity models is that identity itself is always a moving target, never arrived at but constantly being shaped. Nonetheless, what emerges at any point in history are compelling tropes that represent the historical moment or period. Perhaps best captured through fiction or fictional devices, in the visual arts, and currently through film, these formats allow for profound intuitive insights into the nature of a people, society or civilization.

One example comes to mind. A collectively understood trope on the creation of the new world subject – perhaps relevant to both African slavery and to the decimation of the indigenous Amerindian population, has emerged through a reading of the Shakespearian play *The Tempest* (1623). The relationship between the main protagonists Caliban, Ariel and Prospero demonstrates the extent to which ideological assumptions about race and culture that were pervasive in the fifteen and sixteenth centuries could allow a master to assume a deity like superiority over those he enslaved. By setting the scenario of this play in the Caribbean and ensuring that Caliban is taught to speak, Shakespeare vilifies the colonizer and establishes the humanity of those enslaved. Ultimately Caliban, using the same tools he has been taught of language and guile, rises above his master and defies him. Both Aime Cesaire and Kamau Braithwaite draw on *The Tempest* to create philosophies of *negritude* that bridged Africa and the Caribbean, with Cesaire adapting and inverting elements in the play and conceiving "the Prospero-Caliban relationship in terms of absolute interdependency, as in the black-and-white chessboard,"[10] an astute and far-seeing re-interpretation of the play.

Another trope comes to mind, that of *limbo* invoked by Wilson Harris.[11] Wilson drew on the concept of limbo derived from European mythology referring to an intermediate or transitional state of restraint or confinement over which one has no control. He recasts *limbo* as the dismemberment of the African limb of culture, noting that:

> ...the limbo dance of West Indian carnival celebrations is said to have originated on the crowded slave ships of the Middle Passage. Citing the connection between the limbo dancer's spider-like transformation and the Caribbean Anancy fables in Edward Kamau Brathwaite's "Islands," Harris interprets the emergence of limbo as the slaves' subconscious means of "bridging the gap between an outer frame and an inner dislocation. ...For Harris, Caribbean folk traditions such as limbo and vodun are manifestations of creativity as well as intuitive strategies for dealing with historical crises or traumas."[12]

Just as we have metaphorical literatures that recur in the collective analyses of the African middle passage, we can also see patterns emerging in the genres of English literature that is authored by women. The contemporary English female character cannot now be comprehended without the novels of Jane Austen in late eighteenth century and the Bronte sisters in the early nineteenth centuries that have given us typologies for appreciation and for building composite mental pictures of English womanhood. I venture that the mythopoetics of the Indo-Caribbean experience emerged perhaps most in V.S. Naipaul's *A House for Mr. Biswas* (1961) and in other personal narratives of self and exile.

Deliberations on the depiction of Indian womanhood nonetheless still remain elusive, to be teased out of the different sources. An exception that clearly reaches for such a mythopoetics of Indian femininity is Olive Senior's short story set in Jamaica entitled *The Arrival of the Snake-Woman*. "Everything about the Snake-Woman was magical from the start, even the way she arrived without our seeing, though we were all looking." We are drawn into the web of mystery and romance which Senior invests in the coolie-woman.

> Any thoughts I might have had that she was not a true Heathen vanished when I heard this, for Parson

Bedlow had been very explicit about one thing and it was the Heathen's sinful lust for gold - "Their tinkling ornaments about their feet ...The chains, and the bracelets ...the ornaments of their legs ...the rings, the nose jewels" - exactly as it was in the Bible! And yet, I didn't care. I was already half in love with the snakewoman, with her nose ring and tinkling ornaments and her outrageous, barbaric ways; I could hardly wait for Cephas and Son Son to go with Moses to the Bay and bring her back to the hills.

Miss Coolie, as the Snakewoman is called by the villagers, represents a series of stereotypes by which Indian femininity and Indians came to be known, among them a mysterious sexuality coupled with heathenism, a drive for self-sufficiency and agency, an entrepreneurial mindset that has her ultimately becoming one of the richest persons in the village, and a capacity to navigate her way across the complicated race and power relations still embedded in a colonized space. I agree with Ameena Gafoor that the Snakewoman "works her way through the alienation and isolation of the exile, colonial victimization and racial exclusion to the conscious decision to integrate culturally."[13]

ADDING SYMBOLS OF INDIAN FEMININITY

In the absence of an extensively mature fictional literature, rites and rituals of religion and adornment, the meanings invested in kinship titles, and the originary narrative of crossing the *kala pani* all provide metaphors for understanding Indo-Caribbean femininity and, by extension, Indo-Caribbean feminist interventions. Sherry Ann Singh's *The Ramayana Tradition and Socio-Religious Change in Trinidad 1917-1990*, though not focussed on femininity, inevitably examines some of the models that have informed womanhood among Indians, among these the ubiquitous Sita[14] who presented the demeanour of submission, loyalty, support and devotion, including that of walking through fire to prove her virtue.

I focus here on three other symbols - *jehajee, matikor* and *bindi* - that have emerged like an additional rhythmic drumbeat over the last two decades, and consider why these have been absorbed into the treasury of concepts.

Jehajin - Jahajee

The Jahajee Sisters, the group formed in Queen's, New York in 2009, was comprised of primarily but not exclusively Indo-Guyanese women whose parents or who themselves were migrants from the Caribbean to the USA. The invocation of the term *jahajee* signals both a continuity and transformation of the concept of sisterhood of the boat. Here the migration stream being recognised is a second one, signalling the growth of a diaspora, another crossing of the water from the Caribbean to the north, another shedding of skin, another adjustment to a new set of conditions. The group describes its origins in the publication *Bolo Bahen! Speak Sister!*[15]. The goal of the activist group is the empowerment of Indian women, in particular the Indo-Caribbean community in Queens. The activity which brought the women together was an interactive series of workshops held from January to April 2009 in Queens under the Arts & Empowerment (A&E) Program of New York City. The workshops focused on the issue of domestic violence which was explored through poetry, prose, film and dialogue and, like the earlier second wave feminist consciousness raising groups, the programme sought to harness and develop the voices and the power of women and girls by encouraging them to share their thoughts, emotions, experiences and, crucially, their visions for change. I was invited as a keynote speaker in 2010 to one of their events. Upon meeting the group of women, I was impressed by their level of commitment – these were educated, professional women who were striving for personal freedoms as women and were well equipped with a US identity toolkit while retaining a profound concern with the conditions of their populations, such as the plight of the aged in their communities, and emotional links to their origins.

Their use of *Jahajee* clearly still maintained the power of its original meaning in the first crossing from India, a fraternity among those who travelled on the ships together. This was a relationship and kinship system of support that echoes with the sisterhood that migrant women needed of each other. One of the poems in *Bolo Bahen* illustrates these continuities embedded in the symbol of Jahajee, the new leg of the journey that began in India into the Caribbean then continued onto New York, interpreted as another crossing of the kala pani or black waters - this time the Caribbean Sea and the Atlantic Ocean.

VII. My Jahajee Sisters

Pardesi, Pardesi ...I feel you looking for me!
"Don't fret, Coolie Woman, dry your tears"
Riding on the wings of my Jahajee sisters, mothers, grandmas
Gliding over the Indian Ocean, the Atlantic, Kala Pani
Standing firm on their shoulders
Leaning on the strength of my Jahajee Sisters
Leaning on the strength of my Jahajee Sisters

...We were once caterpillars
emerging from cocoons
now butterflies with iron wings
soaring to new heights

This new crossing appears voluntary however, leading to new possibilities. The voyage is thus transformed, not unlike Isaac Teale's *Ode to the Sable Venus* (1765) and Thomas Stothard's visual depiction of this ode in *The Voyage of the Sable Venus* (1794), women's beauty and strength are privileged over the horrors of the journey and the dehumanizing of their femininity. Uniting soft and hard edges of this voyage with images of iron wings and soft cocoons, the Jahajee Sisters envision a world in which sisterhood is so strong it erases the effects of a dominant patriarchy, ends violence against women, and restores balance. Their achievement of justice is dependent on collective power. They have deployed the concepts of sisterhood of the boat, of a shared experience of trauma if you like, the echoes of this message uniting not only generations but Indo-Caribbean populations across diverse societies.

Matikor

The symbol *matikor*, perhaps the most dominant and potentially useful one for interpreting fundamental elements of Indo-Caribbean femininity, is derived from the popular ritual of the *maticore* ceremony which was held the night before a wedding ceremony. "The term matikor roughly means "digging dirt," from Bhojpuri matti, "earth," and khora, "dig". ...The corresponding Guyanese ritual is most commonly called dig dutty (literally, "dig dirty")."[16] The *maticore* ceremony can be likened to the Hindu or Indian bridal shower generally carried out on the Friday night before the wedding. When marriages were arranged between very young women who had just entered puberty, sometimes to young men who were equally inexperienced, the *maticore* was devised as a means of sexual instruction. Here, in a primarily female space, the young bride would be introduced to the pleasures and vagaries she must expect of married life, amidst much ribaldry and teasing, with information conveyed primarily through the form of song. In this gathering of young and old women, stories were shared, experiences passed on through humour, and solidarities built between generations of women. The songs were acted out sensually and sexually. When these were later introduced into the public marketplace they were referred to or became known as chutney songs. In 1999, naming one of the first edited volumes dedicated to Indian women *Matikor: The Politics of Identity for Indo-Caribbean Women*, Roseanne Kanhai anticipated that this concept had begun to signify both a feminist consciousness embedded in Indo-Caribbean ritual practices and an ingredient of mischief, humour and dissidence in Indo-Caribbean feminine identity. As noted previously Drupatie Ramgoonai, the popular female Indo-Trinidadian singer, drew heavily on this imagery, both consciously and unconsciously, to establish a public persona on stage. Rasika Dindial a well-known Trinidadian chutney and classical singer's rendition of "Maticoor Night," is an often played song for weddings in both Trinidad and in the diaspora.

> I goin' in a matikor to see them ladies fête,
> I goin' in a matikor to see them ladies fête
> They goh fxte for so, they goh can't catch-a they breath!
> I goin' in a matikor to see them ladies fête
>
> They don't really care what anybody say
> Matikor night is for ladies to get away
> When they go to dig the dirt, the tassa does play
> As soon as they finish, they does get away...
> They goin' back in the tent, and they still dancin',
> They tellin' the tassaman, "Doh stop playin'!"
> Matikor night is for ladies to get away...[17]

This last ritual fling of freedom around the bride and groom the night before the knot is tied is evidenced in bachelorette and stag parties of the west and seems universal to all groups.

Currently, when brides are no longer assumed to be naive about sexuality among Indians in Trinidad, the ritual continues and plays another function, that of support and celebration, and, as an offshoot, the site for the creation of new chutney songs. As Kanhai has done, other writers have increasingly begun to recognise the *maticore* is a site for bonding and consciousness-raising among Indo-Caribbean women. Ballangee's fieldwork observations well into in twenty first century confirm that the ritual continues to be practiced with some of its features kept intact. For example men, with the exception of the *tassa* drummers or photographers, are not expected to attend the ritual. The expressive sexual freedom of older women is an interesting aspect of the *maticore*, perhaps providing a role for older females to demonstrate their longer experience of sexual knowledge over that of younger women and to demonstrate that despite age they are still sexual beings.

> Women young and old are encouraged to join the dancing. Some wine ("wind") their waists, a typical Trini movement, while others raise their arms and spin gracefully. Most often, the party will form a circle; ...Commonly, older women will be among the first to enter the circle engaging in humorous and sexually suggestive dancing. On several occasions, I have witnessed an aged auntie emerge from the crowd, lift the hem of her dress, slip it through one clasped hand to form a phallic extension about her groin, and proceed to thrust her pelvis in mid-air or against another dancer. Sometimes a cucumber or eggplant serves the same purpose. ...Overtly sexual dancing is meant to mimic and in some way instruct about the sexual act. Moreover, this kind of dancing is expressly done in the safety of women's space. Among older women—who are indeed the most suggestive dancers—the lewdness remains there, though young women might dance equally as suggestively among their peers at parties and nightclubs. Klass noted, for example, "the women of [Felicity], who tend to be demure, shy, and self-effacing normally, become bawdy, raucous, and riotous when they gather together on such occasions.[18]

Attending *maticore* rituals was not a regular experience I had as a young girl growing up in rural Trinidad primarily because of our Islamic background. By the mid twentieth century the reconstitution of Islam had created significant distances in the rituals practiced for weddings in particular. Nonetheless, I recall attending a few of these events and being awed at the ease these women had with each other and with their bodies, some having no doubt taken drink. This confidence and freedom to "breakaway" is a concept of femininity that is not generally associated with Indian femininity yet here was a tradition that not only allowed but expected this licentiousness, while couching it in the art of sexual instruction. Kanhai sums up the values that the *maticore* insidiously ingrained and thus its potential as a symbol for Indo-Caribbean femininity:

> Matikor provided a rare opportunity for plantation and post-plantation women to claim a space of celebration and articulation. Adorning themselves with their best clothing, face decorations, and jewellery – brought from India or acquired during indentureship – women could give themselves the beauty and dignity denied to them in the rigours of daily life. They shared gossip and jokes and sang traditional songs, and performed dances that were celebratory and sexually suggestive. Matikor was a place of healing where women could act out their resistance against degradation and depersonalization imposed on them by a ruling class. ...Matikor exists today, its endurance and transformative capacity providing a lens through which the identity of Indo-Caribbean women can be explored.[19]

Kanhai observed that *matikor* remains a closed, ethnic space against the backdrop of the Afro-Caribbean majority and a reminder of the spiritual strength founded in community and tradition as Indian women continue to enter the wider Caribbean and global mainstreams. Like the concept of *jehajee* above, *Matikor* is presented as a primarily Indo-centric ethnic space, an affirmation of the creative energy and liberatory possibilities that might be derived from the original *maticore* ceremonies. As the ritual became less and less practiced, especially in urban communities, its spiritual message persisted through the public performance of chutney. In the volume edited by Kanhai, a Guyanese and Trinidadian network of women scholars, activists and writers are encouraged to become a part of this new expression of the *maticore* space – another exclusively female Indo-Caribbean circle created for sharing stories and confidences, insights and challenges across time and space with the aim of empowering each other and leaving inscriptions for coming generations. Like the symbol of *jehajee* that is also being extended to embrace additional meanings and symbolisms, the new *matikor* does not replace the original ritual performance that continues to survive in attenuated form in Indo-Caribbean family weddings. Rather it draws on the sentient aspects of a culture that, like all culture, replenishes itself by adding new meanings to the original, drawing its lifeblood from the original source from which it was derived.

The symbol contains possibilities for a recognised concept that might define the unique nature of Indo-Caribbean women's struggles against an Indo-Caribbean patriarchy. It might and should be extended to other arenas of feminist struggles. The more extensive span of history and the demographic and cultural dominance in the Region has given European and African descended women's struggles a longer period of incubation. There was an implicit assumption in the rise of the second wave feminist movement that all women shared similar histories of patriarchal control and social repression so that the difference and diversity of these experiences by class or ethnicity did not surface until well into the late 1990s.[20] Post-colonial thought and intersectionality has allowed a space for different groups, including Indo-Caribbean women to articulate the differences within community or religion, mining the metaphoric and empirical components that speak to these differences.

Bindi
In *Bindi*, Roseanne Kanhai again summons up another icon for Indian femininity – one that is premised not on a ceremonial event but on a decorative tradition that marks status. Derived from the Sanskrit *bindu*, meaning a drop, Kanhai writes that the "traditional *bindi* is a round dot pasted on a Hindu woman's forehead just above and between the eyebrows."[21] The colour and material of the drop signified age and gendered roles, sandalwood for

young girls, vermilion for married women and ash for widows. It is thought that the vermilion for married women signified the menstrual flow that signalled the capacity for childbearing, especially as during the marriage ceremony this was applied as a stripe of vermilion powder along the centre path of the woman's hair, leading to the dot or drop on the forehead. Kanhai notes that in contemporary times the *bindi* has become a fashion statement, highly decorative and multi-coloured and has possibly lost the original intent of defining the stages of womanhood and what was allowed, or not, at each stage. While the *maticore* was a secretive, separate and highly sexualized space, *bindi* as a decorative and now less exclusive practice, allows for another metaphor for Indo-Caribbean femininity to continue its emergence in a western context, perhaps literally "bringing Indo-Caribbean womanhood to the fore." Perhaps what is most fascinating about the metaphoric possibilities of *bindi* is that a decorative device on the body that once signified gender difference and markers of control has been appropriated by women themselves for primarily ornamental use. In its loss of inherent originary meanings, the decorative device has been reinvented as one for embellishment of beauty, and thus sexual power, rather than a signifier of submissiveness to gender definitions of subordinate female status or markers of control.

A DISCURSIVE SPACE FOR SYMBOLS OF INDO-CARIBBEAN FEMINIST IDENTITY

Why has it become necessary for a naming of the Indo-Caribbean female experience that defines both Indo-Caribbean femininity and Indo-Caribbean feminism? The emergence of second wave feminism in the last decades of the twentieth century took for granted a collective notion that we were all sisters under the skin, whether this skin was white or black or brown. The evolution of literature, scholarship, activism and practices has revealed that historical, cultural, class and geographical differences cannot be dismissed. They lead to different access to power, to privilege, to being visible or invisible, to having the confidence of a voice, or having that voice dismissed or, worse, given no hearing. All of the latter are antithetical to the larger feminist goals of empowerment.

The three major tropes *jehajee*, *matikor* and *bindi* selected above for scrutiny are linked but are not exclusive to Hinduism. The early Indo-Islamic population were in the minority compared to the dominant Hindu group and thus the ideas pertaining to an Indo-Islamic presence has been more subdued. I attempted to connect to symbols of Islamic women in an essay entitled *Khadija's Daughters*[22] in which I viewed the Prophet Muhammed's wife Khadija's greater age and financial resources as owner of the household business, as key in providing her with a relative independence and autonomy as a woman. Thus was she able to influence his thinking and teachings as the religion of Islam developed at the time. The idea of the highly controlled or submissive Islamic woman therefore is not grounded in the origins of this religion. I also found one concept in Islam that seems to parallel the ideas of womanhood under Hinduism and apply to most cultures that have sought to contain female sexuality. The concept of *fitna* which derived from an Arabic word meaning to seduce, tempt or lure away was implicitly employed by both the colonial authorities and the male patriarchy in reference to Islamic women to control their sexuality and display of seductive femininity. It is parallel in some ways to the concept of *prakti* in Hinduism.

> The female consists of *shakti* (energy/power, the energizing principle of the universe) and *prakti* (nature, the undifferentiated matter of the universe). The latter is uncultured and therefore dangerous, sustaining the idea that women are impure, easily polluting, and themselves polluted. In metaphorical terms, this has meant that the female, as uncultured nature, must be controlled by the male (Mohammed 2002, 147).

The Indo-Caribbean population were drawn from pre-partition India in the nineteenth and twentieth centuries and there were far more commonalities in their practices and ideas of gender despite religious differences, many of which did not resurface with more clarity until both religions became reconstituted in Caribbean villages and communities. Thus the employment of tropes that derive specifically from Hindu practices do not separate Hindu and Islamic Indo-Caribbean feminism. They relate to more universal ideas of femininity and to the control of women, despite religious difference. There are other symbolic markers in Islam which have emerged in more contemporary times – those of the *hijab* and the *burkha*. The wearing of these cross ethnic divides as many African women also currently cover their heads or faces and bodies when in public. What this signals to us is that newly emerging measures of female control need to be scrutinized even while the older ones such as bindi and matikor spaces have been opened up by women themselves over centuries of whittling away at their meanings.

Inviting a range of concepts and ideas, of practices and rituals into one arena for investigation, rather than seeing each as a different silo, presents a potentially fruitful area for expanding our understanding of the complexity of gender and feminist theory and practice. I have underscored two primary sites where these differences have emerged in the definition of Indo-Caribbean femininity. The first is the burgeoning literary space, the second is the conceptual scholarly space. I see the need for more dialogue between these two spaces and for both to dig deeper into the unconscious as well as spiritual and mythical elements of Indo-Caribbean cultural heritage past and present. In order to capture the wider public imagination and idiomatic use among feminist and popular writers and artists, perhaps the concept of *matikor* which seems most promising needs to be mined for its submerged potential. Why did this ritual emerge? What specific purposes did it serve? What unintended results emerged from this ritual of a separate women's space? How has the ritual been transformed and why has it persisted in the ceremonies of Indians? Most importantly, what is its significance as a symbol that flags independence, uninhibited sexuality and collective consciousness for the Caribbean feminist movement and for Indo-Caribbean women's contribution to the feminist project? All of these meanings must be deconstructed and reinvented by new generations of women who take the concept and the ritual outside of its original site – before nuptials - and into the open, and place it under the scrutiny of a male and a wider non-Indian female gaze. In inviting us to engage with the concepts of *kala pani, jehajee, matikor* and *bindi*, Brinda Mehta, the Jehagee Sisters and Roseanne Kanhai have already begun this task. A collective Indo-Caribbean feminist project has been ongoing over for several decades. What remains on the agenda is that, rather than being viewed as idiosyncratic of the feminist instincts of an ethnic group, these ideas need to become part of a dialogue with all feminisms. The mining of symbols and strategies garnered from a wider cross section of groups may very well be one pathway to invigorating and collectively strengthening the spiritual heartbeat of Caribbean feminism in a new phase.

ENDNOTES

[1] Cited from Ramlagan, Michelle. 2010. "Mehta, Brinda. Diasporic (Dis)locations: Indo-Caribbean Women Writers Negotiate the Kala Pani.," *Anthurium: A Caribbean Studies Journal*, 7 : 1, Article 27.
Available at: http://scholarlyrepository.miami.edu/anthurium/vol7/iss1/27

[2] Kala Pani literally means dark water in Hindi. Discursively it has come to represent the crossing of the the seas to foreign lands and in doing so incurring caste pollution and loss of status and respectability.

[3] Michelle Ramlagan, *Anthurium* Vol 7, Issues 1-2, Spring and Fall of 2000, *Book Review* of Brinda Mehta, *Diasporic (Dis)locations: Indo-Caribbean Women Writers Negotiate the Kala Pani*. Jamaica: The University of the West Indies Press, 2004.

[4] David Dabydeen. 2003, p.19 in *Lutchmee and Dilloo: A Study of West Indian Life*, by Edward Jenkins. This edition Oxford: Macmillan Caribbean.

[5] http://www.jahajeesisters.org

[6] This is true of my own experience as in the village of Lengua, south Trinidad in which I lived for the first eight years after birth; there were a handful of families who had extended households and these tended to be families who were either agricultural or commercial entrepreneurs.

[7] Klass, Morton. 1961. *East Indians in Trinidad: A Study of Cultural Persistence*. New York: Columbia University Press. Reprint, 1988. p 103.

[8] From Sharda Patasar's PhD diss. "Sounding the Landscape: Indo-Trinidadian Musical Identities in Trinidad 1935-2011" Unpublished draft, University of Trinidad and Tobago, 2012

[9] From Roll up the Tassa, Lyrics and rendition by Drupatie Ramgoonai, first released 1988

[10] See https://shakespeare.edel.univ-poitiers.fr/index.php?id=1087

[11] Harris, Wilson E. 2008. "History, Fable and Myth in The Caribbean and Guianas." *Caribbean Quarterly*, 54 (1/2) : 5-38 The 60th Anniversary Edition: Literature and Ideas (March - June, 2008)

[12] https://caribbean.commons.gc.cuny.edu/2012/04/30/reading-wilson-harriss-history-fable-and-myth/

[13] Gafoor, Ameena. 1993. "The Image of the Indo-Caribbean Woman in Olive Senior's 'The Arrival of the Snake Woman'" *Callaloo* 16 (1) : 34- 43, Winter.

[14] This essay might be read as a continuation of ideas on symbolic definitions of Indian femininity started in the previous essay in this section "Negotiating with Myth and Symbols: The Historical Reconfiguration of Indian Mas-culinity and Femininity in Trinidad."

[15] See *Bolo Behen* edited by Kumarie Moteelall, Sasha Kamini Parmasad and Purvi Shah and published by Jahajee Sisters: Empowering Indo-Caribbean Women – Sakhi for South Asian Women in 2009.

[16] Ballangee, Christopher. 2013, "From Indian to Indo-creole: Tassa Drumming, Creolization, and Indo-Caribbean Nationalism in Trinidad and Tobago," PhD Diss., University of Florida, p. 155
[17] *Ibid* p. 156
[18] Ballangee, *op cit* pp 163-164
[19] Roseanne Kanhai, p. xi
[20] From Sharda Patasar's PhD Diss. "Sounding the Landscape: Indo-Trinidadian Musical Identities in Trinidad 1935-2011" Unpublished draft, University of Trinidad and Tobago, 2012
[21] Roseanne Kanhai, *Bindi*, p. i.
[22] Patricia Mohammed "Daughters of Khadija" *The Encyclopedia of Caribbean Religions*: Volume 1: A - L; edited by Patrick Taylor, Frederick Case and Sean Meighoo, Chicago: University of Illinois Press, p. 396

REFERENCES

Espinet, Ramabai. 2003. *The Swinging Bridge*, Phyllis Bruce Books.

Hodge, Merle. 1970. *Crick Crack Monkey*. London and Jamaica: Heinemann.

James, C.L.R. 1936. *Minty Alley*. London and Port of Spain: New Beacon Books.

Jenkins, Edward *Lutchmee and Dilloo: A Study of West Indian Life*, edited with a new introduction by David Dabydeen, first published 1877, this edition Oxford: Macmillan Caribbean, 2003.

Kanhai, Roseanne (ed.). 1999. *Matikor: The Politics of Identity for Indo-Caribbean Women*. University of the West Indies, School of Continuing Studies.

Kanhai, Roseanne (ed.). 2000. *Bindi: The Multifaceted Lives of Indo-Caribbean Women*, Kingston, Jamaica: University of the West Indies Press.

Klass, Morton. 1961. *East Indians in Trinidad: A Study of Cultural Persistence*. New York: Columbia University Press. Reprint 1988.

Ladoo, Harold Sonny. 1972. *No Pain like this Body*. Toronto: House of Anansi Press.

Lewis, Linden. 1998. "Masculinity and the Dance of the Dragon" in *Feminist Review Rethinking Caribbean Difference*, edited by Patricia Mohammed, 59. Routledge Journals.

Mehta, Brinda. 2004. *Diasporic (Dis)locations Indo-Caribbean Women Writers Negotiate the Kala Pani*. Jamaica: The University of the West Indies Press.

Mohammed, Patricia. 2002. *Gender Negotiations among Indians in Trinidad 1917-1947*. England and The Hague: Palgrave Macmillan and Institute of Social Studies.

Mohapatra, Prabhu. 1995. "Restoring the Family: Wife Murders and the Making of a Sexual Contract for Indian Immigration Labour in the British Caribbean Colonies 1860-1920." India: Nehru Memorial Museum and Library.

Mootoo, Shani. 1996. *The Cereus Blooms at Night.* Toronto: Press Gang.

Mootoo, Shani. 2009. *Valmiki's Daughter,* Toronto: House of Anansi Press.

Moteelall, Taij Kumarie, Sasha Kamini Parmasad and Purvi Shah, eds. 2009. *Bolo Bahen Speak Sister* Jahajee Sisters: Empowering Indo-Caribbean Women Sakhi for South Asian Women, Arts and Empowerment Programme, New York, 2009.

Naipaul, V.S. 1961. *A House for Mr. Biswas.* London: Andre Deutsch.

Persaud, Lakshmi. 1990. *Butterfly in the Wind.* Leeds, UK: Peepal Tree Press.

Reddock, Rhoda. 1985. "Freedom Denied: Indian Women and Indentureship in Trinidad and Tobago 1845-1917." *Economic and Political Weekly,* 22 (43) : 79-87.

Rohlehr, Gordon. 1990. *Calypso and Society in Pre-Independence Trinidad.* Trinidad: Gordon Rohlehr.

Singh, Sherry Ann 2012. *The Ramayana Tradition and Socio-Religious Change in Trinidad 1917-1990.* Jamaica and Miami: Ian Randle Press.

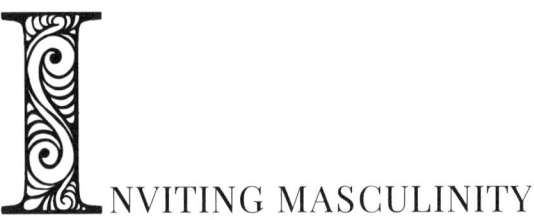

INVITING MASCULINITY

3

11

Deconstructing Patriarchy through Feminist Epistemology[†]

FEMINIST EPISTEMOLOGIES

Identities are never constructed in isolation from our experiences, but our experiences are themselves mediated through the material body. "The material world that surrounds us is one in which we use our living bodies to give substance to the social distinctions and differences which underpin social relations, symbolic systems, forms of labour and quotidian intimacies" writes Henrietta Moore (1994, 71). A male Ghanaian colleague who shared student life with me in the Hague in the 1980s and who came from a prestigious background in Ghana, was appalled

---

[†] Originally presented in the first Caribbean Symposium on Masculinity held in 1996 entitled "The Construction of Caribbean Masculinity: Towards a Research Agenda" hosted by the Centre for Gender and Development Studies, University of the West Indies, St. Augustine, Trinidad, this paper was subsequently published in *Caribbean Masculinities*, edited by Rhoda Reddock. Kingston, Jamaica: University of the West Indies Press as "Unmasking Masculinity and Deconstructing Patriarchy: Problems and Possibilities in Feminist Epistemology," pp. 38-67. It has undergone considerable editing for this collection. I decided to still include the paper as it establishes some of our early ideas and our commitment as feminists in this region of embracing the study of men and masculinity.

that when he entered a tram in Holland, invariably people would clutch their bags and purses closer. Yet black women did not have the same experience. In the relatively sheltered cities of Europe then, as a black male he represented an ethnic group and a sex who are feared for this or that reason. Our material bodies – whether outwardly biologically male or female – our race or ethnic group, the colour of our skin and the class signals we present within a particular culture, constantly inform and mediate our social experiences. Cultural markers influence how we express our masculinity and femininity, as well as how others expect us to perform our gender identities. For example, the black working-class dancehall queen in downtown Kingston is not expected to exhibit the same 'femininity' as the uptown 'browning' of St Andrew, Jamaica.

The relationship between how we daily use and experience our bodies to interact with the social is, nonetheless, more similar than different for any sexed grouping of individuals within a culture and in general, across cultures. Gender identity, nonetheless, is not a static achievement for an individual or group. Age and experience change us within our span of life, as does the way in which cultures collectively or individually shift symbolic interpretations or expectations of ethnic groups, sexes and even classes over time. Experience acts ontologically for all of us, but it does so consciously, through a technique of construction. Our identities, whether racial, ethnic, gender, class, national or political, are constantly undergoing construction. Wars or struggles for independence in a society, poverty caused by famines and drought, political rivalries between ethnic groups, nationalistic programmes aimed at state building, consciousness-raising movements such as black power or the women's movement, all influence the ongoing construction of the multiple parts which make up the identity of an individual. But the material base from which this construction takes place is through our bodies. The body is both a repository of our conscious and unconscious and simultaneously the physical medium through which we experience the world and actively engage with it.

One of the major epistemological tasks that feminist scholarship sets out to do is to reunite the detachment of the individual experience of the body with the collective and continuous process of constructing identities. A preliminary way in which feminist epistemology entered this discourse was to examine how the biological script of the female body gets inscribed with different messages from birth, fashioning a binary narrative between masculinity and femininity. Men and women experience their environment differently and this experience provides the differential knowledge which they formulate about reality, about their life chances, about their sexuality, about themselves. While feminists believe that this difference should not provide the basis for inequality between the sexes, at the same time, they argue that the unequal access to resources or experience, especially in past history, has not been fully incorporated into received knowledge thus far. Joan Scott (1987) writes about the diminishment that feminist scholarship received in its early development:

> In the fall of 1984, I arrived in Paris on my way to a conference at UNESCO on the history of women. At the airport an officious customs officer asked the usual questions about the nature of my business in France, and then queried me on the topic of the conference I was attending. When I replied "the history of women," he responded mockingly, "Do women have a history, Professor? And what might it be?" I was taken aback not only by the hostility, but by the difficulty of answering such questions. Of course women had a history, but one so rich and un-mined that no single phrase or story-line could capture it.

I used this anecdote deliberately, as it echoes the experience for most of us who write and speak on feminism with commitment, whether in North America, Europe or in the Caribbean. Women's absence from historical writing, from the early development of philosophy, has created an omission of not just this group and sex, but has limited our contribution to the ideas which have come to shape all knowledge as we receive it on a daily basis. For example, the idea that women were "imperfect males," as Aristotle in early patriarchal conviction branded the female sex, has long outlived this completely false depiction. Many of the beliefs which shaped femininity as emotional and irrational emerged primarily as a result of women's absence from the process of knowledge-making in the earlier centuries. There was also a marked lack of knowledge of the biology of female bodies, and especially of the contribution that the female sex had in the reproduction of human society. Until the nineteenth century, theories of "embryology attributed to the father's seed the major contribution to the characteristics of the offspring" (Cline Horowitz 1987, 86). The discovery of the existence of the female ovum in 1827 then led to further scientific research on the contribution of the ovum to reproduction and thus the complementary rather than secondary role of the female in reproduction. In other words, according to the received script, women not only did not "make" history, they were also assigned a secondary role in the generation of society itself.[1]

Feminist epistemology or feminist theories of knowledge engage directly in these debates of who determines what is truth and what is important, who creates knowledge and for whom. It proposes that women's experience of life is largely relegated to the domestic sphere, caring for children, the sick and elderly produces new ideas about existence which add to the fount of knowledge creation that is equally important for the survival of human society. In redressing the historical gaps, feminist scholarship does not attempt to replace received knowledge by new knowledge gleaned from only a feminist standpoint of experience. What it attempts to do is to challenge received knowledge and amplify it. Until the middle of the twentieth century, the construction of knowledge in the Western world had been heavily androcentric and Eurocentric. Feminist epistemology began to establish new parameters of thought, to contest what is accepted and valued as admissible levels of knowledge, and to confront the gatekeepers and conveyors of knowledge. And it began by returning first to confront the fact that the roles, sexual division of labour and expectations of women were shaped largely through biology. Women were viewed as closer to nature rather than culture. Culture, "the customary beliefs, social forms, and material traits of a racial, religious, or social group"[2] was assumed to be only created by men.

From the middle of the twentieth century onwards, feminism began a concerted and accelerated search for 'femininity' in opposition to a received 'masculinity'. Man, and manhood were first taken as given, the known factor against which woman and femininity was inscribed as the secondary term, the "Other," the latter coined by Simone de Beauvoir (1949). The project of feminism in the twentieth century after women had won the right to vote and recognition of their civil rights, and had begun what is now referred to as the sexual revolution, was to discover the basis on which the subordination of one sex was justified, in order to understand the origins of patriarchal thought and the persistence of a male dominant ideology. Western philosophical thought set up the binary opposition between masculinity and femininity as two oppositional sets of characteristics, simultaneously positioning masculinity and men as superior and femininity and women as inferior. This opposition is also evident in eastern philosophy although at the metaphysical level the latter is couched in more mediated terms. For instance, women and men are viewed as complementary beings in Hindu philosophy, women are the earth while men are the seed. In essence, the earth lies fallow and barren without the seed and eventually it is the seed that is valued over the earth, which gives it life. This schema of female to male in both western and eastern thought is embedded in language through dichotomies which symbolize woman/man as nature/culture, emotional/rational, passive/assertive/, weak/strong, or private/public. These strategic oppositions continuously privilege men in the superior position of the hierarchy and women in the inferior position, as the second sex.

Dichotomous representation works well for film or literary purposes, rapidly establishing characteristics that present opposing concepts: good and evil, soul and body, real or imaginary, heaven and hell, oppositions that can be easily grasped and provide the basis for tragedy or comedy. The dichotomy of the civilized versus the savage justified the invasive acts of western imperialism from the fifteenth to the nineteenth centuries. The first term generally takes its hierarchy from the position of the second. Dichotomous thought therefore entrenches the superiority of one state of being over the other. The hegemony of these ideological discourses can be traced as far back as Plato and Aristotle, who formulating reason over emotion, and culture over nature, justified the domination of male over female, enslaving women in domestic activities, and excluding them from public life in the voice of reason and objectivity.

Creating a dualism between male and female presents a highly skewed and problematic opposition between mind and body, reason and emotion, culture and nature. If mind, reason and culture are deemed superior, then logically the survival of human civilizations could be traced back to a superior male - the hunter, who conquered nature by producing tools and weaponry and began to control not only women's reproductive labour but the labour and resources of other tribes to ensure the survival of the fittest. The role of woman therefore becomes a minor adjunct – reproduction of the human species being a secondary activity. The domestication of animals, arguably the origins of early agriculture and grain gathering which provided the staple for the tribe, was therefore perceived as inferior to the hunt and chase. The chase involves danger and physical activity, and requires strength and courage, as if these virtues were not also possessed by femininity and woman. A contemporary analogy that comes to mind is the low value attached to housework as compared to labour which is considered skilled, such as driving a truck. As capitalism expanded, housework and childcare were not only considered as non-work, but non-productive work, demanding little skill and no training, somehow natural to women's lesser capabilities, and therefore allocated less wages.

Feminist epistemology has attempted to challenge this dominant classificatory scheme and in doing so has lent support to the contestation of other dichotomies which have affected the development of society – dichotomies which have led to the racial stereotyping designating some races inferior and others superior. For instance, Lady Nugent's diary of Jamaican society in the early nineteenth century depicts a clear distinction between the femininity of the white woman and the "unfeminine" physical strength of the black woman.[3] Childbearing was somehow more "natural and easy" for the black woman who also had to carry out a strenuous workload in the fields. Here it was expected that white women would be frail and feminine while the opposite was simultaneously being proposed for black women. Kimberley Crenshaw (1989) referred to this "problematic consequence of the tendency to treat race and gender as mutually exclusive categories of experience and analysis" as intersectionality providing a trenchant feminist critique of duality from a legal standpoint. Gender must also be deconstructed by class and race and is not a standalone category of analysis.

If in its ongoing dialogues and debates, feminist epistemology presents a paradigm for the study of femininity, how and where do we fit the study of masculinity? The burgeoning interest in masculinity by the last decade of the 20th century is not a coincidental one. For many men it was a reaction to feminism. As Teresa de Lauretis observed by 1987, the construction of gender identities had become a self-conscious one triggering among some theoretical and political activists, claims to sameness and identicality between the sexes. A second insight of De Lauretis, is equally insightful here: the ambiguity of gender must be retained. The articulation of feminine gender identity, framed within concepts of equality in relation to masculinity, does not mean that difference must be denied. To discard the notion of difference between the sexes is dangerous. It assumes that one can disregard the complexity and manifold variety, and thus the richness of the human social experience, including the ontological experience of being masculine, feminine or transgender. Biology establishes the most fundamental difference: only the female mammal can actually physically reproduce the species. This primary difference between masculinity and femininity[4] prompts essentialists to hold fast to an argument that there are different roles for men and different roles for women in society, that the male is naturally the breadwinner and protector and the woman as child-bearer is the dependent sex. Essentialism views male sexuality as aggressive and dominant, with female sexuality as passive and needing to be controlled. Essentialism also holds men as physically stronger and intellectually more agile than women and so on.

Constructivism arose as a reaction to the essentialist school of thought in the latter half of the twentieth century and clearly was informed by shifting notions of class (Marxist analysis), race and sexuality. Michael Foucault's (1976) treatment of sexuality is a prime example of constructivism at work. Foucault demonstrated that sexuality must be conceived of not only as a natural given with drives and instincts, but as also constructed over time by historical and cultural dynamics. As a result of constructivist thinking, to exemplify the point, it is no longer possible to locate rape as a crime stimulated by the instinctual sex drive of a man aroused by a *déshabillé* female. Instead the crime can be viewed as exhibiting the relations of power and dominance embedded in the gender system. Constructivist thinking also influenced writers like Simone de Beauvoir (1949) to express the thought that "woman is made, not born."

Gender theorists immediately latched on to the ideas of constructivism as it allowed the possibility of change. If woman's position was not secondary to man but socially constructed, then there was scope for change. Institutions were viewed as equally responsible for the reinforcement of patriarchal ideologies and continuous construction of gender differences. Most religions rely on essentialist interpretations of the text. If, however, we regard femininity and what is deemed femininity as being constructed over time, then so is masculinity. If what is masculine and feminine is only constructed, then the future vision for feminism is either androgynous societies or the production of Amazonian women.

The dilemma in feminist theory at this point is how do we reject some of the more debilitating aspects of essentialism while still taking account of it? How do we retain the components of constructivism which are relevant - in other words how do we deconstruct femininity and masculinity without falling prey to the idea that everything can be explained by the social and cultural?" What are the boundaries between the social and the individual, both in a psychological and in a sexual sense?" (Wieringa 2002, 18) How do we employ the theoretical frames of essentialism and constructivism without creating further binary oppositions in thought? Essentialism and constructivism should not be seen as oppositional, and "indeed many essentialist arguments are contained in constructivist writing" argues Saskia Wieringa (2002, 18). What is needed is the explanation of difference yet the complementarity of both explanations. Gayle Rubin (1975) proposed the term a sex/gender system to get away from the binary that sex was biological, and gender was socially constructed and culturally specific. The construction of gender identity becomes a rapprochement with biological sex, between essentialism and constructivism and consequently a rapprochement between masculinity and femininity rather than a perceived (natural) opposition.

UNWRAPPING MASCULINITY

It is useful to examine briefly some of ways in which masculinity is viewed by men themselves. Geoff Dench (1994) argues that women have more to lose by attempting to reshape common wisdom of what constitutes masculinity and disrupting the natural harmony between the sexes. For Dench, masculinity is defined by the role of protector and breadwinner, giving men a primary role in society – if that is taken away from them he fears they will become like the frog, ugly and irresponsible, without the kiss of the princess to humanize them and turn them into princes. Dench's argument relies on an essentialist notion that generations of men and women and human civilization thus far have worked out a natural division of responsibility, which if reordered can prove to be destructive to continued social relations between the sexes. He believes that women have more to lose by attempting to be more "like men." Dench assumes here that women are merely trying to ape a dominant man's culture. If women have rejected the paradigm of male power and the limits of patriarchal reasoning then it is hardly likely that they are attempting to replace it by another equally limiting female dominant paradigm?

Michael Kaufman (1987, xiv) puts forward a pro-feminist approach: "Much of the literature by men on male-female relations tends to be at one extreme or another: many look at how men are scarred and deformed by our roles but do not examine men's privileges and power over women." At the same time he places himself candidly in the shoes of men and observes that "What makes feminism a threat for so many men, or at least a source of confusion and struggle, is not only that we have privileges to lose, but that it appears - or at least feels - as if our very manhood is at stake."

Like Kaufman, Linden Lewis (1994) also makes a valiant attempt to situate himself in both male and female perspectives in the Caribbean context, recognizing the power and privileges which masculinity confers on Caribbean men and the resistance they have to losing ground, while acknowledging that analyses of gender in the Caribbean (and elsewhere) which have focussed on women, lack serious examination of masculinity. The result is that masculinity has been conceived primarily in negative terms, in which "Caribbean men are homogenized, and identified as a part of a reactionary backlash against feminist intervention in the region." Lewis notes that this kind of interrogation has failed to promote understanding between men and women, and like Kaufman, he consistently presses for analyses that enhance a relational understanding and not widening the gap with further misunderstandings.

The inquiry into masculinity, as was done with the deconstruction of femininity, requires a precision with terminology. When we speak of masculinity in intellectual discourse are we speaking the same language as the politician, the journalist, the calypsonian, young or older men? What do we mean by the words male, man, manhood, and masculinity? Can they be interchangeably used? Revisiting the etymology of the word gender in feminist discourse, Donna Haraway notes that the equivalent words in the different languages are Gender in English, Geshlect in German, Genre in French, and Genero in Spanish. "The root of the English, French and Spanish words is the Latin verb, *generare*, to beget, and the Latin stem *gener-* race or kind. ...The substantives 'Geshlecht', 'gender', 'genre' and 'genero' refer to the notions of sort, kind, and class. ...The modern English and German words, 'gender' and 'Geshlecht' adhere closely to concepts of sex, sexuality, sexual difference, generation, engendering, and so on, while the French and Spanish seem not to carry those meanings as readily." (Haraway 1991, 130). The words associated with gender in all western languages are entangled with concepts of kinship, race, language, and nationality all of which in contemporary scholarship in gender speak to the politics of identity. Like femininity, masculinity is not simply a descriptive or derivative term but is used discursively in relation to gender identity and must constantly be differentiated by class, race and culture. Given the need to establish both essentialist elements as well as socially constructed ones, a useful differentiation is that "male" is a biological referent, while the terms man, manhood and masculinity are more socially ascribed and weighted with constructed ideas of what it is to not be female. Other nuances come to mind with the treatment of the word. Among men, (and women) there is a difference between youth or childhood which might still be termed boyhood, and manhood in which ideas of masculinity shared by a particular culture or group become more formed and entrenched. This differentiation registers with the association between essentialism and constructivism. While there are shared and universal ideas and concepts of masculinity and manhood, there are also variations from one society to the next, as with femininity. This is fundamental to grasping the deconstructive idea of difference. To unmask masculinity is not to reduce what is deemed masculine or manhood to the known, or to deprive masculinity of its difference from femininity. To unmask masculinity is to remove some of the stereotypes that are assumed to be an implicit blueprint of the generic term.

With the natural division of society into binary oppositions, in the process of writing the history of man into culture, the idea of what constitutes masculinity became fixed. It was assumed that man was the known quantity, with woman the unknown, the more enigmatic of the sexes, and to be defined in relation to man and masculinity. The feminist project had set out first to inscribe the woman as existent and to recover her in history, with an underlying notion that femininity or the feminine gender identity needed to be uncovered through conscious interpretation, and representation, by examining concepts of womanhood and femininity in different cultures. What has become more apparent with this unwrapping of woman and femininity is that the feminine seems much less problematic and more fixed, perhaps even more timelessly inscribed in some way than the masculine. That is, feminine gender identity continues to be rooted in the ontology of the female body.

Definitions of manhood and masculinity were premised on power, status, control. Men were known by their roles as provider and breadwinner. If the male could not fulfil these expectations, then he was not a man. Femininity was linked to childbearing, marriage, sexual partnership and women's class status was generally linked to that possessed by her partner or male kin. The shift in occupational roles and the growing acceptance of women as providers, breadwinners, professionals, leaders in society and so on by the late twentieth century, have challenged notions of masculinity, while allowing an expansion of the gender identity of femininity. This is perhaps at the root of male fear that they are losing ground, and privilege, that manhood is threatened when the "God given and natural role of men" is being whittled away. This apparent losing of ground places an increasing psychological pressure on men to retain the notion of an essentialist masculinity.

The celebrated thesis of man the hunter and woman the gatherer has taken firm root and transformed itself into both an explanation as well as an argument for the timeless persistence of a normative and natural sexual division of labour within society. While the sexual division of labour clearly changes over time - and in keeping with the demands of the existing mode of production, it is uncertain why the task of the hurtling hunter was deemed more important than that of the domestic gatherer and nurturer. Is this an interpretation of contemporary human consciousness and re-ordering of the past? In both the previous modes of production and at the present, the burden of breadwinner must always have been a difficult one for the single individual, either man or woman to bear. The notion of the male breadwinner was an essentialist idea easily appropriated by capitalism to determine the concept of a family wage which assumed that the provider is always male.[5] The status accorded to men was and is based on class and various measures by which men gain power, either over other men or institutions. Poor or working-class men have equally been the victims of other men. In the thirteenth and fourteenth centuries in Europe, the rights of the lord over his tenant extended to *droit de seigneur* – the right of the feudal lord to have sexual relations with the tenant's newly-wedded wife, or *prima nocta*, the semi-historical legal right of a monarch to have sex with any female subject. The dishonouring or diminishment of a man and his masculinity through the female has been and still remains literally a blow below the belt for masculinity. In this sense, masculinity is far more a public arrangement, between men and men, rather than a private one between individual men or the distinction between male and female, man and woman.

Anthropological insights of Maurice Godelier, Margaret Mead and Eleanor Burke Leacock offer a wealth of illustrations on the wide cultural variations of what was considered masculinity in more "primitive" cultures. History also reveals tremendous differences in the trappings of masculinity, in dress style, length of hair, the use of adornment and cosmetics. In the twentieth century the re-emergence of the long hair and ponytails among men signifies either a challenge to bourgeois society, or a willingness to bend gender lines of demarcation. One reading of the rastafarian hairstyle for men is that it reaffirmed biblical notions of manhood, control and power while also being mimetic of the symbolic Lion, the personification of strength as king of the jungle. Hair therefore symbolised among African men the reclamation of identity, of Blackness, of origins, of defiance against a history of denigration through colonization which weakened the patriarchal base, and of regaining control over women of the tribe. Its appeal to men outside the Rastafarian faith, and appropriation by other cultures outside of Jamaica suggest that this message is a universal one for many men throughout the western world.

The willingness to challenge notions of masculinity in a culture seems to also change with experience and with the chronological age of the individual man.[6] While conventional notions of masculinity may be displayed outside the intimacy of the household, within the closed environment, many changes are negotiated; for example, household chores become more shared and some men may openly profess to like cooking. But interestingly, this seems to come with the age, experience and confidence of maleness which a man possesses so that his "feminine" activities will not be misinterpreted by his peers.

Several questions suggest themselves in relation to the study of masculinity in the Caribbean. What is Caribbean masculinity if such a thing exists? What are Caribbean men if they are not marginalized and emasculated as a result of their history of colonization? How do we move away from the stereotypes which have been associated with manhood in the Caribbean and which itself creates the psychological barriers to change in gender relations? Are women in the Caribbean antagonistic to men, or to the system of patriarchy that reproduces gender ideologies that are inimical to both sexes? In my view the ideologies and practice of male dominance, while privileging some men, also keeps masculinity imprisoned behind bars.

DECONSTRUCTING PATRIARCHY

The archetypal patriarch is generally conceived of as the dominant father or powerful man who rules over the household or community – including women, younger men, sons, daughters, workers and slaves. Patriarchy itself can be defined as a prescribed power relationship in which the patriarch or father rules over the others for the benefit of the household or clan. Inbuilt into the notion of power and control by the father or leader of a clan is the idea of a "benevolent patriarchy" at work, someone who undertakes responsibility for provision and protection. Anthropological findings, however, have revealed that the rule of father over sons, or older men over younger men, rather than created for altruistic reasons, in many cases was to ensure that power remained the hands of the older men. In *Sexual Politics* (1970), Kate Millett retained both notions of patriarchy: that of the rule of older men over younger men, as well as the ideology and practices of male dominance as it was manifested in the twentieth century. In subsequent scholarship, patriarchy attained the stature of a key conceptual advance in feminist theory. Radical feminists viewed male control over female sexuality as key in the subordination of women while socialist feminists looked at the intersection between patriarchy and capitalism in ensuring male dominance and control of resources in society. There is ample evidence in global women's studies to suggest that patriarchal ideologies and practices of control are more similar than different across history and nations. An insightful postgraduate student[7] likened patriarchy to an amoeba because of its tendency to change form and alter under different historical conditions. This capacity to adapt, resonant of Darwinian theory, accounts for its continued survival, its reproduction as a system of harnessing power and its control over various historical periods.

It is a fallacy to suggest that elements of Caribbean patriarchy only evolved as a result of the ideologies ushered in by European colonization. Linden Lewis observed: "The nature of social relations of men and women in Caribbean society before the advent of the European is yet to be seriously investigated." He points to the adaptability and plasticity of patriarchy. "…Though excluded from control over resources and from participating in the exercise of power with their European counterparts, African men, and later Indian, Chinese, and Portuguese men were all socialized by, and ultimately internalized, these patriarchal standards" (Lewis 1994).

Two examples, drawn from the histories of two different ethnic groups, demonstrate the retrieval of a patriarchal stronghold despite disruptions caused by migrations. In Trinidad between the nineteenth and early twentieth centuries, Indian men and women were largely brought as individuals, although a minority of migrants came as families, and fewer still created marital bonds on the sea voyage. The dire shortage of women migrants in a system that had initially attracted primarily able bodied men in the nineteenth century allowed a flagrant challenging of the rules of kinship which bound both sexes to family, monogamy and sexual mores observed in the villages and provinces from which the migrants had been sourced. On the estates in Trinidad the authorities recorded a significant violence against women. Indian females were in short supply and women had greater opportunity to choose and desert a male partner who did not fulfil their sexual or material needs. This was a serious challenge to the dominant patriarchy in India that placed Indian women in subservience to the male. The result was a major disruption in Indian family patterns and in the gender system during most of the system of indentured labour which lasted from 1845 to 1917. Women were not the only targets of violence. The suicide rate among Indian men was also very high and worrisome to the colonial officials. Indian patriarchy had suffered a major blow and some of the violence was self-inflicted. Indian women gained greater ground for agency during the system of indenture. This tendency went into reverse late in and post the indenture period when a critical mass of Indians, both India and Trinidad born, reorganised institutions such as religion and began to observe rules regarding the kinship system, some of which reversed the agency women had gained. The *panchayat* – the company of five elders who sat as community leaders, judge, jury and decision makers began to enforce norms which had been established for centuries in Indian society, although these were also undergoing changes in the home society.[8]

As with Indian migrants, the African slave populations who had preceded them as forced labour into the Caribbean, also suffered serious disruptions in their internal arrangements as a result of the uprooting and displacement of norms and traditions. The slave population, like Indians, were gathered from different tribes, with different languages and cultural customs. On plantations neither marriage nor family life was encouraged as the primary purpose was to harness labour potential. Thus gender arrangements and sexual relations among this group were characterized by a marked degree of inconstancy – both men and women changing partners, "baby mothers" and "baby fathers," with consummate ease. There was a startling parallel in the evolution of gender relations among Africans under slavery, to that of Indians in the early stages of indentureship. The breakdown of kinship rules and tradition allowed more flexibility for both men and women during slavery, and insofar that this could be exploited within slave society, African men and women were not indifferent to the possibilities. The re-grouping of the African patriarchal system has however, in my view, been far more complicated by the oppositional dichotomies of black and white masculinity that dominated and emerged in post slavery and into post-colonial systems of governance and control. While African masculinity emerges by the twentieth century as a regrouping of patriarchal authority of this racial grouping, there was no corresponding subservience among African descended women. Instead, African women were viewed as emerging from slavery with greater independence and in charge of their households, even without a male, with males being viewed as marginal to the family, and secondary to a white masculinity which still held the reins of control over commerce and governance.

While this highly schematic reading of gender relations presents one facet of deconstruction, we also need to examine how the interactions and power relations among and between the different ethnic groupings are, as Lewis notes above, continuously restructuring patriarchy. In other words a new patriarchal order between men and men is being formed? In Jamaican history by the late nineteenth century we have the emergence of a white creole society, coloured middle class and black marginal male grouping. In Trinidad, after indenture a similar hierarchy was created with the dominant white male, the French creole grouping, the middle-class coloured group, the emancipated African descendants and the Indian male at the bottom of the ladder. Within each group there are gender relations to be negotiated between men and women, but the dominant patriarchal group provides the rules for the creation of a new order which becomes the meeting ground for new negotiations between men and men for power, status and privilege – all of which eventually define their masculine identity and their overall status in the particular culture.

In deconstructing patriarchy, therefore, we must also see masculinity as being negotiated between men and men in the public spheres where visible signs of power are observed. The most important of these are the preservation of political power, control of money, status, privilege and access to women. Symbols of masculinity in Trinidad and Jamaica were reflected by the song writers and performers of calypso and dancehall. The Mighty Sparrow's famous "Jean and Dinah", released in 1956 is one of the most potent examples of how we can see the patriarchal order in Trinidad recognising itself: "The Yankees gone and Sparrow take over now." Agostino Pinnock (2007) observes: "Masculinity is performed in the Dancehall, …as a self-reflexive and, at times, parodic representation of Jamaican gender wherein nationhood is re/constructed in Dancehall as positively black and very sexual… postures of a rampant and very publicly advertised male heterosexuality as well as a vocal denunciator of male homosexuality."[9] For both the male calypsonian, and the male dancehall artiste, race and class struggles in the society are negotiated around ownership of the female body. Since patriarchy also depends on the control of weaker, dependent or vulnerable men, we might add patriarchy is also very much negotiated around the control of male bodies.

CONCLUSION

An interesting dilemma in feminist epistemology was created in one of the earliest Caribbean texts that focused on masculinity. Errol Miller's 1986 thesis on the "marginalisation of the black male" creates black men as victims of the dominant colonial order. Miller suggested that black men were underrepresented in the teaching profession as they could not be allowed to rise to positions in the Jamaican patriarchy to challenge those who previously had been their masters. Instead women were given access to education and appropriated as the schoolteachers as they would not pose a threat to the prevailing white and creole patriarchy. Women were not viewed as threatening to a male leadership and it was thought they could be more easily controlled. Miller's thesis inadvertently or deliberately placed the burden of emasculating men on the backs of women. While Miller accurately observes that Jamaican women have taken advantage of educational opportunities and have achieved greater mobility than men, he does not question the notion of manhood itself or the assumption of male dominance as the normative ideology for society. Patriarchy is systemic and bolstered by a very gripping ideology that is sustained in most religions. It is essentially a method by which power, whether over race, class or gender is appropriated and maintained. The continued deconstruction of patriarchy remains part of the agenda of a masculinist and feminist struggle and foremost in the project of unmasking and freeing masculinity.

ENDNOTES

[1] The irony of course is that also outside of the public sphere, women thought of themselves as the secondary sex, and with the exception of a few who challenged mainstream views, also bought into their roles as wife, mothers, nurturers etc etc.
[2] https://www.merriam-webster.com/dictionary/culture
[3] Wright, P. (ed.). (2002). *Lady Nugent's Journal of Her Residence in Jamaica from 1801 to 1805*, University of the West Indies, Jamaica.
[4] I am mindful in this statement that biology itself cannot be so neatly divided into male and female and that there exists not only biological possibilities which combine both sexes, but also sexual identities which conflict with biological appearances. How this must be incorporated in the representation of masculinity and femininity into the twenty first century must also be considered part of the feminist project.
[5] This point is made by Michelle Barrett in her book *Woman's Oppression Today*, London: Verso, 1980
[6] See for instance "Steel-Toed Boots" by Tal Peretz, in *Men Speak out: View on Gender, Sex and Power*, edited by Shira Tarrant, New York and UK: Routledge, 2008.
[7] This observation was made by Michelle Rowley, a Trinidadian student who was then one of the candidates in the first MSc in Gender and Development Studies being offered by the Centre for Gender and Development Studies at UWI, Mona, Jamaica in 1994.
[8] See Patricia Mohammed, *Gender Negotiations Among Indians in Trinidad: 1917-1947*. London / The Hague: Palgrave / Institute of Social Studies, 2002.
[9] Agostino Pinnock, "A Ghetto Education Is Basic": (Jamaican) Dancehall Masculinities As Counter-Culture" *The Journal of Pan African Studies*, 1 (9): 53 (August 2007).
https://pdfs.semanticscholar.org/1408/725e9a64a15f91b98267b6c5a52089eed040.pdf

REFERENCES

Best, Steven and Douglas Kellner. 1991. *Critical Interrogations*, Basingstoke, UK: MacMillan.

Burke Leacock, Eleanor. 1979. Engels and the History of Women's Oppression. In *Myths of Male Dominance: Collected Articles on Women Cross-culturally*, Chicago: Haymarket Books.

Crenshaw, Kimberle. 1989. *Demarginalizing the Intersection of Race and Sex: A Black Feminist Critique of Antidiscrimination Doctrine, Feminist Theory and Antiracist Politics*. University of Chicago Legal Forum: Vol. 1989: Iss.1, Article 8. Available at: http://chicagounbound.uchicago.edu/uclf/vol1989/iss1/8

De Beauvoir, Simone. 1949. *The Second Sex* (French edition). 2010; London: Vintage Publishing

De Lauretis, Teresa. 1987. *Technologies of Gender: Essays on Theory, Film and Fiction*, Bloomingdale and Indianapolis: Indiana University Press.

Foucault, Michel. 1976. *The History of Sexuality, Volume One*. France: Editions Gallimard.

Haraway, Donna. 1991. "Gender for Marxist Dictionary." Chapter 7 in *Simians, Cyborgs and Women – the Reinvention of Nature*. London: Free Association Books.

Kaufman, Michael. (ed.). 1987. *Beyond Patriarchy: Essays by Men on Pleasure, Power and Change*. Toronto and New York: Oxford University Press.

Lewis, Linden. 1994. "Constructing the Masculine in the Context of the Caribbean." Paper presented to the 19th Annual Caribbean Association Conference, Merida.

Mohammed, Patricia. 1995. Fragments of the Colonial Legacy: The Representation of Masculinity in Caribbean Thought." Paper presented to the Society for Caribbean Studies Annual Conference, London, July 1995.

Mohammed, Patricia. 1994. *A Social History of Indians in Trinidad 1917-1947: A Gender Perspective*. PhD diss., The Institute of Social Studies, The Hague. Moore, Henrietta. 1994. *A Passion for Difference: Essays in Anthropology and Gender*. Cambridge: Polity Press.

Pinnock, Agostino. 2007. "A Ghetto Education is Basic": (Jamaican) Dancehall Masculinities as Counter-culture." *The Journal of Pan African Studies*, 1(9): 53

pdfs.semanticscholar.org/1408/725e9a64a15f91b98267b6c5a52089eed040.pdf

Rubin, Gayle. 1975. "The Traffic in Women: Notes on the Political Economy of Sex," In *Toward and Anthropology of Women*, edited by Rayna Reiter. New York: Monthly Review Press.

Wieringa, Saskia. 1995. "Essentialism versus Constructivism." Lecture Notes, UWI, Mona Campus, Lecture delivered to MSc Gender and Development Programme, October, 1995.

12

A Very Public Private Man: Sketches in a Biography of Eric Eustace Williams†

When much has been said, and the twentieth century is done, it is useful to prime the canvas of our history and culture again, retaining the texture and hues of the original but adding depth and complexity to the overlay that we must bring with a new age. Such is this attempt to depict aspects of a Caribbean man who has contributed immensely, if controversially, to the life and vision of a society.¹ His intellectual achievement in *Capitalism and Slavery*, published in 1944 and based on his original doctoral thesis of 1938, provided for people of the Caribbean a new way of seeing themselves, not as "weak and backward and in need of a civilizing mission" but as a "productive source of wealth for England and as victims of economic exploitation past and present."² In *The Negro in the Caribbean* (1942), he declared twenty years before both Trinidad

---

† A version of this paper "A Very Public Private Man: Trinidad's Eric Eustace Williams (1911-83)" is published in *Caribbean Charisma: Reflections on Leadership, Legitimacy and Populist Politics*, edited by Anton Allahar, Kingston: Ian Randle and Boulder & London: Lynne Rienner.

and Jamaica would gain independence, that "The Negro's right to decide his own affairs and his life is not a question for argument" (p. 102) Included with other pioneers such as the pan-Africanists and anti-colonial nationalists, he became a major player in a new "new world" enlightenment project which would rewrite Caliban's script – nobility enshrined and savage redefined, and most of all, human.

The bravado, discipline, arrogance and intellectualism with which Eric Eustace Williams confronted family, friend and foe, were his major strengths and major weaknesses. Williams' iconoclastic retaliation and singular vision as an historian prepared him for his later role, an icon for a nation. If he remains a controversial figure in the world of the intellect, he was doubly so in the sphere of politics. This essay does not attempt to assess Williams' contribution to history or to judge his collaborations in public life, other than where I am capable of doing so. I approach this reading of his life and work through the additional lens of gender, attempting to move beyond the public/private dichotomies which artificially separate the home from the world, in an attempt to depict both his humanness and his humanity.

Williams' leadership is primarily associated with race and nationalism, and to some extent with gender politics. A popular interpretation of the first is generally taken as his attitude and that of the party he led, the People's National Movement, to issues of racial difference in the politics of Trinidad and Tobago; the second to his treatment and employment of women in the political sphere. These tired discourses sometimes need deflecting if we are to move ideas beyond the popular and the clichéd. That Williams was black and experienced all the obstacles of both his race and colonial status in England and the United States and as human, he had internalized some of the biases about race and class which pervaded Trinidad society at the time, must enter the analysis of his politics and practice, as it already has been treated by many. This should not detract from Williams as the intellectual, historian and visionary who confronted the issues of race and racial difference at a more discerning level.

The concept of gender appears to apply only to women, as if men have no gender or as if masculinity itself cannot be problematized in the discourse of gender. I deal with Eric Williams as a man among men and among women, and interrogate indirectly, the problem of masculinity and power. I do not deal extensively with theoretical debates on either race or gender. Rather I let the prose communicate its own narrative of gender, class or race relations, as it does in the real lives of men and women in society. What such a reading may contribute to scholarship is still unclear to me at this stage. Power is a common denominator in all social relations. Masculinity and public power have been so intertwined that to understand how power works, is held, traded and manipulated, it may be necessary to understand men and manhood, and to anatomize and dissect the power of patriarchy which operates equally between men and men, as it does between men and women.

THE FATHER OF MODERN TRINIDAD[3]

> Achieving peace at the price of air and sunlight, I deliberately leave the files and reports and grievances and read and write as a private citizen, maintaining his sanity and seeing the daily chores, stresses and strains in clearer perspective, determined to prove that, like Dante's Ulysses, I
>
> > could conquer the inward hunger than I had
> > To master earth's experience, and to attain
> > Knowledge of man's mind, both good and bad
> > (1969: 343)

This is the last and one of the more lyrical passages included in the final version of *Inward Hunger*, the autobiography of Eric Williams. He completed it on July 6th, 1968, two years before the "Black Power" upheavals which would take place in Trinidad in 1970, shattered any illusion of his control or the harmony he had envisioned for the society. He died just over one decade later in March 1981, a private death for one who had all the public facilities at his disposal.

While the full circumstances surrounding his death remain obscure, it is clear from all accounts that he had, as was his usual custom, dismissed the servants and withdrew into the isolation he had sought more and more since 1970. Both his personal secretary at

Whitehall, Madge Lee Fook and his political secretary D. D Dupres[4] agreed that from the middle of the 1970s he wanted to leave office. Dupres observed:

> The security around him became tighter and tighter It was difficult to get to him. I sensed sadness about Eric. ...I think at the time he did want to leave office. I think he did not want re-nomination in 1973. I don't think it was a ploy. The negative things he was hearing about his faithful servants affected him. Who do you believe? Do you bring in a new set of people to trust? I think one thing that disappointed him was that the PNM stagnated with the party officers not moving forward. He made every decision. He was overworked. I don't think the politicians around him were in full political glory.

In March 1981 he slipped into a diabetic coma from which he never recovered. If Williams' rise to fame and power has retained a fascination, his death has left a puzzlement and sadness for people who knew him or experienced part of his reign.[5] "It was difficult to piece. It was almost unreal. It was like it never was going to happen. I don't know if I thought he would die. I think I just walked around in a daze," said a close friend of the family and of his daughter Erica, on hearing of his death.[6] Conrad O'Brien,[7] a businessman and colleague at one time observed that his mood on hearing of Williams's death was

> One of sadness, especially the manner of his death. I thought it was unnecessary, since I too am a diabetic. If you take your medication, diet and exercise, you can live to an old age. I believe he did not take care of himself, went into a diabetic coma and did not recover. Yet by that time in his life he was beginning to experience regret about some things. He was depressed, the country was in turmoil: doctors, nurses, civil service were all in unrest. One of his biggest mistakes is that he stayed on too long.

Eric Eustace Williams had lived his three score and ten years by 1981. His death appeared to those who were not close to him to be very incongruous with the persona he had constructed for the public in the earlier rise to power in the forties, fifties and sixties. Maybe in a final "death where is thy sting, grave where is thy victory" melodrama, he has left an underlying guilt with a nation who called him their father. Madge Lee Fook surmised, "He was probably very unhappy that his policies were no longer motivating the people. There was a movement to replace him. He was not really appreciated ...Whatever he did was never good enough. There were some that supported him through thick and thin, but it was a general malaise among people." Madge had been his personal secretary from 1961 and had obviously been someone who interacted closely with him. Yet she found out about his death from the news reports on television like everyone else. She had no idea that Williams was diabetic. "He liked his sweets, so it never occurred to me." She admitted that she is not a very observant person, but that she saw no real signs that his health was deteriorating, although D. D. Dupres, his political secretary, had noticed and remarked, "he was getting older and his health was deteriorating."

Perhaps most prescient were Eastlyn Bynoe's observations.[8] Bynoe worked at Longman's Caribbean Publishers and came into close contact with Williams in the late 1970s when, with Paul Sutton then at Sussex University, discussions began about the publication of a book, which was to be called *Forged from the Love of Liberty*. "Sutton wanted to place these speeches in the context of Caribbean history, and also to preserve the works of this brilliant man" said Bynoe. She believes that Sutton initiated the proposal. Williams selected four Cabinet officers to liaise between himself and Longman's in this project. "Williams saw this as a special project. He announced that he wanted no memorial on his death. He did want a scholarship fund in his name for children of the PNM. This was about 1978-79. Both my editor and I were very saddened by what we saw at that meeting. Dr. Williams seemed very old and frail." "Was he not planning his memorial?" queried Ken Boodhoo. Bynoe replied: "That is quite possible. That's how he saw the book. He wanted no direct financial dealings on the book. That's why he set up the committee: to do the book and organize the Fund. The book would fund the scholarship through sales and royalties." Eric Williams died before the publication of this book in 1981.

In death as in life, controversy surrounded his attempt to provide leadership and direction. Bynoe noted that the book was completed in 1982, by which time his daughter Erica had become associated with the project: "She (Erica) understood its importance to her father and its meaning as a memorial he had designed" said Bynoe. But there were others who did not. "I had a formal launching to the public and to diplomats. It was unfortunate but the Party (PNM) was not represented. They were in Tobago or somewhere else. After his death, plans for marketing the book fell apart. Thus, we had difficulty selling the quantity of books which had been produced. Stocks of the book have remained in different places (the party had promised to help but did not)."

Charisma on the public stage has a short shelf life. Once this fades, for real or apparent reasons, the good is often interred with the bones, the memory of wrong far easier and usually more convenient to recall. Williams' sudden death left a shock wave for this infant society he had almost literally slapped into political life with its first lung full of fresh air. James Millette points out: "To understand the contribution of Eric Williams in the field of party politics we need to remind ourselves of the fact that Trinidad and Tobago was arguably the most backward political environment in the British West Indies in the first half of the twentieth century."[9] Williams's political heyday was the fifties and the sixties. By the 1970s, in the opinion of one interviewee, he no longer commanded such widespread or intense attention from the masses and the events of the 1970 mutiny affected him deeply and psychologically. Between 1970 and 1973, Trinidad experienced massive economic decline due the fall in petroleum prices. Added to the economic frustrations, Williams's felt that those he had fought for had turned their backs on him. He experienced the defeat of a man who believed and struggled for a concept of political freedom only to see his vision disintegrating before his eyes. Yet even those who were his fiercest enemies on the battlefield of politics did not wish to see him descend so suddenly into the grave. There was disbelief and profound grief on his death, especially on hearing rumours of the circumstances of his death. It deprived some of the opportunity for reconciliation, others of a chance to reflect with him on the successes and failures of the political process. It deprived the society of a period to understand that he was not immortal, and for those who really cared to find redemption with their own ministrations in his hour of need.

Williams' death, whatever the circumstances, seems very consistent with the way in which he controlled and kept apart his private life. This reticence, silence and grief about death and the private side of life have remained almost completely hidden from a generally prying and prurient society which has a tradition and the tried and tested methods of the calypso and weeklies to cut down everybody to size, to make everyone "boil down like *bhaji*."[10] He presented an unusual and enigmatic figure even for this society. There was little outward display of family other than a close and enduring relationship with his daughter Erica. Again the interviews of those who were close to the family and to Erica in particular tell of a different Williams, a warm, generous, almost doting father, who would feed her dog when she was not there, arrange entertainment for her birthday parties, and whose eyes would "light up like an electric bulb" when she came into the room. As a Prime Minister he lived a fairly quiet life, preferring the normalcy of a private existence for himself and Erica as much as this was possible, sending home all household help at nights so that they were generally companionate with each other and with the friends whom he did entertain from time to time.

As a political man who had to keep tabs on the pulse of the society, and as someone who was obviously aware, for a time, of the heartbeat of the society he governed, he was in touch with the popular culture of carnival and calypso, seen often attending calypso tents around carnival time and easily enjoying the humour and mood of the tent. Yet to the majority he was an essentially reclusive personality. During his most popular period, this charismatic leader attained almost super-hero qualities. There was a time, one interviewee remarked about the period between 1956 and the early 1960s, in the height of his fame "you could say nothing about Dr. Williams to the masses in the country." Manifesting the most esteemed characteristics of Trinidadian masculinity, he could out talk and demolish his political opponents with "robber talk" *sans humanite* and transfix crowds who would stand and listen to him for hours. This is no mean feat in Trinidad or in any society at any time and if Williams countered *picong* with *picong*, then it demonstrated his mastery of this mode of delivery, which was understood and respected by the crowd. He records:

> My second lecture was entitled 'An Evening with Hansard'. It was delivered in the 'University of Woodford Square' on September 6 (1956). I had the large crowds convulsed with laughter at the antics of the Members of the Legislative Council. I quoted liberally from their speeches. One member had threatened another. "I will meet you shot for shot, fire for fire'. Another, recalling unsolved murder cases, had told a colleague that he wished to fill the House with cutthroats and murderers'. ...Much fun had been poked at a member whose deficient English had produced "as far as whey I can see" (Williams 1969, 161).

This capacity to engage the crowd in different ways is unique. Not only did Williams get their laughter and support but he also capitalized on their attention in order to raise their level of political consciousness through information. For the first time a politician and leader demystified the political process for those who were daily affected by it. He relieved it of the sacred mask and brought it into the profanity of everyday life. "Particularly in my lectures at the University of Woodford Square, I made a point not to talk down to the people. It was straight University stuff, in content and in form as well as in manner, designed to place the problems of Trinidad in international perspective" (Williams 1969, 149). Without exception, everyone who has reminisced or been interrogated about Williams, particularly those who worked with him or knew him socially or politically, agree that he had an exceptional mind and grasp of scholarship which made him the intellectual and visionary. The latter made him the brilliant leader who put things into perspective and read its implications for the future. The former was part of the charismatic pull he had on an audience hungry for knowledge.

It was not Williams' voice or stature that compelled people. My own memory of his voice, which I heard mainly on the radio and television, and which differed no doubt from the heady days of the University of Woodford Square, was of a barely modulated monotone, crackling like ice and dry humoured. He was a short man, and in private his close friends poked fun at his height. He took this in good humour. Joan Lake, a close friend of his family: "I remember one night my husband saying to Eric, after this you're gonna tell us good night and go upstairs and play your music and conduct your band. You know Eric was short and my husband told him, you know you'll stand on a chair and conduct the orchestra that is playing" "He said, come up and see. He had great humour."

His appearance, even from the early photographs available of him, is that of an intense bespectacled character, whose eyes never look for or straight into the camera. His arrogance, such as it has been described, is not about the body, but the mind. His appeal to people was his capacity to interest others in what he was doing, because he was himself interesting and compelled by it. This charisma was not limited in the decade of the fifties to one class or ethnic group but crossed many barriers. Hugh Simpson, who met Williams in 1946, when he (Hugh) was 17 and Williams was in his thirties, describes his first meeting: "He was sitting smoking his pipe – a forbidding person." Simpson observes later on that he got to know Williams well between 1962 and 1978 and that "He enjoyed a good joke. He appreciated funny things. I told him some and he roared with laughter. We small talked a lot. He enjoyed this – on a wide variety of subjects, not Trinidad simple 'old talk'. ...He and I had common interests in books. He was not consumed by politics. He had a wide interest in politics. He read furiously, mainly history. ...He would sit and ruminate, look at things from different angles. He certainly did not make you yawn[11] Williams had an interest in music as well. According to Simpson "he worked music into his speeches...He enjoyed classical and also pop music. He liked jazz. I believe it is he who interested me in jazz at his home. He had a collection by a jazz violinist Stephen Grappelli Music from the Hot Club d'France – a jazz quintet. My introduction to music was from E. W. That collection remains of great value."

He had the capacity to infect his close friends and colleagues very early on with his enthusiasm and the breath of his understanding of political and social phenomena, clearly a signal that they were also thirsty for such knowledge at the time. In doing so he would also consolidate friendships which were not simply based on political alliances and which would serve him well in the future. Joan Lake,[12] whose father Wilfred Attal was party treasurer and mother Ivy was at one time Williams' housekeeper, recalls in the 1950s that they would sometimes go to Williams' home in Mary Street at about 7.00 at night just to sit and talk. "Eric would come out and talk politics. We were really being taught politics for the first time in our lives. The politics before was something we were not interested in. But this was something that we all started to get interested in" observed Joan. "He was interesting because for one thing, we were being taught politics. This went on until 2 or 3 in the morning, not even realizing the time. In between we'd get something to eat or drink, or maybe not even bother with that. I remember once quite clearly one night we had a feel for ice cream, and we said to John O'Halloran, John you have to go get ice. John very nicely got up and went to get the ice so we could make ice cream."

George Lamming recognised this talent to infuse the lives of others with his passions and remarked on the method by which Williams would begin to rewrite the colonial script. "He turned history, the history of the Caribbean, into gossip, so that the story of a people's predicament seemed no longer the infinite, barren track of documents, dates and texts. Everything became news: slavery, colonization, the forgivable deception of metropolitan rule, and the sad and inevitable unawareness of native production. His lectures retained always the character of whisper which everyone was allowed to hear, a rumour which experience had established as truth."[13] Whatever misgivings we may have about his political practice, there is almost clear agreement that he had the instincts of a great teacher. Ibbet Mosaheb,[14] one of the men with whom he would join forces to form the PNM, acknowledged his gift as a teacher. "He was great, a born teacher, thoroughly prepared. ... He was my first teacher in a large class that included smaller tutorials. He was faced with not having a text. Thus, he prepared volumes of material. I still have one copy. ... He helped me with a paper for my English class, for which I got an A." It must be recalled that William's first goal had been in fact to return to Trinidad after his scholarship and work as a teacher.

This may have been a goal formulated very early on in his life and one which he sustained throughout, even and especially in his politics. In this sense, Williams was always a generous teacher, unstinting in his desire to transfer knowledge and help others. Halsey McShine, who would later become his personal doctor on a trip to Africa, said he met Williams when they were both at primary school. Williams was then eight and Halsey was seven. They lost touch for a few years when Halsey's father moved him to a private school but reunited again in Queen's Royal College where, according to Halsey, they "clashed in Latin, French and Spanish." They were both then competing for the one island scholarship. They studied together nonetheless, and Williams won that year. Halsey recalls: "I was trying to win the scholarship the next year. I told my father my weakest subject in Spanish and I would like to take private lessons. I told him I'd like to take lessons from Eric Williams." His father agreed and at this tender age Williams tutored Halsey at his parents' house once a week for an hour. "He gave me lessons to read, essays to write in Spanish, things like that," said Halsey. "He taught me very well. He brought up my Spanish, that's how I was able to win the scholarship." "What did he tell you at the end of the sessions?" asked interviewer Ken Boodhoo. "He said if you had told me when you started these lessons that this was your weakest subject, I would've prophesied that you would win the scholarship. And I won it," replied Halsey triumphantly.

If conveying knowledge came naturally to him, it is very likely that some of the other kinds of strengths he needed in public life, such as oratorical performance, were learnt on the field and from the others around him, as in these matters experience is generally the best teacher. Williams' training thus far had been in the arena of the academy, classroom and private drawing room. He had to learn how to transfer this passion to a larger and more impatient audience. Williams was a careful and strategic listener, even though this may not always have been obvious to others. Elton Richardson recalls an occasion in 1955 when he (Williams) was speaking at the Public Library in Port of Spain on education and was hemmed in by questions on Christian values and Christian education. According to Richardson:

> The great debater was unable to budge. With instinct but without a sense of drama, I walked up to the rostrum and asked to say a few words. I pointed out

that I had heard a lot of Christian principles and that it seemed to me that the speakers failed to realise that outside of that hall, the country had a nearly fifty per cent non-Christian population. I went on to relate how abroad I had lived with an Indian who was a Muslim, and how once he showed me a letter from his father because he wanted my opinion on a certain aspect of the letter etc etc.... Eric had a brilliant mind, but he failed at times to see the trees in the forest (Richardson 1984, 25).

Richardson felt that Williams was totally bourgeois, that he was opportunistic, remarking that he had an unlisted phone number and that he "drove a big Buick and looked neither to the right nor to the left" (1984, 27).

This assumed 'bourgeois" aspect of Williams' present background would be used to diminish his obvious capacity to connect, and his propensity to disconnect with the "masses" time and time again. Yet the first few chapters of Williams' autobiography clearly places him in the impoverished and dis-empowered middle class of urban Port of Spain in the 1920s. The environment in which his exchange of ideas was carried out in the middle-class milieu of Port of Spain, and into which Williams naturally fitted into on his return to Trinidad, was a comfortable and relaxed one. Here Williams gained the trust and friendship of those whom he would trust most in the difficult days of politics ahead. Joan Lake's interview indicates the kind of trust a leader needed from those close to him. "Well the thing about forming a party was that when that was done, Eric had to go visit various parts of the country. Uncle Harold, his wife and my parents accompanied him in the car. Eric had a habit of sleeping in the car during traffic. So, he had to feel comfortable with people he knew and trusted." Williams possibly recognised the value of such camaraderie for the future. He was always a pragmatic man, despite his outward "bookishness." By the 'Black Power' unrest in the 70s when a threat of kidnapping came, his daughter Erica was housed at Joan's: "She was housed morning, noon and nights as though she were in a prison. I was married at that time. My children and my sister's children were around Erica's age, so she asked to come around and play with the children. They were all around her age and it was a protection. ...Eric came to see her. I think he felt quite comfortable with that."

Whatever misgivings we may have about the ways in which Williams learnt to employ his strengths and draw on others around him towards a political goal, it is clear that he outshone many others in his day, and would have been resented for his capacity, while being used for it. In the masculine world of politics, he had the added advantage of as calypsonian The Mighty Sparrow said "Big Brain" over "Big Belly" to charm a generation of women to work on his behalf and that of the party. This larger than life quality of his political life meant that Williams not only led the party which he had brought to power, but even during his early rule embodied it, becoming and remaining its recognizable icon as much as the symbol the *balisier* has become.

That the private side of life was kept separate and apart from his public engagement with power is most evident in *Inward Hunger*, in both the style in which the final document is presented, and the selective content which is included. The published *Inward Hunger* was until recently the only record of Williams' writing about his personal life and this can be read primarily as a political tool, outlining as it were the early development of his political consciousness, his confrontations and conflicts and how he dealt with them, and his rise to power. When *Inward Hunger* was published (1969) he had completed fourteen years and nearly three terms as Prime Minister. In the published book of 344 pages, Williams had ostensibly devoted barely 28 pages to his childhood and youth in Trinidad before he sets out for, as he terms it, "Negro Oxford." Nowhere was there an acknowledgment of personal compassion or emotions other than anger or political frustration, except briefly in the early chapters describing his youth and his commitment to his father and to his schoolmates. In the first few chapters of *Inward Hunger* however, nonetheless, one can still see the forging of Williams' understanding of race and gender relations in colonial society. The battles he would undertake in life must be seen in relation to a desire to right the wrongs done to his father and as his father's son, those he experienced in his time at Oxford, in the United Kingdom, and in the United States as the colonized black male subject.

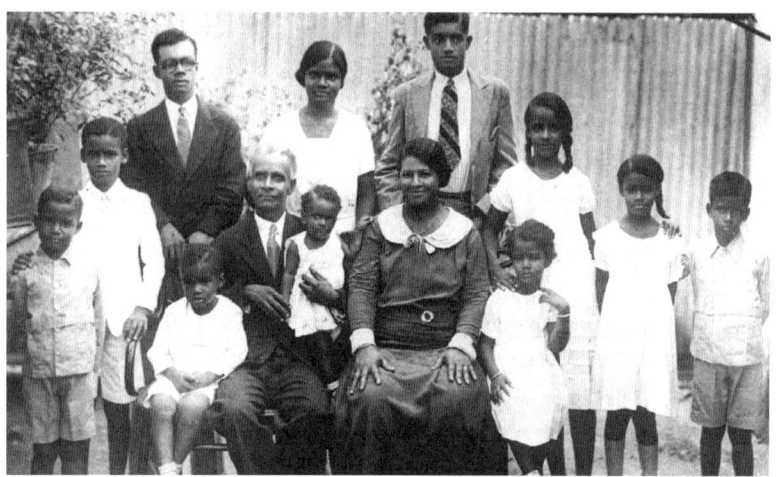

The Williams clan, Eric third from left standing (circa 1939)

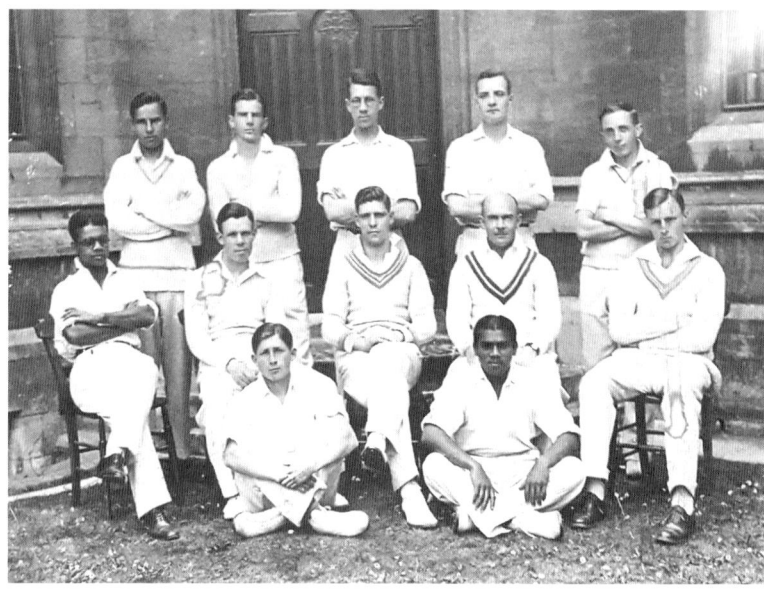

Oxford University Cricket Team (1933-1936) Eric Williams, second row at left with roommate L.A.V. Gobin, cross-legged at right

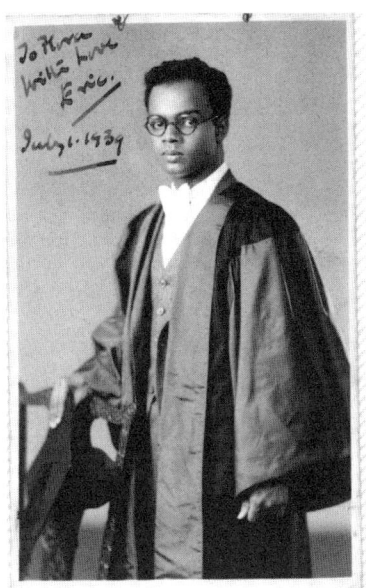 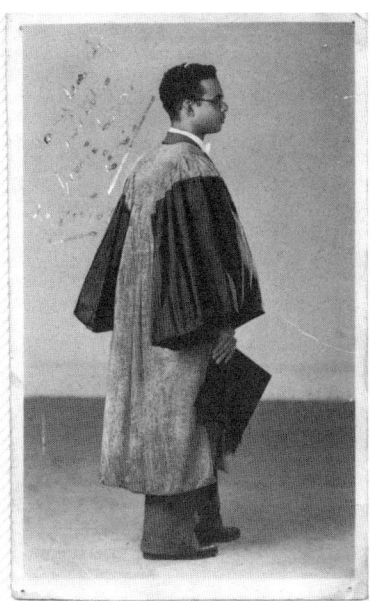

Eric Williams Graduation Photographs Oxford, 1939

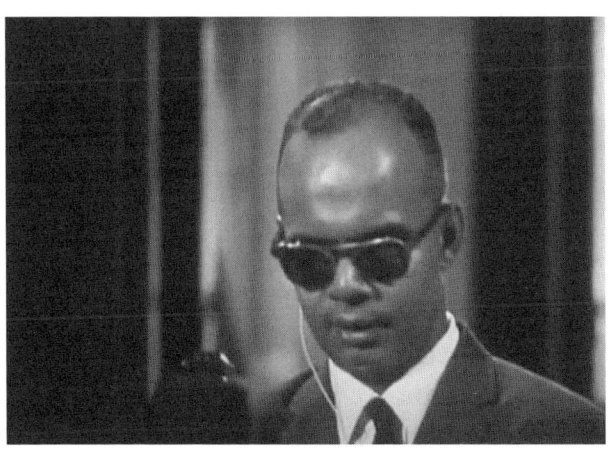

Dr Eric Willams, Prime Minister of Trinidad and Tobago
1962 - 1981

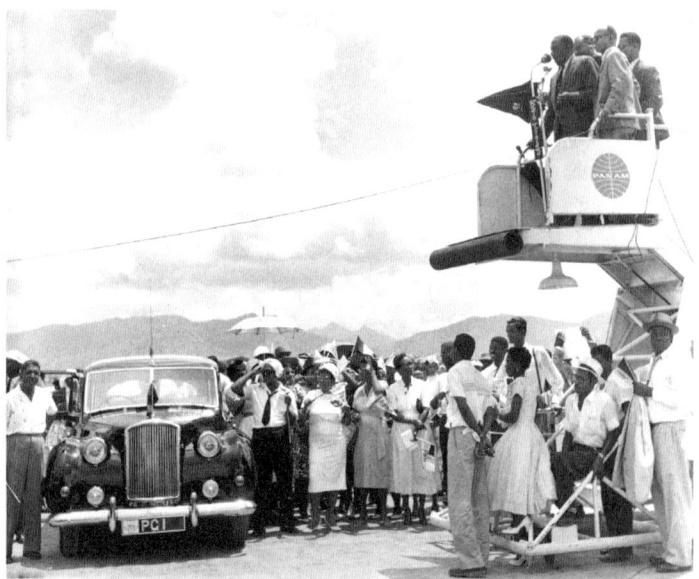

Dr Williams at the airport in Piarco, 1961

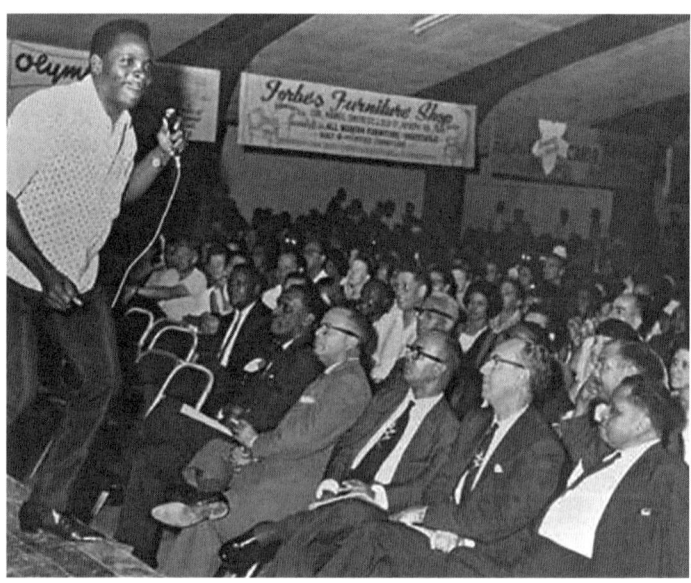

The Mighty Sparrow (Slinger Francisco) performing with
Dr Williams among those in the front row

CHAPTER I
Portrait of a Colonial Society

On the night of April 2, 1911, a census taken in the island revealed that Trinidad, in its 1,860 square miles, supported a population of 312,803. This represented an increase (partly the natural superiority of births over deaths, partly the artificial superiority of immigrants over emigrants) of 57,655 people in the preceding decade. The population, which had increased at the rate of nearly 6,000 per year. In every five people in the island in 1901, there were six in 1911.

There were 168 persons to the square mile in 1911 as compared with 137 in 1901. This seems to have caused no concern whatsoever, except, possibly, a concern with underpopulation.

Indentured immigrants from India during the year numbered 3,200. As compared with 423,443 acres the 552,541 acres of land alienated in the island, of which 423,443 were cultivated. There were 208,346 acres of Crown lands reserved and 472,318 acres of Crown lands available for cultivation. That is to say, for every acre in cultivation, there was more than one acre available for cultivation; comparing and for every acre in cultivation there were nearly one and a half acres of alienated and Crown land lying idle.

Early Draft Chapter 1 I "Portrait of a Colonial Society"
Inward Hunger in hand writing of Dr Williams

CHAPTER 2
Life with Father

My family was typical in a number of ways of the lower middle class families of Trinidad. My parents were themselves typical of the lower middle class of Trinidad. My father's father was a full-blooded Negro, employed in a menial capacity with an aristocratic "real white" family, one of whose daughters decided to elope with him. It was the old problem of the contact between races; however much the philosophers might adumbrate on superiority and inferiority, however much the law might sanction white ascendancy and black subordination, the bed joined together what philosophy and law sought put asunder, and the white planter and black slave, black man and white woman have steadily modified the basic colour scheme of this Caribbean society. The man has only to propose, and woman disposes.

My mother was a product, at a different level, of this racial melting pot. Her family name was French, and she was connected with one of the oldest French creole families — that is to say, connected by blood but not socially. On both my father's side and my mother's, therefore, like so many Trinidadians, I have relatives across that line which, though not discernible to the naked eye, is yet as clear as any visible boundary. One of my sisters, who looks very much like the paternal grandmother, was leaving her office one afternoon with a "white" girl, her colleague, who is, in actual fact, her first cousin; the resemblance was so striking that a Negro labourer in the street commented audibly on it. One can at least understand why the much government land in the past forbade Negroes and mulattoes to take the names of their white parent or of the white family to which they had been enslaved prior to their manumission.

Early Draft of Chapter 2, Life with Father, *Inward Hunger*
in hand writing of Dr Williams

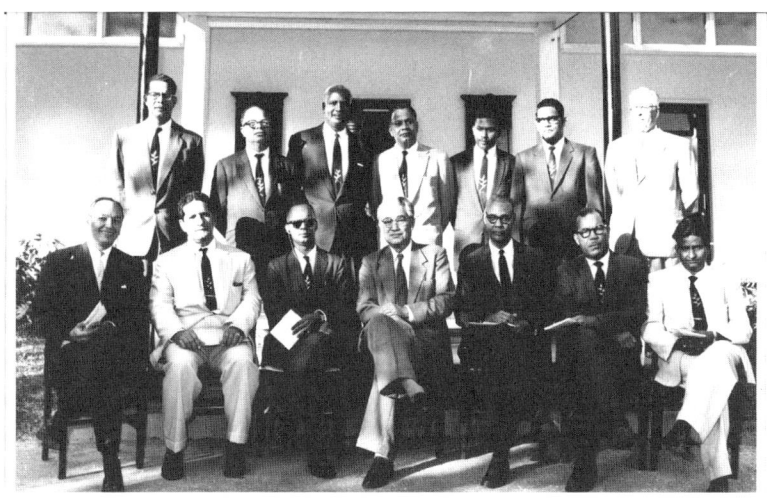

First Cabinet and Governor-General of Trinidad and Tobago, 1962
Standing Donald Pierre, Albert Wallace, Wilfred Alexander, A.N.R. Robinson,
S. Mohammed, Sir Alan Reece. *Sitting* G. Montano, J. O'Hallaran, Eric Williams,
Sir Solomon Hochoy, Dr. P. Solomon, Donald Grando, K. Mohammed.

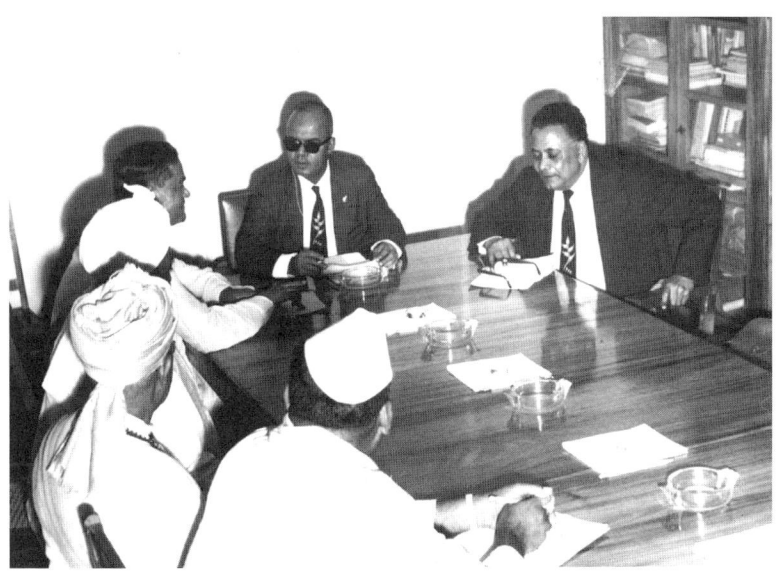

Meeting with Religious Leaders: Prime Minister of Trinidad and Tobago,
Dr Eric Williams (at head of table) meets with Mr. Bhadase Maharaj and
pundits to discuss granting holiday for Divali. 18/05/1966

Working notes and statistics on the Indian population carried out by Dr Williams in writing of *Inward Hunger*

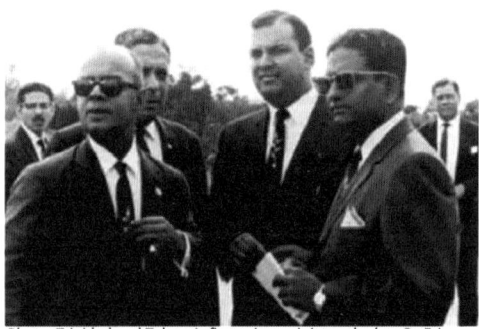

Photo: Trinidad and Tobago's first prime minister, the late Dr Eric Williams (far left, foreground) and long-standing Cabinet member, the late Kamaluddin Mohammed (far right, foreground) flank another Cabinet member, Errol Mahabir (second from right, foreground).

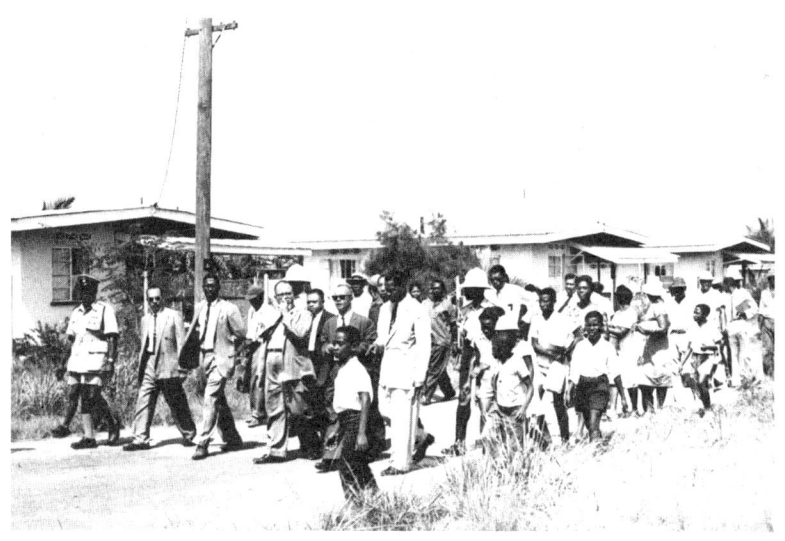

Prime Minister's Tour 100 Rose Block Point Fortin Self Help Meet the People Tour: St. Patrick. 21/03/1963 5th from left: Prime Minister of Trinidad and Tobago, Dr Eric Williams and residents of St Patrick

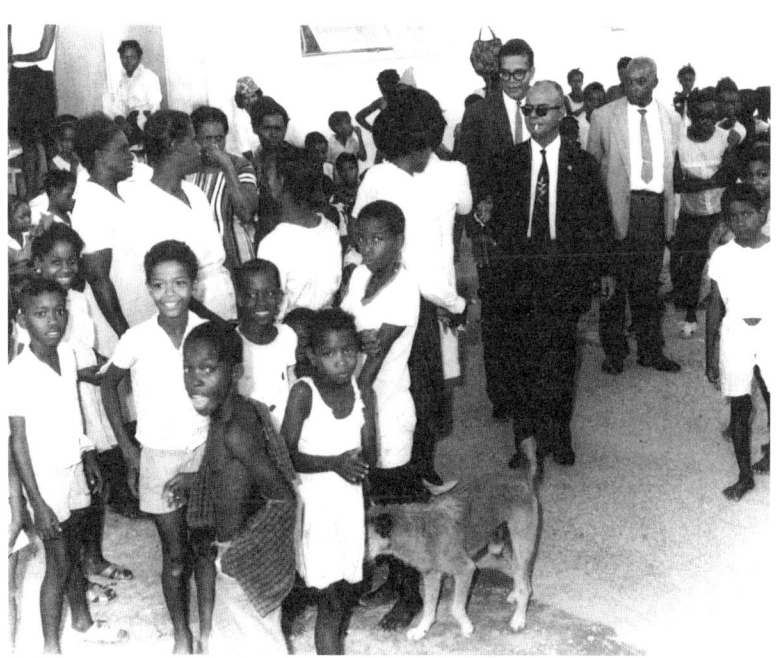

Dr Williams – Meet the people tour Trinidad, circa 1960s

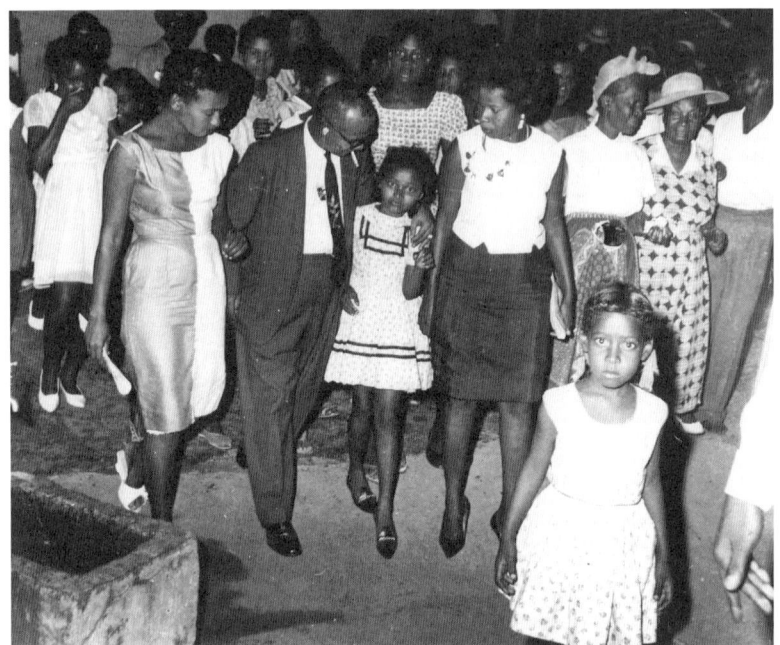

Dr Williams Meet the People Tour, circa 1960s

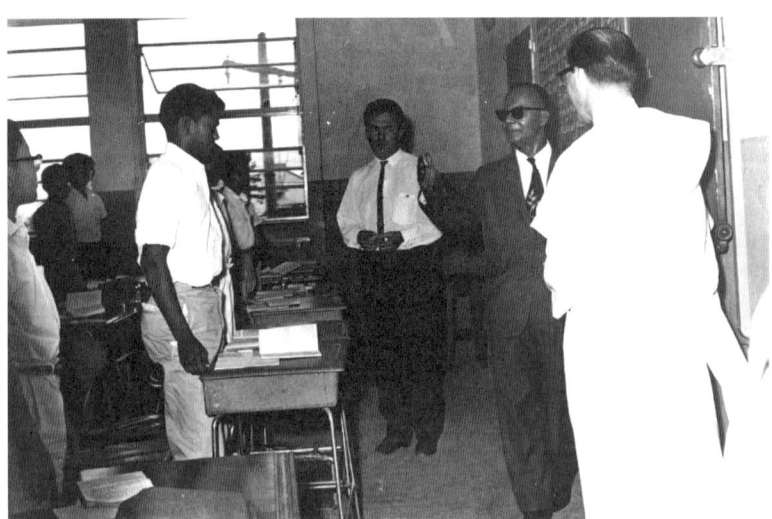

Dr Williams visits a boys school Presentation College, San Fernando,
Date stamp: 13/05/1963

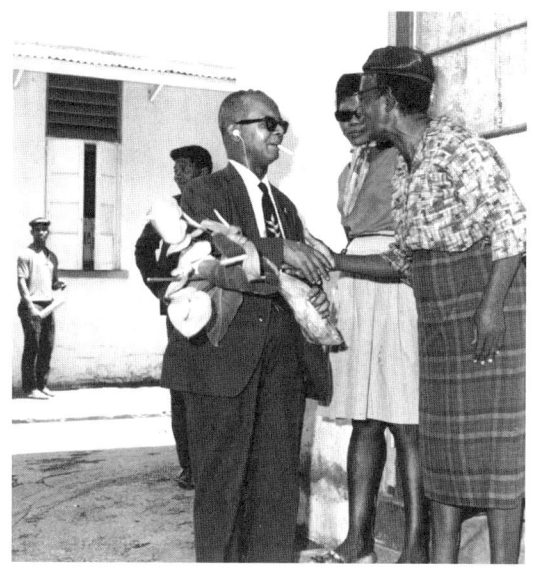

The Prime Minister of Trinidad and Tobago official visit to the City of Port of Spain on September 26th, 1966.

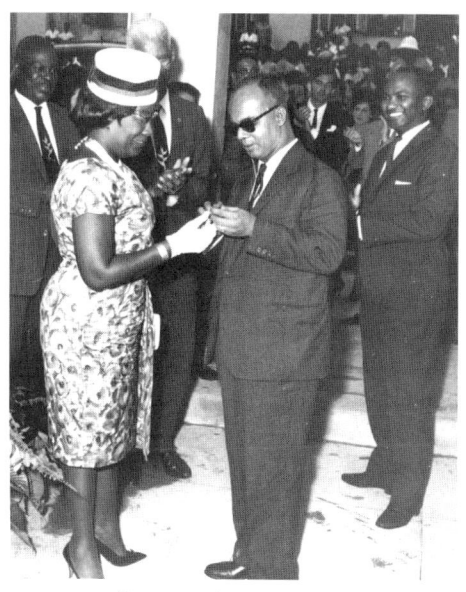

Dr Williams and Mrs Isabel Teshea
Date stamp: 7/06/1963

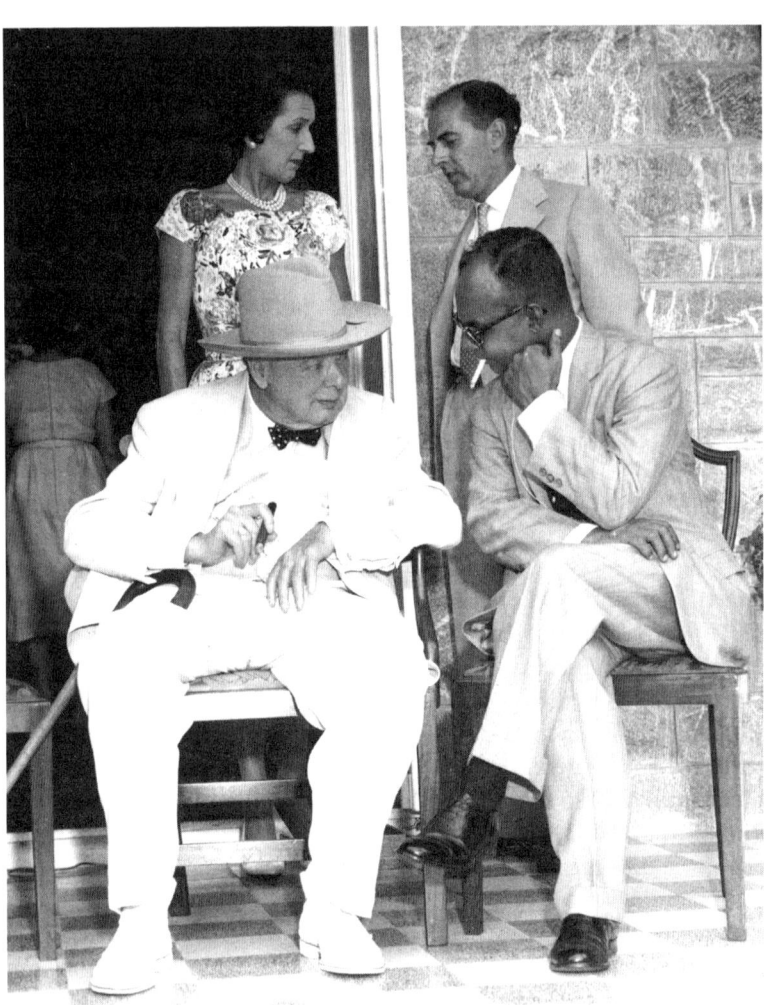

State visit of Sir Winston Churchill. Date: 22/03/1961. *Left-Right* Former Prime Minister of the United Kingdom, Sir Winston Churchill and Premier of Trinidad and Tobago, Dr Eric Williams

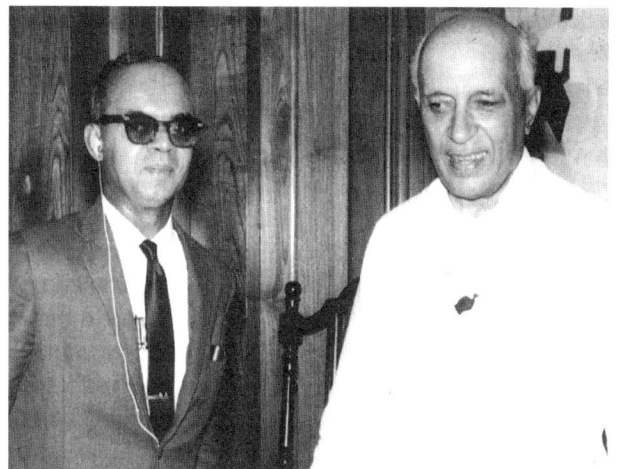

Williams visit to India. Photo with Prime Minister of India, Jawaharlal Nehru. New Delhi, July 1961

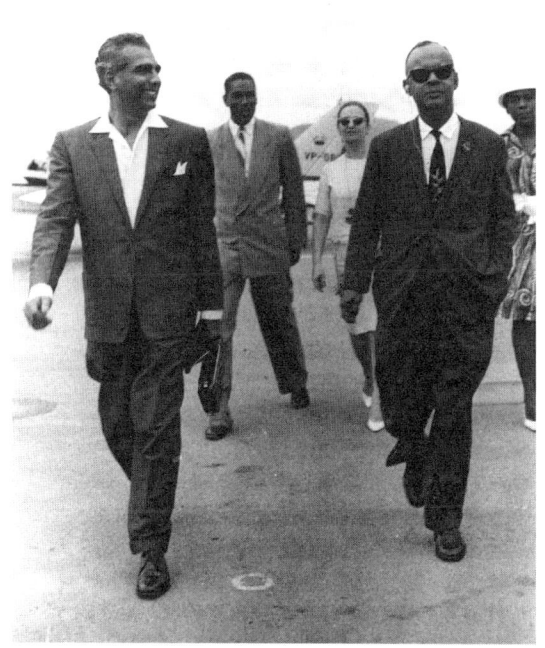

Arrival of Delegates for Conference of Heads of Governments of the West Indies: British Guiana Prime Minister Cheddi Jagan and wife. 23/07/1963

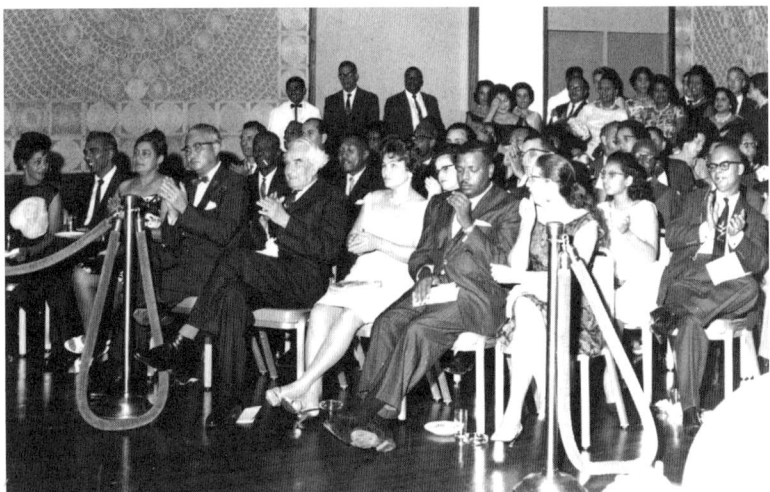

Conference of Commonwealth Caribbean Countries: Trinidad Hilton. Date 22/07/1963. *Left to Right* Premier of British Guiana Dr. Cheddi Jagan, Lady Bustamante, Governor General of Trinidad and Tobago, Sir Solomon Hochoy, Prime Minister of Jamaica, Sir Alexander Bustamante, Lady Hochoy, Premier of Barbados, Sir Errol Barrow, Mrs Cheddi Jagan, Prime Minister of Trinidad and Tobago, *Second row* Dr Eric Williams with daughter, Erica

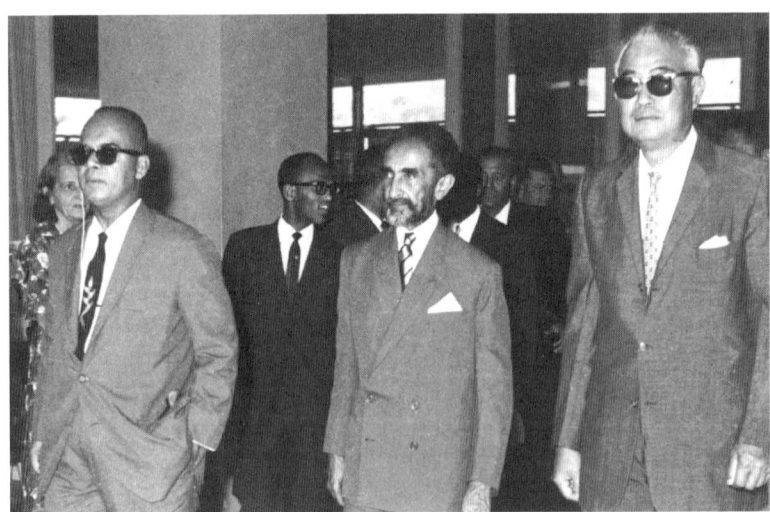

Dr Williams and Sir Solomon Hochoy at visit of Haile Selassie Emperor of Ethiopia to Trinidad and Tobago in April 1966

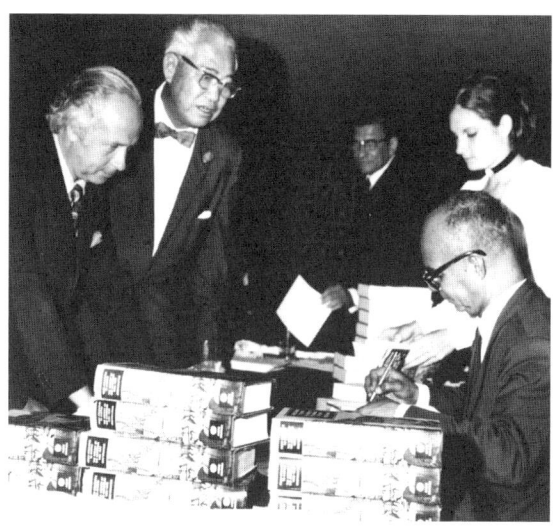

Launch of *From Columbus to Castro: The History of the Caribbean 1492-1969*, in 1970 Sir Solomon Hochoy, Governor General, second from left.

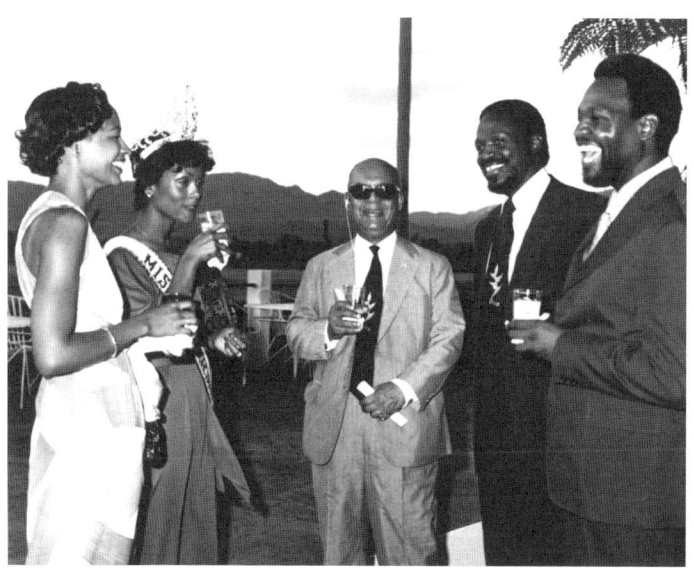

Dr Williams meets the new Miss Universe Penny Commissiong *Left to Right* Margaret Gittens (EW's niece), Ms Universe and John Donaldson, 1977

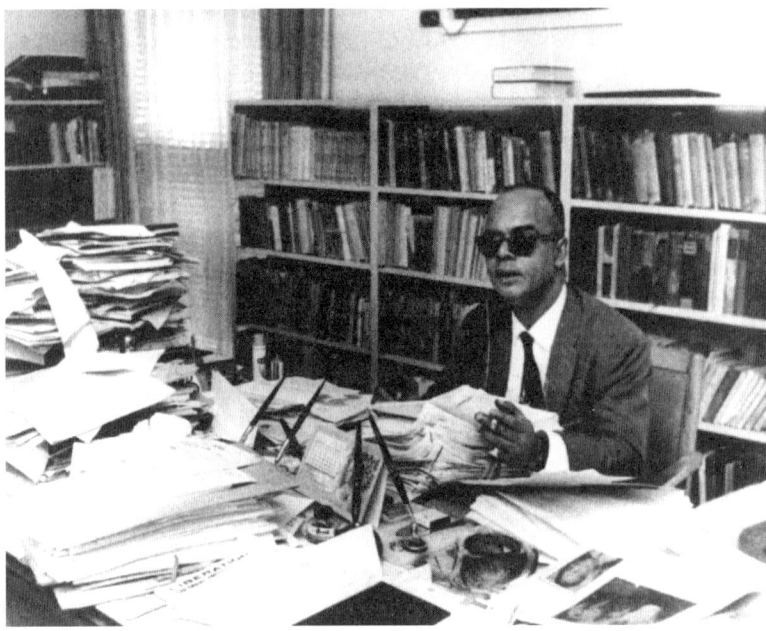

Dr Williams in the Prime Minister's office at Whitehall, Port of Spain

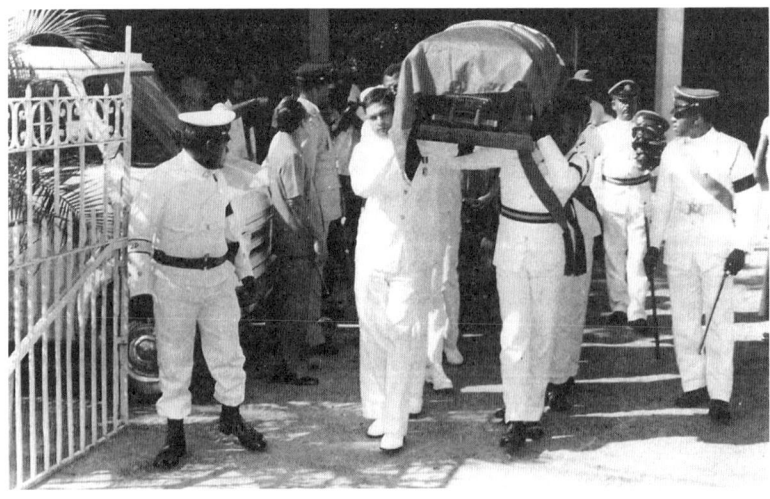

Funeral of Dr Eric Williams 1981

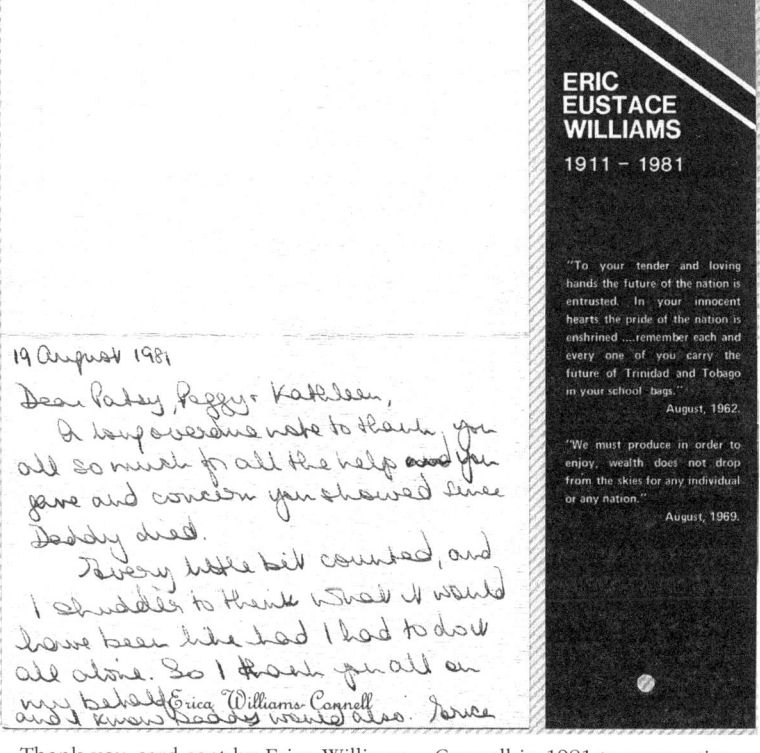

Thank you card sent by Erica Williams – Connell in 1981 to supportive friends after death of Dr Williams

In recently discovered[15] unpublished early chapters of *Inward Hunger*, Williams speaks directly through his writing to us, rather than leaving us to rely completely on secondary sources. This later acquisition of previous drafts of his autobiography, some handwritten, scratches and changes in the prose demonstrating the process of his thought, has produced more evidence for our scrutiny and given us more about Williams himself and the formulation of these ideas. The unpublished drafts of the earlier chapters of his autobiography are far more revealing about the private aspects of his life which he had concealed so well from the public. The drafts show a sentimental, melodramatic side of him, as opposed to a hard-edged, dry-humoured or distant character, which the later political persona suggests. That they are first unedited drafts from the pen of the writer is like being privy to his innermost thoughts. The studied and edited final product may hit at a more calculated truth, another reading of a life, but first drafts are not to be taken lightly. Conceive of them as parallel with the word association technique which psychoanalysts employ to elicit deeper or hidden meanings, tapping foremost thoughts, images and ideas which come to mind when a writer first puts pen to paper, before motive, logic and the artifice of writing is applied. For this reason, it is useful to draw heavily on William's actual phrasing of sentences, and to let the drafts rewrite the script where possible as it moves towards the published version.

In his perception of what motivated his life's work, it is clear that Williams felt quite deeply about the historical role the scholar and activist should play in a developing society that had suffered the pangs of colonization and African slavery. These early ideas hint indubitably at the political nature of this role. He portrays a committed, grandiose, perhaps even an overdeveloped sense of responsibility to his country in these early drafts.

> ...Morally I felt myself obligated to specialize in this neglected field of research because for fifteen years – from 1922 to 1937 – my education was funded by the people of Trinidad and Tobago – no other West Indian, living or dead, is to such an extent the child of his people ...I am convinced that the history of my education and my life can point a moral and ...in one direction in terms of the integration of the Negro in

the western world, in another by throwing light on a quite unnecessarily dark cranny in the history the world, but, more important, in terms of the ideological history of the west, its relation with "backwards peoples, and its often repeated assurances of a better world" (3/140 Ch 4).

This grounded belief in the value and power of education and what he has been able to achieve as a result of a sound education was translated very clearly into his political approach. Good examples are those of his University of Woodford Square lectures and the policies for free secondary and university education that he introduces with Independence in 1962.

William's belief in education and knowledge as delivering people from ignorance was grounded in his own experience, his own "emancipation from mental slavery" as a result of his gift of education. He was confident about his own knowledge and has been described by some as "arrogant" for being intolerant of those who would not listen or learn quickly. He demonstrated nonetheless a remarkable commitment and willingness to learn and share his knowledge with the Caribbean colleagues he encountered in his years abroad. Ibbet Mosaheb recalls about his tutelage at Howard University. "I took one course with him for a year. He corrected the papers of W. I. students. He marked very hard. He took a special interest in W. I. students. He became our mentor. …After becoming friends, 5 or 6 students met regularly with him in our dormitory. Dr. John Martin became a Jamaican surgeon. Henry Fletcher of Grenada, Eric Williams had a Grenadian connection, Clyde Burnett and I were Trinidadians. We also played cards in his apartment." Mosaheb goes on to relate details of Williams visit to McGill University in Canada in 1948, invited by the W. I. Society. According to Mosaheb, this was "largely a black group" in which both himself and Winston Mahabir were active members. "Eric spent a week with us. The Association later produced his speech in a booklet: *State Education in Trinidad.*"

For years before he entered politics formally, Williams had pondered on the value and benefits of educating a population, a proposal he would honour when he did come into power. Having benefited himself from a state-supported scholarship, he wished to return this gift to the people of Trinidad. Maybe this explains a note of deep sadness which one finds in interviews from those closest to him, about his mood after the Black Power riots in Trinidad in 1970, less than two decades after he has struggled to bring education, freedom and a sense confidence to his people. He is devastated by the turn of events, which move him from being saviour and deliverer to oppressor. He seeks out his own company more and more from that time on, perhaps to inwardly comprehend this.

"SOME ACHIEVE GREATNESS, OTHERS HAVE GREATNESS THRUST UPON THEM"

As the eldest son born into a family of twelve, he was burdened by responsibility of one sort or another from quite early, as we glean from both the published and unpublished versions of his biography. On the one hand he helped his father with the figures in auditing the books of friendly societies, on the other he helped his mother with the baking and selling of bread and cakes to earn the extra money dearly needed by the family. His eldest sister, the third child of the family, died at age nine months. He does not dwell on the cause of her death. He describes his childhood in a blend of quasi-Dickensian workhouse ethic of the schoolroom coupled with the pleasures of a reasonably happy and "normal" Caribbean boyhood.

In the first of his draft chapters titled "Life with Father" Williams writes:

> The circumstances of my birth were quite unremarkable and in no way differed from these of other West Indian children of the lower middle class, before or since …I was born in a small house in Oxford Street, a typical house of the lower middle classes in a typical street in Port of Spain. The house still stands, probably very much the same as it was in 1911. As one looks at it today, it reminds one of a square wooden box placed right on the street pavement, with one window on either side of the door, to which one ascends by a few stone steps. The front room is what is called in Trinidad the "drawing room." The dining room is at the back and

two bedrooms behind that. In the backyard were the kitchen, toilet and servant quarters – the smallest West Indian middle class house has some sort of room for the servant, a visible tangible symbol of the ascent of the family in the social scale by, at least, reducing the general amount of work for the female members of the family …My parents were typical of the lower middle classes in those days. My father was thirty-three years old when I was born. I later came to regard him as a strong silent man, reserved, except for the company of close friends, somewhat inclined to asceticism, but as son of his class, partial to a good Sunday table and the usual delicacies at Christmas and other festive seasons. On his father's side he was Negro; my only recollection of my grandfather is a vague recollection of a powerfully built strapping man of some vigour, whom I can remember seeing not more than once or twice, and of whom I can recall little or no mention whatever in the family circle. On his mother's side, my father has some of the Scotch blood which is found all over the West Indies, beginning first with the transportation of the Jacobites in the English civil wars in the 19th century, ending with the stress of young bachelor overseers and drivers brought in for the sugar industry.

"My grandmother, whom I recall, was as is not unusual in West Indian and American Negro families, a very light skinned woman of colour, the "high yallah" type of contemporary American Negro society rather than the café au lait variety so much esteemed in the slavery period in the West Indies. I remember her as an old woman, always dressed in black, wearing the ankle length dresses of those days. At her death she left me, her favourite grandchild, the only legacy I have ever received – 55 Trinidad dollars.

His family moved eight times during his twenty years in Trinidad. In early 1918, the family left Diego Martin and "relocated to a part of the town called Newtown – in a street named after the first governor of Trinidad "Picton," the central figure of a celebrated trial involving his cruelty to a mulatto woman, Luisa Calderon… It was a long rambling wooden house going far into the rear, a drawing room, a dining room, three bedrooms, a large room in the backyard, a verandah ran almost the length of the house, outdoor kitchen bathroom and toilet, and a fair amount of yard space where we could play bat and ball, kept pigeons." At this time his family consisted of himself, age seven, his sister, age three, and his brother, but this would "increase thereafter at the approximate rate of one child every year."

While according to Williams' notes they had a servant who cooked and they gave out the laundry, the family also had "the usual monthly account with the Portuguese grocery where an uncle in law worked." A conception of class respectability of the struggling lower middle class in Port of Spain at this time emerges from the vignettes of his penned notes: "POS was the city of the gay caballero, the bachelor girl and the merry widow. Females exceeded males in the town – 7110 females – three out of every five town inhabitants were females." They had to rent out the backyard

> … due to financial considerations, to a large foot, dark brown skinned woman who was a cook in one of the white families. She was visited by a light skinned married man - later arrested for defalcations at a firm where he worked. …My mother and father had a profound sense of propriety and gentility. The house was always kept clean and I can still recall my exasperation at having to assist, especially on Saturdays, with wiping off the dust from the myriad fine ornaments which decorated what were called the "what nots" tall pieces of furniture about the height of a hat rack.

Despite their straitened circumstances, the lower middle class was prone to petty theft, and Williams describes several occasions when they were almost robbed. "This prevalence of theft from poor people of the lower middle class, desperately struggling to maintain themselves, above the working class, is one of the more pathetic manifestations of poverty of the West Indies."

He draws on anecdotes and characteristics of individuals, in this case those of his extended family, to depict the tenor of class and race relations at the time, very similar in fact to the style which sociologist Lloyd Braithwaite also employs in *Social Stratification in Trinidad*, (1953). In another draft Williams writes, "The few memories which I retain of my aunts afford some insight into the colonial life and society of the time. One married a Negro tram driver and was generally regarded as having lost caste; the light skinned woman might marry 'dark', might go back to the kitchen having reached the drawing room – as the French West Indian proverb puts it, but she must not descend lower than the professions." Of one boyfriend of an aunt he recalls that "he always was in a waistcoat, symbol of the professional class in those days, taking salt in his coffee, a solicitor I believe he was …The fourth sister has a local white as a boyfriend. …He kept a small store in Port of Spain which served as a vantage from which as a small boy, I watched the two days of carnival which preceded the Lenten season for which Trinidad has long been famous and is steadily becoming infamous."

He is aware that not only skin colour, but straightness of hair provided markers of class and breeding at this time, as it perhaps unfortunately still does in the Caribbean. "The pathetic importance attached to the quality and texture of hair in Trinidad affects women in particular, but also men. For example, Trinidadians always commented on my good hair and are surprised to hear that I have no Indian blood in my veins. In the West Indies, light and dark frequently produce dark children with good black hair, and light children with bad light hair. The latter are often called derisively in Trinidad 'shabeen'. He notes that boys were then contemptuous of girls who had "wire hair." The importance of hair and skin colour was brought most clearly into focus when it came to the question of marriage partners as marriage should generally lead to an improvement in one's status. His parents were no exception in this matter. "…When it came to marriage, my parents were adamant. One might come from Africa, but there was no point in going back to Africa, that was their attitude…"

He displays a reasonably good grasp of the status and position which his family held in the society at that time and the choices then and later on that were available to them: "The opportunities open to the lower middle class in the society is here indicated by a consideration of the positions held by my relatives and the occupations of close friends of the family; 2 of my mother's sisters worked as store clerks; 2 of my brothers as civil servants; 4 sisters in private commerce; 1 brother a newspaper reporter; apart from myself and my younger brother, none of us have travelled abroad." Williams was the only one to obtain a university education.

His place of birth in the family, as the eldest child and son, the problems of everyday domestic life, moving from one place to another, struggles with income, all of these would have predisposed any sensitive and sensible child to a sense of responsibility. This was matched by the other major one placed on his still very young shoulders - to fulfil the ambition which his father had had for himself. Never retiring in his own self-aggrandizement, Williams writes "Greatness, Trinidad style, was thrust upon me from the cradle. My father knew that what he had never been given an opportunity to achieve with his brains, he might with his loins. The island scholarship for his son became the dream of his life." He noted in his earlier drafts that his father was educated at Tranquillity school, which represented the best primary and intermediate education offered in those days.

> Secondary education was then – as it still is today, a luxury, available only to the boy – and to a lesser degree to the girl. I can testify to my father's pride in the fact that he was president of the Tranquillity Old Boys Association and I remember the night that he took me to a social function there complete with sweet drinks, soda crackers and cheese. Like most Trinidadians, he thought highly of public speaking, and always welcomed an opportunity for that expression so dear to the hearts of older Trinidadians and not unknown even today "unaccustomed as I am to public speaking.

His father completed his education at Tranquillity and with "the help of some pull" started his first job as a mailing clerk in the Post office, a post Williams describes as "subordinate white collar."

In a subsequent version of this chapter, he describes his paternal grandfather as "a full- blooded Negro, employed in a menial capacity with a well do to local white family, who eloped and married one of the daughters."[16] His father he writes was dark brown, had joined the civil service at age 15 and was passed over because he lacked "social qualifications." These drafts are by the way show full evidence of William's wry sense of humour, his capacity to laugh and not take himself too seriously all of the time, very consistent with the views expressed by those closest to him, that he could also be a funny, engaging and warm person.

Of his mother he writes "His wife, my mother, was ten years his junior, and much lighter in colour than he was. Her family bore a French Creole name, of which both she and my father were quite proud, as it indicated the social importance of the 'French Creole' then." While Williams noted that his father had only one sister, his mother, he writes, had two brothers, four sisters in Trinidad, and a fifth sister, his godmother, who emigrated to New York and married a West Indian from "one of the smaller islands." He clearly recognized the effects of childbearing. "The midwife, for example, could not be dispensed with. Nor could one ignore the effects of repeated childbirths on her health. She became prematurely old, fat, and querulous, a constant victim of headaches." Despite her illnesses she outlived his father by 32 years. In these chapters Williams acknowledges his gratitude to both parents: "My father allowed neither religion nor finance to stand in his way ...and he was warmly supported by my mother." It was, however, his father's opinion which mattered to him, as is patently clear in this extract: "My first wife whose humble antecedents were compensated by a Portuguese father, an education in England and an income of her own, met decidedly with their approval. But my father died before our divorce and I am in no position to say what his attitude would have been to my subsequent marriage to a girl whose sole qualifications were a poor Chinese father, a native intelligence unspoiled by a university education, and a character uncorrupted by a private income. My mother's opinion I have never sought."

In the class and colour hierarchy which defined Trinidad colonial society at the time, masculinities were being pitted, one against the other. It is therefore against and in relation to his father as a black man, unable to comfortably support his family, and humbled by the prejudices of class, race and colour, that Williams proceeds to define his political vision for the Caribbean, and for Trinidad and Tobago in particular. Again, education is the signifier by which vision can be realized. His drafts recount in minute detail and with typical dry humour his appreciation of the cost of education and therefore what it cost the family to educate him. "The most serious consequence of the steady disproportion between population and resources was in the education of the children." Education was costly. While primary education was free, it cost two shillings per month to educate a child at intermediate level, secondary education cost $60 per year per child, fees were $16 per term but the child also needed clothes, books, shoes and so on. Added to that was the almost obligatory $2.40 a month for extra tuition "which all Trinidadian parents believed in and the majority moved heaven and earth to afford on the theory apparently that the child is like the sink in one of those problems in arithmetic I had to do - if one tap could fill the sink in 10 minutes and another in 15 minutes, how long would it take to fill the sink if both taps were turned on simultaneously." At this time Williams's father earned $120 per year.

He suffered no discrimination in his family because of skin colour because he was bright. He describes the precocious way in which his ability was recognized. "No doubt I was a good pupil, perceptive, alert, with a good memory, but looking back on it all, now, I see my precociousness." His father suspended a tricycle from the ceiling saying he would have it when he could recite his alphabet. He earned the tricycle before he was two years old. While he recalls "naturally" very little, this one incident he says, stood out in his mind. He took to learning like a duck to water. "I recall now one of our favourite games, under the house, playing school. I was always the disciplinarian, satisfying ...a pronounced trait in my character. "He was sent to Tranquillity school and not to the Catholic school as was expected. For his father this was "no mere whim of his ... a considerable financial sacrifice was involved ...education cost 5 shillings a month with a reduction for younger brothers." At the time he attended Tranquillity there were 250 boys on role, primarily black and coloured, with few Indians, Chinese and white boys. "The consequence was to make the young child, more particularly the boy in the days of which I write a potential economic and social asset, a possible future professional man... So from as early as I can remember, I was tormented and plagued with these possibilities, awed at being generally regarded as the rising hope of my stern, unbending relatives."

This fact of living up to the investment placed on his young shoulders and the "unbending stern" mien of the adults looming large over his childhood persists in another draft passage. Williams had just won the Charles Dickens novel *Great Expectations* for coming third in examinations. His father sneered at the title. "I should have come first ...little did he suspect how often I would come third in other exams before I came first, or what hard times would have to precede the realization of the great expectations." Nonetheless, it is clear that his father had faith in Williams, choosing Queen's Royal College (secular education) over St. Mary's (the Catholic boys' college) for his secondary education. Caught between church and state, religion and education, Thomas Henry Williams was the true pragmatist, as would Eric Williams also be in his political responses in the future.

That Williams presents his origins in the published *Inward Hunger* primarily from the standpoint of the son of a black man who feels cheated by the French Creole and whites of Trinidad, that the major preoccupation of his work, intellectual and political, is geared to liberating blackness from its secondary oppositional relationship to whiteness, is filled with a particular irony perhaps most meaningful to a Trinidadian audience. By 1991 a French Creole-owned publishing house in Trinidad produces a family lineage for Williams, which now claims him as French Creole-mixed. His ancestry is traced to the 1830s, elaborated along matrilineal descent. His paternal great-great-grandmother, Phillipa Susannah Commissiong, is described as an "apparently light-coloured person reputed to have been rich" who was "married not churched" with the Lt. Col. Sir Charles Felix Smith, Acting Governor of Trinidad in the 1830s. This union gave rise to a daughter Phillipa Susannah Smith who married John Baptist Hunt, illegitimate son of Col. le Hunt. Their daughter Onemia Wilhemenia Jane Hunt was born in Trinidad in 1853 and married Thomas James Williams, Eric's grandfather, who was born in Nevis in 1855.

Onemia is described as looking like a white person but as having coloured blood, she "had long straight, light hair, and a straight long nose, spoke French and French-patois fluently but spoke English with difficulty."[17] According to Besson and Brereton, she was "disowned by her relatives as a result of this marriage" to the Nevisian. Thomas James Williams was the son of Sarah Jane Williams neé James who was said to be of Carib descent with long straight hair, born in Nevis in 1830. Sarah died in Trinidad in 1915. She married a Negro nicknamed "Old King" who was a turnkey at the prison in Nevis. Old King was a Methodist like Sarah and was said to have a good education at that time. He came to Trinidad with Mr. Gaston Johnson who operated a real estate agency. Thomas James Williams and Onemia had two children who survived childbirth, one of which was Thomas Henry Williams, Eric's father, who was born in Trinidad in 1878. Thomas Henry then married Eliza Boissiere born in 1888 daughter of E.Redford and Jules Boissiere (Besson and Brereton 1991), and Eric Williams is the first born of this marriage in 1911. In the published version of *Inward Hunger*, it is not crystal clear whether Williams knew of, or deliberately understated this lighter shade of his ancestry. Some of the above details about his family background scribbled on the hand-written and typed drafts of early chapters, omit the above information that comes to light later on by future historians. Nonetheless, in a society where the battle had commenced about "who was the true indigene, the real citizen"[18] and who had credentials to claim political control, and where these ideas had already entered the debates on the politics of constitutional reform since the first few decades of the twentieth century (Singh 1994, 5), Williams's understood his own place and class/colour position he must be associated with in this struggle to establish the rightful claim for a people. It must be appreciated that by the time he is crafting an autobiography he had also experienced "Negro Oxford" and the black racism of the United States.

Coming from the small island of Trinidad, his father's status as a minor civil servant in the 1930s when this was a position of relative importance, his mother's family name of Boissiere, his urban childhood, his all-rounded excellence in both scholarship and sport, and the encouragement and hopes which his family had in him, all prepared Williams to be a confident and brash rather than retiring young man. This was the only heritage he would receive from his parents and also the only reward he could return, particularly to his father.

He writes in the published *Inward Hunger*:

> It was a day of jubilation that, October 19, 1931, when the news of my scholarship victory was brought to me as I was struggling, as temporary master ...Jubilation, particularly for my father, who arrived home for lunch, bewildered by the congratulations from people on the way. His twenty-year-old dream had come true. Under paid, tired, demoralized by the sight of younger people promoted out of turn over his head, because he lacked the necessary pliancy to ingratiate himself with the powers that controlled his destiny, he looked upon my victory as a decisive proof of his manhood. His bearing was more erect thereafter, his confidence in himself restored, and he often told me that, whatever his rivals had, they had not an Island scholar as their son.

In a society in which the professions of law and medicine were certain avenues to mobility and signals of status, Eric Williams's choice to enter Oxford to read for an honours degree in history, was not, and could not be comprehended by his father. "On this question, the disagreement between my father and myself was sharp, profound, persistent, and destined to strain our relations almost to breaking point." Having consulted two "coloured nominated members of both the Legislative and Executive Councils of the island, one a physician, the other a lawyer" (1969, 39) both of whom agreed with his choice, he reckoned with his father much the same way he would later proceed to do with his tutors and lecturers at Oxford, with his superiors at the Caribbean Commission and later with his opponents and fellow politicians in Trinidad and elsewhere. "I was thus ready for a showdown with my father. Aptitudes, my interest, personal experience, the advice of others, the signs of the times, all cried out in support of my choice. But he was one of those people in Trinidad who cannot draw a distinction between past, present and future ...He was accordingly very angry with me. He protested and remonstrated, argued and sneered, cajoled and persuaded. It was all in vain. I had made up my mind. He gave in with poor grace" (1969, 39). That he had made his decision, stood by it and won even greater glories than his father had anticipated was clearly another victory for Williams. "When I saw him in 1944, after twelve years, having got not only the bachelor's degree but the doctorate in philosophy, he greeted me with: "So you are a doctor after all." From this point on, his autobiography and such notes that exist in draft, become a very public one and in none of his writings or speeches, except in passing, are we ever given a glimpse of his personal life or emotions again. After he returns to Trinidad to live, Selywn Richardson emphasizes that his tastes had become very bourgeois and that he distanced himself from his family and others of his race. "He lived in an exclusive area where Negroes didn't live. He had an unlisted phone so that he could call us, but we could not call him – a fact that I had not known until then. He also said that he had at that time little or no relationship with his family" (Richardson 1984, 27). The implication of individualism and opportunism cannot be missed nor should we deny that Williams might have distanced himself for reasons of his own, had a separate set of friends with whom he associated and as noted before, for his own reasons, trusted more generously than his political colleagues. That he was single minded and focused is no news to us. He had won every battle as a result of this particular trait and applied this with all, *tout monde*. Halsey Mcshine, Williams' friend who trained as a medical doctor at the same time Williams was in Oxford, who later travelled with him abroad as his personal physician, and was also his father's personal doctor for some time, relates an anecdote which reveals William's capacity for focussing on the task at hand and distancing himself from others. "His father was very ill, and I wrote Eric and told him to please come to see his father. But Eric said that he was so busy, he wouldn't be able to come for three weeks. I tried to keep him alive for those three weeks until Eric could get there. I was hoping his father wouldn't die before Eric came. On the day Eric was to come I told his father, but he died one hour before Eric arrived. ...He was very sorry he could not come before."[19]

Williams never mentions his father's death as his autobiography continues. He has been going about his father's business even while his father lay dying. When he finally returns to Trinidad, he replaces the nuclear family and adopts the nation and the society as the larger extended one. He creates for himself, as do we all, the role he must play in the life of this society, given the rewards he has reaped from the same society and from his father. In his father's house there are many mansions, and some he keeps private, the others become his public space. From 1954, when it is clear that he has left the Caribbean Commission, instead of selling out like others, he was back:

> These people were my own flesh and blood. I had been to school with them played cricket and football with them, shared their sufferings, and enjoyed carnival with them. We had grown up on the same food, the same drink, and the same experiences. I had gone away, they had stayed home. I had come back with a University education, they had none. Now I their former classmate, was their teacher, I who had shared their sufferings was explaining their sufferings. I who had been with them passive objects of British imperial history, was telling them of their history, I who had suffered with them the tribulations of colonialism had come back as, so one called me, "the philosopher of West Indian nationalism" (1969, 93).

This relationship of father to son and the promise that the son might fulfil a father's thwarted ambition is a critical one to observe in the construction of masculinity in colonial society of Trinidad at this time. There is a parallel with another Trinidadian who would also attend Queen's Royal College, win a government scholarship 17 years later, go to Oxford and "make good," but who would not return, a parallel also acknowledged by Gordon Rohlehr, "These two Island Scholarship winners and graduates of Oxford, though different generations, have developed similar visions of Trinidad and Tobago society, and similar stances of intellectual detachment from which they delivered equally acerbic judgements on its deficiencies. The single positive element in Williams's assessment of his society at the moment of Independence was his faith in the power of a patriotic and multi-ethnic intelligentsia to function as role models in the new nation" (Rohlehr 1998, 851). There are other differences and similarities between these two sons of the soil, which may be observed. In *Finding the Centre*; "Prologue to an Autobiography" V. S. Naipaul (1984) only then confronts the knowledge that he had achieved what his father could not in Trinidad. He writes:

And it was with a sudden churlishness, a sudden access to my own hysteria, that I had left my father in 1950, not looking back. I wish I had. I might have taken away, might still possess, some picture of him on that day. He died miserably – back at the tormenting *Guardian* – three years later. To become a writer, that noble thing. I had thought it necessary to leave. Actually, to write, it was necessary to go back. It was the beginning of self-knowledge (Naipaul 1984, 39).

In *Letters between a Father and Son* (1999) Naipaul retraces this step again, still from a distance, to lay his father's ghost and his own guilt to rest. Why one returns and the other does not, perhaps is the choice which had to be made between the writer and the activist, at an historical moment in which most writers from small societies were forced into exile to be able to write.[20] It was probably a choice which Williams himself had also deeply wrestled with.

Eric Eustace Williams's demise as a tragic figure in Trinidad, very different to that which he self-consciously constructs through most of his life, is perhaps that he attempted to combine two essentially competing ambitions into one life. To do this he had to separate his "self" into a public figure that belonged to the nation, and a private one who was inaccessible, who distanced himself from his early origins so that he could continue to invent himself. He was also a scholar and thinker and he needed the space to write and reflect without intrusive noises in his head, away from the society and the world. He returned to Trinidad in 1948 after an already phenomenal career of teaching and writing, to enter politics first of one sort with the Anglo-American Caribbean Commission, then on to another which he would sustain for many decades. He continues on his father's business. Whether the driving force behind Williams is his own ambition and wish for power, or the desire to redeem his father's life is pure conjecture on the part of any of us. Nonetheless, the sheer energy and time which he puts into his political and simultaneous writing career needs to be acknowledged and celebrated, much the same way that we do any one individual who dedicates his life to a cause worth fighting for.

That Williams appeared on the horizon at a fortuitous time in the country's politicization is important to acknowledge. The idea of nationalism was not a new invention and the society had already begun to experience the emergence of other sons of the soil. Both Uriah Buzz Butler and Albert Gomes had preceded him, Winston Churchill had declared for the United Kingdom the sovereignty and self-government of the States, and nations of Europe had identified "the progressive evolution of self-governing institutions in the regions and peoples which now owe allegiance to the British Crown" (cited in Williams 1942, 102). Conrad O'Brien comments on William's own reading of the situation:

> We must bear in mind that by then England was ready to get rid of its colonies, now an economic burden, due its large WW11 debt. England was also pressured by the US to disband its empire. It was a two-way street. He grasped the opportunity since England was vulnerable. He also felt impatient that Trinidad should have been independent long ago. He hated colonialism ... At that point he was the only one who could do it with stability. Naturally having been brought up in the colonial era as I was, with the security and safety of the world's leading power at your side, despite its faults, having given you the rule of law and a great educational system, naturally, you are skeptical about what independence will bring. We had seen independence deviate from its course with ruthless dictators and economic decline. ...I think we were fortunate to have Dr. Williams to take us to independence and lead us in the first few years.

The demagogues like Butler in Trinidad and Alexander Bustamante in Jamaica had outlived the new time when the "Negro" must take on "government, legislation and planning" (Williams, cited in Rohlehr 1998, 866). That Williams had a good understanding of the dynamics of class and anti-colonial politics in Trinidad long before he entered fully into the field is clear from his writing. "The "agitators and hooligans" as they were called were men of the people. Uriah Butler, the leader in Trinidad, uneducated, with a queer political concoction of God, Marx and the British Empire, yet withal a man of great sincerity" (Williams 1942, 93).

Added to passion and fury signifying something, Williams also introduced reason and empirical detail underscored by new metaphors for struggle and vision. In an earlier unpublished draft of Chapter Two on *Inward Hunger* he writes:

> Today the Caribbean area is a museum of noble recommendations and political platitudes, hopes denied and promises reneged. The optimism inherent in western democracy has here been interred amid this frustration of colonial realities. Architecturally the symbol is Brimstone Hill in the British Island of St. Kitts, a huge fortress built by slave labour symbolic of the days when Britain and France shared and squabbled over this tiny island, today a monotonous trinity of sea, mountain and sugar, whose entire life revolves around the sugar factory which pays huge dividends to absentee shareholders at the expense of a population whose sex, twenty four yards off, is indistinguishable – flat chested women, ragged trousers suggestion of skirts. The real derelicts of the Caribbean are the Caribbean people. I am aware of them, I who paraphrasing St. Paul, by the grace of the people of the Caribbean am what I am and in whom their grace has not been void. The bells toll for me because it tolls for them. It is because I believe and realize this that I present this account of the education and experience of a colonial Negro, of his hopes and fears, his optimism and pessimism, confidence and scepticism, ambition and futility, aspirations and frustration – in the hope not only that it will be relevant to Africa tomorrow, but that it will be of value to the west today.

He begins writing *Inward Hunger* in Switzerland and recalls seeing the pilgrims come to worship at the church in Einsiedeln. He describes the baroque architecture, the piety of the worshippers and the virgin to which they are praying blackened by the soot of the candles, an image which must have intrigued him as he wrote:

> Einsiedeln is a symbol of faith, hope, peace. It is in other words an anachronism – in a world whose faith

> is the almighty dollar, whose only hopes is 'after me the hydrogen bomb' and whose peace is the cold war …as I looked at Einsiedeln, there passed before my eyes the epic struggles for freedom in the modern world against tyranny …Spinoza's right of private judgement, of Frolius for the freedom of the seas, of P… and Hamfden against royal tyranny, of Milton against the tyranny of priest and Presbyterian, of Locke in England, Rousseau in France and Jefferson in the colonies for the natural and inalienable rights of man, and though of our own times, with freedom slowly narrowing down from precedent to precedent. I thought of the efforts of Louis XVI, Bonaparte the Kaiser and Hitler to become world dictators…

Williams had conceived of political history as a history of consciousness and struggle and geographically, Trinidad and the Caribbean in the New World as the site from which another liberty could be forged. "Thus, for four hundred years" writes Williams, "the Caribbean has been emphatically and unambiguously in the western hemisphere of influence. If ever western civilization has anywhere had a chance to solve the world's problems, that place is the Caribbean. It was for this reason that sixteen (sic) seventeen years ago, I deliberately decided to make the Caribbean area the subject of my special study in research. I had all the necessary equipment for that study, both psychological – technical." A certain confidence is a necessary element in the make-up of those who hold lofty visions – a capacity to believe in oneself and the possibility of one's dreams, even in the face of detractors, the hero must be able to stand outside of the crowd. Williams' track record thus far, his successes and his intellectual reading of a situation must have convinced him of the historical role he must play in the society. At the same time, he was not omniscient and could not have anticipated the rocky path along which history would then take him.

What Williams brought to the society and to the crowds who came to view him as "William the Conqueror" was, as Rohlehr again points out, drawing insightfully on Sparrow's calypso, that of "Big Brain" and book learning. Brilliance and cleverness were important to the society to which Williams returned. What one could not achieve by the station of one's birth, class, or colour, was won through education and intelligence. In *The Middle Passage*, Naipaul (1962) captures the contradiction of the Trinidadian psyche towards those who stand out as different, a characteristic which allows Williams access into all classes and homes, and which he understands and employs well. "For if such a society breeds cynicism" writes Naipaul, "it also breeds tolerance, not the tolerance between castes and creeds and so on – which does not exist in Trinidad anyway – but something more profound: tolerance for every human activity and affection for every demonstration of wit and style" (Naipaul 1962, 82). The latter is perhaps what Williams added to a backdrop already positioned for political independence.

Bukka Rennie's reading from a perspective of the history of working-class organizations in Trinidad is that the society was already primed for Williams. "He did not have to do much to attain success. He did not have to sweat to build a Party, to do field work, testing theory with practice, and suffering the pressures that normally go with boring, painstaking political work. All Williams had to do was walk into the scene and complete the picture that had already been drawn and framed" (Rennie 1973, 163). Williams had to walk many miles up and down the country however, before he would reach centre stage. Apart from the many public lectures he gave before the PNM was launched, "from January to June 1956 he launched the party in 52 different meetings all over the country, following this from July to September, the date of the elections, with no less than 157 election meetings. His reputation for sustained and concentrated hard work, previously known to few, was now known to all" (Sutton/Williams 1981, xxii).

Williams benefited from those who preceded him and from those who worked alongside him and with him, and perhaps this needs to be made clearer and more transparent, allowing others part of the stage on which this play for nationhood unfolded in the fifties to Independence. So far the narratives of each, including that of Williams, may be partial and self-serving. Where and when this has happened also needs to be illuminated by bringing some of these stories together. That Williams did not present himself as a martyr in the struggle against colonialism but as a conqueror, both physically and intellectually, was consistent with his personality and with his confidence, and should not surprise us. Ibbet Mosaheb, one of the earliest partners in the movement that led to the formation of the PNM, noted about Williams that after his wife dies "He went to Europe. Took his gas-guzzling car. I wondered why. It allowed him control. He liked being in charge, very egoistic. He couldn't participate if he was not in charge. He needed to be in command." Williams was not a social historian and his autocratic style of management, as well as total absorption in the struggle, makes it difficult for him to extract himself and see both the forest and the trees. As the leader, brilliant thinker and visionary for the party, Williams depicts in January 24th, 1956, in *Forged from the Love of Liberty* the celebration of the birth of a child, the child was the PNM - to which it appears he alone had given birth, handmaidens of both sexes notwithstanding.

Nothing at this time came between the hero and his crowd. By 1956 Williams devotes himself completely to the nation. His daughter Erica observed:

> One of his favourite sayings was that "a prime minister should never have a wife, he should never have a daughter; and under no circumstances should he ever have both." I made him repeat that statement to many friends over the years because I found it so obviously funny, but I know now he really meant it. I think he was attempting to express the belief that a political man must devote his entire being to politics to his country. Pathetically, when he died, he had neither his wife, his sister, his daughter nor indeed a single relative by his side.

Despite the many who would come to know him and work with him, he remained an enigma, more charismatic because the wall he had constructed between himself and others could not be easily scaled. Elton Richardson observed. "Eric and I travelled together, and this led to a wider feel of the man than would have been otherwise possible. The facts are that I did get to know him well, but not enough. He was always a loner who needed a shoulder" (Richardson 1984, 24). And Williams leaned on and needed the shoulders of both men and women in an effort to rid the society of the colonial menace he deplored.

THE YANKEES GONE AND ERIC TAKE OVER NOW: WILLIAMS, MASCULINITY AND RACE

"Eric was the captain of football at QRC," recalls Halsey McShine. "During the scholarship exams in high school, his father worried that he would hurt himself during one of the football matches. His father was worried that it might ruin his chances for the island scholarship. So, his father asked him not to play one afternoon. So, Eric came to the stands to look at the match. Our team was losing, and Eric said he couldn't stand it. He went home and got his clothes. He played so great that we scored the winning goal." In *Inward Hunger* Williams writes: "I had a distinguished record at Queen's Royal College, both in the classroom and on the playing field. ...For the next five years my examinations provided the island with one of the most extraordinary patterns they have ever taken in their long history; whilst I topped the students in respect of the number of distinctions, I always placed third in order of merit until I won the 1931 island scholarship. I gained both cricket and football colours at school and was the football captain" (1969, 32-33).

Eric Williams did not live up to the image of the bookworm, the weak and unmanly lad who could only "beat book" and did not know how to lime with the boys. The same discipline and perhaps competitiveness that he brought to his studies, was clearly evident in his early sportsmanship. This control over mind and body, which he then exhibited, is evident in the way in which he also brought up his daughter Erica who remembers, "In my early years, he was undoubtedly very strict with regard to my upbringing" (Boodhoo, 1986, 4). Williams, although far thinking along other lines, worked primarily within the expectations of gender roles at the time - that of a deeply entrenched opposition and perhaps complementarity between men and women in society. Erica recalls:

> With my mother now dead, and my father away, I, at age two, must surely have believed that I had lost both my parents. ...He constantly wrote to me whenever he was away, even before I was able to read his letters, ...on one particular occasion I became ill. ...He had left me with some of my mother's relatives who, upon seeing my condition, and knowing the circumstances,

of course, indulged me terribly. When he returned, he was both disturbed by my illness and annoyed that I had been pampered. He then decided that he and I should live apart from relatives, since he thought I needed a more disciplined environment. His rationale for this action was later stated in a letter which I subsequently saw, in which he wrote, with reference to me, "what she lacks in feminine affection, I shall make up for with masculine discipline" (Boodhoo 1986, 4).

This world of masculine and racial and class politics which Williams experienced in both London and the United States, was mirrored, in different proportions in Trinidad. He proceeded to learn the ropes just as he had employed his acumen to every task he had undertaken before. His political shrewdness was a blend of his own remarkable intelligence and the ideas learnt very rapidly from those around him. We know that Eric Williams was no mean learner when he set his heart on it. Ibbet Mosaheb recalls that when Williams and Soy, his second wife, returned from the US where they had got married, he taught Williams (circa 1949-50) who did not then know how to drive on the roads of Debe and Penal. "He learned quickly. I taught him to play poker also, then he began to win the games." If we are to go on some of Elton Richardson's comments and those of others, the insights about mass politics Trinidad-style to which he would add his own brand of doctor politics were learnt primarily from those around him. Richardson related the incident before Williams was to deliver his now famous speech "My Relations with the Caribbean Commission" (1943-1955) in Woodford Square, on 21st June 1955. It had to be read first to the *Bachac* group – a study circle – comprised of Krishna Bahadoorsingh, Elton Richardson, the Montano Brothers, Telford Georges, Norman Girwar, Winston and Dennis Mahabir, Eustace Siegnoret, Claire Sloane-Seales, George Wattley, Eric Williams and Selwyn Richardson among others, and predated the final grouping which initiated the party. Richardson's account of this is as follows: "It was a beautifully done speech, but I felt that it lacked the quality of identification. I said that he ought to couch it so that all poor struggling folks could see their own struggles reflected in his experiences the speech. Eric hesitated long before he accepted but he finally did," responding to Richardson on the night, just before the speech was actually delivered "You were right, I should try to get people to see that my struggle was a replica of the struggles of others." "He was an oratorical type and he knew then what he could do with that crowd. The evening was an outstanding success and Eric was safely launched" (Richardson 1984, 28).

Where the leader stands on his own, and where he is a composite of the group is the thing which most differentiates the public figure from, for instance the writer, who of necessity, must remain the individual. The others around him, primarily men, felt that as a politician he was made in their image, undifferentiated by race, and that this was not fairly reflected. This appears to me to be one of the elements, perhaps a major one, in resentment to Williams as political leader. Ibbet Mosaheb supports some of Richardson's claims that the group, which formed around him by 1955, moulded him into the political persona that was first needed to bring the PNM to victory "When the group was very small, Richardson said to Dr. Williams, "Eric, you are not just another black boy." Williams did not like that. "There are some things you must do if you are going into politics. One, you must get rid of that big car. Two you must move off this hill to join the people." Another party affiliate comments "Well, he certainly responded to our advice and suggestions. Williams was not involved in the Caribbean movement of the masses. He was identified to the masses through his writings. Williams was brilliant, he was able to identify with what the masses wanted. He was leading them, but he was not from among them, so he had to seek support from party members who had the know-how."[21]

Williams sold the car, bought a little gear shift Vauxhall, sold the house on the hill and moved to Cornelio Street, a centrally located middle class suburb in Port of Spain. His journeys thus far had taken him into the belly of the colonial beast, across its various tentacles and their prey, and now back to the island where he was born and where he had decided to "lay down his bucket." He was back to dealing with the problem which had confronted his father two decades ago for fulfilled aspirations, mobility and recognition of worth. The chessboard of national and anti-colonial politics was no doubt fully fathomed and played with the same skill and commitment which Williams had employed in everything he had so far undertaken. The question that one must ask, however, is how in the midst of this group of progressive and obviously learned men, does Williams emerge as the political leader? Why was he as a man among other men, selected to represent them? They, like Williams, had recognized that the "common folk" of Trinidad at the time "looked to a leader to be somebody respected. They themselves did not want to be identified with the activities of the normal man. They saw Williams as a modern-day Christ."[22] In other words what did Williams have to offer in the 1950s which provided the necessary charisma to pull together not only those who identified with him racially, and politically?

Brilliance is an overused word in the Caribbean, and before the twenty first century usually referred to those who had excelled in academic scholarship. In the fifties in Trinidad few could boast the range of achievements of 'de Doc'. Education had provided the masses with some freedom from manual labour. The educated man, the one who could read and write, became the keeper of the books, the paymaster on payday. Williams embodied not only the "brains" needed to deliver people out of the hands of the colonial masters, but he had the oratorical skills from which he could beat Massa at his own game, with empirical data, rhetoric and argument, in his own tongue. As Selwyn Cudjoe observed "Williams grew up in the social environment in which the proper use of language was of utmost importance" (Cudjoe 1993, 43). He now added to this a capacity to move crowds in the middle of a city, village or community centre. This is a feat, as any public speaker knows which cannot be dissimulated. It was clear that in the period between 1955 and beyond Independence, Eric Williams was the man who had all the characteristics to appeal to a wide cross section of the multi-cultural melee of Trinidad and Tobago. At the same time, he also had to be outside of the masses to cross class and racial barriers and again here his breeding, intellect, travel and experience would present him as the best choice. "In fact, he was never identified as one of them. I think for all practical purposes, we didn't want him to be identified with them. They looked upon him with awe – like a charismatic leader. ...One must recall that Williams was a social scientist. He understood more than anybody else the thinking of the black Trinidadian." Williams himself knew only too well why it was necessary and appropriate to be identified with but not identical with them; that they time looked to the leader to be somebody who had achieved more a who would bring something new to the table to be respected. He could not represent the typical man. "They always saw Williams as the modern-day Christ. ... We had to protect that image. It was a nationalist movement trying to embrace the two major ethnic groups in the society who were at the time the oppressed people. While it was necessary to have him identify with a part of the establishment (the whites) it was not politically sensitive to be fully identified with them."[23]

Williams presented more than a politically expedient character. His writing before this time already articulates a vision that needed to be rendered into political practice. His brilliance was also in being able to arrive at the appropriate metaphor for struggle at the time, which was immediately understood by the masses. This is reflected in two forms, first in *The Negro in the Caribbean*, written twenty years before, and in his famous "Massa day done" speech delivered on March 22nd, 1961 at the University of Woodford Square.[24] The analysis of Williams's conscious knowledge of and application of language as a political tool is explored fully by Selwyn Cudjoe (1993) and Gordon Rohlehr (1998). I want to elicit another reading of the language he deploys as metaphor and how this transliterates into the contestation of patriarchy and the construction of masculinity in Caribbean society. The vision that is presented by Williams is a freeing of all colonized men (read Negro) from the control of all-powerful men (read Massa). *The Negro in the Caribbean* already contains "Massa Day done," written in a different script for a different audience. "The Negro in the Caribbean, we emphasize, is primarily an agricultural labourer, working for pitifully low wages. As the saying goes, he produces what he does not eat, and eats what he does not produce" ... (1942, 32). The Massa: "It is the deliberate policy of planters and governments to keep the people ignorant and unlettered. In the words of one planter: "give them some education in the way of reading and writing, but no more. Even then I would say educate only the bright ones; not the whole mass of the agricultural population, you will be deliberately ruining your country" (p. 72). In 1942, his Negro is not differentiated by sex, race or even society necessarily, and represents a pan-Caribbean rather than pan-African vision drawn from a working-class male and female composite.

In his speech on his "Relations with the Caribbean Commission" Williams, convinced that the enemies of the state were the colonial masters and the planter class, also reasons with the crowd about his actions and persuades them to his conclusions. "I stand before you tonight, and therefore, before the people of the British West Indies, the representative of a principle, a cause, a defeat. The principle is the principle of intellectual freedom. The cause is the cause of the West Indian people. The defeat is the defeat of the policy of appointing local men to high office." Paul Sutton summarizes the text of this speech. "Here, Dr. Williams examines his own frustrating and often unrewarding career in the previous twelve years as a senior official of the Caribbean Commission, drawing the inevitable conclusion that colonialism only impedes in every way possible the progress of West Indian people, individually and collectively. To move forward was to confront and destroy colonialism" (Sutton/Williams 1981, 269). Williams' experience mirrors that of his father's struggle over three decades before. They say a man travels the world in order to tell the stories to the people of his village. Only this comprehension of the individual in history allows Williams to understand his growth and prepare for his next journey, as he prepares for his next move. "I have rejected the job, as I shall reject all others like it. I was born here, here I stay, with the people of Trinidad and Tobago, who educated me free of charge for nine years at Queen's Royal College and for five years at Oxford, who have made me whatever I am and who have been or might be any time the victims of the very pressures I have been fighting against for 12 years" (Sutton/Williams 1981, 280).

In Williams's vision, Trinidad and Tobago and the Caribbean must be united against colonialism in order to win the battle. A recurrent fact comes to light from all of those who worked with him closely – that he had a vision of the Caribbean region as a whole basin, undivided by language, and needing to enter the anti-colonial struggle together. Complications arose in the actual working through of this vision, but this is the position from which Williams begins his historical vision. He had a commitment to improving the quality of life of the people in the Caribbean, not only those of Trinidad and Tobago. On entering party politics, however, he becomes one of the parents involved in the birth of a new nation and very consistently again, he becomes focused on the problem at hand. The children of the nation must forget their ethnic and racial differences politically in order to march forward. The nation like the child must be a mixed one, like Williams's himself. These ideas are evident in his concluding chapter of *History of the People of Trinidad and Tobago* (1962), the history book he had written in haste during his first term as Chief Minister to present to the people of Trinidad on Independence Day 1962 with a chronicle of the nation viewed from within. For Williams, deliverance from colonialism cannot be based on backwardness and ignorance of one's history nor from its interpretation by others. He embodies both the hero and the messiah, a latter-day Moses engaged in a task that had been undertaken by Gandhi and Nehru, both of whom he has admired in what he recognizes as a parallel struggle taking place in India.

> And only together can they build a society, build a nation, build a homeland. There can be no Mother India for those whose ancestors came from India; the young Trinidad novelist Ismith Khan, in his recent novel has described the disappointment of the Indians when the first Commissioner of the Government of India arrived in Trinidad some 11 years ago, not to arrange their repatriation as they had hoped, but to advise them to stay in Trinidad and become good Trinidad citizens. There can be no Mother Africa for those of African origin, and the Trinidad and Tobago society is living a lie and heading for trouble if it seeks to create the impression or to allow others to act under the delusion that Trinidad and Tobago is an African society. There can be no Mother England and no dual loyalties (1962, 281).

In a speech delivered to the University of Dakar on the relations between West Africa and the West Indies, Williams distinguishes the West Indian from the West African. "Thus, can we define the West Indian as he has developed during four centuries of colonialism. He is not an African, nor is he an Asian, nor is he a European. He is an African or Asian assimilated to the European. ...His political struggle has not been so much a struggle against Europe as a struggle to be incorporated into Europe, a struggle to oppose Europe's rejection of him on grounds of colour or race or previous conditions of servitude" (Sutton/Williams 1981, 226). In

Williams's vision of race, a nation, like a family, must have one loyalty and be pulled together by a common disloyalty. What he underestimated in this vision was that race is not only skin deep and that the problems due to racial and ethnic difference surface in the day to day relations of people, despite compelling visions of unity and struggle which they may in fact share.

Williams displays in his unpublished draft a good comprehension and sympathy with the different population groups in Trinidad at this time. He had observed in the unpublished draft of Chapter Two of his autobiography that while he attended Tranquillity school "The importance of education was not fully appreciated by the Indian community as it was today – hardly surprising when one recalls that my admission to Tranquillity also coincided with the cessation of the annual importation of indentured Indian immigrant labour." He thought that the Chinese regarded themselves as a distinct group not racially but economically, running small groceries, laundries and restaurants with the coloured people.

The history and process of identity formation of Indians in the Caribbean was a different one to the migrant groups who preceded them, or those who would come later into Trinidad. By the fourth and fifth decades of the twentieth century, many settlers were still India-born and had the memories and longings of first-generation migrants. The majority of Indians lived rural lives, outside of Williams' urban experience of Trinidad, and those whom he comes into contact with are urban or educated Indians. Chapter IX "The Contribution of the Indians" in his *History of the People of Trinidad and Tobago* (1962) and an unpublished set of notes titled "Indian Immigration in the West Indies" both demonstrate his sound intellectual grasp of the issues which affected Indians in the society, whether internally as a group, or externally in their relations with the other groups. He understood fully the deterrent to the political process of nation building caused by incoming immigrant labour. "Thus, it was in the West Indies, while one race was freed, another was indentured, and the task of forming a genuine society was therefore deferred." If political practice has cast a shadow on Williams' presumed use of or attitude to the Indian population, the handwritten or unpublished parts of his autobiography reveal a far greater understanding of and empathy with those who experienced this system of labour migration in Trinidad.[25] That he equated the experience with slavery at one level is very clear in this observation: "The African slave was imported by private enterprise. Indian contract labour was subsidized by the Government, that is to say by the ordinary taxpayer to the extent of one half...The slave was slave for life, indentureship was a five year contract, the slave was exiled permanent from his land, Indians were guaranteed return passage at the expense of the importing country after five years ...If indentured labour was free, it was, to paraphrase Carlyle – freedom plus a constable." He pointed out that Indian immigration, designed to compete with the Negro landowners, resulted in a class of Indian landowners and that "Once the Indian had received his plot of land, he was no more willing to work uninterruptedly and exclusively on the plantation than the former slave had been."

His writing resounds with genuine sympathy:

> There was no St. James in those days. It was known as 'Coolie Town'. The moment you see them in St. James, you arrest them. You arrest them on sight. Everybody knows this was no new law in West Indian society. It was exactly the same for the slaves. Their punishment came in the form of lashes. You could not whip the Indian. No corporal punishment for him. You see a Negro in the town, it was on the Negro to prove that he had a right to be in the town. The Indian was bound to live on the plantation and nowhere else. The moment you saw the Indian off the plantation, he was arrested, arrested on sight by anybody. If found anywhere else without a ticket of leave he was arrested by a plantation policeman – not even an ordinary policeman – or by his employer, or his manager, or overseer and taken to the nearest police station. If convicted the penalty was a maximum of seven days imprisonment with or without hard labour ...The symbol of West Indian society in 1870 was the jail. The Indians packed up the jail. There were not sufficient jails for them.

Williams is very aware of the grim details of indentureship, the conditions of life on the estates, the incidence of diseases such as hookworm and malaria among a labouring population many of whom did not have shoes, that the infant mortality among the Indian population doubled that of the rest of the society, and that Indians were also created as a criminal population by the 1899 Immigration Ordinance. He argues, as have others, that the Indians "introduced one innovation into the life of Trinidad – thrift. "Notwithstanding their pittance wages, many managed to save about 40%." Williams' concern with Indian immigration was a philosophical not antagonistic one: "Indian immigration was responsible for the long delay in grappling with the question of a modern labour code and decent relations in our society. And you understand, I am not apportioning blame… This is the effect. It kept generations of West Indian employers at the moral level of slave owners." While he admits in his schooling and early life, he has had little contact with Indians, there are snapshots here of his capacity to empathise with the plight which this group found themselves in within a new and foreign culture in the nineteenth century.

> To give you an idea of what I mean, this is what happened. Two fellows were found in the heart of the British Guiana forest – when asked where they were going, one said, he was walking back to India. Many Africans said the same thing. And the Indians used to say when they died, they would not remain on the sugar plantations. Their spirits were going back to Calcutta and Madras, just as the Negro slave used to commit suicide saying they would cheat the sugar planters and their spirits would go back to Africa. The Bandung spirit! African and Indian saying the same thing throughout the West Indies, fighting the same enemy, in the same arena of battle, under the same difficulties, both of them struggling…

That Indians may have proved for him to be the "recalcitrant minority" some time in his career should not be conflated with his early intellectual comprehension of the state of indentureship. Perhaps what was not then, and in my view is still not fully grasped about political collision between ethnic groups, is that differences need to be also appreciated from a sociological and psychological lens rather than primarily through political ones. The divergence caused by the juxtaposition of a very different 'eastern' culture onto a "western" space was not understood or interpreted by anyone at this time in the light that they may be now. For instance the internal differences between the monotheism and the secular nature of Islam, compared to the pantheism of Hinduism and consequently the differences between people even within the same cultural/ethnic group, may very well explain why the party Williams led to power was able to attract key Muslim figures rather than Hindus.

As a man who had seen the ignominy experienced by men of his own racial group, Williams could not have been insensitive to the problems experienced by Indian men. This is evident in again one of his unpublished draft chapters and hints at the sensitivity of Williams to an issue that affected all men, regardless of class and race. With the poignancy of the fiction writer he depicts a despair rarely captured in the literature pertaining to masculinity and Indian indentureship: "Jealous and vindictive to the n'th degree, the shortages of women of their own race was a standing incentive and the man who life revolved around the cutlass soon learned that a cutlass could be put to a variety of uses besides cutting cane – he could cut his loaf with it as easily as he could cut his wife's throat or her lover's. The sight of an old Indian man in Port of Spain, leaning against a wall, crying out in dumb despair, 'me want am woman" remains an indelible impression of my boyhood."

Examined through yet another set of lenses, therefore, Williams's struggle can also be viewed as that of the colonized male subject against the presumed superiority of the male colonizer. It must be recalled that women are generally not part of this struggle for political power at this time. In Trinidad this script is differentiated by race even while Williams' vision embraces all groups. "Black men" writes Hilary Beckles, "embarked on a Caribbean experience within the context of institutional environments that reflected the conquistadorial ideological interests of white patriarchy. Outnumbered by black men in West Africa, and the Caribbean, white men privileged the power apparatus of mind over body, appropriating for themselves an iconography of the former and projecting an imagery of black men with the latter. The conquest and control of the black male body, and its denial of a mind, resided at the core of the dichotomised ethnic masculine context" (Beckles 1997, 8).

If the contest between white men and black men appropriated the dichotomy of mind over body, within the iconography of the noble savage, then that between white men and Indians was also rendered in a script of otherness. The rationalization for British rule over the Indians was similarly justified in the difference between the enlightened and progressive civilized nations of Europe and those, which were dark, unscientific and backward, very similar to that of the African. These oppositions between Britain and India justified the rule of the colonizer and kept the colonized, to all intents and purposes, in their subordinate places. The characterization of the gender order between the British and India differed in one way. "We see throughout India a race of men, whose make, physiognomy, and muscular strength convey ideas of effeminacy." The physical difference of Indian men in the spectrum of masculinities had also been shifted to Trinidad (Mohammed 2002) placing Indian men here too at the lowest end of the patriarchal ladder.

This discourse of race and masculinity had its roots long before Williams appeared on the political scene as Singh (1994) develops in his analysis of race and class struggles in the colonial state of Trinidad 1917 to 1945. Cyrus Proudhomme David represented the sole African presence on the Legislative Council as a result of the 1912 Sanderson Commission, but there had already been an outcry from both black and coloured men that Indians would soon swamp the African population. Stephen Laurence, the Coloured Unofficial, in Singh's assessment, "openly voiced what must have been a long-suppressed consideration in the minds of the Black/Coloured intelligentsia." First was the objection to the continued importation of the Indians on the grounds of a population demographics – that Indians were already one third of the population. More importantly was the perception of the space as an indigenously western one belonging to those who had inherited and inhabited the west longer. Laurence felt that "as a 'West Indian', he had a right to object to the colony being converted into an 'East Indian' colony" (Singh 1994: 5).

Why such fears surface between ethnic groups is still not fully understood and remains at the centre of political struggles even more today in Trinidad and elsewhere. A metaphorical discourse on masculinity suffuses the writings and speeches of Williams. The relationship between the 'negro' and the 'massa' is that between a subordinated masculinity and a hegemonic one.²⁶ I think Williams conceived of a composite public hegemonic masculinity representative of one group which functions against all other oppressed and subordinated colonized men. In the practice of translating vision into reality, the struggles of race, class and the complexities of his own personality reproduced another male gender regime (Connell, 1990). This regime comprised first of all Williams and his relations with other men within the party. the second between men of the different ethnic groups where Williams himself takes on the role of the hegemonic male, and all other men become subordinates or subjects of one sort or another: "The Yankees gone, Williams take over now."²⁷ Struggles for political control are never straightforward ones and are complicated by race and class differences within the same society. These internal differences can be further appropriated by external forces to divided and rule a society. In general, these have involved primarily male factions as women were invisible or sometimes completely absent in the deliberations for the highest levels of power. The power broking for political power in a society might also be read as an expression of how masculinity itself is being contested between men and men.

In the struggle for power by the decades of the fifties and the sixties, the contestation of masculinities involved Indian men represented on two sides, those who supported the goals of the PNM, and those who stood outside of this circle. Kamaluddin Mohammed²⁸ records in his autobiography that he was involved in the earliest formation of the PNM. He describes his first meeting with Williams as on 28th May 1954, a chance meeting in which he Kamal, as the youngest County Council Chairman in the country, presided over a function at the St. George's Vocational School. Here Williams, as Deputy Director of the Anglo-American Caribbean Commission, was slated to give a lecture and this he did for ninety minutes. His second meeting with Williams was when they were both invited by Ibbet Mosaheb as President of the Naparima Old Boy's Association to a symposium on Caribbean culture, the other panellists being Beryl McBurnie and Errol Hill. Kamaluddin Mohammed's presence on this platform was also due to his well-known career as a radio broadcaster and cultural impresario of "Indian culture on parade" and therefore ideally suited to represent Indian culture. After this meeting, the presenters at the symposium and some other guests were invited to Dr. Mosaheb's house in San Fernando for some light refreshment, and here the question of uniting for a political cause arose. Other discussions followed and by April 1955. these conversations included Kamal (as he was popularly known), Dr. Williams, Mr. de Wilton Rogers, Mr. John Donaldson Snr.. Dr. Winston Mahabir and Mr. Gerard Montano. Here Kamal recalls, "It was suggested that Dr. Williams should lead such a political movement and he replied that he would give it some thought. A common view was expressed that evening at Dr. Mosaheb's home that since there was such a strong platform to discuss culture of the people, then why not the political development."

Kamaluddin Mohammed places the birthplace of the PNM in the Dil Bahar restaurant in Port of Spain owned by himself and Hasmath Khan. "It was out of the Dil Bahar Restaurant that the first major steps in the formation of the PNM were made. Some months after the meeting organized by the Naparima Old Boys Association, Kamal got a telephone call from Dr. Williams to say that he (Williams) wanted to come to see Kamal. They agreed on a time and Williams came to the Dil Bahar restaurant for lunch. They had paratha roti and curried goat and the meeting went well into the evening and the idea of a political party was born." (Was this the beginning of rum and roti politics!)? One week after his visit to the Dil Bahar restaurant, he called Kamal to invite him to a meeting with a few friends to continue the discussion of one week before" (pp: 67-70). This meeting took place at Williams's house and a few others were present in addition – De Wilton Rogers, Wilfred J. Alexander, Donald Granado, Dr. Elton Richardson and John Donaldson Snr. Later on, it was decided that they needed to have a series of public meetings and that they needed to widen the group, and others were added: Tajmool Hosein, Felix Alexander, Isabel Teshea, Andrew Rose, Harold Duprey, Ulric Lee and A. N. R. Robinson. According to Kamal, the Dil Bahar provided the earliest headquarters for the political activity that was later to be constituted as the PNM and after six months was moved to the party headquarters in Queen Street. So far only two women, Claire Sloane Seales and Isabel Teshea, are mentioned as part of these political discussions although the interviews show that others had been contributing in various supporting roles. Williams had by now become further entrenched in the public's imagination through the medium of calypso. His staunch supporter then, The Mighty Sparrow released a song that would rally popular support for the party and its proclaimed leader. Released in 1955 Sparrow sang:

> Praise little Eric, rejoice and be glad,
> We have a better future here in Trinidad
> PNM, it ain't got nobody like them
> For they have a champion leader William, the Conqueror

William the conqueror was no saint and his human frailties as a public figure have been held up for scrutiny far more than others who, whether by choice or necessity, have remained less public. Ibbet Mosaheb recalls

> After he lost the Federal Elections to Bhadase Maraj, he became very hostile. At a speech in Woodford Square he referred to the East Indians as a "recalcitrant minority" he should not have done this. Many of us went to his home after the meeting and told him so. Yet two weeks later in a meeting in San Fernando he repeated the same things. I thought it was a political blunder. He was hurt by the outcome of the elections. He blamed one ethnic group. He was upset he had lost so he sought to place the blame somewhere."

His outburst was a product of his temper, a blow to his ambitions, perhaps even his political naiveté at the time in assuming that he could convince all of the people all of the time. At an intellectual level he had demonstrated both compassion and a keen political understanding of the situation of Indians in the society. But he was well aware that Indians were not indifferent to the political future of the society. Of the forty-three men who were candidates for the General Election of 1946 to the Legislative Council, fifteen were of East Indian descent. He no doubt blamed Bhadase Sagan Maraj and the political mobilization of the Sanatan Dharma Maha Sabha for racially polarizing Trinidad politics and helping to create a climate of overt political racism between East Indians and Afro-Trinidadians, without understanding that the Indian population who had had a different historical relationship to the society was not as easily convinced by his anti-colonial nationalist rhetoric.

In his 'Massa day done speech' of 1961, Williams represented all of those who stood outside of his vision as the "stooges of Massa." His tone becomes more vituperative, one that has wrestled with practice and experience far more now and perhaps already feeling and beginning to express the dissonance between vision and reality. Nonetheless, still working with these differences of race, Williams inverts race and colour into a class position, and presents himself and the party as cleansing the society and the nation of the backward elements to progress. He clearly expected in the political sphere to have things run his way – and perhaps had got used to this after a fashion. We need not settle this matter of his autocracy or personality here – there is sufficient evidence of his character to deduce that he expected to win, although in facing the death of his loved second wife, Williams would also have experienced grave defeat. Perhaps he had got used to it in the sphere of public life. There were many sides to his character. His political secretary D. D. Dupres noted: "Well, he didn't like to lose and would get vexed. If he lost a seat in the elections, he would sit down and look at the figures to see where he lost. He was interested in what areas he lost and analyze it immediately." Ibbet Mosaheb commented: "He used people and dropped them all the time. People had functions. When those were completed, he dropped them. That was one of the bad things about Eric – the personality of the man" Conrad O'Brien observed that "He was the type of person who having had one complete a duty he would end the relationship, at least for a time. He was not very friendly, did not enjoy the company of others very much. He was very private, not a good mixer. He had to, as Prime Minister, but was not the sort of person to have a real best friend, to sit and chat with for hours, and confide in him." O'Brien also agreed in the same breath that Williams could be tough, charming and belligerent, and that there was the other side of him, the side that had made him a leader of men among other men: "his forthrightness, his defence of democracy and freedoms."

Williams's outbursts in public are well known, but there is little in his writing, which personalizes the anger or disenchantment he feels to anyone in particular. As Paul Sutton has observed, it is not an easy task to decipher Williams from his writings and practice. Sutton agrees that both of these need to be placed temporally and to be analyzed against the purpose for which it was intended.

But Eric Williams was contending with another far more fundamental characteristic within this relatively new society. In *The Middle Passage* Naipaul had analyzed it thus: "Everyone was an individual, fighting for his place in the community. Yet there was no community. We were of various races, religions, sets and cliques; and we had somehow found ourselves on the same island. Nothing bound us together except this common residence. There was no nationalist feeling" (Naipaul 1962: 45). One decade later, in a speech to the 15th Annual Convention of the PNM, Williams repeats the same sentiment; "One of the most serious difficulties we have to contend with is the national character. The sheer individualism of the place is absolutely unbelievable. Everyone is out for his own interest, the interest of a particular constituency, the interest of a particular industry, the interest of a particular village, the interest of a particular family. Nobody ever thinks of the national interest" (September 1971).

From 1970 onwards Eric Eustace Williams grows tired and spends more and more time at his home. He began to withdraw to his private world where he could ensure order and perhaps retain something of his illusions. Madge Lee Fook recalls, "...during the later years he was working more at home. He still came to his cabinet meetings as usual. He just didn't spend that much time at Whitehall, but he still fulfilled his duties ...I think that he was not appreciated. Whatever he did, it was never good enough, there were some that supported him through thick and thin, but it was a general malaise among the people."

The persona of Williams in the 1950s who takes on "massa" and leads this army of men to a victory shifts to a tired and battle-weary warrior, more resigned and distrustful of the same men he once fought alongside with and whom he struggled to defend. He had moved from the benevolent patriarch to the somewhat distant and unforgiving patriarchal father.

"To My Mother, Eric Was A Charmer"
Every school child received, along with other trinkets barely remembered today, chocolate bars from the government of Trinidad and Tobago, to celebrate Independence Day on 31st August 1962. We, the children of 'hewers of wood and drawers of water' were given small bars, individually wrapped in red, of delicious brown

chocolate. In a supreme irony of history and culture, the sugar cane and cocoa[29] that defined plantation life and agricultural labour in Trinidad between the eighteenth and nineteenth centuries were represented in the twentieth century to court the labourers' offspring in their first taste of freedom. The gesture was a magnificent one: both for its calculated political intent and for the bittersweet estate it recalls of the man who would reside in the collective memory of the society as "the father of the nation."

The consummate intellectual, historian and politician, Eric Eustace Williams would have understood the value of this gesture to the children of Trinidad and Tobago. It combined cultured civility along with tenderness; much the way chocolates have come to be treated as a tasteful luxury gift of love. He demonstrates a profound understanding and interpretation of the importance of these two crops, sugar and cocoa in the history of the island. In the handwritten draft of Chapter One of his autobiography he writes:

> ...Agriculture was the backbone of the island's economy, sugar and cocoa vying with each other for pride of place, the difference between them being essentially a difference between the absentee-owned plantation which excluded all the crops and the locally owned estate which encompassed the subsidiary cultivation of food crops. ...There was a further essential difference between sugar and cocoa - the former dependent on contract labour from India, the latter on native labour. Sugar in its essential aspects was, like so many of Trinidad's children, an "outside" child, cocoa was the legitimate first born. Sugar was English, cocoa was Trinidadian, sugar was the symbol of imperialism, cocoa was the quintessence of local autonomy, sugar to revert to a metaphor drawn from family life in Trinidad, was the de facto extra-marital connection, while cocoa was the de-jure wife, like so many wives in Trinidad, fighting a losing battle against the other woman.

The gift-wrapped finished product, to continue Williams's metaphor, was a marriage of the two products each transcending the limits of the other, very consistent with Williams's sense of a future which must exceed the ethnic and racial boundaries of the past.

His message to the Youth of the Nation in the Independence Youth Rally, Queen's Park Oval, on 30th August 1962 also conveys another insight – the value of nurturing youth in building a society. "To your tender and loving hands, the future of the Nation is entrusted. In your innocent hearts the pride of the Nation is enshrined. On your scholastic development the salvation of the nation is dependent." To the politician Williams, we can impute many subtexts and motives to gifts and words such as these. To the visionary, the writer, the private man and father, they should not be taken for granted. Williams succeeded for the brief period around independence in involving almost everyone, those who supported the PNM and those who did not. And that was no mean achievement.[30] Conrad O'Brien, Trinidadian businessman, recalls: "It was a glorious time. The country came together. ...You could feel the spirit of unity and excitement taking place. Despite the odd fears the country was together and everyone was behind Dr. Williams in a peaceful transition. The independence week was a great experience. I cannot forget the ceremony which lowered the Union Jack and raised ours, and the first singing of our national anthem. There was joy and excitement as I walked the streets of Port of Spain that night to absorb it all. It was great to be part of it." As part of the thriving commercial sector in the 1950s, O'Brien, and others like him, was, if not unwelcoming, disturbed when Williams had first come on the scene. O'Brien: "I was concerned, mainly due to lectures Dr. Williams gave in Port of Spain, together with Dom Basil Mathews, who was then a Dominican monk and also intellectual, and in those lectures, in my view Dr. Williams said some worrying things. I suppose being a politician he said things that would capture the imagination of the majority of people who would eventually be voters. To me who was mapping out a business career, and I suppose a conservative, was rather concerned. And therefore, when his party won a majority of seats, in the then colonial era, I was concerned."

O'Brien like many others were eventually persuaded that Williams was a man who meant business and that he had the good of the society at heart. O'Brien relates this anecdote.

I was in Senate from 1967-71. Then I represented the business community making many speeches on the free enterprise system and its importance to Trinidad. A labour leader, Carl Tull was also in the Senate. We got along very well. He requested a meeting at Queen's Park Hotel. He then told me that Williams would like me to join the delegation to the USSR, representing the business community. Dr. Williams wanted to know if I would accept, before making a formal invitation. I said, "When your Prime Minister calls upon you, you must accept. Of course I would accept to join the delegation." The phone rang in my office the next morning. Amazingly it was Dr. Williams, himself. He asked me to come to his residence to meet him. I did. This was one of the few occasions I spent some time with him alone. It was fascinating: two hours at his home. Dr. Williams stood behind the bar at his home. We fired a few 'grogs" during that two hours. It was quite an experience. Naturally he spoke more than I did. He lectured me on politics and world affairs. I saw the depth of his mind, his interest in world affairs. It was quite an experience. ….he can turn on the charm whenever he want to, then his a very much of a human being with great sentiments, kind thoughts, and he did so that afternoon. He spoke with great human feelings, with tact and sympathy towards our country's problems. I saw a side of him one cannot see from the podium or the Parliament.

Williams did not put himself out unnecessarily to be a charming man to either women or men. He was a complex, many-sided character, who had to be understood on his own terms. There were many human frailties that stood glaringly in the public's eye, but we have snapshots of a private self that reveal a likable and humane man. At the same time, he is always studied, controlled and controlling – heightened consciousness leads equally to increased self-consciousness. "He was a very private man," continued O'Brien. "To meet him and to shake his hand was not very easy, especially getting to know him at such a meeting. I doubt whether many got to know him. He had an especially strong personality. When he was ready to turn it on, he was very charming. During that period (around Independence) he was very happy and very charming. The functions where we met, then, he was always on top of the world, full of smiles and warm handshakes. But he could also be the other way."

The charming side was one which was revealed quicker to women; Williams had no need to compete with them. He accepted women as equal, but different. D. D. Dupres, his political secretary for years, speaks of the kind of relationship he had with her mother and here we get an insight into William's understanding of the "fairer sex" at this time:

> My mother Muriel Achong was half Chinese. She was a very gentile (sic) woman. I think she was a very sobering influence. I think he admired that aspect. She symbolized everything that he thought was a woman. In addition I think Eric knew that my mother adored him as a brain. They discussed things. My mother was a very political woman, she would write articles for the PNM newspaper, *The Nation*. He would call her up to get a feel of what was being said in the supermarket, what was being said when she went out to tea with her friends. To my mother, Eric was a charmer. He was able to speak to women young or old and charm them. When he spoke to you, he focused on you; he listened to what you said. Whatever you had to say was important. He would not allow anybody to join in the conversation when he was talking to you. Even with children, he would focus on each child and maintain eye-to-eye contact. He was a woman's man. When he focused on you, you were the important person at the time. He really was interested in what you had to say.

That Williams implicitly understood sexual politics is clear. At the same time he was not unfair to the women he would come in contact with either socially or professionally, because they were women. From his treatment of his daughter Erica and care for her own scholarship and development, one may deduce that he was progressive and was willing to engage women and challenge their intellectual potential. D. D. Dupres recalled as a young girl of seventeen in August 1955, "I was not happy to meet Eric Williams because he was the one who took my mother and father out every night. We talked about school. I had just left school to do commercial lessons. He told me his library needed fixing and he'd pay me to come fix his library with his sister-in-law Kathy. We ended up reading more books than fixing the library. I started attending political meetings."

Williams recognized that women were important and valuable in the private life of things and respected this, but the gendered worlds had to be kept apart. Halsey McShine recalled that he and Williams met up in London during the time they were both studying, and during the final year of his studies, Williams "became friendly with a Trinidadian lady, Elsie Ribiero" who was studying music in London. Despite the fact that they were relatively close friends, Halsey did not realize that Williams was then courting Elsie, and was very surprised and a little bit hurt when he found out that as his best friend he had not been selected to be the best man at his wedding, nor for that matter to attend the wedding. "We all used to go out in a foursome with my now wife. We used to go out to eat and dance. He never let out that it was serious, that they were actually married." McShine only found out later from John Pillai who had been the best man, when Williams and Elsie was safely married and had left for America. Nobody knew whether he got married before or after he finished his degree although Halsey thought it was before but qualified it "I am not sure. Like I said, nobody knew because he was afraid the Trinidadian government would take away his scholarship. He kept it as quiet as possible."[31] This compartmentalizing of his private life continued even when there was no obvious need to do so. McShine remembers about his second marriage to Erica's mother Evelyn (Soy) Moyou: "It was a very private wedding. He didn't let anybody go. It was a shame that she died so early, he was very fond of her. ...I think that was the one woman he truly loved. I think his life would have taken a very different course if she hadn't died. ...He might not have gone into politics. His life changed dramatically after she died." Erica also believes that "he was deeply affected and scarred by the death of my mother. She was the "be all and end all" of his life." (Boodhoo 1986, 4) It is not a simple task to make the distinction between public and private influences on our lives. The relationship between the two is as interwoven as the connection between objectivity and subjectivity. Nowhere is this interface made more evident than in the comments from his closer friends and colleagues as to the reasons why Williams agreed to enter politics. Ibbet Mosaheb in response to Ken Boodhoo, "There is a theory: if she didn't die he would not have gone into politics. I do not agree. If he was not fired from the Commission he would not have entered politics." Later on Mosaheb adds:

> I believe Eric was forced into politics by the firing. The position of Secretary General rotated. Eric believed that when it was the English turn he would be appointed Secretary General. He wasn't and was eventually fired. He called me on that day asking me to come to his home with (Winston) Mahabir. We met Dr. Elton Richardson at Dr. Williams' home. All four began to discuss Eric's future. We looked at the existing parties and deciding that Eric should not join any. By then he decided to enter politics. He may have been planning this for years. He was an opportunist. When the Gomes regime postponed general elections for one year, it allowed the PNM time to organize.

The answer is probably neither fully one thing nor the other.

That Williams fell deeply in love with Evelyn Moyou was obvious to all who knew him. Hugh Simpson recalls that he was seventeen years old and friendly with the Moyou's and knew when Williams was "courting Evelyn." Joan Lake who also knew the Moyou family recalls, "Quite often, I would be at their home. I knew him as Eric, not as Dr. Williams. He would be visiting his fiancé, Soy. ...Apparently she might have been his secretary. She did a lot of typing late into the night. Eric and I played hockey together on the same team. Naturally, we discussed and visited." This was the early fifties and Williams had already started the round of lectures at the Public Library. Although Joan did not attend, she remembers, "My father followed his early lectures at the library and was very very impressed. My father and Uncle Harold followed him very closely."

The picture that emerges of Williams at this time is that of a man just over forty, courting his fiancé, and having a well-rounded life, of sport, lectures and work. The capacity to love, either a partner, or a country, and to create something wholesome out of these attachments, which is lasting, is already an achievement which few will have made in their entire lives in the way in which Williams did. The matter of the race of the women whom Williams married, and his reasons should remain his private business and should not enter the scope of gender scrutiny. In the guise of protecting race and culture, feminist and race politics have done sufficient damage to the relations between men and women, without imposing further limits and constraints on human desire, on the choices that people make in their lives and the reason these choices are available or appeal to them.

Having said this, it is clear that Williams seems to have been in close contact with and perhaps trusted many women from the Chinese community. His secretary for his entire period was Madge Lee Fook; Mrs. Joyce Wong Sang was in charge of the Better Village competition; his political secretary D. D. Dupres was the daughter of Muriel Achong, a Chinese woman and his second wife Soy was also clearly partly or wholly of Chinese descent. There are also pragmatic reasons for this. If we are to go on Wally Look Lai's assessment of the Chinese at this time (Look Lai 1998), it would seem to me that in the fifties, these families were the ones Williams would have had more contact with in middle-class Port of Spain society, and that their daughters were educated and fitted into the range of secretarial and white collar posts, or the social milieu in which he moved and were therefore accessible to Williams.

After Soy's death in 1953 Williams retreated into greater solitude and later on took on the task of bringing up Erica on his own, with help from the women in the families with whom he was close, and from his secretary, Madge Lee Fook. Williams did not choose the convenience of marriage to assist in his political life. D. D. Dupres, his political secretary, commented: "The absence of a female caused a practical problem ...Eric led a very lonely life. He had to plan his own entertainment and get approval from the security people. Once he became Prime Minister, everything had to get planned. It was the nature of the job. I think if he had a wife, things might have been different. When he had a free day he had no one to share it with."

It is difficult for those who were not acquainted with Williams closely to understand the charm he exerted and loyalty he engendered in the women closest to him. Yet there is every evidence that this was a crucial part of his appeal and that he established a base of power among both middle- and working-class women. As he had no wife to deal with the business of entertainment, Joan was asked to assist him in this. At the same time, as a politician he was always astute about the capacities of each of the women he dealt with. She recalls:

> One of the things that was interesting about Eric is that he would say to me, Joan, we're going to have parties and I want you to take care of them. He'd tell me to do everything and just tell him how much it cost. I was none the wiser really why Eric asked me to do the parties, but it was nice, and I did it. ...One Christmas we were invited to Christmas dinner. ...somebody came to me and tells me that Eric wants to see you right away. So I go to him and he says how would you like to go away. It would have been nice, but we were already committed to my sister's children, so it was not possible to go away. Years later it dawned upon me that because we were new, Eric did not have any qualified people in international affairs. We might have been groomed for one of the positions.

The popular gender reading of Eric Williams and the PNM is that his power base has depended largely on the PNM Women's League and their capacity to mobilize at the grassroots and community level on his behalf. Perhaps this is so, but it is likely that any male politician of the time would have done the same, making Williams no better or no worse for not replacing the old patriarchy of the 'massa' by another one. At the same time one must also consistently respect Williams' capacity to engender such loyalty from women who worked with and for him. That he understood the secondary status of women in society and the need to incorporate them as fully as possible into mobilization and decision-making is clear from his speeches and the programmes of the PNM government. He writes in *Inward Hunger*:

> We set up specific units of the Movement as follows: Party Group, Constituency Group, General Council, Central Executive, Legislative Group, Women's League; Youth League, Annual Convention." (1969, 146). "The General Council was the governing body of the Movement. It comprised the officers of the Movement, holding office for a normal term of the Legislative Council, (that is to say 5 years), 18 members elected by the Inaugural Conference for five years (one sixth of these were to be women), one representative elected annually by each Annual Constituency Conference, 12 members elected by the Annual Convention to hold office for one year (one sixth of these to be women), 8 members from the Legislative Group. The twelve officers of the Movement, in order of precedence, were: Chairman; Vice Chairman; Second Vice Chairman, Lady Vice Chairman; Political leader; Education Secretary; Public Relations etc" (1969, 147).

In addition, he notes, "The women and youth were organized on a constituency basis, and provision was made for an Annual Youth Rally and an annual women's conference. The latter elected a Women's League executive. Both Units were represented at the Annual Convention by two delegates each."

The emergence of the PNM predated any second wave feminist activity in Trinidad so that here both the party and Williams were not influenced by contemporary feminist propaganda. Were women merely another constituency through which power would be assured? One does not get that impression from a reading of his private relations with the women he knows or from his treatment of his daughter Erica, but here again he may have been a man of many contradictions. Williams, however, must have known that the issue of sexual equality had emerged as a political one. In the series of lectures in the PNM adult education programme given by C. L. R. James in 1960 at the Public Library in Port of Spain, James devotes lectures to "The Exploitation of Sex" and, "The sex war" placing the exploitation of women within a Marxist reading of class exploitation and, not surprisingly for James, an insightful and succinct reading of the condition of women in capitalist society (James 1960, 82-84). Williams could not have been unaware of some level of feminist politics at the time, having also travelled and been widely read. In *Inward Hunger* he writes "one of my favourite topics was the place of women in Caribbean society. Occasionally I spoke specifically of the place of women in the PNM" (1969, 149).

He courted women for the party as a gentleman and scholar, carefully, wisely, perhaps ruthlessly, and gained the strength that would keep him in power despite dissensions by his male colleagues. In a previous essay on Williams and nationalism I argued that the politician Williams could not and would not have overturned the fundamental belief in the superiority of male leadership. To do this would have "capitulated to a philosophy of equality far beyond its time" (Mohammed 1997, 743). The second wave feminist revolution only grew to universal recognition by the decade of the seventies. Williams drew on the real or imagined capacity of the female for loyalty and devotion. As his political secretary, Dupres would remain, as she phrased it, "in the doghouse" for nine years during which time he never spoke a word to her, had not even told her what caused this, and passed his instructions to her on paper. Yet he obviously trusted her as she remained his political secretary and served him during this time:

> If I did something wrong, he would blast out at me. If it would be over some minor thing, I knew that somebody had vexed him before. Every time I threatened to leave my job, Andrew Carr suggested I write down on a piece of paper his assets and liabilities and see which one outweighed the other, and then make a decision. Andrew always started off by putting down one liability, no wife, second liability, child away at school. He has no one at home. If he gets vexed, he has no one at home to take it out on. Of course I would put down his assets as well. His love for people was a great asset. He had total committed love. He loved his constituents. He was a father to his people. I did this at least once a month. On the balance the job was worth it.

Nesta Patrick, a member of the League of Women Voters and the People's National Movement Women's League, recalls:

> I remember very vividly my days as a young woman going out with the League of Women Voters. We were jeered at and missiles thrown at us in addition to vile abuse. ... Men were not ready to accept us as partners who could think and speak; they felt uneasy with the wife whom the men knew as articulate and other men felt was too involved. I remember too at one time I had to shed my top garments in the porch before I could enter the rest of the house, because it was said that I would bring in germs in the family, having met with all kinds of women. ...It was this strength which entered the People's National Movement Women's League in 1956. Mrs. Isabel Teshea had herself been a member of many of the women's organizations such as the Child Welfare League, Union of Women's Citizens and League of Women Voters, so that it was easy to get this mass following of women to form the women's arms and indeed its feet today in the PNM as it exists (Patrick 1988).

That women benefited from their association with Williams and retained their loyalty and devotion long after his male colleagues did not, seems clear from all accounts. Feminist scholars like Rhoda Reddock have touched on the role and function of women in the PNM[32] but this remains one area of primary research that needs to be undertaken seriously by social historians. The evidence so far leads one to ask the question why did women retain this loyalty to a leader? Do women fit into some stereotyped mould of not questioning or challenging men in power or is it the different mindset about women at the time? What do we really know of the challenges of women within the PNM? So far the data I have uncovered reveal very little.

One way in which he dealt with both women and men, and which in fact came to be associated with a certain Williamesque style of control, was that of being put in "cold storage." This may be a spurious discussion, but it often occurred to me in the reading of both interviews and material by and on Williams that he had a supreme capacity to distance himself from people. Cold storage connotes not just putting a distance, or a demonstration of displeasure, but putting someone in or on ice, to cool down, to think it over, giving one the cold shoulder, to wait on one's pleasure. Williams applied this method indiscriminately with both women and men and was not averse to doing it to other world leaders as well. D. D. Dupres commented that "...I was in the doghouse for the longest. He tried to talk to me about what he had heard, but at that point, I was hurt and wasn't open to it." At the same time, this capacity he had to distance himself and express his displeasure did not affect the commitment of those closest to him. Dupres relates the sequel to this incident "One night, I was called out to tea at Parliament. I walked into the tearoom and there was a meeting going on. He started talking to me as if we had spoken only ten minutes ago and I hadn't spoken to him in eight years."

Conrad O'Brien remembers the time when they visited the Kremlin and Williams had a meeting with Kosygin. According to O'Brien, "Kosygin arrived on one day to lead the delegation. He kept Kosygin waiting for one hour. When he later met Kosygin, he proceeded to read a book! I assume this day followed the day he was pressured to sign the particular agreement. Thus he displayed his displeasure to Kosygin. We all stood around amazed at the disregard for Kosygin and his daughter." There were other reasons why he probably put people in "cold storage." One interviewee noted that "He had the problem of dealing with the rat race and this often offended him in terms of people seeking to get things for themselves and to monopolize him. There was always this situation where people felt he was too close to "John" and "Harry" and that I suppose is the power play that created the problem for him ...If it occurred that you thought you were too important, he would treat you differently. For a period of time you would not be called upon."[33] In other words you would be put in cold storage.

The convenient switching off of his hearing aid was also an extension of this capacity to withdraw. Williams was probably secretly amused that he was aided in this detachment. He figured out that the loss of hearing had to do with a serious fall in playing football as a youth, when his parents could not afford the medical expense of seeing to it, but he observed "Not that I regret – a hearing aid is a powerful weapon against an opposition in Parliament, one can always turn it off." This method of distance, aloofness and detachment may very well be a tried and tested mode of functioning in the public workplace, but an interesting parallel is the way in which it is used most effectively in the domestic sphere. A potent means of control between intimate partners, or parents and children, is that of not communicating or withholding affection because of displeasure. That Williams came to employ this method the most and eventually, in his last few years distanced himself more and more from his nation, remains one of his most serious political errors.

Despite this aloofness and the control he needed, he also had the capacity to admit when he was wrong, although this may have not been frequently observed. Ibbet Mosaheb recalls that he was never a man to say, "I'm sorry." But you will understand by his actions. He would ask you to perform another task. If he realized he had made a mistake he compensated by giving you some responsibility." Others, especially women, commented frequently about his distrust, but by some logic, which may be a very accurate assessment, put it down to the fact that he trusted people too much. It is a plausible contradiction, if one trusts too much then it is difficult to discern the trustworthy from the non-trustworthy and both get painted with the same brushstrokes. D. D. Dupres summed this up: "I always say that he had one fault and one fault only and that was his total trust in people. Eric believed people to his detriment. He could not believe that anybody could openly and bold facedly come and lie to him." Joan Lake also agreed that he had in time become a very distrustful person because he felt that people always wanted something from him. "He didn't trust anybody," she said. "You had to show him you didn't want anything." That this very human trait existed for good reasons is confirmed by the threats which had been made on his life, and in Joan's recollection that during elections "He never sat outside. Security and the police would come look over the place, then he would come. He would only drink from me. He would not drink from everybody or eat from everybody. He was somewhat suspicious. He would eat only from whom he trusted." And clearly, Williams trusted women.

A TIME FOR HEROES AND HEROINES

Eric Williams' early work as a scholar provided a crucial polemic against which a more equal exchange of a kind would begin to take place between the West Indies and the Empire. The continuous debate as to the validity and value of his thesis will continue and necessarily so. We must also concede as Paul Sutton has done, that Williams' *Capitalism and Slavery* (1944) "inaugurated the modern period of West Indian historiography" and that when it was "first published, it was, quite simply, original. The thesis within it, that Britain had directly benefited from the West Indian connection had been decisive, had apparently occurred to no one before, or at least not enough to elaborately set it out in writing"[34] (Sutton 1992: 30). The real victory of Williams is that he had learnt his master's tongue well, as Caliban defiantly speaks to Prospero in The Tempest "You taught me language, and my profit on't is I know how to curse" (Scene 11, Lines 364-365).

Richard Sheridan points out that the "new" school of political economy associated with the Caribbean New World Group emerged in the decade of the sixties, the New World Group attempting to explain why the Caribbean and other similar societies have been characterized by monocrop production for the masses. He observes, "It is of interest that while the theory of plantation economy and society has varied and intellectual pedigree, much of the intellectual inspiration has come from Eric William's historical analysis in *Capitalism and Slavery* of the eighteenth and nineteenth centuries. Not only is this acknowledged within the Region, but Andre Gunder Frank, leading theorist and historian of the dependency approach also arising in the sixties, writes that by comparison with Adam Smith, Friedrich List, and Karl Marx, Eric Williams in his *Capitalism and Slavery* makes perhaps the most forceful argument regarding the connection between the expansion of colonial trade and the development of British Industry" (Sheridan 1987, 336).

Elsa Goveia's review (1966) of William's *British Historians in the West Indies*, in which she argues that Williams had replaced old shibboleths by new ones, is no doubt justifiable. "I cannot help thinking," writes Goveia, "that it is a most unnecessary and damaging waste ...for Dr. Williams to spend his limited time doing badly the kind of detailed monographic work which is being done already by other scholars with competent professional qualifications. ... No one is ever educated or liberated from the past by being taught how easy it is to substitute new shibboleths for old." To read Williams only as a scholar is to do him a great injustice. Such a review understands only Williams the intellectual, and does not consider the energy, political commitment and drive which made Williams continue to write while holding down one of the most demanding jobs in a society, that of leading a nation. The irony here is that Williams' contribution to historiography, even if problematic, and his insistence that university education should be made available within the region, had cut through the underbrush for others to bravely follow.

V. S. Naipaul had written in 1961: "Power was recognized, but dignity was allowed to no one. ...We lived in a society which denied itself heroes. ...Generosity, the admiration of equal for equal – was therefore unknown" (Naipaul 1962, 44). In this biography I came not to bury Williams nor to praise him, but to sift through his remains so that we do not continue to deny ourselves heroes. To recognize heroism is not to disregard that heroes are made of flesh and blood and bones and that they too have felt pain and joy, were arrogant and have been humiliated, have been indifferent and caring, ambitious and retiring, idealist and pragmatist, and neither black nor white but the many colours in between. All culture is built on a certain amount of myth. All culture is also derived from our belief in myths. That Williams is in the process of already being mythologized as a leader of the nation in the history of Trinidad and Tobago demonstrates a measure of progress for a society that was once deemed incapable of ruling itself. This process, through which Williams's legacy must pass onto generations to come, should be prepared to turn the pages back and forth to his vision and to his lived practice, to read between the lines, to paint other heroes and heroines onto the landscape of his terrain, and to redeem the moral in his estate.

ENDNOTES

[1] I have no private and personal allegiance to party politics of one sort or another. I was born in the era which Eric Williams and the PNM ushered in nationalism and independence and benefitted from Williams's vision of the nation by perhaps never fully constituting myself as a victimized colonial subject. I am grateful to Erica Williams for providing me with access to the original interviews carried out by Ken Boodhoo which were used in writing this biography.

[2] This is taken from Solow and Engerman's discussion of William A. Green's chapter "Race and Slavery: Considerations on the Williams thesis" cited in *British Capitalism and Caribbean Slavery: The Legacy of Eric Williams*, edited by Barbara Solow and Stanley Engerman, Cambridge University Press, 1987, p. 2

[3] This is taken from the interview of Williams's secretary Madge Lee Fook, carried out on July 23rd, 1997 by Ken Boodhoo for the Eric Williams Memorial Collection. The full quote is "I think he is Trinidad and Tobago. Wherever you turn, you see evidence that he was there. He was involved in education, roads, schools. His image is everywhere. He's the father of modern Trinidad."

[4] Transcript. Interview with D. D. Dupres, July 26, 1997, Ken Boodhoo, Trinidad. Dupres, was the daughter of Muriel Achong who was a close friend of Eric Williams and a member of the PNM. She became Eric Williams' political secretary as a result of this association and stayed in this position for many years.

[5] I make this obviously subjective point for several reasons. In his interviews with people who lived and worked with Williams, Ken Boodhoo asks several persons whether they knew he was ill, and how did they hear about his death, and what they felt. Secondly, Ramesh Deosaran in the Preface to his study *Eric Williams: The Man, His Ideas and His Politics (A study of Political Power)* (1981) describes his response to the news of Williams's death, noting that he pulled out his file on Williams and for the rest of this week wrote as the nation mourned - among other things clearly an act of immediate cognition and recognition. I remember my own response and that of those around me to Williams's death, first, disbelief and second an indescribable feeling one has on the death of someone you should have paid more attention to, thinking that they had been there for so long, it seemed as if they would live forever.

[6] Transcript of an Interview with friend of the family on September 22nd, 1998 by interviewer Ken Boodhoo, Port of Spain Trinidad, Eric Williams Memorial Collection, whose consent has not yet been given to use this information. Her name has therefore been kept from the records. The quote is used as it is a fairly innocuous one vis-a-vis politics, but it does summarize nicely the mood of people on hearing about Williams's death.

[7] Transcript of an interview with Conrad O Brien, former Trinidadian businessman at his home in Boca Raton, Florida, on Thursday February 20, 1997, conducted by Dr. Ken Boodhoo of Florida University.

[8] Transcript: Interview with Eastlyn Bynoe by Dr. Ken Boodhoo at Hilton Hotel, Trinidad, on 21st July, 1997. Eastlyn Bynoe worked at Longmans Caribbean Publishers on the book Forged from the Love of Liberty with Dr. Paul Sutton and with Williams.

[9] James Millette "The Party of 56. Eric Williams and Party Politics in Trinidad and Tobago," Paper presented to the Conference on Capitalism and Slavery, Fifty Years later: Eric Williams and the Post-Colonial Caribbean," St. Augustine, Trinidad, September 1996, p.3

[10] Naipaul makes reference to this colloquialism in *The Middle Passage* as follows: "And such people had to be cut down to size or to use the Trinidad expression,

be made to "boil down" (1962: 44). Colloquial use of the term as I know it also extends boil down to include *like bhaji*, the latter a (Bhojpuri) Hindi term for spinach, which has a much larger mass before cooking, reducing considerably under heat. While clearly the calypso and weeklies are at one level geared to keep people in their place, (whatever that is), it must also be said that it is useful method of social censuring and social ostracism designed to ensure that people maintain responsibility to each other. Needless to say, it can also be easily abused.

[11] Transcript, Interview with Hugh Simpson good family friend from before the 50s, by Ken Boodhoo, 12th April, 1997.

[12] Transcript: Interview with Joan Lake, July 27, 1997, Trinidad, Interviewer Ken Boodhoo

[13] Williams actually cites Lamming as having written this in the PNM Weekly August 30th, but no date is given for the first publication. It has been reprinted in part in Callaloo, 20.4 (1998) 731-736

[14] Interview with Ibbet Mosaheb, 12th July, 1997, Port of Spain Trinidad, Interviewer, Ken Boodhoo

[15] A portion of Williams' collection of books and papers which are owned by his daughter Erica Williams Connell was made available to the Library of The University of the West Indies, St. Augustine, Special Collections in 1999 and is available now for public use.

[16] All original quotes from the early unpublished drafts are cited in italicized script to differentiate between readings from the later published version, from other authors' work, and from my own interpretations where these occur.

[17] This description of Onemia Wilheminia Jane Hunt is (if one excuses my reading of the subtext) painstakingly provided in this text perhaps to prove that William's heritage is distinctly related to the French Creole of Trinidad who also laid claims to the society as the "true indigene."

[18] Gordon Rohlehr, 1998, p. 56

[19] Transcript of an Interview with Halsey McShine, Williams friend and doctor for years, with Ken Boodhoo, July 24th, 1997, In Port of Spain Trinidad: Eric Williams Memorial Collection

[20] This is not only true of other West Indian writers like George Lamming and Samuel Selvon, but of many other writers in the early twentieth century, among them for instance the Irish writers James Joyce and Samuel Beckett.

[21] Interview with party affiliate carried out on July 20th, 1997 by Ken Boodhoo. The name of the interviewee cannot yet be cited as permission has not been officially received by the Eric Williams Memorial Collection.

[22] *Ibid*

[23] *Ibid*

[24] Though much longer and with less eloquence possible in the brevity of Abraham Lincoln's Gettysburg address, in his "Massa day done" speech Williams packaged both his historical knowledge and practice of the battlefield of politics into this speech to propel him into another victorious term. I began rereading the speech, thought of the parallel between this and Lincoln's address, read it on the internet, and then discovered that William's ended this speech citing "Lincoln who dealt Massa in the United States of America a mortal blow" (Cudjoe, 1993, 264)

[25] In writing this section I recall in one of many conversations with Lloyd Braithwaite, that he felt in his *Social Stratification in Trinidad* first published in 1953, ISER he had omitted the Indian population and he had either drafted or had intentions of doing so, a parallel investigation which placed Indians alongside others in the society. Among Williams' unpublished drafts, there is a chapter entitled "Indian

Immigration in the West Indies" some of which I have drawn on here, and in his actual first drafts of his autobiography there are more insights which did not emerge in the final version. There may be many explanations for this, one being that he and Braithwaite, in the general tenor of the times, still perceived the Indian population as outside of the mainstream of Trinidadian and Caribbean culture and felt that they had to be treated as a specifically different group. Perhaps, as is more likely the case with honest scholars, they did not feel comfortable writing about a population they did not feel they sufficiently understood and were wary of committing the insights of the "outsider" within to paper.

[26] See discussions on masculinity in the work of Linden Lewis, "Masculinity and the Dance of the Dragon: Reading Lovelace Discursively" *Feminist Review*, No 59, June 1998.

[27] A liberal adaptation by the author of The Mighty Sparrow's "The Yankees gone, Sparrow take over now" a line from Jean and Dinah released in 1956 which has endured both as musical history and social history of gender relations in Trinidad.

[28] For the purposes of establishing the objectivity with which I have attempted to approach this reading of Williams, it would be useful to state here that I am not related to Kamaluddin Mohammed, although we of course share the same surname.

[29] Bridget Brereton writes that "For the Trinidad peasantry, cocoa provided a profitable export crop that required neither considerable outlays of capital nor a large labour force. Because of cocoa the peasants were relatively secure between 1870 and 1920, but the attitude of the government towards them tended to remain indifferent or hostile. The local government's policy on economic matters, during the nineteenth century, usually reflected the bias towards the plantation and sugar" (Brereton, 1981, 93-94)

[30] While writing this paper I called several of my friends, family and colleagues in Trinidad to discuss with them various ideas or memories they had about Williams and the era in which he brought the country to Independence. There was unequivocal agreement that this was a moment in which a nation came together, sharing some of the goals and the vision he had presented.

[31] That such ideas of gender and gender relations affected both men and women (perhaps in different ways) needs to be established as part of the ongoing feminist deconstruction of the public sphere.

[32] See Rhoda Reddock, *Women, Labor and Politics in Trinidad and Tobago, A History*, Ian Randle Publishers Jamaica, 1994

[33] Interview with associate 12/7/97 – Eric Williams Memorial Collection, identity may not yet be cited.

[34] Sutton notes here that Williams freely acknowledged his debt to C.L.R. James's *The Black Jacobins: Toussaint L'Ouverture and the San Domingo Revolution* (London, 1938) in conceptualizing *Capitalism and Slavery* which was first published in 1944.

REFERENCES

Various Interviews from the *Eric Williams Memorial Collection*, cited in Endnotes

Beckles, H. (1997). "Freeing slavery: Gender paradigms in the social history of Caribbean slavery", The Elsa Goveia Memorial Lecture. Mona, Jamaica: Department of History, The University of the West Indies.

Besson, G. and Brereton, B. (1991). *The Book of Trinidad*. Port of Spain, Trinidad: Paria Publishing.

Boodhoo, K. (ed.) (1986). *Eric Williams: The Man and the Leader*, Lanham, New York and London: University Press of America.

Brereton, B. (1981). *A Modern History of Trinidad 1783-1962*, Kingston and Port of Spain: Heineman.

Cudjoe, S. R. (ed.) (1993). *Eric Williams speaks: Essays on colonialism and independence*, Wellesley, Massachusetts: Callalou Publications.

Cudjoe, S. (1997). "Eric Williams and the politics of language" In *Eric Williams and the Post-Colonial Caribbean society*, Special issue of *Callaloo*, Vol. 20, No 4, pp. 753 -763

Deosaran, R. (1981). *Eric Williams the man, his ideas and his politics (A study of political power)*. Port of Spain, Trinidad: Signum Publishing .

Ghany, H. (1996). *Kamal: A Lifetime of Politics, Religion and Culture*. San Juan, Trinidad: Kamaluddin Mohammed.

James, C. L. R. (1960). *Modern Politics*. Port of Spain, Trinidad: PNM Publishing Company

Lamming, G. (1997). "The legacy of *Eric Williams*" In *Eric Williams and the post-colonial Caribbean society*, Special issue of *Callaloo*, Vol. 20, No 4, pp. 731 -736

Look Lai, W. (1998). *The Chinese in the West Indies, 1806-1995: A documentary history*, The University of the West Indies, Jamaica: The Press.

Millette, J. (1996). "The Party of 56: Eric Williams and Party Politics in Trinidad and Tobago." Paper presented at the Conference on Capitalism and Slavery, Fifty Years Later: Eric Williams and the Post-Colonial Caribbean, UWI St. Augustine, 28th September, 1996.

Mohammed, P. (1997). "Midnight's Children and the Legacy of Nationalism." In *Eric Williams and the Post-Colonial Caribbean Society*, Special issue of *Callaloo*, Vol. 20, No 4, pp. 737 -752

----. (2002). *Gender Negotiations among Indians in Trinidad, 1917-1947*, The Hague and Macmillan UK: Institute of Social Studies.

Naipaul, V.S. (1984). *Finding the Centre*, London: Penguin Books.

---- (1962). *The Middle Passage*, London: Penguin Books.

Rennie, B. (1974). *History of the Working Class in the 20th century Trinidad and Tobago*, Toronto: New Beginning Movement, Toronto.

Richardson, E. (1984). *Revolution or evolution and other writings including the scholarship of Dr. Eric Williams*, San Juan, Trinidad: Imprint Caribbean.

Rohlehr, G. (1990). *Calypso and Society in Pre-Independence Trinidad*, Port of Spain, Trinidad: Gordon Rohlehr.

Rohlehr, G. (1997). "The Culture of Williams: Context, Performance, Legacy" In *Eric Williams and the Post-Colonial Caribbean Society*, Special issue of *Callaloo*, Vol. 20, No 4, pp. 849-887.

Sheridan, R.B. (1987). "Eric Williams and Capitalism and Slavery: A Biographical and Historiographical essay." In Barbara L. Solow and Stanley L. Engerman (eds.), *British Capitalism and Caribbean Slavery,: The Legacy of Eric Williams*, Cambridge: Cambridge University Press.

Singh, K. (1994). *Race and Class Struggles in a Colonial State Trinidad 1917-1945*, University of Calgary Press and The Press of the University of the West Indies.

Sutton, P. (1992). "The Historian as Politician: Eric Williams and Walter Rodney." In Alistair Hennessy (ed) *Intellectuals in the Twentieth Century Caribbean*. Warwick University Caribbean Studies, Macmillan Caribbean.

Williams, E. (1962). *History of the People of Trinidad and Tobago*, Port of Spain, Trinidad: PNM Publishing Co. Ltd,

---- (1969). *Inward Hunger: The Education of a Prime Minister*, London: Andre Deutsch.

---- (1981). *Forged from the Love of Liberty: Selected speeches* of Dr. Eric Williams Compiled by Paul K Sutton. Trinidad and Tobago: Longman Caribbean.

Williams, E. (1942). *The Negro in the Caribbean*, Westport, CN: Negro Universities Press.

13

The Harder they Fall: Masculinity and the Cinematic Gaze[†]

CASTING EMOTIONS IN DRAMATIC CONFLICT

There are several scenes in *Brokeback Mountain* (2005) that pull you helplessly into an emotional vortex. Some of this is achieved by forcing the viewer to empathize with the dilemma of the main protagonists. Empathy is not easy to achieve in a film that deals with the taboo subject of a homosexual affair between two men, combining the elements of both eros and agape.[1] Perhaps only *La Cage aux Folles (The Birdcage, 1996)*[2] has attempted to reach the widest audience in some ways and even so, it has done this through comedic humour and situated the film within the genre of the "gay" film. The task is an even more difficult one if the primary subject matter of the film challenges a sacrosanct symbol that underscores the dominant hetero-machismo of a nation; in this case destabilizing the persona of the quintessential US

[†] First published in *Love and Power: Caribbean Discourses in Gender*, edited by Eudine Barriteau. University of the West Indies Press, Kingston, Jamaica 2012, 488-513.

western cowboy. Yet insidiously, this film draws you further and further in to its heartbeat. When the director wrests from you a huge gulp of emotion, not a slight tear drop that you successfully hold back in a darkened cinema, but the gut-wrenching kind that leaves you unsettled for the duration of the film, and afterwards - he has already caught you by the seat of your pants.

The first scene in which he does this is when Ennis Del Mar and Jack Twist separate after their initial encounter as sheep herders at Brokeback Mountain, a landscape portrayed as a harsh yet penetrable beauty. Both men are returned to the dusty trailer shed and flat terrain where they had first met some months ago. The parting is a laconic one, in the non-verbal style and temperament befitting that of the cowboy characters that have been inscribed in film grammar for near a century now - a monosyllabic silence. Jack drives off in his beaten down van. He looks at Ennis's lonely receding figure, a visual reference to his spying on Ennis through the wing mirror of his car as they both wait to be considered for the job. This shot foreshadows the intimacies of his later gaze. Ennis walks up the deserted street; he slips into an abandoned doorway, doubles over and explodes in a torrent of grief. The pain of separation is so great that he literally throws up the feeling that has welled up inside, this taciturn character whose emotions have emerged in playful and not so playful violence rather than in words thus far. He punches the walls as if to shift the internal torment that cannot be placated into a physical pain. He transfers the pain into one he could feel, and see, and touch, in bruises and dried blood. A chance male passes by just at this time, again providing another masculine moment for diffusing deep emotion. Ennis curses him violently "what the fuck are you looking at," the intemperate language and mood of anger and pent up frustration is immediately conveyed to the viewer. After all, men don't cry, much less cowboys. At the end of the movie we see that Ennis's contained exterior is a thin skin over his passionate desperation and fear of a public retribution should he choose a redefined manhood. In conveying these ideas, director Ang Lee set the tone for a profoundly destabilizing film, whether you like it or not or even agree with its subject matter and treatment. He has successful recasted the range and boundaries of masculinity in a field that film has not, (although textual fiction has) been able to render with sufficient emotional depth or breadth thus far.

In *The Harder They Come* (1972) - a much earlier film, another play of masculinity unfolds, with multiple roles and stereotypes, culturally borrowed and redefined gender schemas, a brutal landscape of Caribbean gender relations and the classic portrayal of men's continuing inhumanity to each other in a battle for survival of the most cunning and exploitative kind. In this pioneering film, released three decades before *Brokeback Mountain*, director Perry Henzell also culturally situates for this region another construction of masculinity, described by Julianne Burton as Ivan's "attempt to live out the American dream on that colonized Caribbean island"[3] of Jamaica. In the film grammar of the region, the main protagonist in *The Harder They Come* establishes one archetype of masculinity, much the same way perhaps that Charlie Chaplin created the character of the lovable tramp. Ivan has a family resemblance in the region's fiction, like Fisheye without the death wish from Earl Lovelace's *The Dragon can't Dance* or Hat from V.S. Naipaul's *Miguel Street*.[4]

The Harder They Come and *Brokeback Mountain* continue to position manhood as an unfinished project, the pathos of the failure of Ivanhoe Martin's dream of succeeding in the face of all odds and Jack Twist's dream of living together and farming the land with his male partner. Both directors present the raw underbelly of a masculine emotional gamut that is rarely dissected and held up for close scrutiny. The same way in which *Brokeback Mountain* ushers in the scuffling inarticulate Ennis who invites immediate sympathy, so also *The Harder They Come* draws the viewer from the very beginning into the boyish naïveté of country lad Ivanhoe Martin who is at first too easily susceptible to deception and intrigue. When the rickety bus and a more modern flatbed truck encounter each other in a face off on Flatbridge between country and town, (symbolic of all the encounters that would take place between Ivanhoe and the more sophisticated urban men in Kingston) he pulls out a mango from one of his bags. Another passenger asks him for it but he says he is taking this to his mother. This harvest taking of fruit is respected as a sentiment to be honoured in 'country." The mango as the Caribbean fruit of temptation continues to recur in the film as the metaphor, the apple in the book of Genesis, the site of temptation of one sort or another. As soon as Ivan lands in Kingston, he is easily relieved by two conmen of all the worldly goods that he brings with him into Kingston, hoping to make a new life for himself. He goes to see his mother and she asks if he has not brought her anything, not even a mango, from country. He lies. Better the lie than the truth that will hurt and worry her - it was not a good mango season this year he says. Outside her one room barrack flat he runs into the men playing dominoes and meets the man who will contribute to his fall from paradise.

Like Dick Whittington heading for London, Ivanhoe is here to seek his fortune, and if the streets are not paved with gold, at least there is the possibility of adventure or opportunities for earning a living. He is guileless, trusting, innocent and a still gawky outmoded country boy with liquid dark eyes, beginning to acquire a swagger in his walk. He gazes at the world in wonder, greets it openly, and expects that it will return his trust similarly; just like the way on the journey into Kingston when he looks out from the back of the country bus and unselfconsciously waves to the occupants of a small sporty convertible, as if he does not differentiate between the modes of transportation or the conditions in which they find themselves compared to him. This naïveté coupled with shrewdness and innate intelligence, perhaps the hallmarks by which the colonized small islander survives, best describes the mixture found in Ivan's character. Like many colonized subjects before him, he has an unwillingness to remain in the box that others have designed for men of his race and class. The dramatic tension between the two streams of his personality, trusting and optimistic, yet skeptical and wily, will be Ivan's downfall but also his redemption as a tragic hero in defense of Caribbean masculinity.

This essay explores the theme of masculinity in two films,[5] *The Harder They Come* written and directed by Perry Henzell, Jamaican film maker, with the lead role in the film played by Jamaica reggae singer Jimmy Cliff, and *Brokeback Mountain*, directed by Ang Lee, with lead roles by actors Heath Ledger and Jake Gyllenhaal. Over three decades separate the release of the two films. In the intervening years between their making, cinematic styles, film technology and discourses on gender have undergone tremendous change. Yet these films speak to universal and timeless questions of gender and sexual identity, to how one finds a place in the world and make meaning of one's existence in the context of cultural norms or conditions of birth which dictate the boundaries and possibilities of a life. The heroism of both films is found in the complete candor and honesty that the main protagonists demonstrate. As an actor Heath Ledger observed in the making of *Brokeback Mountain* that he liked to give a little of himself in a film, it was therapeutic. This had in fact become one hallmark of his acting and perhaps of his personality – already recognizable in the making of a new screen icon who was unfortunately prematurely taken away in his prime. Jimmy Cliff renders Ivan as an audacious, perhaps overconfident young upstart, poor and almost undernourished in his slim appearance but with hope and a readiness to dream. Ivan represents a kind of purity with which all men and women possibly start off life before they have to acquire the arts of deception of one sort or another. This faculty to give of oneself so consciously unselfconsciously on camera, the capacity of directors, screen writers, cinematographers and editors to elicit this performance from an actor and from the raw material that is cobbled together in no logical sequence, to be made sense of and converted into a seamlessly finished product by visual and sound skills, is itself the magic of the screen, and some of which is untranslatable in words as each viewer brings to it their personal history and experience. Thus there are as many Ivanhoes and Ennisses as there are viewers who have seen and interpreted these characters. Nonetheless, it is possible to read some recurrent metaphors and codes. I concentrate on some of the metaphors that reveal explicit or implicit gender narratives, and the filmic codes that are employed by the director to unwrap or reveal gender schemas or behaviours.

The most compelling reason for the exploration and comparison of these two films is that they are both linked by the idea of the "cowboy" that generations have defined as prototypical of masculinity in the American west. In *The Harder They Come*, the displaced country boy Ivanhoe becomes the outlaw in the rough terrain of music and drug trading in an unvarnished snapshot of urban life in Jamaica in the 70's. He is killed in a shootout on a beach that takes its cues from the spaghetti westerns of that era, the latter well patronized films by cinema-going audiences in the Caribbean. In *Brokeback Mountain*, the real-life cowboy occupation of herding sheep in the mountains of Wyoming in 1963 is converted into the space where compulsory homosociality is transformed gradually and naturally into a site for a homosexual relationship between two men, Ennis Del Mar and Jack Twist. Only *Midnight Cowboy*[6] in 1969 comes close to portraying not only the homosexual encounters that Joe Buck (Jon Voight) agrees to for money, but that the relationship between Buck and Ratso (Dustin Hoffman) may be, if not homosexual, certainly founded on a sincere act of caring between two men. The recasting of the "Marlboro" country image of manhood in Brokeback Mountain is doubly haunting as homosexuality – 'the Love that dare not speak its name[7] – has been named, and by a director who is not American born and is of Chinese origin and descent.[8] The troubled, passionate and secretive relationship that Ennis and Jack would continue for nineteen years and which ends in the tragic death of Jack has parallels in some ways with the death of Ivan in Henzell's Jamaican film, another desire unfulfilled, as if constructs of masculinity must be maintained, even at the cost of self-destruction: perhaps echoing the another subtext of the song which gave the film and this essay its title: *the harder they come, the harder they fall, one and all.*

FEMINIST APERTURES ON GENDER AND SEXUALITY

The essay examines how these themes and ideas are conveyed to viewers through *mise en scene*, plot, symbol, camera work and carefully constructed cinematic effects, arguing that cinema and the visual gaze in their emergence in the twentieth century, are potent in transforming how we look and think about many issues that we were previously unable to sufficiently interrogate. One of the areas that cinema has successfully explored is the multiple masks that men must wear in their quest for living out pre-defined notions of masculinity. Several films, many adapted from novels come to mind: *Death in Venice* (Dirk Bogarde, 1971), *Cruising* (Al Pacino, 1980), *My Beautiful Laundrette* (Saeed Jaffrey and Daniel Day-Lewis, 1985), *Maurice* (James Whilby and Hugh Grant, 1987) and *A Single Man* (Colin Firth, 2009). Of these, *Brokeback Mountain* released in 2005, was described as the first mainstream queer film of the new millennium. How were these films and themes interrogated by feminist studies? Feminism and recently, masculinity studies, have emerged as two distinctive yet interrelated discourses. There is no happy marriage between the two, as some writers place them in opposition.[9] It was inevitable that the centering of and reclaiming of a space for a female voice and position consistently and over three decades in a world that presented itself to women as phallocentric, would evoke a male response. At the same time, the male response has developed alongside and in partnership with advances in feminist thought in the work of postmodern theorists, particularly that of Roland Barthes, (1972) – (differentiating the signifier and the signified in the image); Jacques Derrida, (1978) - (deconstruction of the binary); Jacques Lacan, (1979) - (desire and the signification of the phallus); Judith Butler, (1990) - (gender and performativity) and Luce Irigaray, (2001) - (écriture feminine and the challenge to phallogocentrism). These theorists have allowed for a greater fluidity in thinking through the sameness yet difference between masculinity and femininity and provided far more productive ways in which we can now both understand and critique archetypes.

In *real* life stereotypes do not exist, even if *reel* life needs to use shortcuts to position and flesh out characters in accelerated time. While film depends on rapidly establishing the basic markers for an audience, good and evil, ugly and pretty, ethical and unethical and so on, and the symbols which hold these in place, the medium also allows for refraction of these symbolic representations, just as plays have done on the stage for centuries. For example, one can argue that deconstruction of the western genre began long before it was recognized as disassembly – think of the character Kitty Russell as the kind yet spirited saloon keeper in the long-running series *Gunsmoke* which was aired on television since 1955. *Gunsmoke* to date holds the "distinction of not only being the longest running TV western series, but also the longest-running dramatic series in network television history (and) …can be aptly described as TV's first "adult" western, featuring three-dimensional characters with all-too-human flaws and weaknesses, and stark, austere, realistic storylines."[10]

Queer theory has also challenged the essentialist notion that sexuality is biologically determined, or that it is a product of social construction, that our gender and sexual identities are continuously being defined, forever undergoing change, mercilessly dependent on our minds as well as bodies. Queer theory[11] has upended the cart of theories that could safely position people in one or the other side of the assumed binary, allowing for the multiplicity of human emotions, interactions, decisions and behaviours, contradictions and varied expressions of sexual desire. Next to Neil Jordan's 1992 - *The Crying Game*,[12] the film *Brokeback Mountain* represents one of the finest examples of this nuancing of gender and sexual characterization that was raised in ideas expounded in queer theory.

Gender and the cinematic gaze make a fascinating field of enquiry and in my view one of the areas that is propelling radical thought in progressive, some might argue transgressive directions. It acknowledges the importance of developing our visual intelligence in technologically driven environments where visuality has taken prominence over the text. An early essay by Laura Mulvey "Visual Pleasure and Narrative Cinema" (1975) unwraps the film making process vis-a-vis a gender lens. Drawing in the psychoanalytical viewpoint, Mulvey argues that Hollywood films have depended largely on the "male gaze." She argues that cinema provides visual pleasure through the systemic framing of "the look" as the primary semiotic representation of woman as the sexual objects of men and primarily for the pleasure of men. This dominant feature of cinema across cultures cannot be dismissed or underestimated. At the same time, written over three decades ago, we might also critique this limited percept of radical feminism and point out that directors and film makers also cater to a male audience who look to films for gender roles of all kinds, look to men who desire male bodies, or to women who desire female bodies. In the scopophilic[13] pleasure afforded by the cinema we have to imagine that the film maker consciously plays all audiences like a violin,[14] touching the strings here and there so that the resonances are appropriated differently by each viewer based on personal experience, psychological predisposition and temperament, sexual orientation or the vicarious site that it provides for imaginary pleasures.

VISUAL TROPES OF MASCULINITY IN *THE HARDER THEY COME* AND *BROKEBACK MOUNTAIN*

Not only are both films differentiated by time, space, and cultural distance, but they are vastly different in *mise en scene*, camera movement, editing techniques, lighting and sound. *The Harder They Come* is set primarily in an urban landscape, a profusion of noise, mechanical objects, voices, lyrics, grotty inner city yards and zinc fences, and hemmed in seascapes that hold the city in proximity. When Ivan arrives in Kingston there is the rapid movement of the camera, highlighting the congested nature of the city. Even when we move to natural vegetation, the plane flies over to land on a field where a huge bag of ganja is thrust to the pilot to be transported away, the white plane like a small bird lands and takes off gracefully, but the underlying echo of the drug trade violence dominates the organic feel of green and grass. *Brokeback Mountain* however tells of huge spaces, wide mountainous views, balanced by the domestic turf and streams that the two young men have captured with the mountain for a shelter. The music is soft and meandering, like the stream, lulling you into the love song they have created for themselves. *The Harder They Come* represents a contrast, the antithesis almost to *Brokeback Mountain*. The musical score of Caribbean sounds cannot be ignored in *The Harder They Come*, the transistors are always on, the radio announcers are on the air, the horns screech, the city dominates, raw poverty and cramped overcrowded spaces imprison you as it does Ivan who has come from the country and used to more unfettered oxygen and space. Yet in this setting, the hero refuses to comply and lives out his dream. Like Jack Twist his passions lead him to a dramatic death, rather than a safe regretful life that is only partially fulfilled.

Island style cowboy

Cultural codes may be subject or regionally specific and lost from one film to another. For example, some of the "cowboy" imagery that Ivan takes on in *The Harder they Come* like the clothes he acquires even before he has money to buy food, and after he has made the first record, is symbolic of a masculinity that sets itself up as the dandy (in Jamaica in the 50s the "rude bwoy," in Trinidad the "saga boy"). He is dressed sharply, if flashingly with matching hat, shirt, waistcoat and pants, not unlike the cowboy of the western films except the holster is not slung across his hip. In Jamaica, Ivan has to emulate this dress style to perform and represent the role of the cowboy. In *Brokeback Mountain*, this is the natural garb of the mountaineering shepherd and not out of sync with our assumptions about the early western dress of the film cowboy.

When he enters the film, Ivan's narrow-brimmed pork pie hat is the first sign of his difference and the stylishness he will continue to adopt. It is also the hat of the respectable man from the country. He next wears a serviceable saffron coloured corduroy beret and exchanges this soon enough for the showy shiny white leather beret once his song has been released. White is the colour associated with the good guy and equally associated with the rich who can afford the luxury of frequent laundering. His wardrobe would take on the palette of white more and more as he acquires wealth. But by the last scene when Ivan is shot on the beach, he is hatless. Why is this an important, or unimportant, symbol of masculinity? The cowboy in western fiction is associated with a hat, these can vary according to occupation, status or fashion, with the variations of the Stetson being the most dominant one, its wide brim to keep out the sun from the cattleman's or outback rider's eyes. Wearing the hats sets Ivan apart immediately from the other men he encounters on the streets of Kingston, some of whom who also wear caps and tams of varying sorts. Yet he wears his consciously, sporting it always at a jaunty angle that is consistent with the spring in his step and the confident air he has to present to Elsa, his woman, and to the largely low-life characters he becomes embroiled with. He is constantly adjusting the hat, tipping it this way and that depending on the situation, almost like the way in which Caribbean men hold on to their crotch as a crutch in situations of unease or tension, or perhaps to remind themselves of their manhood constantly. When Ivan is on an upbeat, or in an optimistic space, he is hatted, when he is not, the hat is not evident.

Ivan is the heterosexual Jamaican male. *The Harder They Come* does not admit to any other dimension of sexuality than the heterosexual. This is consistent with Jamaican society where the idea of the homosexuality among men is not only taboo but attracts violent reaction. While the man-woman gender dynamic appears secondary to the main plot of this film, the allusion to a deep-seated Christianity that provides the blue print for gender in Jamaica is replayed in several indexical forms. Ivan meets Elsa the same time he is helped by Preacher. She is both a member of Preacher's flock as well as his ward. Ivan is attracted to her and she eventually shifts her loyalty from the preacher to him. Ivan seduces Elsa with his youthfulness, his sweet talk and high-flying visions of what he wants to become, perhaps she is persuaded by his freedom and willingness to challenge this 'godly' man who keeps a deceptively benign but close control of the females around him. Ivan, like the serpent in the Garden of Eden, allows Elsa the opportunity to break with the cloying and dubious protection of Preacher, who, the other girls say, has his eye on Elsa. But it is eventually to the pastor that Elsa returns as she betrays his whereabouts to the Preacher who then informs on Ivan to the police.

By the time she betrays Ivan, Elsa feels forced to end the fantasy of a possible life with him. It is the act she must take to save the child she is caring for. She never entered the cinematic world of make-believe that Ivan lives in. Elsa was not a light soulmate in this film. She is his saviour and conscience, a replacement for his grandmother and mother rather than a joyful sexual partner who will go to the club the night his first record is being released, to celebrate this moment with him. This play between seduction and betrayal, between church and secular, between competing male lust and the ultimate female betrayal are obvious metaphoric references to Christianity. Men discuss women's sexuality and sexual maturity: who has the right "to pick the ripe fruit" is discussed in the masculine sphere of the shed in Preacher's yard. The apple is replaced by the mango, which Ivan refuses to give up in the bus as he is bringing it for his mother, it is stolen from him as he lands, the fruit that he does pick is from the Preacher himself, i.e. Elsa, it is this same fruit that betrays him back to the Preacher, albeit for an honourable reason, and when Jose goes to see the policeman, a call from the Preacher comes in to complete the triangular betrayal of Ivan. This scene takes place with the policeman sitting in a hammock under the mango tree and the camera lingers on the three or four mangos hanging over his head,[15] inverting fruit and serpent in the biblical text. The mango that he has never brought for his mother recurs as a symbol of the forbidden fruit. Only those like the policeman and the studio manager Hilton who exploit him mercilessly, can savour the taste of this sweetness won through the fruits of corruption of one kind or another.

Ivan is not a rough character although he is capable of extreme and menacing violence, as for instance the time he repeatedly slashes the face of the man working for Preacher who attempts to relieve him of his bicycle. He is soft and well-spoken in his first encounter with his mother. He is a jovial character, not mean streaked. He never becomes a rude rough speaker like Jose, nor does he have the sleazy dishonest tone of Hilton, the record studio magnate who rips him and many others off and monopolizes control of the record industry. Nor does he have the middle-class accent of the policeman whose colour, lifestyle and connections to all ranks of society is important for his upward mobility.

There is a hierarchy of power in the drug trade, the police force and the record industry. All the players presented in the various status layers are male. In the film, the drug trade is a masculine domain and the women are represented as whores, objects to be relegated to the private sphere and to the "collaborative and regressive agency of the Church."[16] The plot revolves around Ivan's quest to raise his status and level in his respective hierarchy, but he must prove his manhood in a system that does not offer promotion easily, if at all. Ivan maintains an almost voyeuristic attitude to the events that are shaping his life, as if he is outside of these inconvenient realities, like the fact that he takes Elsa's last twenty dollars to go out with, as he believes that his record will instantly make him rich and famous. As the plot evolves, we see him change into another, still naïve, but shrewder operator. Like Adam in the book of Genesis, he has lost innocence after tasting the fruit. In the scenes where he becomes involved in the ganja trade and the smoking of ganja, the lighting is clever, his plays with the underworld, its smoke and darkness contrast the scenes with Ivan's previous openness – the darkness feeds his growth into unreality, not unlike the darkened cinema where he escaped pleasurably into the character of the star boy.

Ironically, he fools neither himself nor others, despite the apparent fantasy world in which he functions. His astuteness is obvious - he figures out very quickly that Hilton, the record magnate will exploit him and therefore he tries to create his own market. When he is being used as a middle man who carries out the dangerous part of the trade he knows that he is being paid a pittance, "spit" as he describes it with graphic eloquence. But his initial lack of aggression and innocence and a willingness to earn his keep and his fortune through talent and wit or by selling his physical labour power has brought him nothing but more poverty, and further disillusionment. He walks off the street into a garden in which the front gate has been left open and asks the lady of the house for something to do to earn money - he is prepared to wash her car. She drives him off unceremoniously, inferring that he is unemployed and hungry because he is a lazy good for nothing. The colonial legacies of Jamaica are still tightly embedded in the class relationships that have been formed between those who have and those who do not, and Ivan soon learns this. Poor and unemployed black young men are at the lowest rung of this ladder for if they are not viewed as criminals or intent on crime, their other crime is perceived to be that of laziness.

When the attempt to earn a decent living within the boundaries of the legal does not succeed, Ivan turns back to the influence that men in urban ghettos or inner-city areas are drawn into, without volition. He has already met Jose, (who has an almost predatory feel, as if always looking for raw talent to recruit to the forces of the unsavoury). Jose is the ring leader of underworld crime but also a two-faced character who works as a spy for the police and turns Ivan in when he becomes a wanted man. At their first meeting, it is Jose who treated him to his first outing to the Rialto cinema, which Ivan had only read about before, and subsequently to a gambling house that Jose frequents and in which his girlfriend works. The film that Ivan sees at Rialto cinema is a spaghetti western starring Franco Nero in which the hero kills off the posse who is after him with a blazing machine gun. The posse approaches head on, walking into the trap bravely, without flinching, their faces covered by red bandanas. The red bandanas that the cowboys wear in the film might be read symbolically as the blood and blood-letting that is to come in Ivan's life. Jose berates a heckler in the cinema audience. "You shut your mouth; yuh think hero can dead till the last reel." This throwaway line is ominous.

Ivan begins to disappear from a state of reality gradually in the film as the plot unfolds. But this disappearance is logical. The film starts off with the optimism of a country boy who believes that "*You can get it if you really want it, ...if you try, try and try, you'll succeed at last.* The title song "The harder they come" already portends the denouement of the plot.

Well they tell me of a pie up in the sky,
waiting for me when I die,
but between the day you born and when you die,
They never seem to hear even your cry,
So as sure as the sun will shine,
I am going to get my share now what's mine,
Then the harder they come,
The harder they fall, one and all

Ivan prefers notoriety and his fortune on earth rather than any imaginary reward in an imaginary heaven. As he is being chased by the policeman on a motorcycle, his mind flashes back to the ignominy of being whipped in jail after his first offence of assaulting someone, and rather than endure this again, he chooses to retaliate and takes out his gun and shoots the policeman. When he is a "wanted man" like the westerns, since no posters have been plastered on the walls of the city, the writing is still on the wall – a challenge – *I am everywhere, and I disappear* – graffiti is scrawled on the concrete. He has already disappeared into himself in one sense; he was always elusive and unwilling to play by the rules. He had written his own script and the rules by which he would live his life. Perhaps unconsciously Ivan perceives himself to be the cowboy hero meant to save the people from those who hold the power over the masses.

When he is on the run, dressed in the leopard skin waistcoat, white trousers, shirt and white beret, Ivan goes to the photographer to have his likeness taken to send to the press. He re-enacts a western scene in front of the camera emulating the shootout scene of the cowboy, guns drawn from the holster on his hips. On the streets he is the good guy, the crowd is behind him. Not unlike the Spiderman character who sends pictures to the newspaper to prove that he is on the side of good not evil, Ivan chooses to be his own spin doctor, creating his own mythology of what he represents. It is a foolhardy and dangerous courage, but courage all the same, one of the characteristics of human nature that provides the plots of many a film. The Jamaican men and women know he has challenged the men in power who also rip them off; his rise from poverty is a success story, not a failure. He outsmarted those who would outsmart him first. He is the sung hero of this too consistent tale of power and greed between those who control and earn on the backs of others and through emasculating other men. The story is one of masculinity against masculinity itself, with the various configurations of masculinity all represented in the different key characters, Hilton the entrepreneur is totally unscrupulous and unfair, the policeman will use every informer to get his man, Jose befriends him for his own ends but is essentially a police informer. Even the Preacher, the man of God, shows little compassion for the young man whose masculinity threatens his control of the women of his flock.

Ivan meets his death hardened through reality but by also disappearing from reality, entering the dreamlike state of being himself in a film in which bullets are not real and envisioning that after the scene is shot the hero literally gets up and dusts himself off. He walks unflinchingly towards the group of lawmen who have been stalking him; he comes out like the "good guy" in the western with his two guns asking for a fair fight. The sounds that surrounded him in the first cinema outing in the Rialto become the soundtrack to this final shootout between Ivan and the lawmen. His mind has escaped into the cinema where that first pleasure of the city had embraced him, the notion that the good guy wins over the bad. "We are going to do a frontal assault" the police shout. Ivan has by then lost all hold on the gravity and reality of his situation. "All right, hold on …don't worry with the armour business, one man just come out, who is the bad man who can draw." The soundtrack flashes round and round in his head, he is not on a beach facing death but transported to the darkened cinema in Rialto where Jose's words ring in his ears "You tink hero can dead till the last reel." The symbol on his dark T-shirt is a big star worn like a bullseye on his chest. It represents both the easy target he is for the lawmen, but also the other quintessential hero of the western, the sheriff, the good guy who outshoots the baddies, and who also sports the tin star prominently displayed on his shirt front. Jose is prescient – the hero does not die until the last reel. The final denouement is a fitting end. He has fallen hard but still standing on his own two feet, and this is the way we would have it. We want him to die like a hero, not be captured by the police and be put through the ignominy of a trial and be hung. His death is honourable and one that he has, in a sense, chosen.

While shepherds watch their flocks by night

Director of the film *Brokeback Mountain* Ang Lee focusses on unspoken aspects of gender that he has attempted to tap into. From the very first time that he lays eyes on Ennis, the latter scuffling his shoe, head down, face partially obscured by his Stetson, Jack smiles secretly to himself. Then he peeps at Ennis in his rear-view mirror while he is shaving. Ennis is the shy partner. The die is cast, the idea of sexual attraction is hinted at, if not established. A short time later, after they have begun to work on the mountain, Jack looks through the valley from his cold and lonely moonlit perch from which he oversees the sheep at night and sees the single light that comes from the campsite where Ennis stays. The camera focuses on a close up of his face turned completely toward the audience, then it follows his eyes by briefly moving into a long shot of the glowing light of the campsite in the distance and then moves back to Jack's face. The look has become one of longing for companionship and comfort.

While the trailer for the film posits Jack and Ennis' relationship as a friendship that had to be kept a secret, already branding the film in the genre of queer films, the content is multidimensional and layered as all relationships are. There are sexual relationships that are both heterosexual and homosexual; there are heterosexual marital and parental relationships in the film, there are dynamics between parents and children all of which affect the decisions that Jack and Ennis make or do not make about the choice of their sexual lives. We see the development of the relationship between the two main protagonists change – there are times when it is not primarily a physical relationship but a friendship between two individuals. In "Policing manhood: New theories about the social significance of homophobia" David Plummer talks about the term "compulsory homosociality." He comments that "during primary school, peer culture expresses a strong expectation that boys should socialize only with other boys."[17] The protagonists are employed in a male-dominated occupation of sheep herders and are out in the wilderness with other men, but there is a line that cannot be crossed – yet one might ask when does homosociality turn into or become defined as homosexuality?

The basic rules of the job are established by the foreman played by Randy Quaid, and already set up the paradigm of a typically understood marital household division of labour between the two men he hires to work on this forsaken mountain, guarding sheep for months. One is the camp tender who stays by the hearth creating the basis of domesticity, doing the home chores, cooking the meals, the other, the herder, goes out with the sheep all day and sleeps with the sheep at night to guard them from other animal marauders. A thought is planted. Is this a deliberate rule to ensure separation between the two men during the night? In any event, the arrangement reproduces the domesticity of two heterosexual partners so much so that there are scenes that parodies, ever so slightly the minutiae of a domestic marital scene. For instance, Jack's parting shot one morning to Ennis is simply "no more beans." Ennis orders soup the next time from the supplies deliverer who reminds him that he said he did not like soup. Then Jack returns to the campsite and finds that his meals are not prepared one night and, whisky taken, berates Ennis angrily when he comes in late: "Where the hell have you been, I been up with the sheep all day and when I get down here all I find is beans." As the routine of inside and outside, home and world sets in, Jack complains that it is not fair this division of labour where he is up half the night with the sheep. A role reversal occurs. Jack now becomes the domestic partner, taking on the "feminine" role if you like in the campsite and later on in this relationship until the end of his life. He continues to pursue Ennis, to desire him and to go out of his way to please him, to set up meetings that cannot be kept, to dream about a domesticity with Ennis that will never take place. This role switching is paralleled in the method by which the director diffuses a binary construction of characters. The choice of framing and editing in the film directs us to a combination of perspectives. There are times in the film where the camera's gaze is Jack's and other times when it is Ennis' we are allowed to see the world from their different points of view. By doing this the director also disrupts the dichotomy of characters as active participants in the story with that of the viewer – he invites them/us to judge the events, even if we do so with a different set of values.

Jack and Ennis get to know each other slowly on the campsite by communication about their family histories – in particular they talk about the relationship with their fathers. There is a period of bonding and sharing of confidences over alcohol. Ennis does not go back to watch the sheep one night after a prolonged bout of whisky drinking. Preserving masculine distance he attempts to sleep near the camp fire but wakes up shivering. Jack calls him into the tent to sleep and get warm. The closeness and body heat lead to the first fairly rough sexual encounter between them, sounds of belt buckles opening, heaving and grunting, very little tenderness or emotional connections are established. Ennis rises early and sets off to the mountain top without a word to Jack. The camera angles and shots that follow take on an interesting sexual connotation in the daylight. He rides up the hill and across the undulating ridge of the mountain, the ascendancy and grandeur of the landscape drawing you into a sense of peace that he possibly feels – but as he reaches a point and looks down he sees in the distance one of the sheep has been killed and eviscerated by a coyote that night. He rides down to the body, splayed open on the hillside, in shape and symbol representing the open and raw bloodied vagina or the insides of a body ripped apart. First blood has been drawn. The evidence of blood as sign of deflowering of a virgin, referring in this case to Ennis's first encounter with a homosexual experience, again gets replayed later. When he learns that they are being recalled from the job as the weather has turned nasty and the sheep are being moved, in the only way he knows to express emotional pain, Ennis begins a fight with Jack. Blood is spilt on both their shirts.

Like the symbol of the mango in *The Harder They Come*, blood and the retribution of violence for sexual transgression is a recurrent one in *Brokeback Mountain*. As the plot later on unfolds, Jack is possibly beaten to death by some men and his body left bloodied, to be discovered. The full significance of the bloody shirt is only grasped after Jack dies. Ennis visits Jack's parent's house to pay his respects after his death. Jack's mother allows him to look at the room which she has kept exactly as it was since Jack was a boy. He finds the two shirts, dried blood still on the cuffs, one shirt enveloped by the other on the same hanger in the small cupboard in Jack's room. Only then, we the viewers realize that the shirt that Ennis thought he had left at the campsite was deliberately squirreled away by Jack and kept as a memento for sentimental reasons. This moment of realization and knowledge - the significance of their love, brotherhood/friendship and the extent which Jack was completely consumed by this relationship comes to him in an epiphany of comprehension, with unbearable sadness and regret. It comes too late. Ironically, this is the real moment in which he loses his virginity to Jack and to the value of such a relationship – he has denied the possibilities between them for nearly 20 years.

Heterosexual performances of gender relations

As Jack and Ennis leave the homosocial world of their jobs in the wilderness and return to society they now engage in what Adrienne Rich calls "compulsory heterosexuality." They obey the hetero-normative rules of society and get married and have children. Perhaps this too is just another layer in the multiple masks that men must wear in their quest for masculinity. Perhaps it is a necessary one, that the act of parenthood and fathering or giving birth to a child is a human need despite one's sexual orientation. What is interesting about the women in this film, as with the roles played by female characters in *The Harder They Come*, is the complex and varied nature of these relations. Although the film does not attempt to privilege the viewpoint or perspective of one or the other main protagonists, at the same time, Ennis's bi-sexuality is kept intact – he is actually demonstrated as wanting to maintain a sexual relationship with his wife Alma, while Jack's sexual life with his wife is never made apparent. Alma has been aware of Ennis's proclivities from the first time that Jack visits, four years after the first encounter on Brokeback Mountain. She looks out of the window and catches them kissing at the side of the house. Her silence even then, and for years after when he left to go on the fishing trip in which no fish are ever caught, is more painful to swallow than the angry confrontation which comes much much later. She never reveals or talks about Ennis's relationship with Jack until after they are divorced, at a thanksgiving dinner that she has invited him to with her new husband and with his two daughters. Lureen, Jack's wife, wonders why he always goes up to meet Ennis and he never invites Ennis down to fish in Texas, but she does not seem to be the pondering kind. The friendship between the two men once it involves fishing or hunting or camping up in the mountains is partially understood and accepted as normal, as it were. The heterosexual performance of gender is maintained on both sides. Just as Ivan also lives out other expectations of heterosexual masculinity in *The Harder They Come*. Once he gets into money and the drug running behaviour, he sleeps with Jose's girlfriend who, consistent with the tenor of how femininity is developed in that film, was set up to betray him.

Marlboro Country

The dominant element of *Brokeback Mountain* is the landscape – the raw beauty of craggy mountains and sparkling streams, green hills and lowland, blue skies decorated by just enough clouds to temper the visual clarity of blueness, and the brutality of seasons that shift into cold and wintery chills and monochromatic colours. All of these come to reflect the changing moods and situations of the characters in this film. Unlike *The Harder They Come* it is not an urban movie, despite moments of semi-urban life, but one set in the expanse of the countryside. This breadth of space allows the possibility of escape - to run and hide, to move from one state to another. For Jack Twist it suggests the possibility of living out their lives together separately, perhaps isolated on a farm as partners and lovers. Yet the other elements of the landscape, the large mass of sheep moving like maggots on the hillside, juxtaposed with recurrent flatness hemmed in by well-ordered roads and fields, or the grey urban poverty that Ennis and Alma live in, all add up to constrain the character of Ennis who reciprocates desire but must be guarded about his choices. Throughout the film the camera gives us sweeping vistas of the Western frontier. Although the frontier is supposed to be a savage place, the opposite of the civilized world of man-made towns, in this film it is where Jack and Ennis ironically have the freedom to be together. Even within this vast expanse of land where they have their freedom, there is still need for secrecy. When the foreman comes up one day to give them a message that Jack's uncle is ill he sees them horsing around half naked near the campsite, he immediately draws a knowing conclusion, a correct one for sure. This returns one to a consideration of what is allowed masculinity and where – the football or rugby field legitimizes manly horsing around and bodily contact, not the western outback. Marlboro men are always seen riding on their horses, bedding down camp style for the night around a fire, not safely tucked away together in tents.

If Jack represents the intensity of Brokeback Mountain (his last wish is to have his ashes scattered over this mountain), Ennis's character represents the flatness of the terrain which they both inhabit in the daily round of living, the flatness of emotions kept under control, and his life kept away from prying eyes or worse yet, weapons that hurt. Whenever he lashes out however, there is violence of another sort, he interrupts the structured immobility of his features and expressions - he must hurt himself or another to express anger and frustration. For instance, after Alma discloses that she has been aware of the affair between him and Jack and reduces it to something "nasty," he crosses a road indiscriminately and deliberately starts a fight with a man who nearly runs him over through no fault of the driver himself. Ennis had learnt the tragedy of homosexual love very early in life. When Jack tries to encourage the idea of both of them working a farm as a couple together, Ennis recounts the story of the two men who farmed together in the village in which he lived, one of whom was viciously killed and left on the mountainside for all to see his body – bloodied prey is left to be discovered. Ennis was age nine when he was taken by his father to see this sight as a warning and observes to Jack that it might very well have been his father who had killed the man.

The tragedy of the film and pathos of the plot is fixed with this anecdote. The memory of the dismembered man whom his father had taken him to see serves to restrain Ennis from a commitment to Jack and to hold him aloof as a secondary partner in this love affair. Jack is the more obvious "gay" homosexual character who has pursued Ennis. Ennis is positioned as the heterosexual male who falls against his will in love with Jack but maintains his heterosexual position and status at all costs. Jack crosses both physical and mental borders and goes to Mexico to satisfy his sexual desires. Ennis maintains the semblance of a heterosexual existence; he is a father to his daughters and has a supportive and loving relationship with them. Jack's death is never clearly spelt out and we are left to imagine one of two scenarios, that he is either killed just as Ennis has feared by other men who brutally attack and kill homosexual men, or as his wife told Ennis over the phone, in an unfortunate accident while fixing his car. Either way, he meets with an early death. Like Ivanhoe Martin, and Jim Stark – the latter being the character whom James Dean plays in *Rebel without a Cause* (1955), Jack Twist was the outsider, daring to live beyond the defined safety codes. The penalty is excommunication and death. Desire and imagination are two elements of the human condition that cannot be tolerated if it does not fall within the boundaries of the socially permitted.

CONCLUSION: CONFRONTING MASCULINE TROPES OF GENDER AND SEXUALITY

The two films, separated by over three decades (1972 and 2005), present different constructions of masculinity and in *Brokeback Mountain*, a movement away from the pure binary construction that once predominated. This is not unexpected. During those decades technologies of film production have been revolutionized along with ideas about sexuality itself[18] – the latter perhaps signified by an increasing acceptance of homosexuality as a normative expression of human sexuality at least in the matter of human rights. It is not unexpected (culturally) that *The Harder They Come* would be completely silent on this theme, maintaining heterosexuality as a complicit norm, both because of the time in which it was made and also the cultural setting of Jamaica that is resistant to support of male homosexuality. In any event, this was not the key focus of *The Harder They Come*. *Brokeback Mountain* on the other hand is well situated in time to tackle such issues head on. It does so intelligently. It is not only about homosexuality but about the many sexual worlds that people inhabit, the contradictions and problems that come with each choice and the problems that real life decisions present to ordinary individuals.[19] Jack is driven by homosexual desire but lives out the public part of his life as bi-sexual. Ennis does love his wife and children, and part of him is both happy and committed to a heterosexual frame of reference. He falls in love with Jack. This is the essence – Jack draws him out of a non-responsive exterior ("hell this is more words than I have spoken for a year" he admits to Jack). Sexuality is another site for communication, an opening up of paths in our lives that can remain shuttered forever. The dilemma which the film presents is that sexual desire is both learnt as well as a product of our biological and psychoanalytic drives, the latter over which we may have little control. It heightens the evidence of silences between men and women in marital relationships, the power plays between men and men: for example the diminishing behaviour of Jack's father in law towards Jack and the persistently disapproving eyes of the foreman are presented as "society's" watchful presence on those who do not sit quite right with the unwritten cardinal rules of human sexuality. A parallel might still be drawn to Ivan's transgressive nature, he challenges another set of cardinal rules – the capitalist owner of the music studio, the arm of the law and the assumed code of honour established among thieves. Both films in this sense deal with the pleasures and dangers of living out one's desires on terms set by oneself and not others.[20]

Both films also present different planets for scopophilic pleasure. Ivan's struggle against exploitation is not set within the conventional narrative of the western - the good guys against the baddies. He has challenged and enters a life of crime as a matter of survival as well as establishing his resistance to becoming the underdog. We identify with this character as a heroic one – he is the proletariat hero in Marx *Das Kapital*, he is the new un-emasculated male in post-colonial Jamaica, he is the working class underprivileged, country boy come to town. There is a constant bounce and swagger to his walk, a shifting of scenes from tropical exteriors suffused with natural light, motor cycle chases and stolen car rides to tropical interiors, dark smoky rooms alive with the pungency of ganja spliffs. In its forays into sexuality, there is some success. Burton comments that "In the close-ups of mouth and tongue and hard-to-identify skin surfaces (Ivan's making love to one of Jose's women), we see an incorporation of techniques confined not too long ago to underground cinema."[21] More convincing as a Caribbean method of conveying sexual excitement on the screen are the emotional tensions or playfulness between the characters, the orgasmic gyrations of the choir and congregation in songs of praise, the preacher's dawning suspicion of the attraction between Elsa and Ivan, his invasion of her room and violent accusations and Elsa's sexual fantasies. In the bicycle ride taken by Ivan and Elsa on his handcrafted machine there is the still innocent courting of two young people that is convincingly real, and hauntingly complex, composed of multiple horizontal planes, including two silver bands of water, glinting like a thousand pieces of broken glass in sunlight. When the camera draws away in a long shot only then we see that the scene is another dump full of debris – but the cinematic aphorism is nonetheless apposite – the lotus can grow on a dung heap.

The treatment of sexuality in *The Harder They Come* brought to mind a question that has occupied me in the business of how Caribbean audiences treat with film. There is always audience interaction, especially in emotive moments – as observed by Lloyd Warner, Bruce Paddington and Richard Fung. The audience becomes part of the movie narrative, entering the dialogue at places to either question the filmmaker's veracity or to diffuse a particularly stressful or disturbing moment. The enaction of the sexual act on the screen is one such moment – if it is acceptable behaviour for "foreigners" on screen, by 1972 it would have been at least daring in a Caribbean-based and made film. Displays of emotion, kissing in public and too affectionate behaviour between couples in company have never really been acceptable in the region, although raunchy and sexually expressive dances fill this vacuum even more completely. Even the filmmaker diffuses this moment of frank sexual forays – when Ivan jumps out from the landing after making love to Jose's girlfriend and finding out he has been set up for a fall, he makes his escape with only his underwear on. Then a comic scene plays out in which he steals the clothes from an unfortunate man who is returning home late at night. The filmmaker has anticipated and produces the relief that the Caribbean cinema audience requires to recover from the embarrassment of this scene, even while they are concealed in dark cinemas.

Jack and Ennis, like Ivan, are of working class humble origins, Ennis spends his life struggling to make ends meet – the underbelly of middle America poverty is revealed in Ennis's fulmination against the loss of one month's wages when the job on Brokeback Mountain closes down early due to bad weather, the balancing act of domestic tasks and work that he shares with Alma in the colourless houses that he moves into one after the other. Visually the camera draws us into the monotones of his existence outside of the escapes with Jack. On Brokeback Mountain they constantly recapture the zest of a full bodied life, away from prying eyes both men revel in the clear running streams, horseback riding on trails, naked plunges into lakes combined with the depths and angst of separation at each parting. They are two beautiful looking men, pleasing to the eye. Gyllenhaal's lips and eyelashes are seductively presented to the camera, time and time again, keeping Ledger's more structured features hard edged and masculine – the ying and the yang of it. There is no gratuitous sex in this film – each sexual act either between Jack and Ennis or Jack and Alma, is carefully crafted to achieve a mood, carry forward the narrative and elicit a feeling from the audience. The first time Jack and Ennis copulate, it is cold and grey inside the tent. The second time, they make love; the relationship is one now of volition, the light in the tent changes to gentle browns and hues of candle light yellows. Their light brown bodies merge together at rest. Like the mountains and plains their beauty is equally compelling. Is this the view of all audiences? When the film was first screened in a gender and cinema class I was teaching, it elicited very different responses, with one or two students actually repelled by the film and these enactments of passion between two men. Do men view the film differently to women? What gaze is being compelled here. I return to the critique of Mulvey's seminal article – that the cinematic gaze has refracted the lens with which we must now view gender – the 'subject' and 'object' positions are slowly being merged or becoming interchangeable, just as Jack and Ennis changed around domestic and sheep herding jobs. As Teresa de Lauretis proposes, the re-presentation of gender is itself its deconstruction.[22]

The two films present different soundscapes as backdrops for cowboy films. One is set against the faster rhythmic tones of Caribbean music with changing lyrical scores that are themselves part of the narrative sequencing. The other unfolds against a repetitive theme, a slowly drawn out epic western sound haunting its way back to the peaceful mountainous presence that has quieted the storm of passion and friendship of the two men. Ivan's conception of himself as the cowboy is built on the real-life story of an outlaw in Jamaica, and invented through the myth of cinema. His psychological escape into the celluloid fantasy that leads to his death is a product of both cinema and the social constraints that present such escapism as more palatable than reality. Jack and Ennis are modern day cowboys – with all the appurtenances in dress, occupation, skills and props – horse, camping gear and vittles, and baked beans in tins notwithstanding.

Ultimately, the two films destabilize the basis of another fiction that was itself an invention of the cinema. The west never existed in the way in which both sets of directors conceived of it, yet both build on this cinematic trope as if it originated in some truth or memory that might be preserved. The appeal of the cowboy which influences both films is by definition one of a hard edged, strong, resilient, and resourceful masculinity. This too was the invention of fiction and film – throughout ages human beings have come in every shape and size, some are indoor scholars and some are better geared to outdoor pursuits or skilled labour. What is the appeal of the cowboy that it has persisted with such vigour and why is *Brokeback Mountain* invested in undermining this trope of masculinity in cinematic history? In *The Harder They Come* the western movie itself is revealed as a thing of falsity which can be harmful to those who cannot suspend disbelief outside the cinema. In bringing together gender and sexuality to undermine the cowboy character, Ang Lee is proposing that if the virtual world of cinema can serve to destabilize these myths that have underpinned society and kept many imprisoned for life, then we can destabilize some of these strongly held myths about gender and sexuality that are supremely guilty of many other kinds of imprisonment.

ENDNOTES

[1] If eros is used as erotic love and desire, then agape is used here not as Christian brotherhood but as an unconditional, self-sacrificing, active, volitional, and thoughtful love.

[2] *La Cage aux folles*, directed by Edouard Molinaro was first released in French in 1979. The plot is essentially the story of two gay men living in St. Tropez who have their lives turned upside down when the son of one of the men announces he is getting married. An English production was released as *The Birdcage* in 1996, directed by Mike Nichols and starred Robin Williams, Nathan Lane and Gene Hackman.

[3] Julianne Burton from *Jump Cut*, no. 6, 1975, pp.5-7, copyright *Jump Cut: A Review of Contemporary Media*, 1975, 2004, p.5

[4] Earl Lovelace, *The Dragon can't Dance* London: Longman, 1986 (first pub 1979) and V. S. Naipaul, *Miguel Street*, London: Heinemann, 1982, (first pub 1959).

[5] My thanks to Laura Battersby, research assistant, who carried out some preliminary research for me on both films and shared her insights from the perspective of gender and cinema.

[6] *Midnight Cowboy*, Directed by John Schlesinger, A naive male prostitute and his sickly friend struggle to survive on the streets of New York City. First released 1969
[7] Testimony of Oscar Wilde from under his examination by Counsel Sir Edward Clarke, 1895, http://www.law.umkc.edu/faculty/projects/FTRIALS/wilde/Crimwilde.html
[8] This could be interpreted as the undermining of the icon by an "outsider." So far I have not come across such a critique of the director Ang Lee.
[9] See the description of the different streams of masculinity studies and positions that have emerged in Kenneth Clatterbaugh, *Contemporary Perspectives on Masculinity: Men, Women and Politics in Modern Society* Westview Press, 1997
[10] http://movies.msn.com/movies/movie-synopsis/gunsmoke-tv-series/ Downloaded 17.1.09
[11] Queer theory took its cue from the fields of gay and lesbian studies as well as feminist studies and was influenced heavily by the work of Michel Foucault, particularly his *History of Sexuality, Volume One*. Foucault's remarkable insight that sexuality is itself a product of social construction, what he refers to as the technology of sex, a major challenge of the ideas of what might itself be taken as natural or normal as for instance heteronormativity.
[12] *The Crying Game*, director Neil Jordan, released 1992. A British soldier is kidnapped by IRA terrorists. He befriends one of his captors, who is drawn into the soldier's world.
[13] Scopophilia refers to the pleasure derived from looking itself. In *Three Essays on Sexuality*, Freud defines scopophilia as a component instinct of sexuality that is independent of stimulation of erotogenic zones, in other words, sexual or other desire stimulated by visuality.
[14] See for instance films by Isaac Julien, especially his *Looking for Langston* (1989) 40 mins, Black & White 16mm
[15] Franklyn St Juste, cinematographer on the film *The Harder they Come*, in conversation with the author admits that the fruit hanging over the policeman's head in this scene was purely coincidental. Nonetheless, visually it works to continue the analogy.
[16] Julianne Burton, *op cit* p.7
[17] David Plummer, "Policing manhood: New theories about the social significance of homophobia"
[18] Michel Foucault's *Histoire de la sexualité*, was published in France in 1976, and translated into English in 1977. The last three decades of the 20th century began the revolutions of gender and sexuality that shifted ideas and the concept of sexual rights as human rights, if not attitudes to homosexuality.
[19] *Brokeback Mountain* was based on a short story by Annie Proulx, a very gifted writer who has an amazing capacity to render inarticulate emotional states of being accessible to a reader. Originally published in *The New Yorker*, October 13, 1997, it won the National Magazine Award for Fiction in 1998. Proulx regretted writing the story, having received too many suggestions from film fans who wanted a happy ending for Ennis and Jack. Interviewed on this she said "[They] can't understand that the story isn't about Jack and Ennis …It's about homophobia; it's about a social situation; it's about a place and a particular mindset and morality. They just don't get it." The reviewer disagreed. "Or maybe they do – and more intimately than she realises. There is a clear psychological motive behind "fixing" in works of art the errors we experience in life. That is the very basis of escapism and wish-fulfilment". https://www.theguardian.com/commentisfree/2014/dec/29/annie-proulx-regrets-writing-brokeback-mountain

[20] There are differences in possibilities between men and women in this regard. Do female characters have less options; are they more hemmed in – what boundaries are established for lesbianism that are less blurred? A useful comparative point to pursue in films.
[21] Julianne Burton, *op cit*.
[22] Teresa de Lauretis. 1987. *Technologies of Gender: Essays on Theory, Film, and Fiction. (Theories of Representation and Difference)*. Indianapolis and Bloomington: Indiana UP.

REFERENCES

Films:

A Single Man. 2009. [Film] Directed by Tom Ford. USA: Fade to Black Productions.

Brokeback Mountain. 2005. [Film] Directed by Ang Lee. New York: Focus Features.

Cruising. 1980. [Film] Directed by William Friedkin. USA: United Artists. Lorimar Film Entertainment.

Death in Venice. (original Italian title: *Morte a Venezia*). 1971. [Film] Directed by Luchino Visconti. Italy: Panavision

Gunsmoke. 1955-1975. [Television series] USA: Columbia Broadcasting System.

La Cage aux Folles. 1978. [Film] Directed by Ĭdouard Molinaro. Rome: Da Ma Produzione.

Looking for Langston. 1988. [Film] Directed by Isaac Julien. British Film Institute. Sankofa Film and Video.

Maurice. 1987. [Film]. Directed by James Ivory. UK: Merchant Ivory Productions. Cinecom Pictures.

Midnight Cowboy.1968.[Film] Directed by John Schlesinger. USA: Florin Productions, Jerome Hellman Productions.

My Beautiful Laundrette. 1985. [Film] Directed by Stephen Frears. UK: Working Title Films.

Rebel without a Cause. 1959. [Film] Directed by Nicholas Ray. USA: Warner Bros. Pictures.

The Crying Game. 1992. [Film] Directed by Neil Jordan. UK: Palace Pictures, Channel Four Films.

The Harder they Come. 1972. [Film] Directed by Perry Henzel. California: International Films Inc, Xenon Pictures.

Books and Articles:
Barthes, Roland. 1972. *Mythologies*. Selected and translated from the French by Annette Lavers. New York: Hill and Wang.

Butler, Judith. 1990. *Gender Trouble: Feminism and the Subversion of iIdentity*. New York: Routledge.

Burton, Julianne. 1975. "The Harder they Come: Cultural Colonialism and the American Dream." *Jump Cut: A Review of Contemporary Media*, no.6, pp.5-7.

Derrida, Jacques. 1978. *Writing and Difference*, translated by Alan Bass. Chicago: University of Chicago.

de Lauretis, Theresa. 1987. *Technologies of Gender: Essays on Theory, Film, and Fiction. (Theories of Representation and Difference)*. Indianapolis and Bloomington: Indiana University Press.

Foucault, Michel. 1990. *The History of Sexuality*: Volume 1. New York: Vintage Books.

Irigaray, Luce. 2001. *Democracy Begins between Two*. Translated by Kirsteen Anderson. New York: Routledge.

Lacan, Jacques. 1979. *The Four Fundamental Concepts of Psycho-analysis*. Edited by Jacques-Alain Miller; translated from the French by Alain Sheridan. Middlesex: Penguin Books.

Lovelace, Earl. 1986. *The Dragon Can't Dance*. London: Longman.
Marx, Karl. 1992. *Das Capital: Volume 1: A Critique of Political Economy*. Penguin Classics.

Mulvey, Laura. 1975. "Visual Pleasure and Narrative Cinema." *Screen* 16.3 pp. 6-18.
Naipaul, V.S. 1982. *Miguel Street*. London: Heinemann.

Paddington, Bruce. 2005. *Caribbean Cinema: Cultural Articulations, Historical Formation, and Film Practices*. PhD Diss. St. Augustine: The University of the West Indies.

Plummer, David. *Policing Manhood: New Theories about the Social Significance of Homophobia*. Accessed: http://www.xyonline.net/downloads/policingmanhood.pdf

Warner, Keith. 2000. *On Location: Cinema and Film in the Anglophone Caribbean* Warwick University Caribbean Studies, Caribbean Macmillan.

14

Re-calibrating Male Gender Identity: A Dialogue with Men and Masculinity[†]

> "Honestly I got no choice and I just want better
> But the place where me grow, Jaron, police don't send love letter"
> Mali Dan, *Response to Jaron Nurse, 'Fed up'*, (2018)
>
> Can't man up if masculinity is your only weapon
> Aminé, *Dr. Whoever*, (2018)
>
> I am just a man
> Not superhuman...
> Someone save me from the hate
> Just a step from the edge
> Just another day in the world we live...
> I need a hero to save me now
> A hero'll save me (just in time)
> Skillet, *Hero* (2010)

What issues have preoccupied gender scholars, government agencies, civil society and feminists in treating with the "problem of men and masculinity" in the Caribbean over the last years of the twentieth century and into the third decade of the twenty-first. How much of this is connected with what the male researchers, concerned men's groups, artists, male rappers and young men are saying about their options? In this paper I have attempted to explore, with fairly broad strokes, the main arguments or concerns raised in this gender conversation, proposing logical conclusions that these lead to in the interpretation of Caribbean masculinity and masculinity studies in general. I have added the

---

[†] This paper is an amalgamation of two public lectures and is previously unpublished. The first was a Public Seminar Presentation at the Université des Antilles in Martinique entitled *"The Trouble with Men: Recurrent Themes in the Study of Men and Masculinity in the Caribbean."* The second was a public lecture entitled *"Male Underachievement: Fact or Fiction"* delivered in St. Kitts and Nevis on 15th and 16th November 2016 as part of the Institute for Gender and Development Studies Roaming Professors Lecture Series of this year.

lyrics of various contemporary hip hop artistes and rappers as relatively new voices emerging in this discourse, but rather than analyzing the subtext of music and masculinity which is itself a very rich vein to be mined, I have interspersed their voices as a responsive echo in this dialogue.

With the onset of gender scholarship and activism in the Caribbean from the late 1970s, feminist scholars examined masculinity primarily through a scrutiny and overhauling of the system of patriarchy, providing a necessary critique on its capacity to reproduce power and privilege, not only for men but for particular groups and classes. Many of the early debates and activism in feminism focused on men and masculinity as the perpetrator of gender and sexual violence, as primary forms of control over female sexual freedoms and reproductive rights. As a counterpoint argument to the feminist-centered debates, primarily male scholars and writers, noted that defining male gender was problematic for boys and men, especially during adolescence and early manhood. With the emergence of a masculinity studies movement by the 1990s, there were investigations into men's marginality from the family and from parenting roles of fatherhood, the cultural difficulties of learning to be a man, male underachievement in education, and the indiscriminate perception of all males as perpetrators of crime and gender-based violence. In the Caribbean, the occurrence of these issues was linked to the identity crisis of black men under colonial and in post-colonial society and, less so, on the pressures on masculinity enacted by expectations of hetero-normativity and hypermasculinity. In short, the discourse on masculinity, as on femininity, was primarily one of consistent victimhood. Among some, it was to counteract what is perceived as an increasing female hegemony as a result of the second wave feminist movement of the twentieth century. Admittedly, not all men or male gender scholars shared this perspective. After several decades of the dialogues going back and forth like a tennis ball on an uneven court, the dialogue is largely at an impasse, both sides playing largely for their own gender team. Many women are nonetheless sensitive to and very cognizant of the fact that gender identities are not fixed, are malleable and problematic for both men and women and are very sympathetic to the problems experienced by men and boys. The critique of heteronormality and heightened visibility and the voices of lesbian, gay, transsexual and intersexed groups have made for greater sensitivity to sexual identity issues that are commonly shared between male and female groupings. Similarly, the feminist movement and female empowerment have always had integral support from many men in powerful positions, in private homes, in classrooms and in the wider society. Nonetheless, the debates about men and masculinity are still maintained by both sides as largely oppositional ones: women are viewed as victims of gender violence or alternatively forging ahead of the sex and gender race, while men are depicted as either heroes or brutes, victims or perpetrators.

Was Caribbean masculinity always a fragile thing in the eyes of the region? Perhaps it was? Yet from the middle of the twentieth century Caribbean leaders and statesmen have been primarily men. Among our often-recalled male heroes or great achievers of the Anglophone Caribbean are Marcus Garvey, C. L. R. James, Eric Williams, V. S Naipaul, Derek Walcott, Walter Rodney, Maurice Bishop, Norman Manley, Errol Barrow, Bob Marley and Usain Bolt, while others from the Francophone islands are Toussaint L'Ouverture, Frantz Fanon, Aime Cesaire and Jean Price Mars. There is a host of distinguished men of action, song or letters who shaped the way both men and women have collectively understood regional and national identities. The list has been incrementally added to across the region in the intervening years along with smaller numbers of women whose contributions have been acknowledged, but the increasing voice and visibility of women is a relatively recent phenomenon. It has created disruption in the ideas of what constitutes masculinity globally and has been accompanied by a popular ideology and belief that went viral across the region in the last decades of the 20th century - that male power has waned, that women have taken over the helm, and that Caribbean masculinity is in crisis.

Thus the study of masculinity as it has evolved in the twentieth and into the twenty-first centuries has, perhaps inadvertently, foregrounded the idea that men and manhood as we know it is at risk Apart from trolling the academic and journalistic voices, I tuned in to the lyrics of male singers, particularly rappers of the twentieth to the twenty-first centuries.[1] Although women are one of the easiest targets for reproach in their songs, the male rappers know that the culprits are far more widespread, inaccessible and invisible. Acknowledging the valid concerns that echoes of anger, pain and hurt and self-reproach have raised for a consideration of men and masculinity in Caribbean society, we also need to ask who and what is invested in maintaining this relatively fixed ontology of manhood, and what may be gained by unsettling this paradigm? I look primarily at two overlapping but major themes that have emerged in the study of masculinity: the male victimhood discourse and male underachievement in education and contemplate some of these in an effort to recalibrate the strict dominions of gender that have informed our belief systems about male gender identity.

> He's losing his virility
> And now his masculinity
> Has been compromised
> And his libido down-sized
> The Darkness, *Bald* (2005)

> Man up
> Sit down
> Chin up
> Pipe down
> Socks up
> Don't cry
> Drink up
> Just lie
> Samaritans, *Idles*, (2018)

THE LINGERING DISCOURSE OF MALE VICTIMHOOD

The notion that men are marginal in society began long before in the literature on Caribbean sociology[2] and gained ascendancy through books such as Errol Miller's *The Marginalization of the Black Male* (1986) and *Men at Risk* (1992). Miller established a "marginalization hypothesis" that spread like a virus across the Caribbean. He argued that the marginalization of black men in the family was due to the nature of plantation life during slavery and the role required of men as labourers and sexual stud rather than as parents or live-in partners in a residential household. This fragmentation of men from the family of course resulted in a substantial proportion of female-headed, matrifocal or mother-centered families in the

Caribbean, leading to the idea that Caribbean women were strong, independent, could survive without men and were resilient under any conditions. Miller argued that by the 1980s in the teaching profession in Jamaica, the white elite felt threatened by the rise of black educated men who were vying with them for legislative power, and thus gave women increasing opportunities for education and employment. By the second half of the twentieth century, female teachers were numerically outstripping males in the education system. The idea of marginality then took greater hold and was given more support so that by the end of the twentieth century the number of boys in the education system declined and males were viewed as underperforming and underachieving in the education system.

Another problematic that emerged in the study of masculinity had to do with how men were groomed into their gender identity. Barry Chevannes, in *Learning to be a Man: Culture, Socialization and Gender Identity in Five Caribbean Communities* (2001) found, as did a study in Barbados by Graham Dann, *The Barbadian Male: Sexual Attitudes and Practices*, (1987) that boys and men suffered from being brought up in single-parent families – especially in female-headed families due to the lack of male role models and authority figures in the home. It was argued that boys have more distractions and temptations to contend with than girls, they are more easily sidetracked by sex, gangs, drug culture and street life and the desire to have a "bad-boy image" to prove that they possess the dominant features of masculinity. In the inner-city ghettoes or "hoods" in Jamaica the young adolescent learns that homophobia and macho-ism are essentials of masculinity.

The contemporary Caribbean "Man Box" therefore contains the cumulative legacies of its historical construction: the notion of marginality that has been attached to black men in the past, an assumed male marginality from the family, a perception of indifferent fatherhood, the view of males as underachievers in education, that masculinity has an affinity with violence and men are more prone to crime and criminal behaviour, including that of being the main perpetrators of violence against women. All of these produce the primary narrative of masculinity as pathology, as diseased. The popular renditions and interpretations have led, as Eudine Barriteau says of Miller's male marginalization thesis, "to a deeply flawed one-dimensional reading of manhood in the region. It gives us Caribbean masculinity as victim, wounded and regressive."[3] If we follow this logic, then Caribbean masculinity is always suffering at the hands of someone or some system. I want to frame this pathologizing of masculinity within a concept of deficit gender accounting. By this I mean that masculinity is constantly being accounted for as a deficit and therefore a cost to Caribbean nations.

The deficit model of masculinity has an impact on behaviours and expectations of boys and men in both policy and day to day interactions. Viewing men as marginal from family life, as unable to nurture or be good fathers and father figures has influenced our laws and policies that affect men themselves. It has been customary at divorces or separation to give custody for children to women. Many men who are willing to take on these roles are denied or assumed by the family court to be irresponsible parents[4] What is taking a longer time to change is the idea that men deserve and require paternity leave or can be the first parent of choice. When the subject of male paternity leave comes up for discussion in gender policies there is much hilarity and discussion about how many times might a Caribbean man might request paternity leave in one calendar year.[5]

The expectation of hyper-masculinity and the burdens that have been placed historically on man as protector, as physically strong, macho, objective, not allowed to demonstrate emotion and heterosexual is a heavy one to bear. Not all men are the same, some are artists, some want to do construction work, some like books and reading, some are happy to be house husbands and look after the children and do housework. How do we allow all the choices, including alternative sexual choices, without tampering with the biological difference behind masculinity and femininity? What do both men and women have to gain by accepting that gender identities, like race and class identities, are also malleable and that we possibly have no choice in this matter. In my view, female gender identity over the last half century has been allowed far more flexibility to adapt – women can be both strong and weak, be workers or housewives, be breadwinners or dependents. Has masculinity been allowed this fluid range that has incrementally been allowed femininity?

Is heteronormative patriarchy and macho masculinity the birthright of all males and will the absence of this be collectively damaging to men and to our social communities? By retaining the notion of an unchanging patriarchy that is only able to function with power over women and over other men, and the idea that one sex is diminished if the other ascends or adapts, holds both masculinity and femininity imprisoned. It completely ignores changes in technology, and enlightened ideas of equality about race, class and gender that have emerged in human consciousness by the twenty-first century.

> On the corner with the reprobates
> That you will call your mates for all the years you'll waste
> This toxic masculinity
> It's all that I can see in floods of thirsty streets
> Sam Fender, "*Friday fighting*" (2018)

> Suspended from school, and scared to go home, I was a fool
> With the big boys, breaking all the rules
> Tupac "*Dear Mama*" (1995)

> Everyday me ah brave and me ah put down me gun and pick up meh pen
> But we place where me grow, if me put down my pen, me might just get ten
> Mali Dan, (*Response to Jaron Nurse, Fed up* (2018)

FIGURING OUT MALE UNDER-PERFORMANCE IN EDUCATION

In the census data for Barbados for 1911, the recorded professional occupations by sex were as follows:

	Male	Female
Artists	4	1
Photographers	9	none
Authors	none	1
Dentists	18	none
Editors and Journalists	11	none
Engineers	11	none
Land Surveyors	3	none

Law	32	none
Medicine	59	none
Ministers of Religion	75	1
Reporters	10	none
Total	**232 males**	**3 females**

The professional workforce consisted of 98.71 per cent men and 1.29 per cent women in 1911. There were very likely no discussions in the newspapers that year, in policy documents or public settings about the absence of women or underachievement of females. This imbalance would have been viewed as absolutely normal. Girls where they were exposed to education or training were to be tutored in the art of becoming wives and mothers, eventually becoming the nurturers of children and the family. Money spent on an education or skill training for girls, even for those from middle and upper classes, was not a sound investment. Boys, especially those in the middle and upper classes, on the other hand, were expected to be educated and become the breadwinners, to be the professionals, opinion leaders and innovators for societal development. It was a different time. We did not have widespread medicalized technologies of birth control allowing for planned families that freed up a majority of women to take up jobs that were incompatible with family life. And although girls and women were not exactly unemployed, those professions like cooks, maids, seamstresses, nursing, caregiving, housekeeping and mothering were not assumed to require training or in fact to be considered skilled work at all.

By the last decades of the twentieth century the census data showed a different picture of educational attainment by sex. Males were consistently achieving lower educational attainment rates particularly at secondary and tertiary levels, compared to females. The occupational choices now available to women had undergone major changes and had a massive impact on young women's aspirations. It opened up educational and career choices to girls and women, making academic qualifications more important for their futures. At The University of the West Indies on all three campuses the student distribution rose to 70 per cent female and 30 per cent male. The number of women graduating each year from The University of the West Indies (UWI) began to exceed the number of men. While between 1948 and 1972, over

60% of the university graduating population was male, by the late 1990s over 70% of the graduates were female on all campuses of The UWI. The lower number of males graduating at university level was worrying as societies appeared to be turning out more women qualified to take up white collar and professional jobs, jobs that are usually associated with greater power, prestige and privilege. Coupled with the drop-out rates for boys at the secondary level, there was a desperate concern about this new phenomenon of female predominance and performance at tertiary level education and male dropouts at the secondary level. This was referred to in both the academic and popular literature as the "underachievement" of males.

The resultant societal panic revolved around several axes. Reasons were sought within the education system for why boys were resisting or underperforming in education. In the Caribbean for the first time in the history of the development and rolling out of research in gender and development studies, the Caribbean Development Bank provided research funds for a gender issue and governments stood up and took notice.[6] The Gender and Education Association report commented "In the 1990s a panic started about boys' 'underachievement' in North America, Australia, the UK and some other parts of Western Europe. In 1996, the UK's Chief Inspector of Schools called it "one of the most disturbing problems facing the education system."[7] Male performance in education had been taken on seriously both regionally and globally.

In Jamaica, *The Gleaner* reported that "Every year more girls are sent to high schools than boys, resulting in vastly more women at university than men, and fewer suitable marriage partners for educated women."[8] The carried-over ideology that girls were simply being educated to be suitable marriage partners was ignored for the minute while Cynthia Cooke, Principal of Camperdown High School, took up cudgels with the inaccuracy of the statement. Investigations with the examinations unit had revealed instead that there were equity problems "...in the placement of girls and boys. They said they had to "go down deep into the barrel" to place some of the boys. It was a policy to make sure there is a balance in the numbers of boys and girls. It resulted in many girls who did very well compared to boys not getting a place. Should that have been fixed?"[9]

In 1999 Barry Chevannes had noted in the Caribbean that there was a high drop-out rate for boys. He observed also that boys underperform in English which had increasingly been perceived as a "girls" subject, Chevannes argued that this low performance in English probably handicapped boys much more than girls' lower performance in mathematics handicaps girls. In a study of fourth forms in Jamaica, Barbados and St. Vincent and the Grenadines (2001), Odette Parry (2001) reported that teachers described English as a subject that was "too effeminate," "not macho enough" "nerdish' and "too girlish" for males. One teacher reported that in Barbados "a nerd is a boy who shows academic inclinations." Education itself had undergone a period of "feminization" not only in terms of a greater number of females involved in this profession at all levels, but also in the way schooling itself was perceived in relation to hypermasculinity. It was thought that there were insufficient male students, men as teachers and men as role models in the education system so that the profession of teaching was deemed to have become "feminized." Those boys who remained in education were viewed as bookish and boring. Boys who wanted to read had to hide from their male peers to do this for fear of being seen as "girlie girlie."

David Plummer *et al* tackled the question of why boys were not interested in reading with a comparative study based on interviews carried out in 2005 in Guyana, Trinidad and St. Kitts. They found that for most boys the ability to project yourself as successfully masculine takes center stage as they mature. They aspire to a clearly defined heterosexual masculine status and the peer group polices behaviour to ensure that it conforms to prevailing masculine standards. Unfortunately, these masculine standards according to Plummer *et al* are about "aspiring to be bad: the rise of a hard masculinity."[10] Thus, an easy step to establishing a bad boy image is the movement to gangs and with this a culture of celebrating a rough, violent and virile sexuality that separated real men from assumed effeminate boys. Underachievement of boys in education therefore spoke to the increasing fear of being able to match up to defined gender roles where certain professions and attributes were more gender stereotyped within society. As education itself was, for the boys, becoming more feminized, it became more devalued.

The problems of boys' resistance to reading was also attributed to sex differences between brains, that their brains developed differently from those of girls. It was found that "The different regions of the brain develop in a different sequence in girls compared with boys." In other words, boys learn differently from girls. Should we conclude from such biological differences that one sex has a functional advantage over the other? When did this functional advantage begin? It is ironic that the same biological argument of brain differences was used to keep girls and women out of the education system for centuries. It was thought that women were only fit for reproductive and nurturing roles and that if they strived to develop their intellect then their reproductive systems would be affected and their desire to have children would decrease.[11]

The tables had turned. Because of the competitive advantage that female brain development now appeared to give girls, single sex schools were being proposed as one of the solutions to male underachievement. The Ministry of Education and Information in St Kitts had done extensive homework on the nature of this trend, finding that the performance in the Test of Standards across the four areas of Language, Mathematics, Science and Social Studies across all grades demonstrated that between 2008 and 2011 girls were outperforming boys by over fifty per cent. The report noted "…currently our nation is battling an outbreak of crime and violence like never before with the vast majority being committed by young men between the ages 18 to 25." The solution proposed by the Government of St. Kitts in 2011 as a means of tackling boys' achievement and disciplining was a Single Sex Education Implementation programme.

The Communications Unit of the Office of the then Prime Minister of St. Kitts and Nevis, The Honourable Dr. Denzil L. Douglas announced plans in September 2011 to introduce single-sex education for students from Grades III to VI in three of the larger primary schools on St. Kitts. Dr. Douglas expressed concern on what he termed a gender imbalance at The University of the West Indies, which has been traced to the primary schools. He argued that "This imbalance, (at university level) clearly, is not one that magically emerges when our young people arrive at UWI. It is a trend that has been developing throughout the region over time.

It is a trend that can be seen right here in the Federation."[12] He proposed that the problem should be addressed from primary school level.

"What we have found" Prime Minister Douglas said, "is that up until Grade III, the academic performance of boys and girls is indistinguishable, one from the other. At Grade III, however, a clearly discernable divergence develops. The performance of the girls remains strong, while the performance of the boys begins to lag. And this divergence remains in Grade IV, it remains apparent in Grade V, and it remains in Grade VI. ...This is not something that any society should want. We want both our boys and our girls to have the kind of curiosity, and pluck, and enthusiasm that is needed to fuel their successful course through elementary, secondary, and eventually university itself." They argued that boys' brains were wired to be less attentive at an early age and that single sex schools would increase the boys' concentration, based on the assumption that girls excel at certain subjects over boys and pose too much of a distraction at this age. It was also felt that female teachers who predominated in the education system at primary and secondary level, tended to treat girls more favourably because they were more pliable learners. The jury is still out on how brain differences affect the capacity of sexes to learn or apply themselves although clearly there are differences that are created through social expectations of each sex and gender.

> And who'd think in elementary?
> Hey! I'd see the penitentiary one day
> And running from the police, that's right
> Mama catch me, put a whooping to my backside
> ...I finally understand
> For a woman it ain't easy trying to raise a man
> Tupac, *Dear Mama* (1995)

> On the corner with the reprobates
> That you will call your mates for all the years you'll waste
> This toxic masculinity
> It's all that I can see in floods of thirsty streets
> Sam Fender, *Friday fighting*, (2018)

Apart from not equipping themselves for further education or white-collar jobs, the pressing concern that male underachievement has been associated with is that of increasing male criminality. Remaining in the school system requires discipline, time and mental labour rather than physical prowess. There are quicker, if more high risk returns on working in crime than applying oneself to the rigours and discipline of education or depending on a monthly salary in lower paid white or blue-collar jobs. The statistics of crime and prison population today show that significant numbers of young men are involved in criminal and illegal activities. In his book *Dying to be Men: Youth, Masculinity and Social Exclusion*. Gary Barker notes "On the island of St. Vincent, young men represent about 20 percent of the arrests on drug related charges. Every year several hundred young men enter the prison system or one of the government-funded residential mental health facilities."[13] Apart from other crimes of homicide, burglary, drug pushing and the like, men are viewed as the main perpetrators of rape, incest, sexual harassment and crimes of gender-based violence – this idea of masculinity as violent or un-trustable continues to work against all men and boys trying to not get into the criminal game.

If we argue that boys need to be separated from girls at a certain stage of their learning, then other parallel gender imbalances emerge as a result. Wouldn't the boys fall further behind if girls are not there to present a competitive edge which they now do? How are boys and girls going to learn to socialize with each other and perhaps quell the distance in communication that results in gender-based violence? Should we therefore employ only male teachers to teach male students and female teachers to teach female students? Does this approach not promote gender stereotyping for girls and boys both? How exactly did boys learn in the previous era when they dominated the professions as we saw in the 1911 Barbados census. Is it the problem of brains or application to learning, recognizing education not as a right but as a privilege and that a good education is the pathway to lifelong learning, that education does not end with the classroom. Are the messages being sent out about education as only a means to an end harmful to both boys and girls?

That the problem was named underachievement of boys was itself interesting. The term underachievement attached to one sex seemed to imply that girls and women were overachieving or overextending what was expected of their sex. This interpretation was the simplest explanation of more complex changing gender arrangements due to changes in technologies of production and more equitable access to education. One could also easily have argued that boys were underachieving in relation to their usual performance level within the educational system, and this is a valid concern. What does underachievement really mean? Underachievement can be defined as an inability or failure to perform appropriately for one's age or talents, a state of unfulfilled potential. If girls were not expected to, or given access to certain jobs previously or given access to different levels of education, then there had been no benchmark set for girls and the unusual female who stood out had not posed a threat.

It is not a straightforward task to identify who is an underachiever in education per se especially as book learning should not be the only measure by which we establish human potential. To excel at a craft or vocation of any kind is achievement. What has been unfortunate in this discussion and fictional is, as Barbara Bailey puts this "Claims of 'male underachievement' are relative and emerge by comparing the achievement of boys with that of girls."[14] Based on analyses of secondary-level entry and performance data at two different time periods, 2004 and 2007 in a study carried out throughout the Caribbean, Bailey thought that the phenomenon has more to do with under-participation than it has to do with underachievement. She found that boys who remain in the education system in fact do well, particularly in the critical areas or those that society deems critical, such as science and technology. More so, it has been proven that middle class boys are not underachievers so that this issue as it pertains to masculinity is class-related. Interestingly while the female population at university level education rose to over 70% in most disciplines, as the economists have demonstrated, despite women's higher access to formal and higher education, another truism emerges: "Women Learn – Men Earn."

What exactly has altered in society in the last decades of the twentieth century into the present? First, economic and technological changes in many Western countries have led to a drop in the number of jobs available in manufacturing and other fields which suit young men who could have left school with few or no educational qualifications. As a result, these young, primarily working-class men have become a 'problem' to be addressed by solutions within the education system. The problem was viewed primarily in terms of how systems of education must be adjusted to suit the different learning abilities of boys. My own concern about the diminishing number of young boys in the education system is that we have also seen a rise in violence, male youth gangs and in the co-optation of young boys in crime and criminal-related activities. From an equity perspective therefore, do we need to enforce affirmative action such as single-sex schools where curricula can be adapted to boy's development cycle to ensure that societies absorb boys who have become unemployable due to their educational attainment levels? And if so, what incentives are there for boys to remain in this institution?

Gender scholars and practitioners in the field, including educators themselves have agreed that the under-performance and under-participation of certain groups of boys is problematic. What other kinds of jobs do young men get into if they do not complete their schooling? Are they all drawn into a life of crime? Do they become the freelancers, the new entrepreneurs, the new social media specialists? We need more evidence on how the economy has absorbed them into other areas that perhaps do not require lengthy academic training. How do we begin to harness the potential of boys and young men outside the education system and still ensure that they achieve their own aspirations which may or may not be related to an academic education? What we all agree on is that the solutions lie in many structurally embedded attitudes and practices about gender that stifles masculinity itself. The dialogue that began with the terminology of underachievement merely signaled what had already happened in society, that another seismic shift had begun to take place in gender definitions and identity making.

Perhaps the question that the popular perception of male "underachievement" most raises for me is that it challenges the concepts of equality and equity that are now fundamental precepts of human civilization that we must accept without question.[15] The definition of gender equality and equity is a somewhat abstract one to grasp. Equality establishes the ideological beliefs and philosophy of egalitarianism that underpins the notion that both sexes are indeed equal in the eyes of the legal and judicial systems. The problem with the popular perception of equal is that it is also taken to mean identical. But equal does not and cannot negate the fact that the sexes are differently constructed biological creatures, the effect of which makes for varied cultural belief systems that have led to differences in social expectations, behaviours and attributes of each sex and for those who live in the interstices of the biological continuum, and will continue to do so. Equity on the other hand is the act of fairness, justice, impartiality and parity with which a society must treat with each sex, allowing each through various embedded mechanisms in its constitution and legal framework to avail themselves of opportunities to develop their human potential, earn a living and respect.

RECALIBRATING GENDER: NEW WAYS OF SEEING CARIBBEAN MASCULINITY

The mask
Of masculinity
Is a mask
That's wearing me
Samaritans, *Idles*, (2018)

Drop ah jail 16 years old with three case
Mommy say, "the devil got ya boy, slow down"
Ay, don't cry fuh me Momma, just hold on
Done know the journey ah go go so long
Nuff boy sellout cause dem heart not so strong
But me sorry for the pain, me brought to a new man
Plumpy Boss, *My Journey*, (2018)

"You thought toxic masculinity was a new cologne"
Open Mike Eagle, *Woke as me*, (2019)

I went to his parties as a straight minority
It never seemed a threat to my masculinity
Rush, *Nobody's hero* (2009)

The primeval fear of a realignment of gender roles was the factor that historically restricted women from education and entry into the waged labour force for centuries in western society. Now into the third decade of the twenty-first century, major inequities of the past have been addressed or re-calibrated but currently, both in the region and globally, few countries have achieved gender equity goals that demonstrate equal status for both sexes. The 2015 Global Gender Gap, which is published each year since 2006, is supported by statistics showing that power, privilege, the high-paying jobs and opportunities for promotion beyond middle management, are still enjoyed by men. The World Economic Forum calculates that the gender pay gap could take 170 years to close. It is likely that certain groups of privileged men have not been affected by the male underachievement syndrome. At the same time, the legitimate claims by masculinity of a destabilization due to a shifting set of ideas and practices that are expected of men and boys must be taken seriously.[16] While femininity has historically been on this journey of incremental change in its boundaries for centuries, the current challenge to masculinity has had a shorter time span, perhaps only beginning to show its dimensions from the late twentieth century. What was referred to as "male underachievement" in education was one of the first vibrations that resonated globally. This was followed by the greater visibility of boys and men in gangs and community warfare, and that this sex largely filled the prisons and remand camps. The full message of this upheaval comes home to me largely through the changing song lyrics and beat of the music expressed by men from the late twentieth century, such as Tupac Shakur who died at age 25 due to a drive by shooting deemed to be an assassination.[17] In Trinidad and Tobago the life stories of rap artistes echo a similar refrain and, like their counterparts elsewhere, their influence on masculinity and shaping male identities today remains unmapped – perhaps it is impossible to even gauge this. Plumpy Boss, one of the more influential rappers in Trinidad, currently tells the story of his journey as a young man:

Life wa me live me lucky so me grow big
…Pain inna mi heart wa make me bun dis spliff
…All d wrongs wa me do wa make mi turn who I is
Yow dawg wa dem know bout this?

…Bad juvenile no pussy can't call me no clown
38 with six live rounds to roll round
Young Tali so me never go down

Jump out a Juvey, enter Curepe, in a new land
Marley bro, why it so hard to be a new man
Cyah see me way inna nothing wa me do
Touch Gonzales, jump out with ah plan
So me start sing some song

Friend ah kill friend man
And man get lock up fuh ten years and can't get ah sentence
Ministers fail dem, promises after elections
So me self me depend pon
Can't wait pon no help from anyone
Land ah get savage cause it full of bare oppression
Man have no laws nor no regards fi no man[18]

When masses of younger men are dropping out of the school system by being drawn into organized crime, drug running, assassinations and territorial wars of all kinds, defending the interests of the drug mafias to stay alive and make their songs, they are being viewed as the expendable parts of our populations.[19] The culprits are not primarily women – patriarchy is a relationship between men and women as it is between men and men. Patriarchy or the system of male dominance emerged as a benevolent as well as controlling one, the control of men over the household and family to offer protection and support, alongside the control of older men over younger men, or the elite over the underprivileged. Societies have always seemed eager to dispose of its working-class male population as if this were some strange kind of birth control mechanism. For all the wars that have been fought for millennia, the men who fight on the front lines are rarely the educated or upper class officers. What is the cost to the nation of losing men to crime and prison, as opposed to them becoming more educated, skilled craftsmen and professionals alongside women to advance society's productivity, innovation and invention? How might we replace crime by honest labour and make this the norm instead? Is it possible to do this or is human nature and the relations of gender itself fixed and unchanging? Is society as an organism incapable of adapting for survival and bent on its own self destruction.

Rhoda Reddock (1998) concluded that the issues of gender cannot be understood outside of their relations to other factors such as race/ethnicity, class and socio-economic status, location and even issues of health and ability – so the question of male underachievement cannot be tackled only within the education system. David Plummer reminded us that boys who drop out are influenced by the attraction of "hard masculinity" as described by David Plummer and Stephen Geofroy (2010), and as seen above in the lyrics by Plumpy Boss and repeated by many other rappers, they seem to have no alternatives other than to prove their machismo "Bad juvenile no pussy can't call me no clown." Mark Figueroa concurs that "the solution of the problem of male underperformance must be sought in the transformation of gender relations and not in any measures that would create new exceptionalities for males within the education system.

The problem does not rest specifically with the education system although all systems must be challenged to respond to concerns. It is allied to shifts that have taken place in job markets and the kinds of jobs available to men as compared to women. In the meantime amending curricula choices in schools and a valiant attempt to discourage male drop-outs are all solutions that should be continued. Added to this however as noted by Amanda Keddie (2001, 251) there should be significant corrections "… in the school's gendered and heteronormative infrastructure (such as the dispersion of power within the school, the teachers' and principal's gendered expectations, and philosophies and practices for managing behaviour) in endorsing and perpetuating particular dominant modes of being masculine." Keddie (277) concludes it is unlikely that "…boys will shift their investments while the individuals who excel at combative sports, are publicly glorified as heroes and given a social licence to behave in 'privileged' ways."

The natural law of survival of species is adaptation, not violent rejection. What have men to gain in consciously making this mental leap that can lead to policy and perceptual changes? What do women have to lose? Let's begin another kind of conversation on masculinity, one that does not only focus on the marginality or underachievement of males, but on the potential that might still be released if the configurations of gender allow for fluidity of masculine and feminine identities without each losing face or power in relations to each other. The current definitions have for too long, been restricting to both sexes. The human race cannot be won with only one single-sexed champion at the finish line.

ENDNOTES

[1] In "Refining Gender Methodology: Studying Masculinity through Popular Song Lyrics" published in *Caribbean Masculinities* edited by Rafael L. Ramirez, Ineke Cunningham, and Victor I. Garcia-Toro. San Juan: HIV/AIDS Research and Education Center, University of Puerto Rico. pp.33-56 I suggested that songs sung and written by males were one of the best conveyors of how men expressed emotions. I had then drawn primarily on calypso and early reggae. Looking at the music produced by another generation of men, I am more convinced that this is a masculine gender script that requires very serious analysis.

[2] Peter J. Wilson, Caribbean Crews: Peer Groups and Male Society *Caribbean Studies* Vol. 10, No. 4 (Jan., 1971), pp. 18-34 Published by the Institute of Caribbean Studies, UPR, Rio Piedras Campus

[3] Eudine Barriteau, (ed) *Confronting Power, Theorizing Gender in the Commonwealth Caribbean*, The University of the West Indies Press, Kingston, cited in Introduction, p. 11

[4] From discussion with family lawyer who represents both men and women in family court in matters of separation and divorce in Trinidad and Tobago.

[5] From my experience of introducing paternity leave as an option in family legislation in gender policy consultations in several Caribbean territories between 2000 and 2011.

[6] Regional Gender Differentials Research project led by Professor Barbara Bailey resulting in a policy framework developed in collaboration with the Caribbean Development Bank and adopted by CARICOM Ministers of Education at the 20th Meeting of the Council on Human and Social Development (COHSOD) in October, 2010. See Barbara Bailey, "Boys, Masculinity and Education" *Caribbean Review of Gender Studies*, 8, https://sta.uwi.edu/crgs/december2014/journals/CRGS_8_BoysMasculinity Education_BBailey.pdf

[7] Gender and Education Association, "Boys Underachievement" 2013 http://www.genderandeducation.com/resources-2/the-boys-underachievement-debate/

[8] Cynthia Cooke "Marginalisation of the Male" Jamaica Gleaner Tuesday | February 2, 2010

[9] *Ibid*

[10] Has Learning Become Taboo and is Risk-taking Compulsory for Caribbean boys? Researching the Relationship between Masculinities, Education and Risk David Plummer, Arden McLean and Joel Simpson, *Caribbean Review of Gender Studies*, Issue 2 – 2008, See p. 6 https://sta.uwi.edu/crgs/september2008/journals/DPlummerAMcleanJSimpson.pdf

[11] See Janet Sayers, *Biological Politics: Feminist and Anti-Feminist Perspectives*, Tavistock, United Kingdom, 1982

[12] Single-sex Education to be Introduced in September – My Vue ... www.myvuenews.com › single-sex-education-to-be-introduced-in-sep... 2011

[13] Gary Barker *Dying to be Men: Youth, Masculinity and Social Exclusion*, Routledge, London, 2005, p. 105

[14] Bailey, *Ibid* p 1 Abstract
[15] I admit that this way of viewing equality and equity is the rule of thumb I have used for at least two decades in crafting national gender policies for several societies in the Caribbean. What I have found is that it facilitates popular comprehension of a very complex and layered framework for integrating gender into policy.
[16] While I have always been sympathetic to the real concerns men have raised, I owe further insights to the work I am currently doing in my post retirement working experience with the Corporate Social Responsibility Gender Agenda of First Citizens Group, Caribbean. In setting up the first large scale Boys Symposium in 2019 in Trinidad entitled "Boys will be Boys?: Boys will be what we teach them to be" I worked closely with Peter Weller, Clinical Psychologist and Gregory Sloane Seale, youth outreach officer and motivator. Both of them have supported projects for boys and men for decades. They agree that many men simply do not understand the shifting ground beneath their feet, what is expected of a new masculinity, when they have grown up with old ideas that are constantly also being reproduced.
[17] Tupac Shakur, better known by his stage name 2Pac, was a highly successful rapper and actor known for his violent and shocking lyrics. …Born into a family notorious for their brushes with law, he had no contact with his biological father until he was an adult. Violence was nothing new to the youngster whose mother was imprisoned while pregnant with him. It is no surprise that his music was replete with references to ghettos, street violence, sex, gangs and other social problems he faced while growing up. …Even though professionally he was becoming successful, his life became entangled in violence and he had frequent rifts with the police. In addition to his music career, he had also acted in some films (and) was a voracious reader and a big fan of Shakespeare. https://www.thefamouspeople.com/profiles/tupac-amaru-shakur-3096.php
[18] For full set of lyrics see https://genius.com/18088662
[19] I am grateful to Michael Mooleedhar, filmmaker of Trinidad and Tobago for his references on local rap artistes and explanations on the music they make, the context of its production and its influences on young male listeners.

REFERENCES

Chevannes, Barry. 2001. *Learning to be a Man: Culture, Socialization and Gender Identity in Five Caribbean Communities*. Kingston, Jamaica: University of the West Indies Press.

Dann, Graham. 1987. *The Barbadian Male: Sexual Attitudes and Practice*. London: Macmillan Caribbean.

Figeroa, Mark. "Underachieving Caribbean Boys: Marginalization or Gender Privileging?" http://www.cedol.org/wp-content/uploads/2012/02/23-25-2007.pdf

Keddie, Amanda. 2001. *Little Boys: The Potency of Peer Culture in Shaping Masculinities*. PhD diss., Deakin University.

Miller, Errol. 1986. *Marginalization of the Black Male: Insights from the Development of the Teaching Profession*. Mona, Jamaica: ISER.

Miller, Errol. 1991. *Men at Risk*. Jamaica: Jamaica Publishing House.

Parry, Odette. 2000. *Male Underachievement in High School Education: In Jamaica, Barbados, and St Vincent and the Grenadines*. University Press of the West Indies.

Plummer, David and Stephen Geofroy. 2010. "When Bad is Cool: Violence and Crime as Rites of Passage to Manhood," *Caribbean Review of Gender Studies: A Journal of Caribbean Perspectives on Gender and Feminism*, Issue 4.

Reddock, Rhoda. 1998. "Contestations Over Culture, Class, Gender And Identity In Trinidad And Tobago: 'The Little Tradition," *Caribbean Quarterly A Journal of Caribbean Culture*, Volume 44, Issue 1-2, pp. 62-80.

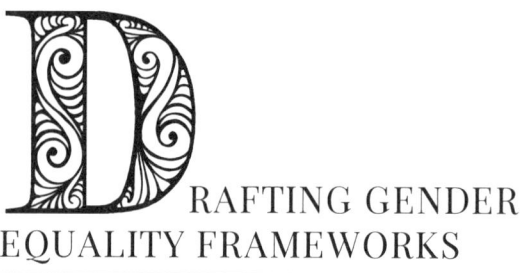RAFTING GENDER EQUALITY FRAMEWORKS

4

15

Gender Politics and Global Democracy: Insights from the Caribbean[†]

INTRODUCTION

Modern democracy centred on the nation-state has invariably inherited the rules of patriarchy.[1] Men are viewed as the natural leaders of nations and continue to dominate in the political arena. Women's roles are relegated to the private sphere of the home and in supportive roles to men in the process of political decision-making. How might contemporary global democracy present an opportunity to overcome patriarchy and work towards gender equity? There have been some promising developments to bring women's voices, participation and control into global politics, such as the Convention on the Elimination of All Forms of

---

[†] This paper has not been previously published but has undergone several reviews. It was originally presented at the annual meeting of the International Studies Association Annual Conference on the panel "Global Governance: Political Authority in Transition", at the Le Centre Sheraton Montreal Hotel, Montreal in March, 2011. My thanks to Professor Jan Aart Scholte for his comments on several drafts. He organized the panel on which it was presented and led an international project on Building Global Democracy at the University of Warwick in which I also participated. The essay thus benefits from the exposure to the discussions with other global partners in this project.

Discrimination against Women (CEDAW) and the Beijing process. Such global initiatives have assisted in the struggles for gender democracy in the Caribbean.

Full integration of gender into global democracy has been largely subordinated in global discourses. Prevailing patriarchal methods of negotiation have insufficiently incorporated women into decision-making and treats gender as a marginal aspect of achieving democracy internally. While political imperatives required that Caribbean states ratify global conventions and draft national policies for gender equality and equity, there appears to be no penalties for parliamentary non-acceptance or rolling out of these draft policies. This is highly regrettable. The persistence of gender inequities undermine democracy in relation to global circumstances as women's voices and the ideas that they propose for change are viewed as subsidiary concessions to popular global discourses rather than inherently instrumental to achieving development goals.

What can be done to correct this situation? Perhaps recent experiences with the drafting and passage of national gender policies could offer important suggestions. This analysis assesses the possible implications for global democracy that might be drawn from the formulation of national gender policies in the Cayman Islands, Dominica, Trinidad and Tobago and the British Virgin Islands between 1999 and 2011. The value of gender policies might be that they stimulate change and initiate a democratic process of actually engaging women's voices and perhaps privileging their voices alongside those of men at the national and local levels. The gains of gender policies that feed directly back into the attempts to achieve global democracy may however be far more delayed.

Comprising primarily small island societies, the Caribbean region was settled from the fifteenth century onwards through a process of decimation of indigenous settlers and forced historical migrations of people from different continents. Anti-colonial and nationalist movements, from the late eighteenth century in the case of Haiti, and from the twentieth century onwards in other states, have produced peoples who are relatively strident about their self-sovereignty and national identities. Yet due to their geographical size and politically dependent histories, the region remains open to "predominant forms of globalization that are severely undemocratic. 'Rule by and for the people' mediates with the impact of global companies, global communications, global ecology, global finance, global health, global knowledge and global migration" (A Cairo Conversation 2009, 2). The postcolonial legacy continues to shape the contemporary problems of gender and democracy in the region. Local political machineries, though outwardly promoting democratic governance, have remained relatively male dominated. Women's empowerment or participation in the governance and decision-making of the state has not seriously made an inroad into an assumed public/private dichotomy of male and female spheres. As observed by Heba Raouf Ezzat, "empowerment" has never been premised on "a notion of power and politics that would be inclusive of women" (Ezzat 2009, 3), although from the 1980s onwards, an awareness of gender has increasingly been placed on the development agenda of the region.

At the same, time cultural constructions of gender in the Caribbean have challenged the traditional hierarchical structure of power that places men at the top of the ladder and women at the base. Gender relations in the Caribbean, can be described as *paradoxical*. Women have traditionally been invested with social and even economic power as breadwinners or heads of households but are restricted in their access to political power (Momsen 1993). The overriding image of Caribbean women is that of exceptional strength and influence in the family (Cuales 1984, 117), assertive characters as heads of households (Massiah 1984), resilient in the face of economic hardship and social disasters (Mohammed and Perkins 1999) and actively supportive to men folk in the social and political movements that have led to emancipation, adult suffrage, independence and the development of social services (Antrobus 1984, 119). Due to its settlement patterns that discouraged legal or stable marriages as the basis of family life, particularly among African descended populations under the system of African slavery from the sixteenth to nineteenth centuries, black men were historically viewed as marginalized, from political power in the rule of Caribbean nations and from the family (Miller 1986, 1991). From the middle of the twentieth century this trend began to be overturned so that by the first few decades of the twenty-first century, most Caribbean societies have internal self-rule and governments largely dominated by black and coloured men. At the same time, capital remained concentrated in the hands of the old/new merchant corporations, an extenuation of the old planter class.

Caribbean women have by no means been invisible or silent as the region matured politically. Women played a central role over time in bolstering political parties, aiding and abetting male leaders in their bid to gain and retain office. Inspired by ideas of feminism, there was a concerted drive from local independent women's movements from the last decades of the twentieth century to magnify the voices of women and to ensure that they would be noticed and counted. Added to this, governments were pressured through the conventions they had signed to produce gender policies and strengthen national gender machineries to fulfill their mandates. Since the first world conference of women was held in Mexico in 1975, states in the Caribbean were either encouraged or forced to establish women's desks, bureaus or gender affairs departments. One of the most fundamental conventions to be ratified was the CEDAW convention formulated in 1979.

By the twenty-first century several Caribbean governments committed to formulating, if not actually implementing, national policies for gender equity and equality, in order to qualify for international loans and treaties. The questions that I explore in this overview however have to do with the impact if any that national policies on gender equality have on the patriarchal control of state governance and a more gender nuanced practice of democracy. By extension we might therefore be able to see how processes of formulating and implementing national gender policies influence the politics and practices of achieving global democracy? Furthermore, by looking at the case study of the Caribbean, we can anticipate what small island states bring to the conceptual understanding of global democracy by engaging in a nation-wide consultation process on gender equality and equity?

This paper fleshes out these questions, with reference to the Caribbean, under four sections. The first section examines how gender inequities undermine democracy, both within a society and in relation to global circumstances. The second section demonstrates some outcomes from the gender policy creation process in the four island states of Cayman Islands, Trinidad and Tobago, the Commonwealth of Dominica and the British Virgin Islands, considering whether these have actually advanced democracy in these states. The third section examines how global circumstances have both furthered and frustrated strivings for gender democracy in the countries selected for scrutiny. The fourth and final section of the paper analyses the lessons that the Caribbean experiments of formulating national gender policies illustrate for rethinking global democracy.

SECTION 1: GENDER AND DEMOCRACY

The common perception of democracy is that there is a level playing field of political involvement where each participant, undifferentiated by sex, gender, race, class, religious and cultural difference or physical disability, has a voice in the decision-making process about how the society is governed. In this notional level playing field it is assumed that the state's funds are channeled fairly and discriminately for the good of the society and that all groups have a say in the kind of arrangements that their governments enter into with other states. Eva Erman points out that "both academics and practitioners have been keen on finding solutions to the global problems that we face today ...(while) conceptual unclarity still reigns concerning what 'the rule by and for the people' means in a global context" (Erman 2009, 1). Taking a lead from Erman, this section examines the gender dimensions of the deliberative account of democracy – that is a consideration of whether gender inequities are themselves absent from both the formal track of democracy, i.e., formal representation, electoral aggregation, and a system of rights, as well as the informal 'track', i.e., civil society engagement, debate and public deliberation, between people as well as between the people and those in power (Erman 2009, 2).

There is a "long-standing feminist claim that women have been consistently marginalized within democracy" (Eschle 2000, 32). Women's claims were first focused around concrete gains that could enhance their status in society, to provide them with both the confidence and wherewithal to enter the tracks where the democratic races are run. By the late nineteenth and into the twentieth century, women first still had to convince societies that the rights they were fighting for were legitimate ones. Although assumed available to all, in reality such rights were controlled by a patriarchal notion of what constituted the inalienable rights of men over women. Among the other issues for which women fought to gain inroads into have been equal treatment in occupational fields, equal access to decision-making in the political sphere, the right to education, to sexual and reproductive control over their bodies, and to freedom from the fear of sexual violence of all kinds, include rape, domestic violence and sexual harassment in the workplace. Of these, from the twentieth century onwards, the accelerated demands of women globally for the vote and for sexual and reproductive rights have been the ones most contained by religious communities and by governments themselves who fear reprisals for their re-election if they confront long-standing spiritual belief systems. The right of women to vote and admit this sex evenly into the public space, has challenged the naturalized notion of male leadership. The struggle to gain sexual and reproductive rights has disputed a fundamental aspect of male control of femininity, that of female sexual freedoms. These areas have traditionally underpinned patriarchal control over women in most societies. Marxist feminists and radical feminists generally used the concept of patriarchy to refer to the institutionalization of male power. Patriarchal control exerted by the state goes beyond the abstract or actual preservation of male power and privilege for men. It persists because of a gendered ideology upheld by most religious belief systems, that there is a natural gender division of society into a male public sphere and female private sphere in which each sex holds rightful power. Ideologies such as this ultimately determine state intervention in policy and legislation over issues such as sex and gender, marriage and family where public and private are conflated (Stearns 2007, 88). Gender inequities and discriminatory practices are experienced at all levels – individual, domestic and private, collective, institutional and public. Efforts to remove such inequities have affected the gender dynamics within households, communities and the workplace and within political machineries as they challenge the gender complicity and complacency with which most societies had functioned until the late twentieth century.

In the Caribbean in particular up until the 1960s, gender inequities remained as marginal issues in the struggle for nationalism and independence. The most important battle that these societies needed to win first, in their estimation, was that of freedom from colonial clutches, disregarding in the heat of the colonial and early post-colonial struggles that inherited gendered beliefs were also an integral component of colonial ideologies. Eric Williams in Trinidad and Tobago and Norman Manley in Jamaica, both of whom were to become the first Prime Ministers of these nations on their independence from Britain, entered as charismatic liberation fighters as well as natural born leaders. Despite the struggles to free themselves from the colonial methods of rule that had "emasculated" them, the same political systems were inherited and introduced by the first male leaders of the nations. The formal track of democracy comprised electoral rules patterned after the Westminster system of party politics, election of candidates and a constitution that accepted the freedom in principle for all persons of right mind to participate and to go up for positions of power. In theory this allowed for any woman to be a full participant in the democratic process. In reality, few women were in a position to do so. Men like Williams and Manley who had access to higher education when most women did not, became the primary leaders of the anti-colonial movements. In the course of the first 50 years of independence and post-colonial rule in the Anglophone Caribbean, by 1980 only one woman had risen to the leadership of a nation, Dame Mary Eugenia Charles, Prime Minister, 1980-1995 in the Commonwealth of Dominica.[2]

There is a mutually reinforcing relationship between the global and local tracks of democracy. If women are viewed as marginal to the public sphere, are barely involved in civil society, public debates and public deliberation, then they have little confidence or backing by political parties to put themselves up for access to the formal track where they might be selected as candidates for political elections. Regina Gathonai Mwatha notes that this absence of women in the political sphere was recognized in the global development discourse in gender. The discourse shifted between 1975 and the 1990s. First it was thought that women had to be brought into development – Women *in* Development (WID). Later it was agreed that women had always been part of development - Women *and* Development (WAD), and finally it was appreciated that gender rather than women had to be mainstreamed in all development agenda and goals – *Gender and* Development (GAD). Despite these incremental perceptions Mwatha points out for the situation of Kenya, that "the women's agenda was only "an add-on," it did not pose any threats and could easily be sidelined" (Mwatha 2009, 6). The question arises therefore about the actual political clout of the global development women's discourse in seriously representing a marginalized sex. Why would a women's global agenda be at the same time recognized and paid lip service, yet continue to be sidelined?

It is possible that the global women's agenda presented another challenge to the concept of democracy. As Erman (2009) points out above, conceptual unclarity pervades when we apply the qualifier of global. The concept of the global is a more modern one and has incorporated the idea of difference. There cannot be absolutes in global democracy as difference needs to be accommodated, including difference of approaches, geography and culture in the struggle to attain democratic processes in any society or region. A good example of this difference is illustrated in the homegrown Pacific perspective of *talanoa* – a cross-cultural process of storytelling at local level that accommodates narratives of both the pain and pleasure that people experience in the introduction of policies that affect their lives and livelihoods (Halapua 2010). This is one of the few examples that exist of local attempts to mediate with the global. We have little hard evidence beyond clichés such as glocalization – "think locally, act globally" on the extent to which the local impacts on the national and global. In addition, Ezzat observes that we do not have the indicators that measure women's present contribution to loçal or global achievements for "where socio-political survival strategies take place, the politics are usually overlooked by dominant quota approaches that are focusing on official bodies" (Ezzat 2009, 7).

How gender inequity undermines the local democratic processes is still insufficiently grasped. The global gender discourses proposed recipes such as increased public participation of women in politics at local levels, the establishment of provisions such as shelters for battered women and access to credit that would lead to the improvement in individual women's lives. But quantitative indicators reported at periodic CEDAW meetings do not appear to signal global political democratic gains, even while they may improve conditions in individual countries. By focusing on certain woman centered measures, the strategies ensure that women stay largely within the private sphere. Anything that pertains to the gender discourse in local politics and development is perceived as a palliative towards enhancing the quality of family life and male-female gender relationships. Global gender indicators need to be challenged, moving them primarily from quantitative to include qualitative indicators that demonstrate transformative ideologies and the changing balance in gendered relations.

Increasing women's participation in decision making at executive and legislative positions or in political parties may be misleading as a singular strategy to enter women in the public space. A demographic presence is not necessarily a sufficient indicator of gendered awareness or commitment to the removal of gender inequities. Women also perpetuate patriarchal ideologies that create and sustain gender inequalities and inequities. There are no easy quick fix indicators on how the formal and informal tracks of deliberative democracy within states make room for further access of gender in global confrontations and dialogues. Gender should be understood as an inherent, inseparable part of global democracy that attempts to achieve the following:

1. The representation and acceptance of women among the decision-makers so that not only is there is greater demographic balance in male and female presence in leadership at different levels but that the different concerns they raise are accepted as inherently important.
2. That gender is understood as needing the commitment of both men and women, that gender issues affect both sexes, and that the mediation of the relations between the sexes is meant to produce healthier and more enriched lives for both and the gains are not exclusive to one sex.
3. That gender interventions by way of state-commissioned gender policies break down the binary divide and appreciate the overlaps between public and private spheres as a natural constituent in the social organization of sexual difference.
4. Ensuring gender concerns are taken into account in the policies and plans that are made

for a population either by the state or industry and are enforced by civil society advocacy.

How these issues have been taken up in the formulation of national gender policies in the Caribbean are examined in Section 2.

SECTION 2: GENDER POLICIES AND DEMOCRACY IN THE CARIBBEAN

I was recruited as a consultant by various governments to work on the gender policies of the islands of Trinidad and Tobago, Cayman Islands, Dominica and the British Virgin Islands in the Caribbean.[3] Unlike Middle Eastern Islamic-based societies (Mostafa 2011) or China (Xu Jiajun 2011), the Caribbean states have evolved within systems of western democracy premised on a separation of the secular from the spiritual, although the valuing of ethnic cultural differences in gender systems and religious differences is embedded in the idea of how each nation is formed and must be confronted in policy and decision-making.

These territories have some similarities and parallels that may be noted. They are all geographically relatively small island territories, and apart from Cayman Islands and the British Virgin Islands, achieved independent status from the British Crown in the twentieth century. Both Trinidad and Dominica have influences of the French under earlier colonization while the Cayman Islands remains decidedly British while the British Virgin Islands, though still under Crown rule, at present has far more daily interaction with the nearby US Virgin Islands. All four countries inherited a form of British parliamentary democracy that promotes participation and consultation in any democratic process of decision-making.

The process of gender consultation with the various stakeholders - individual, communities, civil society, media personnel, commerce and members of the government demonstrates a democratic method of policy formulation. In each sphere of work or occupation examined, participants are asked to break down how male and female, masculinity and femininity are differently affected. For example, if the health sector is approached, how health workers treat with and understand differently the health-seeking behaviours of women versus men, the different diseases or conditions that each sex is prone to because of physical and biological differences and the resources that are made available for each are considered. The idea is always to have a policy that is shaped by the needs of the local community and accepted by the stakeholders within, thus reflecting closely their own sense of gender identity and visions for change in gender relations and gender access. In each of the various gender policies formulated, I illustrate how the above three concerns are interrogated: (1) demographic imbalances in female leadership; (2) the perception that gender is a "woman thing" and (3) that women's defined role is still to nurture the private sheltered space for men and children.

1. A demographic balance in male and female political leadership

An investigation of the rate of female participation in political decision-making in Dominica from 1985 to 2000 revealed that eight per cent of total candidates were female in the general elections of 1985, the percentage rising to 17% in the elections of 2000. This 150% increase emerged totally out of the candidature of a new party that was formed in the interval. The two other entrenched political parties had fielded the exact number of females they did at the previous election. An exploration of the longer history of women in politics in Dominica reveals that the participation rate of women in parliament for the period 1967-1988 was ten per cent. The number of women in parliament advanced by 150% from 1975 - 1979 to 1980 -1984. This coincided with the reign of the Freedom Party under the leadership of Dame Mary Eugenia Charles who was not only the first woman parliamentarian in Dominica but the most well-known and first woman in the Caribbean to become a prime minister.

From 1980 to 1988, eight women, including the speaker of the house, served in Parliament. More than half of them were directly linked to the advent of Mary Eugenia Charles as leader of the ruling Freedom Party. The three women in opposition during that period were all nominees or senators, meaning they had not contested elections. Despite the apparent growth in women's participation in parliament in the 1980's, effective female involvement in government receded, shown by the presence of only one woman with ministerial responsibility and by extension a member of Cabinet – the then Prime Minister Eugenia Charles. Women were increasingly becoming involved in the electoral and leadership process of the society, yet recurrent questions surfaced in gender policy consultations in the island. Why were women still hesitant to be presented as candidates for national and local elections? What were the lingering disabilities women faced when they enter this still male-dominated space? Would their presence and participation make a difference in the programmes implemented by government to move the society to greater gender equity and equality? The emphasis of this government was on the erosion of poverty and the stimulation of economic growth for an island continuously beset by economic challenges and natural disasters.[4] Such questions were common to all four territories considered in the Caribbean and continue to remain on the agenda for each state.

What was also noticeable as an improvement however was the rise of women to the position of permanent secretaries in the various ministries. While women did not always occupy the highest seats of power, they were responsible as permanent secretaries for major decisions in the implementation of policies and advice to ministers and thus to cabinets. They tended to head ministries that had some affinity to household care and nurturing roles, such as Education, Housing, Culture and Health, rather than Finance or National Security. And in general, these female permanent secretaries were sympathetic and aware of the different concerns which men and women had with respect to each of these areas, for instance a sensibility that the challenges of "underperformance" of young males in education compared to young women, recurs in all societies. The consultation process revealed that the effects of the local and global women's movements and efforts at gender awareness had entered the consciousness of these public servants in terms of the contributions that they brought to the table at the levels in which they functioned. It is no longer possible to assume a lack of gender awareness among women and men. In the case of both Trinidad and Tobago and the British Virgin Islands, female ministers with responsibility for "Gender Affairs" were committed to driving the policy process and piloting it through their cabinets. While their motives could be considered "politically expedient" to harness female supporters, it is clear that their defense of a gender policy required some personal commitment to gender equality, in other words, political will. Gender consultants involved in the policy consultation process were useful in guiding them how to sell the goals of gender and gender equality and equity to colleagues and to those in more powerful positions. What the policy consultative process attempted to do was to convert solutions for gender differential problems into economic gains to a society and demonstrate that these solutions relieved social destabilization and enhanced the quality of lives of all citizens in the long run. One example that was often invoked to persuade male ministers or parliamentarians was to consider the cost to the society suffered by poor male health seeking behaviours – many men are resistant to be tested for prostate cancer thus accounting for significant deaths among men.

2. Gender as inclusive of both men's and women's issues.
The still dominant interpretation of gender as rights for and about women and that it deals with "women's issues" only, leads to questions of whether these issues are considered important to local democracy. It is acceptable for a gender policy to take up issues that are understood as gendered ones, those such as violence against women and children, or issues pertaining to female reproductive health. If gender policies attempt to deal with national budgeting priorities in its public negotiations, as the Trinidad and Tobago gender policy did, then it is thought to be out of its depth, venturing into areas that femininity by definition, should not go. Once the struggle for gender equality and equity is kept within the boundaries – i.e. its bargaining with patriarchy to gain ground in the private spheres of household, family, sexuality, its relevance is more easily affirmed. Once gender begins to take up cudgels on behalf of the society itself, on issues of economic and monetary policy, then it must explain an assumed border crossing. The word "assumed" is purposefully used as the question that the insertion of gender has raised remains a pertinent one: Is there a difference between human rights and gender rights? Why are gender issues separated from and seen as a secondary component of human rights? The Universal Declaration of Human Rights by the UN General Assembly in 1948 is quite clear that these rights are indivisible.[5] As humans we live and experience life as gendered beings. Gender has always been marginalized, occupying a "ghettoized" space, when it really is an integral part of being human. Once this parallel is accepted, then it is easier to convince detractors that gender does not exclude men. Human rights are however not gender neutral and must fully accommodate difference.

The example of economic policies is a useful one to illustrate the value of gender equity with difference. In general, economic policy is formulated and executed at a macro level and tends to be viewed as gender neutral. Gender policy is relatively new to the economics discipline and even more so to macro-economic policy-making. The decisions by the Trinidad and Tobago government in 1988 to seek assistance from the IMF and World Bank were made without specific reference to whether the resulting policies would impact males in a harsher manner than females, or that single-headed households headed by females would be made worse off than those headed by males. The adjustment process entered into by 1994 did not take place without major dislocations in the area of social expenditure. In particular the burden of adjustment fell heavily in the area of capital expenditure causing an erosion of health, education and social services, with numerous gendered implications. To counteract this, the Trinidad and Tobago gender policy advocated that gender analysis be introduced as an integral tool in all future national budgetary and planning processes. If accepted, this would commit the government to carrying out the necessary training and extra legwork, dedicating funds and resources to ensuring that national budgets are cross classified by gender.

In another scenario, while gender policies have focused necessarily on the more obvious areas of abuse or discrimination such as threats women and children face through domestic abuse, violent sexual assault and the like, the guiding philosophy of a gender policy is for an all-inclusive democracy to be achieved. Men's issues, women's issues, concerns raised by lesbian, gay, bisexual, transgender and intersexed groups (LGBTI) must not be separated but brought together and perceived as existing relationally and symbiotically. Unlike the two societies of Cayman Islands and Trinidad and Tobago, Dominica presents a completely different topographic and social landscape in the region. Its largely mountainous though lush geography, monopolistic economic base which was devastated by the World Trade Organization (WTO) removal of preferential treatment for the banana trade, and as noted above, a history of consistent natural disasters being in the clear path of hurricanes, have made for high levels of poverty and unemployment. Like all Caribbean societies, Dominica also had a strong matrifocal family base. With the increasing unattractiveness of formal education to boys and men, it turned out that the rhetoric and the reality of "male marginalization" was as dominant a feature of the gender discourse in Dominica as that pertaining to issues such a domestic violence against women. Thus the gender policy consultation process in Dominica involved as many men as it did women at all levels and engaged in serious gender dialogues, ensuring that where an issue affected women, this should be matched for gender balance in terms of how it also affected men and masculinity. Interestingly enough, the problems faced by young men with troubled sexual gender identity were also discussed in committee consultations by a leading clinical psychologist in this society despite the protests by his peers.

The Dominica policy advocated open and frequent public discourse and debates through the media on the question of masculinity and the performance of manhood in Dominican society. Although men are still perceived as the main perpetrators of gender-based violence, the policy admitted to the fact that some men are also on the receiving end of this kind of violence but are less empowered to seek counselling or other forms of assistance. In addition, not all men are violent and the gender stereotyping of all males as prone to violence affects the perception of masculinity in general and the self-esteem of men in society in relation to women. Some might argue that this is an over-compensation for masculinity and a pandering to patriarchy. To address the gaps in the deliberative account of democracy, however, gender policies have to make strategic efforts to examine, perhaps even compensate for areas that are often overlooked in the original centering of women as the primary victims of gender oppression and discrimination.

3. The overlap between public and private spheres as a natural constituent in the social organization of sexual difference

In the Caribbean, the institution of the family has never maintained a static composition or definition and is constantly adapting to the changing occupational and economic demands on both women and men over time. Family members' relationships to each other have also shifted as expectations of gender roles change with new technologies of production and reproduction. Disruptions due to economic downturns, changing cultural messages about modernization, and a perceived growing empowerment of women in the workplace are blamed for an increase in violence and abuse in the household. In Cayman Islands, accelerated economic development from the sixties brought economic prosperity to some if not to all. By the end of the twentieth century, with shifting modes of production, more women found gainful employment away from the home in the public sector, commerce, manufacturing industry or financial sector and in the expanding tourism sector, along with men. This increased demand for women's time in the labour market was unaccompanied by a comparable increase in male responsibility for household tasks such as childcare or by provision of day care from the corporate or public sector.

These employment changes transformed relationships between spouses and between members of households. Households in Cayman Islands became increasingly dependent on the labour of immigrant domestic workers. In 1970, the proportion of Caymanians to non-Caymanians (i.e. those not born in the islands) was 85 per cent; in 1999, the proportion was 53 per cent and in 2008, 56 per cent. In 2000, approximately 44 per cent of the population who lived in the Cayman Islands had non-Caymanian status. The influx of migrant domestic workers changed the demographics and composition of households and altered relations between women and men. The household as a residential unit and site for domestic activities such as food preparation, cleaning and family entertainment, the socialization of the young and cultural transmission of values and traditions, in large measure, inadvertently passed to the domestic helper in the home, while mothers could now take on jobs in the public sphere.

The Cayman gender consultations had recognized the value and necessity of women's economic contribution to both household and economy. It pointed out that help in the home enabled women and men's participation in the paid productive sector of the Caymanian economy. The policy emphasized that the worth of women's economic contributions needed to be enhanced through support services provided by the public and private sectors and by gender-responsive immigration policies. Immigration policies, however, revealed a major contradiction in the democratic process. The existing immigration laws permitted work permits to both professional males and domestic helpers. While professional males were allowed to migrate with their families who lived with them in the Cayman Islands, domestic workers on the other hand, primarily female, many of whom came from the nearby society of Jamaica, were not allowed to live or settle in the society with their own families. The justification for this differentiation in the residency policy provided by the immigration authorities was that domestic helpers were low-income earners and thus a drain on the country's resources if their families entered the country. Professional males were deemed to bring added value, to the economy and society. The value that domestic workers brought to the private sphere by allowing Caymanian women to work in public sector or local industry was not taken into account. The gender policy argued that domestic helpers were important to the stability and functioning of Caymanian homes. As caregivers they ensured environmental hygiene, family nutrition and supervision of children, nursed the elderly and the sick in the household setting. The policy argued that they were key actors in the social reproduction of Cayman society although hitherto they were not viewed as adding to social capital in the public sphere. How societies organize the care and protection of the family and dependent members such as the elderly and infirm is both a private and a public issue that concerns gender directly, particularly because as a sex, women have been allocated this responsibility in the sexual division of labour. By the twenty-first century where women have entered many occupations and professions and when largely female migrant labour absorbs the roles of domestic caregivers and nurses, as have numerous women in the Cayman and British Virgin Islands, the policy argued that it was no longer possible to conceive of the organization of sexual difference into a rigid public versus private sphere. Rather it was necessary to see the role of the private sphere as supporting the public organization of goods, services and governance. Signaling the importance of housework and childcare in buttressing the state and industry is not new to the gender question. It was one of the earliest issues raised by Socialist and Marxist feminist in the 1960s and 1970s and was referred to as the Domestic Labour debate.[6]

SECTION 3: GLOBAL INFLUENCES ON NATIONAL OUTCOMES

By the late twentieth century, global discourses that emerged from WID, WAD and GAD approaches had pressured governments in the Caribbean to commit to formulating national policies for gender equity and equality. The ratification by governments of the CEDAW Convention committed them to national reporting on the status of gender in their society once every four years to the CEDAW commission. The CEDAW was supplemented by other international pressures: a commitment to the United Nations Universal Declaration of Human Rights (1948), the further stimulus of The Nairobi Forward Looking Strategies (1985), and the Millennium Development Goals - MDG's (2000). In June 2000 the United Nations reiterated the need for countries to establish strong institutional machineries for gender by hosting the Beijing+5 Conference in New York. At this conference governments were called upon once again to honour, among other things, their commitment to create or strengthen national gender machineries. Have there been any real gains from this imperative that states must take on the global gender and development discourses and prescriptions?

As signatories to conventions and by observing some of the protocols, governments were also provided with resources by UN and other NGO-related support to deliver on promises to achieve indicators of gender equality. Agencies like the UNDP and UNIFEM supported the production of the gender policies and projects that gender bureaus or gender affairs departments engaged in, among these especially the eradication of gender violence and gender and HIV/Aids intervention. For instance, in both Trinidad and Tobago and Dominica, the UNDP underwrote part of the costs related to the recruitment of consultants to the gender policy research, consultation and formulation process. Other independent initiatives internationally such as the Commonwealth Secretariat in the United Kingdom and global/regional institutions such as the German foundation Friedrich Ebert Stiftung (Jamaica Office) and the Caribbean Policy Development Centre (Barbados)[7] supported regional training workshops for women in political participation and women in governance. Such initiatives were geared to equip women to become confident and skilled political leaders.

In the published global listing, countries who have not been systematically presenting their four-year CEDAW reports are clearly identifiable against those who have done so. The quantitative global monitors, though problematic, allow for comparisons of the status of women *vis a vis* men from country to country and are used as advocacy and monitoring tools for gender-related policy discussions. For instance, the Gender Empowerment Measure (GEM) is a measure of inequality of men's and women's opportunities in three areas: political participation and decision making, economic participation and decision making, and power over economic resources. The Gender-related Development Index (GDI) measures achievement in the same basic capabilities as the Human Development Indicator, focusing on the inequality in achievement between women and men. Not all Caribbean countries commit themselves to producing these indicators. The 2010 UNDP Human Development Report lists Trinidad and Tobago and Barbados with a Gender Inequality Index of 48 and also reports on the percentage of females having seats in parliament at each successive reporting period.

In this sense the global has a continuous role in facilitating the local processes perhaps by embarrassing leaders and governments into ensuring that they measure up to other economies and societies. The exposure to global trends and changes in gender practices creates other positive effects. Whether driven by changing local cultural practices of sharing of housework and childcare by both sexes, or primarily as a result of global influences, many Caribbean societies have become far more conscious of rights and privileges to be accorded to women and men in such areas as provision of both maternity and paternity leave. The Dominica gender policy for example endorsed the need for both men and women to "be allowed to pursue the fulfillment of family life and the conditions under which men might be willing to accept such responsibilities and play equal or complementary roles to women in the nurturing and parenting of children."

Some global influences have not been successfully negotiated and there are specific issues under which the global movements have worked against the local. Sexual and reproductive rights and sexual harassment in the workplace have been two such areas in the Caribbean that resisted successful gender policy interventions. In fact the militancy from other global partners has acted against the transference of such gains locally or regionally. The 2009 Cairo workshop on the theme of democracy noted that global democracy needs to encompass and include many peoples: not only nations, but also communities based in shared class, disability, ethnicity, faith, gender, generation, and sexuality. In the attempt to incorporate issues of sexuality and alternative sexual orientation, gender policies in the Caribbean have had to first overcome major cultural perception hurdles: *first* that such policies were "foreign ideas of feminists (read lesbian) rather than homegrown concerns that were pertinent; *second*, that women in the Caribbean had all the power they could want since they were dominant as heads of households, and *third*, that homosexuality did not exist and was largely an invention of western consumer society imposed on the region by media and a vibrant tourist industry" (Kempadoo 2004). All of these perceptions had to be counteracted, especially among local communities and religious bodies, rather than among professionals who were exposed to the psychological and other effects of these denials. The popular view was that the intrusion of global and foreign ideas was destabilizing if not damaging to local customs, traditions, beliefs and practices of gender. These ideas are surprising for the region given its otherwise openness to western norms and influences of all kinds, including fashion, music and consumer goods, all fueled by consistent migrations in and out to the north. Yet the example of the non-passage of the gender policy in Trinidad and Tobago in 2007 is instructive on how conservative a population might be about ideas of gender and sexuality, even while they admit advancing technologies of communication and other items readily into their households.

The Government of Trinidad and Tobago had only ratified the CEDAW convention in 1990. The International Committee of Experts that received the report in New York in 2000 made a number of responses. Among these, the Committee observed carefully that the proposed Equal Opportunities Act of 2000 excluded sexual orientation and thus explicitly discriminated against the homosexual population. In response to the barrage of critiques resulting from the presentation of this report in New York, the state re-committed itself to the development of a national gender policy as a key instrument to critically review existing legislation and to heighten public awareness of gender related labour issues such as workplace discrimination.

Reference to homosexuality in the national gender policy document created utter havoc when the draft was made available for public discussion in 2004, (as is the democratic custom of the policy process). The policy advocated that *"The state should be proactive in initiating public debate on the discrimination suffered by persons due to sexual orientation with a view to making this a prohibited ground of discrimination under the Equal Opportunity Act and decriminalizing homosexual and lesbian acts under the Sexual Offences Act, 1986.*" The Roman Catholic Church and its associate organizations led an opposition to the adoption of the document by staging prayer and fast sessions under a large white tent for three days on a pleasant savannah green opposite the Prime Minister's office in the main city of Port of Spain. The Emmanuel Community, one of the more vocal groups in this gathering, said the document attempted to "undermine the fabric of our society." Another group named Lawyers for Jesus that had not surfaced at all during the two-year span of public consultations, also joined the camp. The media frenzy which they collectively funneled against the draft policy forced the government to quickly withdraw the document.

Given only snippets of the document by the state, those who had not been involved in the initial discussions which led to the policy choices were ill-informed about the intent of the overall policy and viewed it primarily as a mechanism to open the door to homosexuality, same-sex marriages and to promote the legalization of abortion. While non-governmental associations, particularly a vociferous body called the Network of Women's Organizations, groups such as Advocates for Safe Parenthood Improving Reproductive Equity (ASPIRE), and progressive journalists made a major bid to reinstate the policy document, fear of local political reprisal outweighed the government's commitments to international conventions and since 2006 the policy never made its way out of the cabinet discussion to be adopted and implemented.[8]

In Cayman Islands the policy was equally silent on the question of homosexuality. Like Trinidad and Tobago, Cayman Islands prided itself on being a God-fearing nation and religion plays a key role in the life of the people. As a British Overseas Territory and not a sovereign state it cannot itself ratify CEDAW so it was not duty bound to observe the demands of this convention for reporting on the status of gender under the various categories. More importantly, without a written Bill of Rights or a human rights act as an Overseas UK Territory, Cayman Islands could not undertake to draft a policy without the support of the UK government. Issues such as homosexuality were considered even more taboo if placed in the policy document for this society. The British Virgin Islands policy process echoed then a similar attitude to Trinidad and Tobago about incorporating explicit issues that challenge the heterosexual norm.

The problematic areas of abortion rights, sexual orientation and sexual identity present some of the major stumbling blocks to gender democracy and are perceived as damaging to the conservatism and religious base on which small societies fashion and ensure gendered behaviours deemed acceptable. The fears of the leadership in disavowing any commitment to the policy document in the face of such attacks, hinder the process of democratic consultation and policy making in a society.

SECTION 4 - LESSONS FOR GLOBAL DEMOCRACY FROM THE CARIBBEAN

1. The integration of national and global governance
Global discourses do not filter easily into local processes and are largely viewed with suspicion. The Cairo Global Democracy Project workshop in 2010 led by Jan Aart Scholte noted in its summary that "it is important always to ask who defines global democracy and for what purpose. Definitions always come from somewhere and promote certain interests." There is natural wariness on the part of nations that global governance again pits the more powerful and wealthy against the weaker nations and that global democracy is just another brand of imperialism. Adding to this is the issue of ethnocentrism. Globalization tends to be perceived as perpetuating a specific hegemonic, western gaze that leads to a persistently skewed ethnocentric worldview. From this point of view, global democracy appears to be a bit paradoxical. In an effort to achieve global democracy and equal rights for all, gender issues are flattened, marginalized and homogenized. How do we strive for and achieve global democracy without holding on to an ethnocentric gaze? Despite these considerations, the global watch on gender is important and impacts on the local and regional significantly.

2. Gender consultation as education and consciousness-raising of democratic rights
Although national policies for gender equity and equality are commissioned from top down, that is through international imperatives and governmental directives, the actual process of

consultation and formulation requires intensive capacity building, gender training and gender consciousness-raising internally so that the policy choices are collectively agreed, pragmatic and meaningful to change in the society. The process of consultation is carried out at all levels from the "man in the street" to the highest echelons of society, engaging with different sectors and interest groups who come together to debate gender issues and concerns. Because gender policy discussions enter the domestic space, probe the quality of relations between men and women, young and old, the intimate conditions of people's lives as well as the externalities that determine their legislative rights, entitlements to resources and access to benefits, a gender policy consultation across a society is a seriously enriching and learning exercise on the practice of democratic nation building. How are ideas of democracy conveyed generally to a population? The tendency has been to view democracy primarily in relation to electoral politics, budget, financial and economic issues, international relations and national security concerns. Gender consultations impose another level in which the concept of democracy is itself being recast.

While the incorporation of the issues such as those pertaining to alternative sexualities resulted in the non-acceptance of the policy or non-inclusion of controversial issues, frustrating to those who drove the policy process, at the same time, this must not be viewed as a wasteful exercise in democratic learning and change. What the policy consultation process does is engage opinion leaders in society and groups in discussion and debates. Many of these are sufficiently heated and passionate to alert governments that important gender issues cannot be forever ignored. The process also heightens dialogues about other aspects of human rights and responsibilities that would normally not have surfaced for major discussions, especially those pertaining to disabled populations, children, the infirmed, elderly and LGBTI issues.

3. Questions of gender equity need to lie at the heart of global civil society and associated practices of deliberative democracy
The problems of integrating national and global governance have to do with translating the minutiae of national struggles into issues of global governance. Local experiences are laden with the grounded insights and examples that can affect and infect global policies. They may either stretch or confirm the important indicators of

global democracy. For example, contemporary globalization has involved on a larger scale the movement of workers from one society to the next either as single individuals or individuals with families. What has this meant in terms of provision of citizenship, benefits, access to health services and freedom from fear of expulsion or harassment and so on are issues that need to be fine-tuned from a range of national scenarios to formulate global practices that are more universally accepted. The experiences of the Caribbean show that migration areas are sadly open to many abuses. For instance, although protocols exist for the reporting of sexual harassment by employers or sexual violence, migrant women in the BVI are afraid to report such incidents for fear of deportation. What gender equity calls into question is rooted in the everyday concerns about people's lives and livelihoods. There is a resonance here with Ezzat's point that "there has been a "shifting from a definition of democracy" to the "politics of representation" and to the more relevant and truly aspired "politics of presence" (Ezzat 2009, 12-13)

All aspects of gender equality cannot be legislated since much of this depends on the mutual agreement of trust and responsibility between parties. Arguably it is possible to achieve gender equity by firm measures imposed in workplaces and homes. At the same time the process of creating a national gender policy requires what David Moss (2017) has described as getting people to agree with what is best for them and what is possible in their society at any point in time. Deliberative gender democracy must, however, accept that what is best will vary from person to person and group to group even within the same society. The idea of the democratic decisions being made on the basis of the "collective good" may need some modification. The Caribbean experience has shown that there are differences between one society and the next even within one region and even among relatively small populations. The challenges for rethinking global democracy then have to do with the mediation between the universal and the particular.

4. Prescriptions for treatment of the patriarchal character of national parliaments

The fourth implication is that while the global conventions have tied governments into engaging with a local democratic process, it has not equally imposed penalties to the non-implementation of gender policies. In other words, there continues to be a gap between a concept of what is politically expedient and what is truly democratic. It is expedient for governments to commission policies. It is not crucial for them to honour the process that this has engaged the community in. There is collusion here globally in the lack of penalties for non-compliance with the demands of conventions.

In all of the societies examined, national parliaments retain a patriarchal character and are demographically more male centered. In an effort to ensure that gender is accepted as a legitimate concern, gender policies are called upon to demonstrate the way in which it not only affects women but also men. There is a residual and overarching fear that giving gender affairs bureau or offices more resources will further empower women and thus create a major challenge to male leadership at national levels, thus threatening patriarchy and creating the potential fear of "emasculation" of male leaders. Where women have attained powerful positions, once they can be counted as "one of the boys" who have not really tampered with the masculinity of the parliament, this is acceptable to a contemporary understanding of patriarchy. In the exercise of formulating national gender policies, a recurrent theme of numerous consultations is that men have to be convinced that the gender policy is neither about putting women at the top nor removing male power and leadership, and that it is an effort to create gender power sharing. The consultations in the Caribbean have shown that gender power sharing need not be viewed as a reduction to gender neutrality. Rather the goal is to ensure that gender differences are appreciated and observed in order to fully recognize the concept of equality. The Caribbean experience of carrying out national gender policy formulation and convincing parliaments of their value to the nation has demonstrated that men's ideas about gender, power, leadership and authority need to be specifically targeted as a gender issue in order to scale high ideological barriers that work against both local and global gender and democracy.

5. *Gender needs to be translated into a language that is absorbed in all areas of global governance*
There is a dire need to arrive at meaningful definitions of the concept of gender and the ideas of global governance that are understood

at the popular level by the practitioners and professionals in the field of gender. Academic concepts and textbook definitions are grasped by a minority. In order to make gender an integral concern across all areas of global governance, we need a language and set of ideas and arguments that convince the masses. Such expressions may vary by idiom but share a common thread of meaning that allows for buy-in rather than antagonism. The concepts of gender and patriarchy remain inaccessible and can carry negative overtones so that even beginning a dialogue is impossible. One appreciates that gender and global governance and the concept of democracy are complex and cross cutting but for this reason they must be made more amenable to easy understanding. If not the cultural and personal fears that people possess will become further sites of resistance to global discourses. The conflation of gender with feminism, gay rights movement, gay liberation, homosexual rights, abortion rights, sexual freedoms and sexual liberation for women has been a necessary but unfortunate rite of passage that has dogged a movement intended to bring about radical change. One of the lessons from the experience of the Caribbean is that these symbolic representations embodied in language that spur on rejection even without unpacking meanings have worked against gender and global democracy rather than for it.

CONCLUSION

The marginality of the gendered voice in making these connections still leaves gender democracy as the out-runner in the field of politics and governance. Gender issues are relegated to the sidelines as the question of governance moves back and forth between the local and global tracks.

The issues selected above illustrate the complexity of the relationship between gender and democracy. They demonstrate how gender analyses and demands have shown up the weak underbelly of democracy itself in its unwillingness to take on the most fundamental problems that gender has presented to a rethinking of the human condition - for example a re-consideration of the value of family and household as the core economic and social and decision-making units of society, a theory that underscores Friedrich Engels *The Origin of the Family, Private Property and the State* in the nineteenth century and is still relevant to contemporary thought. At present states seem to be largely invested in a *gender democracy of convenience* – to strategically engage with the process of commissioning policies as a gender spin on democracy, and to ensure they satisfy the growing mass of educated women in leadership positions in professions, industry and public sector, while remaining unconvinced that the policies that are proposed will seriously impact on the collective good of the nation. The experience of crafting and arguing for democratic changes through the introduction of gender policies in the Caribbean again reinforces how marginal gender remains when it was viewed primarily as women's issues and when it did not appear to take on the 'gender' issues that affected men. It also demonstrated quite categorically that the democratic process within internal states could not appreciate that the gap between public and private had diminished considerably since women now occupied both areas fully, perhaps had always done, and that this was a major oversight in the interpretation of the relationship between gender and the democratic process.

In conclusion, it seems to me that despite the problems of arriving at completely shared notions of what global democracy is, people maintain ideas and ideals about good governance. In the Caribbean, perhaps because of the relatively small size of nations, there is a strong view that individuals or groups possess a certain agency and autonomy to shape the national policies that affect their daily lives and to have a say in how they are governed, and by whom. This optimism of democratic intervention by Caribbean people is expressed in the idiom that "better mus come." They recognize the need to fight for the rights of their children, even if they envisage no hope of change in their own lifetimes. Such a sentiment still ensures that within any society, many committed groups and individuals do participate in collective processes that result in some measure of transformation. This optimism is even more exemplary in the sense that, by and large, people eschew a *politics of blame*, opting for solutions out of critiques. The efforts of Cayman Islands, Trinidad and Tobago, Dominica and the British Virgin Islands to implement national gender policies for equity and equality still present good examples of this optimism and belief in an inherent notion of democracy that people honour to preserve human rights and dignities and thus to the worthiness of the concept of democracy even while we continue to reconfigure its parts.

ENDNOTES

[1] See Carol Pateman, *The Sexual Contract*, Bloomington, Indiana: Standford University Press, Ch. 1. "Patriarchal Confusions" and Ch. 3. "Genesis Fathers and the Political Liberty of sons".

[2] By 2018, the effects of women's struggles to gain ascendancy in the Anglophone Caribbean were seen in the elections of Janet Jagan, President, Guyana (1997 - 1999), Pamela Gordon, Premier, Bermuda (1997 - 1998), Jennifer Smith, Premier of Bermuda (1998 - 2003), Paula Cox, Premier of Bermuda (2010 - 2012) Portia Simpson-Miller, Prime Minister, Jamaica (2006 - 2007; 2012 - 2016), Kamla Persad-Bissessar, Prime Minister, Trinidad and Tobago (2010 - 2015), Sharlene Cartwright-Robinson, Premier, Turks and Caicos Islands (2016 - present) and Mia Mottley, Prime Minister, Barbados, (2018 - present).

[3] I was also recruited in 2017 to assist the Government of Guyana with its formulation of a national gender policy. My thanks to those I have worked with closely in various settings, among these Audrey Ingram Roberts, Marilyn Connolly, Rhoda Reddock, Leith Dunn, Rosie Browne, Gaietry Pargass, Deborah Mc Fee, Jane Parpart and Patricia Hackett.

[4] The island of Dominica has continuously suffered set backs in the 20th century from hurricanes and tropical storms, among these David in 1979, Georges in 1998, Dean in 2007, Tropical Storm Erika in 2009 and Maria in 2017.

[5] See https://www.un.org/en/universal-declaration-human-rights/

[6] See https://newleftreview.org/issues/I116/articles/maxine-molyneux-beyond-the-domestic-labour-debate

[7] Friedrich Ebert Stiftung (Jamaica) was led by Judith Wedderburn and the Caribbean Policy Development Centre by Cecila Babb both of whom spearheaded a project on gender policy writing and training of women for public office in 2002-4. I was privileged to participate in this project which was launched in several Caribbean countries.

[8] As an update on this in 2011-12 another draft policy was created and circulated, drawing from the original draft but edited and revised to entertain some of the concerns raised on the definition of gender and on other issues that had surfaced since the first draft. Currently, as I understand it a final version reshaped from the last draft is under consideration by the Trinidad and Tobago Cabinet.

REFERENCES

Antrobus, Peggy. 1984. "The English-speaking Caribbean: A Journey in the Making." In *Sisterhood is Global*, edited by Robin Morgan. New York: Anchor Books, pp 118-125.

Cayman Islands. Compendium of Statistics, Economics and Statistics Office, Government of Cayman Islands, http://www.eso.ky/pages1.php?page=populationandvitalstatistics

Cuales, Sonia. 1984. "The Dutch-speaking Caribbean Islands: Fighting until the End" In *Sisterhood is Global*, edited by Robin Morgan. New York: Anchor Books, pp 114-117.

Erman, Eva. 2009. "Globalizing the Rule by the People: A Deliberative View." Draft Paper presented to Building Global Democracy Workshop, Cairo, 6-8 December, 2009.

Eschle, Catharine. 2000. "Gender and Gobal Democracy." *Gender and Global Democracy, Issue 3*, University of Sussex, p. 32.

Ezzat, Heba R. 2009. "On the Future of Women and Politics in the Arab World." Cairo University.

Government of Cayman Islands. 2002. *Cayman Islands National Policy on Gender Equity and Equality, (draft)*. Consultants: Patricia Mohammed and Audrey Ingram Roberts. Cayman Committee Chair, Marilyn Connolly.

Government of the Commonwealth of Dominica. 2006. *The National Gender Policy for Gender Equity and Equality in Dominica*. Lead consultant Patricia Mohammed with Deborah Mc Fee, prepared by the Consultants with a Committee led by Ms Rosie Browne of the Gender Affairs Desk of Dominica.

Government of the Republic of Trinidad and Tobago, *The National Gender Policy on Equity and Equality for Trinidad and Tobago, (draft)*. Consultant Institution: Centre for Gender and Development Studies, The University of the West Indies, St Augustine. Lead Consultants Rhoda Reddock and Patricia Mohammed

Halapua, Sitiventi and Peau Halapua. 2011. "Global Democracy as Talanoa: A Pacific Perspective." International Studies Association Paper, Montreal.

Xu Jiajun, Ma Ben and Peng Zongchao. 2011. "Cooperative-harmonious Global Democracy from the Perspective of Chinese Culture – The Case of the World Bank's Development Assistance in China." International Studies Association Paper, Montreal.

Kempadoo, Kamala. 2004. Sexing the Caribbean: Gender, Race and Sexual Labor. London and New York: Routledge.

Massiah, Joycelin. 1986. "Women and the Caribbean Project: An Overview," *Social and Economic Studies*, 35 (2): 1-29.

Miller, Errol. 1986. *Marginalization of the Black Male*, Institute of Social and Economic Research, University of the West Indies, Jamaica.

Miller, Errol. 1991. *Men at Risk*, Kingston, Jamaica: Jamaica Publishing House.

Mohammed, Patricia and Althea Perkins. 1999. *Caribbean Women at the Crossroads: The Paradox of Motherhood among Women of Barbados, St. Lucia and Dominica*. Canoe Press, University of the West Indies, Barbados, Jamaica and Trinidad and Tobago.

Momsen, Janet. 1993. *Women and Change in the Caribbean: A Pan-Caribbean Perspective*. Kingston, Indiana and London: Ian Randle Publishers, Indiana University Press and James Currey.

Moss, David. 017. *Democracy: A Case Study*. Belknap Press: An imprint of Harvard University Press, Cambridge, MA

Mostafa, Nadia. 2011. "Beyond Western Paradigms of International Relations: Towards an Islamic Perspective on Global Democracy." Paper presented to International Studies Association, Montreal 16-19 March 2011.

Mwatha, Regina Gathoni. 2009. Gender Empowerment and Global Democracy: Experiences from Kenya. Draft paper presented to Building Global Democracy Workshop, Cairo, 6-8 December, 2009.

Pangsapa, Piya and Mark J. Smith. 2008. "Political Economy of Southeast Asian Borderlands: Migration, Environment and Developing Country Firms" *Journal of Contemporary Asia*, 38 (4): 485–514.

Stearns, Jill. 2007. "Global Governance: A Feminist Perspective." In *Governing Globalization: Power, Authority and Global Governance*, edited by David Held and Anthony McGrew. Cambridge: Polity Press.

Stiglitz, Joseph. 2002. *Globalization and its Discontents*, New York: W.W. Norton. Cited in Richard Sandbrook, Mark Edelman, Patrick Heller and Judith Teichman. 2007. *Social Democracy in the Global Periphery: Origins, Challenges, Prospects*, Cambridge, UK: Cambridge University Press.

Trinidad and Tobago Report to CEDAW. 2000. Government of Trinidad and Tobago.

16

Profiling the Gender Sensitivity of Nations[†]

INTRODUCTION

When men and women go about their daily lives, are gender differences, opposition and discrimination by sex uppermost in their minds? An awareness of oneself as a sex, or a preoccupation with one's sexuality or sexual identity may be the prominently conscious component of gender. It is more than likely that only academics and gender activists or experts probably have a sharpened gender lens and both problematize and define gender with the complexity with which it is used for various applications: as biology, sexual orientation, sexual relations, the encoded set of beliefs, practices and uneven hierarchies that maintain sexual difference in society, or the performance of gender as an identifier of sexual or class or racialized cultural groupings.

[†] This paper was presented at The University of the West Indies Symposium "Research, Enterprise and Impact" on the Panel: *Facilitating Evidence-based Policy Making* (2013). The conference was organized by the Office of the Campus Principal, then Professor Clement Sankat and coordinated by Dr. Stacy Richards-Kennedy. The paper has not been previously published.

Identities are not stable. "All individuals possess multiple identities and different ones come into play at different times. These multiple identities are selectively mobilized as a response to economic, political, social and cultural processes" (Ganneri 2013). As Donna Haraway (1994) observed, some identities are adopted through self-conscious choice. Alissa Trotz noted that some identities are stimulated through the imperatives of globalization and transnationality that force an awareness of one's ethnic, class or gender status differently because of migration and resettlement in another society (Trotz 2007). Gender systems are also not fixed. They are negotiated over spans of historical time and cultural shifts that allow for challenging gender roles and changing conceptions of masculinity and femininity (Mohammed 2002). If as Joan Scott has noted,[1] this might be examined over distinctive periods through the lens of history, Hosein has examined how in contemporary Trinidad society, younger women who have grown up in a more gender sensitive age now begin this navigation of gender identities relatively early in life (Hosein 2004).

When do women or men consider that they have suffered gender discrimination? Are young babies born with a natural awareness of a gendered script? The biological determinist school, convinced that biology regulates such characteristics as ability, preferences and even occupational choices, would have us think that chromosomes, sex organs, hormones and other physical features predispose gendered behaviour. On the other hand social constructivists argue that our gender identities, like our definitions of race and ethnicity, are created through our lived relationship with others and through beliefs and practices in society, rather than shaped primarily by a biological and immutable force (Eliot 2009).

In one of the most revolutionary books published in the second wave feminist movement in 1970, Germaine Greer wrote:

> In order to approximate those shapes and attitudes which are considered normal and desirable, both sexes deform themselves, justifying the process by referring to the primary, genetic difference between the sexes. But of forty-eight chromosomes only one

is different: on this difference we base a complete separation of male and female, pretending as it were that all forty-eight were different. (Greer 1970).

Do nations organize around these assumed natural differences constituted by the single chromosome? Of course they do! Adam Smith (*The Wealth of Nations* 1776) and Karl Marx (*Das Capital* 1867) have established that nations have to be organized around how skilled labour is appropriated, who owns the means of production and who controls the labour power of the working and professional classes, and how the sexual division of labour is understood in a society. Feminist thought, which identified gender as its key concept, has demonstrated extensively, beginning with Friedrich Engels (*The Origin of the Family, Private Property and the State 1884*), continuing with Simone De Beauvoir (*The Second Sex* 1949) and Michel Foucault (*A History of Sexuality* 1978) that the collective term labour must be further disaggregated into the elements that describe and define how human labour and human sexuality are actually appropriated and controlled. To maintain a productive work force, society requires the reproduction of human beings – live bodies whose arms, legs and brains, eyes and ears, are utilized for goods and services. Production requires the care, protection and classification of the sexed body as masculine and feminine within institutions like the family, church and school, along with the disciplining of sexuality in order to regulate work schedules and divide tasks into male and female competencies. It is not difficult to comprehend why such a strict sexual division of labour has required adherence to the idea of a heterosexual norm.

This is not to assume that all nations have organized the sexes in exactly the same way over time, nor to agree that human sexuality can be fully controlled and contained to benefit capitalism. In fact, the cultural variations that have emerged over space and time are proof of the ongoing rapprochement that actually exists between biological determinism and social constructivism in the lived culture of any society: i.e. that people do not live out their lives as dictated only by biological imperatives. For example in India, the creation of the caste system presents a new organization of labour informed by occupational divisions and a strict hierarchy that is preserved through religious belief systems. But even so, castes are still subdivided into male and female roles and sustained by the strict sanctions on caste endogamy that ensured the constant reproduction of the caste system. In the Caribbean, the experience of African slavery under European colonization also demonstrates that a strict sexual division of labour was not observed among the enslaved where both men and women were made to work similarly under the whip.[2] Both men and women worked as field labourers and were equally deprived of the rights to produce a family and live under one roof. In an examination of African labour in the British Caribbean in 1834 Barry Higman calculated that "...81.7% of the slaves were classified as active in the labour force. Indeed the only slaves excluded were children under 6 years of age (13.6% of the population) and those classed as "aged, diseased, or otherwise noneffective" (4.7%)."[3] The category "field labourers" accounted for almost 75% of the active labour force, a category from which women were by no means excluded, although as Higman has demonstrated, a division of labour that established more females as domestic slaves could be found even then. The way in which people are organized in any territorial division in order to ensure the control of wealth, along with the survival of classes, castes, ethnic groups, is a complex one both determined and challenged by sexual difference and the intractability of human sexuality.

What feminism and the evolving interdisciplinary area of gender studies have demonstrated is that the social organization of masculinity and femininity and the continued construction of sexual difference have not been equitable for both sexes.[4] Heidi Hartman (1979) and Michelle Barratt (1980) among many others demonstrated that the relationship between patriarchy (organized male domination) and capitalism was an unhappy one for women. They argued that women's labour and women's childbearing capacity had been appropriated without equitable recompense to ensure the creation of the surplus required for a thriving capitalism. But neither author reduced women's oppression primarily to the terms set out by capitalism or to the idea of a patriarchy that is biologically predestined. Both argue for a full comprehension of the role of ideology in shaping social relations, already pointing to the way in which sex and gender were highly complicated categories of social analysis undergoing further theoretical unravelling with each generation of scholars.

Twentieth century proliferation of ideas on gender performance and queer theory was a further theoretical attempt to grasp how gender and sexual difference can be at the same time culturally diverse in different societies yet possess universal consistencies. Judith Butler (1990, 1993), observed that the gendered division into maleness and femaleness was itself problematic and that human beings functioned on a more subversive plane. Butler argues that gender is a studied or invented performance of maleness and femaleness and that there are legitimate alternatives to traditional gender and sexual identities. These unmapped alternatives had to be accounted for in order to respect the full range of human sexual and social potential. Some known examples of other gender and sexual identities are the *hijras* of India defined as neither man nor woman and allocated a definition of the third sex (Serena Nanda 1999) and the practice of female husbands in the Igbo culture of Nigeria which conferred on daughters the rights to inheritance where there were no sons to inherit (Amadiume 1987). Nwoko (2012) explains that unlike a lesbian relationship "…woman to women marriage or female husbands was more pronounced than might be supposed especially in Africa where it occurred in over 30 societies, including; the Igbo of southeastern Nigeria, the Zulu of Southern Africa, the Nuer of East Africa …suggesting the flexibility and dynamism that have attained gender roles in Africa."[5] He notes, however, that these arrangements unfortunately emerged to bolster a system of patriarchy rather than as a challenge to ideologies of dominance and control.

GENDER INEQUALITY AS A PROBLEM AND A SOLUTION TO DEVELOPMENT

The historical records, literature and criminal records of any nation render up innumerable instances where women demonstrated that they were uneasy with the rule of patriarchy. For instance, in western English literature fifteenth century Chaucer's *Canterbury Tales*, sixteenth century Shakespeare's plays and the early nineteenth century Jane Austen novels have many examples of women's challenges to male control or baulking under the strictures of a limited range of behaviours expected of femininity. The ideology of feminism becomes more evident only from the later nineteenth century when women began to demand equality in various arenas, especially that of the right to vote and to education. Women's struggles for freedoms were not restricted to Europe. The story of Sor Juana Inés de la Cruz born Juana Ramírez de Asbaje (possibly in 1651), in Mexico is an interesting example. According to her biographers, Juana was born out of wedlock and thirsted for knowledge from her early days but as a female she had little or no access to learning and was thus self-taught. Her mother was a Creole and her father Spanish (Mexico was then under the rule of Spain). Juana's mother sent her gifted daughter to live with relatives in Mexico City where, through her intelligence, she attracted the attention of the viceroy, Antonio Sebastián de Toledo, Marquis de Mancera.

> He invited her to court as a lady-in-waiting in 1664 and later had her knowledge tested by some 40 noted scholars. In 1667, given what she called her "total disinclination to marriage" and her wish 'to have no fixed occupation which might curtail my freedom to study,' Sor (Spanish: "Sister") Juana began her life as a nun with a brief stay in the order of the Discalced Carmelites. She moved in 1669 to the more lenient Convent of Santa Paula of the Hieronymite order in Mexico City, and there she took her vows. Sor Juana remained cloistered in the Convent of Santa Paula for the rest of her life. Convent life afforded Sor Juana her own apartment, time to study and write, and the opportunity to teach music and drama to the girls in Santa Paula's school.[6]

Sor Juana served the convent as an archivist and accountant, amassing in her convent cell one of the largest private libraries then held in the New World. As an early renaissance woman of the west she also collected musical and scientific instruments, continued her contact with scholars and powerful persons in the Spanish court and became the unofficial court poet in the 1680s, producing a body of work that included plays in verse, poetry and religious services that were used widely outside of the convent. She died on April 17, 1695, Mexico City as an outstanding poet, dramatist, scholar, and nun, a writer of the Latin American colonial period and of the Hispanic Baroque. Among other examples of unusual women who challenged the strict division of labour allotted to women was the great French-Italian author Christine de Pizan. She was born in Venice but moved to Paris when her father was appointed astrologer at the court of Charles V (1364-1380 CE). According to Pizan's own works, "her father encouraged her literary interests while her mother felt she should restrict herself to 'women's work' such as learning to spin and weave cloth. Left with no means of supporting her family after both her father and husband died, Pizan turned to writing, becoming the first female professional writer in European history."[7]

To assume that a consciousness of gender inequality did not exist in the past is to be blinkered about the many forms of gender inequity found in all cultures and the reasons why these would coalesce into a global movement by the late twentieth century. Christine de Pizan and Sor Juana's stories echo with many other women who have rebelled or navigated freedoms outside of the norm, among them Abigail Adams and Sojourner Truth in the United States, Mary Wollstonecraft and the Pankhurst sisters in the United Kingdom, and Amy Garvey and Audrey Jeffers in the Caribbean. Irene Tinker reminds us that progress is not even. "We all know that women's rights and autonomy have certainly not progressed in a linear fashion throughout history. Like the rise and fall of empires, women's roles have altered as the predominant cultures or beliefs have constructed women's lives to suit their purpose."[8]

By the late twentieth century, gender equality and equity became more integrally linked to the concept of citizenship. Critiques of citizenship came from the work of feminist theorists who sought to expose the male biases inherent in notions of citizenship. Nira Yuval Davis focussed on the distinctive separation between the family/private and the political/public spheres that continued to exclude women from citizenship. She argued for a concept of active citizenship that promoted participation by women and other marginalised groups in decision making either at state or community levels.[9] The advancement of gender equality and gender rights as human rights also began to emerge as an indicator of the development of a nation. The accelerated evolution of ideas from the late twentieth century – referred to as a second wave feminist or "women's liberation" movement – coincides with the emergence of the birth control pill that afforded women more choice in reproduction, and increasing access to education in most societies. Changing philosophies regarding human rights and freedoms and a new media that aided the rapid spread of ideas through the printed word and television allowed for the groundswell of a consciousness that before had been isolated to individuals or groups within countries. This systematic study of gender and exposure of the condition of women in many states provided evidence that societies suffered underdevelopment if one half of their populations remained voiceless. The real accounting of women's labour in society had, however, begun many years before.

Published in 1970, *The Role of Women in Economic Development*[10] by Danish economist Esther Boserup examined what women's labour actually contributed to the economic development of nations. She disagreed that in Africa there was a natural sexual division of labour where women were primarily occupied in domestic and nurturing roles, while men were engaged in actual farming and food production. She pointed out "Africa is the region of female farming par excellence. In many African tribes, nearly all the tasks connected with food production continued to be left to women" (Boserup 1970, 4). Boserup's work highlighted not only the silences about women's contribution but the way in which this undervaluing of women in society led to their further subordination in other spheres. For example, although women maintained the survival of their families, they were not allowed to open saving accounts on their own, to handle their own investments, to make choices about the lives of their children and so on.

Boserup's thesis connecting women to development was very persuasive and influenced policies in economic development, linking these directly to reproductive health. Boserup argued, drawing on but departing from the Malthusian concern with the relationship between population growth and economic development, that women's capacity and decision-making about childbearing was important to their continued efficient participation in development, especially when increasing urbanization impacted more and more on the failure to produce adequate food supplies for a nation. She argued that the way to control family planning was to give women access to educational opportunities that would promote both better health status of families and lead to their choices in a reduction in births. In other words, allow women more agency in these areas of life where they were hindered by cultural practices or social policies. In 1974, at the first United Nations (UN) World Population Conference in Bucharest her ideas were incorporated, anticipating the resolutions made twenty years later at the UN Population Conference in Cairo in 1994.

The United Nations advocacy for global gender justice is central to the way in which gender equality and equity is negotiated currently. "The Preamble to the Charter of the United Nations sets as one of the Organization's central goals the reaffirmation of faith in fundamental human rights, in the dignity and worth of the human person, in the equal rights of men and women."[11] The Commission on the Status of Women (CSW) was originally established in 1946, first as a sub-commission of the Commission on Human Rights, and soon after, pressured by women's activists, as a full commission. The CSW focused close attention to those areas where human rights treaties did not make specific provisions.

> Between 1949 and 1959, the Commission elaborated the Convention on the Political Rights of Women, adopted by the General Assembly on 20 December 1952, the Convention on the Nationality of Married Women, adopted by the Assembly on 29 January 1957, the Convention on Consent to Marriage, Minimum Age for Marriage and Registration of Marriages adopted on 7 November 1962, and the Recommendation on Consent to Marriage, Minimum Age for Marriage and Registration of Marriages adopted on 1 November 1965. Each of these treaties protected and promoted the rights of women in areas in which the Commission considered such rights to be particularly vulnerable.[12]

At the same time that Boserup was producing convincing arguments that influenced policies regarding women's health and reproduction, the CSW were actively engaged in ensuring that there was global acceptance in eradicating all areas of discrimination against women. The CSW was also encouraged by the World Plan of Action for the Implementation of the Objectives of the International Women's Year, adopted by the World Conference of the International Women's Year held in Mexico City in 1975, which called for a convention on the elimination of discrimination against women, with effective procedures for its implementation. In 1974, at its 25th session, the Commission decided to prepare a single, comprehensive and internationally binding instrument to eliminate discrimination against women. This instrument underwent exhaustive discussions and drafting for another four years before it emerged as a binding *Convention on the Elimination of Discrimination against Women* in 1979, referred to as the CEDAW convention. At Copenhagen on 17th July 1980, "64 States signed the Convention and two States submitted their instruments of ratification. On 3 September 1981, 30 days after the twentieth member State had ratified it, the Convention entered into force – faster than any previous human rights convention had done – thus bringing to a climax United Nations effort to codify comprehensively international legal standards for women."[13]

One could argue that attitudes, practices and social policies in gender have been brought about by the coalitions and even antagonisms among three forces. The *first* comprises the individual or small non-governmental organized groups such as the suffragette women in the early twentieth century who militantly argued for the vote for women. Or women like the controversial Marie Stopes who was born in 1880 in the United Kingdom, and Margaret Sanger in the United States, both of whom were pioneers in the history of contraception and in the promotion of family planning clinics, thus allowing women a choice in childbearing. Challenges were not always confrontational but, as that exemplified by Sor Juana above, were demonstrative of the talent that was being wasted if not recognized. The *second* is that which came through organized civil society pressures, the church groups, social workers, professional bodies and so on. For instance, one of the leading forces for change in Trinidad was that of the Coterie of Social Workers led by Audrey Jeffers

(Reddock 1994). In the more recent history of feminist struggle in Trinidad, women's groups aligned along with other supporters were responsible for major changes in attitudes to rape and domestic violence in Trinidad and elsewhere in the Caribbean. Others such as CAISO – the Coalition Advocating for Inclusion of Sexual Orientation formed in 2009 in response to the Trinidad and Tobago Cabinet's unwillingness to admit to the existence of alternative sexualities in the society, also pushed the gender agenda into coalitions with LGBT issues. The *third* force is that of the necessary compliances that have been forced by global UN agencies onto regional blocs and individual governments. While the process of achieving change may appear to be top down, there is an ongoing and symbiotic relationship that takes place between and among all of these levels.

Between 1989 and 1990 eleven Caribbean countries ratified the CEDAW convention and several commissioned national gender policies for equity and equality. The ratification of the CEDAW commits the government to reporting to a global assembly on the status of women in relation to men under various heads such as women's access to political power, the efforts being made to reduce gender-based violence, gendered access to education and employment and the enhancement of legislation that protects the rights of women and children, among others. Deborah McFee notes that "Internal pressures and the desire to fit into the larger regional and international gender and development scripts have led six Caribbean states to engage in the process of developing a national policy on gender. These countries include Cayman Islands, Trinidad & Tobago, Dominica, British Virgin Islands, Jamaica, Bahamas and Belize."[14]

In addition to the progress of nations being examined through the implementation of gender policy actions, there are actual global statistical measures that have been put in place to compare the levels of inequality between societies. The two gender measures are accounted under human development – the first is the Gender Empowerment Measure (GEM) and the second, the Gender Development Indicator (GDI). The GDI is the Human Development Indicator (HDI) discounted for gender inequality. The GEM calculates an index for empowerment by examining the parliamentary representation, managerial and administrative positions and professional and technical positions held by men and women in the society.[15]

What nations are concerned with, in general, by the twenty-first century, is good governance practices that respect human rights. At present some of the key problems that have surfaced and are part of the contemporary movement to ensure gender equality and equity are conventional ones associated with gender-based violence – these include rape, domestic violence, incest, reproductive rights of women and girls and increasingly children, pedophilia, pornography and human trafficking for sexual purposes. The eradication of gender-based violence remains high on the agenda of most societies, as gender violence generally reflects some form of abuse of power. In addition, heterosexism has been challenged and most societies now are involved in some debates that attempt to diffuse this singular assumption of human sexuality. Most societies now also accept education for women and girls as given, such that societies where this right is abused undergo sanctions by others. Women's access to political decision-making has increasingly come under the microscope of gender and there are quotas being allocated for women in political parties and in cabinets in some societies. Gender as a concept once allied only with women and femininity has expanded in usage to fully embrace the condition of both sexes; the different ways in which men live their masculinity and are confronted by gender identity issues is another area that has come under close scrutiny.

WHAT ARE THE RISKS TO NATIONS FOR IGNORING GENDER INEQUITIES?

What if nations did not take this new imperative of gender into account? The 1995 *United Nations Human Development Report* underscores its mandate: "Human Development, if not engendered, is endangered."[16] Ignoring gender problems can seriously impact not only the individual in a society, but collectively, the capacity for nations to realize their potential for development. Drawing primarily on Caribbean examples, this section demonstrates losses to the community, or to the well-being of a sex, if some issues of gender are not confronted with policy or legal remedies.

Child marriages, Teenage pregnancy and policies related to adolescent motherhood
When the problem of child marriages was being debated in India in the nineteenth and twentieth centuries, one of the primary reasons outlined for arresting the early marriage of young girls was the physical and psychological unpreparedness of the young mother. This was a very valid concern. Not only was the young girl not given a chance to develop biologically into womanhood, being herself little more than a child, she was still unprepared to undertake the needs of an offspring. By the twenty-first century, most nations have now outlawed child marriages. In Trinidad and Tobago, until 2017, the Hindu and Muslim Marriage Acts allowed for the legal marriage of young girls. The Muslim marriage act Chapter 8 had established "The age at which a person, being a member of the Muslim community is capable of contracting marriage shall be sixteen in the case of males and twelve in the case of females" while the Hindu Marriage Act 11. (1) recorded the age at which a person, being a member of the Hindu faith or religion, is capable of contracting marriage shall be eighteen years in the case of males and fourteen years in the case of females." On 9th June, 2017 the Parliament of Trinidad and Tobago passed the Miscellaneous Provisions (Marriage) Bill, 2016[17] which amended the Marriage Act, the Muslim Marriage and Divorce Act, the Hindu Marriage Act and the Orisa Marriage Act. The amendment is an absolute prohibition against marriage under 18. In addition the Trinidad and Tobago Parliament rejected an exception proposed by the group - *Coalition against Child Marriage* - which would have allowed marriages of persons between 16 and 18 under limited circumstances and with judicial consent.

"Is it better to build a place for young, unwed mothers than to marry underage girls?"[18] asked the Secretary General of the Sanatan Dharma Maha Sabha (SDMS) in one of the debates in 2013 in Trinidad and Tobago on the legal age of marriage. In the argument of the Secretary General of the SDMS, the law provided an escape route for underage girls who become pregnant. The solution he proposed for teenage pregnancy then was to ensure that girls give birth within marriage. The 2013 State of the World Population report released by the United Nations Population Fund titled "Motherhood in Childhood: Facing the challenge of adolescent pregnancy" had put forward the view that there is need for an "ecological approach" to adolescent pregnancy "that takes into account the full range of complex drivers that conspire against the adolescent girl to increase the likelihood of her pregnancy."[19] Family determinants are high on the list of factors that influence teenage pregnancy. Single-headed households, stability of the family, the degree of conflict or violence between family members, the levels of poverty from which a young girl might be trying to escape, whether she is at school, whether her mother also became pregnant as a teenager, might be some of the key factors that lead teenage pregnancy. All of these are underscored by cultural attitudes. Historically in the Caribbean, heterosexual masculinity and femininity are demonstrated by the fathering or bearing of a child, and some of these legacies remain, particularly in garrison or under-resourced communities. In the former the *droit de seigneur* takes prevalence over age restrictions. In the latter, young girls from unsteady homes seek alternatives to overcrowded households or even to peer pressure to demonstrate evidence of their womanhood. While the target for prevention of teenage pregnancies has been the young girl, the problem, as noted above in the "ecological approach" has to contend equally with masculinity. Nor should we assume that only young boys are responsible for impregnating young girls. In fact it has been proven that girls are more likely to go into sexual relationships with older men who have more to offer in the way of consumer goods and luxuries.

In general teenagers are unprepared for the experience of motherhood. One case study highlighted through the United Nations Fund for Population Activities (UNFPA) in Jamaica demonstrates this.

"Becoming pregnant at such a young age was a terrifying experience. I did not know what to do when I found out,"[20] said 17-year-old Joelle as she recounted the emotional turmoil of being pregnant during her teenage years. "It was going to be my final year in high school. I would have been graduating and making my parents proud," she recalled. "I was so horrified, ashamed and devastated to see that all the things I wanted would not happen." The Adolescent Mothers Programme of the Women's Centre Foundation of Jamaica that Joelle is enrolled in is a "good practice" model for other countries. Through the intervention of the Women's Centre Foundation, Joelle was able to finish high school and end of the year examinations, "Thanks to the Women's Centre, I have a second chance to make things right, to have an education and to make my parents proud again."[21]

The consequence of teenage pregnancy in most societies is expulsion from school, ultimately leading to low education levels of those who become teenage mothers, increased levels of poverty, and the creation of more single headed households. As Esther Boserup had pointed out in the twentieth century, the control of reproduction can be aided through better educational opportunities to women thus producing improved health status of mother and child and enhanced family life. The Jamaican good practices spearheaded for many years by the Women's Centre of Jamaica Foundation and the Ministry of Education, an alliance between civil society and government, was in 2013 approved by its Cabinet as a policy on the *Reintegration of Adolescent Mothers into the Formal Education System*. The policy allows all school-aged young girls to continue their education during and after childbirth. According to the policy, teenage mothers cannot be denied entry to their schools to continue their education while pregnant and must be accepted back or can enter new schools if they so choose after they have given birth.

Confronting teenage pregnancy is a good indicator of how a society comes to terms with gender equality and equity. It demonstrates a regard for problems in femininity at different ages rather than exhibiting a punitive attitude towards those who absorb wrong gender messages or are misguided by cultural norms. An offer of protection and continued support can guard against offspring repeating the cycle. The Minister of Education of Trinidad and Tobago, speaking in the Senate in 2014, noted that for "every 15 new patients in the ante-natal clinic, 10 were teenagers." The statistics he reveals show that most of the teenagers had become pregnant for fathers who were between the ages of 25-40 and that some of the mothers were below the ages of 12. Research from the Faculty of Medicine at The University of the West Indies showed that by age 19, more than 1,000 young women already had four children.[22]

The implications are far reaching. Many men were therefore getting away with statutory rape, as teenage pregnancies were under-reported; among these were girls in primary schools who were summarily dismissed from attending schools. With over 2500 teenage pregnancies reported each year in Trinidad and Tobago, the problem needs a solution that demonstrates that the society does not turn a blind eye to the legal issues involved as well as to the signals it sends about the potential value of these young women as responsible and productive citizens.

Young men at risk
The problem of young males, whether this is referred to as marginalization or underachievement, has become a dominant concern of gender, not only in the Caribbean, but certainly in the west. The news items and headlines about young men and crime have become commonplace into the second decade of the twenty-first century. "In the Caribbean today the number of rapes, armed robbery, assaults and other forms of violence committed by black males has increased significantly from three decades ago. On the other hand, the ratio of female-to-male performance in education is at 65% to 35%. In Dominica, an Eastern Caribbean state, for every five students moving on to college only one is male. The 20% representation of males in higher education is similar to the statistics in the United States amongst blacks. Caribbean governments are concerned about this new phenomenon and are looking for solutions."[23]

The problems of young men and criminality, male unemployment, a *laissez faire* attitude to education, and their increasing marginalization from the family have emerged as a major one leading to numerous studies, reports, programmatic reforms and policies. In four national gender policy consultation processes, in the Cayman Islands, Dominica, Trinidad and Tobago and the British Virgin Islands, this problem was recurrently posed.[24] The changing system of gender relations, wrought by changes in production, technologies, demands for equal rights and opportunities, shifting population and climate issues that require new ways of thinking about survival, have led to a crisis in which masculinity no longer occupies the same position it did in previous eras. Women have challenged the patriarchal right to lead countries and households and, by their visible presence in the public sphere and workplace, the idea that the sexual division of labour is immutable. What this has created for some men is a "crisis" in masculinity; a term that gender itself prefers not to use as the crisis for many seems generated by women's achievement. In framing the problem as a challenge or crisis to masculine gender identity, the reasons for male underperformance have been found in the increased empowerment of women in spheres such as education and employment. Research carried out on the education of males and females for the Dominica National Gender Policy demonstrated that, like many Caribbean territories, Dominica is faced with: a higher repetition rate among boys at primary and secondary school; fewer males than females are selected for and enrolled in secondary school; girls outperform boys in many subjects; a higher dropout rate for boys at secondary level; the lower enrolment of males in tertiary education; and increased tendency to violence among under-achieving males.[25]

The problem of defining their masculinity and understanding gender roles is by no means faced only by young men. The Draft Trinidad and Tobago National Gender Policy (2012) notes in its introduction:

> Men's gender concerns and their capacity to function effectively in society were repeatedly voiced in the consultations held throughout the country for the preparation of this document. Among the recurrent themes were those pertaining to the high levels of incarceration of men in prisons, the underperformance of males in the education system in general, and the rigid expectation of the man as primarily the breadwinner.[26]

The concerns with masculinity, male performance, male criminality, especially that of young black males, male productivity and male gender identity have undeniably surfaced as key issues of contemporary gender texts. While the movement for gender equality was stimulated by women, gender as a concept was always viewed as relational, as connecting the lives and identity of both sexes. Despite this increasing concern with masculinity and the lives of young males, the gender argument warns against preferential treatment for young men. Eudine Barriteau reminded governments that there are no State policies that deny men access to resources or opportunities for economic and social advancement and that "while many public commentators bemoan the fact that girls are taking over academic performance, none of them say to young men that they need to put in 100% effort in school."[27] The unemployment rate for young women still exceeds that of young men in the Caribbean. What is different is that young women are expected to be domesticated and perform household tasks, be mindful of their reputations, while young men are given the kind of freedoms that allow for their absorption into crime and dissident behaviour.

What therefore are the solutions being put forward by gender policies, by governments and by civil society? A joint World Bank and Commonwealth Secretariat high-level *Regional Caribbean Conference on Keeping Boys Out of Risk* was held in Montego Bay Jamaica in May 2009. Participants were policy makers, technical experts, practitioners and civil society organizations representing the education, youth and/or labour sector from 15 World Bank /Commonwealth Caribbean member countries: Antigua & Barbuda, Bahamas, Barbados, Belize, Dominica, Dominican Republic, Grenada, Guyana, Haiti, Jamaica, Saint Kitts and Nevis, Saint Lucia, Saint Vincent and the Grenadines, Suriname and Trinidad and Tobago. They were brought together to share analysis of experiences that focus on boys' underachievement in education, skills development and response to labour market challenges. The key outcome of the Conference was the *Common Platform for Action to Keep Boys Out of Risk*. The Platform for Action included the identification of individual priorities for keeping boys out of risk in the region, as well as opportunities for regional and international cooperation.[28]

In 2011, I was recruited on a Trinidad and Tobago Cabinet-appointed committee to examine the situation of young men at risk in this society.[29] The findings were largely predictable except that there was an attempt to explore more profoundly the context of masculinity in the setting of Trinidad and Tobago. The Report produced by this committee, *No Time to Quit*, sought:

>...to move beyond the narrow concept of sameness and to embrace the concepts of difference in the multi-cultural, multi-class society of Trinidad and Tobago. The report argues that the young male population that is more at risk of directly being caught in the criminal world of drugs, guns and deadly violent crime are of African descent, especially those located in urban "hotspots" such as Laventille. At the same time, it focuses on the different problems which young Indo-Trinidadian males face in areas of Central Trinidad, their predilection to alcohol and related domestic violence abuse. It also addresses the way in which women and young girls are both drawn into crime or become victims of the effects of male involvement in crime.[30]

The solutions put forward, though anticipated as in the 2009 regional conference above, became more focussed on rehabilitation and restorative justice as the problem of criminality was given further attention in this study. It called for an integrated approach:

>...in particular, for a continuation of the work that was initiated by the Ministry of Justice that seeks to liberalize the prison system to make it more humane. ...a comprehensive model of educational reform that features national service and service learning, along with strong parent and community involvement in schooling. Along with the formal system of education, ...We position the media and those involved in popular culture as partners in this struggle to reclaim the lives of young men. The solutions, therefore, privilege restorative justice and creative approaches at both school and community level.[31]

The problem of youth and masculinity persists, even while such studies, discussions and programming of reforms continue at various levels. What have been the gains as a result of such incursions in this area? This may not be quantifiable in this generation but perhaps in the next when again the forces that shape gender relations, none of which can be fully pinned down, will reveal its own changes. What is important now is that these issues are considered sufficiently important for social engineering by governments and their populations.

CONCLUSION: THE OPPORTUNITY COST OF A GENDER DEFICIT

When economists refer to the "opportunity cost" of a resource, they mean the next-highest-valued alternative use of that resource. What is the fall-out opportunity cost of a gender deficit - the impacts of gender and sexual identity discrimination, threats or incidents of gender and sexual violence, the problems of teenage pregnancy and indifferent sexual and reproductive health practices and the particular burdens borne by masculinity among other concerns?

Despite the notion that modern globalization has created a global village which we all inhabit, the onus rests heavily on each society to engage with its own populations to consider cultural specificities and how gender is lived out differently and treated fairly on each terrain, because of and regardless of universal similarities. The impact of gender sensitivity has reverberated in many areas not fully explored in this essay, as for instance in the rights now being won for lesbian, homosexual and transsexual communities, the impact of gender awareness on HIV Aids research, the clampdown of internet child pornography and concern for the rights of the child, the sex-differentiated approaches necessary in medical research and so on. This increasingly complex and complicated unfolding of gender as an analytical category in developmental thinking does not always accommodate policy making at global and societal level as it requires states, groups, individuals, all the players to "think critically about how the meanings of sexed bodies are produced in relation to one another, how these meanings are deployed and changed."[32] To be deemed gender responsive and sensitive each society must examine its practices, legislation and conscience towards all its citizens and residents, and consider the impact of present-day gender problems on current and new generations. Despite the ongoing difficulties that remain in convincing nations and institutions that fairness in treatment and inclusivity of gender difference will reveal sustainable gains, my sincere optimism of the potential of gender as a conceptual field to create social change for the greater good lies in one solid fact. Gender awareness emerged by the early twenty-first century as a marker of the advancement of societies in the space of just over one hundred years. To have gained so much traction in such accelerated time signals the human capacity for accommodating real progress.

ENDNOTES

[1] Joan W. Scott. 1986. "Gender: A Useful Category of Historical Analysis" *The American Historical Review*, 91 (5): 1053-1075

[2] See Chapter 1 Keith Hart. 1996. *Women and the Sexual Division of Labour*, Canoe Press, University of the West Indies, Kingston, Jamaica.

[3] Barry Higman Chapter Title: "Population and Labor in the British Caribbean in the Early Nineteenth Century," In *Long-Term Factors in American Economic Growth* Volume edited by Stanley L. Engerman and Robert E. GallmanUniversity of Chicago. Chapter URL: http://www.nber.org/chapters/c9689 Chapter pages in book: (p. 605 - 640) 1986http://www.nber.org/chapters/c9689.pdf

[4] "Historians agree about two things: that sexual differences were carefully marked in the early modern period, and that theories of difference underwent significant changes in the late seventeenth and eighteenth centuries" http://www.answers.com/topic/theories-of-sexual-difference

[5] Chukwuemeka Nwoko, Kenneth. 2012. "Female Husbands in Igbo Land: Southeast Nigeria." *Journal of Pan African Studies*, 5 (1).

[6] 300 women who changed the world: Sor Juana Inés de la Cruz https://www.britannica.com/women/article-9028065

[7] https://www.ancient.eu/article/1345/women-in-the-middle-ages/

[8] Irene Tinker, "A Tribute to Ester Boserup: utilizing interdisciplinarity to analyze global socio-economic change." Presented at Global Tensions Conference held at Cornell University, Ithaca, NY March 9-10, 2001. A shortened version was published in Lourdes Beneria, ed., 2003, Global Tensions: Challenges and Opportunities in the Economy. London: Routledge. http://irenetinker.com/publications-and-presentations/ester-boserup

[9] Yuval-Davis, N., 1997, 'Women, Citizenship and Difference', *Feminist Review* 57: 4-27 URL: http://www.siyanda.org/docs/davis_citizendifference.pdf

[10] Esther Boserup. 1970. *The Role of Women in Economic Development*, London: George Allen and Unwin.

[11] Short History of CEDAW Convention http://www.un.org/womenwatch/daw/cedaw/history.htm

[12] ibid.

[13] Ibid

[14] McFee, Deborah. "National Gender Policies in the English Speaking Caribbean." In *Politics, Power and Gender Justice in the Anglophone Caribbean: Women's Understandings of Politics, Experiences of Political Contestation and the Possibilities for Gender Transformation* IDRC Research Report 106430-001, by Principal Investigator

Gabrielle Jamela Hosein and Lead Researcher Jane Parpart. Ottawa, ON Canada: International Development Research Centre, 2014, p. 10

[15] Patricia Mohammed, *The Construction of Gender Development Indicators for Jamaica*, UNDP, Planning Institute of Jamaica and CIDA, Kingston, Jamaica, 2000, pp 97-100

[16] UNDP *Human Development Report*, 1995 http://hdr.undp.org/sites/default/files/reports/256/hdr_1995_en_complete_nostats.pdf

[17] http://www.ttparliament.org/documents/2468.pdf

[18] Laurel V. Williams "Sat: Better for girls to marry." *Trinidad and Tobago Newsday*, Friday October 11, 2013

[19] Adolescent pregnancy influenced by many factors.state of the World Population 2013:Friday, November 29, 2013 http://www.jamaicaobserver.com/news/Adolescent-pregnancy-influenced-by-many-factors_15432302

[20] UNFPA27 August 2013 Jamaica Offers a Model for Preventing Adolescent Pregnancies while Supporting Young Mothers. Joelle was one of two girls who shared their experience with the Chantal Compaoré from Bukina Faso and her team, who were in Jamaica to learn about the strategies the government has employed to address adolescent pregnancy in the country. http://www.unfpa.org/public/home/news/pid/14825#sthash.90SNz4vu.dpuf

[21] ibid

[22] http://www.caribbean360.com/news/trinidad_tobago_news/trinidad-and-tobago-records-more-than-2-500-teenage-pregnancies-annually

[23] Donald C. Peters, *Black Males in the Caribbean* http://da-academy.org/blkmales.html

[24] I worked as the Lead Consultant on the National Gender Policies of Cayman Island, Dominica, Trinidad and Tobago and the British Virgin Islands so am more familiar with the material of these societies. However, the problem of young masculinity has surfaced throughout the region.

[25] National Gender Policy Dominica. http://americalatinagenera.org/newsite/includes/fichas/politica/DOMINICA.pdf

[26] Introduction, Draft National National Policy on Gender Equality and Development of the Republic of Trinidad and Tobago Ministry Of Gender, Youth And Child Development June 2012 p.16

[27] Eudine Barriteau, 2000. *Re-examining Issues of 'Male Marginalisation' and 'Masculinity' in the Caribbean: The Need for a New Policy Approach*. Issue 4 of Working Paper Series (Cave Hill)

[28] *Regional Caribbean Conference on Keeping Boys Out of Risk* was held in Montego Bay Jamaica in May 2009.

[29] The committee which was chaired by Selwyn Ryan and Indira Rampersad included members Marjorie Thorpe, Lennox Bernard and Patricia Mohammed. The report produced was entitled *No Time to Quit: Engaging Men at Risk*. 436 pages and is available at http://www.ttparliament.org/documents/2197.pdf

[30] Ibid p.11

[31] Ibid p.12

[32] Scott, Joan W. 1986. "Gender: A Useful Category of Historical Analysis," *American Historical Review* 91: 1053–75

REFERENCES

Amadiume, I. 1987. *Male Daughters, Female Husbands: Gender and Sex in an African Society*, 189. London: Zed Books.

Barratt, M. 1980. *Women's Oppression Today: Problems in Marxist Feminist Analysis*. London: Verso.

Butler, Judith. 1993. *Bodies that Matter*. London: Routledge.

-----. 1990. *Gender Trouble: Feminism and Subversion of Identity*. New York and London: Routledge.

Chukwuemeka Nwoko, Kenneth. 2012. "Female Husbands in Igbo Land: Southeast Nigeria" *The Journal of Pan African Studies*, 5: (1). https://www.questia.com/library/journal/1P3-2672718561/female-husbands-in-igbo-land-southeast-nigeria

de Beauvoir, Simone. 1949 (translated 2009). *The Second Sex*, translated by Constance Borde and Sheila Malovany-Chevallier. Random House: Alfred A. Knopf.

Eliot, L. 2009. "Under the Pink or Blue Blankie." In *Pink Brain, Blue Brain: How Small Differences Grow into Troublesome Gaps -- and what We Can Do about it*, by Lise Eliot, 55-102. Boston, MA: Houghton Mifflin Harcourt.

Engels, Friedrich. 1884. *The Origin of the Family, Private Property, and the State*. First published in Hottingen-Zurich, https://www.gutenberg.org/files/33111/33111-h/33111-h.htm

Foucault, Michel. 1978. *The History of Sexuality, Volume 1: An Introduction*. New York: Pantheon Books.

Gahneri, Namrata R. 2013. "Perspectives on Women and Communal Politics in South Asia July to September 2013, p.2 http://www.isidelhi.org.in/wl/article/namrata1903.pdf

Hartmann, Heidi. 1979. "The Unhappy Marriage of Marxism and Feminism: Towards a more Progressive Union." *Capital & Class* Summer 3: 1-33

Hosein, Gabrielle. 2004. *Gender, Generation and Negotiation: Adolescence and Young Indo-Trinidadian Women's Identities in the late 20th Century*. MPhil diss., The University of the West Indies, St. Augustine.

Mohammed, Patricia. 2002. *Gender Negotiations among Indians in Trinidad, 1917-1947*, Basingstoke, Middx.: Palgrave Macmillan.

Nanda, Serena. 1999. *Neither Man nor Woman: The Hijras of India*. Belmont, CA: Wadsworth Publishing.

Reddock, Rhoda. 1994. *Women, Labour and Politics in Trinidad and Tobago: A History*. Kingston, Jamaica: Ian Randle.

Trotz, Alissa D. 2007. "Going Global? Transnationality, Women/Gender Studies and Lessons from the Caribbean. *Caribbean Review of Gender Studies* Issue 1 April 2007.

17

Gender Metrics: A Guide for Gender Policy Making[†]

INTRODUCTION

The process of policy making can be an impenetrable one to those who operate outside of the fields of public policy, programme evaluation, policy analysis, and public management, although it draws on many sub-disciplines of the social sciences, especially sociology, economics and political economy. Gender is an important dimension of all public policies, but a gender policy incorporates a gender perspective that ultimately promotes gender equality. It requires that both the policy makers and those who are driving or implementing the policy, as well as those who are consulted in the process of policy making have some working knowledge of gender as a concept and an appreciation or what might be achieved as a result of a successfully implemented policy.

[†] This is an unpublished keynote address to the Inter-Parliamentary Meeting for ParlAmericas' Anglophone Membership: *Partnerships to Transform Gender Relations*, Kingston, Jamaica, January 24-25, 2018. It was edited and amended for this publication.

Drawing on hands on experience of drafting national and institutional gender policies, I introduce the reader to several aspects of gender policy making that might demystify the process and make it more accessible to many. *First* I outline the complexity of gender and some conceptual definitions that allow those working in the area of gender to grasp the multi-layered level of analysis required for engineering social change in gender. *Second,* by exploring through a rough chronological overview some of the social actions that have been undertaken primarily in the Caribbean, I establish how and where gender inequality has been and is perceived as actionable thus requiring a policy approach in order to generate collective change. The main thrust of this exercise is to provide a range of persons: students, scholars, policy makers, planners, government officials, civil society, the legal fraternity and media personnel with what is schematically involved in the production of a national and by extension public gender policy. *Finally* I end with some open-ended questions and suggestions for improving the process as there is a constant fine-tuning taking place with all policy making.

1. THE COMPLEXITY OF GENDER

If gender inequality and gender discrimination were simple or straightforward areas to tackle collectively, in over a century of mushrooming attention to women's rights, and several decades of targeted approaches to diminishing gaps in gender inequity, many of the glaring issues would have been resolved. Yet recent events which include the surfacing of sexual harassment claims against high-profiled actors and directors in what is being dubbed the MeToo campaign, (although labelled a whingeing after the fact by feminist Germaine Greer) demonstrate that gender waters run deep and that we perhaps have been merely tapping into surface streams thus far. I have spent much of my working life trying to understand and unravel the complex nature of gender. Admittedly, there have been many gains, which we should acknowledge. Yet it seems that each time we lop off one of the Hydra's heads of gender inequality, another surfaces – for example, the rise of internet pornography against children, the thriving trade in young female and male human trafficking, the persistent homophobia that holds back gender initiatives for policy change, the horrific cultural permutations of gender-based violent acts that are still reported in many societies: these are all palpable evidence that gender inequality remains today a high priority for global attention.

Comprehensive solutions require an understanding of the complexity and insidious ways in which gender inequality is enacted in both the private and public spheres. Because we all live and experience gendered lives, there is an underlying assumption that we are all experts in the subject. Thus, parliamentarians or the man and woman in the street or media personnel do not think they have to inform themselves about the conceptual advances in gender scholarship and global actions, or the multifaceted nuances of how gender works in society. Gender is viewed popularly as man/woman business especially in relation to the domestic sphere, and as women's attempt to cross the invisible glass ceiling in the public sphere. Gender imbalances and inequities are rarely conceived of as sites of underdeveloped or misused resources of an economy or society. How does one quantify gender? How might we create a set of measures, or metrics as I refer to them in this paper, that allow for a robust qualitative and quantitative assessment of gender imbalances in a society, and a generic framework that might be adapted for formulating and tracking national or institutional gender policies. The language of policy making or encouraging uptake of required changes in gender arrangements must be accessible to a range of actors, especially those in government or senior positions who have the power to effect change through policy. This is necessary because the comprehension of gender as a conceptual category of social analysis goes at a slow, sometimes retrogressive pace, and there can be active or passive resistance to gender initiatives.

There is also fear, a collective and perhaps irrational anxiety, that in shifting from viewing gender as a natural order of masculinity and femininity to gender as a constantly negotiated set of roles and attributes that may be better engineered, secular states are tampering with a "god given" edict of what it means to be human.

It is admittedly difficult for many persons, whether by religious persuasion or personal convictions, to accept that the concept and components of gender are fluid. In the last thirty years the term itself has become a shorthand code to refer to the condition of women or men, girls or boys, to define ones' masculinity or femininity, and to refer to the lesbian, gay, bisexual, transgender, intersexed or queer population. When the concept of gender is applied technically, it now automatically incorporates some reference to difference and sexual diversity, power and empowerment, or discrimination and abuse, (and this is just in the English language). The more gender is used as an analytical category, social worlds and perceptions undergo change, and some of these are not always beneficial to the goal of gender parity. I deliberately focus on language and meaning because many of the strategies for change require communication that ultimately is at the core of how we might disrupt accepted cultural gender belief systems, attitudes and practices. One of the most recurrent statements echoed in every public consultation for a gender policy in the Caribbean is, as one man put this in Cayman Islands, that "Women are abdicating their God-given roles by seeking equality with men."[1] Religious belief systems reinforce cultural practices that maintain strict gender roles for men and women, despite changing technologies and demands on both sexes over time, despite changes in the home and workplace and despite the increased access to education and opportunities available to both sexes.

Gender struggles abound daily in the private sphere, within homes, villages and communities where customs that are abusive of gender rights are protected because of cultural norms that are deemed important to sustain cultural, class or ethnic identities. For example in Trinidad and Tobago, the 2017 parliamentary campaign to amend the Marriage Act, the Muslim and Hindu Marriage and Divorce Act, and the Matrimonial Proceedings and Property Act, the latter raising the legal age of marriage to 18, and effectively outlawing child marriage, was met with resistance by men from the Hindu community who benefitted from an out-dated law that allowed marriage of girls from the age of 12. The preservation of young female virginity among the Indian population far outweighed the concerns, drawn attention to for many many decades, that at a tender age young girls are not ready for marriage much less motherhood. The complexity of gender is therefore exacerbated by the fact that it involves negotiating freedoms that protect customs that have historically privileged some. Legal restraints remain one of the primary barriers to gender transformation.

Using a political economy approach to decipher the gender system, Eudine Barriteau created a deceptively simple theory that demonstrates how gender inequality has been normalized through the state and in the public sphere of work, governance and leadership. She defined the gender system as "comprising a network of power relations with two principal dimensions: one ideological, the other material. ...The material dimensions demonstrate how women and men gain access to or are allocated economic and social resources within the state and society."[2] The ideological sustains the cultural norms, ideas and beliefs about sexual difference. In general, the female body is held ransom to biology. But so is the male. For example, in Trinidad it is still not a norm for men to enter nursing and until recently, midwifery was not a path of specialization open to male nurses.

The added complexity lies in the inseparability of sex as biological and gender as social, both of which combine to create an indivisible network of surfaces under which all gender inequality resides. We are born with a biological script but what we make of that script is socially and culturally shaped over our lifetime and varies by society. Thus gender might also be defined as the social organization of sexual difference and sexual diversity. Every society take its units of human labour, human sex and human sexuality and determines the cogs into which each human body is supposed to fit in order to ensure the survival of the family and reproduce economy and society. Admitting to sexual diversity and challenging deeply rooted gender expectations about the role of woman versus man become aberrations for which there are no easily adaptable blueprints for either the organisation of labour or for sexual reproduction.[3]

While the struggle for gender rights proceeds apace, the question of what actually constitutes gender equity remains unclear, perhaps because the meaning of a concept like gender equality is itself indistinct. What does gender equality look like? How measurable is it, particularly when the cultural and social constructs of gender differ from country to country? Gender behaviour is difficult to legislate and depends on individual and collective agreements on practices and expectations. Treating with gender inequality requires a multi- or interdisciplinary approach that is embodied in no one individual or institution so that remedies are invariably partial, (not unlike medicine which selectively treats one part of the human body, sometimes off-setting others).

One example of the innate complexity of gender's cultural specificity - the need for societal remedies that send clear signals about the difficulty of legislating gender behaviour - is that of sexual harassment. It has been a major challenge in most societies to even acknowledge that sexual harassment takes place, underscoring that while in general women and girls are the primary targets, men and boys can also be subjected to sexual harassment both by other males and females. Particularly within the sexualized culture of gender relations in Caribbean societies, where every slap and tickle is not a direct sexual assault and women have grown to expect that their femininity will be noticed, sexual harassment legislation is difficult to enact. For example in the carnival season in Trinidad and Tobago, gyrating on someone's else's body in public fetes or 'wining', is assumed to be acceptable, if not actively expected as many barriers are lowered in this libidinous festival. Yet the Trinidad public had been warned in the 2018 Trinidad and Tobago Carnival by a police spokesman that 'Thiefing a wine,' is behaviour which is now considered assault under the Summary Offences Act in this society, with penalties that could lead to imprisonment for three to six months.[4] There is of course a major problem of how a 'wining' assault, in the midst of sometimes chaotic revelry, can be proved. Nonetheless, the actual passage of such an Act is a signal of how this society is dealing with the increasing demands by women and some men that ultimately, individuals' rights over their bodies are sacrosanct. It builds imperceptibly on the famous Clause Four of the Sexual Offences Act debated in 1986 which created the offence of rape within marriage, a revolutionary step for a Caribbean society to take in this decade of the twentieth century.[5]

2. OVERVIEW OF PAST STATE INITIATIVES IN THE CARIBBEAN

The numerous policies and joint action plans, coalition activities of civil society, sporadic state interventions, and ongoing non-government initiatives that have emerged around gender issues since the 1980s in the Anglophone Caribbean are frankly impressive. Many of these are well documented and archived in various places including at the Institute for Gender and Development Studies at the University of the West Indies whose mandate includes that of preserving records that trace gender advances. Nonetheless, these gains have collectively not undergone a rigorous evaluative analysis over the last four decades to examine what they tell us about how gender inequality is being perceived, or interpreted, or tackled, and whether successfully or unsuccessfully. A rigorous analysis might well reveal a road map of ideological progress and concrete gains in the region and beyond. Gaietry Pargass,[6] human rights lawyer and long-time activist who has been involved in many initiatives since the 1980s, pointed out that even in the absence of national gender policies or action plans, the earliest state-related initiatives can be seen in legislative reform.

Legislative changes have been central to the struggle for gender equality and the most glaring form of inequality to be tackled was gender-based violence. Lauren Zandry comments on the regional knock-on effect of model legislation when "…Trinidad and Tobago created the first Sexual Offences Act in the region and helped establish a regional organization to create a sample Sexual Offences Act for the other Caribbean countries including Barbados, the Bahamas and Guyana to follow."[7] Enacted in 1986, the *Sexual Offences Act of Trinidad and Tobago* consolidated the laws dealing with sexual crimes against children and adults, established protection for minors, both boys and girls, and, among other advances, included heavier penalties for the offences of rape and sexual assault. The CARICOM Model Legislation on domestic violence, passed in 1997, was influential in the development of domestic violence legislation across the region. Earlier reforms are referred to as "first generation" legislation. With increasing advocacy by active women's groups, a "second generation" of domestic violence legislation emerged, among them the Trinidad and Tobago (*Domestic Violence Act* 1999), Belize (*Domestic Violence Act* 2007), and The Bahamas (*Domestic Violence (Protection Orders) Act 2007*, which further improved the CARICOM model legislation by providing a definition of domestic violence and by expanding the range of persons who can seek relief."[8] The avalanche of changes in legislation for sexual offences and remedies for gender-based violence, including rape crisis centres, homes and shelters for battered women, many of the latter supported by business and professional women's groups, signalled the widespread regional agreement on another conceptual interpretation of gender inequality – that underpinned by violence and abuse, including the abuse of children. Another area highlighting what women's groups perceived as a primary site of gender discrimination was that of the lack of access to abortion on demand and the number of deaths caused by the illegal steps women took to relieve themselves of unwanted pregnancies. Here the relationship between the church and the medical needs of women have clashed and most governments have been afraid to tackle this issue for fear of alienating its voters. Michelle Rowley writes that Barbados has remained both "a pioneer and anomaly in its passage of legislation, a pioneer for termination of pregnancy in 1983, long predating the Cairo population meeting of 1994, an anomaly "because of its virulent resistance to homosexuality and the decriminalization of sex work" just under a decade later.[9]

The remedies to assist pregnant teenagers also presented another picture of coordinated action. Jamaica led the way with the Programme for Adolescent Mothers established by the Bureau of Women's Affairs in 1978, a model that is now transformed from early provision of a shelter for pregnant teenagers to a National Policy for the Reintegration of School-age Mothers into the Formal School System.[10] In a gender belief system where motherhood was synonymous with proving femininity, the society also understood that the future potential of young women should not be limited because of persistent cultural signals and errors of youthful judgement.

From the 1980s onwards, the "underachievement of males" was the masculinity flipside of the gender problem which emerged as a necessary but somewhat combative one. Gender concerns before were viewed largely as women's problems. The acknowledgement by states and ministers in various fora was also the first time that the "gender problem" captured the full attention of the region's politicians and male opinion leaders. For some the decreasing male involvement in education was viewed as a "wilful or deliberate" attempt to marginalize men. Well-documented in the literature was a concern that the feminization of education was forcing boys away from book learning.[11] That the universities had nearly 75 per cent female enrolment by the late nineties was evidence that masculinity was being replaced by a dominant and rival femininity.

The responses were varied. Barry Chevannes was a leading founder of Father's Incorporated in Jamaica, "a community-based parenting group established in 1991 to address negative stereotypes of Jamaican fathers."[12] He later carried out a Caribbean-wide study on how men learnt their masculinity.[13] In the latter, while illustrating the challenges that boys had in meeting expectations of Caribbean masculinity, he argued, among other things, that Caribbean men needed to reclaim their role as fathers and patriarchs of the household. The Caribbean Development Bank commissioned a major study across the region of the education system to understand why boys were under-achieving in the education system.[14] In Trinidad in 2013 the then Prime Minister Kamla Persad-Bissessar commissioned a major study into *Youth at Risk*,[15] looking at the growing criminality of primarily young black males and the "lost generation" as young males were referred to in one study.[16] Initiatives such as Second Chance in Belize (and other Caribbean societies), while not focussed only on boys, drew attention similarly to the drop-out rate and associated risks associated with young Belizean males.[17] The question one asks here is if Caribbean men are wilfully or inadvertently marginalized, what measures must be put in place to ensure gender equality or equity for both sexes? Some family and labour laws have undergone reform allowing men easier access to children, have removed the punitive approach to custody payments and concede paternity leave that recognizes the nurturing role of men in parenting.

In the development literature, a growing recognition of gender inequality could be seen in the movement from Women in Development (WID), adding women and stirring, Women and Development (WAD) – the strangely naïve assumption that women had to be brought into development, and Gender and Development (GAD), an affirmation that the progress of a country lagged behind others if primary areas of gender inequality remain untreated. The Beijing conference of 1995 had already signalled the paucity of women in political leadership. The UNDP's Human Development Report adapted to create metrics for country comparison on gender equality status. The GDI or *Gender Development Indicator* was the *Human Development Indicator* now discounted for gender inequality, and the GEM or *Gender Empowerment Measure*, an index for empowerment calculated through an examination of parliamentary representation, managerial and administrative positions and professional and technical positions held by women and men in a society. In other words, these indicators examined how well-placed women were to be decision-makers at all levels compared to men, to bring a gender perspective into development.

Several strategies and coalitions were attempted in the region to ensure female presence in leadership and decision-making. In Guyana, the strategy of constitutional reform, to legislate a quota system of representation by sex, ensuring that women were 33 ¹/₃ per cent of electoral candidates and representatives in the national assembly, emerged from a coalition between women of opposing political parties. In practice, this figure has never been achieved, premised as it were on a feminist activist strategy that was still unfavourable to many.[18] Nonetheless, such signals are far reaching in raising the consciousness of populations. This confidence of placing women in leadership was built on a strong female presence in the region long before this, Dame Nita Barrow and Billy Miller, Minister and Parliamentarian in Barbados, and Prime Minister Eugenia Charles in Dominica. In Jamaica, Women Working for Transformation (WWT) between 1999 and 2003 targeted transformational change at the personal, community and corporate levels, as in Guyana promoting coalitions and cross-party affiliations. In 2003, two development organizations, Friedrich Ebert Stiftung Jamaica directed by Judith Wedderburn and Caribbean Policy Development Centre (CPDC) chaired by Cecilia Babb joined forces to carry out workshops in Jamaica, Dominica and Barbados to train cadres of women from all parties and levels in the understanding of gender policy making and political leadership. In 2005, the Caribbean Institute for Women in Leadership (CIWiL) assumed regional responsibility for training women for public leadership drawing on the resources of the staff of the Institute for Gender and Development Studies. All of these initiatives, (with admittedly many omissions) signalled a new concept that had entered the framework for gender inequality, that of gender justice. Beyond the material encroachment on the female body, there was also the false ideological assumptions about the female mind, that women were still not fit to be leaders of nations. That this coalition struggle against gender inequality would take effect by the late twentieth century might be read from the advent of Janet Jagan, Kamla Persad-Bissessar, Portia Simpson and Mia Mottley as state leaders in Guyana, Trinidad and Tobago, Jamaica and Barbados by the twenty-first century – a signal of the Anglo-phone Caribbean's growing acceptance and confidence in female leadership at the helm.

3. METRICS FOR GENDER POLICY MAKING

The public policy-making cycle streamlines the process of addressing societal problems, identifies objective indicators for creating policy or action plans, and establishes mechanisms for monitoring and evaluation. Most importantly, it ensures that a representative sample of the society, including non-partisan individuals, groups and institutions, are brought together to inform the process and to collectively determine the parameters of policy change that are required. The written policy outlines the methodologies used, the actors involved and establishes in policy statements or numbered paragraphs, what elements constitute the policy. These may relate to changes in legislation, amendments to regulations and defined action plans that are time-bound for delivery. There is no single blueprint for creating national gender policies or national action plans, although gender policies are patterned along the same procedures deployed to create all public policy. Based on political awareness and sensibility to issues associated with gender that obtains in the specific society, or the particular political climate and structure that exists in the society, each policy process might require different groupings or components coming together as an enabling environment for policy advocacy and change.

I draw variously on the experience of drafting four national gender policies and assisting with a fifth national process along with other projects and programmes that I have carried out in this area over a two-decade period in the region and globally to outline schematically how policies are delivered, or not. I came to policy writing not from any formal training in the drafting of public policy and learnt the craft on the ground. But I realize and emphasize that a sound understanding of gender, tools of gender analysis, the history of feminism and women's struggle and experience in the field of activism and outreach are still pre-required knowledge for crafting meaningful gender policy.

The Enabling Environment
There are *seven* main prerequisites that come together at any time, not necessarily in this order but which certainly help to create the right enabling environment for policy creation.
1. Conventions and agreements that governments have signed since 1980 that mandate the commissioning of national gender policies and action plans for equity and equality. Among these are the Universal Declaration of Human Rights, 1948, the Convention on the Elimination of All Forms of Discrimination Against Women (CEDAW) 1979, The Inter-American Convention on the Prevention, Punishment and Eradication of Violence Against Women (Convention of Belém do Pará) 1994, The Beijing Declaration and Platform for Action, 1995, the Commonwealth Plan of Action for Gender and Development and the CARICOM Plan of Action to 2005 and its Framework for Mainstreaming Gender. Relevant sections of a country's constitution, national development plans, visions and strategies are all invoked as underscoring drivers of a gender policy.
2. Funding for research, consultations, consultants, training and outreach activities are a necessary part of the process of finding consensus and building cadre within the society. In at least three national scenarios in which I worked, the policy was underwritten through funds sourced through UN or other global development agencies with supplemental government support.
3. Identification of a well-supported national machinery charged with the responsibility of spearheading and coordinating gender responsive development. In Cayman Islands in 1999 the Ministry of Community Services, Women's Affairs, Youth and Sports led the process. There was no bureau of women's affairs at this time although there was a gender focal point within this

ministry and the Permanent Secretary in the Ministry had oversight, while the policy was championed by the Minister with this collective portfolio. Some ministries, organizations or individuals begin the groundwork long before the policy is commissioned. In the British Virgin Islands for instance the preamble to the policy consultation began a decade before it was actually commissioned in 2010. In 1992 a Women's Desk was established and renamed the Office of Gender Affairs. In 1998 organizations and individuals in the Virgin Islands concerned with women's advancement and gender equality set up a Women's Focal Point as an umbrella body to pressure the VI government. The final policy was submitted to the Minister in 2011.

4. A network of government ministries, non-governmental agencies, civil society organizations or individuals, religious institutions, professional bodies, media, legal professionals, community leaders and communities who are willing to be part of the consultation process. Some pressure groups may lend support, or they can arrest the passage of the policy even after it is written and presented to Parliament. Consultations require that even the loudest detractors must be heard and documented.

5. The selection of the Consultant and Consultant Team – a policy is rarely a single authored document - with clearly mandated Terms of Reference and deliverables to the government within a set time frame that is also agreed by the line ministries and expectations of the Cabinet.

6. The political willingness of a champion minister who will ensure that the policy process is resourced and respected and that colleague ministers are kept apprised. In the British Virgin Islands, the then Minister for Health and Social Development, Minister Dancia Penn who also held the position of Deputy Premier, together with the Permanent Secretary in her ministry, were major drivers of the policy process.

7. The rallying of parliamentary support for transitioning the policy from written document to adoption and implementation.

The Research, Consultation and Sensitization process
This period may be longer or shorter depending on the groundwork that has been covered before within the society, the legislation that has already been tackled outside of a policy framework, and the level of education or sensitization of a population – the latter includes the level of education and awareness of gender among ministers and public servants and services. In all of the policies I reference, these processes were in-depth and involved wide-ranging consultations with communities, religious groups, civil society organizations such as rotary clubs and business and professional groups, traditional men's associations such as sports groups and so on. Most of these were carried out over a full year and in some cases more than one year to ensure that sufficient time was given for consultations with as many groups or individuals as possible.

In some societies certain issues were more developed than others. For example, the engine room of the process in Cayman Islands was located in the Women's Resource Centre because this Centre had militated for homes for battered women, against child and sexual abuse, and thus had become synonymous with driving the gender agenda in the society. In order to broaden the scope of the policy to sectors such as immigration, a major area for attention in Cayman Islands, a Research and Development Team comprising representatives from almost every public sector and profession, roughly about twenty-five persons in all, became part of the training and sensitization team who would in turn convey information to others. In addition large national consultations and site visits were carried out in all the islands comprising Cayman Islands. In Dominica, years of groundwork including workshops particularly on domestic violence and abuse had been previously carried out by Rosie Browne, the then Gender Affairs director. The Gender Affairs Ministry similarly again brought together again a very qualified team of experts from the society, education experts, psychologists, priests and public servants who were subdivided into sectors which conformed with policy areas designated by the Consultant as possible policy areas for attention. Gender Training sessions and workshops were carried out by the Consultant team on various issues such as gender and agriculture, or education, meetings were held with permanent secretaries from many ministries, with ministers and other experts identified by the Gender Affairs Bureau. The designated country team prepared position papers and provided some of the research data from which the policy could be crafted by the consultant.

There are six key areas that need to be emphasized in the formulation of a gender policy.

1. Gender policies are first and foremost research driven documents
2. Gender policies signal fundamental areas requiring legislation
3. The role of non-governmental bodies in supporting or responding to drafts of a policy is key
4 There is unimaginable value to be gained by sensitizing cabinet ministers and political referees who will drive the policy process
5. The roll out success of the policy depends on anticipating and setting up a strong implementation and action plan that has advisory or committee oversight
6. The policy should anticipate mechanisms for monitoring and evaluation of the successes and weaknesses when it is implemented in anticipation of another policy cycle.

First – as with all policies, a gender policy is a research-driven document. Each of the sectors advocated for policy intervention must be researched for data – both quantitative and qualitative, with secondary and primary sources that establish the nature of the problem, when and where it makes for gender inequality, the remedies that have been sought or programmes adopted if any, and statistical or directional indications that the policy should advocate. Although some policy areas are easily identified through statistical inferences, e.g., domestic violence cases reported, recurrences of health issues that either men or women suffer that need attention in the health sector and so on, there are other gender indicators that have to be gleaned from qualitative assessments. A Cayman Islands example is a useful one that has a bearing on how material and ideological gendered data need to undergo interpretative analyses from a gender perspective. The Caribbean Single Market and Economy (CSME) was designed to represent a single economic space within which people, goods, services and capital would be able to move freely between states, but this also required the harmonisation of social, economic, and trade policies among the participating member states. Existing immigration laws in Cayman Islands then favoured male professional immigration over that of female domestic labourers. Male professionals were allowed to settle in the society with their families. Female domestic labourers, most of them from Jamaica, were prohibited this right.The policy research established the integral value that these women workers brought to the private sphere. As caregivers they ensured environmental hygiene, nutrition, care of the young and elderly all of which allowed professional men and women to produce goods and services, earn a decent living and develop Cayman Island society, while the children and families of the domestic workers suffered because they did not have access to similar care. This example demonstrated the transactional value placed by the state on the work of one group over another, and the artificial division of the life of a nation into public and private spheres, an intersection that a gender policy often has to traverse. Thus each gender policy has to be prefaced by a rigorous situational analysis of the society that establishes from a gender perspective, the condition and status of women vis-a-vis men in all sectors, education, health, labour, employment, crime and violence, along with a rich cultural understanding of gender belief systems, how social concerns are rated, and what remedies would best suit the society.

The *second* area is that of legislation. One of the primary functions of Parliaments is the development and implementation of laws, policies and practices that promote democracy and good governance. Legislative changes that correct gender anomalies are a primary focus of gender policies, but this may pertain to some societies more than other, as some may have consistently updated laws outside of a policy framework. In this respect, the contribution of legal experts to the research, consultation, and crafting of a gender policy is vital. The Trinidad and Tobago gender policy, or lack thereof, has now become legendary in the Caribbean for its attempt to confront legislation that is in contravention of human rights treaties that this country has signed.

In an earlier draft, this policy advocated for public education on the decriminalizing of homosexual and lesbian acts under the Sexual Offences Act, 1986 in an effort to confront these barriers to freedoms. To date the issue of gender and multiple sexualities remains the key area that has restricted the passage of the policy as patriarchal or parochial attitudes remain entrenched, and due to the highly mediatized debates, the gender policy became an incendiary issue in this society.

The *third* area emphasizes different spaces where actors from outside of government can be involved, the role of pressure groups, be they from health and education professionals, police and judiciary, from women's groups and from religious and cultural bodies and the media. These are all key in providing expert opinion, evidence of discrimination or areas for shaping public opinion. As in the case of Trinidad and Tobago, the involvement of the Interreligious Organization and Lawyers for Jesus, a coalition who felt that the term gender was a smoke screen for legalizing homosexuality, proved to be a major deterrent. Nonetheless, if we argue that gender equality is achieved by recasting the material context through the ideological, then public discourse that begins to educate and inform becomes a vital function outside of the passage of a policy itself and in fact is one of the most dynamic periods of policy creation in a society. During consultations and media debates, the levels of gender consciousness become raised and heightened and admit personal and institutional sites of inequality that are normally not confronted in public.

The *fourth* area of focus is awareness, consultation and sensitization in particular of cabinet ministers and political referees in this process. The effective communications skill of the Consultant is key in bringing persons on board. Much of the insider trading of the policy merits however is carried out by the line minister and permanent secretaries to bring fellow parliamentarians on board. Despite all the advocacy and media sensitization that may occupy the gender policy process at this time, the real challenge is to convince those who will debate and accept the policy when it is presented to Cabinet. The case of Dominica and British Virgin Islands offered best practices in this respect. In Dominica, a small and relatively accessible society, as Consultant

I was able to meet with and have discussions with a range of permanent secretaries, with some ministers and found an ally in the permanent secretary of the line ministry in which the Gender Affairs Bureau sat. Not only were these one-on-one discussions useful for reaching minds, but in addition close interaction with these lawmakers helped to guide the writing and presentation of the policy to Cabinet, to lay a finger on the attitudes and concerns that these decision makers had at the time and to present studied data and arguments that responded to the issues they raised. It is also crucial to convey to political regimes that gender policies are time-bound, and it is important to strategically select and establish what can be achieved in its own time and propose that policies are to be monitored and evaluated to improve their potency in the next round of policy making.[19]

The *fifth* area has to do with the implementation stage of the policy which must be put in place while the policy research, consultation and formulation is in progress. Successful policy implementation requires identifying within an existing governmental structure the mechanisms that will ensure efficient the implementation, of the gender policy. The best practice has shown that an independent Advisory Board drawn from persons who are very familiar with gender, with policy making and with government processes and also reflecting representation of non-government organizations and civil society is created for oversight of the implementation process.

Policy monitoring and evaluation (M&E) has a critical role to play in effectively delivering public policies and services that the policies have promised and is the *sixth* key area that must be factored in preparing a gender policy. Each policy is time-bound and establishes deliverables during its lifetime. M&E is a central tool to manage interventions, improve practice and ensure accountability to stakeholders. These need not be prescriptive but can be developed in tandem with the frameworks adopted for implementation but they should definitely not be an afterthought. M&E demonstrates the success of the policy implementation and provides quantitative and qualitative metrics that measure the gains of the policy, while signalling weaknesses or strengths for the next cycle.

CONCLUDING INSIGHTS AND QUESTIONS

Although gender policies will remain a strategic method by which a society presents its philosophical positions and solutions to tackle gender inequality and equity, we need to also challenge the use of the mechanism of a gender policy as a primary or only instrument for achieving gender equality in a society.

First the commissioning and acceptance of a policy by Cabinet does not automatically lead to resource allocation for ensuring implementation of policies. Policies are presented with a time-bound action plan that outlines deliverables. Is gender budgeting factored into it as a priority of governments?

Second, over time many changes have been brought about by coalitions on specific gender issues. How has coalition politics, which can include the demand for legislative reform, for programmatic action and for dedicated resources to specific areas, also be considered as an alternative mechanism for difficult areas that will never have consensus, particularly those related to human sexualities and human rights? In the passage of gender policies or legislation relating to gender, how might the system of Joint Select Committees which is an established part of some parliaments in the Caribbean, be better utilized and given teeth to respond to complex and very sensitive areas such as gender?[20]

Third, the model of mainstreaming gender, adopted at the Beijing Platform in 1995, while fundamental to conceptually spreading gender into each layer of governance, has met with difficulties in its actual application. How might we revisit strategies that reconfigure and stream gender differently in actions plans for national gender transformation and into a range of institutions that provide other models and mechanisms for handling gender inequity and inequality?

The twenty-first century has brought with it a plethora of other problems and prospects into which gender issues and analysis provide good allies for transformation of thought and action. Climate change issues, migration, wars, and communicable viruses along with the increased expectation of the human life span and the changing landscape of employment, referred to as the future of work. All of these areas require the joint wisdom of women and men, young and old. The frameworks and metrics identified in this paper might I hope be useful in planning and delivering all policy or public programmes for change that involve a gender-dimensional analysis.

ENDNOTES

[1] This was actually one of the statements made at a Public Consultation Grand Cayman in 2000. Since then in almost every public consultation this statement is echoed in different words.
[2] Barriteau, Eudine. 2001. *The Political Economy of Gender in the Twentieth-century Caribbean*. Basingstoke, Hampshire and New York: Palgrave.
[3] Clearly the controversial issues of same sex marriage are ways in which societies are grappling with these issues, so there has been fundamental change over the years.
[4] http://newsday.co.tt/2018/01/20/reckless-outburst-by-machel/
http://newsday.co.tt/2018/01/18/you-could-get-charged-fined-for-wining-like-that/
[5] I insert this reference as I was involved as the Coordinator of the Rape Crisis Centre in Port of Spain in the debates and discussions that would eventually lead to the passage of the Sexual Offences Act in 1996. The public deliberations and outbursts defined a distinctive gender consciousness moment and growth in Trinidad and Tobago society.
[6] Personal conversation with Ms. Gaietry Pargass, Attorney at Law.
[7] http://berkeleytravaux.com/creating-regional-organizations-to-support-the-adoption-of-sexual-offenses-acts-in-africa/
[8] http://berkeleytravaux.com/creating-regional-organizations-to-support-the-adoption-of-sexual-offenses-acts-in-africa/
[9] Michelle Rowley. 2011. *Feminist Advocacy and Gender Equity in the Anglophone Caribbean: Envisioning a Politics of Coalition*. London and New York: Routledge.
[10] See https://www.unfpa.org/news/jamaica-offers-model-preventing-adolescent-pregnancies-while-supporting-young-mothers (Accessed 5/1/2020)
[11] There is a prolific academic and popular literature available on this subject in the region, see especially Errol Miller. 1986. *The Marginalisation of the Black Male: Insights from the Development of the Teaching Profession*. Kingston, Jamaica: Institute of Social and Economic Research and Barbara Bailey: *Boys, Masculinity and Education*, https://sta.uwi.edu/crgs/december2014/journals/CRGS_8_Pgs283-288_BoysMasculinityEducation_BBailey.pdf
David Plummer "Is learning becoming taboo for Caribbean boys?" http://siteresources.worldbank.org/INTLACREGTOPPOVANA/Resources/PLUMMERLearningTabooforCaribbeanBoys.pdf
Anna-Lisa Paul. Worry over why girls are learning more. https://www.guardian.co.tt/article-6.2.362336.38d7931107, Fri Mar 27 2015
[12] See https://dogoodjamaica.org/organization-search/item/fathers_incorporated/
[13] Barry Chevannes. (2011). *Learning to be a Man: Socialization and Gender Identity in Five Caribbean Communities*. Kingston, Jamaica: University of the West Indies Press.
[14] https://sta.uwi.edu/crgs/december2014/journals/CRGS_8_Pgs283-288_BoysMasculinityEducation_BBailey.pdf

[15] *No Time to Quit: Engaging Youth at Risk.* Report of the Committee appointed by the Government Trinidad and Tobago to examine the situation of Young Males and Crime chaired by Professor Selwyn Ryan with members Professor Patricia Mohammed, Dr Indira Rampersad, Dr Marjorie Thorpe and Dr Lennox Bernard. 2013. http://www.ttparliament.org/documents/2197.pdf

[16] Bailey, Barbara, and Suzanne M. Charles. "The Missing Generation: A Situational Analysis of Adolescents (10-14) in the Caribbean Community." UNICEF. September 2008. http://www.unicef.org/barbados/ spmapping/ Implementation/youth/2008_ LitReviewCaricom.pdf (accessed May 1, 2012).

[17] https://ambergriscaye.com/forum/ubbthreads.php/topics/21834/friends-give-boys-a-second-chance.html. See also https://www.cxc.org/a-second-chance-is-waiting-for-you/

[18] See Hosein, Gabrielle Jamela and Jane Parpart. 2017. *Negotiating Gender, Policy and Politics in the Caribbean: Feminist Strategies, Masculinist Resistance and Transformational Possibilities.* London: Rowman and Littlefield.

[19] Mohammed, Patricia. 2011. "Gender Politics and Global Democracy: Insights from the Caribbean" in *Global Democracy: An Intercultural Debate*, in project led by Jan Aart Scholte, University of Warwick, Building Global Democracy Project

[20] My thanks to Dr. Hamid Ghany, Political Scientist and Constitutional expert and Director of the Sir Arthur Lewis Institute for Social and Economic Studies at The University of the West Indies, St Augustine whom I interviewed for insights into parliamentary processes.

SELECTED REFERENCES

Hosein, Gabrielle and Jane Parpart, eds. 2016. *Negotiating Gender, Policy and Politics in the Caribbean: Feminist Strategies, Masculinist Resistance and Transformational Possibilities*, London: Rowman & Littlefield International.

Mohammed, Patricia. ed., 2000. *The Construction of Gender Development Indicators for Jamaica.* Kingston: Planning Institute of Jamaica / United Nations Development Fund / Canada International Development Agency, 100 pp.

Mohammed, Patricia. 2015. "Gender Equality and Gender Policy Making in the Caribbean," In *Public Administration and Policy in the Caribbean*, edited by Indianna D. Minto-Coy and Evan Berman. New York: Taylor and Francis.

Mohammed, Patricia, Lead Researcher/Consultant. 2011. *National Policy for Gender Equity and Equality for the British Virgin Islands to the Government of the BVI.* The policy team also comprised Ms. Deborah McFee, Professor Jane Parpart of the IGDS and Ms. Gaietry Pargass (Attorney at Law.

Mohammed, Patricia and Audrey Ingram Roberts. 2002. A National Gender Policy on Equity and Equality for The Cayman Islands, Final Policy Document submitted to the Ministry of Community Development, Women Affairs, Youth and Sport Government of the Cayman Islands. 80 pp

Mohammed, Patricia. 2017. Concept paper, Methodology and time frame for the development of a national gender policy for the Co-operative Republic of Guyana.

National Policy for Gender Equity and Equality for the Commonwealth of Dominica, Policy Document written for the Government of Dominica. Research Assistant to Project, Deborah Mc Fee, 2005, pp. 120,

No Time to Quit: Engaging Youth at Risk. Report of the Committee appointed by the Government of Trinidad and Tobago to examine the situation of Young Males and Crime chaired by Professor Selwyn Ryan with members Professor Patricia Mohammed, Dr. Indira Rampersad, Dr. Marjorie Thorpe and Dr. Lennox Bernard. 2013, 438 pp. Published in limited hard copy and posted on the website of the Trinidad and Tobago Parliament *http://www.ttparliament.org/documents/2197.pdf*

Trinidad and Tobago National Gender Policy and Action Plan, submitted to the Government of Trinidad and Tobago, Senior Technical Expert, Policy document co- written by Patricia Mohammed, Rhoda Reddock, Camille Antoine and Gaietry Pargass. 2004. The University of the West Indies, St. Augustine: Centre for Gender and Development Studies.

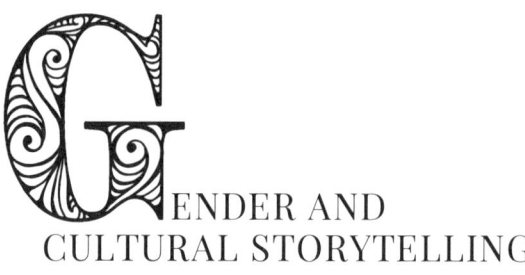
Gender and Cultural Storytelling

5

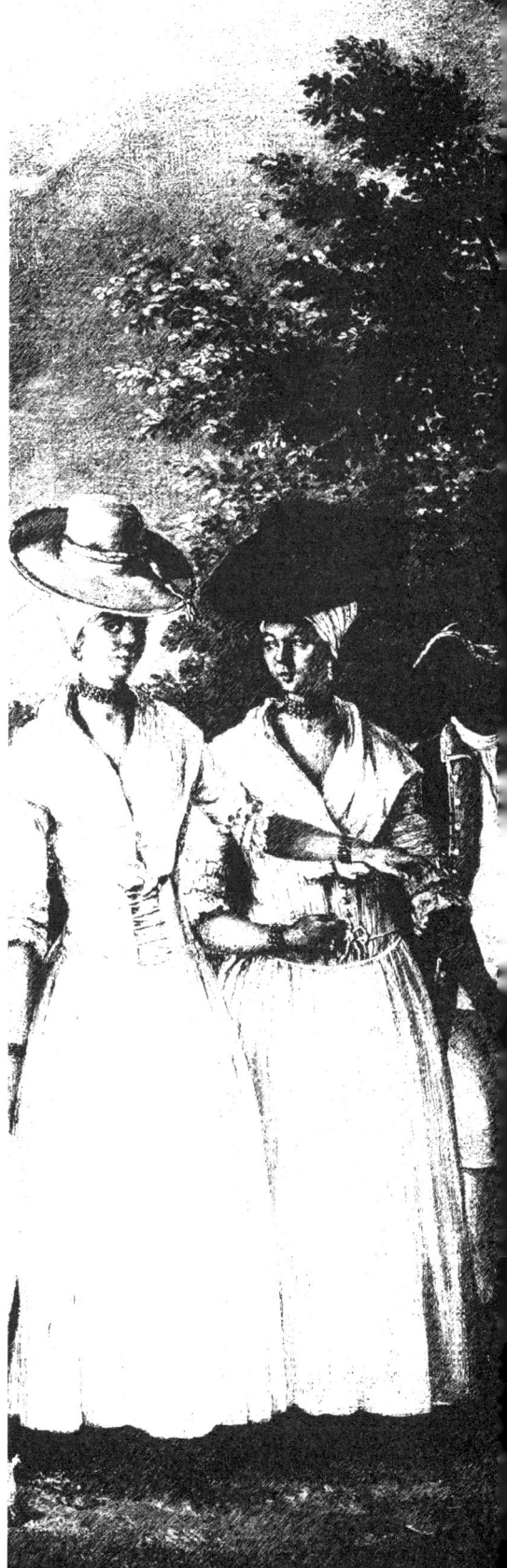

18

A Blueprint for Gender in Creole Trinidad: Exploring Gender Mythology through Calypsos of the 1920s and 1930s[†]

THE CALYPSO AS CREOLE AESTHETIC

The calypso is one of the products of creole society as it emerged in the Anglophone Caribbean as a result of Spanish, French and British colonization of the region from the fifteenth century onwards. Trinidad[1] society was populated mainly with freed African slaves from the other Caribbean territories, particularly the French Antilles and Haiti, and the indentured labour of other ethnic groups from China and India. The calypso form is constantly undergoing change. There are vast differences between the early origins and the calypso of the late twentieth century. Gordon Rohlehr (1990) suggests that to fully appreciate the emergence of calypso in Trinidad during the nineteenth century one would need to consider the complex blends of musics and dances of French Creole slave society before emancipation, the various African

[†] First published in Linden Lewis, ed. 2003. *The Culture of Gender and Sexuality in the Caribbean*, 129-168. Gainesville: University Press of Florida. It was based on a paper first presented at the Caribbean Studies Association Conference, Barranquilla, Columbia, 1997.

influences on the evolution of French Creole society, the musics and dances of the Anglophone West Indian migrants between 1840 and 1900, the musics and dances of the groups of liberated Africans during the post-emancipation period, the small Hispanic element in Trinidad which persisted through contact with Venezuela and Curacao, and "the ritual celebration of all these things in the annual Carnival as well as their simplification into a few predominant forms by 1900."[2] Maureen Warner-Lewis's work confirms the hypothesis that the expressions of African culture was primary in the development of the calypso form, lending itself readily to adaptation and mixture with the various elements which generated creole society in the West Indies.[3]

By creole aesthetic I am making reference to the calypso as a major channel through which the people of Trinidad from the late nineteenth, and certainly in the twentieth century, began to configure a value system denoting good and bad, admissible or unacceptable behaviour, concepts of beauty and ugliness, and to determine the mechanisms by which these values are collectively accepted and observed by the population. My use of aesthetic here refers largely to notional concepts of beauty, taste and other values that become archetypal in a specific culture. How these shared notions evolve in any society is difficult to trace historically or delineate in textual analyses. In this essay I attempt this task nonetheless by an unwrapping of the complex process by which various identities - national, cultural, ethnic, class and particularly gender – are cumulatively being fashioned, through an examination of an important expression of this society's culture, the calypso.

The emergence of any popular art form in a society is, in part, determined by the material conditions to which the creative instinct responds. For instance, the evolution of the dance hall and disk jockeys in Jamaica with parallel forms of hip hop in the United States, in Britain as a rap culture and into India as "bhangra" in the last few decades of the twentieth century, is the response of groups in society who feel they have been short changed in the process of "development." They have generated not only alternative musical and lyrical styles, but, inadvertently or deliberately, created another language and mode of struggle. The calypso in Trinidad society emerged initially out of slavery and colonialism, as entertainment combined with social protest. Through *double entendre*, the singer conveyed ideas of rebellion and resistance to the indignities of slavery and post-slave society, disguising his or her outspokenness behind laughter and innuendo. As an art form, the calypso continued to offer the singers, generally men in the earlier part of the twentieth century, the space from which to articulate the grievances of the individual, class or community to which they belonged. The success of the calypso depended on the extent to which the singer or song writer had tapped into the sentiments or popular ideas of people in the society.

The 1920's and 1930's in Trinidad were fraught with economic hardships and a profound dissatisfaction with colonial rule. A spate of workers' riots during this period led by 1937 to the Crown Colony Moyne Commission Inquiry into conditions in various West Indian territories and resulted in trade unions, among other directives, for the first time in the region. The angry and debilitating tenor of working-class life at the time is captured in Arthur Lewis's *Labour in the West Indies: The Birth of a Workers Movement* (1938). Music was not yet recognized as a legitimate form of protest, so that Susan Craig's afterword to the 1977 edition of this book is an insightful one. Lewis, an economist, could not appreciate the social roots of popular music in the New World. "Popular music is in part produced by the changes in social structure" wrote Craig. "The growth of the unemployed to between 20% and 30% of all Caribbean workers, their struggle for survival and recognition and against repressive organs of the State, this is what is mirrored in the development of the steelband movement (and its struggle for survival), and in the musical explosion of West Kingston in particular."[4] This reading of both the calypso and the steelband are after the fact of their evolution from early twentieth century history.

The calypsos of the nineteenth and early twentieth century concentrated on glorifying physical prowess and were primarily concerned with display of courage and skill of men in a situation of physical encounter. Gordon Rohlehr (1990) analyzed the calypsos of the 1930s in relation to the "sociology of food acquisition in a context of survivalism." He suggested that the lyrical content of the calypsos of the 1930s accurately demonstrates the extent to which the calypsonian literally sung for his supper. The calypso form is to social commentary as butterflies are to pollen, and the themes and lyrical content change to suit the occasion and particular grievance of the moment. The actual shifts that may occur in the form of the calypso result from the changes in economic and social conditions. As one would expect in a creative musical form, it is also continuously influenced by changes in musical ideas, tastes and instrumentation. The calypso as an art form is versatile and resilient within the culture, particularly because it is in continuous dialogue with itself. Not surprisingly, some general themes such as economic survival, social exclusion, and the ubiquitous man-woman story are persistent and recurring, if not favourite themes of the calypsonian.

To examine the calypsos of the 1920's and 1930's in Trinidad, one needs to envisage the moment in its economic, political and social context. The period was characterized by growing unemployment, increasing urbanization, internal migration and sudden occupational shifts owing to the discovery of significant oil reserves in south Trinidad. The distinctive features in the migrant groups that comprised the society were also becoming more visible, and perhaps beginning to create the mosaic that was recognized as a 'Trinidadian' culture. Indian indentureship, the last organized labour importation system into the island, which ended in 1917, had brought thousands of Hindi-speaking Indian migrants each year since 1845 onto a space where Amerindian languages, then African languages, Spanish, English and French had been blended into a "French creole patois." That English was by then acknowledged as the language of the masses, could be recognized further from the emergence of the first Indian journalist, Seepersad Naipaul, who had begun in 1926 a twice weekly column entitled "Indian News and Views" for the English-owned and managed *Guardian* newspaper. Here the news from Indian villages was reported; religious celebrations such as Ramleela and Eid ul Fitr, and Indian marriage ceremonies were photographed, and published in the newspapers, along with news items of other segments of the population slowly gaining English literacy. A survey of the newspapers and writers of this period demonstrates that people were not only absorbed with poverty and survival that affected the man in the street. They were equally concerned with understanding the different ethnic beliefs and practices contained within this relatively small island, a quarter of the size of Jamaica.⁵ Calypsos were being used at this time to confront and make sense of the varied messages of masculinity and femininity that different groups and social classes introduced, at times uncharitably; calypso relies on rhetoric, humour and clever wit to bring the message home.

LANGUAGE AS AN INSTRUMENT OF THE MASSES

To acknowledge the importance of the English language in the development of calypso into the twentieth century, Raymond Quevedo (1892-1962), sobriquet Atilla the Hun, who would later become a political figure in the society, observed that from 1903 until about 1921, the oratorical skill of the calypsonian was celebrated, especially the calypsonian who could extemporize and thus impress his audience with his command of language. It was thought by Quevedo that in this period the calypso was influenced by the great public speakers of the time, among them Sir Henry Alcazar, M'Zumbo Lazare, Maresse Smith and Bishop Hayes.⁶ The performance being rendered more and more from the beginning of the twentieth century, the calypso and calypsonian could only now begin appealing to a public sensibility. The importance of the growth of the English language to calypso as the latter developed a greater mass appeal from 1920's onwards, cannot be underestimated in a cultural art form which relies on the word to carry the message. Bridget Brereton (1979) supports the argument that a shared language increased the impact of calypso as mythmaker from the early twentieth century. She writes:

> At the end of the [nineteenth] century, the majority of lower-class Creoles spoke creole habitually among themselves and as their native tongue. Most peons spoke Spanish among themselves. A large number of blacks who had come from the other islands spoke English mainly, though many learned patois in order to communicate with Creoles. The older Creoles and peons, those over forty or fifty by 1900, usually spoke little or no English, though they often understood it. Their children under the age of about forty usually had been exposed to English-language elementary education, and so both spoke and understood English, though they might not use it in their homes.

English was spreading fast; but patois remained the language of the Creole masses at the end of the century (Brereton, 1979, 166).

Thus it would take another generation born into this island, roughly into the second decade of the twentieth century, before English was more widespread in the society. Language has always been a major instrument of control, a fact well appreciated by the various European colonizers who wrested control of the various landmasses from each other.[7] By the end of the nineteenth century, the English language predominated, replacing patois - a dialect influenced by Spanish, African, French and English. As the language of British colonial rule and of government, English also became the language of the elite and the well-educated, offering the speaker of English a pathway to social mobility in a society now unfolding and requiring new talents. Eloquence and verbal skill became as powerful as the physical weaponry of the erstwhile stick fighter, a means by which power could be wielded against another. Since this power was usually traded between men, the calypso singer began to use the word as "power" adding this to working-class men's signifying attributes of masculinity in the society.

From the twentieth century, calypsonians in Trinidad were increasingly perceived as echoing the *vox populi*. The ruling class and the educated were viewed as being removed from the day-to-day experiences of the man in the street, whom the calypsonian appeared to represent. But this perception must be accepted advisedly. The calypsonian largely expressed the views of the class and ethnic group from which he originated and the sentiments of his sex. For the most part from the working class, calypsonians were men who, according to Ray Lucas, "...were supposed to be outcasts of society, and so was anyone who dared to sing the calypso in public"[8]. Up to the last decade of the twentieth century, if a young woman from the middle class fell in love with a singer in this category, she still had trouble persuading her parents to accept the legitimacy and decency of the occupation or the status of the profession of her young man. While there has been some change in attitudes towards calypsonians who have certainly gained more respectability in the twentieth century, some element of their *déclassé* status still persists. There are also class barriers erected around the singing of calypsoes, and until the eighties it was difficult for women and persons of different classes or ethnic groups to enter this arena. The idea that popular culture is fomented from the masses and reflects a widely shared aesthetic is nonetheless indisputable, and the messages carried over in the most popular, witty and clever calypsos, those that captured the imagination and appealed to the collective consciousness, attained classic proportions within the society and even throughout the Caribbean, appearing to represent the sentiments of the region as a whole.

In the development of Trinidad society in the twentieth century, there is an inseparable relationship between calypso and music (both local and externally influenced), linguistic idiom, and ethnic and gender relations. Such influences on the continuing evolution of calypso are numerous and complex. I make no pretence here of exhaustively examining this complexity. Much of this is done in Gordon Rohlehr's pathbreaking *Calypso and Society in Pre-Independence Trinidad* (1990) and in his many other publications and public addresses which deal with this theme. My concern in this essay is a specific one. Among the various forms of popular culture, song is, perhaps in many societies, the most potent one through which ideas pertaining to gender and sexuality are transmitted and debated. The emphasis that calypso of the early twentieth century placed on lyrical skill, humour and "*picong*" – "derived from the French *piquant* (stinging, insulting) and referred originally to the stinging insults that were traded during the exchanges by rivals *chantwelles*" (Warner 1982: 11) – has made it a persuasive and convincing vehicle for transmitting ideas and ideology, particularly with regard to gender. The *chantwelles* were groups of women and men, boys and girls from the stick fighter bands of the *diametré* class who moved around all year in the yards of Port of Spain. The role of the *chantwell* was to insult the rival yards, to egg on the stick fight and the stick fighters. Needless to say, everything became fodder for the wit and provocation of each yard, and undoubtedly, as always, gender and sexuality provide some of the sauciest material for the lyricism of singers.

Humour in calypso is a crucial part of its makeup and undeniably part of its entertainment appeal to a mass audience and to arousing popular consciousness. The relevance of humour, as it is employed in calypso, may be interpreted through the insights of Sigmund Freud: humour allows the unpalatable to be evoked and easily digested, and moreover dislodges repressed thoughts and images that influence conscious interaction. In the performance of the calypso, the cleverness of the lyrics impresses and amuses the listener even while it may address something contentious, distasteful, or perhaps taboo in the society. At the same time, by bringing these images or ideas to the surface, neither the singer nor the audience has allowed them to be conveniently forgotten. The humour or witticism is repeated for its insights and cleverness, easily recalled again in company away from the calypso tents, lending to discussions whether on the street corner or around the dinner table. The music, though important to the calypso, is the sauce that whets the appetite for the calypso dish and makes it palatable despite the controversy it evokes.[9] This mixture of humour and license allowed to the calypso has made this popular art form a primary one through which ideas of gender and sexuality are conveyed and debated (very often in heated exchanges between men and women) and eventually accepted in this society.

By the second decade of the twentieth century, the singers of calypso in Trinidad were primarily drawn from the majority ethnic group, those of African descent. The remainder of the population were Indians, Chinese, Europeans, Portuguese, Lebanese, and peoples from other Caribbean islands. Despite variations of ethnicity which eventually formed the total population, there persists a collective idea of regional identities and racial stereotypes - constructions of masculinity and femininity and male and female sexuality which typify, not only Trinidad but are often extended to the wider Caribbean. Racial stereotypes are not reducible to psychological traumas. Amina Mama's approach to the study of racialized identities of the post-colonial black subject is a useful one to draw on here. In *Beyond the Masks, Race, Gender and Subjectivity* (1995), Mama employs the concept of 'subjectivity' instead of the psychological terms of "identity" and "'self." She rejects the "dualistic notion of psychological and social spheres as essentially separate territories: one internal and one external to the person."[10] She analyzes the psychological and social spheres as mutually connected, each advancing in a recursive relationship with the other. While her analysis deals primarily with the production of subjectivities of contemporary black women in the 1980's and 1990's in Britain, her approach of deconstructing the psychologically weighted term "identity" and 'self' into 'subjectivity' allows a more nuanced interpretation of the role which the calypso and calypsonians play in the creolization process in Trinidad at least.

The idea of subjectivity admits the emotional integrity of the subject's own experience, the class from which he or she emerges. To admit to subjectivity as a valid process in the construction of our reality valorizes the particular expression of gender or ethnic identity portrayed by the singer, as well as those of the listeners. The calypsonian and the audience are simultaneously engaged in the production of racial, gender and class identities, each actor or participant in the production positioned in a shared subjectivity, supporting or perhaps denying the dominant models produced by bourgeois society. The fact that a particular set of cultural values is selected and transformed in the colonial process by a people is not accidental. The perceived differences among people in any community are constantly being reinforced to accommodate social or economic demands, as for example, the caste/occupational divisions in India, the class/status hierarchy of Britain, or the colour/ethnic hierarchy of the United States. At the same time, one must recall that these are being shaped alongside the ideological struggle of the ruling class to project the notion of a dominant cultural elite system, thus guaranteeing the economic and political interests of that class. This process of changing class and status has often involved radical, violent and revolutionary struggles. The problems of class, ethnicity and gender definition that the calypsonian draws attention to in his songs allow combative positions to enter into a dialogue, thereby airing grievances and settling some differences without the additional complications caused by physical confrontations.[11]

GENDER AS A THEME IN CALYPSO

By the 1920s the main language of the calypso was of English. Its schematic form allowed and included witticisms and a relative freedom of speech. There was also an audience receptive to this kind of performance. We need to consider the role of the calypso song in creating mythologies related to gender and sexuality, in Trinidad in particular and the Caribbean in general. Messages of gender in a society are transmitted in oblique ways, such as scripture, proverbs and the like, lending an air of timeless truths. In that sense the meaning of calypsos past is immortalized as truths.

Between the dominant ideas embodied in cultural aesthetics, and the pragmatic day-to-day lives of a people, we know there is a distance. Yet popular culture inscribes through its very popularity, a mythology that is continuously reproduced in the semiotics of each art form. How do symbols of maleness and femaleness, ideas of gender and difference, of separate male and female spheres, distinct and indistinct male and female sexualities, and concepts of masculinity and femininity, surface as representative of any society's population? Are these accepted or rejected by the society? Does acceptance reflect the condition and sensibility of the majority of men and women in the society at the time, and should it reflect the sentiments of the majority? In other words, how and why are ideas of gender – masculinity and femininity, and male and female sexuality in a society becoming mythologized through popular culture itself? What is the logic of this myth within this society?

To analyze both the how and why in the mythologies of identity created by the subjects themselves, I examine a selection of the calypsos written and performed during the decade of the twenties and thirties. Apart from my argument that by the turn of the century the English language has become the shared tongue of the society, I have chosen to focus on the calypsos until 1939 for three other reasons. *First*, by 1900 the oral and scribal evidence made the task of the ethnomusicologist a simpler one, and the research by Rohlehr (1990), Quevedo (1983), Warner (1982) and others who record in excellent detail the calypsos from the 20s onwards, has made possible the systematic analysis of gender construction through calypso. The calypsos that are recorded and recalled from the 1920s appear to be the most critical ones in constituting contemporary mythologies. "My experience of the calypso goes back to somewhere around 1927, but vivid memories start only in the early 1930s when 44 Nelson Street was the hub of the calypso, and where the late Atilla, Douglas and later Lion, all appeared," writes Ray Lucas. "The centre of Carnival and of course Calypso was at that time Henry to Duncan Streets, and Duke and Marine Square, with Frederick Street as the borderline. ...And since calypso tents were put up in backyards, under roofs of bamboo and coconut branches, one can see at once why this uptown area was the centre of activity."[12] The working class of urban Port of Spain was at the heart of this construction of an art form and aesthetic of calypso and carnival in this period.[13]

The *second* reason has to do with the emergence in Trinidad society in the twentieth century of an articulated ideology about class and gender.[14] In his published book *Atilla's Kaiso*, Raymond Quevedo (1983) or Atilla the Hun writes that the calypsonian was inseparably bound up with the ritual of stick-fighting or *kalenda* and thereby with working class male culture. These bands of men were "often accompanied by a retinue of women,"[15] some of the chantwelles referred to before were of working-class background. Quevedo writes that "the participation of the upper strata of society, including lawyers, in the covert practice of *kaiso* and *kalenda* is in a large measure attributable to the attraction that the women of easy virtue wielded." The men from the upper strata were referred to as Jacketmen, literally men who wore jackets. One nineteenth century singer, Lord Hannibal, had a famous song which was both a road march and kalenda stick fighting song during the era 1870 to 1890. The subject was Peti Belle Lily, a tourist woman of great beauty. The rivalry between men for Peti Belle Lily entered into a song. Congo Jack, a gravedigger and famous police spy, was ostracized by the *diametré* or jammette world but aspired to win her affections. Andrew Pearce (1988, 157-158) writes "Hannibal was jealous and angry that she had fallen so low and attacked her in this song:

Peti Belle Lily   Peti Belle Lily
Peti Belle Lily   Peti Belle Lily
Lom Kamisol   Jacket man
Lom sa Kamisol   Man without jacket
Tut mun kase bambirol   Are all making free with her

Peti Belle Lily jen fi du Peti Belle Lily sweet young girl
Peti Belle Lily se yo fu   Peti Belle Lily she crazy
Peti Belle Lily maliwe   Peti Belle Lily she's unfortunate
Su la jam-li mete dife   They put fire to her legs

In the last line of the song, Hannibal referred to an incident in which Congo Jack assaults Peti Belle Lily by attempting to set her dress afire with some inflammable liquid.

Though the double standard of Victorian morality forbade the active participation of their women in carnival before the thirties,[16] it allowed middle-and upper-class men the opportunity to indulge in illicit liaisons with working class women. The lingering legacy of gender relations - the white master/female slave sexual relationships which had existed during slavery – persisted into the early twentieth century. By the early twentieth century, however, the calypso provided one means by which black working-class men could legitimately respond to what they viewed as the trespass of the upper classes on their territory and their women. One calypso of this period goes:

> Point pour point
> Moen si miex point youn jacketman
> Jacketman pas ka ba moen bois en la rue-la
>
> Point for point
> I prefer a jacketman
> Jacketman don't beat me with the stick in the street

The author is unknown but the patois in which the calypso is written dates it as the first decade of the twentieth century. What is interesting is that it immediately situates working class masculinity in opposition to that of the middle and upper classes, and in relation to an explicit idea of femininity. The persona of the song is female, but while the song addresses the desire of women, it actually stirs up the resentment that these working-class men felt about the incursion of more privileged men invading the space and having greater access to "their women." Nonetheless, the female voice speaks not on the presumed monetary gain which the working-class woman will benefit from being in a liaison with a "jacketman," but on the idea that she will not be battered and humiliated in public.

Johnson (1977) has observed that there are great lacunae in our knowledge of sexual mores of the black urban working class during the late nineteenth and early twentieth centuries, but from what is known, the "relationships between the sexes have been coloured ...by a mutual suspiciousness." He observes that black working class culture was less sexually inhibited than that of the upper and middle classes, but at the same time there was the tradition of an aggressive masculinity, a tradition that in his view represented a social change from the previous period, in which women were not on the margins of creating song and dance.[17]

Rohlehr (1990) and J.D. Elder (1966) agree that the stick fighters, chanterelles or chantwells, and jamettes of the late nineteenth century, the precursors to twentieth century carnival and calypso culture, included women. "The women who were an inseparable element in all stick fighting bands did contribute to the singing, and during the intervals between stick fights would sing their carisos: lewdly erotic songs accompanied by exotic dancing."[18]

The nature of female participation in carnival and calypso and its impact on the gender relations, and female gender identity in particular was interesting to note. Bridget Brereton (1979) comments that "carnival as a whole was purged after the 1880s but this purging affected men and women, but maybe men more as Canboulay was always a male domain."[19] She disagrees that there was a decline in female participation in calypso and carnival from the nineteenth to the twentieth century or that there was a major shift in gender identities where women become the onlookers and property of men, as there is insufficient evidence as yet to make such claims. Brereton summed up that although jamettes became less conspicuous in Carnival, they were central to the urban carnival scene in the first half of the twentieth century. The slums of Port of Spain and the sub-culture that emerged based on the barrack yards was "dominated by the jamets or *diametrés*, the singers, drummers, dancers, stickmen, prostitutes, pimps and badjohns in general."[20] The term jamettes was the creole evolution of the *diametré*, similar to the Parisian *demi monde*, referring to those who lived on the diameter of respectability, the outcasts as it were of society. "The jamets," writes Brereton, "boasted their skill in fighting, their bravery, their wit and ability at 'picong', their talent in song and dance, their indifference to the law, their sexual prowess, even their contempt for the church. In short they reversed the canons of respectability."[21] Women emerged more visibly again in the steelband movement of the 1930s-40s as the flag women, the "Jean and Dinahs" of that era. "One of the interesting things about urban working-class Afro-Trinidadian culture" Brereton agrees, "is that it always tolerated, at times celebrated, open female sexuality – a countervailing value to the hegemonic gender identities of the time."

Between the late nineteenth and early twentieth centuries, however, while women are avid participants in the world of carnival and calypso, at the same time, they were becoming the butt of male conversation through calypso. The early calypso cited above "Jacketmen," begins to lay down a blueprint for notions of gender and sexuality between different classes of men in the society, and hints at the brooding antagonism and violence between working class black men and women.

The *third* reason for choosing calypsos from the decades of the 1920s and 1930s is that in this period the calypsonians are possibly increasing in numbers, coming from different classes and ethnic groups in the society. For instance, Raymond Quevedo or Atilla, whose father was Venezuelan, had a secondary school education and would have emerged from the then middle class. The calypsonians themselves were known and differentiated by personality and style. Their calypsos had begun to be recorded, and the rest of the society, especially the ruling class, had begun the process of censorship and control over the voice of the calypsonian. Between 1929 and 1939, the number of calypsos available for analysis is adequate to provide us with a clear blueprint for gender drawn up for the most part by the male performer. By 1940, the politics of the Second World War had led Winston Churchill to sign an agreement for the establishment of US naval and air bases in Trinidad in exchange for fifty old US destroyers. There was a consequent influx of American soldiers and sailors which added another layer of masculinity to the struggle for patriarchal control and racial identities in the society. While this essay limits itself to the period prior to 1939, before another rupture to the gender system occurred, the period after 1939 still requires close and careful analysis.

SETTING THE BOUNDARIES FOR MASCULINITY AND FEMININITY IN THE TWENTIETH CENTURY

Point for point
I prefer a jacketman
Jacketman don't beat me with the stick in the street

The jacketmen having some claim to their women, Quevedo constructs the successive notion that must then arise among black working-class men to let them reclaim masculine pride. He suggests that, possibly as a result of the class rivalry, the ordinary man, or *negue jardin* (field slaves) as he was called on Carnival day, "renewed his interest in his personal appearance (and) ...took to being dandily attired"(Quevedo, 1983: 23). The press, directed by the upper echelons, began to complain about a labour shortage on the estates and the calypsonians retorted:

> Ah wouldn't work, Ah rather lahay
> Ah wouldn't work, Ah rather lahay
> For when ah don't get no pay
> So ah rather walk about every day
>
> Ah eh working no way
> But knocking bout in me serge and me flannel
> Ah eh working no way
> People want to know how ah living

The "serge and flannel" of the calypso clearly parodies the dress of the leisured upper-class man. The impunity of the working-class man to announce that he was not working is itself a slap in the face of the system which forced the labour of the slave at one time, a labour which could no longer be coerced through violent means.

When the calypsonian engages with the crowd, either by mirroring its idiosyncrasies or depicting recognized sexual personae, his success encourages subsequent performances. The public performance of the calypso and the affirmation through the response of the audience are in tandem with one of the origins of this form of song, the call and response of slave work songs. Inasmuch as gender and sexuality were topics ripe for ribaldry and social observation and were very popular with the crowd, they emerged as two of the major and ongoing themes selected by the calypsonian for commentary and performance. By playing and replaying the ideas which were popular with the crowd, the calypsonian helps to sustain the aesthetic and the mythologies regarding gender.

A spate of calypsos dealing with gender themes began in the late twenties and burgeoned in the decade of the thirties. The calypsonians who were more or less engaged in this dialogue were: Atilla (Raymond Quevedo), The Roaring Lion (Hubert Raphael Charles), Lord Beginner (Egbert Moore), Lord Ziegfield (Eric Belasco), The Growling Tiger (Neville Marcarno), King

Radio (Norman Span), The Young Pretender (Aldric Farrell), The Growling Growler (Errol Duke), Lord Invader (Rupert Grant), Lord Executor (Phillip Garcia), Houdini (Wilmoth Hendricks/ Edgar Leon Sinclair), and Lord Caresser (Rufus Callender). The sobriquets chosen by the calypsonians are themselves indicative of the masculinity with which they identify. There were very few women calypsonians. Rohlehr cites three women involved in calypso performance: Lady Beginner – Mrs. Egbert Moore, Lady Iere and Lady Trinidad (Thelma Lane).

The verbal skill of calypso by the 1920's was by no means only directed against another class of men. Calypsonians attacked each other equally. Rohlehr notes that there was no personal enmity in this give and take between calypsonians, rather masculine reputation was at stake. "Calypso humour existed not so much to annihilate identity as to remind the over-reacher that his identity lay within the group, and that however high he might ascend, he could be levelled" (Rohlehr, 1990, 4). This levelling was symptomatic of the newness of the society, a struggle between the individual men representing various ethnic groups and the working class to assert their social space, while setting up psychological defenses against other groups of men more privileged within the society. It must be recalled that the society is relatively small, that there were a handful of calypsonians within the entire society, and that they are becoming the eyes and ears and voice of their sex, their race and their class. While calypso lyrics projected ideas about femininity, the contest was essentially that between men and men vying to outdo and out rank each other. This is a critical idea to be retained in a consideration of calypso as it frames gender mythology in its continued development in Trinidad.

Rohlehr's treatment of the calypsos of the thirties which deal with gender is to be found in his comprehensive essay, "Images of Men and Women in the Calypsoes of the 1930s: or the Sociology of Food Acquisition in a Context of Survivalism."[22] Male ego retrieval in the face of adverse economic conditions, if not outright poverty of the 1930s, was carried out at the expense of women. Women were depicted as malicious and promiscuous, yet also virtuous and strong, they were to be feared while being idolized. The calypsonians, almost uncritically, reproduced the stereotype of femininity espoused by Christianity and other western and eastern ideologies – in other words the contradictory depictions of femininity: woman was either virgin or whore, mother to be largely trusted and glorified, or wife to be mistrusted, brutalized and kept in place.

In the 1920s calypsos, Atilla, Executor, Lion and Caresser waged war against calypsonian Houdini. Houdini appears to be a very slippery character. From the biographical entries found on his life history, Houdini – Edgar Leon Sinclair, claimed two birth dates 1895 and 1902, and established that he had a reputation both at home and abroad, with thousands of songs to his name. While he was no doubt prolific, fewer than 250 songs had actually been attributed to him by 1945 and he did not author some of those. Two calypsos written and sung by Houdini constructed ideas of femininity and masculinity which were popularly believed in the island: *Sweet Like a Honey Bee* (1928) and *Woman Sweeter Than Man*, (1929). In *Sweet like a Honey Bee* Houdini sings "The Blacker the woman the sweeter she be," predating the genre of calypsos which began to extol the virtues of one race of women in contrast to another. Not only did this begin a commentary on physical attributes, but also set up the opposition between black and the other, whereby the other could be White, or later, Indian and Chinese.

King Radio or Norman Span is described by Quevedo in 1929 as "the slim, darling figure" who "in the tradition of the art, ...sent bouquets to himself, extolling his sexual prowess, handsomeness and ability to surmount (questionable though it appears) the economic rigour of the time." All of these themes were pursued by the various calypsonians as the signature of masculinity. A calypso which King Radio sang in 1933 *Country Club Scandal*, used a woman's honour to dishonour the husband and established the calypso form as the airing ground for sexual grievances of one man against the other, while it also permitted the space for the victim to publically gain revenge. In one version of the story, the taste for revenge was stimulated by the double standards of sexuality of bourgeois society. Working class men were supposed to practice what was preached to them, not what they observed, and they resented the privileges and double standards set by men of property or those in positions of power. Radio's calypso was transparent in challenging the double standard:

From the swimming pool
To the servant's room
That is where Mrs. X met her doom
The Country Club scandal
Was a hideous bacchanal

This began the travails of calypso censorship in Trinidad. Quevedo/Atilla in a speech to the Legislative Council in 1951 (by which time he had entered politics and won a seat in the Port of Spain City Council), revealed the details behind this calypso which led to state censorship debates, a debate which persists to this day. "It was alleged that a certain high-placed lady, the wife of distinguished officialdom, made the unforgivable mistake of allowing herself to be caught *in flagrante delecto*. The correspondent was the then Inspector General of Constabulary, a highly placed Government Officer." Another version of the story, an account by Albert Hicks reported in Rohlehr (1990) cites that the affair was supposed to have taken place between the Inspector General of the Constabulary and another man's sweetheart. The aggrieved partner complained to a calypsonian in order to revenge the insult to his masculine pride. The calypsonian's (Radio's) many performances of this story led to the eventual seclusion and banishment of the Inspector, and offending wife, from the colony.

In 1933 Radio was billed to sing this calypso at the Silky Millionaires tent. This scandalous subject attracted huge crowds who were prurient about the personal lives of the white and upper-class population. Quevedo writes that a message was brought by a policeman on stage to say that this calypso must not be sung. At this point the calypsonians appealed to Captain A. A. Cipriani, a member of the Legislative and Executive Council and leader of the largest political party in the country whose response was "Put a chair for me on the stage and sing your song. Let the police do their damnedest. I am by your side" (Quevedo, 1983, 281). Censorship continued to be a concern of the state, however, and Rohlehr notes that in 1944, eleven years after he had permitted the stage performance of this song, Cipriani himself stopped the performance of a Calypso drama being staged at the Victory Tent by Atilla and Lion (Rohlehr, 1990, 294).

Cipriani's initial support of this washing of high society and eminent professionals' dirty linen in public set the stage for two features which were built into this creole aesthetic. First it safeguarded a certain degree of freedom of speech and therefore the way in which the calypsonian as the *vox populi* ensured that no scandal, by rich or poor, politician or priest, would be suppressed from public gaze and commentary.[23] One result of this freedom of speech is that it also gave license to the male calypsonian to comment unfavourably, if he so desired, on subjects such as femininity. With the absence of women from the field, it was an open stage for calypsonians to air their grievances about bad experiences they may have had with individual women, or to play on the fantasies of masculinity in a colonial setting where different ethnic groups of men are competing for prestige, jobs and women. The corollary of course was that femininity was therefore being shaped and controlled by men in their own interests in an uneven forum.

For the year 1933 there were fewer calypsos that figure gender relations, but an interesting duet between Atilla and the Roaring Lion confirms some of the theoretical ideas raised in this essay about the continued evolution of calypso, language, humour, stage performance and subjective involvement of men in creating mythology. Atilla and the Roaring Lion recorded two calypsos in 1933, *Grenadian Girl and Doggie Doggie Look Bone*. There are no lyrics cited for the former in any of the texts consulted but the lyrics found for the latter, the coincidence of the year, and the form of presentation, suggest that these two were perhaps the same or the second calypso an extension of the first. In *Doggie Doggie Look a Bone*, Lion first sung:

> Once I met with a Grenadian
> In whom I had all my affection
> But for all I do and for all I try
> I couldn't win her heart, friends, I don't know why
> For every time I go to her home
> De woman tell me, doggie doggie look a bone

Lion and Atilla were performing this calypso for a small party in a city restaurant, a shift from performing primarily at the calypso tent where the competition was becoming acute.[24] One of the patrons commented on "the lack of that usual gay abandon" which they had in the tents which he felt could be resolved by extemporizing between them. Thus it became a duet between the two calypsonians, and he who was paying the piper called the tune. Atilla's extempore response to Lion was immediate, such was their skill at wordplay:

> Why don't you get mosquito heart and lye
> Jumbie bird liver and roucou dye
> Crapaud mild, bat-face and saltfish wing
> A young keskidee that never sing
> Guinea pepper, salt, blue and a match box
> Mix them together and wear in your socks
> And whenever you go to her home
> She never tell you doggie doggie look a bone
> (Quevedo, 1983, 46)

While much of this extempore performance was done to elicit satisfaction from the guests, extemporizing calypso is also more successful if it relates to familiar or collectively shared notions. The idea in the Caribbean that spells can be cast on the unwilling victim is based on popular belief in obeah or ritual magic of African religions and also resonates with the age-old idea of witchcraft in western traditions - for instance the role of the three witches in Shakespeare's Macbeth. What is interesting in this calypso is that the male figure is the undesirable, the female desired. Tiger in *Marjorie*, undated but likely to be sung before the fifties, reverses this gender equation with "Yes sir, a girl named Marjorie, Giving me things in me food for matrimony" and by 1966, in one of his most well-known calypsos *Obeah Wedding*, The Mighty Sparrow continues this mythology. Melda, his protagonist, is castigated for using obeah to catch and marry the unwilling man who states that "All you do, you can't get through, Ah still eh go marry to you." *Doggie doggie look bone* at the same time draws another line in the blueprint for gender relations as laid down by calypso: the calypsonian's propensity to locate characteristics of femininity according to society or country, in this case the Grenadian woman, and later on according to race or profession. An analysis of calypso from the 1920s to the present reveals numerous songs which stereotype women by race and/or society. These stereotypes have amazingly long-lasting appeal in the public sensibility.

By 1934 we see a calypso dialogue between Lion and Beginner which debates the virtues of the Ugly Woman versus the Pretty Woman. This was one of the first instances where the calypsonians, Lion and Atilla, travelled to the USA to record "Trinidad's own national song and music." Quevedo writes that "Lion simply took New York by storm with his *Ugly Woman*:"

> If you want to be happy and live a king's life
> Never make a pretty woman your wife
> All you've got to do is just what I say
> And you'll be always happy and gay
> From a logical point of view
> Always marry a woman uglier than you
>
> An ugly woman gives you your meals on time
> And will always try to console your mind
> At night when you lie in your cozy bed
> She will coax, caress you and scratch your head
> And she will never shame her husband at all
> By exhibiting herself with Peter and Paul
> So from a logical point of view
> Always marry a woman uglier than you

Bill Rogers/Augustus Hinds in 1934 contributed to this dialogue by composing and recording in this same year *Ugly or Pretty Woman Paseo*:[25]

> It matters not your friends may say this and that
> Tit for tat and butter for fat
> The nice woman face might be soft as silk
> And the ugly woman own like sour milk
> But ugly or nice you all men should know
> Is woman a 'ready and you must get blow
> So it quite plain to understand
> A nice woman pass off an ugly man

Rogers is suggesting that the entire debate is meaningless because, ugly or pretty, the woman would be unfaithful to her husband. A remarkably fixed set of ideas and a syllogistic equation on femininity emerges from this exchange between the calypsonians. Pretty women are not to be trusted, ugly women are not to be trusted, therefore all women are not to be trusted. Subtly proposed is the possibility that perhaps ugly women are to be trusted more than pretty women who are more attractive to other men. The yardstick for measuring beauty is not clear as yet from the calypsos in question, but we can assume, based on the ideas built into creole society, that the lighter coloured more sought after women would be deemed the pretty ones, whereas, the dark skinned women with the broader noses and curly hair - the uglier. In this parry between calypsonians of the virtues of the ugly versus the pretty woman, the concept of prettiness is subjective and relative yet its popularity suggests a taken for granted meaning of the terms pretty and ugly shared not only by the calypsonians engaged in the dialogue, but the larger audience who respond positively to this message.

Whether real or imagined in the milieu in which these calypsonians lived, womanhood is painted with the brush strokes of the biblical Eve in the garden of Eden, capable of great deception of men. Men on the other hand portray themselves as the unwilling victims of a female culture premised on duplicity and cunning, or also capable of guile by using women to satisfy their sexual needs and desire for security.

Duets led to trios and another construction of femininity is born in *Marian leggo me man*, sung by Atilla, Roaring Lion and the Growling Tiger in 1935. This situates another dimension of the feminine personality, that women are constantly in competition for men. In 1935 as well, Lord Beginner introduces the persona of the Hispanic woman in the form of the Spanish prostitute Anacaona, possibly an allegorical play on the anaconda, a very large nonvenomous snake of South America which kills its prey by constriction. The snake as metaphor for woman is clichéd in both religion and literature and therefore not unlikely to be incorporated into the calypso blueprint for gender. Certainly, the lyrics Beginner sings about the Hispanic dancer describes the snake: "How she slip and she slide up/And she dip and she glide up." Hispanic prostitutes and Hispanic dancers were part of Trinidad's *diametré* in this period and no doubt the contradictory relationship between woman as dancer and prostitute, disreputable yet desired, and the thinly veiled ideas of exploitation of the man by such immoral women, were all evoked in the name Anacaona. This obliqueness of speech has not augured well for the construction of femininity and female sexuality.

Atilla more prosaically outlined a persistent yet underlying male fear of women in 1935 when he sung a calypso *Women will rule the world*. This calypso appears remarkably prescient for its time, more suited to the late twentieth century progress of women in Trinidad. It was a particularly interesting calypso regarding women since both in Trinidad and globally, women were still largely perceived as the 'weaker sex' and in many societies were underprivileged and unexposed. Despite the efforts of the Suffragettes in Britain at the turn of the century and the strident voices of female comrades in the dawning of Soviet Russia, by 1935 very few countries had given women the right to vote. In Britain and the United States, two women, Marie Stopes and Margaret Sanger had begun not more than a decade before to champion the virtues of contraception for women, which at the time were promoted to ensure planned motherhood and racial hygiene. The Second World War had not yet demanded the employment of women in the United States and Europe in factories and shipyards. Yet, in Trinidad, Atilla wrote and sang:

> How different the ladies of long ago
> To the modern woman that we all know
> If you've observed, you are bound to see
> That sex has changed entirely
> Long ago their one ambition in life
> Was to be a mother and a wife
> But now they go out and imitate the males
> By smoking cigarettes and drinking cocktails
>
> Girls used to like to be schoolteachers
> Gradually becoming stenographers
> We next hear of them as lecturers
> Authors and engineers
> There is no limit to their ambition
> They've even gone in for aviation
> And if you men don't assert control
> Your women will rule the world
>
> If women ever get ascendancy
> They will show us no sympathy
> They will make us do strange things, goodness knows
> Scrub floors and even wash clothes

> If these tyrants become our masters
> We'll have to push perambulators
> And in the nights when they go out to roam
> We'll have to mind the baby at home

Rohlehr (1990) comments that: "Politically aware, conscious of every current in his society, Atilla retained a blind spot on the subject of woman's role, and jealously warned men about women's trespassing on male preserves of power and prerogative." In the 1930's, the apex of women's achievements in the eyes of society was marriage and motherhood, with a small minority becoming educated to achieve more than these careers in Trinidad. Between 1930 and 1940 the largest proportion of women who had even migrated to further their education were doing so in areas such as nursing and teaching. The only known progressive organization of women in Trinidad at this time was the League of Social Workers led by Audrey Jeffers (Reddock, 1994).

Atilla sang at least twenty calypsos between 1911 and 1955. Of these I have identified ten probably written and sung between 1930 and 1940 that dealt with the theme of feminine dangers to the male. Atilla (Raymond Quevedo) was born to a Venezuelan father and Trinidadian mother in 1892 and died in Trinidad in 1962. He attended St. Mary's College, the prestigious Roman Catholic secondary school in Port of Spain where he had won a scholarship. This schooling prepared him for either higher studies abroad or at least a professional white-collar occupation in business or in government service. Instead, Quevedo decided to become a calypsonian, a choice which was very unusual for a man of his class, colour and ethnic mixture at this time in Trinidad. The subjects of the majority of his calypsos signal a shrewd interest in the political government of Trinidad society and he established himself over the years as a social reformist with an empathy for the poor and downtrodden.[26] Despite this progressive outlook, he became "the mouthpiece for some of the most reactionary anti-feminist ideology, and the spokesman for a rigid patriarchy that was incapable of transcending the narrow sexism of the age."[27] One undated calypso which emerged possibly in the 30s and is attributed to Atilla has become legendary in inscribing a model for female sexuality and a prescription for male behaviour in gender relations. Entitled *Treat em rough* or *Turn em down*, the calypsonian suggests:

I've discovered a new philosophy
How to live with women happily
What Socrates and Zeno and Plato didn't know
I'll explain to you in calypso

Chorus
Every now and then turn them down
They'll love you long and they'll love you strong
You must be robust, you must be tough
Don't throw no punches but treat them rough

I had a pretty little mopsy and
She left me for a robust man
I followed her and said, darling I care a lot
What this fellow has that I haven't got
Then she said, Atilla confidentially
He does things you never did to me

Chorus
Every now and then he turn me down
So I love him long and I love him strong
When he kiss or squeeze, he does it brutally
That's why I love him eternally

Look around any place and you will see
Faces radiating virginal purity
But, boys, please don't misunderstand
Don't play the fool and act like no gentleman
Don't let the aura of their sweet passivity
Paralyze your judgement of evoke your sympathy

Chorus
Every now and then push them round
They'll love you long and they'll love you strong
You must be robust, you must be tough
Don't throw no punches but treat 'em rough

Even in the bridal chamber
Teach them, yes, who is the master
Don't be swayed by sentimentality
Or they'll tell their friends that you are a sissy

These are the things you must never forget
I mean the ethics of your boudoir etiquette

Chorus
Every now and then turn them down
They'll love you long and they'll love you strong
You must be robust, you must be tough
Don't throw no punches but treat 'em rough

A variant of the calypso, which was included by another calypsonian, Duke of Albany in 1947, changes the chorus a bit but retains the same message:

Every now and then cuff them down
They love you long and they love you strong
Black up the eye and bruise up the knee
And then they love you eternally

Slinger Francisco or The Mighty Sparrow who attained massive popularity as a calypsonian from the fifties onwards, revived and included this version of the calypso in his repertoire in the 1970s. Now in a climate where a contemporary western feminist consciousness could not be disregarded, he changed the last line of the chorus to "Then they leave you eternally." This advice on the rough treatment which women apparently desire has become so mythologized into gender relations in the Caribbean context that it is presented as folk wisdom rather than the witty ditty of a misogynistic calypsonian in the thirties. Its recurrent rendition by other calypsonians through the decades appears almost part of the rites to manhood in the society, a form of instruction to the younger men. This message is so gripping, that by 1984, calypsonian Penguin (Seadly Joseph), employing more contemporary idiom and less violent language, repeated the same mythology in *Woman don't like soft man*, a song, over-weighted with *double entendre* and sexual innuendo, but which earned him great popularity in the calypso halls of fame.

In 1935, Lady Trinidad made her debut at the *Crystal Palace Tent* on Nelson Street in Port-of-Spain as the first female calypsonian to sing in a tent. She was soon followed by two more female calypsonians in 1936: Lady Baldwin (Mavis Baldwin); and Lady

MacDonald (Doris MacDonald).[28] However, in 1935 we have what is possibly the first female response to Atilla's *Treat me Rough* in Lady Iere's calypso *Love and Affection* sung in 1935. Interestingly, Lady Iere (Edna Pierre) is not combative but urges women: " ...if you love your man and your man love you, you have a right to be honest faithful and true. Love was ordained by the Almighty for creation, for the male to love the female species."[29]

In 1936 King Radio sung one of the calypsos which gained immense and classic popularity, *Man Smart Woman Smarter*, a calypso which was recorded as jazz entered its swing phase which made it accessible to a much wider audience. The title again posits the female as the more deceptive or more ingenious of the two sexes. What is clear from its popularity is that calypsos that created stereotyped gender identities were fast becoming fashionable in the calypso repertoire. Included in this set of calypsos which comment on gender is The Roaring Lion's, *The Fall of Man*, recorded in April 1936, and The Growling Tiger's, *Money is King*. Rohlehr notes that the last calypso addresses the idea that the possession of money is the yardstick by which a man's value is assessed in society. The calypso focusses on the way in which society will overlook a man's disabilities or criminal records as long as he has money. Money and masculinity go hand in hand, as Tiger proposes in his refrain in *Money is King*:

> If you have money and things going nice
> Any woman will call you honey and spice
> If you can't give her a dress, or a new pair of shoe
> She'll say she have no uses for you
> When you try to caress her, she will tell you, "Stop
> I can't carry love in the Chinee shop"
> Ah sure most of you will agree it's true
> If you haven't money, dog better than you

The reference to the "Chinee shop" has specific relevance to the poorer classes where much of the goods are taken on credit or bought from the local store owned generally by a Chinese man. Tiger infers that the man cannot even feed his woman therefore she has no time for him. This theme of "no money no love" is continuously replayed in calypsos and attained classic proportions by the 70s when The Mighty Sparrow sang *No Money No Love*. In Sparrow's calypso, the female protagonist is explicit about her needs, and as with Tiger's innuendo, it is implied that women are the more mercenary and pragmatic of the two sexes:

Yuh cyar love without money
Yuh cyar make love on hungry belly
Darling, you see, you are the only one for me
Your'e my turtle dove
but no money no love

"THE FIGHTING CONTINUES, WOMAN VERSUS MAN"[30]

Between 1937 and 1939 there is an increase in the number of calypsos dealing with gender-related themes. Some of this increased interest in gender must be attributed to the interplay between calypsonians themselves whose call and response to each other spurred on a dialogue within the group. By 1937, however, we see the emergence of Lady Trinidad who begins to outline a female viewpoint in her *Advice to Every Young Woman*. She warns young women not to be taken in by the guile of faithless young men. Lady Trinidad sang a duet with Rass Kassa or Inveigler entitled *I can't live on Macafouchette* this same year. Caresser's *Macafuchette* sung in 1938 suggests that Macafouchette refers to the leftovers from a rich man's plate.

One of the dominant themes which signal a persistent idea of femininity versus masculinity, and the relation between the two, is that of woman as prostitute, played out in the song version as the classic biblical temptation of the helpless and hapless male. This idea rears its head in Cobra's *Mamaguy me* and Growler's *In the Dew and the Rain*. These were among a cycle of calypsos sung only by men which castigated prostitution and prostitutes. One reason is that with increasing urbanization more young girls were being forced into prostitution as a profession. The calypsonian whose milieu would have exposed him to seedier aspects of urban nightlife, would have been aware of the growth of this profession among women. The presence of the Social Welfare League founded by Audrey Jeffers in 1920, which, among its other aims, worked on the eradication of prostitution and the protection of young girls who had left their homes and boarded in working girls hostels in the city, also indicates that it was a growing phenomenon in urban life. The imagery of the prostitute was a savage and unrelenting one.

Growler visits retribution on the prostitute *In the Dew and the Rain* with:

> Too late too late shall be the cry
> When St. Peter put water in their eye

He reinforces the biblical injunction against harlotry in the Old Testament, the fault of course lying in the low flying birds of the night, rather than the prowlers who preyed on these birds.

Cobra's imagery of the woman as predator is more graphic in *Mamaguy me*:

> I couldn't believe the girl was like that
> But she prove to be a vampire bat
>
> But when you take them down to Teteron
> You will be frightened to see the size of they craw

The woman is the devourer of men, the man the innocent who is misled by first appearances hence "Mamaguy" me. The term *mamaguy* is a colloquialism used in Trinidad generally to describe men who are fooled by women. Phonetically and syntactically it suggests a commonsense notion of the man or 'guy' who is ruled by his mother or woman, harking back to the idea of the man who cannot stand on his own two feet due to his dependency on his mother, therefore a "softman" who is easily fooled, in this case by a prostitute. The logic is consistent, the woman does the fooling, the man is always being misled.

The warning for the female whose path led to prostitution is found in Ziegfield's *Advice to Young Ladies* to "Remain with Mamie in her decent home." Like Growler, Ziegfield also brings biblical retribution onto women who go astray:

> If you should upkeep your prestige in life
> Some day a gentleman will make you his wife
>
> But the seed you sow such fruit you shall reap
> And like your mother, some day it's your turn to weep
> But too late: don't cry, for now it's no use
> Prepare for Maracaibo or Lapeyrouse

Woman as prostitute persists in Roaring Lion *Girls of Today* and Beginner's *Second Hand Girls*, the latter in its idiom of 'second hand' is eloquent about a male perception of sexual encounters with prostitutes as goods already used by other men.[31]

This theme of woman the temptress is embellished through revisiting of a mythological creature called La Diablesse, the female devil. The female devil is a popular figure in western mythology, and a foundation myth in Caribbean folklore. According to the myth, La Diablesse is disguised as a beautiful woman who entices the man into the forest, away from his home and village, and when he has been led astray, far from his familiar terrain, he realizes he has been fooled as one of her feet is that of a cattle hoof. So gripping was this tale that in my own childhood in the fifties in village Trinidad this was one of the myths which we were weaned on and frightened into good behaviour. It also clearly established the dichotomy about good and bad women, and an empathy for the misguided men who were deceived. The other mythological female creature was that of the Socouyant, the blood-sucking witch who shed her clothes at night and flew through the village preying on other women's blood. In both myths, the female is depicted as avaricious, thirsty, predator, the qualities of a loose woman as opposed to the good wife, and always, the temptress of the unwary male or the virtuous female. In 1937 Lord Invader renders a literal interpretation of this myth in La Ja Blesse woman, where he is led into the metaphoric forest of temptation:

> She had a pair of magnetic eyes
> That's what had me hypnotize
> As she was walking by herself alone
> I said "Young lady, may I accompany you home?"
> And with the lady then I made self-introduction
> She said, "Invader, there is no objection"
> Still I insisted and I chat her to my very best
> Yet I didn't realize she was a La Ja Blesse

Rohlehr writes that this is the classic story whose version in English poetry is Keats *La Belle Dame Sans Merci*. "It belongs to that body of Western mythology through which female sexuality is demonized and male sexual inadequacy rationalized ...The Diablesse is the Caribbean version of the most powerful anti-feminist European myth and merits close ethnological study, if just as a means of exploring how Europe transported not only economic, political and social structures but also her deepest phobias, embedded sexual fears and patriarchal fears" (Rohlehr 1990, 170-1). This would be true if the mythology of woman as temptress, possessed by strange and mythical qualities which men fear, did not evolve similarly, yet independently from each other, in all cultures, both east and west, north and south. The answer, therefore, seems to me to lie not primarily in the legacy of colonialism, but in the essentialist biological and psychoanalytic differences between the sexes which have given rise to these myths in the early development of human consciousness in most known cultures. By the time they are inherited in colonial Trinidad, the package includes the symbolic fears of western society, the imagery of African mythology, and a blending of indigenous and recent history in the new society.

A second calypso on *Lajabless Woman* by Executor in 1938 supports the argument that new mythological features are grafted on to the old ones and given their Trinidadian peculiarities. More poetic and allegorical in his presentation, Executor's calypso brings into the foreground the Indian male, another masculine presence in Trinidad society. The protagonist here is Nabadeen, a poor Indian lad of St. James who is innocently entrapped by the demonic woman but manages to free himself from her clutches and escape unscathed:

> She led him over mountains and plains
> If he missed a step, he'd smash his brains
> She led him over precipitous rocks
> To fill his body with electric shocks
> There must have been some good angel by his side
> Or otherwise he would have died
> This was the rumour we hear next day
> Lajablesse sha ya le alla

The next verse in this calypso continues with no sexual temptation, but the fear of physical danger as well the "black magic trick" which "gave him a fright." Granted, the protagonist is a young rather than experienced older man which may account for the undercurrent of fear which is laced throughout the calypso. In my view, however, this calypso is also about a contest between different masculinities in the same society. Thus far the working-class man of African descent symbolizes the aggressive masculinity in the society. The newcomer, the Indian male is generally viewed as physically not his equal, and must therefore not tangle with his female counterpart, the black woman. While all men are drawn together in this web of brotherhood against the female of the species, yet the "poor Indian lad Nabadeen" is not sexually aroused, has no opportunity to consummate the sexual act, he is simply afraid for his life in the face of the "black magic." This interpretation on the perception of Indian masculinity in Trinidad society in the first half of the twentieth century is not an impressionistic one. In my research on Indians for this period, I encountered several instances where the aggression of the black man was the overpowering symbol of masculinity, while that of the Indian male was a more introverted, not sexually charged, yet violent, not to other men, but towards Indian women. While the history of the black male slave as stud and marginal to the family has left its own mythology of black masculinity, the indentureship system which transported far more Indian males than females, and isolated them on estates, has made for a different ideology regarding Indian masculinity in the society.[32]

By 1939 the range of women's vices as prostitutes or loose women is extended in Ziegfield's *Bad Girls* and Roaring Lion's *Badwoman*. It was not until 1943 when Invader's *Rum and Coca Cola* "both mother and daughter working for the Yankee dollar" and 1956 The Mighty Sparrow's *Jean and Dinah*, "Rosita and Clementina, round the corner posing, bet your life is something they selling" were released that the female prostitute in calypso became indelibly inked into the framework of indigenous gender mythology in Trinidad society. As mentioned before, an in-depth analysis of gender relations during and after the Second World War is sorely needed to continue this thematic enquiry.

The spate of calypsos between 1937 and 1939 firmly establishes not only the symbolic fear of woman as temptress and sinner, but the literal fear of women in day to day life. Radio proclaimed *Tell the world I don't want no wife*, Lord Invader sang about *Sweet Man Bachelor* and *A Bachelor's Life*, and Lord Ziegfield says categorically *I don't want a young girl*. In the last calypso Ziegfield states a preference for older more experienced women to the younger girls who humiliate men in public. Older women tolerate indifferent or bad treatment from men because of their own anxieties that the younger man would abandon them. Ziegfield describes the young women as tyrants, the older women as more tolerant:

> You got to stay silent in front of the tyrant
> Or she'll send you in L'Hospice for a month
> You could do them what you like, they won't get enraged
> They fraid you may strike for a higher wage

This fear of women was not restricted to the loving and leaving of men, but also designated the particular class and race of women who must be feared. One of these is typified in Lord Caresser's Madam Khan, (by no means an Indian as the name might suggest in the setting of Trinidad). Madam Khan is depicted as a black woman, physically very strong and ruthless in her attitude to men:

> I never see a woman with a right hand so
> One from she, nail me to the door
> I really thought that I was dead
> When a nail in the door went right through me head
>
> *Chorus*
> Hold your hand Madam Khan
> You'll hear the same from woman and man
> Talk about a woman bad like a crab
> Your heart and soul all she would grab
> Cut out your pocket and leave you to groan
> Beat you with a big stick, bottle and stone
>
> Not me in this kind of thing
> Friend, I rather walk about daily and sing
> I could make my living in an easier way
> Than to have a woman licking me every day
>
> I never see another human like that
> She boast how she big and she strong and she fat
> The female Carnera, a heavy weight
> Breaking down the scale at ninety-eight
>
> Such a desperado can't tackle me
> She'll be coming to meet her own destiny

Though if I slip I slide or lose my post
She'll give me all the blows I want, God knows

She got the heart of an octopus
That nigger woman too dangerous
When she saw she couldn't put an end to my life
She even tackle me with an old grass knife

THE EMERGENCE OF FEMININE AND MASCULINE ARCHETYPES

It is useful to compare the archetypes presented by the calypsonians of the varied groups of women in Trinidad in the decades of the 1920s and 1930s. If Madam Khan was to be the feared female, an image of the ideal feminine beauty that was desired is contained in Caresser's *Rubina* sung in 1937. Rubina is the daughter of a wealthy Spanish family:

Rubina was the girl I saw
One morning standing in front her door
She gazed at me with eyes of blue
Then she gave me a fine how-d'ye-do
You can imagine how I really felt
By receiving such a greeting from a girl of wealth
Whose family was in Spain
She would like to get a sweetheart
But one who is native to Trinidad
Hoping that he will not treat her bad

Rohlehr comments that the ideal woman had to be white, rich and stupid. This theme is also reproduced in Lord Pretender's *Yo no quiero trabajo* where the Spanish woman, Margarita, buys him a victriola and promises him a car. Pretender boasts:

Even friends they envy
But I am idealized by the family
And sooner or later I'll buy a car
To drive round the circular

The Growling Tiger's *Panchita* of 1938 continues the theme of the stereotype: rich white Spanish woman who falls in love with the black working-class man. The somewhat ambivalent relationship between Trinidad and the neighbouring society of Venezuela has made the Spanish woman or "payol" (a bastardization of español) consistently one of the favourite subjects of the calypsonian. For instance, in 1959, The Mighty Sparrow proclaimed his undying love for a woman called *Maria* – "Maria girl I love you so bad" he croons, making the calypso into a heart-rending love ballad. At the same time, Sparrow also sang one of his more derogatory songs against a Venezuelan prostitute named Rafaela. The "payol" woman does not always get elevated treatment as the desired in Trinidad society, nor does any other class or group of women, for that matter. By the 1980s, however, in another deft twist to a Latino curve, David Rudder would unconditionally elevate the Bahia Girl who combines voluptuous sensuality with the free expression of her sexuality. The times had changed, and so had some of the men who sang calypsos.

Two other themes have been recurrent ones in Trinidad calypsos since the 1930s. The first is depicted in the Growling Tiger's *In Love with Foreigners*, sung in 1938:

> Some girls always promise to take them far
> To England, France or America
> And she is undoubtedly a girl with personality
> And parents with big properties
> But you could see them when the Carnival gone
> Escorting a big ugly barefoot one

The foreign woman, generally Caucasian, is portrayed as rich and personable, and usually attractive. An attachment to a woman like this promises enhancement in status and pocket, and a possibility of travel, the modern Caribbean gigolos dream. Growler already is prescient of what has become a stereotype in Caribbean society today, the practice of men latching on to foreign women or tourists during and out of Carnival season with the hope of future rewards in travel and upkeep, the goal being "survivalism" through women.

The second set of archetypes address other ethnic groups who are outside the circle of writers and singers of calypsos but who generally came in for a harsh or uneasy time. As we have seen,

Indian men and women, the second largest group in the society by this time, were also unwilling subjects of the calypsonian. If the Indian man was construed in calypso as aggressively guarding Indian female sexuality, the Indian woman has been painted in different tones. Two calypsos emerged in this period that demonstrate the general tenor of treatment of these women: Atilla's *Dookhani* and Lord Executor's *My Indian Girl Love*. Atilla presents in *Dookhani*, a portrait of a beautiful and no doubt overly romanticized Indian woman:

> She was the prettiest thing I ever met
> Her resplendent beauty I cannot forget
> With her wonderful dark bewitching eyes
> I used to gaze at them hypnotized.
> Then she had the kind of personality
> That tempted one to behave ungentlemanly
>
> She was exotic kind and loving too
> All the charms I could never describe to you
> When she smiled her face lit up rapturously
> Radiating joy, love and vitality
> The most reserved was bound to feel
> The power and force of her sex appeal

Executor's *My Indian Girl Love* is also named Dookhani, but in this instance his desire s reciprocated, and she is willing to confront her father for the sake of love, another expression in the realm of fantasy, although it is not altogether unlikely that this kind of situation had happened once or twice in the society, particularly in the urban area of St. James where the festival of Hosein had encouraged freer mixing of peoples. The majority of Indian women in the society were, however, not available to non-Indian men. By this time, unlike the earlier period of indentureship in the nineteenth century, fewer women were able to challenge the patriarchal norms re-established in Indian society, with the reconstitution of villages, family life, kinship observances, religion and marriage customs. The western notion of romance was still relatively new to the Indian community, and marriages were largely arranged by parents, or with parental consent between the two families involved, and with the same religious background. Executor nonetheless sings convincingly:

> It was on the night of the Hosein
> That gala Indian fete I mean to say
> Pretty Indian belles was seen around
> Happy consolation there I found
> Music, dancing and drum beating
> All the time her love she was repeating
> Me tell am papa
> Me love am Lord Executor

Two fairly accurate ideas about Indian femininity can be gleaned from the two calypsos. Indian indentureship had just come to an end in 1917 and in general Indian women were relatively inaccessible, particularly in an urban environment, the milieu of the calypsonian. Her unattainability, the fact of her not being accessible itself creates the illusory beauty as embellished by Atilla. Executor alludes to the over protection of Indian men and to his one upmanship by her confrontation on his behalf. These calypsos reinforce the point that different masculinities were being confronted in the society, and that this art form provided one means by which differences were articulated between the groups.

If ideas of femininity were constantly being invoked by the male calypsonians, then we can also read into a myriad of calypsos by this time, the way in which masculinity was perceived or being fashioned by the men themselves. In their competition to outdo each other on stage through invention and illusion, a persistent theme was the idea of the male outsmarting the female by making use of her, and in this way outdoing his male peers. In 1937 The Growling Growler sang *I want to rent a Bungalow*. This was immediately followed by King Radio's *I am going to buy a Bungalow*, and not to be outdone, Atilla responded with *I don't want no Bungalow*.

While the virtues of owning or renting a bungalow, itself a fantasy for the working-class man, are being debated, the lyrics of Growler's calypso in fact suggest that the female adjunct is part of this acquisition of property. Growler sang in his calypso:

> I want to rent a bungalow:
> I want to rent a bungalow

> I want a guitar, a banjo, a cuatro, piano
> To practice calypso
> Yes and I want a pretty Jane
> The only thing is she must not make me shame
> If I make a mistake and I charge a blow
> She must call me Papito

Invader's *Maharaj Daughter* sung in 1939 was originally entitled *My ambition is luxury* and in similar vein he tells us:

> And if my wife doesn't like my disposition
> She'll have to leave me and get another husband
> That time I know I have my money and property
> I'll get plenty girls and live luxuriously

Another aesthetic of female beauty and behaviour had also emerged in the society. A direct descendant of slavery, a product of the mixture between black and white, we see the evolution of the brown skin woman, and in cases where she was of very light complexion, she was referred to by the calypsonians and others as high brown. In singing about the high brown, the male calypsonian was accentuating the importance of his virility despite lower class status, and his capacity to attract a woman who, elevated by the colour of her skin, was desirable to other men, especially to men of the upper classes.

In *My High Brown*, Atilla sings:

> I got a high brown working for me
> That's why I'm happy as can be
> The acutest depression can't trouble me
> I have a high brown working for me

Growler, however, debates the merits of aspiring above one's means, in *No High Brown Again*:

> The high brown believe in only two things
> Plenty rouging, plenty dressing
> Every new fashion dress that they see
> This is they talk: "Honey buy one for me"
> And when you give them, this is what they would do

> Charge a pretty kiss to mamaguy you
> "Doo doo, darling," and patting you head
> Until you catch Mr. Jamesie under your bed
>
> With a high brown woman you have plenty trouble
> Don't ask how they would have you miserable
> They won't wash your clothes, they won't cook your food
> And when you speak to them, they want to be rude
> And if you hit them they will bawl for murder
> Run in the Station for the Super
> And when he come because she pretty and she skin brown
> He will rough you, beat you and carry you down
>
> My darkie will work and give me a help
> Flannel pants, buff shoes also Wilson felt
> And pretty rings to wear on my hand
> And a Raleigh bike to ride all over the land
> She will clean my nails also comb my hair
> And bet her sweet life her love is sincere
> But the high brown would not do that for me
> So you see I bound to love my darkie
> Although her hair is pickie and hard
> Above everything she won't treat me bad

A pattern of gender relations was becoming clear to working class men in the society. Although the familiar and known were commonplace, aesthetically unappealing and denoted a reduction in status in the eyes of other men, at least the black female counterpart was dependable as a partner. Beauty was inextricably linked to colour and mixture of race. The high brown woman, later to be dubbed "red woman" in Trinidad, was more desirable and brought higher status to the man who courted her, but the black woman, "although her hair is pickie and hard" was valued for her good treatment of her man. This love/hate contradiction in the relations between men and women within a particular ethnic group, however, must not be reduced entirely to the legacy of colonialism While the binary opposition of the colonizer and the colonized, forms the basis of much of the sexual subjectification of the colonized woman as treated in such texts as Robert Young (1990), Ann McClintock (1995) and Carolyn Cooper (1993), I am unconvinced that these arguments fully explain the patterns persisting in society in post-coloniality. These need to be analyzed in the context of more complex ideas pertaining to difference and sexual fantasy that the dialectic of gender involves.

CONCLUSION: A BLUEPRINT FOR GENDER

The calypso has allowed the evolution of a creole aesthetic and a popular culture that, though provincial in its appeal, at the same time has fostered the growth of indigenous ideas and imagery possessively claimed by islanders at home and abroad. This rootedness of the calypso in local affairs supports my notion of its function as creole aesthetic. It explains in part the lack of universal appreciation of the lyrical calypso, and the almost incestuous relationship which Trinidadians in particular, and Caribbean islanders in general, have with this musical tradition. Precisely because of this closeness to the art form, their personal relationships with calypsonians and idiosyncratic preferences for calypsos and the issues they address, the medium of the calypso is puissant, conveying ideas and concepts that have far reaching and long-lasting appeal. They became the verbal icons of an emerging society.

The idea of the calypso as creole aesthetic is also supported by its versatile hallmark of *creolite*. Born initially out of difference it continues to be accommodating of differences in musics, dances and lyrical experimentation, as the society develops. With the absence of the more dominant means of communication which would emerge in the later decades of the twentieth century, the calypso in the 1920s and 30s provided an avenue through which ideas were transmitted and debated. My description of it as "creole" is a very fundamental one - it is a form native and unique to the society and the region. It has evolved within the society as a medium through which the miscreant, be it the errant husband, the unfaithful wife, or the corrupt politician, can be publically shamed. It developed both as a mechanism through which social change could be achieved, and to ensure that unacceptable behaviour did not go unnoticed.

What are some of the lines of the blueprint for gender established by calypsos of the twenties and thirties? The patriarchal contract between men of different races was being drawn up. White men, the jacket men, must not assume control over the women of other races. Black men, unsure of their social status and weakened by the poor state of their pockets, are nonetheless a force to reckon with by virtue of their sexual prowess, or physical strength. There is an uneasy tension between the latecomer Indians and working-class black men; the control over women became part of the struggle for maintaining power and status. Masculinity is a battle fought between men in relation to women. It is equally a demonstration of the power which one group of men have over another, the source of power deriving not necessarily from money or privileged positions, but the capacity of the less privileged male to resist or rebel. The labour power of black men would no longer be violently coerced as it was during slavery. There were other ways of making a living, such as a liaison with the rich man's wife or daughter, or the temporary flirtation with the rich female tourist.

Masculinity is multi-dimensional, plural, allowing a range of possibilities for men of the different races and classes. Femininity is depicted through male eyes and voices, construed as contradictory, yet its boundaries are relatively fixed – good or bad women, desirable or undesirable, pretty or ugly. In debating the virtues and attractions of women of different societies, the idea of otherness and therefore of the cultural identification is being processed. By stereotyping the Venezuelan, Grenadian or women of other countries, the calypsonian is also distinguishing the difference of this island's cultural and gender identity. Concepts of beauty are determined by colour, race and availability, and are consistent with the values which emerged in colonial society, the fairer the skin the more beautiful the woman. This is contradictory, however, for the less attainable white or foreign woman may be beautiful, but the working-class male, dependent on his female counterpart also acknowledges that "The blacker the woman, the sweeter she be." Adding further to the uneasiness which masculinity has with femininity, beautiful women are not to be trusted and the ugly/black woman is the more trustworthy, the assumption here being that she is more unlikely to have a choice of anxious partners. The Indian woman also represents the unattainable at this time, guarded as she is jealously by father and family. The struggle however is between the black and Indian men, to win mastery over each other's women. Indian men are unequally placed to deal with black women, so the struggle is at first asymmetrically balanced in favour of the black man. Eventually the high brown begins to epitomize the mixture which aesthetically appeals to all men, but being desirable, she is still untrustworthy. She represents a mixing of blood as well as class, and perhaps, in the aesthetic of beauty, which is evolving in the society, she presents a more socially acceptable cultural alternative to the dominant bourgeois and European ideal, which is ideologically rejected, while secretly remaining desirable.

The double standards in male and female sexuality are firmly entrenched. The virtuous woman is the faithful wife and good mother, the bad woman is the prostitute, La Diablesse - the temptress, the Soucouyant - the blood sucker. Women are deceivers ever, they will trick the always unwilling men into marriage, "tying they foot" by fair or foul means. Men are allowed many sexual partners but are helpless against women who set out to trap them. Female sexuality is unknown, desired but feared. There is an apprehension towards femininity and its potential in the society, especially echoed in Atilla's calypso, *Women Will Rule the World*. Women must therefore be controlled. The formula for control is a physical one, "every now and then cuff them up, they love you long and they love you strong." The ideas about love are tossed around by calypsonians like a dog playing with a favourite bone. "You cyar love without money, you cyar make love on hungry belly" Sparrow's calypso sung in the sixties, sums up one notion of love. Yet black women will love you for what you are. Following the doctrine according to Atilla, if you beat your woman then she knows you love her, hence it follows that women like to be beaten into submission. The relations between black men and women are couched in violent and antagonistic terms and love is merely a honeyed battle of the sexes. These messages remain potent in the history of gender relations within this society and in the Caribbean in general. As calypso continued its commentary on the society into the twentieth century, many male calypsonians and more females began to fill in the text between mythology and reality, between stereotypes and experience, to change the aesthetic of early creole society and to erase some of the lines in the early blueprint.

ENDNOTES

[1] Although part of the twin island stage of Trinidad and Tobago, both islands have had very different colonial histories up until 1800 when Tobago was annexed to Trinidad. The calypso as it continued its evolution then of course incorporated Tobago from which there emerged several very significant calypsonians. The time period which this essay deals with however, focuses on its evolution primarily in Trinidad.

[2] Gordon Rohlehr. 1990. *Calypso and Society in Pre-Independence Trinidad*, 8. Port of Spain, Rohlehr.

[3] Gordon Rohlehr (op cit. pp 16-17) makes this crucial point drawing on the path breaking work carried out by Maureen Warner-Lewis. He cites several of her publications, among them, *The Yoruba Language in Trinidad*, Kingston: UWI, 1984, *Yoruba Songs from Trinidad*, Kingston: UWI, 1984 and "The Influence of Yoruba Music on the Minor Key Calypso" in *Papers: Seminar on Calypso*, UWI/ISER, 1986.

[4] Susan Craig, "Germ of an Idea." Afterword, in Arthur Lewis, 1977. *Labour in the West Indies: The Birth of a Workers Movement*, 75. London: New Beacon Books. This comment of Craig in relation to the development of the steelband movement which together with calypso continued to define notions of masculinity and femininity in Trinidad, is clearly the next step for textual analyses of gender identity through popular culture in this society

[5] This preoccupation with ethnic and language variations and the different religious festivals of the eastern peoples proved to be a recurrent theme in my newspaper research of this period.

[6] Raymond Quevedo, 1983. *Atilla's Kaiso - A Short History of Trinidad Calypso*, 20. Department of Extra-Mural Studies, University of the West Indies, Trinidad. These references to public speakers refer largely, to my knowledge, to men prominent on the local scene.

[7] Kim Johnson develops this argument extensively in a manuscript entitled *The Fragrance of Gold*, Extra-mural Department of the University of the West Indies, St. Augustine, 1977 which examines the period of Spanish invasion in to the Americas and into Trinidad, in particular in the fifteenth century. Johnson points out that since this time it was clearly recognized by the imperial powers that the full control of a people was only possible through language. This explains the struggle which took place in the nineteenth century in Trinidad where both English and French competed for economy and society also through the dominance of their language.

[8] This and other quotations by Ray Lucas are located in a brief and insightful printed article entitled "The Great Calypsonians" which is included among a series of song lyrics and musical sheets of Sparrow's calypsos. Full reference for this publication is unknown.

[9] As calypso continued its evolution the musical accompaniment became more sophisticated, evolving with technologies of instruments, reproduction and trends in music. Integrated into Carnival by the mid 20th century, and its introduction to public and private fetes or parties calypso would also influence dance. While I have not explored this fully, I would hazard that it is this combination - the call and response between bodies on the streets to the rhythmic beat of the music - that produced the "wining" dance typical of Trinidad and Tobago

[10] Amina Mama, 1995. *Beyond the Masks: Race Gender and Subjectivity*, New York: Routledge, p. 1, Chapter 1, Introduction.

[11] This is one explanation, in my opinion, for the *laissez faire* attitude ascribed to Trinidadians and Trinidadian culture. The social conflicts between groups

became resolved differently, possibly through less violent means. It was necessary in a society which had been constantly populated since the fifteenth century by new groups of migrants, each bringing a different set of ideas and traditions and competing for social space within a relatively small geographical area.

[12] Ray Lucas, *op. cit.*

[13] I am not completely convinced of this statement, since it is probably truer to say that there were many currents at work in the villages and smaller towns in Trinidad and Tobago. Nonetheless, for the purposes of constructing a dominant mythology, I imagine that the centre, which was undoubtedly Port of Spain, was the most influential.

[14] Gender as it is being used in this essay refers to the social organization of sexual difference and specifically to the way in which masculinity and femininity are continuously being presented and represented over different historical periods. Masculinity and femininity are therefore always undergoing construction and deconstruction, nonetheless, retaining the universality which defines the difference of the essential male body from the essential female body. What changes overtime are the values and attitudes as well as the range of possibilities for each sex. This process is a dialectic one, masculinity and femininity shape and define each other. The existing imbalanced power relations between male and female in society, however, generally means that this process is not an equal one for each sex, and the configurations of class power and ethnic differences interact with gender identification.

[15] Kim Johnson, "The Social Impact of Carnival." Institute of Social and Economic Research, University of the West Indies, St. Augustine, Trinidad, mimeo, 1983 p.184

[16] Kim Johnson *op. cit.* notes that when middle- and upper-class women began participating in carnival around the 1930's they were closely chaperoned and segregated in trucks, removed from the crowds. p. 179

[17] Kim Johnson, *op. cit.* 1982, p. 185

[18] Cited in Gordon Rohlehr, Chapter Two, p. 54, taken from D. Epstein. 1977. *Sinful Tune and Spirituals*, 32. University of Illinois Press, Urbana, Chicago.

[19] Bridget Brereton. 1979. *Race Relations in Colonial Trinidad, 1870-1900*, 166. Cambridge University Press, Great Britain.

[20] *Op. cit.* 166

[21] *Op. cit.* 166

[22] Rohlehr, *op. cit.* pp. 213-277. Also published in Patricia Mohammed and Catherine Shepherd (eds), Gender in Caribbean Development, UWI, St. Augustine, Women and Development Studies Project, 1988.

[23] An interesting consequence of this freedom allowed the calypsonian is the way in which a culture of free press including a rampant degree of picong has also developed alongside the calypso in Trinidad. An early newspaper of this type was the Bomb and later the TnT Mirror, both of which perform a similar function as the calypso in some ways.

[24] Calypso singers had to make their money as "troubadours" essentially. It was not always a good living, and although the calypsonian may have been popular with the masses, he was by no means considered an eligible match for unmarried young impressionable girls. Up to the last decade of the twentieth century if a young woman from the middle class fell in love with a calypso singer, her parents still had problems accepting the legitimacy of the occupation or the status of the profession of her young man.

[25] Rohlehr notes that between 1912 and 1934, American recording companies began to record and sell Trinidad's music as a genre of Latin American music. This

clearly made economic sense to Bill Rogers who advertises this openly in the title of the song (Rohlehr, 1990, 147).
[26] Quevedo formally entered politics in 1946 and won a seat in the Port of Spain City Council, eventually serving a term as Deputy Mayor. He was President General of the now defunct Trinidad Labour Party and among his other activities, in 1950 he was elected to the Legislative Council of the colonial government then existing in Trinidad and Tobago.
[27] Gordon Rohlehr, *op cit*. 1988
[28] Calypso 1900 – 1949. http://www.bestoftrinidad.com/calypso40s.html
[29] Compared with the male calypsos denigrating women Lady Iere's calypso was very conciliatory. See https://www.youtube.com/watch?v=-8vAS5uc6KA
[30] This title is a line appropriated from a song *Woman versus Man* by David Byrne of the American pop group Talking Heads, released in 1989.
[31] By the next few decades, the litany of words will evolve in Trinidad to describe the "loose" woman such as the ever persistent jamette, wabin, jagabat and many others. A useful study will be to examine the origins of these idioms in Trinidad society and to see if they are in any way linked to calypso or the way in which singers and songwriters latch on to the vernacular and create popular idioms.
[32] These ideas are well developed in Mohammed, Patricia. 2001. *Gender Negotiations among Indians in Trinidad: 1917-1947*. London and The Hague: Palgrave / Institute of Social Studies.

REFERENCES

Allsopp, Richard. 1996. *Dictionary of Caribbean English Usage*. Oxford: Oxford University Press.

Brereton, Bridget. 1979. *Race Relations in Colonial Trinidad 1870-1900*. Cambridge: Cambridge University Press.

Cooper, Carolyn. 1993. *Noises in the Blood: Orality, Gender and the "Vulgar" Body of Jamaican Popular Culture*. London: Macmillan.

Craig, Susan. 1977. "Germ of an Idea." Afterword to *Labour in the West Indies: The Birth of a Workers' Movement*, by W. Arthur Lewis. London: New Beacon Books.

Elder, J. D. 1966. "Evolution of the Traditional Calypso of Trinidad and Tobago: A Sociohistorical Analysis of Song Change," PhD diss., University of Pennsylvania, (University Microfilm, Ann Arbor. Mich.)

Johnson, Kim. 1983. "The Social Impact of Carnival." Mimeo paper to Conference on Carnival, hosted by the Institute of Social and Economic Research, University of the West Indies, St. Augustine.
Johnson, Kim. 1977. *The Fragrance of Gold: Trinidad in the Age of Discovery*. St. Augustine, Trinidad: The University of the West Indies, Department of Extra-Mural Studies.

Mama, Amina. 1995. *Beyond the Masks: Race Gender and Subjectivity.* New York: Routledge.

McClintock, Anne. 1995. *Imperial Leather: Race, Gender and Sexuality in the Colonial Context.* New York: Routledge.

Mohammed, Patricia. 2001. *Gender Negotiations among Indians in Trinidad: 1917-1947.* London and The Hague: Palgrave / Institute of Social Studies.

Mohammed, Patricia. 1994. "A Social History of Indians in Trinidad 1917-1947: A Gender Perspective." PhD diss., The Hague.

Pearse, Andrew. 1988. "Mitto Sampson and Calypso Legends of the Nineteenth Century," In *Trinidad Carnival*, edited by Gerry Besson, 140-63. Port of Spain: Paria Publishing.

Quevedo, Raymond 1983. *Atilla's Kaiso: A Short History of Trinidad Calypso.* St. Augustine: The University of the West Indies, Extra Mural Studies.

Reddock, Rhoda. 1994. *Women, Labour and Politics in Trinidad and Tobago.* Kingston, Jamaica: Ian Randle Publishers.

Rohlehr, Gordon. 1990. *Calypso and Society in Pre-Independence Trinidad.* Port of Spain, Trinidad: Rohlehr.

Warner, Keith Q. 1982. *Kaiso! The Trinidad Calypso: A Study of the Calypso as Oral Literature.* Washington: Three Continents Press.

Young, Robert. 1990. *White Mythologies: Writing History and the West.* London and New York: Routledge.

19

'Who taking advantage ah who': Sparrow and Caribbean Man/Woman Relations[†]

INTRODUCTION - THE MIGHTY VOYEUR

Music and song allow us to archive and retrieve events, people, places and emotions that are stored in time. The Mighty Sparrow's repertoire is not a minor but a major key into our collective memory of Trinidad and Tobago and the Caribbean. These songs, especially for those of us who are of a generous age, prompt both a personalized soundtrack of our lives, as well as a slideshow of political, economic and cultural moments from the late fifties to the eighties, a period I refer to as The Mighty Sparrow's golden years of kingship. Like the bird after which he is named, Sparrow flitted from subject to subject. The songs are

---

[†] This essay is an edited version of the performance lecture for Canboulay Productions led by Rawle Gibbons in 2014 at Daaga Hall, The University of the West Indies, St. Augustine, Trinidad. It was the last of five lectures in a tribute to Sparrow entitled, "If Sparrow Say So." Selected verses in the presentation were performed by David Bereaux and Friends of Trinidad. The lecture was reprised with some amendments and with the same performers in Barbados for the 21st Caribbean Women: Catalysts for Change lecture in honour of Dame Nita Barrow, which I delivered on November 13th, 2015 at The University of the West Indies, Cave Hill Campus. It was filmed by the Caribbean Broadcasting Corporation for screening on Barbados television.

vignettes of a nation claiming its independence and personality, a region grappling with language and establishing its vernacular. If we think for instance of the irony in "Dan is the man in the van" (1965):

> The poems and the lessons they write and send from England
> Impress me they were trying to cultivate comedians
> Comic books make more sense
> You know it is fictitious without pretence
> Cutteridge wanted to keep us in ignorance

The songs tell us of a rigid class-based society trying to level off differences as is evident in "The Governor's Ball" (1967):

> The Governor had a ball
> I never see nothing so yet
> Ah mad woman jump the wall and invade the fete
> Prospect with the baton in hand conducting the police band
> He say the woman shake she waist, in the Governor face

The Grenada-born calypsonian was brought by his mother to Trinidad when he was twenty-one months old and was made never to forget his Grenadian origins. He occupied the insider/outsider position in the society in which he grew to manhood. This gave him the vantage point of multiple identities from which to speak to provincial, political and economic decisions as, for instance, his critique in "Federation" (1962):

> ...if they know that they din want federation
> And they know that they doh want to unite as one
> Independence was at the door
> Why they didn't speak before
> This is no time to say you eh federating no more

Apart from his political and social commentary which makes up the subject matter of over one third of his songs, Sparrow is perhaps best known for his undressing of the anatomy of the sexual politics of the region – by the latter I mean how men and women negotiate the boundaries between sexual profligacy and harmonious gender relations. I focus primarily on Sparrow's treatment of man/woman relations in Trinidad and Tobago and the Caribbean. The title of the essay "Who taking advantage ah who" is extracted from his calypso "Stella" (1959):

> No no no no no no no Stella
> Darling have some behaviour
> Darling have some behaviour
> You had too much drink in the christening
> Now you don't know what you doing
> Get out of me place I will tell you flat
> Is advantage for me to do a thing like that
>
> *Chorus*
> Go ahead and take yuh advantage
> Go ahead I give you privilege
> I could take care of myself
> Sparrow darling bring the whisky from the shelf
> Only give me one or two
> And we go see who taking advantage ah who
>
> Girl it's getting late I want to go
> Move let me shut the window
> Remember I know your family
> And we all very friendly
> It won't be nice when they get to hear
> I took advantage of you my dear
> So for heaven sake get out go for a walk
> When you sober up tomorrow Stella we go talk

As with many of Sparrow's calypsos, while there is a story being told, there is also a lesson to be learnt. He ends "Stella" on a high moral note:

> Well I could not stand this thing no more
> I decided to throw she out the door
> She came to my bar drunk already
> Its advantage to sell her more whisky
> Her family and I are very good
> And we live in the same neighbourhood
> Don't mind she give all privilege to me
> I will never take advantage on a young lady

While absorbing the superb stretching of a metric rhyme to fit snugly with voice, intonation and musical accompaniment, are we convinced that this is not just another ploy of male seduction? "Darling have some behavior," says the upstanding older male neighbour/bar-keeper. His very restraint seems to further fuel Stella's desire. Why is Stella at this gentleman's place after the christening? The language and setting challenge our belief that this is all above board and suggests a grey area of gender subterfuge and complicity. I have used the calypso "Stella" as an example in Sparrow's oeuvre to persuade many who have found his repertoire offensive to the current feminist spirit, that Sparrow is in fact quite catholic in his gender calculations. He targets both sexes, although we might argue perhaps not equally.

On stage Sparrow presents the persona of a mischievous child, not up to harmful malice, but naughty and playful, and ready to shock us into confronting our sensibilities and psychoses. I first saw Sparrow on stage in 1971 at the carnival event held each year in Naparima Girls High School. I imagine Sparrow was invited as one of the judges for the calypso competition, with the expectation that he would also perform. Sparrow had won the road march already six times, with "Jean and Dinah" in 1956, "Pay as you earn" in 1958, "Mae Mae" in 1960, "Royal Jail" in 1961, "Melda" or "Obeah Wedding" in 1966 and "Sa Sa Yea" in 1969. The lyrics of these calypsos were not exactly the kind of delicacy we were served up in our polite finishing girls school curriculum. Our Principal, a well-meaning but straitlaced Presbyterian woman, had been skeptical about having a troubadour who sang bawdy lyrics in her school. The head girls and house captains who organized the event had nonetheless persuaded her to allow this smooth talking, handsome and rakish calypsonian into our midst. I am sure he knew the politics around his presence in that large assembly hall. With rows and rows of impressionable ears hanging on to his every note – what would Sparrow choose to sing from his repertoire – but "Sa Sa Yea" and "The Lizard" (1969) "The lizard ran up she leg and she tay lay lay," he demonstrated provocatively, belting out the French *patois* chorus of "Sa Sa Yea" with meaningful pauses that had our Martiniquian teacher Mrs. Alert who was on stage as Emcee, literally blushing and simpering coyly at the same time.

If Sparrow slurs women's sexuality, he is also castigating of male behaviour. He treats with both sides of the man/woman story. For example in "Who she go cry for now," the protagonist has lost his woman to another man named Dennis. Here Sparrow is unsympathetic with men who poach:

> Well you take away mi woman
> And you put a ring on she hand
> And you feeling down in your heart you so smart
> You thought was an angel cake
> But you tief a bake
> You know she eh love you
> You damn stupid conoomoonoo
> Dennis pay for your damn fastness

Of course we can argue that he is again protecting male patriarchal interests, but The Mighty Sparrow is a complex package and not lyrics dismembered from performance. His wicked lopsided grin, clever and endearing wit, and incredible command of the vernacular: "You thought was an angel cake/But you tief a bake," makes even the politically incorrect, palatable. Even while mentally rejecting some of the images the songs convey, we sing along with tunes like "Congoman" (1964) and "Saltfish" (1976). His ribaldry and lasciviousness reveal the contradictory nature of sexual politics in a region that is known more for its portrayal of antagonistic rather than supportive relations between the sexes.

PART ONE - A LITERARY GENESIS

I will return to Sparrow's preoccupation with gender and sexuality, but first I want to suggest that when we read Sparrow's cultural production, not as reductive, single sound bytes extracted from the whole repertoire, but as a call and response between this calypsonian and Caribbean society, it places him as an important contributor to the West Indian literary space that emerges from the fourth decade of the twentieth century. While the origins of calypso remain relatively obscure, researchers have claimed that the word 'calypso' first appeared in 1890 and at that time was spelled 'calipso'. It is also argued that it was the French who originally brought the idea of Carnival to Trinidad, along with the calenda or Kalinda - carnival songs that were sung in French Creole by *negre jardin* stickmen and their followers.[1] Half a century later, Sparrow had experienced the patois mix of Trinidad's 'callaloo' of ethnicities, race and gender relations, languages and linguistic expressions. He had an eye for what was trending and, like a sponge, absorbed it all and returned them to the society with a poet's versatility. But he was also innovative and incorporated his own style, lengthening for the first time the shorter repetitive chorus of the traditional calypso into a form more consistent with the literary genre of poetry.

He had learnt his craft from an honourable oral tradition. He absorbed much from the great calypsonians who predated him in the thirties and forties, among them Lion, Atilla, Growler and Caresser. Of nearly 200 calypsos written and sung by him that were examined, 20 are distinctly political, 43 can be described as economic and social commentary, 40 are party and carnival songs and 93 deal with themes of gender and sexuality.[2] Looking at the entire body of his work, one can trace a poetic theatre of the streets scripted into song, a balladeer whose storytelling can be compared to the contribution that Chaucer makes to English literature. This likening of Sparrow's verse to the literary arts is not a new idea. Warner (1983) describes the calypso as oral literature and makes extensive use of Sparrow's songs to illustrate this point in his path breaking work. Both he and Rohlehr (1990) agree that we should allow Slinger Francisco the distance "between the e.y.e. (EYE) and "I" personal pronoun – the separation between perception and fiction that "creates out of what it has seen or imagined."[3]

By the late fifties Sparrow begins a systematic storytelling of characters that have become archetypal in our imagination. Like Geoffrey Chaucer he is the scribe of verse for a new era - post war, independence, nationalism, feminine ploys and masculine confidence. *The Canterbury Tales* by Chaucer is a collection of stories written between 1387 and 1400 of a group of 30 pilgrims travelling to Canterbury (England). The pilgrims, who come from all layers of society, tell stories to each other to kill time on the journey, and in doing so relate the minutiae of everyday life and human frailties. Chaucer developed his vision of an English poetry that would be neither obedient to the court - whose official language was French, nor to the Church - whose official language was Latin.

Instead, he wrote in the vernacular, the English that was spoken in and around London in his day. *The Canterbury Tales* is written in Middle English, which bears a fairly close visual resemblance to the English written and spoken today.

I illustrate the parallels with only one example of Chaucer's work. "The Miller's Tale" is about a carpenter of more advanced age who marries an 18-year old wife. The couple takes in a young male clerk as a boarder in their spare room - clearly an arrangement fraught with possibilities. Here is Chaucer's picture of the wife:

> A brooch she wore upon her collar low,
> As broad as boss of buckler did it show;
> Her shoes laced up to where a girl's legs thicken.
> She was a primrose, and a tender chicken

Here is Chaucer's depiction of the carpenter's state of mind.

> For she was wild and young, and he was old,
> And deemed himself as like to be cuckold.
> He knew not Cato, for his lore was rude:
> That vulgar man should wed similitude.
> A man should wed according to estate,
> For youth and age are often in debate.

Sparrow is a storyteller of tall tales that have to do with love and politics; like Chaucer and other good storytellers, he panders to our prurience for a rumour. And like the griot entrusted with preserving the genealogies of the tribe, he also provides the moral twist as seen at the end of "Tobago girls" (1980). This is sung in the middle English of the period in which it was written, demonstrating the mastery of English 'big words' blended with the local idiom. There is a cocktail of references to place, people and situations, well laced with a Caribbean tongue in cheek humour. Like all poets he could stretch the meter of a line to ensure that it met both the rhythm of the music and the rhyme.[4]

> Dis old man from Ohioho
> Spend the holiday in Scarborough
> Time up, he eh want to go
> Why bredda I really don't know

Immigration told the old man
You are now a prohibited immigrant
Listen sire the time expire
We would like to know, wey your really want

All them Tobago girl
Thick thick thick like a new sponge ball
Them from Mason Hall eh easy at all
Pretty as a doll
Me I love them Tobago gyul

I have been east west north and south
I have seen women all about
But they cannot compare
With these you have down here
When they walking, background shaking
Pretty teeth and eyes that just seem to glow
What they eating, what they drinking
have them looking so I would like to know

All them Tobago girl
Sweet sweet sweet like a Kaiser ball
Burrows you could call
Or ring Interpol
Meh eh going at all
Furst I love them sweet Tobago gyul
Look at each in their Bikini
On the beach bathing in the sea
God take he own two hand
To shape Tobago woman
So much beauty, all around me
This place have me heart controlling meh head
Deportation is no solution
Gimme permission to stay till I dead

All dem Tobago gyul
Nice and round like a butterball
Doh meh money small
I go wuk bobol
Just to gie them all
Cos I love them Tobago gyul

In "Tobago Girls," Sparrow presents the archetypal tourist, not unlike the anthropologist of the 1930s and 1940s gone native, his reference to Robinson Crusoe and utopia in verse four (unquoted here), is a parody of the mythologized history of these islands.

In "Lying Excuses" (1996), he also depicts another masculine archetype: the smooth talking husband who could get away telling his wife glaring untruths:

> Maggy darling, sugar dumpling
> Don't get so mad. Please let me explain
> Doo doo darling, sugar dumpling
> Don't get so mad
> Please let me explain
> If you see me with some woman
> I doh want you misunderstand
> Whatever you might see me do
> Know my love is true, I'm not being unfaithful to you
>
> De woman you catch me with in de bed
> Really didn't have no place to rest she head
> Business close down, she lost she wuk
> Disappointed, suffering from shock
> So ah take she home just to relax and cheer she up
> Exhausted she said to me
> Boy ah so tired and so sleepy
> Casually she sat on de bed
> And ask me to massage she leg
> That's all, that's is all, that is all
>
> Troublemakers will spread rumours
> For confusion, oh no doh take dem on
> Just be trusting and doh dig nothing
> Try and understand, I'll never do you no wrong
> Darling you I'll never deceive
> There is no need to disbelieve
> Keep your trust and your faith in me
> And I promise you there'll be no infidelity
>
> De lady you saw me with de other night
> She and she husband just had a fight

Ah fine it was really looking so bad
How de hell she clothes was in de yard
She sit down dey and start to cry like she going mad
De two thousand dollars ah give to she
Was to buy a sandwich and a coffee
Not another ting eh happen
Me and de gyul eh in nothin
That's all, that's is all, that is all

Let nobody cause you to be jealous and confused
Doh mind dem and dey news
Dey want we to mash up
So dey could come and shack up
And when you refuse
We'll be like two fools singing the blues
Doo doo, why these women doh stop
Always try to set me up
Trying to give you de impression
Somethings wrong when my darling nothing eh going on

De gyul ah was with behind de lamp-post
Doh get vex cause ah was holding she clothes
She's ah old tief from in de east
Is somebody earring she tief
Ah was only trying to hold she for de police
De reason me hand was in she bosom
Ah was feeling to see if she had a gun
She didn't have no gun by she chest, Is why ah was searching under she dress
That's all, that's is all, that is all

Just because I am such ah nice guy
Somewhere, somehow it always leave me in row
Helping people, seem to be my trouble
Ah seeing it now
No more will it be allowed
After all meh go help mehself
Give meh problems to someone else
Is too much conquer and confusion
And ah know to mehself I am an innocent man
Ah know dey go tell you me and Miss Leach

> Was seen making love on Maracas Beach
> Well de fact dat she had on a bikini
> And was attacked by African bees
> And very bravely I cover she with meh whole body
> Well she lock meh neck and she grab meh hand
> And with dat she pull meh down in de sand
> Ah bee sting meh on meh behind
> Ah couldn't help it, ah had to grind

Naipaul (1969: 90) observed that "It was characteristic of a Trinidadian sense of humour to turn grave international incidents into private jokes". "Congo man" was another example of this. Sparrow explained in an interview with journalist Wayne Brown that

> The Congo Man came to me on a subway in New York - just the melody. And the lyrics came from the many activities in Africa at the time. So many nuns and priests were being ambushed and beaten, you know... And I got the idea that this was probably happening there: white people were just traveling through and found themselves in the hands of head hunters, ...who put them in a pot, had a fire at the bottom, and had a chant.[5]

Rohlehr (2005) is not convinced that this calypso was "purely humorous and completely unsuggestive" as Sparrow claimed, particularly because the conditions that led to this violence were so distressing. "What Sparrow calls "the activities in Africa at the time" writes Rohlehr, "was really the tragic disintegration of the Congo in the years after Belgium on the 30th of June 1960, suddenly thrust Independence on the over two hundred ethnic nationalities whose land Belgium had invaded, exploited with barbaric ferocity and left completely unprepared for the challenge of independence and nation-building."[6] Despite the licence that was generally allowed to Sparrow in other songs that crossed an imaginary line of acceptability, "Congo Man" was banned from radio airplay until 1989. Underground however, it remained a favourite, its popularity resuscitated with new cover versions, reflecting for Regis (2013) "the divide between the few thoughtful and the numerous thoughtless in Trinidadian society."[7]

Sparrow had cottoned on to the irreverence of the Trinidadian psyche, a coping mechanism adopted by the population for matters that could not be confronted openly, yet if remembered as humour served as a distorted mnemonic device for recollection. Incidents, whether local or foreign, are captured and politicized in ways that are themselves not deemed political. On closer inspection, however, these strategies demonstrate profound identity politics, very similar to the way that Chaucer is grappling with the class and gender politics of England at the time.

In 1982 Michael Fagan, an Irishman who apparently bet his friends at the pub that he could breach security and enter the Queen's bedroom, successfully managed this feat. The fact that the queen was sleeping alone in her double bed and Phillip was absent from the chamber was too much grist for the Trini mill of salacious innuendo. Sparrow's "Phillip My Dear" is a good example of irreverent humour spun through an embellishment of the facts.

> Phillip, my dear, last night I thought was you in here
> Where did you go? Working for good old England
> Missing out all the action. My dear, do you know
> There was a man in my bedroom wearing your shoe
> Trying on the royal costume, dipping in the royal perfume
> I telling you true
> There was a man in my bedroom
> Anxious for a rendezvous and I thought it was you
>
> *Chorus*
> He big just like you but younger
> He thick just like you but stronger
> He lingay like you but harder
> He laylay like you but badder
> A man in my bedroom
> He came on the bed, doudou, and I took him for you
>
> The palace guards were playing hopscotch in the yard
> Abandoned the throne, me with this perfect stranger
> The jewel was in danger for I was alone
> With a man in my bedroom loaded with brew
> Yes, this malodorous urchin on top of my bed was perching like a cockatoo

A man in my bedroom
Sorry, dear, I misconstrued when I took him for you

Evidently I've suffered great indignity from this commoner
Instead of being free in London
He should be put in a dungeon under the Tower
There was a man in my bedroom enjoying the view
This vicious, immoral scoundrel
Son of a common mongrel, scared me through and through
There was a man in my bedroom
Your input was overdue and I thought it was you

Sparrow paints an image of the grandeur of Buckingham palace, diminishing the guards with furry hats that the intruder eluded, and with a sleight of hand, bridged gaps between royalty and commoner. The satirical twist of the intruder's presence is told from the Queen's point of view, the shifting of her voice between middle English and Trini idiom humanizing her for the Caribbean audience. He blends nuances of not only the irreverence of the Trinidadian but an iconoclasm bred from years of skepticism about the promises made by those in power. Iconoclasm nonetheless co-exists quite comfortably with admiration for the privileges that power allows. Apparently, (well, so I heard somewhere), Trinidadians were quite upset that this song was not performed for the Queen's jubilee celebrations. While making fun of the bedroom incident Sparrow had reflected the ambiguous regard that is generally held for the English monarchy. Thus, ironically, the song is the quintessential Trinidadian tribute to its one-time colonial status – placing it in the dispatches as akin to Barbados's encouraging message to Britain during the outbreak of hostilities in the imperial war "Go ahead England, Barbados is behind you."

An interesting area of comparison in the works of Sparrow and Chaucer are the use of rhyme and meter. *The Canterbury Tales* of Chaucer is composed in iambic pentameter, the latter a type of poetic meter that is deemed similar to the cadence of regular speech in English, and refers to the number of stressed and unstressed syllables in each line of a poem.[8] Sparrow's poetry does not fit snugly into categories of rhyme or meter and differs according to the particular song. He has been described as producing "adventitiously structured" verse, absorbing and generating slang and creating nation language.[9]

A marked correspondence between both is that they are bawdy and lascivious and largely nonjudgmental of human foibles. Like Chaucer, Sparrow is the traveller in time telling other people's stories or fables, some of which project a moral ending, and all capturing the lives of the people who inhabit a place and time. "It is only in the calypso that the Trinidadian touches reality" writes Naipaul (1969: 75). While Belafonte's universalizing of the island ditty "This is my island in the sun, where my people have toiled since time begun" was valuable touristic public relations verse for the region, it nonetheless conveyed a romanticized version of colonial history and claims to heredity. The calypso form was more authentic to this history, exempted from the photo-realist postcard image. The frequent references and use of Sparrow's calypso by Naipaul's *The Middle Passage* and *Miguel Street* is as much a homage to calypso as it is to Sparrow himself.

Sparrow's repertoire has been described as pre-literary. Perhaps pre- in the sense of its precocious anticipation of pastiche and postmodernism. Adding the prefix again in another allusion to Sparrow, John Thieme comments that "The Mighty Sparrow's "Dan is the Man in the Van" (1963) takes as its departure point the pre-text of Captain J. O. Cutteridge's *"West Indian Readers,"* diminishing its didactic capacity through his comic approach while parodying the educational curricula first afforded to West Indian children. This calypso is probably one of the earliest trenchant critiques of the primary school curriculum, allowing the listener the range of emotions – entertainment and laughter combined with an appreciation of originality, while conveying a serious message. Sparrow's repertoire of calypso inherits from all of those who filled the stage before him and literally spans the gamut of the oldest traditions in calypso's call and response, simple re minor key, to the ballad form, but he adds to it a consistent experimentation with the form, a changeability in the content and music, a shifting between substance and moods as seen for instance the song range between "The Slave" (1963) and "Sandra" (n.d), and his unrivaled ear for the cadences of speech and accent. If we return to the last verse in "Tobago Gals":

> Will you incarcerate a man
> Wid honourable intention
> Your country is pure bliss

> For ah polygamist
> Oh what rapture
> The thrill of capture
> Robinson Crusoe was the smartest man
> I see hope here
> This is utopia
> Perfectly, try and understand

Sparrow seamlessly incorporates the way in which a Trinidadian would actually speak the word – not incarcerate but in - caarcerate, not honourable but honour…raabble in - tentions. In stretching the syllabic meter to ensure a recurrent rhythm he transmits other meanings of words or phrases. In the example cited, nonetheless, we question the honourability of the visitor's motives, gently finessing the *double entendre*. In doing so Sparrow picks up on the intonations of accents which he clearly listens to acutely, he is familiar with the slangs and idioms of the street and can combine these with the "good English" that a colonial education and Cutteridge's/Nelson's *West Indian Readers* were trying to inculcate. I would argue that this capacity of Sparrow to reflect back to a nation how it had appropriated another language forges a modern acceptance; perhaps even more, a delight in being able to switch dialect and language codes and thus create a style of speaking and public delivery that has become firmly accepted as typical of Trinidadian speech and language composition of the labouring classes.

Much remains to be done on the linguistic deconstruction of his style and his particular method of bringing together a rhythm of his speech - prosodic, with the music and performance. I suggest that, like C. L. R. James, Albert Gomes, Sam Selvon, V. S. Naipaul, Edgar Mittelhozer, Wilson Harris and other writers at the time who are introducing the vernacular into dialogue and fashioning a literary Caribbean sensibility, Sparrow has the advantage. He was able to comfortably and unapologetically use the colloquial form of poetry that combines an intricate verbal texture, local imagery, honing into the psyche and psychoses of a society, and establishing the network of psychological relationships between characters and a narrative structure, to relay the sequence of actions in a plot. Sparrow, like Chaucer, has constructed a new folkloric space – capturing the archetypes like Jean and Dinah, Elaine and Harry, Melda, Mr. Walker, members of high society, the village Casanova and Carlton the peeping tom, those who fill the life of the streets of his familiar, the people and events that now shape our imagination of a time that has already passed. Perhaps in the future these will become the mythological characters who inspire our theatre, film and novels.[10]

PART 2 - WHO TAKING ADVANTAGE AH WHO

The conventional view of male calypsonians is that their calypsos have been largely patriarchal, misogynistic, controlling and violent to women. Sparrow's repertoire in this respect, despite his likable and commendable qualities, places him as one of the primary culprits. Of approximately 200 songs he recorded, 93 deal directly with women and matters related to man/woman relations. Hodge (1975) argues, "The violence, verbal abuse and humiliation of women advocated in calypso is an emulation and appropriation of the hostility the black man learned within the plantation system." Rohlehr (1990, 216) had pointed out also that since the 1920s and 30s, "in the process of fictionalizing domestic lower-class situations, calypsonians brought into focus the confrontation of males and females in a context where both were battling for economic survival." The dominant script about love Caribbean style presented by the calypso therefore was primarily that of lust with implicit mistrust.

To hold the ideas that colonial imbalances of power, poverty and a natural opposition between the sexes are the primary sculptors of a gender and sexual culture, makes cardboard characters of real life people who are constantly engaged in re-inventing their sexuality, gender role attributes and identities. All women are not natural victims and all men are not natural perpetrators. Gender and sexuality are, like all other aspects of human society, multi-dimensional, contradictory and chaotic. Calypsonians and song-writers continue to offer some of the best insights into this unfathomable area of social life.

About a decade ago, I had interpreted the calypsos of the 20s and 30s as creating a blueprint for gender relations in the creole aesthetic of Trinidad (Mohammed 2003: 129: 168). By this, I meant that in those tent and radio days, the calypso provided an accessible means by which men and women could debate and sanction acceptable or unacceptable sexual norms, concepts of good and bad behaviour, which physical attributes were considered beautiful or ugly, and who was desirable or undesirable. How else could one explain the calypso dialogue between Lion and Beginner in 1934 that debates the virtues of the Ugly Woman versus the Pretty Woman. Lion's song "Ugly Woman" goes like this:

> If you want to be happy and live a king's life
> Never make a pretty woman your wife
> All you've got to do is just what I say
> And you'll always be happy and gay
> From a logical point of view
> Always marry a woman uglier than you

Those were the days when the word gay had a completely different meaning of course. "Ugly woman" took New York by storm, hitting it seems a universal chord among men. The debate was then primarily among men and men. Women's voices were silent – a situation that changed from the sixties onwards when more female singers like Singing Francine could retaliate "dog does run away, cat does run away, woman put two wheels on your heels and you could run away too" a tradition that was picked up by others like Singing Diane and Singing Sandra.[11]

I have read Sparrow's oeuvre or legacy of male/female encounters as a dialogue between men and women and with the society, rather than a one-sided masculinist position. Sparrow was a product of a post-war era that was the precursor and usher of a second wave feminist movement of women, women like Rosita and Clementina who possible migrated from Venezuela in search of work, women in trousered suits with padded shoulders smoking cigarettes that Atilla had sung about,[12] like those seen in the black and white movies that had presented a post-war era femininity. With the newfound confidence of a black masculinity that had confronted, although not erased, the colonial spectre, Sparrow took the performance stage and the airwaves with an assurance. This command of the stage had been earned from years of apprenticeship and study of those that preceded him. He gained a dedicated following and was poised to present the primer on love Caribbean style.

Citing Sparrow's "Benwood Dick": "Tell your sister to come down here I have a message for she," Naipaul (1969: 70) comments that this is Trinidad's version of the Emily Post's Advice on dating, a column for the lovelorn published in the *Trinidad Guardian* at the time. One can read Sparrows songs on love and sex as defensive of a male patriarchal control of "we women." But Sparrow's women by and large, as we see already from Stella's response in "who taking advantage ah who," are not without agency and men are also fully equipped with their masculine wiles.

In "Benwood Dick" (1960) for instance the silent Mildred is no lady in waiting. Sparrow relates the story of "a boy's bewilderment at the sudden appearance of his sister's shabby ex-boyfriend who expects to awaken her affection with the memory of his peculiar anatomy."[13]

Benwood Dick
Aye, little boy, let me tell you this
Don't be afraid. I ain't the police
You wouldn't know me, but I want you to show me
A girl around here they call Mildred
When I tell you mister, Mildred is meh sister
He jump up and then he said

Chorus
Tell your sister to come down quick
I have something here for she
Tell she is Mr. Benwood Dick
The man from Sangre Grande
She know me well
I gih she already
She must remember me
Go on, Go on, tell she Mr. Benwood come

Sorry old man, that won't do for me
I don't carry message for anybody
If you want to see she, doh worry to send me
Climb up the step. You won't fall
It have a bell on the gate. Ring it and wait
She must come after you call

Curiosity, had meh head confused
I wonder what Mildred doing with a man who cyah buy shoes

> They start to talk and talk, then they went for a walk
> If you see them, hand in hand
> When he gone I ask she, who is he?
> She tell me, is she compere but was she man

Apart from the *double entendre* encoded in the caller's name Benwood Dick, Sparrow depicts him as up to no good, trying to get Mildred's attention through her brother rather than going directly to her house. By introducing himself as Mr., he invokes some notion of respectability to the young boy, with the allusion "she know me well. I gie (give) she already" suggesting to us the listeners, knowledge in the biblical sense. He renders both character parts of this song in a rapid delivery, while "shaping the lyrics with a relaxed, lilting voice that rises and falls effortlessly, managing to make fun of the hapless suitor while expressing his yearning."[14] Do we sympathize with Mr. Benwood Dick who has come all the way from Sangre Grande or pass judgment on Mildred for walking out with a suspicious financially challenged character. While the underlying message is the power of the phallus, the song leaves the judgment open to us. What Emily Post advice to men is Sparrow giving here? In Benwood Dick, unlike Stella, we are not privy to Mildred's side of the story, as we are in another song "Monica Dou Dou" (1959), where the protagonist complains that her husband leaves her alone for weeks on end and she has to depend on a seaman friend. Monica says in her defence "When the seaman friend bring a friend is then I have cash to spend." The narrator commiserates with her: "Darling that's a shame, your husband is the only one to blame, he shouldn't get on so. …you may not have quality, but you got personality, your husband stupid like hell, if was me, I eh letting a next man smell." Sparrow's raunchy and wicked wit rescues the song from too much moralizing but he has laid out the cards on the table for us to see both sides.

The calypsonian in the society therefore is merely the mouthpiece for echoing the emotional and sexual transactions that are continuously taking place around him. Women are viewed as manipulative and trying to tie men's foot through fair or foul means as we see in the song "Obeah wedding" which has come to be seen as the quintessential advice on how (Caribbean) women attempt to entice men through other worldly means.

Obeah wedding (Melda)
You making youself a pappy show Melda
You making youself a bloody clown
Up and down the country looking for Obeah
And your perspiration smell so strong, well
Girl you only wasting time
Obeah Wedding Bell's don't chime
And you can't trap me with necromancy

Chorus
Melda oh you making wedding plan
Carrying me name to Obeah man
All you do can't get through
I still ain't go marry to you

The amount of incense that you burn at night
Lard and garlic stinking up me place
So much different colour candles that you light
Rubbing red lavender in your face, well...
Nastiness gone cause your death
Girl no man can stand your breath
You too damn nasty, get away from me

If you really want a wedding ring Melda
There are many other ways and means
Like scrubbing your teeth and bathing regular
Soap and water keeps you fresh and clean
Dress up in the latest style, always wear a charming smile
Some koonoomoonoo bound to say I do

Look how many nights we hug up tight tight tight
All we ever know was love and peace
Now every minute is only fight fight fight, till you using
Obeah man for priest, well...
You don't seem to understand
Obeah can't upset my plan
For Papa Nisa is me grandfather

My sympathies for any young woman named Melda in Trinidad after this calypso became popular, such is the power of art. "Obeah wedding" together with others like "Congoman" and "Jane" are often used to invoke Sparrow's misogyny. Women in these calypsos argue that they are adopting coping strategies, and for obvious reasons. The unmarried childless woman was considered a failure in society; the unmarried woman with children needed to find a provider. In singing about women however, Sparrow also immortalizes different stereotypes. Even if their roles and morality are depicted as questionable, they are visible and given voice. I for one am happy that we have such echoes of women in our history and the kind of agency that we see in Jean and Dinah, Rosita and Clementina, Monica, Sandra, Mildred and Teresa, Melda, Raphaela, Maharajin and Matilda, Dorothy, Elaine, Eve and Gloria, Jane, Lucy, Maria and May May, Miss Mary, Miss Ruby, Rose and the ever willing Stella.

To compensate or define what has, since slavery, emerged as a transcript of black male sexual prowess, Sparrow is selling metaphors of Caribbean sexuality packaged in *double entendre* that continue to signify place and space, demystifying these "islands in the sun." Earl Lovelace (2014) argues that Sparrow's "lyrical prowess made him the Anansi of T&T, a "master trickster,"[15] who could be both a hero and a villain and he used his music to reflect the reality of society as he saw it." I would add that he is also a chameleon, a shape shifter, he moves in and out of each calypso, even geographically, having convinced you that the persona of Sparrow and the protagonist of the song is one, we are forced to suspend disbelief during his live performance or while listening to him on the airwaves. This shape shifting is not only in the character imagery but in his ease with language, to reinforce a former point, sliding between the dialect and polite English, from one tongue to another, investing his character with archetypal persona. When he grunts like the Congo man he signifies a popular movie borrowed image, as politically incorrect as this is, of the African cannibal; in "Teresa" he is the Spanish lover saying *yo te quiero mucho*, in "Lying Excuses," the smooth talking husband who could fool his wife and in "May May" (1959), he becomes the female character, expressing the sensibility of a syrupy *femme fatale*.

May May
Making love one day, with a girl they calling May May
Making love one day, with a girl they calling May May
I pick May May by the railway

And we take a taxi straight to Claxton Bay
Before we lay down on the carpet
She start catching fits
Well she bawling
Darling don't bite me
Don't do that honey
I never had a man who ever do dat to me
Ay ay ay yay doo darling
Look meh pores raise up
You making me feel so sweet
Stop Sparrow stop

Dis time if you see
How she hook me and ah hook she
Like two snakes roll up
She so deceitful, she bawling stop
But she like it, I know dat
By the way she start to scratch me like a cat
Leggo leggo
Stop Sparrow stop

Darling don't bite me
Don't do that honey
"I never had a man who ever do dat to me
Ay ay ay yay doo doo darling
Look meh pores raise up
You making me feel so sweet
Stop sparrow stop

Sparrow does not take the easy linear path. He may understandably identify more with men, but can we grudge him his masculinity? In continuing to configure the anatomy of sexuality and gender relations for the region he contributes some of the metaphors that may now have lost their appeal but were compelling in their time.

A generation of Caribbean folk, especially those in the diaspora who grew up in the Sparrow era still quote his verses as if they present home truths about life and love in the Caribbean tropics.[16] The sustained affection for his verse, despite the sometimes politically incorrect allusions was also owed to his skill at word play. Sparrow is the master of the sustained *double entendre*. His wit, salaciousness, accompaniment of sounds and vocal gutturals, a wicked glint in the eye and his lines delivered poker face to an audience, has allowed him to relay graphic metaphors and practices of sexuality without being censored. One YouTube listener in 2012 responded to his song "Ah fraid pussy bite me" with this comment: "If you study and teach English Literature you will marvel at the genius – the puns, analogy, double meaning – straight poetry that puts you on the spot! Is it literal or subliminal? Then the moral dilemma stares you squarely in the face as you snicker at the humour."[17] This tradition of wordsmith has of course continued in the calypso, soca and chutney arena. Unfortunately wit and *double entendre* are often absent, as if the lack of censorship and freeing up of sexual mores have also diminished the gift of intelligence that one absorbed with delight in the lyrical sentences of Sparrow's calypsos.

Among the sustained *double entendre* of Sparrow that has entered the realm of folk classic are:

Big Bamboo (1957)
I asked my woman what must I do,
To make her honest and keep love too,
She said Sparrow all I want from you,
Is a little little piece baby of the big bamboo

60 million Frenchmen (1969)
You say that you love and you'll give your heart,
But you have a whole body why not give each part
When a love is true there ain't nothing that you wouldn't do
The French people know the trick so they have everybody licked

Ah fraid pussy bite met (1969)
From since I small I hear them say
With pussy cat you mustn't play
A pussy cat always look vex vex vex
You never know what they will do next
Ah fraid ah fraid pussy bite me

Saltfish (1977)
Saltfish stew is what I like
So doo-doo, give me day and night
I like your food, so don't find me rude
My favorite, I sure every man in here already eat it

Sparrow also ingrains the implicit archetype of Caribbean masculinity that reveres sexual male prowess in:

The Village Ram (1964)
Is me the village ram
I eh give a dam
Is me the village ram
I eh give a dam
I cutting down black is white
Man I working day and night
If you have a job to be done
See me, I eh making fun

And not a woman ever complain yet
With me
I eh boasting but I got durability
And if a woman ever say that I
Ever left her dissatisfy
She lie
She Lie
She lie

Beware when I drinking rum
I eh like to done
And I bad like a cobra snake
Doh try to escape
When I put you in a clinch
Don't care how you bite and pinch
And I got meh hand on your mouth
The way I does lock you neck
You cyar shout
And not a woman ever complain yet
With me
I eh boasting but I got durability
And if a woman ever say that I

> Ever left her dissatisfy
> She lie She lie She lie

The idea that sexual performance takes precedence over all else in a relationship, the act of boasting about one's sexual "durability" or exploits, the explicit violence "The way I does lock you neck you cyar shout" - one cannot in all honesty dismiss the critique that the calypso has been used as form of control over women, as it has over all miscreants of one sort or another, the politician and priest alike. Gottreich (n.d.) sums up the contradictoriness of the calypso form with regard to Caribbean femininity: "In virtually every subject area, such as politics, unemployment, or social injustices, the (male) calypsonian seeks to tell the truth, to reflect the public sentiment. Curiously, it is only in the domain of female representation that woman has been chauvinistically distorted, fabricated, constructed and fictionalized in ways that do not reflect reality."[18]

What is *reality* for femininity and masculinity? What is this ideal male/female equity and balance that exists out there somewhere to which we aspire? Sparrow is no philosopher asking the question. He is the bard singing the conundrum into our subconscious. He knows that the power relations between masculinity and femininity are waged on every level. His renditions are an honest representation of his encounters, the psychoses and fears that each sex has of the other, the need for gender relations to be constructed on so many layers of truth and half-truths, the mutations in arrangements between the sexes again in many forms. Think for instance of the meme song "I go be single forever" that won Kris Veeshal Persad, sobriquet KI – chutney soca monarch of the year 2012 in Trinidad and Tobago.

> I don't have to stay at home
> I don't have to answer phone
> I could have any girl in my car …
> When meh partners have it hard
> I doh have to clock no card
> I go be single forever

The battle continues, women versus men, even unto a new generation.

Whether we admit to it or not, there are home truths in Sparrow's songs that undergird any sexual relationship, as for instance in "No Money no Love" (1969), where the true pathos of sexual desire and economics meet up.

> Ivy pack up she clothes to leave
> Because John was down and out
> All alone he was left to grieve
> She had a next man in South
> She said openly
> She say I really love you Johnny
> But you ain`t have no money
> So what will my future be Even though you say you love me?
>
> *Chorus*
> We cyar love without money
> We cyar make love on hungry belly
> Johnny you`ll be the only one I`m dreaming of
> You`re my turtle dove
> But, no money no love
>
> If you hear how he plead with she to get her to understand
> Listen, mister, she tell Johnny
> Leggo me blasted hand
> And make up your mind
> We got to break up this lime
> She said poverty is a crime
> You got no money
> Still you tanglin` me all the blinkin` time
>
> Gentleman let me tell you plain
> She say I don`t want to make a scene
> But if you only touch me again
> The police got intervene
> You ain`t got a blasted cent
> I couldn`t even pay the rent
> I had to give up me apartment
> You give me nothing to eat
> Now you want me to sleep on the pavement?

>Johnny nearly killed she with blows
>Poor Ivy bawl like a cow
>Rip up she wig and he tear down she clothes
>The South man ain't want she now
>Oh, Lord, what a fight
>They roll until broad daylight
>Charlotte street was hot that night
>She get some good lick but she let go kick and some bite

The arrangement of this song is almost dirge like. The calypsonian's pathos extends to both men and women. Poverty is the crime and one that contributes to the violence of sexual relations. In the last verse, with the usual Sparrowdian twist, Johnny nearly kills Ivy with blows, and she ends up worse for the wear, even losing the south man because of this brawl. Love in the urban tropics is lived out in the streets where much of life takes place, outside of small and overcrowded rooms. As the narrator says, "Charlotte Street was hot that night, She get some good lick but she let go kick and some bite." Women are never only victims, men are rarely absolute winners.

I hope this bird's eye view of The Mighty Sparrow has convinced you sufficiently that Mr. Slinger Francisco's extensive catalogue deserves much closer scrutiny for its literary value as well as its complex representation of gender. Behind the mischievous smile and wicked pelvic thrust, Sparrow represents one of the best attempts of Caribbean men to serenade women and to express the *tabanca*[19] of unrequited love. He recognized the transitory nature of existence that many relationships must part because we remain temporary residents and travellers in islands too small to absorb all of its talent, indiscretions, desires and ambitions. In the tradition of the old folk songs like " Jamaica Farewell" (1957),[20] and "Come back Liza, Come back Gyal" (1952),[21] we also have Sparrow's legacy of love ballads like "Rose" in which he confesses "Girl ah want you bad Girl, ah want you bad! I'm going staring mad," (mind you characteristically still promising her blows for leaving and deceiving him) and "Maria" (1959). These two songs from his repertoire speak to the pain of love and loss and have become, like many in his richly varied repertoire, classics to be recalled and sung by generations past and those to come. Let Sparrow have the last word on the ubiquitous bittersweet pathos of love and man/woman relations.

Maria
Maria darling I must go
But remember I love you so
Unfortunately, we must part
Girl you don't know how it breaks my heart

I wish I coulda stay with you
And gie you what is yours dou dou
But until we meet again
I know, right now we got to say ayo
Woa oh oh oh oh Maria
Woa oh oh oh oh Maria

I like the way you walk Marie
And I like the way you talk Marie
I like the way you smile Marie
You know you have me going wild Marie

It's very plain to see Marie
How much you mean to me Marie
I don't care if I starve Marie
You'll get all the money I have Marie
Woa woa woa oh oh oh Maria
Woa woa oh oh oh Maria

I went home to Marie last night
But somebody nearly out meh light
I don't know what was his reason
Now the police have him in prison

I don't know if what he says was true
He says he love Maria too
But now I cyar see what to do
Because he have meh eyes black and blue
Woo oo oh oh oh Maria
Woo oo oh oh oh Maria.

ENDNOTES

[1] See Gordon Rohlehr and J. Cowley. 1996. *Carnival, Canboulav and Calypso*. UK: Cambridge University Press and Everard Phillips. 2005. *Recognising the Language of Calypso as "Symbolic Action" in Resolving Conflict in the Republic of Trinidad and Tobago*. PhD diss., London School of Economics.

[2] I thank Dr. Sue Ann Barratt of the Institute for Gender and Development Studies for her assistance with the research on discography of Sparrow for this paper.

[3] Gordon Rohlehr. 1990. *Calypso and Society in Pre-Independence Trinidad*, Gordon Rohlehr, Tunapuna, Trinidad, p. 216

[4] Think of T. S. Eliot's line from *The Lovesong of J. Alfred Prufrock* (1915): "In the rooms the women go, speaking of Michelangelo" and compare this with Sparrow's similar capacity in verse redering.

[5] *Trinidad Guardian*, 2 October 1966, Interview Sparrow with Wayne Brown.

[6] Rohlehr, Gordon. 2005. "Carnival Cannibalized or Cannibal Carnivalized: Contextualizing the "Cannibal Joke" in Calypso and Literature," *Anthurium: A Caribbean Studies Journal*: Vol. 3 Iss. 2, Article 1. Available at: https://scholarlyrepository.miami.edu/anthurium/vol3/iss2/1

[7] Louis Regis. 2013. "From Apocalypse to Awakenings" *Tout Moun, Caribbean Journal of Cultural Studies*, 2 (1): 4, October.
https://journals.sta.uwi.edu/toutmoun/papers/oct13/Tout_Moun_2_REGIS.pdf

[8] Chaucer's poetic language has been well documented and I am certainly no expert in this area. This reference is primarily to stimulate more imaginative interpretations of Sparrow's poetry in song into this discussion, but certainly not a definitive or fully informed set of statements.

[9] See "Sparrow and the Language of the Calypso" by Gordon Rohlehr, in *Caribbean Quarterly*, 14(1–2), March-June 1968; *The Future in the Present—Selected Writings by C.L.R. James*. Westport, Connecticut: L: Hill, and London: Allison & Busby, and Edward Kamau Brathwaite. 1984. *History of the Voice: Development of Nation Language in Anglophone Caribbean Poetry*. London: New Beacon Books.

[10] Some of this replaying of calypso-created characters is already found in the theatre of Tony Hall. 2002. *Jean and Dinah*, Bloomington, In: AuthorHouse, and in crime fiction by Laurence Waldron 2015. *Gypsy in the Moonlight*, Floodwood, Minn: Four Rivers Press.

[11] I discuss the retaliations of these female calypsonians to the masculine gaze of calypso in a paper entitled "Reflections on the Women's Movement in Trinidad: Calypsos, Changes and Sexual Violence" *Feminist Review*, 1991, No 38, pp. 33-47.

[12] See Raymond Quevedo. 1983. *Atilla's Kaiso: A Short History of Trinidad Calypso*, University of the West Indies Extra-Mural Studies. Atilla had a series of calypsos that deplored what he considered the modern trends of women, their new fashions in "The Modern Girl" p.138 and "Women is not the weaker sex" p. 159. In his 1935 calypso "Women will rule the world" he demonstrates a prescience of the future: "Long ago their one ambition in life, Was to be a mother and wife, But now they mean to be males, Smoking cigarettes and drinking cocktails."

[13] Harris, Mark and Carmel Buckley. "Calypso Picaresque: The Particular Genius of Mighty Sparrow" https://archive.ica.art/bulletin/calypso-picaresque

[14] *Ibid*.

[15] Reshma Ragoonath Tue Feb 18 2014
http://www.guardian.co.tt/article-6.2.378745.4d68585640

[16] I should also note that this is not just restricted to Trinidadian or Caribbean-born peoples. Many colleagues and friends who have visited Trinidad or

were exposed to Sparrow's wit still recall and sing verses of his songs as an identification with this culture. And then of course there is a new second and third generation of listeners and fans who discover Sparrow through You Tube and in other digital media.

[17] Sandy Bradshaw, https://www.youtube.com/watch?v=jUJ-yTp0-Os; Accessed January 3rd, 2020

[18] Anna S. Gottreich "Whe she go do": Women's Participation in Trinidad Calypso. Undated paper https://ufdcimages.uflib.ufl.edu/CA/00/40/01/29/00001/PDF.pdf

[19] Caribbean/Trinidadian word to describe lovesickness, sadness as a result of unrequited feelings for someone.

[20] The origins of this song are unclear although credited to Irving Burgie (American of Barbadian birth) who admitted that it was culled from a Jamaican mento song. It was recorded and made popular by Harry Belafonte in 1957. See https://mudcat.org/thread.cfm?threadid=61495 for a conversation thread on the possible origins of this and other folk songs.

[21] Specific origins of "Come back Liza" in Jamaican dialect, with musical score and chords, edited and arranged by Tom Murray, 1952, Folk *Songs of Jamaica*, Oxford University Press. Sung by Edric Connor and the Caribbeans, 1952, *Songs from Jamaica*, track 6. Revised and arranged by Irving Burgie and William Attaway, *Come Back Liza*, sung by Harry Belafonte 1955.

REFERENCES

Gottreich, Anna S. (n.d.) "Whe she go do": Women's Participation in Trinidad Calypso." Undated paper, https://ufdcimages.uflib.ufl.edu/CA/00/40/01/29/00001/PDF.pdf

Hodge, Merle, 1975. "In the Shadow of the Whip: A Comment on Male-Female Relations in the Caribbean." In *Is Massa Day Dead?* edited by Orde Coombs. New York: Anchor Books.

Mohammed, Patricia. 2003. "Blueprint for Gender in Creole Trinidad: Exploring Gender Mythology through Calypsos of the 1920s and 1930s." In *The Culture of Gender and Sexuality in the Caribbean*, edited by Linden Lewis, 129-168. Gainesville: University Press of Florida.

Naipaul, V. S. 1969. *The Middle Passage*. Harmondsworth, UK: Penguin Books (first published by Andre Deutsch 1962)

Regis, Louis. 2013. "From Apocalypse to Awakenings." *Tout Moun, Caribbean Journal of Cultural Studies*, 2 (1): 4. https://journals.sta.uwi.edu/toutmoun/papers/oct13/Tout_Moun_2_REGIS.pdf

Rohlehr, Gordon. 2005. "Carnival Cannibalized or Cannibal Carnivalized: Contextualizing the "Cannibal Joke" in Calypso and Literature," *Anthurium:*

A Caribbean Studies Journal: 3 (2):; Article 1. Available at: https://scholarlyrepository.miami.edu/anthurium/vol3/iss2/1

Rohlehr, Gordon. 1990. *Calypso and Society in Pre-independence Trinidad.* Tunapuna, Trinidad: Gordon Rohlehr.

Warner, Keith Q. 1983. "Kaiso! The Trinidad Calypso – a Study of the Calypso as Oral Literature." *Caribbean Quarterly*, 29(1) : 72-75.

DISCOGRAPHY FOR SPARROW – SLINGER FRANCISCO

"Congo Man" in *More Sparrow More*. Recording Artists, 1969. LP

"Ah Fraid Pussy Bite me" in *Mighty Sparrow: The Renaissance*. BLS Records, 1996

"Benwood Dick" in *Calypsoes*. RCA, 1960. LP

"Big Bamboo" in *Tatooed Lady*. NRC, 1957. LP

"Congo Man" in *Trinidad Heat Wave*. Mace Records, 1965. LP

"Dan is the Man in the Van" in *Sparrow at the Sheraton, Kingston*. WIRL, 1962. LP

"Federation" in *This is Sparrow*. Balisier, 1959. LP

"Lying Excuses" in *Mighty Sparrow: The Renaissance*. BLS Records, 1996. LP and CD

"Mai Mai" Road March (1960), in *16 Carnival Hits*. Ice Records, 1992, CD. (First recorded in 1959)

"Maria" in *Mighty Sparrow*. RCA, 1959. LP

"No Money, No Love" in *Hotter than ever*. Recording Artists, 1972. LP

"ObeahWedding" (Melda) in *The Calypso Genius Volume I*. NRC, 1966. LP

"Philip My Dear" in *Mighty Sparrow: The Greatest*. Dynamic Sounds, 1982. LP

"Rose" in *Sparrow: Calypso King*. RCA, 1961 LP

"Saltfish" in *Sparrow vs the Rest*. Tysott, 1977. LP

"Sandra" in *Sparrow at the Hilton*. Recording Artists 1966. LP

"Stella" in *Calypso Carnival*. Balisier, 1959. LP

"The Governor's Ball" in *Sparrow at the Hilton*. Recording Artists 1966. LP

"The Lizard" in *More Sparrow More*. Recording Artists, 1969 LP

"The Slave" in *Mighty Sparrow: The Slave*. NRC, 1963. LP

"The Village Ram" in *Sparrow Sings the Outcast*. NRC, 1963. LP

"Tobago Girls" in *Mighty Sparrow: 25th Anniversary*. Charlie's Records, 1979. LP

"Who She Go Cry for now?" in *More Sparrow More*. cc, 1969. LP

20

The Indian Snake Charmer and Other Tales: The Image as Story[†]

FAMILY ALBUMS

Every photograph is a true moment captured in time, even when the photograph is a staged collusion between the photographer and the subjects. Born in 1931 and perhaps fascinated with the relatively new media of his era, my father Ayoob Mohammed clearly had an interest in photography. Before the advent of the home-owned instamatic and now the ubiquitous digital cameras, he made us dress up in our finest clothes and marched us off reluctantly to the photographer's studio in Princes Town, south Trinidad at regular intervals during our childhood and into adolescence. Thanks to his passion for the photographic image, we have an intermittent portrait chronicle that stimulates memory and bears witness to our family life since the 1950s as the examples in Figure 1 show. The first photograph (dated circa

---

[†] An unpublished paper revised in 2020. The original was presented to the "The Indian Diaspora: Identities, Trajectories and Transnationalities Conference", The University of the West Indies, St. Augustine, May 2015.

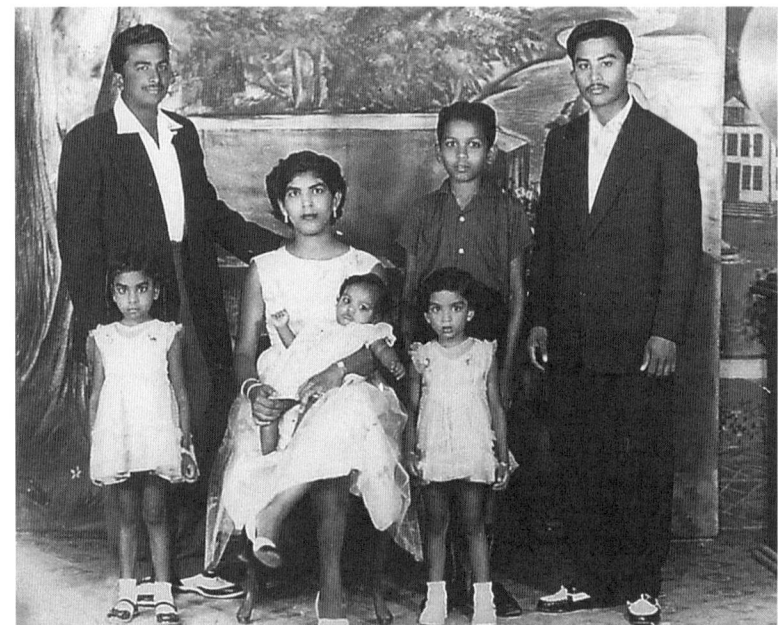

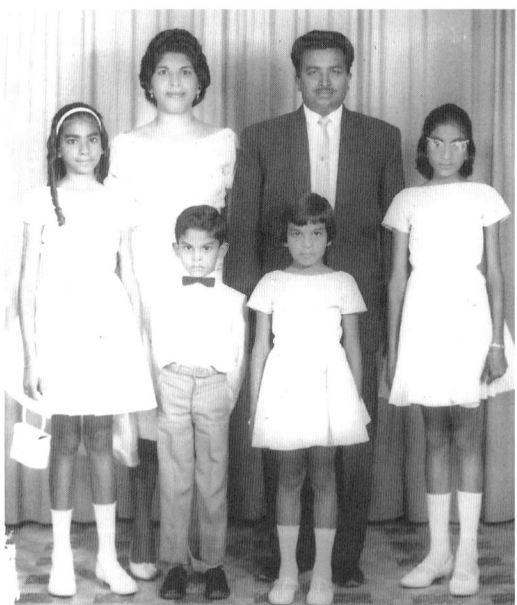

Figure 1: Family Photos – Trinidad 1957 and 1962 (Author photos)

1957) was one of the earliest photographs taken of the family. My father is standing on the far left with his brother and nephew to the right. My mother is seated with her then youngest child. She had joined a readymade family. As the eldest brother with both parents deceased, my father had the responsibility for the welfare of his older brother and on request, his sister's son. As I write this, three of the persons in this photograph have already died. In the second photograph, (1962) taken after my uncle had migrated to Canada permanently and my cousin no longer lived with us, the family had expanded and my brother was made to wear his first tailor made long pants. The photographs have become more treasured. I recognise in the faces of my parents their likenesses to their grandchildren. I only now recognise the natural beauty of their youth in the moment when they were healthy and strong, and to use an old fashioned but appropriate word, in retrospect to 'cherish' this time that I could not comprehend as a child. I see in the stances of all my siblings the characters we would each grow into as adults. Such images that visually capture familiar faces or events are now more valuable because they are few. The grainy texture of the images we save, their faded or scarred surfaces add meaning and depth as they reflect the technology and aesthetic of the period. They are poignant reminders that much else has disappeared both materially and from memory: objects that once made up our everyday lives – books, childhood toys, written correspondence, birthday cards, household furniture and crockery. The photographs serve to fill huge tactile gaps that one longs with age to remember.

This desire to preserve the personal photograph and family chronicle is a compelling one, more so today when we have iPhones at our finger tips. The domestic family photograph or portraiture is still an underused source in writing histories in the Caribbean and family albums are a rich vein that remains to be mined.[1] Capturing the facial features, dress styles and other minutiae of daily life, the private and public events around individuals and groups, can preserve social memory while also providing insights into the performance of gender and ethnic identities. Elements of family or community identity, passages in the cultural life of a family like marriages or births allow family genealogies to survive or to reveal new knowledge. For example, from my husband's family photo albums kept religiously by his mother who was born in 1913, one is able to trace back two generations of English men who fought in the first and second world wars (Figure 2). Roshini Kempadoo points out that "The early and rapid development of photography technologies from the 1850s to 1930s meant photography emerged as a significant part of a European visual economy" both as a "peculiarly modern arrangement of knowledges," and a "compulsion to order and construct taxonomies."[2] There are probably very few families, certainly those in the working and lower middle classes in the Caribbean, who currently have

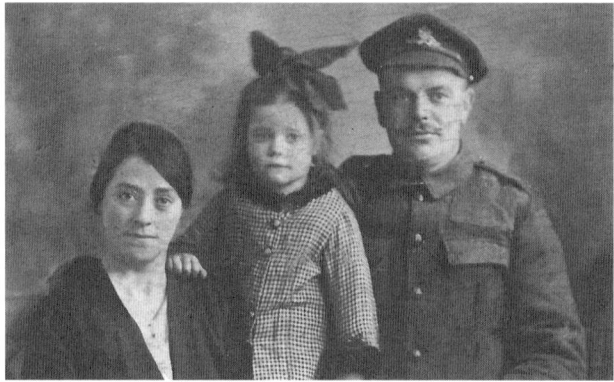

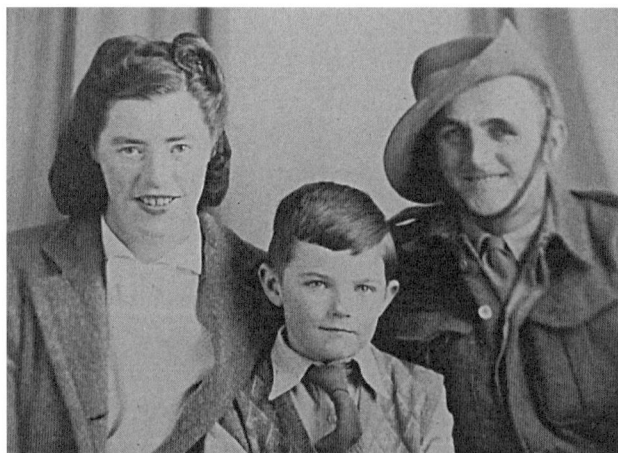

Figure 2: Family Photographs taken in 1918 end of World War 1, Dixon's mother with her parents and 1945 Dixon at 5 years old with his mother and father just returned from the second world war (Photos courtesy of Rex Dixon)

personal photographs that date back to the early twentieth century although photography was introduced into the Caribbean since 1840 with the Duperly studios in Jamaica. If they do then these might very well be primarily wedding photographs, a tradition that perhaps crossed many cultures.

In the same way that we might be able to reconstruct family histories or insights from photographs and glean information that gets lost in translation if transmitted primarily through oral or written communication, it is also possible to create narratives around groups, institutions or organizations. In this essay I am interested in the project of reviving social memory and widening the breadth of interpretation around Indo-Caribbean ethnicity and culture. I read these sources "against the grain of the archives."[3] Margriet Fokken writes that the process of reading deliberately against the conventional archival grain of assumed truth of the image that has passed into posterity and becomes historical baggage, allows for the deconstruction of stereotypes and for telling new stories. By stories I do not of course mean creating fictional narratives. Rather I use insight into a culture, verification of data and other tools to interpret the movement and settlement of a people and to imagine how we can alter the perceptions and the telling of the 'story' conveyed only through a one sided lens. In this approach I am also taking cues from Alberto Manguel's *Reading Pictures* as a "spectator of an eternal display of images."[4] Like Manguel I am drawn to story telling, to disrupting the silence of subjects in a painting or photograph, sometimes in inventive ways rather than primarily writing "history" based on unearthed data. Much of history writing in any event depends on the interpretation of the individual researcher and the conceptual framework that shapes this reading and is generally a partial view. Steven Lubar and W. David Kingery have also pointed out that we seldom use the artifacts that make up our environment to understand the past. Arguing for a "history from things" they remind us that artifacts provide data about history and serve as signs.[5] When we read photographs in a sense we are reading another object or artefact produced by technologies, a technology that sought to capture light and likeness, among many other reasons to extend the life of the moment or the subject captured into posterity and to make this image available to others. It seems to me that in reading photographs we are equally compelled to read between the lines and make connections that have to do with human consciousness and confidence – to discern conditions and states of being. This essay is an experiment in my own reading of images to tell stories of and about the people who still speak to us behind light sensitive paper and now the digital image unto which they have been transferred.

The hundreds of postcards, photographic images and original artworks that make up this visual record of Indians in Trinidad and in the West Indies by their 170th year in this territory is an imaginative geography, configuring a visual map of the past into the present. All images are not created equal. Some of these are postcards that were produced under a colonial regime with a deliberate intent, others are taken from family albums, and still others are creative interpretations by three generations of painters and sculptors. My focus in this essay is on the photographic image. Apart from the family albums I have used, I draw particularly on postcards or those that found their way into travel writings and other printed records.

THE SNAKE CHARMER

Trolling repeatedly through this assemblage of postcards that represent the Indo-Caribbean presence, the recurring Indian huts, slender limbed Indian families, female street sellers stooped alongside a sparse display of sidewalk goods, turbaned Hindu priests, and Indian men in dhotis caught like a different species on a street of western-clothed characters, I came across two that stopped me in my tracks because of the questions they raised. The first, Figure 3, undated, is that of a man dressed in a plaid sarong and kurta pyjama top holding on to two boa constrictors. In Trinidad these are known as macajuel and they are also found in South and Central America. The snake heads protrude from the palms of his hand in which they are caught, presumably in a tight grip. The various fowl at the back seem amazingly nonchalant in the presence of the snakes and the barefooted man holding them. He is posed for the camera looking straight at the photographer as if displaying his goods for sale. The caption is *"Snake Charmer": Trinidad. B.W.I.* Why is he holding these snakes and why was the caption snake charmer selected? Was there

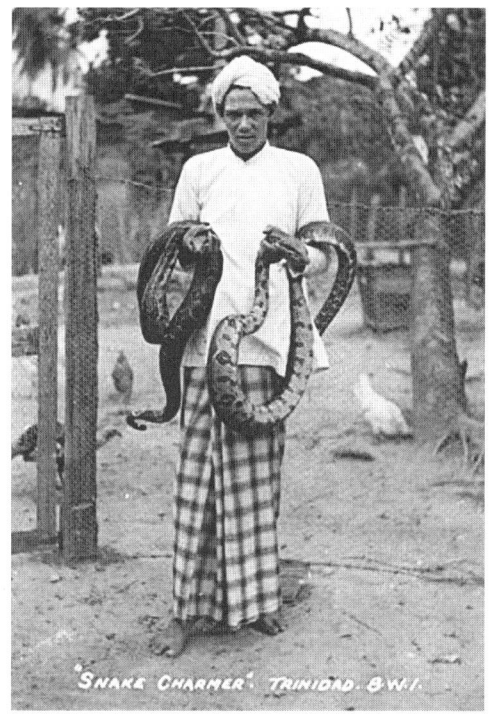

Figure 3: Snake Charmer. Trinidad B.W.I. Michael Goldberg Postcard Collection, University of the West Indies Collection

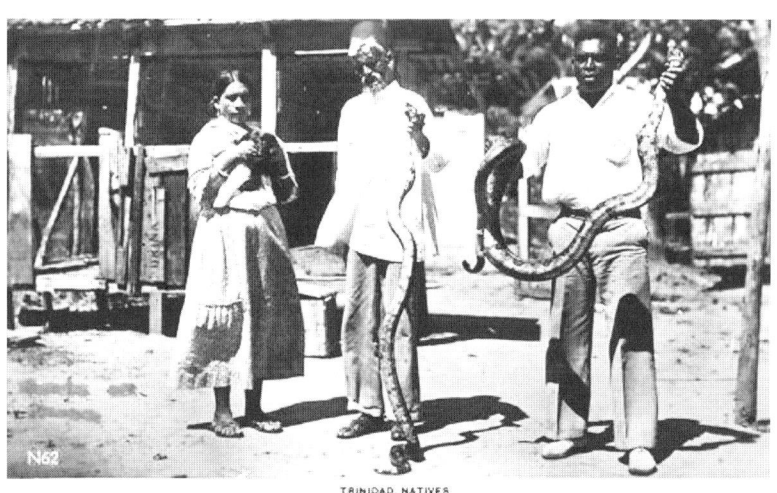

Figure 4: Trinidad Natives – Postcard

such a tradition transferred from India to Trinidad? This was something that either in my childhood or in my close reading of Indo-Caribbean history I had not encountered.

The second image (Figure 4) is titled *Trinidad Natives*, one of the many in a long list of Caribbean postcards that employed the word "natives" somewhat carelessly.[6] Here two men display snakes – boas again – deduced from the patterns on the snake skins, since Trinidad does not have the cobra species that were the dancing snakes used by snake charmers in India. The third person in the photograph is a woman who also appears to be holding a snake in her hands and quite close to her chest. All of them position the snake heads firmly away from their bodies. The boa constrictor or macajuel does not possess a deadly bite but uses its large body to constrict prey, suffocating the victim to death.

While the men are wearing western-styled trousers, the woman's mid-calf dress length, *orhni* or scarf around her shoulders, earrings and bayras around both wrists, suggest a conventional dress of Indian women in Trinidad circa 1940s. Figure 3 might be dated at least two decades earlier than Figure 4. In the former image the man with the sarong is barefooted while in the second image, all of them wear sandals. These two photographs were rather unusual finds in this collection, particularly as the classic visual tale of imperialism, while accentuating migrant differences, more precisely served to establish the exotic activities of "natives" and the distance of civilization they represented from those in the seat of empire. As Ryan (1997) comments, none of these photographs "speak for themselves or show us the world through an innocent historical eye. Rather, they are invested with meanings, framed by and produced within specific cultural conditions and historical circumstances." What the photographs demonstrate are the silences in our knowledge. Who were these people and what were their occupations? Were they actually snake-charmers or were the snakes being harvested and sold as a commodity and if so for what purpose?

Were any of the photographs in the nineteenth or early twentieth century taken by Indian photographers, visitors to the island or "natives" themselves? Who were the earlier and later

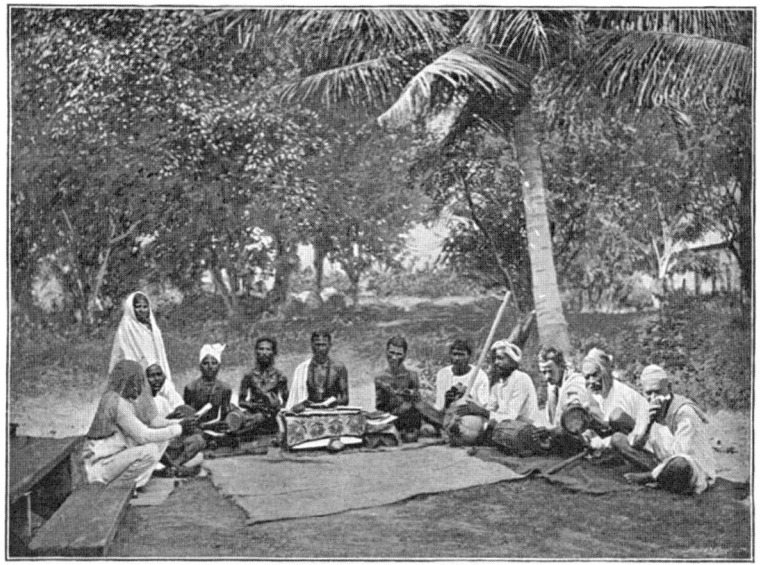

Figure 5: Reading The Sacred Book Of India On Trinidad 1897
(Antique Print)

photographers? Unfortunately we do not know the answers to these questions. By the twentieth century some locally-born photographers and local companies producing the advertising or touristic image had appeared on the scene. From the growing number of books and articles that have been produced about the image from a postcolonial deconstructive angle, we can agree that these were "composed, reproduced, circulated and arranged for consumption within particular social circles" and "reveal as much about the imaginative landscapes of imperial culture as they do about the physical spaces or people pictured within their frame" (Ryan 1997).

Sometimes the visual image was accompanied by a written text reinforcing the imperial script as in this print produced for commercial sale shown in Figure 5: "...*Three continents - Europe, Africa and Asia - have each contributed their share: the white man who rules from Europe and the two dark races, the negro and the Hindu, from Africa and*

Asia. Here we see a group of unmistakable Asiatics, natives of India, who sit round while a Sadhu reads from the Ramayana ...Thus strangely do the races of the Empire shift and mingle under the equal protection afforded by the British flag." The tale being spun here is harmony under a palm tree. That disrupted cultures have been peaceably revived.

As both Mohapatra's (1995) and my own work (Mohammed 2002) have demonstrated, from the remnants of disrupted migrant lives the colonial authorities sought to ensure that family life was resurrected and the instability of labour controlled. The tasks left for the travel writer and roving photographers of the twentieth century were:
(a) to continue to record this experiment of successful migration from a system of transported labour
(b) to depict the difference of Indians on the landscape, to frame the "exotic" - the east meets west.
(c) to romanticise poverty and ignore the signals that the image conveyed of docility, disempowerment and rurality.

Cesaire's *Discourse on Colonialism* (1972) originally published in 1955, long before and prescient of "post-colonial" thought, offers an insightful reading here. There was no civilizing mission inherent in western expansionism nor is the "West" however this is now constituted, invested in relieving the past and present of this mystification. Despite contemporary globalization, an element of mystique is maintained, perhaps necessary for global tourism, but also because major differences do in fact co-exist between geographies, histories, cultures and nations.

I am not concerned with writing back to the empire about our pre- and past history. Rather I am interested in how we who live and work in the Caribbean (and perhaps those from the diaspora) take possession of an imaginary past that these stationery image vignettes reveal. Rather than viewing them primarily as evidence of our victimization by a colonial machinery I am interested in what else they convey about our knowledge of a past and of those of us who would become the inheritors of settled colonies. Visual perception involves thinking and thinking makes subliminal use of visual imagery (Arnheim 2004). As we write the script so must we reconfigure the *percept*.[7] The abundant media at present recycles the recurring images or word plays as a soup of signs. But these, as Baudrillard suggests, are already "crossing into a space whose curvature is no longer that of the real, nor that of truth ...When the real is no longer what it was, nostalgia assumes its full meaning" (Baudrillard 1994). Is this glossing over past images a project of nostalgia or new proclamations of identity? One is not sure? What it still is nonetheless, is a system of representation, an algebra of the past, a visual language of patterns, a shorthand for cultural history and a method for defining and coming to terms with difference whether of ethnicity, class or gender.

Suspend the intense moral outrage of the twenty-first century for a moment and consider that each photograph is a legitimate vignette of the past. I am interested in what they reveal about the people pictured within the frame, outside of the emblematic and problematic colonial narrative, despite the myopic picture taking and image making. My approach is similar to the exercise of re-examining past family photographs to see what the photographer might have inadvertently exposed. For example, to return to Figure 1, Family Photo I see details that a first look does not always reveal - the two-toned shoes of my father and uncle who were both primary school teachers and fashion-conscious young men of their time, youthful likenesses of my uncle and cousin both of whom are now deceased. The cleverness of my mother with the needle - she sewed all our clothes from childhood and took great pride in ensuring that we were, as the school teacher's daughters, the best-dressed children in our village, always in matching outfits. The painted backdrop or drapes in the photographer's studio that provided a grand setting for a humble family photograph. That in the 1957 photograph, apart from my father who has the glimpse of a smile, the rest of the party are all wide eyed and serious, in my case, to the left of my mother staring straight into camera open mouthed, and vaguely recalling that I was possibly afraid of the sudden flash of bright light which accompanied this experience.

READING PICTURES IMAGINATIVELY

"As photographs give people an imaginary possession of a past that is unreal, they also help people to take possession of space in which they are insecure" wrote Sontag (1973) in *On Photography*.

In this allusion to insecurity, while Sontag is referring specifically to the touristic gaze, the outsider appropriating a visual slice, one can apply a different sense of insecurity to the subjects who are being photographed. The snake charmers above begin a visual trail – images of a people and culture whose religious practices, cultural performance and festivals, housing and occupations, musicians and musical apparatus, women's and men bodies as instruments of labour or advertisements of wealth acquisition – all vindicated the system of transported labour. These snapshots were turned into postcards, some hand-coloured and prettified as colour photography.[8] They uncover members of an ethnic group who, in the early twentieth century, were still viewed as outsiders into a society whose colour-coded and class-based hierarchy had already been intransigently blue printed. On their arrival Indians occupied the lower occupations and had distinctive differences in their cultural and social lifeways. Have these images, selective and deliberately chosen for exposure by the earlier photographers, continued to shape how the Indian population sees itself in the Caribbean diaspora? Have they been used to keep a notion of Indian-ness in place, the idea of rural eastern peoples who are not quite yet adjusted to the style and demands of western society? In many of these photographs there appears to be a complicity with the subjects' gaze of the photographer, and understandably so. In the relations of power between the photographer and the subject, the box camera was still a rare and expensive object, a thing of wonder; the idea of the image being used for propagandistic purposes or economic gain perhaps did not enter the subject's mind, there might even have been money passed, and for some, a pride in being made visible and noticed on the landscape.

Figure 6, *A Coolie Priest in Port of Spain* brings to mind the passages from historical records and travellers' books that talk about the strangeness of the Indian presence in Port of Spain in the late nineteenth and early twentieth centuries. If we look closer into the blow ups of the image towards the middle distance, some of those on the sidewalk may have been destitute perhaps or simply waiting around, on their haunches, stooped on the ground bringing the knees towards the chest to hold the balance and thus maintain the position for some duration. The man standing against a tree is separated by an unpaved roadway. At the far back

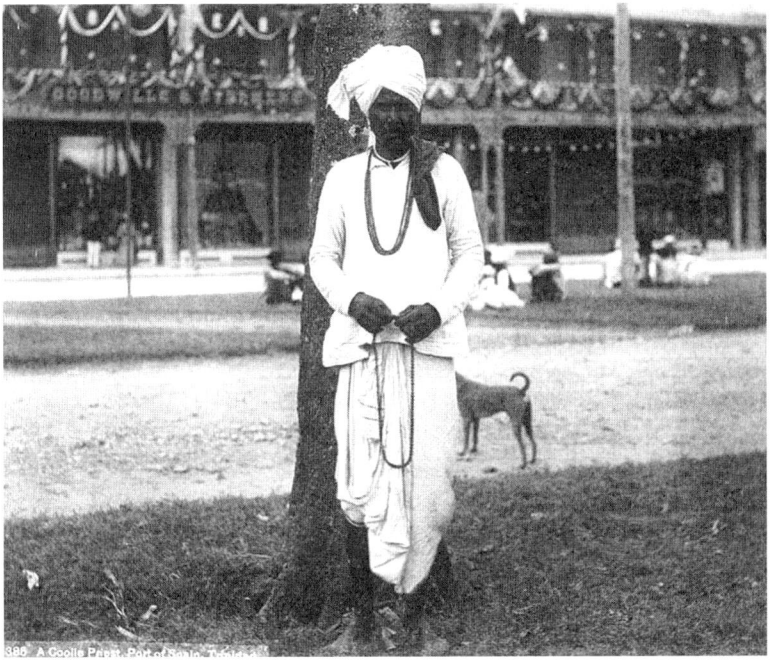

Figure 6: A Coolie Priest Port of Spain Trinidad, possibly late 19th century.

three figures against the shop window, one man, hatted with dark jacket and white trousers and two women, well dressed from the distance, the women's clothes and head wraps signify them as of African descent. The seated female may or may not be a street vendor. There is a curious figure in the row of seated men who is not dressed in the conventional dhoti-styled trousers and he wears a hat unlike the others who are turbaned. Is he of East Indian descent even? And if so what is he doing with a group of Indians on a main street in Port of Spain – the shop at the back is Goodwill & Stephens – its verandah front is hung with decorative streamers, a string of lights. What is the occasion? Is this a celebration of Empire day? Are they on a day pass from the estates? It is a curious grouping and moment that this photograph, examined more closely, invites the viewer to imagine, and to contemplate a time in the city of Port of Spain when people sat around on the grass verges. The central figure of the Hindu priest looks staged, he is even holding a set of beads to emphasise his pious status. He is obviously the focussed subject of this photograph.

Attempts to date the photo more accurately through the history of the store and its location were not very rewarding but both the architectural resemblance to Stephens and Todds on Frederick Street and the name Stephens suggest that this may have predated the previous Stephens and Todds which was only formed after the great fire of Port of Spain in 1895. This places the photograph possibly before 1895, borne out by the style of dress worn by those visible in the image.

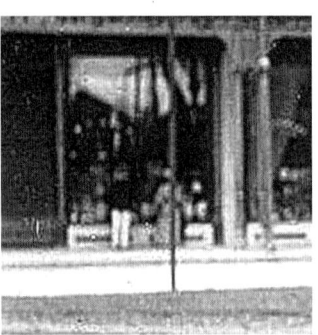

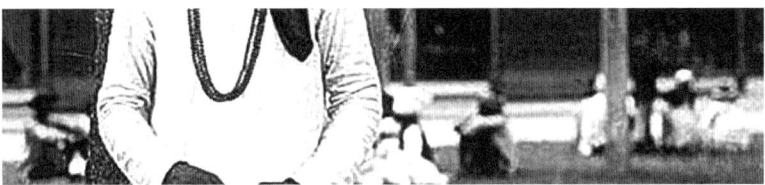

Blow ups from Figure 6

If the above photograph was taken by an itinerant street photographer, many others show signs of studio photography. This deliberate posing for the camera is especially apparent in the photographs of women in Figures 7 and 8. From the feminist perspective, these fit into genre of photographs and postcards that represent the exploitation of women's bodies – jewelled women who carried the wealth of their husbands on their person, women as milk-sellers, women in canefields, woman as mother with child, woman with terracotta pitcher, woman with partner and so on. Surprisingly, although I have come across a similar set of photographs of African women such as street sellers or

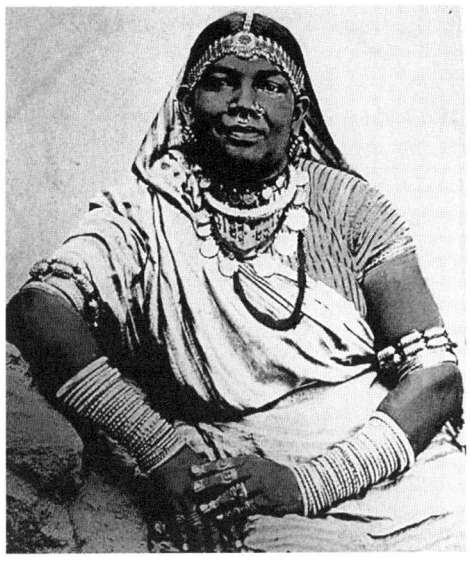

Figure 7: Coloured postcard – Indian woman (undated)

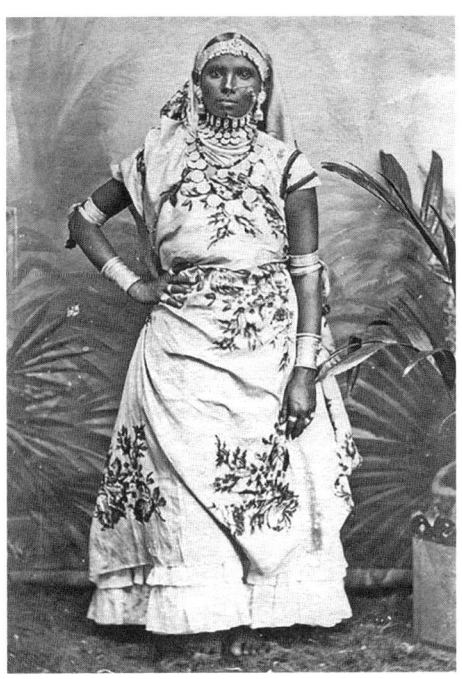

Figure 8: Studio photograph and postcard Indian woman (undated)

market women in postcards in Trinidad and Tobago I cannot recall a genre that scrutinized costume and jewelry so closely as was done for Indian women in the late nineteenth and early twentieth centuries. The travel books have generally illustrated "creole" especially mulatto women at this time with Madras headgear and blousy skirts for example. For the photographer, Indian women represented a new species on this terrain.

What are we to make of these women who posed for the camera? They were clothed and displayed their finery and jewellery to advantage. The woman in figure 7 is mature and apart from the jewellery around her fingers and arms, the string of coins, possibly gold, around her neck, attests to her prosperity which she wears confidently in her smile and expression. How old is the woman in Figure 8. She is barefoot as was the custom of the time, but she is well adorned, *nakphools*, earrings, *bayras*, rings, highly embroidered scarf. Were these her own jewels or, like the models of today, were they borrowed for the occasion? The hand resting on the hip and self-conscious gaze are not unlike the stance of the model posing for the camera. Whatever the reasons, I venture that these photographs illustrate the agency and sexual confidence that my fore-mothers felt in the context of this society, a point again that has been emphasised in the feminist literature, that the shift to the Caribbean in lower proportions than men provided women with the conditions for freedoms of different kinds compared to that which they had experienced in India (Mohammed 2002; Reddock 1985). I am pleased that they were thus captured in their finery and they demonstrated the aesthetic that my female ancestors brought from India. The latter, interestingly by the twenty-first century, is being revived again due to the widespread importation of Indian goods, especially fashion accessories and clothing, into the Trinidad market. Ollivierre (2019) has been examining this new development by looking at how individual women have absorbed historical constructions along with exposure to Bollywood films and the media and in doing so created hybrid re-assemblages of their Indo-Caribbean Hindu and Islamic dress and identities.

A second group of photographs, which includes the snake charmers above, are those who appear indifferent to or who do not meet the photographers' eyes. The subjects are almost emotionless – the camera is a temporary inconvenience to be suffered, and correctly so in that it makes no difference to their daily lives. It is here ironically that the camera is the more intrusive. How and where people work, whether they are tradesmen or farmers, what kinds of festivals they commemorate, the conditions of crowding or overcrowding and the kinds of houses they live in, how these measure up with others in the society, to those who do not live in mud huts – all of these are being presented in this soup of signs through the recurrence of the themes themselves. There is an unspoken assuredness in putting together this jigsaw puzzle of images, a confidence that we can chronologically represent the fragmented and broken histories, regain traditions and plant the footprints of arrival and belonging. And some of this is clearly possible in that we can chart changes in dress styles, housing and occupations overtime. But what else might we see in these photographs?

In Figure 9 the intimacies of family life are interrupted for a photographic moment. Was the photographer invited in for a meal to visit and share an occasion or were these photographs in Figures 9 and 10 conscripted by the colonial public relations

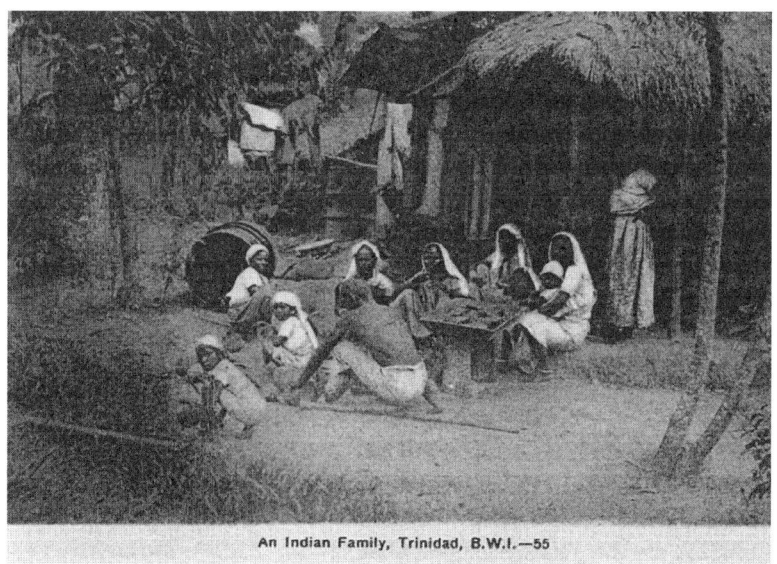

Figure 9: Family in rural settings

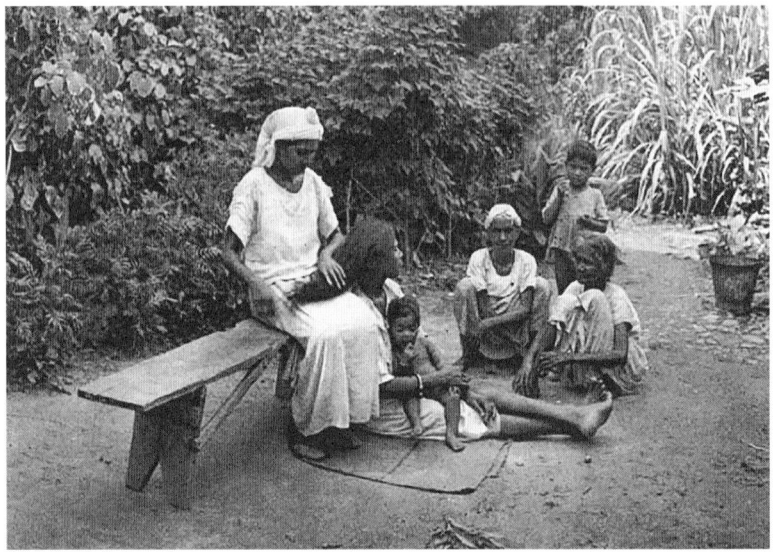

Figure 10: Rural settings

machinery of the time? There is no record of the characters' names or locations or ages. By its very generalization it is assumed to represent the sum of the whole. Figure 9 is a hand-coloured photograph, clearly used as a postcard. Figure 10 has a casualness, like a stolen moment glimpsed into the activities of a next-door neighbour over the fence, the communication between women and generations, the grooming of hair and the nurturing care of women with their children, the roughly constructed wooden bench that was rudimentary furniture in poor households. Examined from a chronological distance, these scenes have come to represent the untroubled more primitive past of the countryside, the unhurried nature of life, a sensibility of simple communal living illustrating the shared compounds that housed the Indo-Caribbean extended family system.

RETELLING THE PAST

A decolonizing of the gaze cannot be done by focussing only on persistent, repetitive and painful reminders of a narrative that was calculated to diminish. How do we deal with the retelling of the past as a form of empowerment, while still recognising the forms of disempowerment that shaped histories and that will continue to prevail? We are always at risk of being mis-represented.[9]

There is no formula for unveiling the past differently. What is invested in this exercise is conscripting an imaginative tale that does not place the "western" eye as the primary and only authoritative one. Images, like smells, are elusive triggers that can help to revive a memory where there is one, or connect ideas that lead to another and another, a kind of visual intelligence, perhaps a more liberating one. This is perhaps akin in medical terms to the role of visual association cortex in the formation of associative memories.[10] I am employing this idea of associative memory as the capacity to connect information conveyed through visual data that one would see as previously unrelated, and in doing so, make sense and meaning from that information.

I want to return to the snake charmer photographs of Figures 3 and 4 and deliberately allow the triggers of memory and imagination to take its unconscious path. Memory also has sound which images evoke. As I looked at these photographs I connected the snakes and the snake charmer with the image of Indian snake charmers I had seen in the Indian film *Nagin*. I recalled the sinuous dancing of the film actress Vijanthimala, and the mesmerising flute accompaniment of the song "Man dole mera tan dole mere dil ka gaya qaraar re, Yeh koun bajaaye baansuriya – (*My mind dances and my body dances, my heart is not in peace. Who plays this tune in the flute?*). In 1954, the popular motion picture *Nagin* was released in India and later in Trinidad.[11] The major protagonists are from two warring Adivasi tribes, the Nagis – the snake charming tribe and the Ragis. The quintessential moment that is recalled in this film is the meeting of the two star-crossed lovers and the interplay between dance and music, the seductive flute played by Sanatan, the son of the Ragi's tribal chief whom Mala, a daughter of the Nagis is sent to kill. Instead of approaching her prey with bow and arrow, Mala's sways in time to the music, not unlike the snakes which are similarly being manipulated by the flute player.

Although the roots of snake charming may be traced to Egypt where the reptile also figures as a mythical one, snake charming as we understand it today is thought to have originated in India.

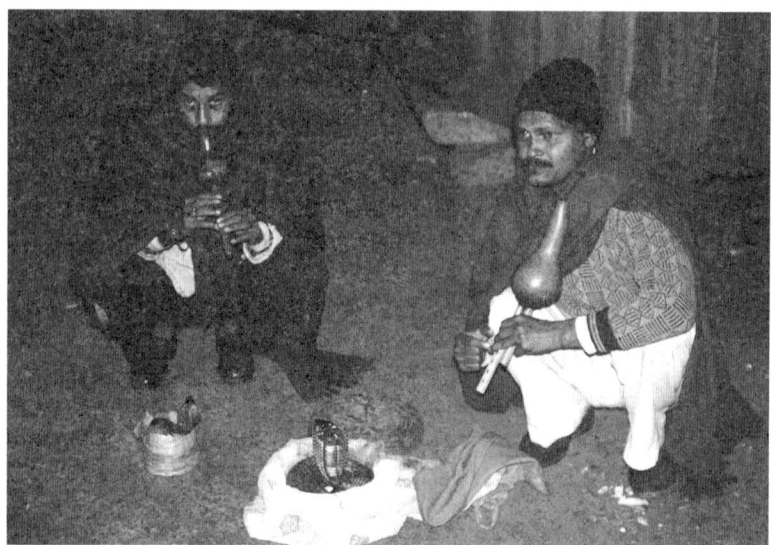

Figure 11: Snake charmers en route to Agra, India, 2010 (Author photo)

Hinduism has long held serpents sacred; the Nagas are a group of serpent deities. In pictures, the cobra sits poised ready to protect many of the gods. By inference, traditionally Indians tended to consider snake charmers to be holy men influenced by the gods. The mysticism surrounding the fear of snakes is grounded in the evolution of human society. Studies have suggested that the brain evolved to pay greater attention to the presence of snakes than other creatures, because snakes were among the earliest human predators and posed a daily threat.[12] Thus the emergence of a tribe of snake charmers, or another derivative of this, medicine men who could capture and extract the snake's venom as the antidote for bites, would have been venerated in the past, and respected in the present. Is this why these snake charmers in Trinidad were thought to be obviously remarkable enough to be found and photographed. Among the various tribes and castes that migrated to Trinidad, did any of these belong to the Nagis? They still exist in India today perhaps primarily for touristic purposes.

In a trip to New Delhi in 2010, not unlike the travellers of the past who focused their lens on the unusual or in this case a recognition of an archetype that existed in our sensibilities of the "west," I could not help similarly jumping out of a car in a fog-ridden early morning drive to Agra to take photographs of the snake charmers shown in Figure 11. Have I, in doing so, not unlike the photographers who focused their lens on the snake charmers in Figures 3 and 4, exploited an image or drawn on a sensibility of India that had been infused primarily through film. Another reference to Indians and snakes surfaced from West Indian fiction. Olive Senior (1989) writes in the short story, *The Arrival of the Snake-Woman*, "Everything about the snake-woman was magical from the start, even the way she arrived without our seeing, though we were all looking." "That is how they call them," Moses said, "from the way their body so neat and trim and they move their hip when they walk just like a snake and they wear no proper clothes just these thin little clothes-wrap, thinner than cobweb, you can see every line of their

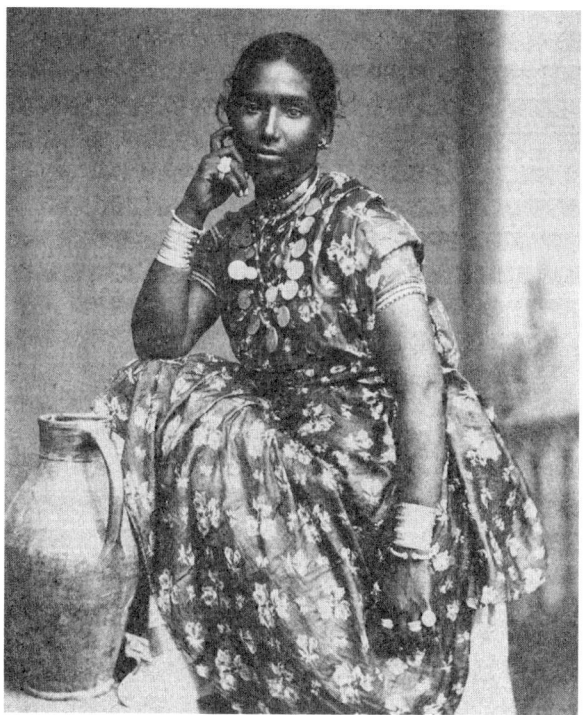

Figure 12: Studio postcard of Indian woman

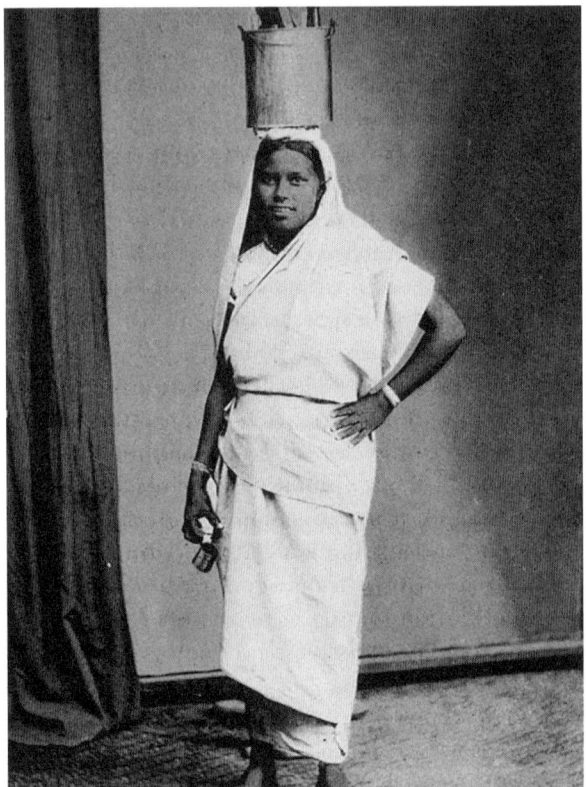

Figures 13: Studio postcard of Indian woman

body when they walk." Thus the mysticism of the snake is feminized in Senior's capturing of Indians in Jamaica and tied to female seduction and heathenism. The association of woman as serpentine beauty as opposed to colluding with the serpent herself, the root of evil in Christianity, appears in ancient Greek mythology as Lamia, the female demon who sucks children's blood. In his poem by the same name, the poet John Keats romanticises Lamia as a symbol of female beauty, sexuality and fearsome erotic power (Huang 2010). This was not the reading of Indian women in Trinidad judging from the photographs of women as water carriers and the like (See Figures 12 and 13), but as hinted above, the proliferation of this subject, the "come hither" expressions that were solicited by the photographer, the display of jewellery, their way of sculpting fabric on the body are still markers of seduction of one kind or another. In their faces and postures I see the women of today, dressed differently but confronting both the ever-ready digital camera and the society with a new found confidence.

A FABLE

Revisiting photographs with different lenses leads us to make connections that widen our world views, expand our imaginative comprehension of the collective histories of events, ritual, tradition and creativity that we share with an ethnic group or a nation or a family. While ethnicity is a result of the external social and economic forces that define the boundaries or possibilities for a group, it is equally the product of actions undertaken by individuals within ethnic groups who continue to reconfigure their self-definition of a culture and the messages this sends to the external. The image and photographs in particular generate rich and vibrant passages from which we can define our existence, drawing on the inalienable right we possess - to construct the personal narratives of our being.

I asked my father, now 89[13] years old why he felt it was important to take the family photographs (as shown in Figures 1 and 2). It must have been both an effort of time and costly in those days. His responses were at first the predictable ones; he said it was to see his family, to have a sense of how, as we grew, he could retain the image of the child in each of us, that my mother who was skilled at sewing and very creative at designing our clothes had us all looking special in the village and he was proud of her skill and of us and that he wanted perhaps to preserve evidence of this. But there was another side to his story that emerged with further prodding. He had lost both parents by the age of 21, two sisters had died under tragic circumstances. One, still a child, had been taken by a *jehajee*[14] family friend to spend vacation with them some distance away and had fallen sick, died and been buried without their knowledge. I think he still feels puzzled and hurt about it to this day, an act unthinkable in the contemporary world to us. He possessed only one surviving image of his mother, who looked not unlike the seated woman on the bench in Figure 10 above. At age 21 he was orphaned with no images of his father or of the two sisters who had died earlier. By the fifties, with a family of his own, he was now able to preserve new memories. Instamatic cameras were available but he did not have one. My father had been trained in the teaching of art as a primary school teacher by M.P Alladin[15] and thus had a sensibility about the visual that was perhaps different to his counterparts. He could not recall any of his friends who made this pilgrimage to the studio almost annually. The family photographs he began to have taken was his security against loss that he had experienced with his own past and a legacy that he felt he was leaving to future generations of grandchildren who would be able to look back to their past and to him as a grandfather. In this sense, his attitude and valuing of the photograph was a sophisticated and modern one. Born as a second generation Indian in this society, and uninhibited by any sensibility of how Indians were framed by the earlier imperial lens, he had, since the fifties, already configured a new narrative history of his identity, his legacy, his place and belonging in Trinidad.

ENDNOTES

[1] See Roshini Kempadoo 2013. "Defining Women Subjects: Photographs in Trinidad (1860s–1960s)." *CRGS*, no. 7, 2013, edited by Kamala Kempadoo, Halimah DeShong, and Charmaine Crawford, pp. 1-14 for discussion on historical photographs and insights on how photographic technologies have visualised Trinidadian women. She uses the historical photographs to demonstrate how these practices persist in contemporary visual culture.
[2] Kempadoo, *ibid* p. 10
[3] Margriet Fokken, *Beyond stereotypes: Understanding the identities of Hindustani women and girls in Suriname between 1873 and 1921*, https://www.rug.nl/research/portal/files/49894094/Beyond_stereotypes.pdf
[4] Alberto Manguel. 2000. *Reading Pictures A History of Love and Hate*. Random House, New York, p. 286
[5] Steven Lubar and W David Kingery, (Eds.) 1993. *History from Things: Essays on Material Culture*, Smithsonian Institution Press, Washington and London. p.viii – xvii.
[6] See Patricia Mohammed *Imaging the Caribbean; Culture and Visual Translation*, for discussion on the use of the "native" as pejorative or descriptive of lower class status in Caribbean society.
[7] I use *percept* here as a visual concept that depends on recognition by the senses, such as sight, of some external object or phenomenon.
[8] Although first introduced in France in 1907 by Auguste and Louis Lumière, the modern era of analogue colour photography was not invented until 1935 by the Kodak Research Laboratories in the United States. The early coloured postcards were thus hand-coloured or tinted using a range of methods and materials.

[9] This conundrum of how we re-present the past is clearly an ongoing one and I must admit here that the history and imagery of African slavery and the Jewish holocaust are two examples that present far more complexities than the migration and resettlement of Asians overseas.
10 See for example Maya L. Rosen, Margaret A. Sheridan, Kelly A. Sambrook, Matthew R. Peverill, Andrew N. Meltzoff, and Katie A. McLaughlin, 2017. "The Role of Visual Association Cortex in Associative Memory Formation across Development" https://www.ncbi.nlm.nih.gov/pmc/articles/PMC5792361/
[11] This song and music probably echoes in the minds of the Trinidad Indian movie-going population since the late 1950s when it was screened here.
[12] http://www.wsj.com/articles/ Wall Street Journal article "Why we are afraid of snakes"
[13] As I revisit and edit this paper in 2020 he has turned 89 years.
[14] *Jehajee* or brotherhood of the boat: those who came over on the same shipment from India were considered family.
[15] Born in Tacarigua, Trinidad and Tobago in 1919, Mohammed Pharouk Alladin was one of the first visual artists to emerge from the country's large Indian population. He was most influential as an art educator. Alladin founded Trinidad's Art Teachers' Association and also served as Director of Culture in the Ministry of Education and Culture for many years.

REFERENCES

Arnheim, Rudolph. 2004. *Visual Thinking*. Oakland, CA: University of California Press.

Baudrillard, Jean. 1994. *Simulacra and Simulation, 2 and 6*. Ann Arbor, MI: University of Michigan Press, p. 2 & 6.

Cesaire, Aime. 1972. "Discourse on Colonialism." New York: *Monthly Review Press*.

Chiung-Ying Huang. 2010. "A Tale of two Lamias: The Representation of Lamia's Passions and Transformations in John Keats and J. W. Waterhouse."
http://www.lancaster.ac.uk/luminary/issue2/issue2article2.htm

Mohammed, Patricia. 2002. *Gender Negotiations among Indians in Trinidad 1917-1947*. Basingstoke and New York: Palgrave.

Mohapatra, Prabhu P. 1995. "'Restoring the Family'. Wife Murders and the Making of a Sexual Contract for Indian Immigrant Labour in the British Caribbean Colonies, 1860-1920." *Studies in History, 11*(2): 227-260.

Ollivierre, Jillian. 2019. "(Un)Veiling "Tradition": Fashioning Multifaceted Oorhni and Hijab Assemblages in Trinidad". *Asian Diasporic Visual Cultures in the Americas*, 5 (1-2): 79-104

Reddock, Rhoda. 1985. "Freedom Denied: Indian Women and Indentureship in Trinidad and Tobago, 1845-1917," *Economic and Political Weekly*, 20(43)

Ryan, James R. 1997. *Picturing Empire: Photography and the Visualization of the British Empire*. Chicago, IL: University of Chicago Press.

Senior, Olive. 1989. *Arrival of the Snake-Woman and other Stories*. Jamaica: Longman Caribbean Writers, p. 1-3.

Sontag, Susan. 1973. *On photography*. New York: Dell Publishing, p. 9.

21

Morality and the Imagination: Mythopoetics of Gender and Culture in the Caribbean: The Trilogy[†]

1 THE TALE OF A PERIPATETIC SCHOLAR

The idea of humanity emerging from the mists of past barbarism into civilisation and progress achieved through European enlightenment and science seems further away today. The world has become both united and divided by different notions of what civilisation entails, that economic might is right, and on the self-righteous morality that my god is greater than yours. We face the real threat of a nuclear holocaust—one nuclear bomb dropped on New York will literally drown all these islands in the Caribbean Sea. I see these same schisms, writ differently but equally destructive, in the society in which I was born. We are blessed and cursed at the same time with natural resources, being propelled along a path that is increasingly mythic in its grand narrative – here every creed and race finds an equal place,

---

[†] Converted from my Professorial Lecture, UWI, St. Augustine, Trinidad delivered in 2005 this essay was first published in *South Asian Diaspora*, March 2009, 1 (1): 63-84. Routledge, UK.

and may God bless our nation. But what if, as Gabrielle Hosein (2004) once asked, borrowing a line from Walcott (1980), "all the gods have been killed by electric light?"

In my search for a language of inclusiveness by which we can speak to and of this narrative, I build on and pay homage to all the work of many writers and artists in the Caribbean region thus engaged. Earl Lovelace observed that the responsibility of the writer is to lead society out of despair, to constantly provide hope.[1] He used the example of *Tales of One Thousand and One Arabian Nights* (McCaughrean 2000).

Mythical king Shahriyar discovers that his wife has been unfaithful and has her put to death. He then starts marrying virgins whom he beheads the following morning. With the lives of all the girls in the kingdom under threat, the clever and beautiful Shahrazad volunteers to be his next wife. But she strikes a bargain (a pre-nup, if you will): he will spare her life until she has told him a story. Each morning Shahrazad leaves him on the edge of anticipation, dying to hear the next instalment. Her story lasts for almost three years. In the end, Shahriyar, impressed with Shahrazad's courage, makes her the queen. This tale of human survival through wisdom, intelligence and compassion is a far more optimistic one about woman than that found in the Greek originary myth of Pandora and Prometheus (Bulfinch 1998). Pandora represents the archetypal inquisitive female. She opens the marriage box from which all evil escapes, unleashing a multitude of plagues for the hapless man: envy, hatred, revenge and spite. Realising what she's done, Pandora quickly replaces the lid, preserving only hope.

The Arabian Nights is viewed as a valuable source of Middle Eastern social history. It originates from three distinct cultures and storytelling traditions – India, Persia and the Arab world. It is an imaginative blend of Arabian classical and colloquial languages.

The tale took root in the imagination of a diasporic East Indian in this part of the world when my father named three of his five children after its characters – two daughters Badura and Zaphura, and his son, Kamral. His name, Ayoob, is another version of Job. As a child I read *The Arabian Tales*, Grimms fairy tales, children's versions of Greek and Roman mythology, and the tales of Brer

Rabbit, the lovable Anancy trickster from whom our "nancy story" was derived. Later, I would come to realise that the Quran, the Bible and some Hindu scriptures – the Ramayana and Bhagavad Gita – more than the divine word of god, were syntheses of past histories of peoples of different nations, recorded to create unity out of disparate groups. Like folk tales and legends, they were cultural signifiers of geography, serving as parables of human behaviour to teach a sense of morality, and inspire hope. Their beautiful prose and poetry continue to be retold and reinterpreted in many different contexts, providing continuity to people's existence and meanings for our lives.

For instance, when Indians came to Trinidad, they saw the place as a temporary exile. Their journey was likened to banishment of Ram and Sita from Lanka as told in the Ramayana. Indentureship represented the tribulations they had to undergo in this separation from India, such is the power of the myth. This is why the enactment of the story of Ram and Sita in the Ramleela performance became a dominant festival in the reconfiguration of Hinduism in Trinidad (Figure 1).

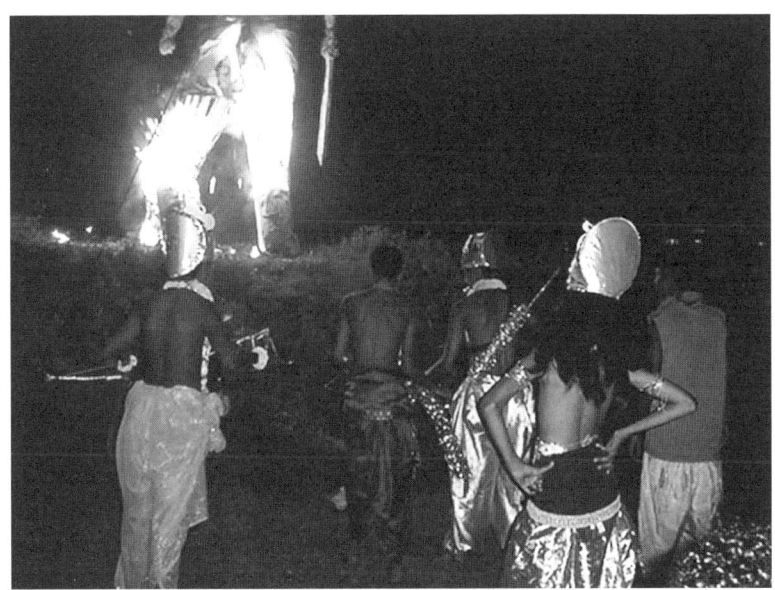

Figure 1: Ramleela the burning of Rawan, Trinidad, Author photo, 2001

Derek Walcott recognised its symbolic value. "The (Ramleela) performance was like a dialect, a branch of its original language, an abridgement of it, but not its distortion or even a reduction of its epic scale. Here in Trinidad, I discovered that one of the greatest epics of the world was seasonally performed, not with the desperate resignation of preserving a culture, but with the openness of belief that was as steady as the wind bending the cane lances of the Caroni plain...I am only one eighth the writer I might have been"...says Walcott, "had I contained all the fragmented languages of Trinidad" (Walcott 1992).

Another fragment of this language of myth is the legend of Gang Gang Sara of Tobago, as collected and retold by Gerry Besson (1989).

Gang Gang Sara, an African witch blown from her home across the sea, lands safely in the village of Les Coteaux. She journeys

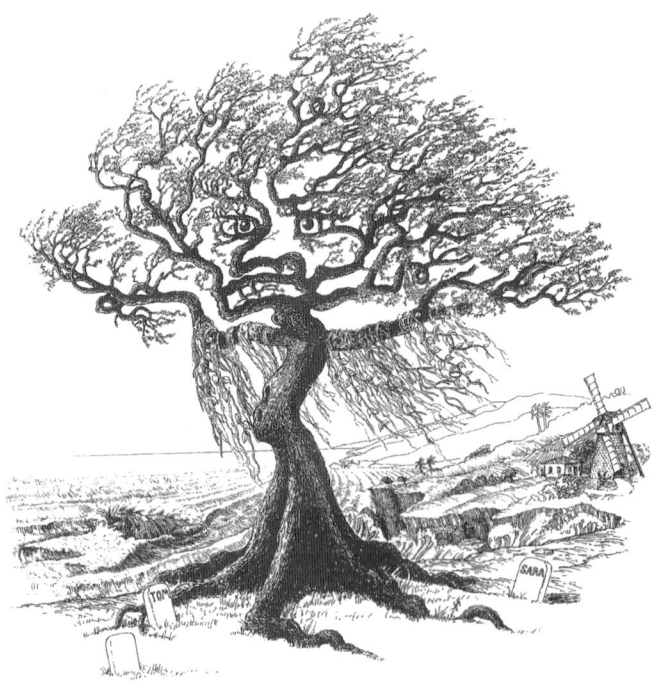

Figure 2: The Silk Cotton Tree. Source: Besson (1989, p. 33).

to Golden Lane to search for her family transported there years before. She marries Tom whom she knew as a child in Africa, and lived a long, happy life, becoming known for her wisdom and kindness. When Tom dies, Gang Gang Sara wants to return home to Africa. She climbs the silk cotton tree and tries to fly, forgetting that she has eaten salt and lost the art of flight. She falls to her death and the villagers bury her next to Tom in Tobago (Figure 2). This legend is another movement of the phantom limb—as Guyanese writer Wilson Harris (1999) calls it—that has become archetypal of New World culture in the Caribbean, the myth of return to the native land, or read differently, a search for the root of tradition.

Despite their symbolisms, these varied narratives have not yet undergone the necessary transformation to create the epic dramas that will in time be constituted as our New World myths. Paget Henry points out in *Caliban's Reason* that Harris focuses on the poetics of the "symbolic world that can be created out of the imploded world views of the Caribbean colonial experience."[2] He agrees with Harris that a cleavage exists between the realism that has been scripted into the historical conventions, and those that inspire the arts of the imagination. For theorist Mircea Eliade, myths are "human documents that express typical human situations and form an integral part of the history of the spirit."[3] Only through the imagination can they release other possibilities for literary and artistic traditions from the limiting paradigms in which they are coffined. This is how I translate Harris's insight that "a philosophy of our history might well lie buried in the arts of the imagination."[4] His ontology requires an access to the unconscious, beyond the notion of conscious reason, to overturn the "straitjacketed condition of ego and surrender to the objective process involved in accessing intuitive connections" (Eliade 1965). His use of the word buried may be allied to the straitjacketing imposed by the colonial experience of othering, of defining god in monotheistic terms, of structuring societies on notions of race, gender, colour, hair texture. As Olive Senior (1990) puts it in 'Colonial Girls School": *Borrowed images willed our skins/pale muffled our laughter and/lowered our voices/let out our hems/dekinked our hair.*

It is in the nature of mythic creation that matter must lie underground. Stories are rebuilt through excavated fragments that are mythmaking poiesis or imaginative truths, rather than presented as historical fact. The activist role of the modern citizen constantly attempting to realise historical projects built on logical frames of reference and a linear conception of progress is another myth that has been constructed. Anthony Burgess (1999) says that history is a cycle divided into four arcs. The first is theocratic, when the gods speak through thunder or oracles; the second is aristocratic, when rulers do not seek divine sanction for their laws; the third is democratic, when "our demagogues are feeble parodies of aristocracy and certainly less than gods," according to Burgess. At this point, Yeats (1961) says, "things fall apart; the centre cannot hold" – anarchy rules and we flounder in chaos. I would say this describes our present phase quite aptly.

If we look at history less as a parade of facts, and more as a pattern which seeks to explain those facts, how do we begin to divine another philosophy of our history that exhumes and brings together its fragmented pieces and silenced passages into a new social order? How can we imagine a New World history that eschews ethnocentricism and the constipated concepts of race, class and gender we have inherited?

Can there emerge a new human view, Sylvia Wynter (1995) asks, that places the event of 1492 within a new frame of meaning, not only of natural history but also of a newly constituted cultural history specific to and unique to our species? "The Caribbean may not have created the Leaning Tower of Pisa," as Rex Nettleford pointed out, "or the pyramids of Egypt and the Taj Mahal in India (though some would insist that their forefathers did). ...but they have created thought systems, ontologies, and cosmologies and a Caribbean way of knowing, a Caribbean way of seeing, nurtured not out of magic, but out of the empirical experience of a collision of cultures ...It makes sense, then, that Europe's "other people" tenanting the Americas should not waste psychic energy on the problems of Europe's ethnocentric view of world history" (Nettleford 1995, pp. 284, 278).

Speaking on "The Caribbean in the Age of Modernity," Bhoendradatt Tewarie (2006) asked: "Should the discussion that has, traditionally, centred around a Eurocentric Enlightenment view, based on the pre-eminence of science and technology, secular notions and rational thought, be broadened? The experience of other societies has shown that there are other modernities …the great civilizations other than the European/Christian – the Islamic, Hindu and Confucian – have been equally successful in modernizing their philosophies to address modern issues."

New World narratives of morality may be divined through origin stories that unite rather than divide, that tell of a people who have come together rather than been rendered asunder. I am not reducing morality to any one religion or to a specific code of conduct put forward by all rational persons in a society. I am attempting to link the idea of "morality' to the imagination, an imagination which gives primacy to the visual, and which makes it possible for us to envisage beyond our present experience and perceptions. The term mythopoetics speaks to imaginative truths that are pre-philosophic, that have not yet attained the status of myth, far less that of philosophy. Whereas philosophy is grounded in rational and reasoned argumentation, myths are self-justifying and allow for a multiplicity of *explanations* that are still being contested, but they form the basis of how a set of philosophical ideas may be reasonably argued. There are no originary narratives without the archetypes of masculinity and femininity, there is no culture without gender, and no gender without culture.

The second and third parts of this trilogy are two parallel yet overlapping narratives of the same history, but scripted from two different viewpoints. So having dispensed with premises, let us move on to the second instalment of my story, lest you, like King Shariyar, grow weary and wish to cut off my head.

II THE FIRST MYTHOLOGY

At the time of the Renaissance, when Italy sought to recapture the former glory of Rome, the classical myths became popular among the educated. Sandro Botticelli's *The Birth of Venus* (Figure 3) was painted for Lorenzo de Medici. The painting is a classical symbol of the way in which the divine message of beauty came into the world. Botticelli's Venus is depicted as emerging from the sea on a shell driven by the wind gods. The wooded shore on her left is verdant, heralding the spring. The Horae were Greek goddesses of the seasons, associated with rebirth; the rose was created by the

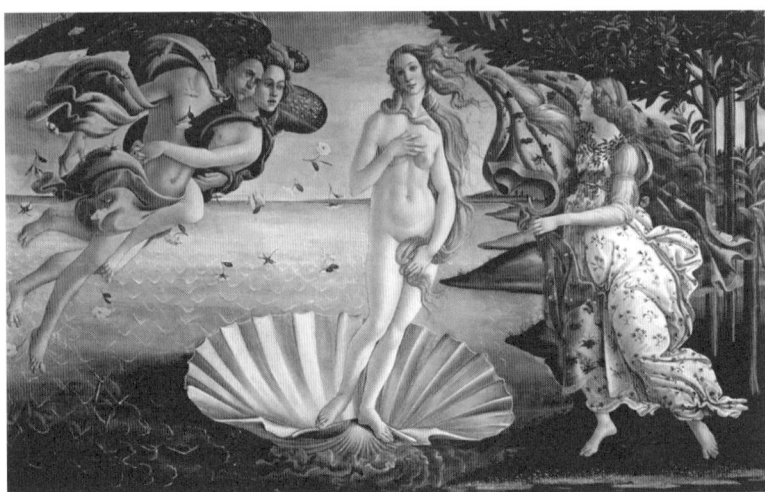

Figure 3: Sandro Botticelli, Birth of Venus, Uffizi Gallery, Florence, c1485, Tempera on canvas 172.5 x 278.5 cm (67 7/8 x 109 5/8 in.)

goddess of flowers, Chloris; Aphrodite added beauty; Dionysus added fragrance; Zephyrus was the god of the West Wind; Apollo, the sun god. The painting is an allegory for the rebirth of Italy itself, and Venus the nubile symbol of this rebirth.

In *Caribbean Sea of the New World*, Germán Arciniegas (1946) connects the Italian High Renaissance with the Caribbean encounter, uniting, like Walcott's *Omeros*, the Caribbean with themes from classical Greek mythology. He connects visually *The Birth of Venus* or the return of Italian glory with Europe's discovery of the Caribbean Sea. "In the very year of the death of Lorenzo the Magnificent, in 1492," he writes, 'Columbus reached Guanahani. What did the men see from the bridges of the three caravels? Copper-coloured Indian girls who peered fearfully out through the tangled jungle. The Caribbean Venus walked naked, as god had sent her into the world."[5] What are the artistic expressions and allegorical metaphors that define this Eurocentric founding moment? There are hundreds of depictions by artists, imagined from reports by the Europeans who came here.

The process of "enlightenment" required that knowledge, meaning customs and habits of others be recorded and categorised.

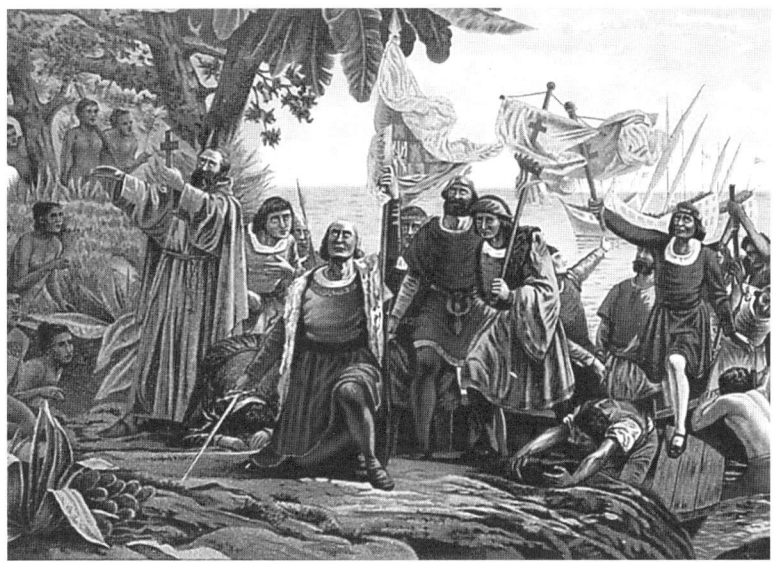

Figure 4: Interpretation of The Landing of Columbus on the Island of Guanahane, 12 October 1492. Painting by Dioscore Puebla, Source: Courtesy Ramsay Antiques, Nassau

Paintings, sketches, drawings, lithographs and engravings, along with maps and textual descriptions became powerful media for control in a pre-photography period. Examine these images closely. The metaphors abound: the stylised flora is abundant, the natives are naked—read uncivilised— so they are modestly placed behind trees, peering through the lush greenery with a mixture of fear and awe. They are made the silent, secondary partners by artistic distancing on the canvas's flat plane. The clothed priestly figure and the flags are echoes of the drapery worn by the nymph in *The Birth of Venus*. The birth of the new civilisation is symbolised through the emblems of nation – flags, crests and the sword. The ship replaces the shell in Botticelli's Venus, the naked wood nymphs must now be clothed and brought knowledge and religion as the cross signifies, by those who have arrived. While Botticelli has returned to the pre-Christian, pagan Greek past, the iconography of enlightenment, conquest and Christian conversion are made dominant features of the New World. The explorer Columbus is the central figure kneeling on the ground (Figure 4). Land and church are conflated. This image represents the New World as barren of mythologies or cosmologies in the European mind.

If discovery was the dominant discourse of the fifteenth to the seventeenth centuries, from the eighteenth to mid-nineteenth centuries Mimi Scheller (2003) writes, there was an "exponential growth of the system of slavery in which Europeans consumed enslaved human bodies in the coerced production of both plantation commodities and domestic and sexual services...". In Thomas Stothard's *The Voyage of the Sable Venus from Angola to the West Indies* (Figure 5), Botticelli's *Venus* is transferred to the slave trade and its carriage. The shell is retained as a vessel of transport.

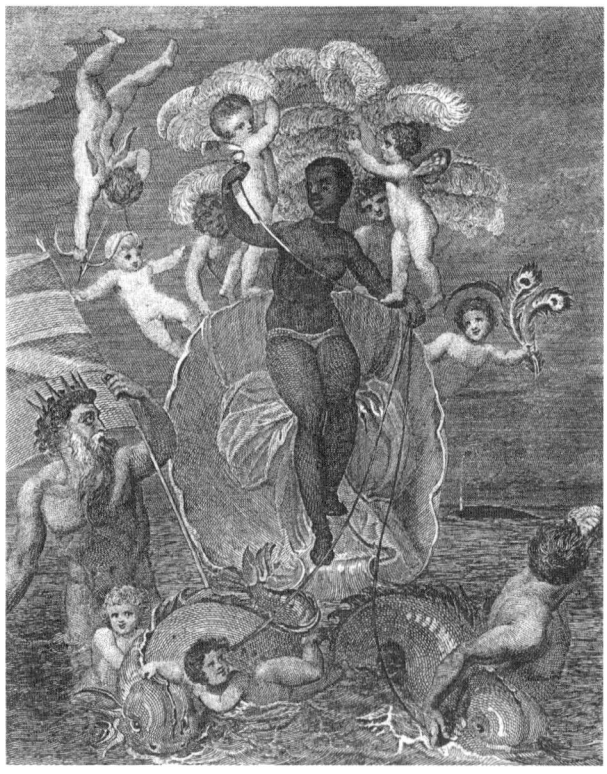

Figure 5: Thomas Stothard, Voyage of the Sable Venus from Angola to the West Indies, 1793, from Bryan Edwards History, Civil and Commercial, of the British Colonies in the West Indies, University of the West Indies Library, Mona

The nymphs and the Horae are replaced by cherubs and Tritons. This is a conscious attempt to transform the image of the slave trade from abject abuse to a leisurely voyage across the Atlantic. Meanwhile, fiction, another masterly device was also constructing other parallel metaphors and myths. Shakespeare's *Tempest* is the quintessential iconic text for the region's philosophy of history. Many more were written.

Specific to the islands is Daniel Defoe's *Robinson Crusoe* (1719), which essentialised the European gaze on territories of the New World. Robinson Crusoe and Man Friday reinforce the original myth of human-eating savages, Friday having been rescued from cannibals by Crusoe and taught how to survive on the island. Crusoe establishes his character in relation to the speechlessness of Friday. Complicit in this definition of human is the privileging of the rational thinker over the "natural" or native thinker. Crusoe is the voyeur, a temporary interloper. Economic individualism drives his purpose – "I came, I saw, I conquered" – and he moves on, having civilised his Man Friday, the original butler and manservant of the islands. Crusoe's successor is the planter and Friday is now the enslaved black labourer. One blueprint for masculinity has been inscribed.

The one for womanhood is also being drawn up. In *Blind Memory* Marcus Wood says of Stothard's Black Venus: "The rape of slave women is reconstructed in terms of a triumph of the slave Venus over the slave owners and traders, who are ironically portrayed as her powerless victims ... the slave ship is transformed into a beautiful scallop shell pulled by frolicking dolphins."[6]

Consider then the advent of the painter Agostino Brunias to Dominica in 1773 as the painter of the first governor, Sir William Young. His *West India Washerwoman* (Figure 6) is evocative of the two previous depictions of Venus.

The stance of the lighter-skinned woman is similar. In the sexual freedoms which the European scripts of primitivism have ascribed to the "natives", she stands in the midst of similarly bare-breasted women folk. Brunias recreates the shell-shaped motif by placing the washerwomen and stones in a circle around the mulatto – a painter's device to rivet the eye on the central object.

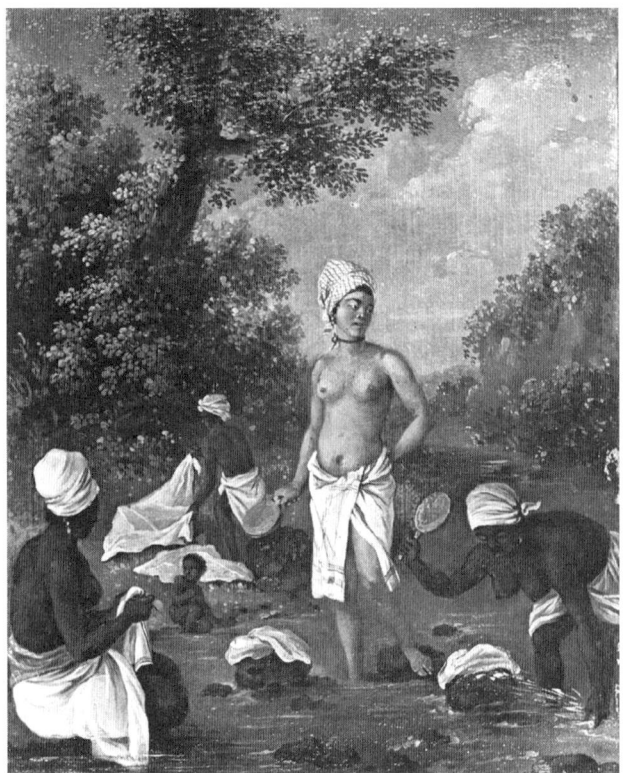

Figure 6: Agostino Brunias, West India Washerwoman, oil on canvas, 1763-1796

This Venus is olive skinned, mulatto, her hybridity reflected in the hybridity of the painting that combines neoclassical and romantic styles, pastiche and abstraction. Brunias's paintings had begun to illustrate this mixing, further exercising the European imagination on the subjects of racial purity and inter-racial desire. In *The Kingdom of This World*, Alejo Carpentier (1957) suggests how the New World had been imagined by Utopian thinkers meeting in Paris in the Café de La Regence. Absinthe made the heart more compassionate. "How easy it is to dream of the equality of men of all races …from the views of the harbors of America decorated with compass cards and Tritons with wind-puffed cheeks, from pictures of indolent mulatto girls and naked washer women, of siestas under banana trees engraved by Abraham (sic) Brunias and exhibited in Paris."[7] With Brunias's painting, the new Caribbean Venus is born, but she is placed in a setting virtually barren of allegorical references, while defining the aesthetics of gender, race, class and colour which have begun to shape the region's ontologies.

In this script of enlightenment and progression, the Cartesian order has been fixed. The idea of progress for the New World is formulated through an idealisation of history and order. But as Walcott points out: "an obsession with progress is not within the psyche of the recently enslaved ...The vision of progress is the rational madness of history seen as sequential time, as a dominated future" (Walcott 1998, p. 41). Historiography in the Caribbean emerges as a linear history of revolution among them the Haitian revolution of 1804, the Maroon revolt in Jamaica in 1865, the Grenada revolution in 1983. Cartesian thought as Barry Chevannes (2001) points out does not embrace the power of ambiguity and contradiction.

The immorality of the first recorders of the region, by and large, was the erasure, silencing and ethnocentric interpretations of the phenomena they encountered. Out of this, to quote Wilson Harris (1970), 'We have the enigma of the divided personality." Rereading Walcott's honest yet abrasive critique of V.S. Naipaul's *Enigma of Arrival*, this phrase, resounds. But I understand Naipaul's enigma, if not his choice, for my generation also accepted European literature as great world literature and its art as great world art. My youngest sister was born when I was 14 years old. I had the pleasure of naming her. I gave her the name Ramona Lisa, derived from Da Vinci's Mona Lisa. I knew more about Da Vinci and Michelangelo than the great Indian painters, and an Indian aesthetic in Trinidad had been reduced to a derided "coolie pink and green."[8]

There is a morality implicit in the act of remembering, reinventing, renaming. As a Trinidadian, I am part Asian, part African, part European and part of everything else that has made up this small space during my lifetime. All the revolutions, upheavals and changes wrought across the Caribbean are part of my history. But the aesthetics of racial anger only limit the potential for creativity that can absorb all of these into the collective unconscious.

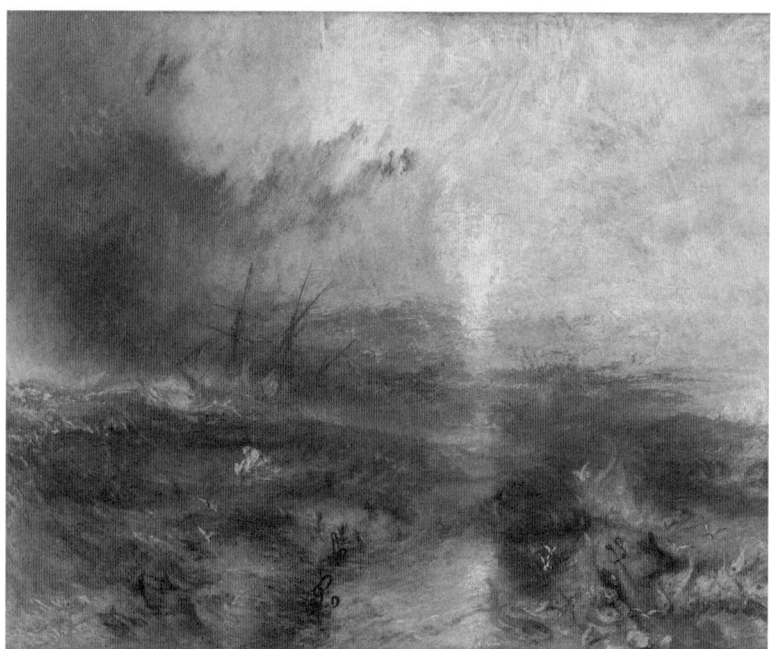

Figure 7: William Turner, The Slave Ship, 1839, oil on canvas, 91x 21cm, Boston, Massachusetts, Museum of Fine Arts (in Gatt 1968)

So, how do we build bridges across this divided conception of humanity? It is part of an all-too-consuming search for identity, in which we think we must choose between modernity and tradition, between Europe and the Caribbean, between Africa and Asia. Such a bridge might be found in William Turner's work.

Turner, a modernist before his time, began painting neo-classical landscapes that won him many clients. His style evolved into a study of atmospheric conditions of cloud, steam, vapour, spume, spray, sunlight and diffused light, reflecting what he saw as the need to change the terminology of art itself, to articulate the ideological changes taking place in Europe. In my view Turner was representing the slipping away of an old order that was clearly defined by lines and structures which had served to preserve certain hierarchies and knowledge. By blurring the composition and figurative elements he allowed the viewer a greater emotional response, personal interpretations and unrepressed consciousness about the subject. In *The Slave Ship* (Figure 7), Turner already prefigures the problems of the Enlightenment myth, by evoking the gruesome nature of slavery, and the inability of classical styles to present such a critique. This is Turner's version of the *Voyage of the Sable Venus from Angola to the West Indies*.

III THE SECOND MYTHOLOGY

In 1813, Michel Jean Cazabon was born on Corynth Estate in south Trinidad to Spanish/French landowning parents. He was sent to boarding school in England at the age of 13. On returning home he dabbled in painting for a while. At 24, he went to Paris to study art. Geoffrey MacLean writes that in Paris, "his philosophy and style followed closely that of the landscape school" (1999, p. 26). Emerging from a class more attuned to an elite culture, Cazabon continued erecting the stage props that would entrench European conventions of painting in the Caribbean. He evokes the Barbizon school of uncluttered pasteurised landscape and portraiture, but also casts a sympathetic, if selective, eye on what he does encounter, for the first time capturing the normalcy of different groups and ethnicities co-existing in a personal, romanticised vision of this landscape as virgin territory. European-trained painter Rex Dixon raises the question: How do we unlearn to see in a particular way? How does a European-trained eye deal with a tropical setting with its different palette of light?

Cazabon's paintings, according to Kim Johnson, are those of a relatively passive onlooker, "showing no hint of Trinidad's wildness at the time, not even the wildlife is wild" (Johnson 2006). While other painters such as Isaac Bellisario in Jamaica had captured the Jonkunnu festival, none of Cazabon's work records "the ecstatic religions, the brilliant, noisy, impassioned ferment of cultures" which, from the mid nineteenth century, had gained greater confidence of expression (Johnson 2006).

By the 1930s there emerged in Trinidad a Society of Independents who formed the first Trinidad Art Society, later comprising painters like Amy Leon Pang, Sybil Atteck, M. P. Alladin and Carlisle Chang, who began to search for a new vocabulary in art. In Hans Guggenheim's thesis (1968), he argues that in the construction of nationhood there should have evolved a body of work in which

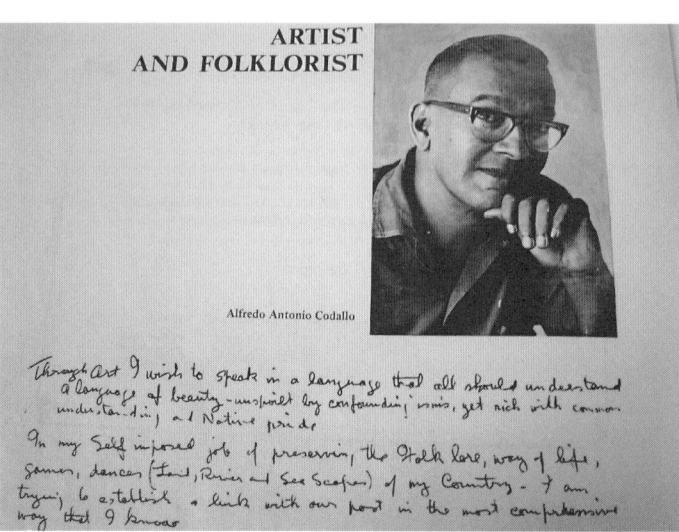

Figure 8: Alfred Codallo (in Gayadeen 1980)

local painters eschewed European formal values and traditions of painting and produced new concepts in the search for a local identity.

In Figure 8, we locate Alfred Codallo, born 1913 to a Venezuelan father and East Indian mother in Arima. When Codallo was a boy, the family moved to Prince Street in Port of Spain. Soaking up the stories which the characters of the rich nightlife told, Codallo became fascinated by folk tales, a passion that would consume him for much of his life. His friend and colleague painter, Tunapuna-born Holly Guyadeen, recalls: "Alf was a man who would find himself out of his home for the entire weekend. People invited him ...there is something taking place in a village, a wake, a shango feast, an Indian katha, firepass or chaathi ceremony – he was a man who was very open to and had a nice kind of interest in what country folk would say. He knew all the folk dancing."[9]

Codallo became a staff artist with the *Trinidad Guardian* from 1935 to 1952, during which time he produced a folklore portfolio executed with caricaturish lines. Hand Arnold and Fernandes Distillers commissioned his pictures for adverts in local newspapers. In promoting flour and rum, he captured life in the streets, backyards,

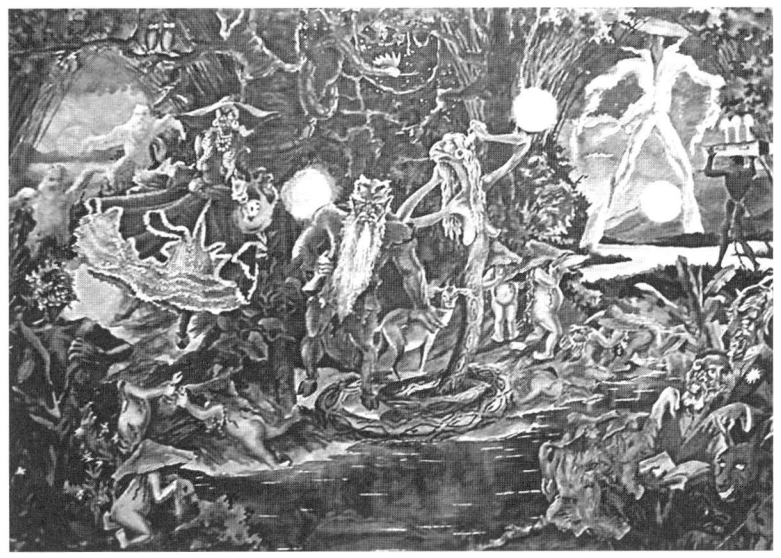

Figure 9: 'Trinidad Folklore' (original title in French "Nous ca sortir au soir" [We are going out tonight]). National Gallery and Art Museum of Trinidad and Tobago, 1958

shops and homes of Trinidad. For the Public Library he drew six of the popular folklore characters. Though everyone knew and spoke about Papa Bois, Soucouyants, Douens and Lagahous, Codallo is the first to give them a visual existence. How we now imagine these characters is a result of Codallo's listening to stories and embodying them.

Guggenheim sees Codallo as a continuation of Cazabon, but where the Paris-trained French-Creole water-colourist was a serene landscapist, Codallo invested the landscape with its pre-history anthropomorphism. In the painting titled *Trinidad Folklore* (Figure 9), which hangs in relative obscurity in the art gallery of the National Museum, Codallo takes the virgin landscape rendered by Cazabon and imagines onto it the ghosts of the human spirits.

The painting was done for the Federal Arts and Crafts Exhibition in 1958 and later donated to the National Gallery. One day, in 2001, I came across a group of 20 or so primary school children seated in front of it. They seemed enthralled by the stories being told by the museum guide about its characters. For these children, who were born into a world of computers, cable TV and cell phones, he was describing the inhabitants of a shadowy moonlit world where "when current gorn," (electricity black out) la diablesse and soucouyant came to life at night.

Many of the characters Codallo depicted represent an archetype of gender. La diablesse, one of the most popular of the archetypes, is the quintessential woman as devil, the temptress who leads the unwitting men astray into the forests at night, the cloven hoof character who disguises her animal instincts with a pretty dress. Like Papa Bois and Mama d'Leau, she is only part human. Mama d'Leau, on the other hand, is the good mother of nature, the life giver.

La Diablesse has an etymology in Greek art and mythology which conflates her with the Sirens, the bad girls of the sea. According to Greek myth, Odysseus escaped the Sirens by having his sailors plug their ears with beeswax and tie him to the mast, for it was the song of the sirens, or the lure of women's wiles, that caused sailors to run their ships aground. In later history, Sirens were depicted as beautiful women whose bodies, not just their voices, are seductive; or as mermaids, half woman, half fish. This troubles the distinction between La Diablesse and Mama d'Leau, the snake woman of the river, of the good woman versus the bad. For Mama d'Leau or Mami Wata is the watery counterpart of Papa Bois; if he looks after the land, then she is the life giver through water. She represents, according to Darwinian theory, the fact that all organisms are related to each other through common descent, the symbol of our amphibian antecedents.

Papa Bois is placed in the centre of the painting, between the two dominant female characters. He is the benevolent patriarch, his beard signifying wisdom, his religiosity and humility signified by the deer, a parallel to the lamb of Jesus. These are the markers of his closeness to nature. He is the old man of the woods, the keeper of the forests, the protector of the animals, and thus the provider of food. He is always to be found under, in or near the silk cotton tree, an important symbol in African and Amerindian cosmologies. He is Adam before the fall of man. He has the cloven hoof of the Bull of Minos, the Minotaur; he is Zeus of Greek

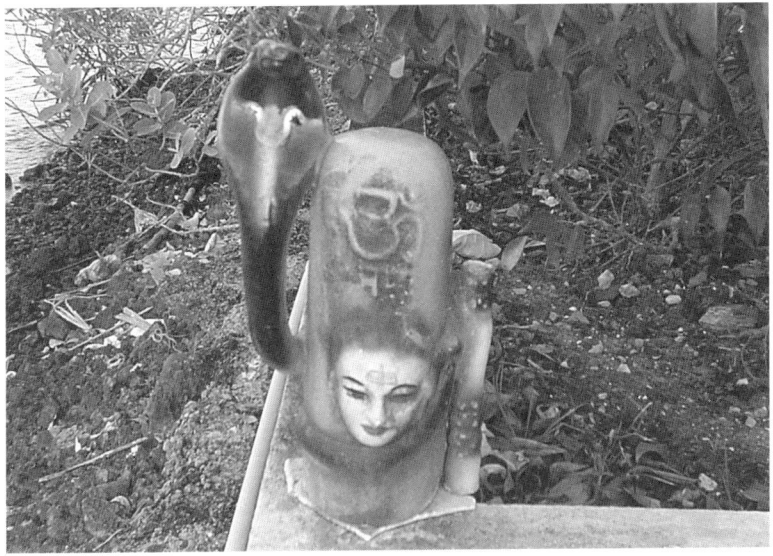

Figure 10: Shiva Lingam found at site of the Temple in the Sea, Couva, Trinidad, author photo 2000

mythology and according to Taino myth, Yaya the supreme spirit. Papa Bois can be traced to the south of France. In Basque mythology, the *basajaun* are 'Lords of the Woods," an ancient race of hairy wild men with animal characteristics and knowledge of magic. Papa Bois is Shango in Trinidad Orisha worship and Chango of Cuba, due to Yoruba influences. In Haiti, because of its Dahomean influence, he is Dambalah, the venerable father god, who takes the form of the snake. In Hinduism the roles performed by the trimurthy of gods Brahma, Shiva and Vishnu may be relocated in the archetypes of Papa Bois, Ligahoo and the Phantom (Figure 10).

But here, the plot thickens. Holly Guyadeen says that the original title of the painting was 'Nous ca sortir au soir' [*We are going out tonight*]. The title is an intended *double entendre*. This is the first time Codallo has put all the individual characters of the folk tales together. He dresses them to return them to the night. This is, if you like, a precursor to Michael Jackson's MTV *Thriller*. In the body language of the painting, placed head and shoulders above the aging Papa Bois both La Diablesse and Mama D'Leau are competing for his attentions tonight. La Diablesse, disguised as a beautiful woman in crinolines and tantans that reflect the French creole dress style of Cazabon's mulatto and negresses, is betrayed by her cloven hoof and handbag containing a skull. But Mama d'Leau is no virtuous opposite – she sinuously eases her half reptilian body closer to Papa Bois while coyly combing her hair.

Signifying the archetypal origin story of the fall of Adam is the plumed serpent above Papa Bois's head. In Aztec mythology, Coatl is a serpent. Quetzalcoatl is the Plumed Serpent known in meso American mythology as one of the creators and forefathers of the earth.

If man, as represented by Papa Bois, is caught helplessly in a trap between the two women, the Christian tale is already embellished sufficiently from other originary narratives and cosmologies to defy a binary signifier of woman as either good or bad. Codallo's Mama D'Leau represents the combined serpent and woman and is visually parallel to several other mythological characters that are universal archetypes. Always in some affinity with the snake, Mama D'Leau is configured in Blakes's rendition of Milton's *Eve*. Minoans worshipped the snake goddess as a mother goddess; archaeological finds suggest that in her importance in their pantheon, the society was either matriarchal or matrilineal. In ancient European demonology, a "lamia" was a monster in woman's form who preyed on humans. In Keats' 1819 poem *Lamia* she is the femme fatale, she is "la belle dame sans merci." He establishes an archetypal figure that would recur throughout Romantic poetry. But lamia has also meant "a witch who was supposed to suck children's blood, a sorceress, a fish of prey"[10] thus leading to yet another split in the imagery of woman as the socouyant or the blood-sucking vampire woman, personified as three balls of fire in Codallo's painting (Figure 11).

> Mama D'leau is Erzulie Dantor in voodoo,
> goddess of love who mates with Dambalah,
> the venerable father.
> Mama d'Leau is Yemaya in Cuban Santeria,
> goddess of universal motherhood,
> queen of the sea and salt water.
> Her dances, when she possesses a devotee,

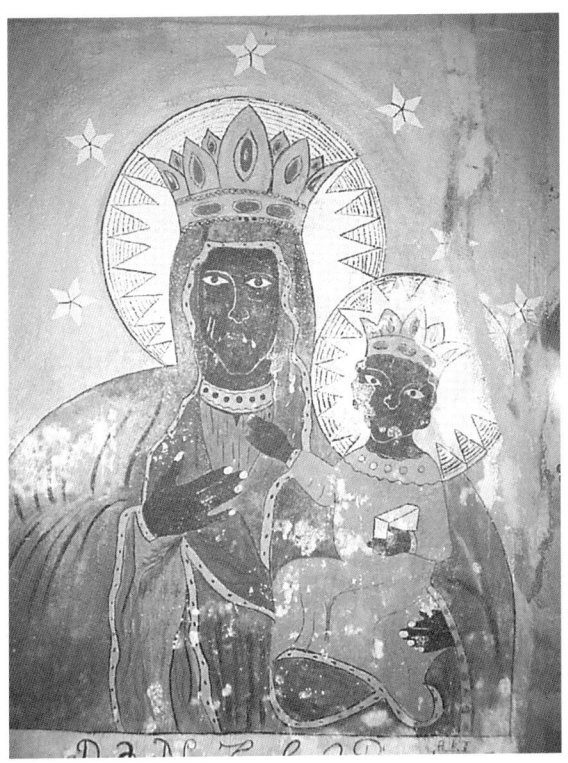

Figure 11: Erzulie Dantor wall painting taken from Petro section of a voodoo temple in Port au Prince Haiti, author photo, 2001

are lively and undulating, like the waves of the sea...
Mama D'leau in modern mythmaking is...
The singer Shakira in the music video "hips don't lie"
Shakira, Shakira, oh baby when you move like this
You make a man want to speak Spanish...(Shakira and Wyclef 2005).

For the Aztecs, she is Tonantzin, lunar mother goddess, who is conflated with the Taino snake woman, Cihuacoatl, a fertility goddess. Cihuacoatl was especially associated with midwives. She created the current race of humans by grinding up bones from previous ages, and mixing it with her husband Quetzalcoatl's blood. Cihuacoatl abandons her child, Mixcoatl, at the crossroads. It is said that she often returns there to weep for her lost son, only to find a sacrificial knife. She is thought to haunt crossroads at night to steal children. The obvious allegory would appear to be the taboo against abortion, just as Sigmund Freud draws from the Greek myth of Oedipus to interpret incest as the primary taboo.

Though focusing on folk characters, I want to guard strongly against a now spent Germanic idea of celebration of the folk as a pure space. While I have used Codallo's painting, it is not to enter another mythical space where tradition is privileged over modernisation and the real gains of science are denied. To confine the trajectory of my narrative thus smacks too much of the Enlightenment search for the untarnished native, or the belief that the authentic self can be found in the pre-industrial being. Instead, I want to reinvent for us the words pagan and heathen as they were transcribed by the Eurocentric pen. In this mythopoetic space, we find a window for the reconfiguration of memory and reinvention of a past without the idea of *limpia de sangre* – purity of blood – which was so important to the construction of race or raza by the Spanish conquistadores.

There is no uncontaminated survival in the tangled nature of our lived experience. Nor is this space fixed in time, for mythopoesis grows into mythology and forms the basis of philosophic references for Caribbean civilization. I have in a sense juxtaposed two Caribbean thinkers and their traditions, Wilson Harris – interior, looking backwards to the primordial past, shaped by the still unexplored terrain of Guyana. And Sylvia Wynter, Jamaican, steeped in the modernity of the United States where she works and writes.

The folk characters cast by Codallo remain unexplored. Gordon Rohlehr recognises this in his comment that "The Diablesse is the Caribbean version of the most powerful anti-feminist European myth, and merits close ethnological study."[11] Meanwhile we have begun to reinterpret mythical narratives so that they lose their original derogatory meanings. In a poem entitled *Picture the Diablesse*, Niala Maharaj makes *la diablesse* a woman pursued by her own sexual desire, which, like the cloven hoof, is hidden under her frilled skirt. Twinned with the Devil, she is always left alone after attempting to snare the hapless man. In Maharaj's clever rendition, she becomes the modern woman:

> ... As she sadly closes the file on this season
> And starts preparing for the next prospect
> In the dry daylight when the forest is no longer a
> myth to be feared
> Does she then, maybe
> sit down and write poetry?[12]

The persona of La Diablesse has never been static in the evolving femininity of this terrain. She is constantly transforming herself, shedding layers of clothing and dispensing with the cloven hoof, as the much sought-after jammette of Port of Spain carnival in the nineteenth century, the ambiguous Jean and Dinah heroines of American occupation of the nineteen fifties, and in the Bacchanal woman celebrated by David Rudder (1988). Mama D'leau is also busily appropriating new resonances as the universal life-giving force. She might now be linked with Hinduism through Ganga Mai, or Mother Ganges, the reference to water is obvious. And in other fiction, Olive Senior's short story, *Arrival of the Snake Woman* (1989), tells the story of Miss Coolie, whose sinuous hips and unknown nature earn her this nickname when she moves to a village in Jamaica.

In Isaiah Boodhoo's high chromatic style, we see the influences of Impressionism evoking an Indo-Caribbean landscape with mythical characters. In his depiction of Krishna, the finely ornamented detail of an Indian aesthetic bridges artistic worlds. His kartik ceremony reverberates with photographs of this ritual by Noor Kumar Mahabir. But Mahabir's lens also takes us back to Cazabon, again a mapping and peopling of the landscape. Now art in the age of mechanical reproduction begins the cycle of reinvention. Mahabir's photographs of people bathing and cooking by the riverside are not the idealisation of the picturesque, but the knowing gaze of the insider.

The archetypal male is also made more ambiguous. Walcott's play, *Ti Jean and his Brothers* (1986), is an obvious allusion to and dialogue with Milton's *Paradise Lost* (1988). Papa Bois changes form and appearance, alternating between the Devil who sometimes takes the guise of the master, and sometimes the truculent but helpful old man of the woods. One can also read into Codallo's painting the alter ego of Papa Bois, Legba as the Phantom of the crossroads and

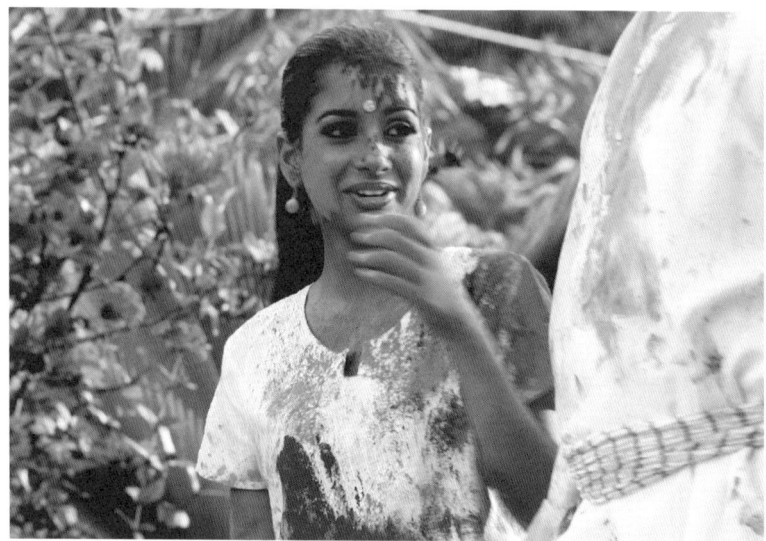

Figure 12: Phagwa festival from the documentary film "Coolie Pink and Green" 2009, Author photo.

the Ligahoo as the classic shape changer, the man who becomes a werewolf with the full moon, the sweet man dressed in his white threads, tall, dark and striding purposefully, like a Mills and Boon hero, or Saga Boy or even perhaps Sean Paul.

This is my imaginary rendition of Codallo's work. As an illustrator he is literal; it is not his forte to be imaginary. He worked within the traditions in which nationalism had already limited the capacity for the imaginary. These are not frightful tales say as the ideas of heaven and hell and damnation, and the fearful creatures in a Hieronymous Bosch painting or a Gustave Dore illustration. The monsters of the Caribbean are not those which the Old World carried around in its head.

This band of characters, produced by Codallo, are the opening act in the jour'overt of our own origin stories, with characters that are neither European nor African, with roots and branches in many cosmologies and offering a free space for our imagination. It captures the collective unconscious, the stirrings and morality plays of Codallo's age. Just as Peter Minshall's *Callaloo* in 1988 reinterpreted Mama D'leau as the pristine washerwoman, and Papa Bois's duality as Mancrab and Saga Boy in a *fin de siecle* performance of Codallo's mythological other world coming out to daylight on the carnival stage.

The cascading colours that despoil the purity of the washerwoman's white are, with the optimism of the artistic voice, transformed into another form of beauty, a beauty drawn from the wildness and wetness every young man and woman experiences subconsciously in phagwa or holi, the Hindu festival of spring, of fertility and thus always of rebirth (Figure 12).

ENDNOTES

[1] Earl Lovelace, Comment from the floor at a CARIFESTA 2006 panel on the responsibility of the artist in society.
[2] Henry, Paget. 2000. *Caliban's Reason: Introducing Afro-Caribbean Philosophy*. London: Routledge. p. 15.
[3] Eliade, Mircea. 1965. *Mephistopheles and the Androgyne: Studies in Religious Myth and Symbol*, translated by J. M. Cohen, 12. New York: Sheed and Ward.
[4] Harris, Wilson. 1995. *History, Fable and Myth in the Caribbean and the Guianas* (revised updated edition), 18. Guyana: Callaloux Publications.
[5] Arciniegas, German. 1946. *Caribbean Sea of the New World*, translated by Harriet De Onis, 11. New York: Alfred A Knopf.
[6] Wood, Marcus. 2000. *Blind Memory*, 20. New York: Routledge.
[7] Carpentier, Alejo. 1957. *The Kingdom of this World* (1949, translated 1957), 51. New York: Knopf.
[8] By 2009 I produced an experimental art documentary film entitled "Coolie Pink and Green" which won the Trinidad and Tobago Film Festival most popular film award in that year.
[9] Author interview with Holly Gayadeen, also cited on the website of the National Library and Information Service of Trinidad and Tobago, http://www.nalis.gov.tt
[10] https://www.gutenberg.org/files/2490/2490-h/2490-h.htm
[11] Rohlehr, Gordon. 1990. *Calypso and Society in Pre-independence Trinidad*. Trinidad and Tobago: Gordon Rohlehr, p. 171.
[12] Poynting, Jeremy. 1987. "East Indian Women in the Caribbean: Experience and Voice." In *India in the Caribbean*, edited by David Dabydeen and Brinsley Samaroo, 247. London: Hansib Publishing.

REFERENCES

Arciniegas, German. 1946. *Caribbean Sea of the New World*, translated by Harriet De Onis. New York: Alfred A Knopf.

Besson, Gerard. 1989. *Folklore and Legends of Trinidad and Tobago*. Trinidad and Tobago: Paria Publishing.

Bulfinch, Thomas. 1998. *The Age of the Fable*. New York: Random House.

Burgess, A. 1999. Introduction to *Finnegans Wake* by James Joyce. USA: Penguin.

Carpentier, Alejo. 1957. *The Kingdom of this World* (1949, translated 1957). New York: Knopf.

Chevannes, Barry. 2001. "Ambiguity and the Search for Knowledge." Inaugural Professorial Lecture, University of the West Indies, Mona, 22 March 2001.

Eliade, Mircea. 1965. *Mephistopheles and the Androgyne: Studies in Religious Myth and Symbol,* translated by J. M. Cohen. New York: Sheed and Ward.

Gatt, Guiseppe. 1968. *Turner: The Life and Work of the Artist*. London: Thames and Hudson.

Gayadeen, Holly. 1980. *Forty Artists of Trinidad and Tobago*. Trinidad and Tobago: Government Printery.

Guggenheim, Hans. 1968. *Social and Political Change in the Art World of Trinidad during the Period of Transition from Colony to new Nation*. PhD diss., New York: New York University.

Harris, Wilson. 1970. *History, Fable and Myth in the Caribbean and Guianas*. Georgetown, Guyana: National History and Arts Council.

Harris, Wilson. 1999. *The Unfinished Genesis of the Imagination*. New York: Routledge.

Henry, Paget. 2000. *Caliban's Reason: Introducing Afro-Caribbean Philosophy*. London: Routledge.

Hosein, Gabrielle. 2004. "Suppose all the gods were killed by electric light." President's Committee for National Self-Discovery Symposium 'Being here: now and then', Trinidad and Tobago.

Johnson, Kim. 2006. *Cariforum*. Arts Journal of Santo Domingo.

MacLean, G. 1999. *Cazabon: the Harris collection*. Trinidad and Tobago: McLean Publishing.

McCaughrean, Geraldine. 2000. *One Thousand and One Arabian Nights*. Oxford: Oxford University Press.

Milton, John. 1998. *Paradise Lost*. London: Longman.

Nettleford, Rex. 1995. "Afterword: a 'New World' View from the Periphery." In *Race, Discourse and the Origins of the Americas*, edited by Vera L. Hyatt and Rex Nettleford. Washington D.C.: Smithsonian Institution Press.

Poynting, Jeremy. 1987. "East Indian Women in the Caribbean: Experience and Voice." In *India in the Caribbean*, edited by David Dabydeen and Brinsley Samaroo. London: Hansib Publishing.

Rohlehr, Gordon. 1990. *Calypso and Society in Pre-independence Trinidad*. Trinidad and Tobago: Gordon Rohlehr.

Rudder, David. 1988. *Bacchanal Lady*. Album: London Recs.

Scheller, Mimi. 2003. *Consuming the Caribbean*. London: Routledge.

Senior, Olive. 1989. *Arrival of the Snakewoman and Other Stories*. Essex, England: Longman.

Senior, Olive. 1990. "Colonial Girls School." In *Creation Fire: a CAFRA Anthology of Caribbean Women's Poetry*, edited by R. Espinet, 193-4. Toronto: Sister Vision.

Shakira and Wyclef, J. 2005. *Hips Don't Lie*. Album: Oral Fixation, Vol. 2.

Tewarie, Bhoendradath. 2006. "The Caribbean in the Age of Modernity." Address to the Caribbean Studies Association 31st Annual Conference at The University of the West Indies, St. Augustine, Trinidad and Tobago.

Walcott, Derek. 1980. "The Saddhu of Couva." In *The Star-Apple Kingdom*, by Derek Walcott. New York: Farrar, Straus & Giroux.

Walcott, Derek. 1986. "Ti Jean and his Brothers." In *Three Plays: the Last Carnival; Beef, no Chicken; a Branch of the Blue Nile*, by Derek Walcott. New York: Farrar, Straus, and Giroux.

Walcott, Derek. 1992. *The Antilles: Fragments of Epic Memory*. Nobel Prize in Literature speech, Sweden, http://nobelprize.org (unpaginated document).

Walcott, Derek. 1998. "The Muse of History." In *What the Twilight Says*, by Derek Walcott. New York: Farrar Strauss and Giro.

Wood, Marcus. 2000. *Blind Memory*. New York: Routledge.

Wynter, Sylvia. 1995. "1492: A new world view." In *Race, Discourse and the Origins of the Americas*, edited by Vera L. Hyatt and Rex Nettleford. Washington D.C.: Smithsonian Institution Press, 5-57.

Yeats, W. 1961. "The Second Coming," In *W.B. Yeats: His Poetry and Thought*, by A.G. Stock. London: Cambridge University Press.

The text of this book is set in Garamond 10.5 point. Garamond is an old-style serif typeface that was created by engraver Claude Garamond in the 16th century.

Making the first letter in a chapter or paragraph larger than the rest of the type is a tradition in book design that predates printing. The practice references the monks who would enlarge the letter large enough to create an intricate illustration.